CW00909594

THE OXFORD HANDBOOK OF

MEANINGFUL WORK

THE OXFORD HANDBOOK OF

MEANINGFUL
WORK

Edited by

RUTH YEOMAN, CATHERINE BAILEY,
ADRIAN MADDEN,

and

MARC THOMPSON

OXFORD
UNIVERSITY PRESS

OXFORD
UNIVERSITY PRESS

Great Clarendon Street, Oxford, OX2 6DP,
United Kingdom

Oxford University Press is a department of the University of Oxford.
It furthers the University's objective of excellence in research, scholarship,
and education by publishing worldwide. Oxford is a registered trade mark of
Oxford University Press in the UK and in certain other countries

© Oxford University Press 2019

The moral rights of the authors have been asserted

First Edition published in 2019

Impression: 3

All rights reserved. No part of this publication may be reproduced, stored in
a retrieval system, or transmitted, in any form or by any means, without the
prior permission in writing of Oxford University Press, or as expressly permitted
by law, by licence or under terms agreed with the appropriate reprographics
rights organization. Enquiries concerning reproduction outside the scope of the
above should be sent to the Rights Department, Oxford University Press, at the
address above

You must not circulate this work in any other form
and you must impose this same condition on any acquirer

Published in the United States of America by Oxford University Press
198 Madison Avenue, New York, NY 10016, United States of America

British Library Cataloguing in Publication Data
Data available

Library of Congress Control Number: 2018945549

ISBN 978-0-19-878823-2

Printed and bound by
CPI Group (UK) Ltd, Croydon, CR0 4YY

Links to third party websites are provided by Oxford in good faith and
for information only. Oxford disclaims any responsibility for the materials
contained in any third party website referenced in this work.

ACKNOWLEDGMENTS

THE editors gratefully acknowledge an award from the University of Oxford's John Fell Fund which assisted in establishing the editorial team.

CONTENTS

PART III THE EXPERIENCE OF
MEANINGFUL WORK

PART IV CONTEXTS AND BOUNDARIES OF MEANINGFUL WORK

List of Figures

LIST OF TABLES

List of Contributors

Catherine Bailey (née Truss) is Professor of Work and Employment at King's Business School, King's College London and a Fellow of the Academy of Social Sciences. She has previously held posts at the Universities of Sussex, Kent, and Kingston, and at London Business School, where she completed her PhD. Her research focuses on meaningful work, temporality, employee engagement, and strategic human resource management.

Ron Beadle is Professor of Organization and Business Ethics at Northumbria University and Visiting Professor at the National Centre for Circus Arts. His research attempts to defend, apply, and extend Alasdair Macintyre's moral philosophy in the context of organizations, and specifically the traveling circus. Ron has published in *Business Ethics Quarterly*, *Organization Studies*, the *Journal of Business Ethics*, and the *American Catholic Philosophical Quarterly* among others.

Laura Boova is an organizational consultant at McKinsey & Company. She works with clients across a variety of industries to improve organizational design to maximize efficiency as well as to address multiple drivers of organizational health such as organizational culture, employee engagement, and leadership. Laura has an MS in Organization Studies from Boston College and an MBA from the University of Notre Dame.

Norman E. Bowie is Professor Emeritus at the University of Minnesota. He is past president of the Society for Business Ethics and former Executive Director of the American Philosophical Association. In 2009 the Society for Business Ethics honored him with an award for scholarly achievement. His primary research interest is business ethics, where he is best known for his application of Kant's moral philosophy to ethical issues in business.

Keith Breen is a political theorist lecturing at Queen's University, Belfast. His general research areas are contemporary political and social theory, the current focus of his research being questions of political ethics and philosophies of work and economic organization. He has published widely in peer-reviewed journals and is the author of *Under Weber's Shadow: Modernity, Subjectivity and Politics in Habermas, Arendt and MacIntyre* (2012). He is also co-editor of *After the Nation? Critical Reflections on Nationalism and Postnationalism* (2010), *Philosophy and Political Engagement: Reflection in the Public Sphere* (2016), and *Freedom and Domination: Exploring Republican Freedom* (2018).

Katherine Brown-Saltzman is co-director and co-founder of UCLA Health Ethics Center. Her clinical practice originated in pediatric oncology and end-of-life care. Her research centers on timely assessment of and interdisciplinary interventions in clinical ethics issues. As the president and co-founder of Ethics of Caring, she established an annual National Nursing Ethics Conference. Katherine develops innovative programs, including Circle of Caring celebrating over twenty-five years of engaging clinicians in an experiential self-care program, Writing the Wrongs, an intervention for healing moral distress, and a clinical ethics fellowship. Katherine now writes poetry, allowing her to transform the suffering and grief she witnesses in the world.

Elizabeth Cavallaro is Assistant Professor, Leader Development, at the US Naval War College (USNWC), College of Leadership and Ethics, in Newport, RI. She is a Certified Professional Coach, credentialed by the International Coach Federation, and is certified in a wide variety of assessment and facilitation tools. Her research interests include a range of topics, such as employee well-being, eudaimonia, mental complexity, and human development.

Neal Chalofsky is an Associate Professor and Chair of the Human and Organizational Learning Department at the George Washington University, Washington, DC. His research and teaching focuses on meaningful work, workplaces with a values-based organizational culture, and increasing capacity for learning in adults. He is the author of *Meaningful Workplaces: Reframing How and Where we Work*.

Jiatian (JT) Chen is an Assistant Professor of Human Resource Management at California State University, Bakersfield. The work of this chapter was completed while he was a PhD student at the University of Kansas. His current research includes career calling, meaningfulness at work, and organizational climates. For leisure, he enjoys running and traveling.

Joanne B. Ciulla is Professor of Leadership Ethics and Director of the Institute for Ethical Leadership at Rutgers University. A BA, MA, and PhD in philosophy, she has published extensively on leadership ethics, business ethics, and philosophy of work. Some of her books include *Ethics, The Heart of Leadership, Honest Work: A Business Ethics Reader*, and *The Working Life: The Promise and Betrayal of Modern Work*. She has also served as president of both the International Society for Business, Economics, and Ethics, and the Society for Business Ethics.

Matthew D. Deeg is a PhD student in management at the University of Kansas, with an emphasis on organizational behavior. His research interests include positive organizational scholarship, the work/non-work interface, and the influence of multiple roles on human functioning and flourishing. He enjoys reading, refereeing soccer, cooking, and the company of his cats in his leisure time.

Bryan J. Dik, PhD, is Professor of Psychology at Colorado State University and also co-founder and Chief Science Officer of jobZology. His undergraduate degree is from

Calvin College and his PhD in Counseling Psychology is from the University of Minnesota. His primary areas of research include meaning and purpose in the workplace, calling and vocation in career development, and the intersection of faith and work.

Ryan D. Duffy is an Associate Professor of Counseling Psychology at the University of Florida. He graduated with a BA in Human Development and Philosophy from Boston College and an MA and PhD in Counseling Psychology from the University of Maryland. His primary areas of research are in vocational psychology and positive psychology, and specifically studies work as a calling and the psychology of working.

Jessica W. England is a third year PhD student in the counseling psychology program at the University of Florida. She graduated with a BA in Psychology from the University of Maryland, College Park, and a MS in Counseling Psychology from Loyola University Maryland. Her primary areas of research are in vocational psychology, and she is currently studying the psychology of working.

Duncan Gallie CBE FBA is an Emeritus Fellow of Nuffield College, Oxford and Professor of Sociology in the University of Oxford. His research has involved comparative European studies of the quality of employment and of unemployment. Most recently, he has published on issues of inequality in work conditions, job insecurity, and participation at work. He has advised the French government as a member of an expert group on psychosocial risks at work. He was a member of the advisory committee of a recent OECD initiative to provide guidelines to national governments for monitoring the quality of work.

Matthew Hall is Professor of Accounting at Monash University. His research interests relate to management accounting and performance measurement, with a specific focus on measuring value in difficult-to-measure contexts, such as in mutuals and cooperatives, nonprofits, and social enterprises. His work has been published in a variety of leading international journals in the accounting, management, and nonprofit fields. Prior to returning to Australia in 2016, Matthew worked for ten years at the London School of Economics and Political Science.

Nancy Harding is Professor of Human Resource Management at University of Bath School of Management, UK, and director of its Future of Work research center. Nancy's research is focused on working lives, which she studies from a broadly critical management studies perspective. She is interested in moving beyond traditional critical approaches that explore exploitation and control and resistance, and argues that we need to develop a language that allows us to be critical of the sheer tedium to which many people are subject while at work, and the effect of hierarchy (e.g. management/staff; leader/follower) on identities.

Heather Hofmeister is full Professor for Sociology with a specialty in Sociology of Work at the Goethe University Frankfurt, Germany, and is co-director of the Center for

Leadership and Behavior in Organizations. After receiving her PhD from Cornell University, USA and before Frankfurt, she worked at Ithaca College, Bielefeld and Bamberg Universities, and accepted a professorship and vice-rector position at the RWTH Aachen University. She specializes in gender and life course research with special foci on science and leadership, using both qualitative and quantitative methods. She is also a CTI-trained Co-active coach.

Thomas Höge works as a senior scientist at the Institute of Psychology, University of Innsbruck (Austria). He studied psychology and sociology at the University of Frankfurt/Main (Germany) and received his PhD from the Technical University of Munich (Germany). His research activities include psychological aspects of workplace flexibilization and subjectification of work, occupational health and well-being, and organizational democracy.

Jason Hughes is Professor and Head of Media, Communication and Sociology at the University of Leicester, UK. His research interests include problematized consumption; drugs, addiction, and health; emotions, work, and identity; figurational sociology and sociological theory; methods and methodology; moral panics and regulation. Recent authored and co-authored books have focused on the sociology of Norbert Elias, visual methods, and archival research.

Roberta J. Hunt is Professor Emeritus from St. Catherine University in St. Paul, MN. Her clinical background focused on maternal child health and public health. She has published research, articles on program evaluation, and two textbooks, one published in five editions. Roberta's passion has been to help nurses understand, appreciate, and address disparity in healthcare.

Douglas A. Lepisto is an assistant professor in the Department of Management at the Haworth College of Business at Western Michigan University. His research explores social and cultural processes that generate meaningfulness, trust, and identity in organizations and occupations. He received his PhD in Organizational Studies from Boston College.

Marjolein Lips-Wiersma has studied meaningful work for the past two decades. This research, while initially concentrating on individual career journeys, is increasingly focused on how to live a good life in response to eroding communities, increasing inequalities, and environmental degradation, and the role of paid work in this. She is Professor of Ethics and Sustainability and has published in journals such as *Journal of Organizational Behavior, Leadership Quarterly*, and the *Journal of Business Ethics*. She is also co-director of the Map of Meaning International, which aims to help people do work worth doing in organizations worth having.

Evgenia I. Lysova is Assistant Professor of Careers and Organizational Behavior at the department of Management and Organisation at Vrije Universiteit Amsterdam, the Netherlands. She is director of the VU Center for Meaningful Work. Her research primarily concerns calling, meaningful work, and careers. In addressing these research interests, she focuses on understanding how to create conditions that enable individuals to thrive in their careers and organizations and therefore to make meaningful contributions to their organizations and society as a whole. Her research has appeared in international peer-reviewed journals such as *Journal of Vocational Behavior* and *Career Development International*.

Adrian Madden is an Associate Professor at the University of Greenwich Business School where he is also Director of the Leadership & Organizational Behaviour Research Centre. Adrian's other research interests include time and temporality in organizations; gender and the informal economy; and workplace mediation. He is a member of the editorial board of *Work, Employment & Society*.

Douglas R. May received his PhD from the University of Illinois at Champaign-Urbana and is a professor and the Bob Billings Director of the Center for Positive Ethics in Business at the University of Kansas. His research interests include positive organizational scholarship topics and ethical decision-making. Most recently, he has been exploring the meaningfulness experienced in client–regulatory interactions, the ethics surrounding meaningful work, and the ethical determinants and outcomes of job crafting. In his leisure time, he enjoys his cats, native plant gardening, and visiting botanical gardens.

Todd S. Mei is Senior Lecturer in Philosophy at the University of Kent (UK). His area of specialization is philosophical hermeneutics (Heidegger and Ricoeur), with interests in the philosophy of work, economics, and ethics. His current project focuses on understanding the production of meaning in work by way of an analogy to speech acts. He has two monographs: *Heidegger, Work, and Being* (Continuum 2009) and *Land and the Given Economy* (Northwestern University Press 2017).

Christopher Michaelson's first experiences of meaningful and meaningless work took place in the New York office of the Big Four firm where he began his career advising clients about business ethics. He is now Associate Professor and David A. and Barbara Koch (pronounced "coach") Distinguished Professor of Business Ethics and Social Responsibility at the University of St. Thomas, on the Business & Society faculty at New York University, and a member of the World Economic Forum's Expert Network on Arts and Culture. His recent research examines meaningful work and capitalism using texts and methods from the humanities.

Carol L. Pavlish is currently an Associate Professor in the University of California Los Angeles, School of Nursing and Professor Emerita at St. Catherine University in the United States. She was elected as a Fellow into the American Academy of Nursing. Her clinical background includes critical care and oncology nursing. She has published several research studies on preventing ethical conflicts and moral distress in clinical practice. Carol has also conducted research on gender-based violence and women's health and human rights in South Sudan, Rwanda, and Uganda for the American Refugee Committee.

Michael G. Pratt is the O'Connor Family Professor in the Management and Organization Department at the Carroll School of Management at Boston College. His interests include how individuals connect with the work that they do, as well as to the organizations, professions, occupations, and other collectives in which they find themselves. He earned his PhD in Organizational Psychology from the University of Michigan.

Johannes Jacobus Redelinghuys is a postdoctoral research fellow at Optentia Research Focus Area at the North-West University in South Africa. He holds a PhD in Industrial/ Organizational Psychology. His research interests include flourishing at work, meaningful work, person–environment fit, intention to leave, and performance.

Silke Roth is Associate Professor of Sociology at the University of Southampton in the Department of Sociology, Social Policy and Criminology. Her research interests include humanitarianism, development, social movement, and gender studies. Her book *The Paradoxes of Aid Work: Passionate Professionals* (Routledge 2015) analyzes the biographies and careers of people working in aid. Her articles have appeared in journals including *Gender & Society, Interface, Journal of Risk Research, Social Politics, Third World Quarterly*, and *Sociological Research Online*. In addition, she has published various edited volumes and book chapters. She belongs to the editorial board of *Sociology*.

Sebastiaan (Ian) Rothmann is a Professor in Industrial Psychology and Director of the Optentia Research Focus Area at the North-West University in South Africa. Ian's research interest is the assessment and development of human potential and flourishing in institutions in multicultural contexts. He is author or co-author of 197 peer-reviewed journal articles and chapters in handbooks.

Hui-Wen Sato is a pediatric critical care nurse at Children's Hospital Los Angeles, California, US. She has also conducted research in long-term care facilities seeking to improve quality of care and quality of life for residents by demonstrating the need for greater staffing. She is passionate about bringing to light the inner heart experiences of nurses, and speaks regularly at various nursing conferences. Her writing has been published in the *American Journal of Nursing* (*AJN*), and she is a regular contributor to *AJN*'s blog, "Off the Charts." In September 2017, she gave a TEDxTalk entitled "How Grief Can Enable Nurses to Endure."

Tatjana Schnell is Associate Professor of Psychology at the University of Innsbruck (Austria) and Adjunct Professor at MF Norwegian School of Theology, Oslo (Norway). She studied Psychology, Theology, and Religious Studies in Göttingen (Germany), London (UK), Heidelberg (Germany), and Cambridge (UK) and received her PhD from Trier University (Germany). Her research is in existential psychology, with a focus on the conceptualization and measurement of meaning in life and the nexus of meaning and health, well-being, worldview, work and civic engagement. She is co-editor of the *Journal of Happiness Studies* and member of several editorial boards.

Catherine E. Schwoerer received her PhD from the University of North Carolina at Chapel Hill. An Associate Professor in the School of Business at the University of Kansas, her research interests include careers, learning, and well-being. She teaches organizational behavior, training, research methods, and business sustainability. Enthusiasms beyond academic life include cats, bees, and books.

Brad Shuck is Associate Professor and Program Director of the Health Professions Education and Human Resources and Organizational Development programs in the School of Medicine and College of Education and Human Development at the University of Louisville. His primary areas of research include the application, meaning, and measurement of employee engagement, emerging areas of positive psychology, and leader development. Shuck is a Commonwealth Scholar, a member of the Honorable Order of Kentucky Colonels, and holds faculty affiliate status with the Department of Counseling and Human Development (UofL).

Ruth Simpson is Professor of Management at Brunel Business School. Her research interests include gender and organizations; inequality and 'dirty work'; and gender and careers. She has authored, co-authored, and co-edited several books including *Gendering Emotions in Organizations* (2007); *Men in Caring Occupations: Doing Gender Differently* (2009); *Emotions and Transmigration* (2011); *Dirty Work: Concepts and Identities* (2012); and *The Oxford Handbook of Gender in Organizations* (2014). She has had several editorial roles and has published in leading journals including *Human Relations, Organization, Work Employment & Society, The Academy of Management (Learning and Education), Management Learning*, and *Gender, Work & Organization*.

Natasha Slutskaya is a Senior Lecturer at the University of Sussex's School of Business, Management and Economics. Her research interests can be divided into two broad areas: stigma management (with a focus on 'dirty work' occupations) and equality, diversity, and inclusion at work (with a focus on social class). Natasha has published a co-edited book (*Dirty Work: Concepts and Identities*) and a co-authored book (*Class, Gender and Occupation: Working Class Men doing Dirty Work*) with Palgrave. Other publications include articles in *Work, Employment & Society, Organization*, and *Gender, Work & Organization*.

Michael F. Steger, PhD is Professor of Psychology, and the Founding Director of the Center for Meaning and Purpose at Colorado State University. He conducts research and provides keynotes, lectures, workshops, and consulting around the world on the topics of meaning and purpose, leadership, psychological strengths, meaningful work, and creating a happy workplace.

Rebecca Taylor is a Lecturer in Sociology at the University of Southampton in the Department of Sociology, Social Policy and Criminology. Her research interests are in work and organizations, and in particular conceptual debates about the nature of work, blurred boundaries between paid and unpaid work, and between work in different sectors and fields. She also has expertise in qualitative research methodologies and research ethics. She has published widely in journals such as *Work Employment & Society*, *Policy and Politics*, *Sociological Review*, and *International Journal of Social Research Methodology*.

Marc Thompson is a Senior Fellow in Strategy and Organisation, Saïd Business School, University of Oxford, and Official Fellow, Green Templeton College, Oxford. He has a DSc from Helsinki University and MSc (Econ.) from the London School of Economics. His research interests include workplace change, high performance work systems, reward systems, the digital transformation of work, meaningful work, and strategic renewal and innovation. He held posts in Sussex University and the LSE before joining Oxford as a Research Fellow. He is Academic Director of the Executive Masters, Consulting and Coaching for Change program at HEC/Oxford.

Dennis Tourish is Professor of Leadership and Organization Studies at the University of Sussex. He is the editor of the journal *Leadership*. He is also the author of *The Dark Side of Leadership: A Critical Perspective*, published in 2013, and is currently working on a new book entitled *How Management Research Lost its Way*, due to be published in 2019. He is currently conducting research into research fraud and malpractice in management studies, economics, and psychology.

Wolfgang G. Weber is full Professor of Applied Psychology, Institute of Psychology at the University of Innsbruck (Austria). He is a co-founding member of the Organisational Participation in Europe network (OPEN) and of the journal *Psychology of Everyday Activity*. His research activities include publications about employee participation and democracy in organizations, socio-moral work climate, socialization of prosocial and civic behavior, humanization of work, and the development of work analysis instruments. He has also published on phenomena of social alienation based on concepts of Critical Theory and cultural-historical Activity Theory.

Laura Anne Weiss works as a Postdoctoral Research Fellow at the Optentia Research Focus Area at the North-West University in South Africa. She received her PhD degree in Positive Psychology on the topic of improving well-being in vulnerable groups at the University of Twente, the Netherlands. Her research interests are developing and evaluating positive psychology interventions, in line with self-determination theory, with the final goal to improve well-being in vulnerable groups.

Ruth Yeoman is a Fellow of Kellogg College, University of Oxford. Her current research portfolio includes Ownership, Leadership, and Meaningful Work (British Academy/Leverhulme), Values to Shared Value Creation in Sustainable Supply Chains (John Fell), and the Meaningful City (Hermes Investment Management and the University of Tampere). She writes on the importance of meaningful work and researches the ethics and practice of mutuality in co-owned and conventionally owned enterprises. Her book, *Meaningful Work and Workplace Democracy: A Philosophy of Work and a Politics of Meaningfulness* (2014), was published by Palgrave. She is a member of the HM Treasury Council of Economic Advisers, an adviser for the Fabian Society's Changing Work Centre, and a Fellow of the UK's Big Innovation Centre. She is currently writing a monograph for the Routledge Business Ethics series called *Ethical Organizing: Meaningfulness and Mutuality in Organization/System Design*, to be published in 2019.

INTRODUCTION AND OVERVIEW

RUTH YEOMAN, CATHERINE BAILEY, ADRIAN
MADDEN, AND MARC THOMPSON

WITH organizations under pressure from new business models, technological change, and globalization, the prospects for meaningful work appear uncertain. Despite this, scholarly and practitioner interest in meaningful work continues to grow. In part, this attention has been stimulated by critical reflections on the causes of the 2008 financial crisis, leading to a search for ways to improve the relationship of business to society, as well as efforts to raise productivity and efficiency by connecting organizational practices, employee engagement initiatives, and experienced meaningfulness. Even so, work for many seems pointless. In a 2015 YouGov Poll, 37 percent of UK workers said their work makes no meaningful contribution to the world (25 percent of US workers).[1] Such results have led to a heightened corporate interest in the meaningfulness of work, and its relationship to a worthy purpose. For example, Satya Nadella, Microsoft's CEO, aims to create a "100-year old company where people find deep meaning at work,"[2] and IBM's 2016 Employee Experience Index includes meaningful work as one of its measures.[3] Overell (2008) reports McDonalds' UK Director of People asserting that if the company could offer more meaningfulness to its employees then 55 percent would be more motivated, 42 percent would demonstrate greater loyalty, and 32 percent would experience more pride.

This Handbook examines the conceptualization, social practices, and effects of meaningful work. Taking an interdisciplinary approach, the collection reflects the many scholarly perspectives on understanding meaningful work from philosophy, political theory, psychology, sociology, organizational studies, and economics. Representing some of the most up-to-date academic research, this Handbook illustrates how meaningful

[1] https://yougov.co.uk/news/2015/08/12/british-jobs-meaningless/
[2] https://www.nytimes.com/2014/02/21/business/satya-nadella-chief-of-microsoft-on-his-new-role.html?_r=0
[3] See IBM. https://www-01.ibm.com/common/ssi/cgi-bin/ssialias?htmlfid=LOW14335USEN

work, while being a rich field of study, has yet to reach its full potential. Hence, our aim is not only to provide a summary of the current state of knowledge, but also to inspire and equip researchers by identifying new directions, questions, and methods through which they may deepen their examination of the topic.

In philosophy and political theory, treatments of work—and particularly meaningful work—have been shaped by debates over the tension between work as unavoidable and necessary, and work as a source of self-realization and human flourishing. The continued centrality of work in modern societies puts us in a double bind, whereby "we see ourselves both as *working to live* and as *living to work*" (Shershow, 2005: 13, original emphasis). Work is either expressively human or oppressively degrading. The work we do shapes the people we become. In extreme cases of bad work, the worker "generally becomes as stupid and ignorant as it is possible for a human creature to become" (Smith, 1999 [1776]), resulting in "a crippled monstrosity" (Marx, 1978 [1867]). In order to improve the prospects for work which is consistent with human dignity, autonomy, and flourishing, theorists of meaningful work have turned to the philosophical literature on "meaning in life" to conceptualize meaningful work, and to political theories of justice, recognition, and human flourishing to clarify what is at stake in meaningful work and what public policy innovations may be justified to encourage the spread of meaningful work. For these scholars, Frankl's classic statement concerning the human will to meaning remains a touchpoint when arguing for social arrangements which enable people to satisfy their search for meaning (Frankl, 1984). Consequently, contemporary scholarship in the philosophy and theory of meaningful work has become increasingly diverse, encompassing: theories of justice, theories of human flourishing including human capability development, Kantian concerns for human dignity and reason, critical theories of power and social recognition, virtue theory, and organizational ethics.

In the management arena, meaningful work arguably became a focal subject when Hackman and Oldham (1976) proposed their job characteristics model of motivation, in which experienced meaningfulness constituted one of three critical psychological conditions. They defined experienced meaningfulness as "the degree to which the employee experiences the job as one which is generally meaningful, valuable, and worthwhile" (p. 162). Much empirical work has focused on meaningful work from the perspective of positive psychology, but more recent research has increasingly considered meaningful work as a complex phenomenon, socially constructed from interactive processes between individuals, and between individuals, organizations, and society.

The conceptual basis of meaningful work is complicated by the presence in the literature of "meaning*ful* work," "meaning *of* work," "meaning *at* work," and "meaning *in* work." These terms are distinct while at the same time being interconnected when scholars seek to understand the experience and organization of meaningful work. The "meaning *of* work" includes debates about the social value of work as a human activity, and the centrality of work as part of the good life (Brief and Nord, 1990). This discourse focuses on ethical concerns regarding whether work is "good" or "bad," and whether the meaning of work as compulsion has crowded out the meaning of work as free, expressive, and creative action (Spencer, 2009). Pratt and Ashforth (2003) associate "meaning *at* work" with the organizational context, and in work itself with the meaningfulness of roles and tasks. "Meaning *in* work" is concerned with the different meanings which people attach to their experience of work as meaningful or meaningless. For example, Rosso, Dekas, and Wrzesniewski (2010: 94) suggest that "meaning" is "the output of having made sense of something," which can potentially yield a wide range of meanings both positive and negative (see: Budd, 2011; MoW, 1987). The generation of meanings in this sense is related to studies emanating from the meaning in life literature examining "sources of meanings" (Schnell, 2011), which encompasses both positive and negative meanings. The concept of "meaningful work" itself is by implication positive, although there remains considerable uncertainty about its precise conceptual definition (Rosso, Dekas, and Wrzesniewski, 2010), and how it is to be distinguished from other positive concepts of work such as good work or decent work. This may be connected to the concern of critical theorists to identify a concept of work which embodies at its core an emancipatory ideal, capable of helping us to distinguish between normatively desirable and undesirable work. Positive concepts of work—meaningful, good, decent work—are candidates for providing this critical standpoint, as well as for being sources of regulative ideals suitable for policy innovations and for organizational initiatives to improve the quality of work. Scholars adopting a critical approach offer proposals for improving the organization of work through the reform of the institutional (economic, political, and normative) environment, leading for example to calls for a citizen's income or economic democracy. This opens up opportunities for specifying the institutional features which will foster organizational and individual-level meaningfulness. Despite some inroads into the institutional framing of meaningful work, this remains a neglected topic.

Efforts to describe a concept of meaningful work which is useful for theoretical and empirical inquiry have frequently drawn from multiple disciplines. Given the resulting conceptual diversity, meaningful work may be considered to be an "essentially contested concept" (Gallie, 1956), which is likely to produce further variation and debate as scholars expand their conceptual understanding and accumulate new evidence. Gallie (1956) argues that an essentially contested concept can be identified when the scholarly debate "inevitably involve[s] endless disputes about their proper uses on the part of their users" (p. 169). He further characterizes such concepts as an "achievement [which] must be of an internally complex character" where "its worth is attributed to it as a whole" (pp. 171–2). Gallie (1956) identifies several criteria of an essentially contested concept which focus on links between the normative content of the concept and other empirical features. These criteria are: internal complexity, diverse desirability, openness, reciprocal recognition of the concept's contested character among contending parties, an original exemplar that anchors conceptual meaning, and progressive competition. Meaningful work may be considered to be an essentially contested concept because the body of work to date is characterized by the achievement of an internally complex character through a process of progressive competition, as well as scholarly openness to new conceptual development. Framing meaningful work in this way creates scope for new approaches, which acknowledge the multifaceted and complex character of meaningful work and its contribution to meaningful lives.

Some scholars have sought at least some temporary "practical closure" (Care, 1973) by specifying a conceptual structure underpinned by a hybrid account of meaningfulness (Wolf, 2010), or the integration of the objective/ethical-moral and the subjective/cognitive-emotional dimensions of meaningfulness. This yields a conceptual structure for meaningful work which combines the emotional and cognitive experience (subjective) of meaningfulness in work with a moral and ethical perspective (objective) on the significance of the work. Within this understanding of meaningfulness, individuals are more likely to experience meaningfulness when the content of their work is structured by normatively desirable features: for example, dignity, autonomy, non-alienation, respect, recognition, and freedom (Yeoman, 2014a, 2014b). Such normative features are conducive to fostering the interactive processes required for the social construction of meaningfulness, and similar characteristics are captured by decent and good work standards, such as the DGB Good Work Index developed by the German Confederation of Trade Unions which contains dimensions of meaningful work (Eurofound, 2016).

Exploring the interactions between the objective and subjective dimensions of meaningful work, including the extent to which meaningfulness reduces to subjective preferences or requires objectively valuable goods, stimulates intellectual thinking in both the theoretical and empirical disciplines. This debate is addressed in different ways by our various contributors. While Schnell, Höge, and Pollet (2013) characterize meaningful work as "inherently subjective," other scholars argue that the objective/moral-ethical dimension of meaningful work sets limits on subjective interpretations of meaningfulness by requiring that meaningful work be "morally worthy work in a morally worthy organization" (Ciulla, 2000). Bailey and Madden (2016) have shown that workers report a sense of meaninglessness when they are given pointless work, as well as when work disconnects them from their values, rendering a sense of futility and despair. Pointlessness and futility indicate an absence of the objective dimension of meaningfulness by marking out work which fails to provide a valuable or morally significant purpose, and is therefore unworthy of emotional and cognitive involvement. Furthermore, in objective accounts of meaningful work, pointless work may be judged to be pointless work, irrespective of people's subjective preferences or interpretations. Here, important theoretical connections can be made to psychological processes involving adaptive preferences (Elster, 1983), whereby people adjust their preferences to the constraints of a choice-set which is shaped by more powerful actors. Drawing on adaptive preferences and forms of constrained choice suggests that future research on meaningful work could usefully consider the role of power imbalances in shaping subjective interpretations of meanings and the incorporation of meanings into a sense of meaningfulness.

In addition, understanding meaningful work to be an essentially contested concept allows for engagement with related literatures such as job crafting (Wrzesniewski et al., 2013) and sense-making (Maitlis and Christianson, 2014). These have yet to incorporate a specific account of meaningful work into their treatment of work meanings and meaning-making in work. Relational approaches offer promising resources for bringing together meaningful work, sense-making, and job crafting. For example, Grant (2007) found a connection between the relational architecture of jobs and the motivation to make a prosocial difference. Thus, a relational approach to meaningful work may lead to proposals that jobs designed to produce normatively desirable relationships, for example, based on mutual respect, dignity, and fairness, are more likely to support meaning-making capabilities and generate a sense of meaningfulness (Bailey and Madden, 2016).

Linked to this, a critical approach to the study of meaningful work will consider theories of power and asymmetric power relations in interpersonal processes of meaning-making, as well as examining how elite groups may appropriate meaning-making through ideology or failing to provide organizational practices such as voice. Questions related to power have yet to be fully explored in constructivist accounts of meaningful work. Partly, this reflects a need in the broader sense-making literature to include theories and practices of power. Here, Maitlis and Christianson (2014) have identified the considerable research potential to advance our understanding of power in sense-making processes. Finally, this suggests that concerns related to the misuse of power may put limits on the legitimacy of corporate initiatives to promote meaningful work. Scholars warn of the ethical and practical limits of efforts by management to deliver meaningfulness to their employees (Bailey et al., 2017). Unlike other constructs in organizational studies, the involvement of the whole person in meaningfulness may ultimately put meaningful work beyond the reach of management ambitions to deliver meaningfulness as an instrumental tool of organizational effectiveness, especially when managers focus on short-term performance or illusory teamwork (Lips-Wiersma and Morris, 2009).

Thinking about the relational aspects of meaningful work may require scholars to attend to how efforts to integrate the objective and subjective dimensions of meaningfulness involve individual-level intra-psychological processes (Isaksen, 2000), as well as intersubjective processes shaped by relational characteristics of mutual respect and being treated as a dignified person (Bailey and Madden, 2016, 2017). These indicate an emergent, process-oriented perspective on meaningful work in which employees wrestle with the wider significance of their subjective experience through interactions with self, others, organization, and society, and how they relate these struggles to moral and human values. This could extend to consideration of how affective engagement with meanings and things of value is generative of the experience of meaningfulness. Few studies have attended to the emotional content of the social construction of meaningfulness, including the connection of affect and emotion to materiality and technology.

The increase in constructivist accounts of meaningful work indicates the potential for combining empirical studies of meaningful work with theories such as the human capabilities approach developed by Nussbaum (2011) and Sen (1993) (see Yeoman, 2014a). Through conversion factors such as organizational belonging and resources, capabilities turn innate and trained abilities into functionings, or the beings and doings that constitute a human life we have reason to value. Capabilities preserve a space for human freedom and agency because individuals retain the choice regarding what functionings they consider to be important, and hence what capabilities they will activate. Applied to the social construction of meaningful work, individual meaning-making capabilities could be specified which are realized through the activation of individual abilities for meaning-making in an institutional setting that provides resources for experiencing meaningfulness, such as a valuable purpose and appropriate organizational practices.

This would require studies taking the constructivist route to pay more attention to theorizing and evaluating our ontological status as relational beings. Smith and Seward (2009) have argued that a relational ontology grounds Sen's capability approach, which is relevant to considering the role of capabilities for meaning-making. Sandberg and Tsoukas (2015) refer to the "holistic and relational character of sense-making" which is of particular importance to an emerging, processual approach to meaningful work. Meaning-making is constructed through a complex interaction between individual intra-psychological reflection, appraisal, and judgment, and integrative processes of social construction which are conditioned by intersubjective relations of respect, esteem, and care (Honneth, 1995; Held, 2006). The quality of social relationships, and the opportunity to engage in social interactions through organizational practices such as voice will influence the formation and exercise of capabilities for meaningfulness.

In the empirical literature, meaningful work studies, including Rosso, Dekas, and Wrzesniewski (2010), have to some extent drawn on social identity theory (Tajfel and Turner, 1986) to examine connections between social relationships and experienced meaningfulness. Further insights can be drawn from the critical social theory literature on intersubjective recognition (Honneth, 1995; see Yeoman, 2014a). Although Rosso, Dekas, and Wrzesniewski (2010) and others have discussed the self–other relation, along with prosocial issues, this remains underexplored territory in the empirical literature. Honneth's (1995) theory of social recognition argues that social progress arises from a struggle for recognition, in which individuals and groups make claims for social recognition of their ways of living or contributions. Individual self-realization depends on positive self-relations which foster self-confidence, self-respect, and self-esteem. Such relationships to the self are more likely to emerge when an individual experiences positive relationships with others who recognize both a person's status as a human being and his or her particular contributions. Recognitive relations in meaningful work permits an examination of how diversity in sources of meaning may act to protect an individual against losses in self-esteem (Crocker, 2002), provided that an individual enjoys the status respect needed to achieve recognition of the meanings they incorporate into experienced meaningfulness. The role of esteem and respect in meaningful work may therefore extend to an examination of how the status of employees as meaning-makers underpins their capabilities for meaningfulness and provides the ethical basis for advancing claims related to their production and interpretation of meanings.

Meaningless work, and the interaction between meaningful and non-meaningful work, is under-researched. Nair and Vohra (2010) associates higher levels of meaningful work with reduced alienation. Bailey and Madden (2016, 2017) have adopted a broader understanding of social recognition in the context of interactional meaningfulness, where negative interactional experiences arising from a lack of respect or recognition can produce experiences of meaninglessness. The authors make a further connection between unfairness and injustice and the experience of meaninglessness. Their observation can be supported by the literature on organizational justice, which identifies the importance of interactional justice—that is, being treated fairly and with respect—for positive individual and organizational outcomes (Cohen-Charash and Spector, 2001).

There is considerable untapped potential to explore meaningful work beyond the level of the organization, including institutions, large-scale economic and social entities, and public policy formation. The absence of research on the links between meaningful work and the level of political economy, policymaking, and state regulation, including political, economic, and normative institutions, would suggest new avenues for research. Further research would also be welcome on how meaningful work is related to attachments to specific communities of practice that transcend the organization, and how occupational identifications lead to a sense of meaningful work. This includes how, beyond the level of the organization, employees' assessments, appraisals, and judgments of their work as more or less meaningful are influenced by the diversity of wider ethical-moral frameworks, the values embedded in national cultures, and in broader meaning-systems.

Finally, in the context of rapid technological change, there is a need for studies which explore prospects for meaningfulness where work is automated, redesigned to incorporate collaborative working with robots and forms of artificial intelligence which enable human–machine learning, or even eliminated entirely. Such "future of work" considerations return us to the fundamental philosophical and moral concerns related to the centrality of work in modern societies, including: what work means to us, what effect the disappearance of work may have on our being able to experience meaning in life, whether we can create new sources of positive meanings, and what kinds of institutional or policy measures may be needed to promote meaningfulness in life and in work. The future of meaningfulness as a moral and ethical value will continue to depend on the prospects for meaningful work.

OVERVIEW OF THE CONTRIBUTIONS

The Philosophy of Meaningful Work

The chapters in Part I reflect a variety of philosophical perspectives on meaningful work. In Chapter 1, Joanne Ciulla notes that the characterization of meaningful work as objective or subjective is subject to considerable scholarly disagreement. While broadly agreeing with Susan Wolf that meaningfulness has both objective and subjective aspects, Ciulla seeks to transcend the debate by separating the moral conditions of work from the concept of meaningful work. She associates the moral conditions of work with features such as whether an employer respects the autonomy of employees, treats them fairly, pays a living wage, offers reasonable working hours, and does not engage in practices that cause physical or mental harm to employees. Workplace ethics are important pathways for experiencing meaningfulness in work and in life. Although she agrees that having to do non-meaningful work harms the prospects for meaningfulness in other spheres of life such as action, Ciulla does not believe that only those who do meaningful work can have meaningful lives. Meaningful lives are possible even when people are doing meaningless work. Indeed, people may do non-meaningful work but still be treated with respect and dignity in their work. In Ciulla's account, most of the objective features of meaningful work are related to the moral conditions of work. These include, for example, being treated fairly and with respect, having personal autonomy on the job, and working in safe environments. When the moral conditions of work are present, then work becomes worthy of a human being. Finally, Ciulla shows that teasing out the moral from the meaningful helps us to see how advances in humanizing the conditions of work arise out of struggles between employers and workers over who controls the work process and who gains or loses from doing so.

In Chapter 2, Norman Bowie explains the central importance of dignity for meaningful work, which he argues justifies an obligation to provide meaningful work. This is because people have intrinsic worth as "dignity beyond price" and also because, through meaningful work, people experience themselves as dignified persons. In the Kantian formulation, people have dignity because they have the capacity for autonomy and self-government, and therefore can be held to be responsible. Bowie takes dignity to be based on such universal characteristics, and argues that since meaningful work is a route to dignity then we must pay attention to the ways in which we can ameliorate struggles to experience our dignity in work. Bowie's Kantian account of meaningful work identifies the normative characteristics of work which is designed to promote the development of rational capacities, including freedom to choose and to exercise autonomy while at work, as well as the conditions for independence such as sufficient pay. Bowie goes on to highlight examples of management practices which meet such normative conditions. These range from open book management to recruiting, training, and participating for the development of rational capacities.

Dignity is grounded in our capacity for self-governance. In Chapter 3, Keith Breen reminds us that autonomy as self-determination or self-governance is just one dimension of freedom. He identifies two further dimensions of freedom which are important for meaningful work: freedom as self-realization, or the ability to develop one's human capacities in pursuit of one's valuable purposes, and freedom as non-domination, or freedom from arbitrary interference. Meaningful work is associated with a plurality of goods. These can be divided into either external goods, such as money or status, or internal goods, such as a sense of purpose or contribution, high-quality interpersonal relationships, the exercise of intelligence and creativity, and the opportunity to develop one's character. While holding the three aspects of freedom to be distinct, Breen argues that all three are at risk when we find ourselves in dominative relationships arising from conditions which foster arbitrary interference. Constant fear and anticipation of the harms resulting from domination stunt a whole life. Breen applies this moral concern to a critique of capitalist firms where managers are permitted by law to exercise authoritarian rule over employees. Although such power is at present weakly accountable, dominative relationships can be checked via measures which support an effective right to exit, a workers' bill of rights, and the institutionalization of worker voice.

In Chapter 4, Ron Beadle uses a MacIntyrean virtue perspective on meaningful work to examine contested issues in philosophical debates concerning the provision of meaningful work and in social sciences concerning the antecedents and consequences of meaningful work. In the former, there is no agreement on the concept of meaningful work, or on how prioritization in public policy or organization design might impact other valued goods, such as rights, efficiency, and welfare. In the latter, despite assumptions that jobs requiring skill and challenge are meaningful work, these jobs are not, on further empirical investigation, always experienced as such. Conversely, a sense of meaningfulness may be reported by those performing jobs from which these characteristics are absent. Beadle reminds us that in virtue-based accounts of work, good work is privileged over meaningful work, and that, in turn, good work is set within a wider account of human goods. Through efforts to create human goods—where such efforts are organized in practices—we acquire ethically desirable qualities of mind and character, and it is only via the meanings and meaningfulness embedded in such practices that the concept of a meaningful life makes sense. Meanings supervene on activities: rather than being mediators in pre-existing psychological needs and desires, they are formative of needs and desires, and part of our ethical learning and development. In this way, our role as practitioners provides us with a standpoint from which to assess different kinds of work, as well as the organizations in which they are housed. Beadle concludes with a virtue-based account of meaningful work which proposes an examination of the provision and distribution of practices able to foster the development of virtues.

Western philosophical accounts of work tend to focus on necessity as its chief defining attribute. The relation of work to the question of the meaning of being is therefore circumscribed by the ways in which work can be said to fulfill necessary ends. In Chapter 5, Todd Mei argues that there are two consequences of this view which delineate the philosophy of work. Work is either *merely* necessary for existence in order for us to be able to engage in higher activities—a view attributed to Aristotle. Or, work is the principal activity defining human existence as such—the thesis advocated by Karl Marx. Mei examines the arguments of each view. He concludes with an alternative account attempting to forge a more substantial role for work in relation to the meaning of being: work is essentially metaphorical in nature as opposed to being only necessary.

In Chapter 6, Neal Chalofsky and Elizabeth Cavallaro draw on Aristotelian thinking to differentiate between hedonic and eudaimonic understandings of well-being. A sense of purpose and meaning are fundamental to the more profound experience of eudaimonic well-being which is associated with authenticity and living in accordance with one's "true self." A framework for well-being and meaningfulness is proposed which highlights the interactive effects between the two. Fundamental to both is a sense of self, the work performed by individuals, and the workplace itself. Eudaimonic well-being can only be achieved through the performance of meaningful work.

Processes of Meaningfulness

The chapters in Part II consider the processes through which meaningfulness may be manifested and experienced. In Chapter 7, Christopher Michaelson explores the problems associated with the observation that not enough people have decent work in the world today. Fewer still have work they consider to be meaningful. Even among those who have the power to choose their work, the absence of work that they consider to be meaningful adversely impacts their physical and emotional well-being—and most adults' waking hours are spent at work. Accordingly, work is a primary means by which most of us can experience meaningfulness in life. This chapter offers two arguments for why we have a moral obligation to pursue and practice meaningful work if we have the autonomy to choose it.

In Chapter 8, Nancy Harding draws on labor process theory to argue that the discourse of meaningfulness in the context of neoliberal capitalism may represent a means for organizations to control and manipulate individual identities. However, she extends this critical perspective by proposing a "politics of meaningful work" that demonstrates how individuals move between abject alienation and the proud identity associated with meaningful work, based on the thinking of Butler and Foucault. Drawing on Marx's notions of the alienated self who is denied identity through the capitalist mode of production, she argues that meaningless work is alienated work since it is associated with the production of a commoditized self. However, recalling her own early work experiences, she shows how both meaningful and meaningless work can coexist through the notion of emplacements. Thus, where the individual is subject to the managerial gaze and work is routinized and controlled, then alienation is the outcome. In other emplacements, where the self is constituted as a social self, engaged in interaction with co-workers, meaningfulness and a non-alienated self arise outside formal organizational constraints. In this way, a sense of meaningfulness may arise even in the face of neoliberalist attempts to quash it.

In Chapter 9, Adrian Madden and Catherine Bailey explore the idea of self-transcendence—a concept often evoked in different approaches to meaningful work, and which also surfaces in other chapters of this Handbook, but which lacks clarity. Drawing on different literatures as well as empirical research, the authors consider how the subjective experience of meaningful work, centering on significance and purpose, gives rise to the idea of meaningfulness as the realization of human potential, by connecting the inner and the outer life along spiritual and social dimensions. This points to a conceptualization of self-transcendence that places greater emphasis on the intersubjective nature of meaningfulness rather than on the "self-oriented" mechanisms often featured in the meaningful work literature. Highlighting the intersubjective nature of meaningfulness raises questions about the experience of meaningful work, which the authors explore: if meaningfulness is self-transcendent, where and how is meaning created; if transcendence denotes "beyondness" of the here and now, what does this mean in terms of the nature of work tasks and roles; and if self-transcendence is an ineffable, transitory state, what might this mean for future research into meaningful work? The authors suggest a shift in the emphasis of future research is necessary if we are to more fully understand the self-transcendent nature of experienced meaningfulness.

Meaningfulness is related to the human experience of feeling part of something larger than ourselves, consequent on a sense of belonging. In Chapter 10, Tatjana Schnell, Thomas Höge, and Wolfgang G. Weber explore the connections between belonging, meaningful work, and the ability of people to fulfill their potential. Drawing on the nexus of two core human qualities, the social and the productive, the authors propose that meaningful work constitutes an arena of practice where this sense of belonging is evoked. Belonging can arise from being part of a group or team at work, where acknowledgment and recognition arise. Although psychological studies have thus far not focused extensively on the construct of belonging, research has examined similar notions such as relatedness, social support, and psychological ownership. Research in these areas has confirmed the importance of belonging, support from co-workers and managers, and identification as internal motivators linked to meaningfulness. However, changes in the workplace, such as the growing flexibilization of work and growing economism, pose challenges to experiencing this sense of belonging and mean-ingfulness. Finally, the authors outline the potential "dark side" to belonging, such as the risk of over-identification, the propensity to unethical behaviors, and manipulative managerial strategies.

In Chapter 11, Laura Boova, Michael G. Pratt, and Douglas A. Lepisto explore work orientations and cultural accounts of work. The authors address the question of what makes work worth doing, and argue that accounts of meaningfulness should be more closely based in societal culture and the dominant work orientations that are manifest in varying cultural settings. They differentiate between a "realization" perspective on meaningful work which emphasizes need fulfillment, and a "justification" perspective which equates meaningful work with worthy work. This latter perspective is particularly relevant for understanding how culture influences meaningful work through promoting particular orientations that foster a sense of meaningfulness. Culture can "push" individuals by promoting specific cultural values and beliefs, or alternatively enable indi-viduals to "pull" particular perspectives from a range of options. Finally, it is possible for individuals to create a shift in larger cultural meanings at the collective level. Based on their analysis, the authors identify some important unanswered questions about meaningful work to guide future researchers in the field.

The relationship of meaningful work to a meaningful life is underexplored. Michael Steger takes up this challenge in Chapter 12. He reminds us that the idea of meaning in life (MIL) is crucial to almost every measure of human wellbeing or flourishing. Yet there is much less consensus over the idea of meaningful work (MW). Although the two ideas are often used interchangeably, the author reviews different conceptualizations of these ideas to see how they are related and takes a "theoretical turn" to consider some shared themes and character strengths, such as "significance," "coherence," "transcendence," "purpose," and "empathy". Based on these themes, the author proposes two workplace models intended to make it easier for workers to find meaningful pathways in work and for leaders to create the conditions for the meaningful organization. He suggests that when these two models work together they can operate to produce social as well as economic value, and to personalize work even when faced with dehumanizing effects of robotics.

The Experience of Meaningful Work

The chapters in Part III consider the different ways in which work may be experienced as meaningful. In Chapter 13, Ruth Simpson, Natasha Slutskaya, and Jason Hughes explore the provocative nature of "dirty" or "tainted" work as a source of meaningful work. The authors consider different sources of meaningful work, including work characterized by intersubjective, self-actualized, or stigmatized dimensions. To explore this further, the authors draw on Bourdieu's concepts of *habitus* (predispositions), *hexus* (character), and *doxa* (beliefs) to propose a scheme of meaning-making in which tainted work serves as a source of meaningfulness. However, where many approaches often focus on the career choices people make, the authors look at the wider contextual factors, as well as two "dirty" jobs in the UK—street sweeping and refuse collecting. They examine not only the traditional meaning-systems in these roles, which echo agential choices, but also the structural constraints within a neoliberal system that places less symbolic value on this work and those who do it.

Chapter 14 by Carol Pavlish, Roberta Hunt, Hui-wen Sato and Katherine Brown-Saltzman is a reflective exploration into the experience of meaningfulness in nursing, which seeks to reveal the meaning of care work, as well as what makes caring work meaningful. Through a series of provocative narratives, the chapter exposes deeply personal explorations of meaningful moments in caring work, challenging basic assumptions about the link between meaningfulness in work and happiness, and the importance of "opportunity structures" for worker and patient interaction. Meaningfulness is eroded where work becomes overly centered on tasks rather than relationships, as well as through struggles over the value and primacy of patient care as opposed to patient medicalization and bureaucracy. Resonating with Frankl's claim that people find meaning through suffering, the authors discuss the power of meaningful work in helping nurses to find their vocation and a meaningful life.

In Chapter 15, Rebecca Taylor and Silke Roth examine meaningfulness in voluntary work. Contemporary debates about meaningful work have drawn on ideas of autonomy and freedom, vocation or calling, dignity, and self-realization, informed by classical sociology. The third sector appears to offer an ideal space for meaningful work, given its social, political, and environmental aims and its assumed independence from state and market. This chapter takes a sociological approach to exploring the ways in which it fulfills this ideal. The authors review what is known about the sector's paid and unpaid workforce and then focus on three different fields within the sector: social service, political activism, and humanitarian aid. Drawing on empirical studies of workers' subjective experiences and motivations, the authors examine what makes this work potentially meaningful. They highlight diversity in how meaningfulness is experienced, how understandings are shaped by social identity and life course, and the paradox that meaningful work in the sector can also be the source of stress and burnout.

A considerable body of literature has been built up which explores callings in work. In Chapter 16, Ryan D. Duffy, Jessica England, and Bryan J. Dik write about the meaningful nature of callings by separating the idea of perceiving a calling from actually living one. The authors argue that callings, whether prompted from within the person or externally, underpin meaningful engagement with work at the social or personal level because they provide people with purpose. Those who pursue a calling are shown to experience more meaningful outcomes such as well-being and work satisfaction, but are also exposed to the "dark side" of callings too often manifest in workaholism, burnout, and exploitation. Those who perceive a calling but who choose not to pursue it can access sources of life meaning through job crafting opportunities, and also through workplace interventions such as critical consciousness training that may empower them to enact their perceived calling, and thus more easily find meaning in work.

There is an equally important literature on employee engagement. In Chapter 17, Brad Shuck articulates the link between employee engagement and meaningful work, acknowledging the complexity of this task against a backdrop of confusion over the precise meaning of engagement, which remains a contested and potentially exploitative construct. Shuck highlights the limitations of the predominant conceptualization of engagement as a positive, active, work-related psychological state, arguing that this encourages a focus on performance-related outcomes at the expense of a deeper under-standing of the individual experience, context, and processes of engagement. Reverting to William Kahn's original theory of personal role engagement as being fostered by the experience of meaningfulness, Shuck argues that individual engagement is associated with the fluctuating interpretation of whether or not a situation can be construed as meaningful. Thus, engagement and meaningfulness, while not synonymous, are symbiotically linked.

In Chapter 18, Heather Hofmeister examines the important topic of gender and meaningful work. Hofmeister argues that the definition of work broadens when using a gender perspective, and the meaningfulness potential of work broadens as well. The historical legacy of gender differentiation in work results in blindness to the range of activities that are work, and to gender inequality within kinds of work. Thus work meaningfulness may vary based on the worker's gender identity or societal values con-nected to gender appropriateness of the work. A gendered view of "work" would be activities or thoughts that affirm life and growth, imagine or create the future, or that abate or delay death and decay. Hofmeister identifies at least nineteen types: paid work; informal labor market work; crowdwork; unpaid on-call work; networking; volunteer-ing; political advocacy; informal helping; caregiving; emotion work; kinkeeping work; housework; consumer work; archival work; hired work; aesthetic work; self-branding; self-care; and slavery. She argues that research on meaningful work could consider gendered aspects of each of these and their relations to each other. A gender-sensitive definition of meaningful work would be activities that are consciously experienced as aligned with deeply held values, and it must consider that values and gender norms are both socially constructed.

Critical theory has a potentially important contribution to make to meaningful work research. In Chapter 19, Dennis Tourish adopts a critical stance toward meaningful work and leadership theory and asks whether it is feasible or desirable for leaders to be positioned as architects of purpose and meaning. He points out that current evidence suggests that work is, for many, a dissatisfying experience with little opportunity for voice and agency, rather than constituting a source of fulfillment and meaning. Leadership theories such as leader–member exchange theory, authentic leadership theory, or transformational leadership theory fail to account for leaders' lack of authority over meaning-making for their followers, and reify organizations as sources of uncontested and unproblematic meaningfulness. Leaders may end up threatening, rather than strengthening, employees' existing sense of meaningfulness, since employees may not "buy in" to the dominant discourse and goals of the organization or the leader. Similarly, spiritual leadership approaches are founded on the unitarist notion that leaders are uniquely placed to provide employees with a sense of meaningfulness, purpose, and community, which fails to take account of the potential "dark side" of managing meaning such as the abuse of power, work intensification, and the colonization of the employees' inner world. For many, meaningfulness may arise from resistance to prevailing ideologies.

Contexts and Boundaries of Meaningful Work

The chapters in Part IV consider what kinds of contexts promote the experience of meaningful work and look at neglected topics such as families, corporate social responsibility, national cultures and broader meaning-systems, the institutional level, and larger scale economic and social units, such as cities. In Chapter 20, Douglas May, Jiatian Chen, Catherine Schwoerer, and Matthew D. Deeg introduce a positive ethical framework for supporting the experience of meaningfulness at work. They identify three specific virtues within this framework that they argue are conceptually linked to meaningfulness (humanity, courage, and transcendence) and a number of character strengths that these encompass (such as morality, gratitude, and spirituality). The authors argue that meaningfulness is more likely to result in the experience of positive emotions, contributing to a positive ethical culture at work and producing a "virtuous upwards spiral" of positive agency. This in turn is more likely to engender meaningful work. Yet the link is more than conceptual and they cite evidence to substantiate their claim. Positive emotions attract more support and facilitate positive social relations inside and outside the workplace; compassion in the workplace can reshape organizational cultures, while other virtues contribute to a self-perpetuating positive culture of meaning at work. Evidence about the links between meaningfulness and volunteering are explored in turn to consider what organizations might do to foster the positive work culture associated with these work orientations. The authors recognize the potential for conflict and paradox between virtues and character strengths, however, such as the need for kindness and a requirement for honesty that may feature in client work. However, what is proposed is that even paradoxes and conflicts of this kind can generate positive experiences.

In Chapter 21, Duncan Gallie connects the quality of work and meaningful work literatures. He considers two aspects of the meaningful work context—task discretion and organizational participation—and argues that these provide opportunities for values associated with meaningful work to be realized at both an intrinsic and instrumental level. Drawing on both theoretical arguments and empirical evidence, he explores the extent to which meaningful work values are realized in both domains. Evidence points to employees' greater control over the immediate job task but less expressed need for wider organizational participation. However, he notes that the demand for involvement at this level has been increasing over time. Gallie also finds that the two types of direct participation are complementary: task discretion is particularly important for increasing the scope for informal learning, while organizational participation is a stronger lever for securing higher levels of training provision. The most controversial issue with respect to direct participation has been whether it promotes or undermines good health. There is moreover substantial evidence that participative decision-making, particularly in the form of control over the work task, moderates the impact of work pressure and reduces its negative effect on health. Gallie presents substantial evidence that participation in decision-making, both at the level of the work task and in wider organizational decisions, is an essential precondition for meaningful work. It allows people to lead work lives that are congruent with values that are widely prevalent in the advanced societies— values of self-determination, self-development, and competence—and the preservation of health. Further, there is some evidence that it is particularly vital to those who are in positions of disadvantage, such as the low skilled, for whom the exercise of influence through market power (or the threat of exit) are highly constrained.

In Chapter 22 Matthew Hall explores the connections between meaningful work, financial value, and accounting systems. Although the concept of meaningful work has not been addressed in accounting research, accounting scholars and practitioners have long grappled with how to reflect the value of employees and human capital in organizational accounts. This chapter examines how the features of a typical accounting system are likely to impact the treatment of meaningful work in organizations, including consideration of only its potential financial value, the exclusion of unpaid forms of meaningful work, and the limits on recognizing meaningful work as an organizational asset because quantifying its value is typically considered too subjective. It also explores how internal accounting and control practices, such as performance measurement and reward systems, tend to ignore the possibility of meaningful work or focus on controlling and harnessing its instrumental value to improve organizational performance, thus downplaying its role in expressing values, fulfilling personal needs, and generating and sustaining meaning in our lives. A stronger engagement with meaningful work would require more fundamental changes to organizational accounting systems premised on recognizing employees as central stakeholders and addressing meaningful work as a human need rather than (only) a means for enhancing organizational performance.

As accounting systems provide a particular and thus partial representation of activities and events, whether these changes eventuate will have important implications for how meaningful work is made visible and potentially valuable in organizations.

In Chapter 23, Evgenia I. Lysova examines how the pursuit of meaningful work impacts families. Experiencing one's work as meaningful is often regarded as beneficial to the individual, yet some scholars suggest that it can also create challenges for individuals requiring them to make sacrifices, including sacrifices concerning their families. This chapter reviews and integrates research on meaningful work, career calling, and the interplay of work and family, to better understand how the pursuit of meaningful work impacts family life. The author draws on work–family enrichment and work–family conflict perspectives to explain how meaningful work can contribute to or be detrimental to family life. In so doing, the chapter challenges the prevailing overly positive perspective on the outcomes of meaningful work, while revealing the scarcity of empirical research on this topic. To stimulate future research, this chapter discusses the role of person-related conditions such as family role salience and identification, and harmonious passion versus obsessive passion, which play a role in facilitating spillover, both positive and negative, between the work and the family domain with regard to work meaningfulness. Lysova concludes with a discussion of additional organization-related conditions that could shape how meaningful work influences a person's family, and a critique of the absence of family in the contemporary discourse on meaningful work, which leads to a further disconnection between individuals and their families.

In Chapter 24 Marjolein Lips-Wiersma examines the argument that corporate social responsibility (CSR) creates opportunities for meaningful work. She develops a conceptual framework that integrates five different perspectives: personal responsibility, meaningful job characteristics, dignity and freedom, worthy work, and strong sustainability. While these conditions are necessary they are not sufficient, in themselves, to create more opportunities for meaningful work in a CSR context. She argues that specific contextual features need to be in place to support meaningful work. These include an ethical corporate culture, embedded CSR, bottom-up CSR, CSR driven by human and planetary well-being, and an intent to move to a post-CSR paradigm.

The connection of meaningful work to national cultures and broader meaning-systems is under-researched. In Chapter 25, Sebastiaan Rothmann, Laura Anne Weiss, and Johannes Jacobus Redelinghuys lay out the territory for researchers in this aspect of meaningfulness through an exploration of cultural, national, and individual diversity and their relationships with meaningful work. They argue that differences between countries, cultures, and individuals might affect people's beliefs, feelings, and values. Most of the theory-building and empirical investigation relevant to meaningful work has originated in Western cultures and developed countries. Moreover, few studies have focused on the relationship between cultural and national diversity and meaningful work. It is crucial to focus on equivalence and bias of measures when comparing meaningful work and its antecedents in different countries. The study of relationships between meaningful work, values, and organizational practices on individual, organizational, and national levels is challenging, given different methods to aggregate data, as well as the different levels involved. Both individual-level and multilevel studies are required to study the complex relationships between diversity and meaningful work. Assessing meaningful work from a national culture perspective could be problematic, as national culture fails to account for factors such as within-culture variability, acculturation, the changing nature of cultural aspects (e.g. values), and cultural tightness or looseness. The authors propose that longitudinal and experimental designs should be used to study the relationship between cultural, national, and individual diversity and meaningful work, and thereby address our gaps in knowledge regarding meaningful work and cultural, national, and individual diversity, including different countries and contexts.

In Chapter 26, Marc Thompson argues that the current literature on meaningful work underplays and mostly overlooks the importance of institutional arrangements in structuring opportunities for people to experience meaningful work. When there are greater opportunities for meaningful work, this can have spillover effects, both in terms of civic participation and also subjective experiences of meaningfulness. He sets out different theories of comparative institutionalism—rational choice, historical, sociological, and constructivist—and explores their implications for future research on meaningful work. He then considers empirical evidence from comparative institutional studies that focus on specific attributes of meaningful work such as autonomy and involvement. This consistently shows that Nordic regimes have institutional arrangements that support greater opportunities for meaningful work, raising issues about how to generate institutional change in regimes which are not as good in creating opportunities for meaningful work. He identifies three important pathways: (1) develop institutional arrangements that encourage social actors to cooperate to create meaningful work as a societal goal, supported by an enabling state, (2) strengthen collective bargaining and employee representation to redress power imbalances at organizational, sectoral, and national level, and (3) develop social movement strategies drawing together academics, policymakers, employer organizations, consultants, social media, and commentators to shape a new discourse and wider societal narrative on the importance of opportunities for meaningful work.

In Chapter 27, Ruth Yeoman applies the value of meaningfulness to a philosophy of the city. Philosophies of the city have been neglected in recent scholarship on urban studies and by political theorists, even though classical political theory originated in the city. At the same time, there has arisen an abundance of techno-bureaucratic city initiatives based on the use of smart technologies aimed at sustainability and participation. Yeoman argues that philosophies of the city can supply such approaches with the human values and attention to the common good which they currently lack. To this end, she brings the value of meaningfulness into a description of city-making, showing how city people have responsibilities to make the city, but only when the activities of social cooperation associated with discharging these responsibilities are constituted by freedom, autonomy, and dignity, and when the social interactions which are generative of positive meanings are just. She specifies the features of an ethico-normative architecture which is capable of promoting city-level meaningfulness. This includes three core elements: first, *public meaningfulness* or a common-pool resource of positive meanings, bounded by a horizon of liberal democratic values, from which people draw to make the city and to craft meaningful lives; second, membership of *the society of meaning-makers* which invests people with the status and capabilities needed to be world-builders; and third, *agonistic republicanism* to foster positive difference-making, and encourage a culture of civic emotions which goes beyond respect to knowing one other as whole human persons. Yeoman argues that city-making which is organized to manifest these features will generate a rich diversity of positive meaning from which people can draw to craft meaningfulness in life and in work.

References

Bailey, C. and Madden, A. (2016). "What makes work meaningful—Or meaningless." *MIT Sloan Management Review*, 57(4), 52–63.

Bailey, C., and Madden, A. (2017). "Time reclaimed: Temporality and the experience of meaningful work." *Work, Employment, and Society*, 31, 3–18.

Bailey, C., Madden, A., Alfes, K., and Fletcher, L. (2017). "The meaning, antecedents and outcomes of employee engagement: A narrative synthesis." *International Journal of Management Reviews*, 19, 31–53.

Brief, A. P. and Nord, W. R. (eds.) (1990). *Meanings of Occupational Work: A collection of essays*. Issues in Organization & Management series. Lexington, MA: Lexington Books.

Budd, J. (2011). *The Thought of Work*. Ithaca, NY: ILR Press.

Care, N. S. (1973). "On fixing social concepts." *Ethics*, 84, 10–21.

Ciulla, J. B. (2000). *The Working Life: The promise and betrayal of modern work*. New York: Random House.

Cohen-Charash, Y. and Spector, P. E. (2001). "The role of justice in organizations: A meta-analysis." *Organizational Behavior and Human Decision Processes*, 86, 278–321.

Crocker, J. (2002). "Contingencies of self-worth: Implications for self-regulation and psychological vulnerability." *Self and Identity*, 1, 143–9.

Elster, J. (1983). *Sour Grapes: Studies in the subversion of rationality*. Cambridge: Maison des Sciences de l'Homme and Cambridge University Press.

Eurofound. (2016). *Germany: Latest findings from DGB Good Work Index*. Available at: https://www.eurofound.europa.eu/observatories/eurwork/articles/working-conditions-industrial-relations/germany-latest-findings-from-dgb-good-work-index [accessed May 30 2018].

Frankl, V. E. (1984). *Man's Search for Meaning*. New York: Washington Square Press.

Gallie, W. B. (1956). "Essentially contested concepts." *Proceedings of the Aristotelian Society*, 56, 167–90.

Grant, A. M. (2007). "Relational job design and the motivation to make a prosocial difference." *Academy of Management Review*, 32, 393–417.

Hackman, R. and Oldham, G. R. (1976). "Motivation through the design of work: Test of a theory." *Organizational Behavior and Human Experience*, 16, 250–79.

Held, V. (2006). *The Ethics of Care: Personal, political, and global*. Oxford: Oxford University Press.

Honneth, A. (1995). *The Struggle for Recognition: The moral grammar of social conflicts*. Cambridge: Polity Press.

Isaksen, J. (2000). "Constructing meaning despite the drudgery of repetitive work." *Journal of Humanistic Psychology*, 40, 84–107.

Lips-Wiersma, M. and Morris, L. (2009). "Discriminating between 'meaningful work' and the 'management of meaning.'" *Journal of Business Ethics*, 88, 491–511.

Maitlis, S. and Christianson, M. (2014). "Sensemaking in organizations: Taking stock and moving forward." *The Academy of Management Annals*, 8, 57–125.

Marx, K. (1978 [1867]) "Capital, volume one." In Robert C. Tucker (ed.), *The Marx-Engels Reader*, 2nd edn., pp. 294–438. New York and London: W. W. Norton & Company.

MoW international research team. (1987). *The Meaning of Working*. London: Academic Press.

Nair, N. and Vohra, N. (2010). "An exploration of factors predicting work alienation of knowledge workers." *Management Decision*, 48, 600–15.

Nussbaum, M. C. (2011). *Creating Capabilities: The human development approach*. Cambridge, MA: Belknap Press.

Overell, S. (2008). *Inwardness: The rise of meaningful work*. Provocation series, vol. 4, no. 2. London: The Work Foundation.

Pratt, M. G. and Ashforth, B. E. (2003). "Fostering meaningfulness in working and at work." In K. S. Cameron, J. E. Dutton, and R. E. Quinn (eds.), *Positive Organizational Scholarship*, pp. 300–27. San Francisco: Berrett-Koehler.

Rosso, B. D., Dekas, K. H., and Wrzesniewski, A. (2010). "On the meaning of work: A theoretical integration and review." *Research in Organizational Behavior*, 30, 91–127.

Sandberg, J. and Tsoukas, H. (2015). "Making sense of the sensemaking perspective: Its constituents, limitations, and opportunities for further development." *Journal of Organizational Behavior*, 36, S6–S32.

Schnell, T. (2011). "Individual differences in meaning-making: Considering the variety and sources of meaning, their density and diversity." *Personality and Individual Differences*, 51, 667–73.

Schnell, T., Höge, T., and Pollet, E. (2013). "Predicting meaning in work: Theory, data, implications." *The Journal of Positive Psychology*, 8, 543–54.

Sen, A. K. (1993). "Capability and wellbeing." In M. C. Nussbaum and A. K. Sen (eds.), *The Quality of Life*, pp. 30–53. Oxford: Clarendon Press.

Shershow, S. C. (2005). *The Work and the Gift*. London and Chicago: Chicago University Press.

Smith, A. (1999 [1776]). *The Wealth of Nations*. London: Penguin Books.

Smith, M. L. and Seward, C. (2009). "The relational ontology of Amartya Sen's capability approach: Incorporating social and individual causes." *Journal of Human Development and Capabilities*, 10, 213–35.

Spencer, D. A. (2009). "The 'work as bad' thesis in economics: Origins, evolution, and challenges." *Labor History*, 50, 39–57.

Tajfel, H. and Turner, J. C. (1986). The social identity theory of intergroup behavior. *Psychology of Intergroup Relations*, 5, 7–24.

Wolf, S. (2010). *Meaning in Life and Why It Matters*. Princeton, NJ: Princeton University Press.

Wrzesniewski, A., LoBuglio, N., Dutton, J. E., and Berg, J. M. (2013). "Job crafting and cultivating positive meaning and identity in work." *Advances in Positive Organizational Psychology*, 1, 281–302.

Yeoman, R. (2014a). *Meaningful Work and Workplace Democracy: A philosophy of work and a politics of meaningfulness*. Basingstoke: Palgrave Macmillan.

Yeoman, R. (2014b). "Conceptualising meaningful work as a fundamental human need." *Journal of Business Ethics*, 125, 235–51.

PART I

THE
PHILOSOPHY
OF MEANINGFUL
WORK

CHAPTER 1

THE MORAL CONDITIONS OF WORK

JOANNE B. CIULLA

Neither Famine nor disaster ever haunt men who do true justice; but lightheartedly they tend the fields which are all their care.

Hesiod, eighth century BCE (Hesiod, 2008)

THERE is little that is self-evident about the concept of meaningful work. What is it? Is it something you get or something you find or make? How do you know when you have it? Does everyone want it? Does everyone need it? Does everyone have a right to it? Is it unethical to not have meaningful work? Moreover, who decides what it is? Is it something that rests in "the eye of the beholder"? Such questions drag us into a maze of philosophical speculation. Yet, wandering in this maze can be quite useful for understanding what separates meaningful work from ethical work. While some aspects of meaningful work are socially constructed and dependent on context, the values of a culture, and the values and preferences of individuals—the basic ethical conditions of work—are not. No matter who you are, where you are, or what kind of work you do, certain moral conditions apply.

In this chapter, I argue that by separating ethical work or the moral conditions of work from the concept of meaningful work, we avoid some of the problems with objective and subjective characterizations of it. By ethical work or the moral conditions of work, I am talking about such things as whether an employer respects the autonomy of employees, treats them fairly, pays a living wage, offers reasonable working hours, and does not engage in practices that cause physical or mental harm to employees. I want to show how the ethics of a workplace, while related to meaningful work, are neither necessary nor sufficient conditions for meaningful work. They are, however, important for being able to seek meaning in work and life.

THE MEANINGS OF WORK

Let us begin by examining the meaning of work. The problem with the word "work" is that it can mean just about any activity and any product of an activity. It comes from the Old English noun *woerc* and verb *wyrcan*, which date back to the tenth century. A now obsolete definition of work characterizes it as "Action (of a person) in general; doings deeds conduct" (OED, 1933: 285). *The Oxford English Dictionary* offers nine pages of definitions of work. Its first definition is only a bit more specific: "something that is or was done; what a person does or did; an act, deed, proceeding, business" (OED, 1933). *The Random House Dictionary* weighs in with fifty-four definitions and starts with a more physical definition, "exertion or effort directed to produce or accomplish something; labor; toil" (Random House, 1987: 2188–9), while *Webster's New Unabridged Dictionary* gives forty-five definitions. Its first one portrays work with a teleological twist: "bodily or mental effort exerted to do or make something, purposeful activity; labor; toil" (Webster's, 1983: 2107). These tallies of definitions do not even include compound words, such as workday, workbook, work bag. Since work refers to so many kinds of activities, determining what constitutes meaningful work can be daunting. Furthermore, the same activity can be work for one person and play for another. A group of children playing soccer is play, whereas a professional soccer team playing a match is work. Aristotle characterizes work as a necessary activity and leisure as a free activity. Work is an activity that has to be done, for a particular reason and often at a particular time and in a particular place. The necessity may also be internal to the person—"I must express myself through my art"—or external—"I have to be at work between 9 and 5."

Slavery represents the most extreme form of necessity. Free people work for a living; the slave works to stay alive. Aristotle says slavery makes people less than human because they are unable to exercise the capacities that make humans distinct from brute beasts, such as the ability to make choices, deliberate, and plan for the future (Aristotle, 1984c: 1999). Slaves, he says, have no share in happiness because they have no control over their lives (Aristotle, 1984c: 2032). Despite his chilling description of a slave, Aristotle notes that the most effective way to motivate slaves is to offer them their freedom as a prize sometime in the future (Aristotle, 1984a: 2132). He says that once slaves gain their freedom, they recover their humanity, which includes their ability to choose and plan for the future. How many workers in the world today lack the ability to decide and deliberate at work? And among them, how many are engaged in employment that is so tenuous and pays so little that they lack the ability to plan for the future?

Aristotle also realized that personality affects how people approach life. He observed that some people have slavish personalities because they do not want to make their own choices (Aristotle, 1984c). Henry Ford made a similar point when he said that some people are not cut out to do creative work (Yeoman, 2014). This raises some of the same questions we find in the philosophical discussion of meaningful work. Is there meaningful work for people who simply want to be told what to do and get paid at the end of the week? What if some people simply neither want nor need meaningful work? Are they misguided? Do they need to be set straight, or are there external factors that made them this way that need to be changed? Moreover, can such people lead meaningful lives?

THE MEANING OF LEISURE

Leisure offers us another way to think about the nature of work. According to Aristotle, leisure consists of activities that are freely chosen and good in themselves and for no other purpose. Listening to music for pure enjoyment is one such pursuit. Aristotle believed that leisure was necessary for human happiness. He said we conduct business (or are "unleisurely") so that we can have leisure (Aristotle, 1984b: 1861). Leisure brings out what is best and most distinctive about our humanity, such as our ability to think, feel, reflect, create, and learn. He said we need education to learn how to use our leisure and we need leisure to develop wisdom. Aristotle's ideal of leisure sounds a bit like meaningful work.

The word "school" is derived from the Greek word for leisure, *skolé*. The Latin word for leisure is *otium*. In both languages, the word for work is simply the negation of the word for leisure, *ascholia* and *negotium* or "not leisure" (Pieper, 1952: 27). This is also true in contemporary Spanish where *negocio*, the word for business, means "no leisure." The Greek, Latin, and Spanish words compare work to leisure as if to say that leisure is the center of life. The English word "leisure" captures its association with freedom. It comes from the Latin term *licere*, which means "to be permitted." It is as if work is the center of life and leisure is when we are "permitted" to stop working and do what we want. As the British essayist G. K. Chesterton quipped, there are three parts to leisure. "The first is being allowed to do something. The second is being allowed to do anything and the third (and perhaps most rare and precious) is being allowed to do nothing" (Chesterton, 1929: 130). Looking at language reveals how culture can determine where people look for meaningful things to do in life.

This takes us back to the original problem with the meaning of work. It refers to all types of activities, whether they are part of paid employment or free time. Sociologist Sebastian de Grazia notes that few people know how to use their leisure to do meaningful things because they need the structure of employment, education, or other factors (de Grazia, 1962: 266). The other reason people today may not cultivate meaningful work in their free time is because they spend most of their waking hours working and lack the energy and perhaps the will to do meaningful work on their days off. Maybe the inability of people to use their free time as Aristotelian leisure is why we look to work for meaning.

FREEDOM AND NECESSITY

This discussion of work and leisure offers a way to narrow down the idea of meaningful work. The reason why it is such a complicated idea is because when most people write about it, they write about paid employment, which is an activity that is always tied to necessity in a way that leisure activities are not. Paid employment involves necessity but it is also associated with three freedoms—freedom to work, freedom at work, and freedom from work (Ciulla, 2000: 75). We may freely choose to work for a company, but in doing so, we do not always freely choose to do everything that is required of us—i.e. some days we may prefer to sleep late rather than show up on time. We also need to have the freedom to not work, something that the slave and sometimes even employees do not have because they fear getting fired.

The question here is whether the necessity of most work arrangements is a serious constraint on a person's freedom (such as not being able to sleep late), or simply a characteristic of moral action, such as having a duty to show up on time. Christine Korsgaard characterizes the latter this way: "when we actually choose the particular actions demanded of us, we often manifestly do not want to do them. And yet we do them, all the same: the normativity of obligation is, among other things, a psychological force," which is what Kant calls necessitation (Korsgaard, 2009: 3).

The nature of the job limits our freedom and autonomy, and the agreements that we make with employers create a moral obligation to live up to the terms of employment. Hence, the real challenge of characterizing meaningful work is not about work that we might freely do during our leisure, it is grappling with the constrained autonomy of paid work and how these constraints affect our ability to lead meaningful lives (see Brief and Nord, 1990: 171–99). The question of meaningful paid work is important today, first, because we spend most of our lives working. Second, not everyone has the time and the ability to use their freedom to engage in the Aristotelian ideal of leisure. And third, people have different values, capacities, and live in different social contexts.

OBJECTIVE AND SUBJECTIVE MEANINGS

The idea of work is easier to pin down than the idea of meaningful work. Meaning is internal or subjective—people differ on what they find meaningful. Yet it is also external or objective in that what goes on in the world shapes what we do and do not find meaningful. A subjectivist approach to meaning says that people determine meaningful conditions and that they have a favorable attitude toward wanting, getting, or setting a goal of achieving something (Metz, 2001). Richard Taylor (1991) uses the example of Sisyphus to illustrate the subjectivity of meaningless and meaningful work. Sisyphus is condemned by the gods to spend his life pushing a large stone up a hill. The stone is so big that he never gets it to the top and it rolls back down. His punishment is meaningless work and a meaningless existence. The basic story of Sisyphus focuses on the nature of his task and the way that he experiences the task as punishment.

Taylor then offers two other variations on the story. Suppose the stone gets to the top of the hill and then it is used to build a temple that will last for the ages. Then Sisyphus's labor has a purpose, but Taylor says purpose is not enough—building the pyramids did not make the lives of slaves meaningful. Taylor and others agree that you need more than purpose to make work meaningful (see also Kekes, 1986: 81). Even with a purpose, there is still a problem with all of that rock pushing. Yet, sometimes understanding what your task means to others strengthens your sense of purpose and perhaps makes the work meaningful to you too.

Researchers have studied how purpose motivates workers. In a longitudinal field experiment, Adam Grant et al. studied callers in a fundraising organization. They had one group of callers meet with the grateful beneficiaries of the organization's work, while the control group simply read thank you letters from them. The group that met with the beneficiaries spent 142 percent more time on the phone and raised 71 percent more money than the control group (Grant et al., 2007). Meeting the recipients and hearing their stories animated the purpose of the callers' work and influenced how they went about their work. Their relationship with the recipients made them see what their job meant to others but it may or may not have made it meaningful to the callers.

We might also imagine a woman who is bored with her life, which she has dedicated to running a charity. She only continues with her work because she has nothing else to do. An admirer writes a book about her that extols her dedication and the good that she has done for society. The woman reads the book and discovers that other people think her work is meaningful, but it still does not make it meaningful to her (Ciulla, 2000: 214). This raises the question: if meaningful work is objective, is it possible for someone to do meaningful or meaningless work and not know it? Some humanistic psychologists might say "yes," because their research has found that a "surprisingly high percentage of the population" are what they call existentially indifferent. They do not know, seek, or maybe even care about meaning. Psychologist Tatjana Schnell characterizes existential indifference as "a state of low meaningfulness that is not associated with a crisis of meaning" (Schnell, 2010: 351). The mental health of these people is not worse than that of others and they do not report depression or anxiety. Explaining to existentially indifferent people that their work is meaningful still may not make it so for them.

Taylor's third and more interesting case asks us to imagine that the gods implant Sisyphus with an obsession for rolling stones up hills. Rock pushing becomes his sole desire. He finds it intrinsically good and he is now able to get what he wants out of life. Philosopher Susan Wolf argues that even if Sisyphus finds his work meaningful, the task is still pointless and hence it has no value because it does not "contribute to something bigger than oneself" (Wolf, 2010). For Wolf, meaningful work is objective in the sense that it must have a purpose and a value. She says Sisyphus may be happy but he is not doing meaningful work. Robert Nozick agrees that meaning is not strictly a personal matter. He believes that it depends on how well people connect with things outside themselves that are valuable. For Nozick there are "opportunity costs" to leading a valuable life, however a valuable life leaves something behind (Nozick, 1981: 596). So according to Nozick, the woman who spends her life doing charity leads a valuable life, even if she doesn't think so. Wolf might say that the woman does meaningful work even if she does not find her work meaningful.

Of course, if meaningful work were only objective, then we could say Sisyphus and the charity worker are simply wrong about their assessment of their work. While other people may influence what is meaningful to us, they certainly do not determine it. This is why I agree with Wolf and others that there are subjective and objective aspects to meaningful work, or as Wolf neatly puts it, meaningful activity "occurs when subjective attraction meets objective attractiveness" (Wolf, 1997: 224). In the above cases the subjective attraction does not meet the objective attraction. Whether people find their work meaningful depends on what they bring to the table and where their table sits in the world. It depends on personal values and personal qualities such as personality, emotional makeup, education, imagination, curiosity, etc. When something is meaningful, we use our energy and resources to do what we think is important to us—actions that help us understand who we are (Wolf, 1997: 212–13).

THE MEANING OF A PAYCHECK

Some people care more about the meaning of their paycheck and the life that it allows them to live than the meaning of the work that they do. This leads us to the question: does pay compensate for meaningless work? To answer this, consider yet another variation of the Sisyphus story. Suppose the gods pay Sisyphus to push the rock up the hill every day and Sisyphus uses the money to support his family. He is still not free, his work is still pointless, but his compensation has a point. This gets us much closer to what "meaningless work" means for many people. Women employed in a sweatshop may do the same task over and over again but the problem with sweatshops is not the meaningless work, it is the poor treatment of employees and wages that barely keep them and their families alive. These are problems with the moral conditions of work, they are not about meaningful work.

The instrumental value of a meaningless job raises the question of whether it is possible for someone to do meaningless work and use the pay from it to lead a meaningful life? Philosopher Ruth Yeoman argues that this kind of compensation argument fails (Yeoman, 2014). She thinks that there are objective conditions for meaningful work and points to numerous studies that show how meaningless work deprives people of the opportunity to develop their capabilities, which can lead to a variety of social, physical, and mental harms. She says that meaningless work affects an employee's autonomy, their ability to exercise judgment, and it undermines their sense of self-efficacy in the world. Lastly, Yeoman draws on literature on the psychology of work and organizational studies to argue that meaningful work is important for our ability to experience well-being and engage in respectful and meaningful relationships with others. Yeoman says that meaningful work should provide people with dignity, autonomy, and freedom, and concludes that meaningful work is a fundamental human need. I agree with Yeoman that work that inflicts the harms that she outlines is wrong, not because the work is meaningless but mainly because of the way these employees are treated on the job. While I agree that people find dignity, autonomy, and freedom in meaningful work, we can also imagine an employer who treats employees with dignity and gives them freedom and autonomy on a job that involves doing a mindless and repetitive task. You can have the moral aspects of Yeoman's meaningful work without actually engaging in interesting or meaningful work, and the reverse is also true.

Yeoman also points out that because of various social factors, there is an unfair distribution of meaningful work that affects the development of capabilities in people and diminishes their well-being. In a similar vein, Adina Schwartz argues that if "a just society respects all members as autonomous agents," then society should not allow mind-numbing industrial labor that undercuts self-esteem, personal autonomy, and the ability of people to pursue good lives (Schwartz, 1982: 635). Samuel Arnold also makes a social justice argument that it does not matter whether you are talking about white- or blue-collar work; he believes that there can be permissible occupational equalities as long as workers can share in the goods of job "complexity, authority, and responsibility" (Arnold, 2012). He focuses on changing what John Rawls calls the "powers and prerogatives of offices and positions of responsibility and authority in the workplace" (Arnold, 2012: 95). This too gets at questions about power, justice, respect for persons, and the morality of the way that work is structured. Arnold believes that work can be rearranged so that employers eliminate division of labor that makes a job mindless, hierarchy that makes workers powerless, and provide autonomy over their work which gives them responsibility. By changing the moral conditions and power structures of organizations, Arnold thinks even boring jobs can be made better, but he also wants to make the work itself more complex or interesting.

The arguments against pay as compensation for meaningless work center on the concern that meaningless work diminishes the development of our capabilities and our ability to lead meaningful lives. While I agree that meaningful work can make life better, I am not ready to say that its absence keeps people from leading meaningful lives. In real terms, what people get paid for their work often has more of a positive impact on their lives than what they do on the job. It is interesting to note that Schwartz's paper, written in 1982, uses empirical studies from the late 1970s and early 1980s to support her arguments. Back then, there was still a large number of unionized industrial workers in America. It is ironic that in the twenty-first century, some of these former industrial workers long to go back to the "meaningless work" in those factories because they were paid better than the jobs that are available to them now and they were protected by unions. Many of these displaced industrial workers even voted for a president who unrealistically promised that they would get their old jobs back. With what they earned, twentieth-century American industrial workers were able to buy houses, send their children to college, and go on vacation. While their lives might have been better if they did not have to do mind-numbing work, these industrial workers did not appear to lead meaningless lives.

Writing in the later part of the twentieth century, psychologist Frederick Herzberg found that job satisfaction and dissatisfaction are not opposites, but separate things. Job satisfaction is a function of the content or the intrinsic value of the job that you do—this is related to meaningful work. Dissatisfaction with work is usually a function of external factors, which he called hygiene factors, such as inadequate pay, dirty or unsafe working conditions, and mean and disrespectful managers—this is related to the ethical conditions of work (Herzberg, 1966). If you improved the hygiene factors of the workplace, offered better pay and benefits, a physically pleasing workplace, and understanding managers, workers would *not* be dissatisfied. Unions addressed these hygiene factors, which are the moral conditions of work such as safety, fair pay, work hours, and benefits. When managers abused employees, the unions stood up for them. While not morally perfect, unions mitigated the asymmetry of power between employers and employees.

THE MORAL CONDITIONS OF WORK

The case of industrial workers in America and Herzberg's distinction between the intrinsic value of the job and hygiene factors lead to what I think is the real problem with understanding meaningful work. If you set aside the factors related to job design such as complexity, creativity, and discretion over the tasks of work, most of the factors in the objective assessment of meaningful work are really about the moral conditions of work. They include everything from being treated fairly and with respect, to having personal autonomy on the job, to working in safe environments. When an employer exploits employees and forces them to work sixty hours a week, when managers harass employees and treat them like mindless children, and when employees have no say in how they do their job, they go home beaten and broken, not because their work is meaningless but because the conditions of their employment are mean (Arnold and Bowie, 2003).

Yet, we still cannot underestimate the meaning of earning a wage and, more importantly, earning a living wage. Consider the immigrant who works two meaningless full-time jobs to build a better life for her children. If the two jobs yield a living wage, there is hope. The fact that one full-time job does not allow her to live is a far more serious problem than the nature of her job. The nineteenth-century designer William Morris said that work can be either a "lightening to life" or a "burden to life." The difference lies in the fact that in the first case there is hope, while in the second there is none. According to Morris, hope makes people want to work and it makes work worth doing. He says, "Worthy work carries with it the *hope* of pleasure in rest, the *hope* of pleasure in our using what it makes, and the *hope* of pleasure in our daily creative skill" (Morris, 1985 [1885]: 21). We can translate this list as time off, or freedom from work, the ability to buy things, and freedom at work. Of the three, the last is about meaningful work while the first two are about the moral conditions of employment and wages. On Morris's account, the immigrant does not do worthy work, but she does it for a worthy reason.

The moral conditions of work make a job worthy of having a human being do it. The practical and/or moral value of a job make it worthwhile or worth spending time doing. Yet, as I have been arguing, while worthy and worthwhile work may facilitate or accompany meaningful work, they are not always necessary and they are never sufficient conditions for it (Ciulla, 2012: 115–31). As Metz notes, "it is plausible to think that Van Gogh's life was made more meaningful by posthumous recognition and appreciation, but that the later did not make his tormented life any more worthwhile" (Metz, 2012: 446).

Moreover, some of the same harms of doing meaningless work are even worse for people who do not have the freedom to work because of the economy, the limitations of their education, or other factors. Sociologist William Julius Wilson observes that when work is scarce, people not only suffer from poverty, they "lose their feeling of connectedness to work in the formal economy; they no longer expect work to be a reg-ular and regulating force in their lives" (Wilson, 1996: 52). Wilson says when jobless people live in low-employment neighborhoods, they lose their perception of self-efficacy or their belief that they can take steps to achieve goals required in a certain situation (Wilson, 1996: 75). So according to Wilson, work itself means more than just meeting material needs. It also satisfies various psychological and social needs such as disci-pline, connectedness, regularity, and self-efficacy. Hence, when we consider the idea of meaningful work, we should not ignore the meaning of working. Getting paid a living wage for work and working forty hours a week or less has significance in that it opens up a space for hope and maybe something more (Ciulla, 2000).

THE MORAL AND THE MEANINGFUL

I have been illustrating why many of the factors that philosophers discuss in regard to meaningful work are really about the ethical conditions of work. The ethical factors of meaningful work are objective and universal. It is always wrong to treat people unfairly and without respect, make them do things or work long hours that are dangerous to their physical and mental health, and place excessive constraints on their freedom and autonomy. This is true for workers who are employed to do interesting, valuable, and creative tasks and those who do mindlessly boring ones. Most theories of meaningful work are normative theories about the conditions of work in addition to subjective and objective assessments of the types and aspects of work that make it meaningful (see, for example, Roessler, 2012).

The moral conditions under which people work have always had an impact on people's lives—from the forced labor of slaves, to the deskilling of labor during the industrial rev-olution, to today's on-demand and contract workers (Todolí-Signes, 2017). Throughout history, employers have intentionally or unintentionally undercut, eliminated, or tried to manipulate meaningful work. As Karl Marx said, labor under capitalism alienates people from their work and their species essence (Marx, 2005). Employers rarely design jobs so that they require the intelligence, creativity, and judgment of employees unless they are convinced that this will up productivity, lower costs, and/or increase profits. While some employers have the imagination to see beyond the narrow confines of efficiency into the ways that they can get profit by making the work interesting, this has not always been the case (Barley and Bechky, 2017). Our technology created what used to be called "labor saving devices." The steam engine eliminated skilled weavers, computers and robotics and disruptive technologies have the potential to put out of work everyone from teachers and hospital caregivers to fast-food workers and taxi drivers (Veltman, 2015). Jean-Jacques Rousseau said man fell from the golden age when he learned to use the labor of others (Rousseau, 1968). Work is and always has been a struggle for employers to control workers and the work process and get the most amount of work out of the least number of people. Many of the moral problems with work come from this struggle. Employers seem to have been moving toward machines and robots ever since the time when slaves were referred to as "*instrumentum vocale*" or talking tools.

Conclusion: Meaningful Lives

Perfectionist accounts of meaningful work implicitly or explicitly include a vision of what it means to be human, the good life, well-being, and morality. Some perfections focus on human goods. They hold "that what is good for its own sake for a person is fixed independently of her attitudes and opinions toward it, that it constitutes an ideal way to live that an individual might attain to a greater or lesser extent, and that in principle cardinal interpersonal comparison of the amount of good that different individuals achieve for themselves over the course of their lives is possible" (Arneson, 2000: 38). The problem with all forms of perfectionism comes down to two basic questions: Who says so? and What if I don't want to live this way? (Hepburn, 1999). As academics who write on this topic, we have to keep in mind that not everyone wants a job like ours.

What I have been doing in this chapter is separating the moral conditions of work from the tasks of work, the subjectivity of the people who do them, and external assessments of meaningful work based on purpose and value. The reason why this is important is because the moral conditions of work are not subjective—they apply to all kinds of jobs whether they involve pushing rocks up hills or saving children's lives. The moral conditions of work determine whether people go home from work feeling like they have been treated fairly, in good health, and with their self-esteem, autonomy, and dignity intact. Earning a living wage and having time off to do other things with their lives are also moral conditions because they respect the right of people to do more than merely keep themselves alive. When the moral conditions of work are met, people are capable of engaging in the pursuit of meaning. Whether they pursue or find meaning inside or outside of work, is up to them.

Because of the subjectivity of meaningful work, the primary obligation of employers is to provide the moral conditions for employees to be capable of finding meaning in their work and/or outside of work in their lives. The question of what makes certain types of work meaningful in itself is partially an empirical and objective question about job design, purpose, what people and society value, and the types and aspects of work that they find meaningful. How and what we find meaningful is a philosophical and psychological question about value, purpose, and how we make sense of ourselves as we interact with and affect the world around us. When we find something meaningful, it lights up and enriches our lives (Ciulla, 2000).

One of the questions that still needs to be explored is: What will meaningful work be like in a future where work is scarce and meaningful work is scarcer (Smith and Anderson, 2014)? Imagine that technology becomes so advanced that robots and computers do almost everything and countries give their citizens a guaranteed basic income because it is no longer possible to give everyone a job (Van Parijs, 2004). If that were to happen, what kinds of social and educational institutions would we need to help people develop the capacity to use their freedom from work to structure their lives and engage in activities that they find meaningful?

In his delightful book *The Grasshopper*, philosopher Bernard Suits imagines a utopia where people are treated well and no longer have to work. He argues that without work, we would eventually end up inventing work games (Suits, 1978). The carpenter would invent house-building games and the scientist would invent discovery games, even though there was no need to build houses and all scientific discoveries had already been made. Suits believes that in this utopia, work activities would become like games because people would freely choose to do them, for their own sake and not for some outside purpose. Would these intrinsically engaging activities be meaningful work or go beyond the goals of the game? For example, the game of golf has a goal not a purpose. The goal of golf is to win or do well by hitting balls into eighteen little holes using the fewest number of shots. Suits's example reminds us that work, unlike games, is necessary in that it is done for some broader purpose. So, even though meaningful work is mostly subjective, we see that purpose is fundamental to the concept of work and by extension, it is a fundamental part of meaningful work as well. By separating out the moral conditions of work from meaningful work, we are better able to focus on the objective and subjective ways that people experience and evaluate purpose and meaning in their work.

REFERENCES

Aristotle. (1984a). "Economics," translated by E. S. Forester. In J. Barnes (ed.), *The Complete Works of Aristotle*, Vol. II, pp. 2130–51. Princeton: Princeton University Press.

Aristotle. (1984b). "Nicomachean ethics," translated by W. D. Ross. In J. Barnes (ed.), *The Complete Works of Aristotle*, Vol. II, pp. 1729–1867. Princeton: Princeton University Press.

Aristotle. (1984c). "Politics," translated by B. Jowett. In J. Barnes (ed.), *The Complete Works of Aristotle*, Vol. II, pp. 1986–2129. Princeton: Princeton University Press.

Arneson, R. J. (2000). "Perfectionism and politics." *Ethics*, 111(1), 37–63.

Arnold, D. G. and Bowie, N. E. (2003). "Sweatshops and respect for persons." *Business Ethics Quarterly*, 13(2), 221–42.

Arnold, S. (2012). "The difference principle at work." *Journal of Political Philosophy*, 20(1), 94–118.

Barley, S. R. and Bechky, B. A. (2017). "The changing nature of work: Careers, identities, and work lives in the 21st century." *Academy of Management Discoveries*, 3(2), 111–15.

Brief, A. P. and Nord, W. R. (1990). "Work and non-work connections." In A. P. Brief and W. R. Nord (eds.), *Meanings of Occupational Work*, pp. 171–99. Lanham, MD: Lexington Books.

Chesterton, G. K. (1929). "On leisure." In G. K. Chesterton, *Generally Speaking*, pp. 127–31. New York: Bernhard Tauchnitz.

Ciulla, J. B. (2000). *The Working Life: The promise and betrayal of modern work*. New York: Times Business.

Ciulla, J. B. (2012). "Worthy work and Bowie's Kantian theory of meaningful work." In D. Arnold and J. Harris (eds.), *Kantian Business Ethics: Critical perspectives*, pp. 115–31. Cheltenham: Edward Elgar.

de Grazia, S. (1962). *Of Time Work and Leisure*. New York: Twentieth Century Fund.

Grant, A. M., Campbell, E., Chen, G., Cottone, K., Lapedis, D., and Lee, K. (2007). "Impact and the art of motivation maintenance: The effects of contact with beneficiaries on persistence behavior." *Organizational Behavior and Human Decision Processes*, 103, 53–67.

Hepburn, R. W. (1999). "Questions about the meaning of life." In E. D. Klemke (ed.), *The Meaning of Life*, 2nd edn., pp. 261–76. New York: Oxford University Press.

Herzberg, F. (1966). *Work and the Nature of Man*. New York: T. Y. Crowell.

Hesiod. (2008). *Hesiod, the Homeric Hymns, and Homerica*. Urbana, IL: Project Gutenberg. Available at: http://www.gutenberg.org/ebooks/348 [accessed April 5, 2018].

Kekes, J. (1986). "The informed will and the meaning of life." *Philosophy and Phenomenological Research*, 67(1), 75–90.

Korsgaard, C. M. (2009). *Self-Constitution: Agency, identity, and integrity*. New York: Oxford University Press.

Marx, K. (2005). "Economic and philosophic manuscripts of 1844." In F. Engels (ed.), *Karl Marx and Frederick Engels, Collected Works*, Vol. 3, pp. 229–346. New York: International Publishers.

Metz, T. (2001). "The concept of a meaningful life." *American Philosophical Quarterly*, 38(2), 137–53.

Metz, T. (2012). "The meaningful and the worthwhile: Clarifying the relationships." *The Philosophical Forum*, 43(4), 435–48.

Morris, W. (1985 [1885]). "Useful work and useless toil." In *Socialist Platform Number 2*. London. Socialist League Office.

Nozick, R. (1981). *Philosophical Explanations*. Oxford: Oxford University Press.

OED (1933). *Oxford English Dictionary*, Vol. 12. Oxford: Clarendon Press.

Pieper, J. (1952). *Leisure: The basis of culture*. New York: Pantheon Books.

Random House (1987). *Random House Dictionary of the English Language*, 2nd edn. New York: Random House.

Roessler, B. (2012). "Symposium: Political Philosophy at Work: Meaningful Work: Arguments from Autonomy." *Journal of Political Philosophy*, 20(1), 71–93.

Rousseau, J.-J. (1968). *The Social Contract*, translated by G. D. H. Cole. New York: Penguin Books for Philosophy.

Schnell, T. (2010). "Existential indifference: Another quality of meaning in life." *Journal of Humanistic Psychology*, 50(3), 315–73.

Schwartz, A. (1982). "Meaningful work." *Ethics*, 92(4), 634–46.

Smith, A. and Anderson, J. (2014). "AI, robotics, and the future of jobs." *Pew Research Center* [website], 6 August: http://www.pewinternet.org/2014/08/06/future-of-jobs/ [accessed July 10, 2017].

Suits, B. (1978). *The Grasshopper: Games, life and utopia*. Toronto: University of Toronto Press.

Taylor, R. (1991). *Good and Evil*, rev. edn. New York: Prometheus Books.

Todolí-Signes, A. (2017). "The 'Gig Economy': Employee, self-employed or the need for special employment regulation?" *Transfer: European Review of Labour and Research*, 23(2), 193–205.

Van Parijs, P. (2004). "Basic income: A simple and powerful idea for the twenty-first century." *Politics and Society*, 32(1), 7–39.

Veltman, A. (2015). "Is meaningful work available to all people?" *Philosophy and Social Criticism*, 41(7), 725–47.

Webster's (1983). *Webster's New Unabridged Dictionary*, 2nd edn. New York: Simon & Schuster.

Wilson, W. J. (1996). *When Work Disappears: The world of the new urban poor*. New York: Alfred A. Knopf.

Wolf, S. (1997). "Happiness and meaning: Two aspects of the good life." *Social Philosophy and Policy*, 14(1), 207–25.

Wolf, S. (2010). *Meaning in Life and Why it Matters*. Princeton, NJ: Princeton University Press. Available at Google Books: https://books.google.com/books?id=_eoPB9zLXFoC& printsec=frontcover&dq=meaning+in+life+and+why+it+matters&hl=en&sa=X&ved= 0ahUKEwiYhKGvs_HbAhXQx1kKHUn3Bf4Q6AEIJzAA#v=onepage&q=meaning%20 in%20life%20and%20why%20it%20matters&f=false [accessed June 26, 2018].

Yeoman, R. (2014). "Conceptualizing meaningful work as a fundamental human need." *Journal of Business Ethics*, 125(2), 235–51.

CHAPTER 2

....

DIGNITY AND
MEANINGFUL WORK

....

NORMAN E. BOWIE

FOR many, work is something unpleasant one must do in order to obtain the necessities of life as well as the goods and services one needs for a life of quality. This view of work as a necessary drudgery has a long history. The Bible reports that when Adam and Eve are expelled from the Garden of Eden, one of the burdens Adam would have to bear is hard work—"by the sweat of your face you shall eat bread." At the beginning of the industrial age, when manufacturing could take advantage of the division of labor, none other than Adam Smith, who had extolled the efficiency of the pin factory, had this to say about work in such factories.

> The man whose life is spent in performing a few simple operations, of which the effects are, perhaps, always the same, has no occasion to exert his understanding, or to exercise his invention in finding out expedients for removing difficulties which never occur. He naturally loses, therefore, the habit of such exertion, and generally becomes as stupid and ignorant as it is possible for a human creature to become. The torpor of his mind renders him, not only incapable of relishing or bearing a part in any rational conversation but of conceiving any generous, noble, or tender sentiment, and consequently of forming any just judgment concerning many even of the ordinary duties of private life. Of the great and extensive interests of his country he is altogether incapable of judging... His dexterity at his own particular trade seems, in this manner, to be acquired at the expense of his intellectual, social and martial virtues. But in every improved and civilized society, this is the state into which the laboring poor, that is the great body of people, must necessarily fall, unless government takes some pains to prevent it.[1]

Clearly the workers Smith described have neither meaningful work nor dignity.

Even in the twenty-first century, many throughout the world labor at jobs which provide neither dignity nor meaning. Even in advanced societies, an unfavorable attitude to work is captured in such phrases as TGIF (Thank God it's Friday), Blue Monday, and

---

[1] Smith (1976 [1776]: part II, 303). For those using other editions, see Book V Chapter 1, article 2nd "Of the Expense of the Institutions for the Education of Youth."

Hump Day (Wednesday is half way to Friday). Thus, despite the vast of amount of time that most human beings spend at work, work is seen by many as without meaning.

WORK AND DIGNITY

But does it have to be this way? There are many occupations, often identified as callings, where work is meaningful because it gives a sense of purpose to one's life. The professions, first responders, healthcare providers more generally, teachers, and even athletes find their work to be meaningful and to provide them with dignity. The key to a change in perspectives about work is dignity. Dignity holds a central position in any consideration of meaningful work. On the one hand, dignity provides a normative justification for an obligation on managers and others to provide meaningful work. Because persons have, as Kant said, a "dignity beyond price," (Kant, 1990 [1785]: 51) and because work holds such an essential place in the lives of most people, workers are entitled to the most meaningful work that can be practically provided. On the other hand, meaningful work allows people to achieve dignity, and thus meaningful work is a key component in individual self-actualization. Thus dignity provides the ground for an obligation to provide meaningful work and dignity is what workers achieve when they have the opportunity to engage in meaningful work. Understanding what human dignity is and how it can be achieved helps provide criteria as to what constitutes meaningful work. These essential points about the relation between dignity and meaningful work are well recognized by a number of leading classical and contemporary thinkers.

Despite the Biblical injunction that you must earn your bread by the sweat of your brow, Catholic social teaching has insisted that work can be a means to human dignity so long as the workplace is organized so as to be supportive of meaningful work. In 1891 Pope Leo XIII issued his encyclical *Rerum Novarum* (On Capital and Labor). That document is primarily addressed to the rights and duties regarding the ownership of property. However, with respect to the relation between the employer and the employee the document says:

> The following duties bind the wealthy owner and the employer: not to look upon their work people as their bondsmen, but to respect in every man his dignity as a person ennobled by Christian character. They are reminded that according to natural reason and Christian philosophy, working for gain is creditable not shameful to a man, since it enables him to earn an honorable livelihood; but to misuse men as though they were things in the pursuit of gain, or to value them solely for their physical powers—that is truly shameful and inhumane.
>
> (Pope Leo XIII, 2002 [1981]: paragraph 20)

The papal encyclical that is most explicit concerning the dignity of work is Pope John Paul II's 1981 papal encyclical *Laborem Exercens*:

> it [work] is a good thing for man. It is good not only in the sense it is useful or something to enjoy; it is also good as being something worthy, that is to say, something

that corresponds to man's dignity, that expresses this dignity and increases it... Work is a good thing for man—a good thing for his humanity—because through work man not only transforms nature adapting it to his own needs, but he also achieves fulfillment as a human being, and indeed, in a sense, becomes "more a human being."

(Pope John Paul II, 1981: #9)

Classical philosophers throughout the eighteenth century did not write much that was explicitly about meaningful work, although they wrote a great deal about human dignity. One could choose from a number of authors, but given Kant's emphasis on dignity, perhaps an exploration of Kant's position on dignity and work deserves special emphasis.

KANT'S ACCOUNT OF DIGNITY

Kant is famous for saying that a person possesses a dignity that is beyond all price. Specifically, Kant says:

> In the realm of ends everything has either a price or dignity. Whatever has a price can be replaced by something else as its equivalent; on the other hand, whatever is above all price and therefore admits of no equivalent, has dignity.   (Kant, 1990 [1785]: 51)

But, first, why do persons possess a dignity that is beyond all price? Kant argues that persons have dignity because human beings are capable of autonomy and thus are capable of self-governance. As autonomous beings capable of self-governance, they are also responsible beings, since autonomy and self-governance are conditions for responsibility. A person who is not autonomous and who is not capable of self-governance cannot be responsible. That's why little children or the mentally ill are not considered responsible beings. Thus there is a conceptual link between being a human being, being an autonomous being, being capable of self-governance, and being a responsible being.

Autonomous responsible beings are capable of making and following their own laws; they are not simply subject to the causal laws of nature. Human beings are different from billiard balls. Anyone who recognizes that she is autonomous should recognize that she is responsible for her actions and thus she should recognize that she is a moral being. From this Kant argues that the fact that one is a moral being enables us to say that such a being possesses dignity.[2]

> Morality is the condition under which alone a rational being can be an end in himself because only through it is it possible to be a lawgiving member in the realm of ends. Thus morality, and humanity, insofar as it is capable of morality, alone have dignity.   (Kant, 1990 [1785]: 52)

---

[2] This interpretation of Kant's rationale for attributing dignity to persons is consistent with that of Michael Rosen (2012) and with George Kateb (2011).

This emphasis on dignity and respect undercuts the notion that Kant's ethics is primarily an austere ethic of duty. As T. E. Hill puts it:

[For Kant] moral conduct is the practical exercise of the noble capacity to be rational and self-governing; a capacity which sets us apart from the lower animals and gives us dignity. Kant's ethics is as much an ethics of self-esteem as it is an ethics of duty.

(Hill, 1992: 36–7)

But why should a person recognize the dignity of other persons? Now as a point of logic a person who recognizes that he or she is responsible and thus has dignity should ascribe dignity to other people who have the same capacity to be autonomous and responsible beings. As Kant says:

Rational nature exists as an end in itself. Man necessarily thinks of his own existence in this way, and thus far it is a subjective principle of human actions. Also every rational being thinks of his existence on the same rational ground which holds also for myself; thus it is at the same time an objective principle from which, as a supreme practical ground, it must be possible to derive all laws of the will.

(Kant, 1990 [1785]: 36)

This quotation provides Kant's argument for the necessity of including all other persons within the scope of the respect for persons principle (treating the humanity in a person as an end and never as a means only) and for the assertion that all human beings have a dignity that is beyond price. The argument is based on consistency. What we say about ourselves, we must say about similar cases, namely about other human beings.

THE MOST RECENT PERSPECTIVES ON DIGNITY

Although the publication of John Rawls's A Theory of Justice in 1971 legitimized serious philosophical work in normative ethics and political economy, little was written on meaningful work. An exception is Adina Schwartz's 1982 article, "Meaningful Work," where she argued that menial jobs such as those described by Adam Smith in the passage quoted earlier were morally unacceptable because they violated the autonomy of the individuals who performed them (Schwartz, 1982). Although Schwartz did not explicitly adopt a Kantian framework for her analysis, her focus on the violation of individual autonomy is certainly compatible with Kant's account as articulated above.

In her American Philosophical Association presidential address, Professor Linda Zagzebski paid special attention to Kant's account of dignity. She noted two different ways of looking at dignity embedded in Kant's account (Zagzebski, 2016). A person can have dignity because a person has value that is beyond all price. A person has dignity because he or she has infinite value. But a person can also have dignity because each is irreplaceable, since each is unique. Zagzebski then considered whether these two strains are consistent, since the former bases dignity on a common characteristic of human beings while the latter bases dignity on each person's uniqueness. In this chapter we have limited our account of dignity to some common characteristic such as the ability to reason morally as the basis of dignity.

Michael Rosen's contemporary analysis of dignity lists three strands of dignity: 1) dignity as status, 2) dignity as intrinsic value, and 3) dignity as dignified manner or bearing.[3] Kant's account is clearly in the second strand, which is the strand that is most relevant to a discussion of meaningful work. Rosen emphasizes that all three strands have moved toward equality. With respect to the first strand, where dignity was reserved for people of a certain rank or social class, as Rosen points out, as early as Cicero that status was given to all human beings. Thus for our concerns here the first strand collapses into the second. The third strand points to the fact that people who struggle against adversity are described as having dignity.[4] Given the emphasis on providing meaningful work as a means to dignity, our discussion seeks ways to eliminate or at least ameliorate the struggle to obtain dignity in one's job.

George Kateb's (2011) contemporary analysis of dignity, which is very much in the second strand, defends dignity for all individual human beings and for the species of humanity as well. Although Kateb's arguments for the dignity of the species of humanity are interesting and worthy of discussion, our focus on meaningful work can proceed by limiting dignity to individual human beings. With respect to individual human beings, Kateb is very much in the Kantian tradition that the dignity of human beings applies to all human beings equally.

The notion that it is a person's ability to act on grounds of morality (the categorical imperative) that gives human beings dignity has been endorsed by contemporary business ethicists as well. Joseph Margolis recognizes that there are many pressures in business that inhibit employees from doing the right thing. As difficult as it is to overcome these pressures, some employees do in fact resist them. Margolis refers to the moment of resistance as the moment of dignity:

> Human beings must be capable of responding deliberately to ethical challenges even amid tremendous social and psychological pressures. That is what it means, quite literally, to be responsible. Proposals for preserving moral responsibility thus attempt to rescue the moment of dignity: the possibility that in any given episode, a person can still exercise those faculties that identify a human being as distinctively human—faculties that endow each human being with the capacity to develop and pursue purposes.   (Margolis, 2001)

The task for business ethicists and ethical managers is to find and develop those conditions that support action at the moment of dignity. Margolis's analysis is very much in the spirit of Kant, who argues that it is free action motivated by morality that gives a person the dignity that is beyond price.

---

[3] Rosen (2012). See section 1 for a full account.
[4] Rosen (2012). See his discussion of the aesthetic dimension of this strand in his section, "Grace and Dignity," pp. 31–8.

A Kantian Account of Meaningful Work

There is a need at this point to tie Kant's account of dignity and respect for persons to work. First, Kant argues that work is necessary for the development of selfhood:

> Life is the faculty of spontaneous activity, the awareness of all our human powers. Occupation gives us this awareness...Without occupation man cannot live happily. If he earns his bread, he eats it with greater pleasure than if it is doled out to him...Man feels more contented after heavy work than when he has done no work; for by work he has set his powers in motion.   (Kant, 1930 [1775]: 160–1)

Thus it appears that work is a duty that one has to oneself. It contributes to independence and to our self-conception. Although Kant does not say so explicitly, one can infer from his remarks that working provides self-respect.

In addition Kant actually endorses wealth and the pleasure it brings. However, to work simply in order to earn money is to display the vice of miserliness, a vice that is even worse than avarice. So long as work is required to make money so that one can provide for one's needs and pleasures, and in so doing make oneself independent, work has value. Selected comments of Kant's will establish his view.

> A man whose possessions are sufficient for his needs is well-to-do...All wealth is means...for satisfying the owner's wants, free purposes and inclinations...By dependence on others, man loses in worth, and so a man of independent means is an object of respect...But the miser finds a direct pleasure in money itself, although money is nothing but a pure means...The spendthrift is a lovable simpleton, the miser is a detestable fool. The former has not destroyed his better self and might face the misfortune that awaits him with courage, but the latter is a man of poor character.   (Kant, 1930 [1775]: 177, 181, 185)

These selected quotations are from Kant's brief remarks, which amount to less than ten pages and represent student notes from his lectures on ethics in the 1770s, before he had written his more critical works on ethical theory. Nonetheless, they provide a starting point for a Kantian theory of meaningful work and for the obligations of employers with respect to providing it.

In his recent book, *The Thought of Work*, John Budd provides a number of traditional views on the nature of work (Budd, 2011). Many, such as work as freedom, as personal fulfillment, and as identity all provide insights into why work is essential to human dignity. Budd's account of work as occupational citizenship is especially compatible with the Kantian account of meaningful work given here. Budd contends that under the occupational citizenship view:

> From this perspective, workers are citizens who are entitled to decent working and living conditions that are determined by standards of human dignity, not supply and demand, and to meaningful forms of self-determination in the workplace that go beyond the freedom to quit. In other words, workers are entitled to equity—fairness

in the distribution of economic rewards, the administration of employment policies, and the provision of economic security—and voice, which means meaningful participation in workplace decision-making.   (Budd, 2011: 59)

Budd's occupational citizenship view is incompatible with a straightforward market efficiency view that sees workers simply as factors of production that can be hired or fired as their price in the marketplace falls or rises. In Kantian language, workers cannot simply be used as a means to profit for the stockholders. Human beings possess a dignity that makes it immoral to use them simply as a means for the purposes of others.

Given Kant's remarks on work and his ethical philosophy grounded in human dignity, I propose the following conditions of a Kantian theory of meaningful work:[5]

1. Meaningful work is work that is freely chosen and provides opportunities for the worker to exercise autonomy on the job.
2. The work relationship must support the autonomy and rationality of human beings. Work that unnecessarily deadens autonomy or that undermines rationality is immoral.
3. Meaningful work is work that provides a salary sufficient for the worker to exercise her independence and provides for her physical well-being and the satisfaction of some of her desires.
4. Meaningful work is work that enables a person to develop her rational capacities.
5. Meaningful work is work that does not interfere with a person's moral development.
6. Meaningful work is work that is not paternalistic in the sense of interfering with the worker's conception of how she wishes to obtain happiness.

I emphasize that these conditions are not descriptive of how employees or employers would define meaningful work. Rather, these characteristics are normative conditions for meaningful work that I believe can be derived from Kant's moral philosophy and from his explicit comments on work.

Management Practices that Support Meaningful Work

If this definition of meaningful work is accepted, then we must ask what management practices would contribute to providing meaningful work to all employees.[6] What is sought here is a description of a business organization that provides dignity through meaningful work. In their 2015 article, Thomas Donaldson and James Walsh have made

---

[5] These conditions were originally advanced in Bowie (1998).
[6] This section is closely adapted from Bowie (2017), which in turn is adapted from Bowie (1998).

dignity one of the intrinsic values central to the purpose of business. They argue that for a business to honor dignity as an intrinsic value it ought to treat each participant with respect in accordance with what they call a dignity threshold, which they define as "the minimum level of respect accorded to each Business Participant necessary to allow the agglomeration of Benefit to qualify as Business Success" (Donaldson and Walsh, 2015). In what follows I describe a number of business practices that would enable a business to meet and perhaps surpass this dignity threshold.

One practice is open book management—a practice that goes far in giving employees autonomy on the job. This technique, developed by Jack Stack at the Springfield Remanufacturing Company, is not new. Stack's book *The Great Game of Business* was published in 1994, however the book was not a fad. It was updated, expanded, and published again in 2013. The underlying philosophy of open book management is that persons should be treated as responsible autonomous beings. A precondition of such treatment is that employees have the information needed to make responsible decisions. The author of an early book on open book management, John Case, called this "empowerment with brains" (Case, 1995: 85–96).

Under open book management employees are given all the financial information about the company. They are also under a profit-sharing plan where what they make is in large part determined by the profit of the company. With complete information and the proper incentives, employees behave responsibly without the necessity for layers of supervision.

> How does open book management do what it does? The simplest answer is this. People get a chance to act, to take responsibility, rather than just doing their job… No supervisor or department head can anticipate or handle all… situations. A company that hired enough managers to do so would go broke from the overhead. Open book management gets people on the job doing things right. And it teaches them to make smart decisions… because they can see the impact of their decisions on the relevant numbers.   (Case, 1995: 45, 46)

The adoption of practices like open book management would go far toward correcting the asymmetrical information that managers possess and that gives rise to the charge that the employment contract is often deceptive. Any time the firm faces a situation that might involve the layoff of employees, employees as well as managers would have access to all the relevant information. Deception in such circumstances would be much more difficult. Open book management also greatly increases employee autonomy, including autonomy with respect to company ethics programs. Put this all together and what open book management does is to enhance workers' dignity.

Early adherents to open book management at the end of the twentieth century included Herman Miller, Allstate Insurance, and Intel. Toward the end of the first decade of the twenty-first, John Case informed *The Economist* that 100 US firms practiced some form of open book management (*Economist*, 2009).

Does a commitment of providing meaningful work for employees require companies to adopt open book management? "No." There may be other management techniques that contribute to the dignity of employees. For example Jeffrey Pfeffer in his 1994 book, *Competitive Advantage Through People*, identified sixteen human resource practices for managing people successfully. In listing the sixteen practices, it is easy to see how they would make work more meaningful. They include 1) employment security, 2) selectivity in recruiting, 3) high wages, 4) incentive pay, 5) employee ownership, 6) information sharing, 7) participation and empowerment, 8) team and job redesign, 9) training and skill development, 10) cross-utilization and cross-training, 11) symbolic egalitarianism, 12) wage compression, 13) promotion from within, 14), a long-term perspective, 15) the measurement of practices, and 16) an overarching philosophy (Pfeffer, 1994: 100–4). Let us see more specifically how these conditions make work more meaningful and enhance dignity.

So long as business firms provide jobs that provide sufficient wealth, they contribute to the independence and thus to the dignity and self-respect of their employees. The true contribution of capitalism would be that it provides jobs that help provide self-respect. Meaningful work is work that provides an adequate wage. High wages are obvious as a means to this goal. Job security is important for providing job stability, which means that employees with an adequate wage will likely continue to have an adequate wage. Job security is essential because it is necessary for achieving the characteristics of meaningful work as outlined in our definition. Wage compression refers to a policy that reduces large differences in pay between the top officials in the corporation and other employees, as well as differences between individuals at roughly the same functional level. If wage compression were adopted horizontally, the Vice President for Finance would not earn a premium over the Vice President for Personnel as is now the case in most United States companies. The ratio between the pay of top executives and the least well paid in the firm has steadily risen. Wage compression is a way of reversing that trend. Profit sharing is a practical way of helping to achieve that. Another important component of meaningful work is autonomy and independence. Advocates of participation and empowerment in the workplace speak directly to the issue of how autonomy and independence are to be achieved. Participation is a requirement in decisions regarding layoffs if the employment contract is not to be viewed as coercive. That is why a technique like open book management is so effective in supporting meaningful work.

Another requirement of meaningful work is that the work should contribute to the development of employees' rational capacities. Selectivity in recruiting, information sharing, training, and participation either directly or indirectly in the running of the business all contribute to the development of employees' rational capacities. By selecting the right people in the first place, you do not get people who are overqualified for the job. Working on a job for which you are overqualified is usually boring and frustrating because it does not make the best use of your rational capacities. One technique for promoting information sharing is open book management. Providing all employees with the numbers makes them more informed and better decision-makers. Information sharing is facilitated through teams. Teamwork enables us to learn skills and perspectives from other team members. All contribute to tackling a business problem, and as a result of team effort the knowledge base of team members is increased.

Cross-training is a technique that allows employees to do many different jobs. Routine assembly line work is often work that is dull, boring, and repetitive. By training a worker to do many different jobs a firm can eliminate or greatly mitigate the drudgery of assembly line manufacturing. Cross-utilization makes teamwork possible and vice versa. Japan has successfully practiced cross-utilization in its auto plants for decades and this practice has increasingly been adopted by automobile manufacturers in the United States.

One of Kant's imperfect duties is the duty that each of us has to develop our talents. All the management practices discussed in the previous paragraph contribute to skill development which is both valuable in itself and helps meet the obligation to develop our talents.

Symbolic egalitarianism is also necessary for self-respect and is a condition of fairness. It breaks down some of the class barriers that say not only is the work that I do different from yours, but it is more valuable than yours, and thus I am a more valuable person. The person who is doing what is perceived to be inferior work thus loses self-respect and loses it unjustly. A business firm is a cooperative enterprise and thus every task is valuable to the enterprise. Market conditions, and other legitimate factors, may justify the fact that we pay one job category more than another, but these conditions do not justify inequality of respect. Open book management and the use of teams help implement symbolic egalitarianism. Jobs are renamed to provide more respect. Garbage collectors become sanitation workers. Some may think changing the names of jobs is frivolous and so it is if the name changes are not accompanied by many, or at least some, of the human resource practices that contribute to meaningful work. But sensitivity to what a job is called is one aspect of treating employees as an end, and thus one aspect of treating them with respect.

OTHER PERSPECTIVES ON DIGNITY AND MEANINGFUL WORK

This chapter has treated dignity as a quality that human beings possess as a result of being human—usually as a result of having a certain trait such as being created in God's image or possessing reason and free will. Special emphasis has been placed on Kant's view that the capacity for moral reasoning is the trait that provides human dignity.

But there are other views. Some scholars also refer to a dignity that is earned through some action or actions of an individual. In the context of work, dignity would be earned through hard work; dignity is not simply something that human beings possess without any action on their parts. Some have referred to this as contingent dignity (Pirson, Goodpaster, and Dierksmeier, 2016: 466). No doubt one can achieve a kind of dignity in this way. A losing sports team can regain dignity if it defeats a superior team and it is common for an outmatched team to play hard just for the sake of dignity. I would even argue that one should work hard to obtain contingent dignity. Contingent dignity is well accepted in society and is relatively uncontroversial. I have chosen to emphasize the dignity that all human beings have just because they are human because I believe this way of understanding dignity provides dignity even to those who cannot achieve contingent dignity, and that concept of dignity places responsibilities on employers that they would not have if our notion of "dignity" was limited to contingent dignity.

Not everyone would accept the definition of meaningful work proposed here. Let us consider some other possibilities. First, there is a division between those who propose an objective definition of meaningful work and those who provide a subjective definition. The issue between these two camps can be explained as follows. The objectivists argue that work can be meaningful whether or not the worker finds it so. Thus a worker who finds meaning in jobs that violate the criteria for meaningful work is mistaken and he or she is wrong in his or her point of view. Similarly a worker who has a job that meets the criteria for meaningful work but nonetheless does not find the job personally meaningful is mistaken. The subjectivists accuse the objectivists of imposing an account of mean- ingful work on workers and thus disrespecting the viewpoint of the person who is actually experiencing the work environment on the job. The objectivists counter by saying that the conditions that create respect and dignity are empirically determinable and morally grounded. If a person finds meaning in a job that is degrading, the person's consciousness needs to be raised. The happy slave is not engaging in meaningful work that supports dignity and self-respect.[7]

There is also a division among the objectivists; some propose a relatively "thin" theory of meaningful work. The definition used in this chapter is an example of a "thin" theory of meaningful work. Others, such as Joseph DesJardins and Joanne Ciulla support a "thicker" theory of meaningful work. Those supporting the thick theory argue that work is really meaningful only if it is socially useful or "worthy." Two quotations will illustrate the position of the "thick" theorists.[8]

DesJardins says the following:

> I would suggest the following three standards for judging goods and services to distinguish meaningful work from less meaningful work. Meaningful work pro- duces: (a) goods and services that satisfy human needs (rather than preferences); (b) contributes to the common good; and (c) is of high quality.   (DesJardins, 2012: 145)

Joanne Ciulla describes worthy work as follows:

> Worthy work is work that is morally and/or aesthetically valuable. It is objective... Worthy work has a purpose that most people can see is good in some way...The most worthy jobs are those that have worthy purposes. They are jobs in which people

---

[7] Susan Wolf has tried to incorporate elements of both the subjectivist and the objectivist view in her important book *Meaning in Life and Why it Matters*. She calls her position the Fitting Fulfillment View. On that view "a life is meaningful insofar as its subjective attachments are to things or goals that are objec- tively worthwhile" (Wolf, 2010: 34–5). Interestingly, *Meaning in Life and Why it Matters* has nothing to say about "meaningful work" nor much to say about "dignity." Neither term appears in the index of that work.

[8] This discussion of DesJardins and Ciulla is taken from Bowie (2012).

help others, alleviate suffering, eliminate difficult, dangerous, or tedious toil, make someone healthier and happier, aesthetically or intellectually enrich people, or improve the environment in which we all live.   (Ciulla, 2012: 126, 127)

A supporter of the thin theory might find much to be sympathetic with in the DesJardins and Ciulla accounts. For example, many business ethicists have always thought that some occupations were noble, in the sense that the work contributed to a broader social good even if it did not result in high pay. Those who have positions in occupations with the characteristics Ciulla identifies are in fact doing worthy work. Indeed critics of the capitalist wage system would like to see some of those occupations have more respect, which would provide those in these occupations the dignity they deserve. Public school teachers in grades K through 12 are sometimes referred to as mere babysitters—a characterization that demeans both teachers and babysitters. We have all heard the phrase, "If you can't do, teach." Yet teachers are surely doing what Ciulla would characterize as worthy work. Moreover, reformers want more people engaged in worthy work and perhaps technological changes might increase the number of occupations that provide worthy work.

However, supporters of a "thin" account would be reluctant to substitute Ciulla's notion of "worthy work" for a thin concept of "meaningful work" like the one provided here. The "thin" theorists believe the class of meaningful work is larger than the class of worthy work.[9] In the article quoted above, DesJardins speaks disparagingly of those who produce junk food rather than nutritious food and those surgeons who operate to enlarge breasts rather than repair a heart valve. I think DesJardins's negative comments here show the dangers of a more thick theory of the good. When carried to an extreme, it can sound elitist and paternalistic. In the world of business, there is a place for McDonalds isn't there?

But my real disagreement with DesJardins is that his notion is too restrictive. Not all work can meet the thick theory criteria for meaningful work. Surely some jobs need to be directed at satisfying human preferences. Some people make snowmobiles and others make chocolate candy. One could argue that neither of these occupations satisfies human needs as opposed to preferences. Yet these occupations, along with similar ones, can be made more meaningful by having management adopt practices like those outlined earlier. Worthy work is a worthy ideal. Meaningful work is a practical goal—at least that is what the objectivists would argue. To some extent an objectivist could adopt the best of both positions. Nearly all jobs can be made more meaningful but there will always be a wide range of jobs that are not worthy jobs as Ciulla defines "worthy jobs." What I find attractive about the list of business practices that recognize the importance of people for competitive success is that they are nearly universal in the

---

[9] Of course the notion of "worthy jobs" can be stretched to include nearly all jobs. The job of bank teller provides an opportunity for discussion. A bank teller does help people complete business transactions, but is that sufficient to fall under Ciulla's definition of worthy work? Arguably the job of bank teller does not fall under her definition. If so, the kind of business practices endorsed by Pfeffer could make the job of a bank teller more meaningful even if not more worthy.

sense that nearly all jobs can be managed accordingly and when managed in that way nearly all jobs would become more meaningful, and thus the dignity of all workers would be enhanced.

THE FUTURE

Recently there has been an explosion of interest in the impact of robots and artificial intelligence on jobs. What happens to meaningful work and dignity in a world where a large number of people do not have to work at all? Two articles from a Wharton Business School publication point out the stark reality. A piece from November 30 points out that manufacturing output in 2015 was at an all-time high but over the last three and a half decades manufacturers have shed more than 7 million jobs (Wharton Business School, 2016a). Much more stuff was produced with 7 million fewer workers. Of these lost jobs, 80 percent were the result of technology rather than the result of moving facilities overseas. What is true regarding the United States is also true with respect to most developed countries (Wharton Business School, 2016a). Robots endowed with artificial intelligence would be assigned to do much of the work that human beings do now. Recently a *New York Times* piece described a military that used drones with artificial intelligence to track down enemy combatants. No human soldiers would be involved. Technology is far along on driverless cars and trucks. What is the implication of this for commercial truck drivers and insurers who sell auto insurance? (Presumably the self-driving cars are safer than human drivers.) Not even fast-food workers are safe. A San Francisco robotics company has built a robot that can make a hamburger from scratch without any human intervention (Clifford, 2016). What are the implications of all of this? More details are presented in the December 6, 2016 interview with venture capitalist Art Bilger (Wharton Business School, 2016b). Bilger argues that we could lose 47 percent of all jobs within twenty-five years. He asks what our society would be like with a 25 percent, 30 percent, or even 35 percent unemployment rate (Wharton Business School, 2016b).

Some, like Nietzsche, simply find no dignity in work, perhaps because Nietzsche saw workers as necessary slaves for those who use leisure to provide culture.[10] As Nietzsche said: "The misery of toiling men must still increase in order to make the production of the world of art possible to a small number of Olympian men,"[11] If Nietzsche's view were correct, then substituting robots for people and providing a decent standard of living for all would be a plus. However, the contention here is that meaningful work can—and even now in some jobs does—provide people with dignity. If jobs disappear, replacing income is not sufficient because it is not income that provides meaning. One of Budd's frameworks for conceptualizing work was work as identity. Tracing the idea back to Hegel, Marx, and Heidegger—among others—Budd points out that to a great extent our

---

[10] For details on this see Rosen (2012: 42–6).
[11] Nietzsche (1964), quoted in Rosen (2012).

conception of ourselves—our identity—is in large part determined by the job we have. "Thinking about work as identity allows us to consider what makes humans distinctly human" (Budd, 2011: 153). The title of a work by John Danahar (2017) gets the issue exactly right: "Will Life Be Worth Living in a World Without Work?" Another way to make the point is to recognize that work is a source of psychological and social meaning (Budd, 2011: 145). Beyond giving workers a sense of identity, meaningful work is the satisfaction one gets in work whether through the creation of a socially useful product, teamwork, or just the feeling of independence that a meaningful job provides. In that way meaningful work provides dignity and a purpose to life. As Bilger pointed out, "Having a purpose in life is, I think, an important piece of the stability of a society" (Wharton Business School, 2016b).

Suddenly people are asking the right question. Even if the government provided everyone with a basic standard of living—a big if—could those without work still find a path to dignity and self-respect? Is work so essential to a meaningful life that people without work could not obtain self-respect—in part because they could not obtain respect from those who do work? Answers to these questions are elusive and create a major challenge to those who would link work, meaningful work, and dignity.

References

Bowie, N. E. (1998). "A Kantian theory of meaningful work." *Journal of Business Ethics*, 7, 1083–92.

Bowie, N. E. (2012). "A reply to my critics." In D. G. Arnold and J. D. Harris (eds.), *Kantian Business Ethics: Critical perspectives*, pp. 175–90. Cheltenham: Edward Elgar.

Bowie, N. E. (2017). *Business Ethics: A Kantian perspective*. New York: Cambridge University Press.

Budd, J. W. (2011). *The Thought of Work*. Ithaca, NY: Cornell University Press.

Case, J. (1995). *Open Book Management*. New York: HarperCollins.

Ciulla, B. J. (2012). "Worthy work and Bowie's Kantian theory of meaningful work." In D. G. Arnold and J. D. Harris (eds.), *Kantian Business Ethics: Critical perspectives*, pp. 115–31. Cheltenham: Edward Elgar.

Clifford, C. (2016). "The real reason for disappearing jobs is not trade—it's robots." *CNBC.com* [website], November 21: http://www.cnbc.com/2016/11/21/the-real-reason-for-disappearing-jobs-isnt-trade-its-robots.html [accessed June 23, 2018].

Danahar, J. (2017). "Will life be worth living in a world without work? Technological unemployment and the meaning of life." *Science and Engineering Ethics*, 23, 41–64.

DesJardins, J. R. (2012). "Meaningful work." In D. G. Arnold and J. D. Harris (eds.), *Kantian Business Ethics: Critical Perspectives*, pp. 132–47. Cheltenham: Edward Elgar.

Donaldson, T. and Walsh, J. (2015). "Toward a theory of business." *Research in Organizational Behavior*, 35, 181–207.

Economist. (2009). "Open-book management." *The Economist*, June 8. Available at: http://www.economist.com/node/13809344 [accessed March 4, 2016].

Hill, T. E. Jr. (1992). *Dignity and Practical Reason in Kant's Moral Theory*. Ithaca, NY: Cornell University Press.

Kant, I. (1930 [1775]). *Lectures on Ethics*, translated by L. Infield. Indianapolis: Hackett.

Kant, I. (1990 [1785]). *Foundations of the Metaphysics of Morals*, translated by L.W. Beck. New York: Macmillan.

Kateb, G. (2011). *Human Dignity*. Cambridge, MA: Harvard University Press.

Margolis, J. D. (2001). "Responsibility in organizational context." *Business Ethics Quarterly*, 11(3), 439.

Nietzsche, F. (1964). "The Greek State." In F. Nietzsche, *Early Greek Philosophy and Other Essays*, translated by M. A. Mügge, pp. 5–11. New York: Russell and Russell.

Pfeffer, J. (1994). *Competitive Advantage Through People*. Brighton, MA: Harvard Business School Press.

Pirson, M., Goodpaster, K., and Dierksmeier, C. (2016). "Human dignity and business." *Business Ethics Quarterly*, 26(4), 465–78.

Pope John Paul II (1981). *Laborem Exercens* [On Human Work]. London: Penguin Books.

Pope Leo XIII (2002 [1981]). *Rerum Novarum* [On Capital and Labor], new edn. London: Catholic Truth Society.

Rosen, M. (2012). *Dignity*. Cambridge, MA: Harvard University Press.

Schwartz, A. (1982). "Meaningful work." *Ethics*, 92, 634–46.

Smith, A. (1976 [1776]). *The Wealth of Nations*, edited by Edward Cannan. Chicago: University of Chicago Press.

Wharton Business School (2016a). "Can Trump-or Anyone- Bring Back American Manufacturing." *Knowledge@Wharton* [website], November 30: http://knowledge.wharton. upenn.edu/article/can-trump-anyone-bring-back-american-manufacturing/ [accessed June 23, 2018].

Wharton Business School, (2016b). "Why the Coming Jobs Crisis is Bigger Than You Think." *Knowledge@Wharton* [website], December 6: http://knowledge.wharton.upenn.edu/article/ why-the-coming-jobs-crisis-is-bigger-than-you-think/ [accessed June 23, 2018].

Wolf, S. (2010). *Meaning in Life and Why it Matters*. Princeton, NJ: Princeton University Press.

Zagzebski, L. (2016). "The dignity of persons and the value of uniqueness." *Proceedings and Addresses of the American Philosophical Association*, 90, 55–70.

CHAPTER 3

....

MEANINGFUL WORK AND FREEDOM

Self-realization, Autonomy, and Non-domination in Work

....

KEITH BREEN

INTRODUCTION

....

WORK matters in contemporary society, just as it did in earlier societies. It matters, as pointed out by Herbert Applebaum, because work "is basic to the human condition, to the creation of the human environment, and to the context of human relationships."[1] Work's role in the human condition inevitably gives rise to questions that reveal and shape our core ethical values. We engage in such questions when we ask how we should understand work as an activity and its connection with other spheres of life, its appropriate place in our social order. We engage in such questions when we seek to determine what we should expect from each other in terms of work, reflecting on the allocation of work in society and the advantages and disadvantages accruing to it. And we engage in such questions when we reflect on the ideal of "meaningful work," work that facilitates and enhances our sense of self and broader personal life.

In considering the ideal of meaningful work, we cannot but stress the contribution of work to collective life, the cultivation of occupational identities through work, and the values of equality, fairness, and justice in the organization of work. Yet we also necessarily have to stress the value of freedom across a number of its dimensions. In this chapter, I aim to underscore the centrality of freedom to the experience and achievement of

---

[1] Applebaum (1992: ix). For similar claims as to the centrality of work, see Arendt (1958), Budd (2011), Deranty (2015), Muirhead (2004), and Weil (2002 [1952]). For varyingly dissenting views, see Chamberlain (2018), Srnicek and Williams (2016), and Weeks (2011). Note that when thinking of work, we should not reduce work to having a "job," which is only one manifestation of work.

meaningful work. My basic claim is that work cannot be genuinely meaningful unless it exemplifies and sustains our freedom along (at least) three dimensions. The first dimension, which underpins many of the most significant arguments for institutionalizing meaningful work, is the positive notion of freedom as self-realization, of actualizing our talents and potentialities as persons through work. Under this dimension, work that has some claim to being meaningful must substantially allow for the personal development of workers through their work activity. The second dimension of freedom that is key to meaningful work is again a positive notion of freedom, but one conceptually distinct from freedom conceived as self-realization. This is instead freedom understood as autonomy or self-determination, of being able to decide on and control one's work. Work in which individuals lack discretion over their actions is, along this dimension, ethically impoverished in offending against our equal status as decision-making beings. The third dimension of freedom essential to the experience of meaningful work is that of freedom from arbitrary interference and domination, namely freedom as non-domination. While the notion of freedom as non-domination does not give expression to the positive good of meaningful work captured by the first two dimensions, it does represent a necessary condition for reliably enjoying meaningful work.

In the following, I first briefly explore the concept of meaningful work, the goods associated with it, and their relation to the value of freedom. I then explore meaningful work in light of the three main dimensions of freedom, aiming to show that attention to these helps properly explicate the meaningful-work ideal and provides arguments for its institutionalization which are ethically compelling. I also endeavor to show that these arguments are not undermined by counterclaims to the effect that meaningful work is not an appropriate public policy concern, or that the values of self-realization and autonomy can be harnessed to legitimize exploitative work arrangements.

Work, Meaningfulness, and Freedom

To appreciate the links between freedom and meaningful work, we need to recognize the varieties of meaningfulness appealed to in the meaningful-work ideal. At a base level, all work activity has meaning. For instance, work consisting in endless data entry or shelling of nuts is replete with meanings, among these being tedium, frustration, and even absurdity. The meaning of work and the meaningfulness of work are therefore not the same thing. What distinguishes meaningful work from work whose meaning consists wholly in tedium or frustration is that it involves the acquisition or cultivation of intersubjectively acknowledged goods.

The different sorts of meaningfulness attaching to work thus reflect the plurality of goods pursuable through work.[2] These goods can be divided roughly into two types. The

---

[2] On the levels of meaningfulness or goods ideally attaching to work, see Gheaus and Herzog (2016), Veltman (2016: 4–9, 115–35), and Yeoman (2014: 8–38).

first type comprises "external" goods for which work functions as a means. Goods of this sort include money, power, and social status. In being genuine goods without which life would be marred by poverty, vulnerability, and social exclusion, these represent important aspects of the meaningful-work ideal. However, external goods are only contingently related to the work people do. Money, power, and status can be achieved through any work activity—mindless drudgery or clever manipulation of others, as much as committed effort in a craft or profession—depending on the vagaries of labor market conditions and prevailing economies of esteem. In this, external goods differ from goods that are "internal" to the content and conduct of work.[3] Indeed, internal goods are of prime importance to the meaningful-work ideal, since they concern not merely contingent, instrumental ends but rather the intrinsic performance and experience of work itself.

The goods internal to meaningful work are, like external goods, plural and varied. One obvious internal good concerns the social worth of the work being undertaken: its point. When aware of the integral goal of their work—being a good carpenter or administrator, and not simply making money—when that goal is thought worthy, and when they know their role in facilitating that goal, individuals experience a sense of making a difference, making a communal contribution, which lends purpose to their lives. Another obvious internal good relates to the quality of interpersonal relationships at work, whether these are defined by equality and mutual regard and a genuinely cooperative spirit, or by hierarchy, disregard, and hostility. To this we can add the internal good of work allowing for the exercise of intelligence and creativity. These three goods are preconditions of a further internal good pursuable in work, that of the positive development of one's character through increased knowledge and prolonged reciprocal engagement with others in shared ventures. When appropriately configured, these four goods can likewise function as grounds for the vital internal good of self-respect—a good without which a successful life cannot be lived—nurtured by work in which workers are valued and deem themselves valuable.[4]

We could, of course, make additions to this list of internal goods, given the heterogeneity of work activity. In doing so, however, we must not assume that, because people's understandings of a particular job will vary, the intrinsic meaningfulness of work is merely a matter of individual subjective preference. Contrary to this assumption, which would render work unamenable to intersubjective assessment, the internal goods achievable through work appear as objectively ascertainable as any external good (Hsieh, 2008a: 75; Walsh, 1994). This becomes clear once we consider the experience of work under the modern "detailed division of labor." First set out with precision by Adam Smith,

---

[3] The distinction between "external" and "internal" goods here is drawn from MacIntyre (1985: 187–97). See also Keat (2000: 23–7) and Moore (2017: 55–74).

[4] Writers emphasizing the connection between work and the cultivation of self-respect include Arnold (2012), Moriarty (2009), Rawls (1996: lix; 1999: 462–4), Meyers (1987), and Young (1979). Of course, the sense of "self-respect" we can gain from work in which we are treated with regard and concern is intimately connected to, though distinct from, the sense of "self-esteem" we can gain in making recognized excellent or somehow laudable contributions to society, etc, through our work. On the distinction between respect and esteem, see Darwall (1977) and Honneth (1995).

in the detailed division of labor work processes are broken down into separate tasks and individuals assigned to a small number of these tasks.[5] In work structured according to this division of labor—including line assembly and manufacture, warehouse packaging, many service and clerical jobs, etc—the internal goods described earlier are largely unattainable, regardless of anyone's preferences. Limited to performing a few routine tasks, individuals cannot easily form a view of the integral goal of the overall work process and find little outlet for their intelligence or creativity. Controlled by preset operating procedures or machines, they enjoy limited scope in work for fostering relationships, and even less for personal growth. And being interchangeable units of production, there is scant chance that the content of their work might contribute to their self-worth.

The detailed division of labor signifies, therefore, the objective antithesis of meaningful work. Moreover, attention to its historical genesis reveals the profound link between meaningful work and freedom insofar as the rise and expansion of this mode of productive organization hinged on a fundamental denial of that value. As explained by Braverman (1998 [1974]: 77–83) in his critique of Frederick Taylor's (1947 [1911]) theory of scientific management, the detailed division of labor rests on principles each of which undermines a dimension of individual freedom.[6] The first dictates the detachment of work from the skills and knowledge of workers, and, thus, the superfluousness of worker expertise and a concomitant rejection of freedom as self-realization. A second principle prescribes the separation of "conception," the design of work processes, from "execution," the act of carrying these out, and a parallel separation between managers and engineers, on the one hand, and the majority of workers, on the other. Gainsaying the decision-making powers of the majority, this tenet necessarily offends against freedom understood as autonomy. A third principle demands exclusive managerial authority over all aspects of the work process. The result is the subjection of workers to managerial rule and the contravention of freedom understood as non-domination. Key to the dearth in many contemporary occupations of the internal goods definitive of meaningful work is, then, a concerted and conscious attempt to eliminate freedom from work.

MEANINGFUL WORK AND SELF-REALIZATION

We can resist that attempt if we better appreciate the different ways meaningful work both embodies and advances our freedom. Many who have examined the ethical significance of work have stressed its role in the development of workers' powers and abilities,

---

[5] Smith (1979 [1776]: 13–24). It is certainly not true that all contemporary work conforms to this division of labor. However, following its introduction first in industrial manufacture, it increasingly encroached onto other occupations, among them retail, food processing, hospitality, public and private bureaucracies, and some educational professions. On this, see, for example, Carey (2009), Garson (1988), Pruijt (1997), and Ritzer (1993).

[6] Further accounts of the detailed division of labor and Taylorism are provided by Budd (2011: 97–100, 118–23), Crawford (2009: 37–47), Merkle (1980), and Murphy (1993: 19–45).

as well as their personalities as a whole. We see this in John Ruskin's and William Morris's reflections on work in the industrial age, as we do in the writings of Marx, Émile Durkheim, and Max Weber.[7] Even where their analyses strike a pessimistic tone, as when Weber (1992 [1930]: 123–4) condemned the "iron cage" of modern work for its grossly stultifying and alienating effects on our persons, the idea of work as a potential means to freedom as personal self-realization remains. Indeed, it is this very idea that motivates and lends sense to their analyses of the modern economic order.

But what is meant by freedom as self-realization? Unlike negative ideals of freedom, which center on the absence of constraints and interference by others, self-realization is a positive ideal of freedom connoting the ability to develop one's capacities and to reflectively achieve valuable ends and purposes.[8] Underlying this ideal is the Aristotelian notion of *eudaimonia* or "happiness." Following Aristotle, happiness consists not in pleasure (though pleasure is a part of happiness), but rather in flourishing, in actualizing the powers and ends characteristic of a good human life, a life lived well.[9] To enjoy freedom as self-realization means, under this view, to have and make real the possibility of living a recognizably good life in the major domains of human action. As with the idea of flourishing, freedom as self-realization is a multidimensional notion. It entails the exercise and refinement of our capacities, capabilities, and talents over time. The exercise of our capacities requires, in turn, the acquisition of knowledge and skill, as well as the gradual cultivation of perceptiveness and judgment. The cultivation of judgment necessitates increasing awareness of ourselves—our strengths and successes, weaknesses and failures—brought about by interaction with others in common endeavors, that ideally prompts attempts at affirmative self-transformation. Such affirmative self-transformation, when genuinely expressive of freedom, further presumes our exercise of deliberation and reasoned choice between the competing ends open to us at key points in time, that is, between the different paths we can take and the different persons we therefore might become.

Freedom as self-realization thus amounts to a normatively rich ideal. It entails striving and effort, a desire to be somehow accomplished, even if only in modest ways. It requires specialization, devoting ourselves to some activities rather than others, insofar as realizing all our potentialities is ruled out by human finitude. It is attainable in myriad activities, from raising a family, through leisure pursuits, to participation in politics. Furthermore, it is of particular relevance to work in all its varieties—whether in the formal or informal economy, whether involving employment or not, whether paid or unpaid—since work

---

[7] See Durkheim (1964 [1893]), Marx (1975 [1844]), Morris (1884), Ruskin (2007 [1853]), and Weber (1992 [1930]). Detailed discussions of Marx's understanding of self-realization and work can be found in Elster (1986) and Wood (2004). On Durkheim, see Honneth (2014), and on Weber, see Löwith (1993).

[8] Carter (2016: 1). For robust defences of the positive ideal of freedom, see Christman (1991, 2015b) and Taylor (1985).

[9] Aristotle (1980, Book I). For explicit appeals to flourishing as central to meaningful work, see Gomberg (2007), Murphy (1993), Sayer (2009), Veltman (2016), and Walsh (1994). I don't have space here to explore alternative romantic and existentialist understandings of self-realization, which equate it with individual "self-creation" rather than flourishing.

is a prime domain in which we not only can but are called upon by others to exercise our capacities toward diverse social ends.

We can get a clearer view of what self-realization can mean in work if we turn to the idea of "practices" expounded in Alasdair MacIntyre's ethical theory. Although the primary aim of MacIntyre's treatment of the idea of practices is to show how we acquire the virtues, this idea also helps reveal the conditions and features of self-realized work.[10] The range of activities identified by MacIntyre as practices is broad, including sciences, arts, games, and childrearing, as well as occupations such as farming, manufacture, and construction. Yet not all activities can be so identified insofar as they lack the internal structure definitive of practices, properly understood. For MacIntyre, a practice is:

> any coherent and complex form of socially established cooperative human activity through which goods internal to that form of activity are realized in the course of trying to achieve those standards of excellence which are appropriate to, and partially definitive of, that form of activity, with the result that human powers to achieve excellence, and human conceptions of the ends and goods involved, are systematically extended.   (MacIntyre, 1985: 187)

The main terms here are "coherent and complex," "cooperative human activity," "goods internal," and "standards of excellence," terms which further illuminate the *sui generis* goods of meaningful work discussed earlier. Unlike routine work in the detailed division of labor, which exhausts itself in the execution of a limited set of tasks, practices involve the performance of a complex set of interrelated tasks in an effective fashion. Successful performance depends, therefore, on practitioners having an overview of the entire work process—what it means to build a house or nurture crops to harvest—and an ability to see that process through. As cooperative human activities, practices represent communal endeavors involving not merely the participation of individuals, but also their immersion in a tradition or history that informs and guides their actions. All practices, from architecture to joinery, are therefore inspired by principles, standards, and bodies of expertise transmitted from one generation to another. Additionally, each practice has internal goods specific to it, that is, goods that can be achieved only through sustained engagement in the practice itself. The "aim internal to productive crafts" is "never only to catch fish, or to produce beef, or to build houses" in the hope of becoming wealthy or powerful, as one would do if external goods were all that mattered. Instead, it is to strive "in a manner consonant with the excellence of the craft," so that "not only is there a good product, but the craftsperson is perfected through and in her or his activity" (MacIntyre, 1994: 284, my emphasis). These internal goods of quality products and of the gradual perfection of practitioners necessitate attentiveness to shared standards of excellence that establish the goal of a practice, its ultimate purpose, and regulate how it is carried out. Moreover, such attentiveness presumes, over and above regard for established standards, the cultivation of personal virtues—honesty in conceding

---

[10] Here I draw on earlier discussions of MacIntyre (Breen, 2012; 2016). See also the discussions of MacIntyre and work in Keat (2000) and Muirhead (2004).

one's shortcomings, justice in acknowledging the successes of others, and courage in experiencing setbacks—which sustain trust and enable future progress in that practice.

The idea of practices vividly captures the promise of work open to freedom as self-realization. Experienced as a practice, work allows for intelligence and judgment in its performance, facilitates the acquisition of discipline-specific skill and knowledge, and enables a positive transformation of character, our movement from novice to master practitioners through an extended educational process undergirded by shared values. Attending to these integral features of practice-like work, we can appreciate the ethical significance of this activity and understand why having substantive opportunity to engage in meaningful work should be thought a reasonable expectation. Just as importantly, the idea of practices furnishes us with criteria for assessing the extent of freedom as self-realization to be had in existing work arrangements and for critically evaluating the institutions underpinning them.

Much work in modern society does not conform to MacIntyre's idea of practices—certainly not in full—but there may nevertheless be potential for it to have more of a practice-like character if it were suitably ordered (Muirhead, 2004: 165). In some cases, comparison with the practice ideal will reveal little present chance for self-realization in our work; in others, it will confirm that we do currently enjoy considerable freedom in this sense. In the latter cases, the practice ideal can empower us to preserve that room for self-realization from constriction and debasement. In the former, the ideal provides a spur for strategies directed toward reasserting individual freedom through institutional reform. One obvious and important strategy would be to try to reinvest our work with possibilities for personal development through job redesign, as has occurred in some industries at the core of the modern economy.[11] This strategy would not find success, of course, without a number of preconditions having been satisfied. Sustained investment in public education systems that are equally accessible by all, at all levels, would be required to ensure an educated youth with the ability, wherewithal, and desire to demand work worthy of their talents. Fundamental here, as well, would be a reorientation of economic policy toward prizing not just the quantity of jobs available in society, but also the quality of these jobs. With work that remains stubbornly closed to freedom as self-realization and attempts at job redesign, but which nonetheless fulfills an essential social purpose, a different solution might be the sharing of this work, as proposed by Paul Gomberg (2007: 75–90) and mooted by Walzer (1983: 165–83). The burden of routine labor now being more fairly apportioned, it might then be possible to ensure that all have sufficient opportunity to pursue complex, engaging tasks in the workplace. Or, failing this, we might provide significant compensations to those performing freedom-deficient yet purposeful labor, granting them a decent income coupled with a much reduced working week so that they have the discretionary time to pursue freedom as self-realization in other domains of their lives (Gheaus and Herzog, 2016: 84; Walsh, 1999). With work

---

[11] Consider here, for example, Volvo's radical restructuring of car assembly in its Uddevalla assembly plant, as set out in depth by Berggren (1992; see also Breen, 2012: 623–7). On the principles guiding job redesign in general, see Littler and Salaman (1985).

inimical to freedom as self-realization and lacking any real social purpose—rote telesales, the production of gadgets without function, administration spent tracking pointless KPIs, etc—the practice ideal gives us reason to seek its diminution, since it benefits nobody in any worthwhile sense and squanders human potential.

MEANINGFUL WORK AND AUTONOMY

Just as central to the experience of meaningful work is freedom as self-determination or autonomy. Broadly Kantian in inspiration, the ideal of autonomy is again a positive notion of freedom, yet one which turns on our faculty for reasoning and deliberating over alternative ends and courses of action. Autonomy therefore concerns our status as decision-making beings, a status basic to human dignity and the normative demand that our relations be defined by mutual respect. There are many conceptions of autonomy, but for our purposes here autonomy is best viewed as "personal autonomy."[12] Autonomy in this sense generally signifies, in the words of Young (2002: 45; see also Raz, 1986: 369–78), being "able to determine one's own projects and goals, how one will live one's life, without...having to obey the orders of others about how one will live." In cooperative endeavors, which necessarily involve engagement with others toward joint ends, personal autonomy can be more specifically understood as the possession of discretion, having a voice others must heed, and being able to contribute to collective decisions.

Autonomy and freedom as self-realization are mutually implicated concepts. A person cannot be said to be genuinely self-determining without her having somehow developed her capacity for autonomous judgment, just as she cannot, as we have seen, herself realize her various capabilities and talents without exercising deliberation and reasoned choice between competing ends. However, these dimensions of freedom remain distinct and can at times diverge to a considerable extent. For example, a worker might attain mastery in a rewarding practice she did not originally decide to enter—think of caste and other traditional societies where occupational choice has limited purchase—or over which she lacks discretion in crucial regards, as in rigidly hierarchical workplaces. Conversely, individuals may autonomously reject self-realization as an ideal, opting instead for lives devoted to idle consumption. This choice might strike us as mistaken, since it would likely have deleterious consequences for their autonomy subsequently, but they would not be truly self-determining were that option unavailable (Raz, 1986: 375). Thus, while autonomy and self-realization will often go hand-in-hand, they need not, with advances on one dimension sometimes coming at the expense of the other.

Setting this issue aside, it is important to register the ways in which autonomy relates to the ideal of meaningful work. As explained by Andrea Veltman (2016: 77–84), we should distinguish between three different levels of this relation. The first is that of

---

[12] On the different conceptions of autonomy, see Christman (2015a).

"autonomously chosen work." This is work whose purpose forms part of one's own conception of the good life, as when people committed to educating the young or protecting their community choose to become teachers or police officers. Opposed to this is work having little connection with individuals' life plans and which they are constrained to do in order to obtain the external good of money to fulfill basic needs or on account of social pressure or a lack of alternatives. The second level is "autonomy as economic independence." Work facilitating autonomy in this sense provides individuals with the financial, as well as social, status that enables them to pursue autonomously chosen ends in other domains of life and to resist attempts at controlling them by other people, whether family members or fellow citizens. These two levels are assuredly very weighty, but of prime significance to the enjoyment of meaningful work is the third level stressed by Veltman, that of "autonomous agency *in* work" (Veltman, 2016: 82). Autonomous agency in work represents a vital part of the meaningful-work ideal because it is only through exercising this agency that our work can become truly "ours" and exemplify our status as persons capable of making informed decisions.

Enjoying autonomous agency has a number of requirements. One condition for individuals exercising autonomy is their possessing the capacity to actively set aims and goals.[13] That capacity presumes their having an adequate range of valuable options to choose from and a sufficient degree of personal control over their circumstances. Another condition is planning how they will effectively achieve their aims, namely deciding between different means. In addition to the ability to plan is a third requirement of reflectively revising their goals and the means to them in light of the results of their previous decisions and actions. Together these three conditions provide the basis for personal responsibility, for giving an account of one's actions to other actors and being deemed accountable by those actors. In turn, personal responsibility implies the acquisition of a "practical identity" expressing the persons we are that makes sense to us as uniquely ours and is lent some basic degree of coherence by the choices we make about our lives over time (Roessler, 2012: 82; Schwartz, 1982: 635–6).

Of course, the requirements of exercising autonomy in work are all violated by the separation of conception and execution, and the related hierarchical demarcation between those who plan and those who merely follow through, distinguishing the detailed division of labor. Hired to perform actions predetermined by others, this division of labor treats workers as human tools and thus denies their status as decision-making beings in fundamental ways. The most rudimentary relates to work tasks. Denied the opportunity to plan their work, individuals have scant possibility of setting aims and goals, of thinking about the best means to these, or of determining how they should be shared. Instead, they are controlled spatially in terms of their bodily movements and temporally in terms of the sequence and pace of their work. Limited in this way, they are likewise denied the knowledge and overview of the work process that would allow them to rationally revise goals and means. As with work tasks, so, too, as regards the

---

[13] My discussion here draws from Adina Schwartz's (1982) classic account of autonomous agency in work, but see also Bowie (1998) and Roessler (2012).

organization of the workplace and the overall end and direction of the productive enterprise. Under the detailed division of labor, the workplace is an institution created by others into which workers must simply fit, and the overall end of their productive activity falls again under the exclusive discretion of their managerial superiors. As a mode of organizing work, this division is therefore inherently disrespectful, conveying to workers that they are not worthy or deserving of making decisions and that they are fitted to routine, predetermined activity.[14] Furthermore, it hinders the maintenance of a healthy practical identity, insofar as it impedes rather than augments most reasonable life plans, and, when endured over lengthy periods, can have potentially serious negative formative effects on our personalities.

Despite being suppressed in routinized work, the capacity for autonomous agency nevertheless endures. We see this in acts of worker resistance, the most conspicuous being strikes, sabotage, and go-slows. However, the more interesting of these acts are those where individuals seek to positively reclaim discretion over their work and contest its alienating content. This manifests itself in many ways, from informal modifications of job schedules to the reconfiguration of production goals and work constraints. These reclamations are noteworthy in showing that the organization of work is always under-determined—that is, open to change and revision. Accepting this truth, the question then is how we might reconfigure work so that it necessitates, rather than inhibits, our autonomous agency.

Such reconfiguration would demand institutional reform first on the level of work tasks and processes. As with efforts to facilitate freedom as self-realization, this requires redesigning work so that individuals can gain discretion over their jobs—how they are devised, sequenced, and carried out. Essential here is a recombination of conception and execution that would be made feasible by the enhancement of worker skill and knowledge via an equalization of the opportunities for professional education and specialized on-the-job training (Braverman, 1998 [1974]: 307–9). A further level of reform concerns the organization of the workplace. For workplaces to be amenable to autonomous agency, there must be a concerted attempt to abolish (Schwartz, 1982: 641) or, perhaps more plausibly, to substantially blur the division between workers and managers (Young, 1990: 224–5; Dahl, 1985: 128). Thus, workers should not just exercise discretion over their work tasks, but also jointly determine the composition of work teams, supervisory functions, and the physical work environment, as well as hiring and training policies. The call for autonomous agency would be incomplete, however, without workers having the additional right to contribute to collective decision-making as regards the purposes and direction of the productive enterprise as a whole: in other words, the democratization of workplace governance.[15] Now co-authors, rather than mere

[14] Disrespect for workers' autonomy finds stark expression in Henry Ford's (1924: 103) ill-informed claim that "to the majority of minds, repetitive operations hold no terrors. In fact, to some types of mind...the ideal job is one where the creative instinct need not be expressed."

[15] There is much agreement between those concerned with increasing autonomy in work that some form of workplace democratization is indispensable. See, among others, Breen (2015a: 39–42), Cohen (1989), Gould (1988: 133–59, 247–61), Murphy (1993: 230–2), O'Neill (2008: 36–7), Pateman (1970: 22–44),

addressees, of enterprise policies, workers would have an actionable say, for instance, over promotion procedures and scales of remuneration, the appointment of senior managers and the extent of their authority, the allocation of internal roles, the products to be produced or services provided, and so forth. Considered together, these institutional reforms might appear utopian. Yet, whether utopian or not, it is only through reforms of this kind that our dignity as autonomous persons can acquire substance in our working lives.

MEANINGFUL WORK AND NON-DOMINATION

In the previous sections, I emphasized the tight connections between meaningful work and freedom as self-realization and autonomy. However, a precondition for realizing one's capacities and exercising autonomy in work is having freedom along another of its dimensions, that is, freedom conceived as non-domination. This is a long-standing conception of freedom, which has been further explored and defended by contemporary republican thinkers.[16] Freedom as non-domination is not a positive notion of freedom because it does not center on actualizing capacities or being self-determining, but rather on the *absence* of arbitrary interference by others and of dependence on them. You lack freedom in this sense when you find yourself "having to live at the mercy of another, having to live in a manner that leaves you vulnerable to some ill that the other is in a position arbitrarily to impose"—in other words, being subject to arbitrary or uncontrolled power (Pettit, 1997: 4–5; see also Pettit, 1999: 165; 2012: 7, 50). Archetypal examples include masters dominating slaves, men dominating women, adults dominating children, as well as employers dominating employees. In assessing these dominative relationships, we should distinguish freedom understood as non-domination from the more minimal negative conception, advocated by liberals such as Isaiah Berlin (1969 [1958]), that equates liberty with "freedom as non-interference." This is because having freedom as non-interference—not currently being interfered with in your activity—remains compatible with being vulnerable to another's dominating control. For instance, you may as an employee enjoy considerable non-interference from a kindly or lethargic manager, yet not enjoy non-domination, since that manager could, should she have a bad day, decide to impose her will upon you. Non-domination is thus a more robust notion of freedom than freedom as non-interference insofar as it requires not simply the actual non-interference of others in your life, but also their *inability* to arbitrarily exercise power over you (Lovett, 2010: 152–6; Pettit, 1997: 50, 63–4).

Yeoman (2014: 166–84, 198–201), and Young (1979; 1990: 214–25). For an autonomy-centered perspective falling short of recommending democratic governance, see Bowie (1998).

[16] On contemporary republicanism, see Honohan (2002), Lovett (2014), and Laborde and Maynor (2008). Of course, domination is not a concern unique to republicans, but also crucial for socialists and liberal egalitarians.

But what is the precise link between the meaningful-work ideal and non-domination? Although freedom as non-domination differs from self-realization and autonomy, which underpin many of the internal goods definitive of meaningful work, these other dimensions of freedom and the goods associated with them stand jeopardized when we find ourselves in dominative relationships. They stand jeopardized because without resilient enjoyment of basic rights and liberties, that is, being free from domination to a significant degree, a personally meaningful life cannot be reliably pursued. It cannot be reliably pursued on account of our exposure to evils that distort and demean our lives, as clarified by Philip Pettit (1997: 82–90). Subject to arbitrary power, our lives suffer distortion in two ways. First, in "constant fear of unpredictable interference," we endure endemic "uncertainty" and "anxiety" that impede our ability to securely plan our futures. Second, when vulnerable to others' caprice, we have an attitude of "strategic deference and antic-ipation" foisted on us, are compelled to guess what those others might want and take steps so as to either please or avoid them in the hope of minimizing their potential future interference. The inevitable result is a constriction of our range of choice and options. Our lives, differently, are demeaned by dominative relationships because they entail an "asymmetry of power" that is recognized by all as consigning us to a subordinate social position and, *ipso facto*, an inferior status. This status is inimical to our sense of personal worth, as well as the core republican demand that we should relate to one another as equals. Exposed to these evils, we might with luck, cunning, or humiliating flattery achieve some of the goods definitive of meaningful work, but we can never be sure this would be the case and it would involve repugnant costs.

Believing freedom simply means non-interference, classical liberals and libertarians contend that the evils canvassed above are sufficiently dealt with by maintaining a free labor market in which people have the right to voluntarily enter a workplace and exit it should they subsequently find their work unsatisfactory (Epstein, 1992; Nozick, 1974). Freedom of contract and consent are, in short, all that are required for us to seek work that is meaningful by our lights. While freedom of contract is an essential freedom, this stance appears seriously deficient from a republican perspective. One reason is that for many people freedom of contract is in reality hollow. They may not be directly coerced into a job, but poverty and a lack of alternatives may nonetheless compel them to take up that job and stay in it, rendering them dependent on others.[17] Another reason is that contracts oftentimes contain legally permitted stipulations—"non-compete" clauses, for instance—which are difficult to contest and by design expose anyone taking up such contracts to future domination.[18] This is quite apart from the fact that all contracts, because they cannot hope to cover every circumstance of the work to be undertaken, are necessarily incomplete and indeterminate, which again allows for wide uncontrolled discretion.[19] Yet the gravest concern as regards the libertarian celebration of freedom of

[17]   See Dahl (2001: 251–2), Gourevitch (2015: 178), Lovett (2010: 196), and Pettit (1997: 62, 164).
[18]   For academic and journalistic discussions of non-compete clauses, see Anderson (2017: 66, 162), Jamieson (2014), Marx (2011), and Woodman (2015).
[19]   On the assignment of "residual decision-making rights" to employers on account of contract inde-terminacy, see Hsieh (2005: 121–3; 2008a: 81–2, 90; 2008b: 63–5).

contract is that it neglects the institutional setting in which most workers find themselves in contemporary societies: the capitalist firm. Correcting this institutional myopia, we should, with Elizabeth Anderson (2015: 50, 60), not view the labor contract "as an exchange of commodities on the market"; instead, it is better viewed as the mechanism through which "workers get incorporated under the governance of productive enterprises," that is, inserted into an organizational hierarchy and subordinated to the authority of employers.

Brought into existence by state-sanctioned corporate, employment, and property law, the capitalist firm is an authoritarian form of government in which employers and managers rule over employees.[20] While circumscribed by legal restrictions in diverse ways, the scope of their rule is wide-ranging, controlling workers' behavior both within and beyond the workplace. As discussed previously, managers have discretion over the performance of work, determining its pace and intensity, the allocation of responsibilities and targets, as well as the time permitted for rest and even toilet breaks. In addition, they enjoy control over work relations, deciding how employees should dress and comport themselves, with whom they can have intimate relationships and whom not, the monitoring and security procedures they will submit to, and the restrictions on individual expression to be observed in work. Managers also have discretion over employment conditions, determining overtime, training, promotion, and firing policies. This discretion, should they wish to exercise it, enables managers to regulate—often quite legally and using sanctions such as reprimands, fines, and dismissal—employees' lives outside of work through mandatory drug or medical testing, surveillance of online and email communications, and prohibitions on numerous activities, whether religious, sexual, political, etc.[21] Similarly, it is managers, or rather senior managers, who have greatest say over matters having potentially severe consequences not only for employees, but also for their families and communities, including redundancies, relocations, and the closure of firms.

Two points warrant attention here. First, while a number of these workplace policies and controls are not objectionable in themselves—for example, having clearly defined rest breaks or codes of conduct designed to prevent the sexual exploitation of junior employees—they do become objectionable when one group alone determines their form. Second, it is no doubt true that many employers and managers will not routinely use their discretion in oppressive, heavy-handed ways, since doing so would contravene shared norms of civility and contribute to serious organizational inefficiencies and an unsavory corporate reputation. However, from the perspective of freedom as non-domination, what matters is not whether they will act oppressively, but instead whether they *can* act in that manner. If they can, even if only intermittently, then they pose a threat to employees, who may, in consequence, experience their work more as a hazard than a good.

---

[20] For arguments supporting Anderson's (2017: 14) claim that the firm represents a "state-licensed private government," see Ciepley (2013), Dahl (1985), Néron (2015), and Walzer (1983).

[21] On these measures, see Bertram, Robin, and Gourevitch (2012: 1–2), Budd (2011: 40), Gourevitch (2015: 174–7), and Maltby (2009).

How might the threat of arbitrary employer power be successfully countered? Employer power can be countered by forcing employers to answer to those they claim authority over and obliging them to take employees' interests into account in all major decisions. To this end, republicans recommend various strategies. One strategy is to ensure not merely a formal but an *effective* right of exit. If they had a sufficient measure of economic independence, workers would be less reliant on specific employers for their income and would thus enjoy greater power to negotiate terms of employment that respect their interests, since their option of exiting firms would now appear credible. Hence the demand for state-supported educational, welfare, and social security provisions, and, in recent republican thinking, the granting of a universal basic income to all citizens.[22] Although this strategy does promise to lessen employers' hold over employees, allowing the latter to change jobs with greater ease, it overlooks the substantial costs employees unavoidably face when exiting jobs—loss of intra-firm capital, the expense of transitioning to new jobs, the possibility of falling into sustained unemployment—that would still play into employers' hands, and does little to challenge the internal governance of the capitalist firm itself.[23] A second strategy, therefore, is to tame workplace governance through the establishment of a "workers' bill of rights" via state and industry-specific regulation of firms (Anderson, 2017: 68–9). Like a bill of civil rights that secures protection for citizens from arbitrary state interference, a bill of workers' rights ensures the same for employees against unchecked employer discretion. These rights uphold basic labor standards, as set out, for example, in the International Labour Organization's "decent work agenda" (ILO, 2013, 2015; see also Gilabert, 2016) and progressive domestic workplace legislation, by imposing legal duties on employers as regards wages, safety standards, dismissal, freedom of expression, harassment, discrimination in hiring and promotion, modes of redress, etc.

In providing a constitutional framework for workplace governance enforced by external bodies such as employment tribunals and labor courts, this regulatory strategy has, as seen in many jurisdictions, salutary disciplining effects on employer behavior. Yet, while necessary, it remains insufficient in countering workplace domination, partly because recourse to external bodies often proves a costly, protracted process, but also because employers have leeway to arbitrarily apply regulations within firms, as well as the fact that there will exist opportunities for unchecked discretion which no existing regulatory measure could be expected to anticipate (González-Ricoy, 2014: 246–7). To address this, many go further and call for the institutionalization of worker "voice" so that employees would themselves have the possibility of changing workplace governance. Worker voice is realizable externally through worker unions and professional bodies, which use their independent power to, among other things, influence state labor policy and negotiate collective agreements across sectors and with individual employers. It is

---

[22] For republican justifications of universal basic income, see Dagger (2006: 166–7), Lovett (2010: 201–3), Pettit (2007; 2012: 112), and Raventós (2007).

[23] On exit costs, see Bertram, Robin, and Gourevitch (2012: 4–5) and Hsieh (2005: 127–32; 2008a: 89–90). On the failure of the exit strategy to properly challenge enterprise governance, see Gourevitch (2016: 23–4).

also, and just as importantly, realizable internally when employees possess the right to contribute to enterprise decision-making processes. This internal organizational voice can be construed as a right to contest enterprise policies, or, more ambitiously and echoing autonomy-based arguments for workplace democratization, as a right both to contest and jointly determine these policies.[24] No matter its construal, the point of ensuring internal employee voice is to disrupt workplace domination on all levels, from the performance of work, through the setting of employment conditions, to the determination of overall corporate policy.

Should these strategies have success, the interests of all would receive appropriate institutional register. No one would have to bow or bend the knee at work, given that all would be free from unjustified interference and endemic uncertainty. Work hierarchies having been curbed, no one would possess the power to treat others as mere subordinates to be ordered about at will. In such circumstances, the goods of meaningful work, as with other personal ends, could then be more reliably sought.

A REPLY TO TWO OBJECTIONS

The thrust of the arguments presented here is that freedom in its various dimensions is central to meaningful work, just as enjoying meaningful work makes for lives that are significantly freer than those without it. I wish to conclude, however, by replying to two objections that challenge some of the main claims in this chapter. Although these objections largely grant my arguments as regards work and freedom as non-domination, they take issue, first, with the assumption that ensuring greater self-realization or autonomy at work is an appropriate public policy concern and, second, with the belief that work in contemporary societies can be a genuine vehicle for self-realization and autonomy.

The first objection is advanced by liberals who believe the state should maintain strict neutrality between different conceptions of the good and avoid questions of ethics, or the worthy life, generally (Arneson, 1987; Kymlicka, 2002). Meaningful work forms part of many individuals' idea of the good life, and it is entirely proper for them to seek it, should they wish. However, there are various other activities that people value, and these activities may be reasonably thought by some to be more valuable than meaningful work: "I may value unalienated labour," Kymlicka (2002: 191) argues, and "yet value other things even more, such as my leisure. I may prefer playing tennis to unalienated production." Given the fact and desirability of value pluralism, it would be inappropriate to politically promote meaningful work or any conception of the good, insofar as doing so would involve the state illegitimately pronouncing on what makes life worth living and interfering with people's choices. To protect individual choice, governmental action

---

[24] On internal voice as contestation, see Dagger (2006: 162–3) and Hsieh (2005: 136–7; 2008b: 67–73); on internal voice as requiring contestation plus the determination of policy, see Breen (2015b: 279–82; 2017: 432–6) and González-Ricoy (2014: 244–8).

and political discourse should eschew perfectionist policies and be limited instead to ensuring justice as regards work, that is, respect for individual rights and liberties, equality of opportunity, fair wages, etc.

The truth to this objection is that many activities conduce to meaningful human lives, work being one of them. Nevertheless, as an argument against the promotion of meaningful work, it fails and this for a number of reasons. The first concerns the formative effect of work. I suggested earlier that work in which people have limited freedom may have serious negative consequences for their lives in general. Attention to the sociological and psychological literatures on work bears out this contention, revealing non-complex, routinized work as a cause of physical and mental ill health that can profoundly impact on workers' personalities and relationships within and outside the workplace.[25] Given work's effect on well-being, the promotion of meaningful work would seem as much a legitimate question of justice as of ethics. A second reason why this objection fails is that questions of ethics are politically unavoidable. As pointed out by Keat (2008) in his discussion of the relative ethical merits and demerits of the "liberal market economies" of the Anglophone world and the "coordinated market economies" of Germany and other continental European countries, economic policies inevitably shape the world of work, making it less or more likely that people will have access to engaging, purposeful occupations. Accepting this truth, it would appear permissible to wish to increase the amount of meaningful work available rather than deliberately surrendering it—itself an ethical decision—to the play of unaccountable market forces. A further reason for dismissing objections based on state neutrality is that there is nothing morally offensive about a moderate perfectionism that promotes work open to self-realization and autonomy while also respecting people's basic liberties and the fact of value pluralism (Breen, 2016; Roessler, 2012). None of the institutional reforms discussed in this chapter—whether encouraging job redesign, increasing educational and training opportunities, or granting workers an actionable say in workplace governance—entail the state coercively imposing one conception of the good or treating citizens without regard to their fundamental interests. In point of fact, these reforms more securely enshrine their fundamental interests and bolster individual choice by expanding the opportunity to avail of an important social good.

A very different complaint comes from radical Marxists and others who challenge the capitalist economy and existing modes of work as a whole. For these critics, the meaningful-work ideal, while admirable in intent, substitutes a "humanist work ethic" for the earlier "Protestant work ethic" whose purpose was to discipline workers into accepting their role in capitalist accumulation. Encouraging people to think that they can, and should expect to, attain self-realization and autonomy through their work, this humanist work ethic is easily co-optable by human resource managers and consultants

---

[25] On work and ill health, see Kornhauser's (1965) landmark study of Detroit car workers, as well as Tausig and Fenwick (2012), among many others. On the negative impact of routinized work on individuals' functioning across their lives, see Kohn and Schooler's (1983) influential findings. For discussions of these and other empirical studies, see Hauser and Roan (2007), Lane (1991: 240–50), Schwartz (1982: 635–7), and Veltman (2016: 50–61).

attempting to extract ever greater productivity from workers (Gorz, 1999: 39–43; Maskivker, 2012: 33; Weeks, 2011: 37–77, 104–9). Work now imagined as the path by which to fully realize their powers and identities, people's very sense of self becomes the means for their own self-exploitation. In a context where appeals to freedom perversely enable tighter managerial control, we should call "not for a liberation *of* work" but instead for "a liberation *from* work," and strive toward a "postwork" world in which work ceases to be a prime value and is subordinated to proper human ends (Weeks, 2011: 26).

This objection certainly picks up on established trends in contemporary, post-Fordist capitalism. Many scholars have shown how a celebration of flexible and adaptable "network" workers, whose freedom is said to consist in realizing their inner selves through moving seamlessly from one project to another, has gone hand-in-hand with strengthened employer power and the erosion of employee entitlements, economic security, and workplace protections (Boltanski and Chiapello, 2007; Sennett, 1998). However, it is one thing to recognize these regrettable (though resistible and by no means uniform) trends, and quite another to dismiss the meaningful-work ideal as misguided. While the values of freedom informing this ideal are vulnerable to co-option, they are likewise vulnerable when appealed to in other major life domains. Just as the ideal of free work is harnessable toward perverse ends, so, too, is the ideal of free citizenship, but this ambiguity— that visions of free work or citizenship can be invoked to emancipate or oppress—gives us no reason for giving up on them (Deranty, 2015: 118–19). On the contrary, that ambiguity gives us grounds for insisting on them more adamantly than before, insofar as they provide, as I have suggested, key standards by which to critique and judge our present circumstances. The humanist work ethic underpinning arguments for meaningful work does not encourage us, in the manner of the old Protestant work ethic, to slavishly commit to any form of work as an end in itself, but instead enables us to more clearly distinguish worthwhile from worthless work so that it might better fit our aspirations and wider lives. Should a form of work be deemed deficient from the perspective of the meaningful-work ideal—perhaps because it promises only a simulacrum of freedom which none but a fool would fail to detect—this justifies reorganizing it or lessening its impact and significance, not relegating the value of work overall. Indeed, the "postwork" call for liberation from work, based on a totalizing critique of current social relations, might itself be thought to have troubling disempowering effects, since it neglects how work, when suitably ordered, augments people's lives, and thereby screens from view real opportunities for transforming the present.

REFERENCES

Anderson, E. (2015). "Equality and freedom in the workplace: Recovering Republican insights." *Social Philosophy and Policy*, 31(2), 48–69.

Anderson, E. (2017). *Private Government: How employers rule our lives (and why we don't talk about it)*, with introduction by Stephen Macedo. Princeton, NJ: Princeton University Press.

Applebaum, H. (1992). *The Concept of Work: Ancient, Medieval, and Modern*. Albany, NY: SUNY Press.

Arendt, H. (1958). *The Human Condition*. Chicago: Chicago University Press.

Aristotle. (1980). *Nicomachean Ethics*. Oxford: Oxford University Press.

Arneson, R. (1987). "Meaningful work and market socialism." *Ethics*, 97(3), 517–45.

Arnold, S. (2012). "The difference principle at work." *The Journal of Political Philosophy*, 20(1), 94–118.

Berggren, C. (1992). *The Volvo Experience*. New York: ILR Press.

Berlin, I. (1969 [1958]). "Two concepts of liberty." In I. Berlin, *Four Essays on Liberty*, pp. 118–72. Oxford: Oxford University Press.

Bertram, C., Robin, C., and Gourevitch, A. (2012). "Let It Bleed: Libertarianism and the Workplace." *Crooked Timber* [website]: http://crookedtimber.org/2012/07/01/let-it-bleed-libertarianism-and-the-workplace/ [accessed September 22, 2017].

Boltanski, L. and Chiapello, E. (2007). *The New Spirit of Capitalism*. London: Verso.

Bowie, N. E. (1998). "A Kantian theory of meaningful work." *Journal of Business Ethics*, 17(9/10), 1083–92.

Braverman, H. (1998 [1974]). *Labor and Monopoly Capital: The degradation of work in the twentieth century*. New York: Monthly Review Press.

Breen, K. (2012). "Production and productive reason." *New Political Economy*, 17(5), 611–32.

Breen, K. (2015a). "Freedom, Democracy, and Working Life." In A. Azmanova and M. Mihai (eds.), *Reclaiming Democracy*, pp. 34–49. New York: Routledge.

Breen, K. (2015b). "Freedom, Republicanism and workplace democracy." *Critical Review of International Social and Political Philosophy*, 18(4), 470–85.

Breen, K. (2016). "In Defence of Meaningful Work as a Public Policy Concern." In A. Fives and K. Breen (eds.), *Philosophy and Political Engagement: Reflection in the Public Sphere*, pp. 139–61. Basingstoke: Palgrave Macmillan.

Breen, K. (2017). "Non-domination, workplace Republicanism, and the justification of worker voice and control." *International Journal of Comparative Labour Law and Industrial Relations*, 33(3), 419–39.

Budd, J. W. (2011). *The Thought of Work*. Ithaca, NY: Cornell University Press.

Carey, M. (2009). "'It's a bit like being a robot or working in a factory': Does Braverman help explain the experiences of state social workers in Britain since 1971?" *Organization*, 16(4), 505–27.

Carter, I. (2016). "Positive and Negative Liberty." In *Stanford Encyclopedia of Philosophy*. Stanford: CSLI. Available at: https://plato.stanford.edu/entries/liberty-positive-negative/, pp. 1–19 [accessed September 22, 2017].

Chamberlain, J. A. (2018). *Undoing Work, Rethinking Community*. Ithaca, NY: Cornell University Press.

Christman, J. (1991). "Liberalism and individual positive freedom." *Ethics*, 101(2), 343–59.

Christman, J. (2015a). "Autonomy in Moral and Political Philosophy." In *Stanford Encyclopedia of Philosophy*. Stanford: CSLI. Available at: https://plato.stanford.edu/entries/autonomy-moral/, pp. 1–22 [accessed September 22, 2017].

Christman, J. (2015b). "Freedom in times of struggle: Positive liberty again." *Analyse & Kritik*, 37(1/2), 171–88.

Ciepley, D. (2013). "Beyond public and private: Toward a political theory of the corporation." *American Political Science Review*, 107(1), 139–58.

Cohen, J. (1989). "The economic basis of deliberative democracy." *Social Philosophy and Policy*, 6(2), 25–50.

Crawford, M. B. (2009). *Shop Class as Soulcraft: An inquiry into the value of work*. New York: Penguin Books.

Dagger, R. (2006). "Neo-republicanism and the civic economy." *Politics, Philosophy & Economics*, 5(2), 151–73.

Dahl, R. (1985). *A Preface to Economic Democracy*. Berkeley: University of California Press.

Dahl, R. (2001). "A right to workplace democracy? Response to Robert Mayer." *The Review of Politics*, 63(2), 249–53.

Darwall, S. (1977). "Two kinds of respect." *Ethics*, 88(1), 36–49.

Deranty, J.-P. (2015). "Historical objections to the centrality of work." *Constellations*, 22(1), 105–21.

Durkheim, É. (1964 [1893]). *The Division of Labor in Society*. New York: Free Press.

Elster, J. (1986). "Self-realization in work and politics: The Marxist conception of the Good Life." *Social Philosophy and Policy*, 3(2), 97–126.

Epstein, R. (1992). *Forbidden Grounds: The case against employment discrimination laws*. Cambridge, MA: Harvard University Press.

Ford, H. (1924). *My Life and Work*. London: Heinemann.

Garson, B. (1988). *The Electronic Sweatshop: How computers are turning the office of the future into the factory of the past*. New York: Simon & Schuster.

Gheaus, A. and Herzog, L. (2016). "The goods of work (other than money!)." *Journal of Social Philosophy*, 47(1), 70–89.

Gilabert, P. (2016). "Labor human rights and human dignity." *Philosophy & Social Criticism*, 42(2), 171–99.

Gomberg, P. (2007). *How to Make Opportunity Equal*. Oxford: Blackwell Publishing.

González-Ricoy, I. (2014). "The Republican case for workplace democracy." *Social Theory and Practice*, 40(2), 232–54.

Gorz, A. (1999). *Reclaiming Work: Beyond the wage-based society*. Cambridge: Polity Press.

Gould, C. (1988). *Rethinking Democracy*. Cambridge: Cambridge University Press.

Gourevitch, A. (2015). *From Slavery to the Cooperative Commonwealth: Labor and Republican liberty in the nineteenth century*. Cambridge: Cambridge University Press.

Gourevitch, A. (2016). "The limits of a basic income: means and ends of workplace democracy." *Basic Income Studies*, 11(1), 17–28.

Hauser, R. M. and Roan, C. L. (2007). *Work Complexity and Cognitive Functioning at Midlife*. CDE Working Paper No. 2007–08. Madison, WI: University of Wisconsin-Madison Center for Demography and Ecology. Available at: http://www.ssc.wisc.edu/cde/cdewp/2007-08.pdf [accessed September 22, 2017].

Honneth, A. (1995). *The Struggle for Recognition: The moral grammar of social conflicts*. Cambridge: Polity Press.

Honneth, A. (2014). *Freedom's Right: The social foundations of democratic life*. Cambridge: Polity Press.

Honohan, I. (2002). *Civic Republicanism*. London: Routledge.

Hsieh, N. (2005). "Rawlsian justice and workplace Republicanism." *Social Theory and Practice*, 31(1), 115–42.

Hsieh, N. (2008a). "Justice in production." *Journal of Political Philosophy*, 16(1), 72–100.

Hsieh, N. (2008b). "Workplace democracy, workplace Republicanism, and economic democracy." *Revue de Philosophie Économique*, 8(2), 57–78.

International Labour Organization (ILO). (2013). *Decent Work Indicators: Guidelines for producers and users of statistical and legal framework indicators*, 2nd version. Geneva: International Labour Office.

International Labour Organization (ILO). (2015). *Decent Work* [web page]: http://www.ilo. org/global/topics/decent-work/lang--en/index.htm [accessed September 22, 2017].

Jamieson, D. (2014). "Jimmy John's Makes Low-Wage Workers Sign 'Oppressive' Noncompete Agreements." *The Huffington Post* [website], 15 October: http://www.huffingtonpost. com/2014/10/13/jimmy-johns-non-compete_n_5978180.html [accessed September 22, 2017].

Keat, R. (2000). *Cultural Goods and the Limits of the Market*. Basingstoke: Palgrave Macmillan.

Keat, R. (2008). "Practices, firms and varieties of Capitalism." *Philosophy of Management*, 7(1), 77–91.

Kohn, M. L. and Schooler, C. (1983). *Work and Personality: An inquiry into the impact of social stratification*. Norwood, NJ: Ablex Publishing.

Kornhauser, A. (1965). *Mental Health of the Industrial Worker: A Detroit Study*. New York: John Wiley & Sons.

Kymlicka, W. (2002). *Contemporary Political Philosophy: An introduction*, 2nd edn. Oxford: Oxford University Press.

Laborde, C. and Maynor, J. (2008). "The Republican Contribution to Contemporary Political Theory." In C. Laborde and J. Maynor (eds.), *Republicanism and Political Theory*, pp. 1–28. Oxford: Blackwell.

Lane, R. E. (1991). *The Market Experience*. Cambridge: Cambridge University Press.

Littler, C. and Salaman, G. (1985). "The Design of Jobs." In Craig Littler (ed.), *The Experience of Work*, pp. 85–105. Aldershot: Gower Publishing.

Lovett, F. (2010). *A General Theory of Domination and Justice*. Oxford: Oxford University Press.

Lovett, F. (2014). "Republicanism." In *Stanford Encyclopedia of Philosophy*. Stanford: CSLI. Available at: https://plato.stanford.edu/entries/republicanism/, pp. 1–18 [accessed September 22, 2017].

Löwith, K. (1993). *Max Weber and Karl Marx*. London: Routledge.

MacIntyre, A. (1985). *After Virtue: A study in moral theory*, 2nd edn. London: Duckworth.

MacIntyre, A. (1994). "A Partial Response to My Critics." In J. Horton and S. Mendus (eds.), *After MacIntyre: Critical perspectives on the work of Alasdair MacIntyre*, pp. 283–304. Cambridge: Polity Press.

Maltby, L. (2009). *Can They Do That? Retaking our fundamental rights in the workplace*. New York: Portfolio.

Marx, K. (1975 [1844]). *Economic and Philosophic Manuscripts of 1844*. In K. Marx and F. Engels, *Collected Works, Vol. 3*, pp. 229–346. New York: International Publishers.

Marx, M. (2011). "The firm strikes back: Non-compete agreements and the mobility of technical professionals." *American Sociological Review*, 76(5), 695–712.

Maskivker, J. (2012). *Self-Realization and Justice: A liberal-perfectionist defense of the right to freedom from employment*. New York: Routledge.

Merkle, J. (1980). *Management and Ideology: The legacy of the International Scientific Management Movement*. Berkeley, CA: University of California Press.

Meyers, D. (1987). "Work and Self-respect." In Gertrude Ezorsky (ed.), *Moral Rights in the Workplace*, pp. 18–27. Albany, NY: SUNY Press.

Moore, G. (2017). *Virtue at Work: Ethics for individuals, managers, and organizations*. Oxford: Oxford University Press.

Moriarty, J. (2009). "Rawls, self-respect, and the opportunity for meaningful work." *Social Theory and Practice*, 35(3), 441–59.

Morris, W. (1884). *Useful Work versus Useless Toil*. The William Morris Internet Archive [online]: https://www.marxists.org/archive/morris/works/1884/useful.htm [accessed September 22, 2017].

Muirhead, R. (2004). *Just Work*. Cambridge, MA: Harvard University Press.

Murphy, J. B. (1993). *The Moral Economy of Labor: Aristotelian themes in economic theory*. New Haven, CT: Yale University Press.

Néron, P.-Y. (2015). "Social Equality and Economic Institutions: Arguing for Workplace Democracy." In George Hull (ed.), *The Equal Society: Essays on equality in theory and practice*, pp. 311–31. Lanham, MD: Lexington Books.

Nozick, R. (1974). *Anarchy, State, and Utopia*. New York: Basic Books.

O'Neill, M. (2008). "Three Rawlsian routes towards economic democracy." *Revue de Philosophie Economique*, 8(2), 29–55.

Pateman, C. (1970). *Participation and Democratic Theory*. Cambridge: Cambridge University Press.

Pettit, P. (1997). *Republicanism: A theory of freedom and government*. Oxford: Oxford University Press.

Pettit, P. (1999). "Republican Freedom and Contestatory Democratization." In I. Shapiro and C. Hacker-Cordón (eds.), *Democracy's Value*, pp. 163–90. Cambridge: Cambridge University Press.

Pettit, P. (2007). "A Republican right to basic income?" *Basic Income Studies*, 2(2), 1–8.

Pettit, P. (2012). *On the People's Terms: A Republican theory and model of Democracy*. Cambridge: Cambridge University Press.

Pruijt, H. D. (1997). *Job Design and Technology: Taylorism vs. Anti-Taylorism*. London: Routledge.

Raventós, D. (2007). *Basic Income: The material conditions of freedom*. London: Pluto Press.

Rawls, J. (1996). *Political Liberalism*. Columbia, NY: Columbia University Press.

Rawls, J. (1999 [1971]). *A Theory of Justice*. Oxford: Oxford University Press.

Raz, J. (1986). *The Morality of Freedom*. Oxford: Clarendon Press.

Ritzer, G. (1993). *The McDonaldization of Society: An investigation into the changing character of contemporary social life*. Thousand Oaks, CA: Pine Forge Press.

Roessler, B. (2012). "Meaningful work: Arguments from autonomy." *Journal of Political Philosophy*, 20(1), 71–93.

Ruskin, J. (2007 [1853]). *The Stones of Venice: Volume II, The Sea Stories*. New York: Cosimo.

Sayer, A. (2009). "Contributive justice and meaningful work." *Res Publica*, 15(1), 1–16.

Schwartz, A. (1982). "Meaningful work." *Ethics*, 92(4), 634–46.

Sennett, R. (1998). *The Corrosion of Character: The personal consequences of work in the New Capitalism*. New York: W. W. Norton.

Smith, A. (1979 [1776]). *The Wealth of Nations*. Oxford: Oxford University Press.

Srnicek, N. and Williams, A. (2016). *Inventing the Future: Postcapitalism and a world without work*. London: Verso.

Tausig, M. and Fenwick, R. (2012). *Work and Mental Health in Social Context*. New York: Springer.

Taylor, C. (1985). "What's Wrong with Negative Liberty." In Charles Taylor, *Philosophical Papers: Volume 2, Philosophy and the Human Sciences*, pp. 211–29. Cambridge: Cambridge University Press.

Taylor, F. W. (1947 [1911]). The Principles of Scientific Management. In F. W. Taylor, *Scientific Management*, pp. 1–144. New York and London: Harper & Row.

Veltman, A. (2016). *Meaningful Work*. Oxford: Oxford University Press.

Walsh, A. (1994). "Meaningful work as a distributive good." *The Southern Journal of Philosophy*, 32(2), 233–50.

Walsh, A. (1999). "Factory work, burdens, and compensation." *Journal of Social Philosophy*, 30(3), 325–46.

Walzer, M. (1983). *Spheres of Justice*. New York: Basic Books.

Weber, M. (1992 [1930]). *The Protestant Ethic and the Spirit of Capitalism*. London: Routledge.

Weeks, K. (2011). *The Problem with Work: Feminism, Marxism, antiwork politics, and postwork imaginaries*. Durham, NC: Duke University Press.

Weil, S. (2002 [1952]). *The Need for Roots*. London: Routledge.

Wood, A. W. (2004). *Karl Marx*, 2nd edn. London: Routledge.

Woodman, S. (2015). "Amazon Makes even Temporary Warehouse Workers Sign 18-Month Non-Competes." *The Verge* [website], 26 March: https://www.theverge.com/2015/3/26/8280309/amazon-warehouse-jobs-exclusive-noncompete-contracts [accessed September 22, 2017].

Yeoman, R. (2014). *Meaningful Work and Workplace Democracy: A philosophy of work and a politics of meaningfulness*. Basingstoke: Palgrave Macmillan.

Young, I. M. (1979). "Self-determination as principle of justice." *Philosophical Forum*, 11(1), 30–46.

Young, I. M. (1990). *Justice and the Politics of Difference*. Princeton, NJ: Princeton University Press.

Young, I. M. (2002). "Autonomy, Welfare Reform, and Meaningful Work." In E. F. Kittay and E. K. Feder (eds.), *The Subject of Care: Feminist perspectives on dependency*, pp. 40–60. Lanham, MD: Rowman & Littlefield Publishers.

....

CHAPTER 4

WORK, MEANING, AND VIRTUE

....

RON BEADLE

INTRODUCTION

....

THIS chapter will consider the distinctive contributions that a MacIntyrean virtue perspective offers to enquiries about meaningful work. These enquiries have been conducted on the one hand by political philosophers interested in whether priority should be given to the provision of meaningful work by individual, organizational, and state agents (e.g. Bowie, 1998) and on the other by social scientists interested in understanding the relationships between the "antecedents, processes and outcomes of meaningful work" (Lepisto and Pratt, 2016: 3). While these debates have often been conducted in isolation, this chapter will outline how a virtue perspective might address contested issues in both.

In debates in political philosophy, the priority that should attach to meaningful work has been contested in both liberal (e.g. Maitland, 1989; Bowie, 1998; Yeoman, 2014) and welfare/socialist traditions (e.g. Schwartz, 1982; Care, 1984; Arneson, 1987). While advocates of meaningful work (broadly understood) argue that jobs should be designed to encourage the use of skills, task variety, autonomy, challenge, contribution, feedback, and relatedness, these are contested by those in both traditions that question the conceptual validity of meaningful work and the impact its prioritization might have on other valued goods including rights, efficiency, and welfare.

The welfare/socialist Arneson (1987), for example, listed seventeen different categories of meaningful goods that derive from work (Arneson, 1987: 528–9). He argued that their prioritization would be so subjective that, unlike employment, housing, health, and so on, meaningful work cannot be analyzed in terms of its distribution (e.g. efficiently or inefficiently; justly or unjustly); and it therefore fails as the type of good that should or even could be effectively promoted by the state. Many liberals concur with this conclusion but on the basis of different determinate criteria: that the positive liberties encouraged by the provision of meaningful work would be bought at too high a price, namely that of undermining the liberties of market agents to trade on the basis of their preferences and resources (Maitland, 1989; Nozick, 1974). To make the case for meaningful work in these traditions requires that such internal objections are themselves addressed, as attempted by the liberal Yeoman (2014) and the welfarist Schwartz (1982), among others. These debates appear unlikely to be resolved.

In the empirical literature, two related conundrums repeatedly demand attention. The first is the oft-repeated finding that jobs involving challenge and requiring skill—those considered most likely to be understood as meaningful—are not always so experienced (Fried and Ferris, 1987; Behson, Eddy, and Lorenzet, 2000). The second is that jobs that do not share such characteristics may be experienced as meaningful by some workers who undertake them (e.g. Wrzesniewski and Dutton, 2001, re cleaning; Isaksen, 2000, re catering; and Kreiner, Ashforth, and Sluss, 2006, re "dirty work"). These conundrums have recently led Lepisto and Pratt (2016) to challenge the basic conceptualization of meaningful work. Their central proposition is that "scholars implicitly or explicitly conceive of the core problem of meaningful work" (Lepisto and Pratt, 2016: 6) in different ways. They suggest that these be disentangled to address the design of jobs which maximize opportunities for the experience of meaningful work in a different way, and perhaps with different tools to those we should use in discussing how people come to justify the meaningfulness of work (Lepisto and Pratt, 2016). Traditionally those who have focused on the problem of alienation have pursued the solution of job redesign, whereas those who research the problem of "uncertainty and ambiguity regarding the value or worth of one's work" (Lepisto and Pratt, 2016: 8) focus on:

> enriching social meanings and individuals' meaning-making such that individuals can develop an account or justification regarding why their work is worthy or valuable.
>
> (Lepisto and Pratt, 2016: 8)

On Lepisto and Pratt's (2016) account it is only if there were agreement on the features that render work meaningful that we could begin to make a case for designing jobs around such features. Despite his doubts as to the reasonableness of that possibility, this conclusion parallels that of Arneson (1987), writing for a quite different audience and in a notably different idiom. But what if the relationship between such meaning-making and the experience of work were more intimate than this shared analytical distinction suggests? Such is the contention of the neo-Aristotelian virtue tradition, and hence the distinctive resources that it brings to our understanding of meaningful work.

This tradition holds that there is an intimate relationship between participation in practices (which include but are not limited to the context of employment) and the discovery of goods (Beadle and Knight, 2012). Sustained participation is required in practices as diverse as surgery, farming, and portrait painting if the goods they produce are to be realized and enjoyed, that is, to be experienced, as genuinely common goods. Such ongoing engagement creates the conditions necessary for the development of relevant technical skills, the extension of our understanding of these goods, and of the virtues that such realization both develops and requires. Undertaking work that pursues common goods in the company of others (MacIntyre, 2016; Knight, 2007) is necessary if we are to learn to order our desires and develop virtues (Anscombe, 1958).

The chapter proceeds as follows. First, it illustrates some of the conundrums that have attended research on meaningful work. Second, it provides an outline of the neo-Aristotelian virtue tradition that accords a significant place to the design and experience of work in the development of the very virtues that enable us to judge well. Third, it argues that this account provides resources that explain the conundrums besetting research on meaningful work. Begin then, with meaningful work.

MEANINGFUL WORK

Meaningful work has undergone a renaissance as an area of enquiry, research, and public policy interest (Breen, 2016; Yeoman, 2015). For example, the number of papers that include "meaningful work" in their titles has grown from 51 between 2002 and 2006 to 81 between 2007 and 2011, and 161 between 2012 and 2016 (Google Advanced Scholar, 2017). This resurgence is apparent across disciplines and includes research in psychology, organizational behavior, and business ethics.

A wide array of theoretical and operational frameworks have been applied to conceptualize and measure the antecedents, experience, consequences, and associations of meaningful work. These include Hackman and Oldham's (1975) classic measure of the relationship between job characteristics and the experience of meaningful work (Fried and Ferris, 1987), Grant's influential accounts of relational job design (e.g. Grant 2007), and accounts from eudaimonic self-determination theory (Ryan and Deci, 2001). Few who observe this growing literature, however, fail to note its range of conceptual disputes and the absence of "overarching structures that would facilitate greater integration, consistency, and understanding of this body of research" (Rosso, Dekas, and Wrzesniewski, 2010: 91).

Researchers have regularly called for improving the conceptualization of meaningful work by highlighting distinctions between, inter alia, studies of worker orientation and studies of work (Michaelson et al., 2014); sources of meaning and mechanisms by which work becomes meaningful (Rosso, Dekas, and Wrzesniewski, 2010: 91); between meaning in work and meaning at work (Pratt and Ashforth, 2003); and between task and relational aspects of jobs (Grant and Parker, 2009). Part of the problem is the complexity of a construct whose dimensions include antecedent conditions, a phenomenology of ascription, and claims around consequences. For the purposes of this chapter, however, the antecedent condition through which agents are able to understand their work as meaningful, and to justify this ascription, are particularly pertinent. In their review, Rosso, Dekas, and Wrzesniewski (2010: 95) "identified four main sources of meaning or meaningfulness in work: the self, other persons, the work context and spiritual life," each of which comprises a variety of potential avenues for meaning fulfillment—your desire for social status, mine for financial security, his for relationships of mutual trust and regard, hers for the relief of suffering (Care, 1984) and so on.

Much work on sources of meaning has drawn on Bellah et al.'s (1985) account of three distinctive work orientations. In this schema, those with a "job" orientation approach work as a means to other desired ends while a second group with a "career" orientation value work inasmuch as it contributes to a wider narrative of the self, organized in terms of career. The third "calling" orientation animates those who desire to undertake intrinsically meaningful work (e.g. Bunderson and Thompson, 2009; Hall and Chandler, 2005). The "called" seek tasks, relationships, and conceptualizations of their work that are invested with meaning (Wrzesniewski et al., 1997; Wrzesniewski and Dutton, 2001; Berg, Dutton, and Wrzesniewski, 2013), even in the most mundane and routine of task environments.

This latter observation has led some to suggest a further distinction between "callers" who craft any job in sometimes discouraging contexts to enable the experience of meaningful work to be realized and the "called" who invest whatever work role they happen to occupy with meaning (Hall and Chandler, 2005; Pratt, Pradies, and Lepisto, 2013). Bunderson and Thompson (2009) suggest a slightly different distinction between two potential sources of meaning—in the first, agents are called to realize what they take to be their particular talents, and in the second they are called to serve some greater good. For the "called" but not the "callers," individual responsibility was "not to decide but to discover and dutifully embrace" their role (Bunderson and Thompson, 2009: 51).

Lepisto and Pratt (2016) argue for another distinction between vocational callings which "emphasize the personal engagements and enjoyment that callings bring" (Lepisto and Pratt, 2016: 3) and those which "emphasize duty and obligation" (ibid. and see also Madden, Bailey, and Kerr, 2015). It is worth noting however that Lepisto and Pratt's distinction requires a bifurcation between self- and other-regarding goods that is rooted in the modern conception of the self, and that Bunderson and Thompson's distinction adheres to a Kantian bifurcation between duty and self-actualization. While both are at home in a post-Enlightenment understanding of the self, both are highly questionable when considered from the perspective of the virtue traditions (MacIntyre, 2016). They also contrast markedly with Bellah et al.'s (1985) initial conceptualization of "calling" in which vocational and communal goods require each other as they do for the virtue traditions. On this account, work provides for those who are "called":

> A practical ideal of activity and character that makes a person's work inseparable from his or her life. It subsumes the self into a community of disciplined practice and sound judgment whose activity has meaning and value in itself, not just in the output or profit that results from it. But the calling not only links a person to his or her fellow workers. A calling links a person to the larger community, a whole in which the calling of each is a contribution to the good of all...The calling is a crucial link between the individual and the public world. Work in the sense of calling can never be merely private.   (Bellah et al., 1996 [1985]: 66, cited in McPherson, 2013: 289)

For Bellah et al. (1985) we cannot describe vocational orientations to self-actualization as expressions of "calling" even if their experience is understood as deeply meaningful, because such orientations are "merely private." Bailey and Madden (2017) concur, and suggest that work should only be understood as meaningful "when an individual perceives an authentic connection between their work and a broader transcendent life purpose beyond the self" (Bailey and Madden, 2017: 4).

While disputes as to the nature of calling are prevalent, there is little divergence in respect of its consequences. In their oft-cited study, Bunderson and Thompson (2009) found American zookeepers to be exemplars of employees for whom work was experienced as deeply meaningful despite a number of structural obstacles. These included being significantly underpaid against comparably qualified professionals, undertaking manual tasks in unpleasant conditions, and having to work second and even third jobs to sustain their income levels. Zookeepers' understanding of the importance of their work was the source of their experience of deeply meaningful work. Justifications took the kind of teleological form associated with vocation (McPherson, 2013) provided, in this case, by animal welfare (Bunderson and Thompson, 2009). Their belief that "one's employing organization also has a moral duty related to the work" (Bunderson and Thompson, 2009: 43) is consistent with other research findings from marginal environments, including the travelling circus (Beadle and Könyöt, 2006; Beadle, 2013). Dempsey and Sanders's (2010) study of narrative accounts of social entrepreneurs found similar relationships as a range of purposive objects animated their particular missions and their willingness to sacrifice economic and other important goods, including those of health and family relationships.

In these studies, the pursuit of work purposes was prioritized over conventional preferences for satisfactory levels of income and work–life balance. Bunderson and Thompson (2009: 32) characterize such work as "double-edged" while Dempsey and Sanders (2010: 437) find their participants' accounts to be "troubling," and indeed the consequences of such an orientation to work are far-reaching. Bunderson and Thompson's (2009) finding that zookeepers who understand themselves as "called" are more likely to resist managerial initiatives that they perceive harm animals than those that impact on their own terms and conditions at work, indicates that this distinction may have implications for employment relations more widely (see also Dutton, Roberts, and Bednar, 2010).

The importance of work orientation to the experience of work is consistent with Malka and Chatman's (2003) longitudinal study. This found that variation in job satisfaction among their sample of MBA graduates was largely explained by pre-existing extrinsic and intrinsic work orientations. While the satisfaction of those who sought extrinsic goods was positively associated with income growth, the intrinsically motivated reported a small negative relationship between income levels and job satisfaction so that as they earned more their satisfaction marginally declined.

In relating such disparate sources of meaning to the experience of meaningful work, Michaelson comments that:

> There is often an implicit logic in this literature that meaningfulness involves a sort
> of "fit" or alignment between the individual and the tasks, job or work he or she

performs. That is, to the degree that work fulfils one's needs or matches one's values or beliefs, then work is often seen as meaningful." (Michaelson et al., 2014: 79)

Critically, such a conceptualization of meaningful work is processual rather than substantive because there is no standard by which "meaningful" work might be distinguished other than its fulfillment of the individual's "values or beliefs." And while this provides an account through which to understand the phenomenology of meaningful work, it does little for those who seek to prioritize the provision of meaningful work as a "public policy concern" (Breen, 2016: *passim*) or as "a fundamental human need" (Yeoman, 2014: 235) in liberal or welfare accounts. For liberals, "meaningful work" thereby reduces to just one more preference to be satisfied (Maitland, 1989) while for welfarists "It is morally arbitrary for the state to put its thumb on the scale to further some of these purposes over others" (Arneson, 1987: 523).

Lepisto and Pratt's (2016) argument that the field has been marred by a failure to distinguish between the phenomenological realization of meaningful work and the justifications that enable workers to distinguish between work that has meaning and work that does not is also thrown into sharp relief. For both liberals and welfarists, matters of personal preference are, as Arneson puts it, "morally arbitrary"; the state should not "put its thumb on the scale" for it has no stronger grounds so to do than one individual has in claiming the superiority of their "values or beliefs" over those of any other agent. You might value work that helps others (Care, 1984), I might value work that pays well, and there is no non-arbitrary basis through which either of us might seek to persuade the other of the merits of our position. The only role for justification is in the means–end reasoning that enables us to align the ends provided by our preferences with the means afforded by the opportunities open to us. Lepisto and Pratt's (2016) examples of the type of anomie into which individuals who are unable to justify the meaningfulness of their work are liable to sink, are to the point. Such individuals are at home in a contemporary social order in which the types of justificatory accounts that might provide such an argument are not only absent, but must be absent, because any such argument is held to be arbitrary and therefore without warrant. This relationship between the crisis of meaning in individual lives and the lack of a shared public standard of meaningful work may only be overcome if we can provide an account of the good that provides a background against which particular claims—those of meaningful work, but also of other goods— might be judged. Arneson recognizes this possibility but dismisses it:

> If one rules out the grounding of pre-modern metaphysics and theology, the prospects for a rationally compelling perfectionism look dim. (Arneson, 1987: 584)

On Arneson's account and that of liberals such as Maitland (1989), the types of justification which Lepisto and Pratt (2016) seek are arbitrary—we might collect them, but in so doing we would be engaged in an activity that had more in common with philately than social science. Arneson's (1987) argument requires the denial of the distinction between preferences and goods and hence renders questions such as: "Should I desire X?" to be unanswerable. Nevertheless, a moment's reflection on our own lives suggests that we not only consider which preferences to act on and in which circumstances, but also whether particular desires (for money, fame, the next cigarette, the downfall of our rival, or whatever) are worth pursuing. To do this requires us to have at least an implicit understanding of the good against which to judge our preferences. Let us turn, then, to the neo-Aristotelian virtue tradition that attempts to provide a grounding for such questions to be asked and answered.

NEO-ARISTOTELIAN VIRTUE ETHICS

It is worth beginning this section with a clarification of language because the idea of "meaningful work" is simply not at home in a virtue tradition. Precisely because this tradition is concerned with the justification of claims to "good" and goods as they apply to whole classes of existents, "meaning" is something to be judged against such an understanding rather than being in any sense primary. To focus on "meaning" is to admit precisely to that form of relativism in which preferences trump goods. MacIntyre outlines this distinction when he states that:

> Aristotle meant by "eudaimonia" a state such that there is nothing better that we could wish for ourselves or anyone else, a state in which the life of a rational animal is completed and perfected. There is no concept of a "meaningful life" in Aristotle or indeed anywhere in thought, I am inclined to say, until the nineteenth century. It is only when people are unable to conceive of human lives as having by their very nature some *telos*, the achievement of which perfects and completes such lives, that they ask "What could give meaning to a human life such as mine?" The question of the meaning of human life, as distinguished from the question about the ends of human life, is posed only when it can no longer be answered.   (MacIntyre, 2015)

An account of good work is therefore privileged over that of meaningful work, and in its turn must find its place in a wider account of human goods. Virtue-based accounts, found across pre-Enlightenment societies and in some contemporary marginal groups, are many and varied (MacIntyre, 2007 [1981]). They shared and share a common understanding of the relationship between the acquisition of virtues, those qualities of mind and character that enable us to identify and achieve goods, and the type of work we do.

This is the work of particular practices, human activities through which, among other features, distinctions become available that were at first obscure to us and their use becomes familiar through undertaking successively more challenging tasks; we may even develop or discover distinctions once we have become experienced practitioners ourselves. Meaning develops with such distinctions as those between colors in portraiture or some other practice in which a color palette is essential (MacIntyre, 1992). On this account, the concept of meaning, and the derivation of meaningfulness as its active attribution, is available only to the extent that we participate in relevant practices. To abstract "meaning" and "meaningfulness" from practices is to render them unintelligible; for it is only in the context of practice that such distinctions become available. It is this conceptualization of meaning and meaningfulness that informs MacIntyre's contention that the concept of "the meaning of life" is unintelligible.

Our education as practitioners—as farmers, painters, acrobats, nurses, and many others—develops our virtues and enables us to learn how to make distinctions around the goods internal to them, and the standards of excellence they seek. On this account, meaning supervenes on practices so that distinctions around the goods and excellences of both practices and practitioners become available to us only as we learn. Such activities as the expression of an emotion through the painting of a particular type of shadow falling over the planes of a face, the critique of such expression, the development of traditions through which the delineation of and relationships between artistic styles is to be understood, and even the isolation of the *sui generis* are all meaning-making and meaning-contesting activities whose intelligibility derives from participation in relevant practices as practitioner or learned observer (Garcia-Ruiz and Rodriguez-Lluesma, 2014). It is only, for example, through an extensive familiarity with literature that the achievements of a Joyce or an Eliot might be understood, a familiarity with mathematics that enables an appreciation of the achievement of Ramanujan, but equally only through a familiarity with the soil and history of particular fields that a farmer can learn how best to manage them.

This understanding of meaning as supervening on activity takes us far from accounts in which work becomes meaningful only to the extent of fulfilling pre-existing psychological needs or motives. One consequence is that we acquire a dynamic understanding of preference and desire, not as surd facts, but as stages in the development of our learning about our own good; stages that may be frustrated by inadequate education, resources, and opportunities. But if things go well, virtues such as temperance and patience are acquired as we develop in becoming farmers, painters, acrobats, and nurses such that:

> desires we initially bring to these tasks—often desires to please parents or teachers and to obtain goods that are the external rewards for success in this or that particular activity, prizes, fame, money, are displaced by and transformed into desires for the goods internal to each particular activity, and more especially, for the good of excellence in performing those tasks.   (MacIntyre, 2000: 124)

Practitioners' development not only actualizes excellence in products but also in ourselves because an intimate relationship holds between our experience of work and the development or frustration of our virtues. As we become able to better discern quality distinctions, identify the skills that we lack and work to overcome them, we develop a rank-ordering of relevant goods that directs our attention and effort:

> It is not only the conception of such ends that may be unexpectedly transformed in the course of our activities. We too, while developing those skills and qualities of mind and character needed to achieve those ends, may discover that the transformation of ourselves that is involved is significantly different from what we had

expected, in part perhaps because of the particularities of our circumstances, but in part because what such virtues as courage, patience, truthfulness, and justice require can never be fully specified in advance. Hence, as Aquinas emphasized, in the life of practice there are no fully adequate generalizations to guide us, no set of rules sufficient to do the work for us, something that each of us has to learn for her or himself as we move toward the achievement of the ends of our activities and the end of excellence in those activities.   (MacIntyre, 2016: 51)

The pursuit of a practice enables the achievement of: "the good of a certain kind of life…the painter's living out of a greater or lesser part of his or her life *as a painter*…is the second kind of good internal to painting' (MacIntyre, 2007 [1981]: 190; original emphasis). This relationship between our own development and our ability to achieve the goods internal to practices characterizes our apprenticeship and introduces us to the necessity of teleological reasoning; that is, reasoning toward the achievement of goods, both as individuals and with fellow practitioners and teachers. Denied this kind of education we are unlikely to acquire such an understanding of ourselves and our goods. While such an apprenticeship might occur at any stage in our lives, our virtues and moral agency will have to be recovered if they are not achieved in early education (MacIntyre, 2000). What is it that we would have lost?

Virtues involve intellectual, emotional, motivational, and behavioral dimensions (Alzolo, 2017) so that, for example, the benevolent person not only acts in a particular way with appropriate understanding of her purposes but is informed by appropriate emotions. The person who saves the child from the on-rushing car is courageous only if their action is inspired by the desire to save the child rather than to impress onlookers or because they are careless about their own lives (Alzolo, 2017: 775). Inasmuch as they are virtuous, however, they will be disposed both to recognize that this situation requires action and to take the action. According to MacIntyre the virtues are:

> just those qualities that enable agents to identify both what goods are at stake in any particular situation and their relative importance in that situation *and* how that particular agent must act for the sake of the good and the best.
> (MacIntyre, 2016: 190; original emphasis)

The virtues enable us to exercise our judgment around the application of tools, materials, means, and arguments as we encounter obstacles to the achievements of the harvest, the painting, the somersault, the administration of medicine and those countless other actions we need to perform at the right time and in the right way. Such virtues serve to guard against undue haste and to reduce the anxiety of waiting; they prevent us from attempting either to dominate or to withdraw from those decision-making contexts in which we reason about and toward common goods (MacIntyre, 2007 [1981]). The virtue of patience, alongside the other virtues developed through participation in practices, prepares us to reason about goods as a whole; and to be denied participation in such practices is to risk becoming the victim of untutored desires, those which are not put to the question. To engage in dialogue around the meaningfulness of our work, rather than simply to state a preference, is to be able to account for the reasons why our work is meaningful in light of an account of good reasons as such. Meaningful work is thus epiphenomenal of the directedness of our lives:

> For individuals cannot define or redefine their place in achieving the common goods of home, school and workplace without also defining and redefining the place in their lives of those various goods through the achievement of which they direct themselves toward that good which would complete and perfect their lives. We go, that is, from asking "What is my good qua family member, qua student or teacher, qua apprentice or master of this set of working skills?" to asking "What is my good qua human agent?" In answering this latter question, we decide how the various aspects and relationships of each role are to be integrated into a single life and how the unity of that life is to be understood in terms of the various stages through which we pass from conception to death.   (MacIntyre, 2016: 192–3)

It follows from the centrality of participation in practices to the development of the virtues that a neo-Aristotelian understanding distinguishes between work with which we are engaged as practitioners and work whose organization excludes us from such activities and relationships. The relationship between practices and the institutions in which they are housed is thus pivotal to the neo-Aristotelian understanding of work, for the institution is both prerequisite to and constantly in tension with the practices it houses (MacIntyre, 2007 [1981]; Moore, 2017).

This truncated account of the neo-Aristotelian understanding of the virtues may provide a coherent theoretical framework, but what evidence is there for its contentions? While the scale of the type of longitudinal enquiry into virtue development that would test neo-Aristotelian contentions about habituation, practices, and the exercise of virtue has not been undertaken, evidence consistent with many of them may be found in empirical studies inspired by virtue ethics traditions, in increasing numbers of studies into particular virtues, and in work from experimental psychology.

Evidence of the relationship between experience of the goods produced through our work and changes in both behavior and subsequent preferences is found in the field experiments of Grant and his co-workers (see especially Grant, 2007, 2008a, 2008b; Grant et al., 2007; Grant and Hoffman, 2011). These demonstrate that the magnitude, frequency, and scope of prosocial job characteristics are positively correlated with affective commitment to beneficiaries (Grant, 2008a: 29). Whether hospital workers improving hand washing (Grant and Hoffman, 2011), fund-raisers improving revenue (Grant et al., 2007), or lifeguards' enhanced sense of the meaningfulness of their work, experience of the impact of work on others has consistent positive and persistent (Grant, 2007: 403) effects on a range of outcomes. Grant argues that conventional understandings of orientations to altruism or self-interest should be replaced by the question, "*When and under what conditions* do employees care about others?" (Grant, 2007: 406, original emphasis). This account supports the traditional Aristotelian notion of habituation through which the work that we undertake encourages particular behavioral and affective responses.

A second source of evidence is found in the now extensive body of survey data (Beadle, Sison and Fontrodona, 2015) in which individual virtues have been found to predict such outcomes as organizational citizenship behaviors (Morse and Cohen, 2017). While there are critical differences between the understanding of virtues, and in particular their individuation and measurement in psychological studies and those of classical accounts (Alzolo, 2015), these studies are largely consistent with an association between both self- and peer-reported virtues and persistent behavioral traits.

A third source of empirical evidence is found in distinctly MacIntyrean studies into workers' resistance against institutional pressure to undermine internal goods of practices. These include von Krogh et al.'s (2012) study of open source software engineers resisting the commercialization of code and Robson's (2015) account of Scottish bankers who undertook career-limiting opposition to the imposition of sales targets on business clients.

A Virtue-based Account
of Meaningful Work

Finally, we turn to how neo-Aristotelian virtue ethics understands the wide divergence between preferences that has been so regularly noted in the empirical studies into meaningful work and how, unlike those approaching meaningful work from liberal of welfarist traditions, such findings are not probative to virtue-based arguments for "meaningful work." On the account presented in this chapter, the type of work that develops the virtues involves tasks whose difficulty increases over time, thereby ensuring challenge; in which apprentices receive ongoing feedback, first from their teachers and later from peers (see Hall, 2011 for an example from surgical practice); in which they enter into relationships not only with other practitioners but with those of the past and the future (see Bailey and Madden's 2017 account of stonemasonry); and in which progress is marked by gradual increases in the ability to exercise autonomy and discretion.

While not using the language of meaning, for reasons considered earlier, these features of the practices that develop virtue echo those that characterize the realization of meaningful work in both classic (Hackman and Oldham, 1975) and contemporary accounts (Lepisto and Pratt, 2016). For the virtue tradition it is only in such contexts that workers may experience the type of calling which directs career choices and relationships—such as Bunderson and Thompson's (2009) zookeepers. The divergence in contemporary preferences is consistent with the decline of such skilled work. It is not to be understood in terms of character traits alone but is socially and historically situated in an environment in which practice-based work is marginal (though see Breen, 2007 for counterarguments).

The availability and distribution of work requiring exercise of the virtues is therefore an ethical concern for a virtue-informed notion of the good. Unlike those liberal and welfarist accounts that deny a substantive notion of human good (MacIntyre, 2016), a virtue-based account argues that our preferences must be educated if they are to make a contribution to our deliberations. Our ability to reason, individually and with others, about goods, is itself imperiled if we have not been introduced to teleological reasoning and to the virtues through which the conclusions of that reasoning might be enacted. Without such an education, our preferences will be ill-formed.

The availability and distribution of the work of practices is therefore a central concern of virtue traditions. It is perhaps then unsurprising that those most concerned with justice in the allocation of tasks and their distribution have regularly contributed ethical critiques of work organization (Breen, 2007; Hsieh, 2008; Sayer, 2009; Walsh, 1994). Walsh, for example, argues for a robust definition of meaningful work based on the extent to which workers control goals and the design of tasks (Walsh, 1994: 243) while Sayer argues that workers should engage in both conceptual and operational tasks which are understood in terms of the larger projects to which they contribute (Sayer, 2009: 5–6), and Breen (2007) lauds the experiments in cellular production by Volvo's Udavella plant. For all of these researchers the observation that workers may be ostensibly satisfied in work that is routine and monotonous does not provide justification for a distribution of tasks that concentrates challenge and contribution in the work of others. One consequence of this virtue-based critique is that the allocation of work tasks is never merely a matter of technical disposal by those armed with the rationale of efficiency but always an ethical question in which the virtue of justice should be central.

REFERENCES

Alzolo, M. (2015). "Virtuous persons and virtuous actions in business ethics and organizational research." *Business Ethics Quarterly*, 25(3), 287–318.

Alzolo, M. (2017). "Virtues and their Explanatory and Predictive Power in the Workplace." In A. Sison, G. Beabout, and I. Ferrero (eds.), *Handbook of Virtue Ethics in Business and Management*, pp. 773–87. Dordrecht: Springer.

Anscombe, G. E. M. (1958). "Modern moral philosophy." *Philosophy*, 33(124), 1–19.

Arneson, R. (1987). "Meaningful work and market socialism." *Ethics*, 97(3), 517–45.

Bailey, C. and Madden, A. (2017). "Time reclaimed: Temporality and the experience of meaningful work." *Work, Employment and Society*, 31(1), 3–18.

Beadle, R. (2013). "Managerial work in a practice-embodying institution: The role of calling, the virtue of constancy." *Journal of Business Ethics*, 113(4), 679–90.

Beadle, R. and Knight, K. (2012). "Virtue and meaningful work." *Business Ethics Quarterly*, 22(2), 433–50.

Beadle, R. and Könyöt, D. (2006). "The man in the red coat: Management in the circus." *Culture and Organization*, 12(2), 127–37.

Beadle, R., Sison, A., and Fontrodona, J. (2015). "Introduction: Virtue and virtuousness: When will the twain ever meet?" *Business Ethics: A European Review*, 24(S2), S67–77.

Behson, S. J., Eddy, E. R., and Lorenzet, S. J. (2000). "The importance of the critical psychological states in the job characteristics model: A meta-analytic and structural equations modelling examination." *Current Research in Social Psychology*, 5(12), 170–89.

Bellah, R. N., Madsen, R., Sullivan, W. M., Swidler. A., and Tipton, S. M. (1985). *Habits of the Heart: Individualism and commitment in American life*. Berkeley, CA: University of California Press.

Bellah, R. N., Madsen, R., Sullivan, W. M., Swidler. A., and Tipton, S. M. (1996 [1985]). *Habits of the Heart: Individualism and commitment in American life - updated edition with a new introduction*. Berkeley, CA: University of California Press.

Berg, J. M., Dutton, J. E., and Wrzesniewski, A. (2013). "Job Crafting and Meaningful Work." In B. J. Dik., S. Byrne, and M. F. Steger (eds.), *Purpose and Meaning in the Workplace*, pp. 81–104. Washington, DC: American Psychological Association.

Bowie, N. (1998). "A Kantian theory of meaningful work." *Journal of Business Ethics*, 17(9–10), 1083–92.

Breen, K. (2007). "Work and emancipatory practice: Towards a recovery of human beings' productive capacities." *Res Publica*, 13(4), 381–414.

Breen, K. (2016). "In Defence of Meaningful Work as a Public Policy Concern." In A. Fives and K. Breen (eds.), *Philosophy and Political Engagement*, pp. 139–61. London: Palgrave Macmillan.

Bunderson, J. S. and Thompson, J. A. (2009). "The call of the wild: Zookeepers, callings, and the double-edged sword of deeply meaningful work." *Administrative Science Quarterly*, 54(1), 32–57.

Care, N. S. (1984). "Career choice." *Ethics*, 94(2), 283–302.

Dempsey, S. E. and Sanders, M. L. (2010). "Meaningful work? Nonprofit marketization and work/life imbalance in popular autobiographies of social entrepreneurship." *Organization*, 17(4), 437–59.

Dutton, J. E., Roberts, L. M., and Bednar, J. (2010). "Pathways for positive identity construction at work: Four types of positive identity and the building of social resources." *Academy of Management Review*, 35(2), 265–93.

Fried, Y. and Ferris, G. R. (1987). "The validity of the job characteristics model: A review and meta-analysis." *Personnel Psychology*, 40(2), 287–322.

Garcia-Ruiz, P. and Rodriguez-Lluesma, C. (2014). "Consumption practices: A virtue ethics approach." *Business Ethics Quarterly*, 24(4), 509–32.

Google Advanced Scholar. (2017). Available at: https://scholar.google.co.uk/scholar?as_q=Meaningful+Work&as_epq=&as_oq=&as_eq=&as_occt=title&as_sauthors=&as_publication=&as_ylo=2002&as_yhi=2016&btnG=&hl=en&as_sdt=0%2C5 [accessed February 16, 2017].

Grant, A. M. (2007). "Relational job design and the motivation to make a prosocial difference." *Academy of Management Review*, 32(2), 393–417.

Grant, A. M. (2008a). "Designing jobs to do good: Dimensions and psychological consequences of prosocial Job Characteristics." *The Journal of Positive Psychology*, 3(1), 19–39.

Grant, A. M. (2008b). "The significance of task significance: Job performance effects, relational mechanisms and boundary conditions." *Journal of Applied Psychology*, 93(1), 108–24.

Grant, A. M., Campbell, E. M., Chen, G., Cottone, K., Lapedis, D., and Lee, K. (2007). "Impact and the art of motivation maintenance: The effects of contact with beneficiaries on persistence behavior." *Organizational Behavior and Human Decision Processes*, 103(1), 53–67.

Grant A. M. and Hoffman, D. A. (2011). "It's not all about me: Motivating hospital handwashing by focusing on patients." *Psychological Science*, 22(12), 1494–9.

Grant, A. M. and Parker, S. K. (2009). "Redesigning work design theories: The rise of relational and proactive perspectives." *Academy of Management Annals*, 3(1), 317–75.

Hackman, J. R. and Oldham, G. R. (1975). "Development of the Job Diagnostic Survey." *Journal of Applied Psychology*, 60(2), 159–70.

Hall, D. E. (2011). "The Guild of Surgeons as a tradition of moral enquiry." *Journal of Medicine and Philosophy*, 36(2), 111–32.

Hall, D. T. and Chandler, D. E. (2005). "Psychological success: When the career is calling." *Journal of Organizational Behavior*, 26(2), 155–76.

Hsieh, N. (2008). "Survey article: Justice in production." *The Journal of Political Philosophy*, 16(1), 72–100.

Isaksen, J. (2000). "Constructing meaning despite the drudgery of repetitive work." *Journal of Humanistic Psychology*, 40(3), 84–107.

Knight, K. (2007). *Aristotelian Philosophy: Ethics and politics from Aristotle to MacIntyre*. Cambridge: Polity Press.

Kreiner, G., Ashforth, B., and Sluss, D. (2006). "Identity dynamics in occupational dirty work: Integrating social identity and system justification perspectives." *Organization Science*, 17(5), 619–36.

Lepisto, D. A. and Pratt, M. G. (2016). "Meaningful work as realization and justification: Toward a dual conceptualization." *Organizational Psychology Review*, 7(2), 99–121.

MacIntyre, A. (1992). "Colors, cultures and practices." *Midwest Studies in Philosophy*, 17(1), 1–23.

MacIntyre, A. (2000). "The Recovery of Moral Agency." In J. Wilson (ed.), *The Best Christian Writing 2000*, pp. 111–36. London: HarperCollins.

MacIntyre, A. (2007 [1981]). *After Virtue—A study in moral theory*, 3rd edn. London: Duckworth.

MacIntyre, A. (2015). "Interview with Alasdair MacIntyre" (interviewed by Andrius Bielskis). *Aplinkkeliai* [website]. Available at: http://aplinkkeliai.lt/musu-tekstai/tekstai-kitomis-kalbomis/interview-with-alasdair-macintyre/ [accessed March 31, 2017].

MacIntyre, A. (2016). *Ethics in the Conflicts of Modernity*. Cambridge: Cambridge University Press.

Madden, A., Bailey, C., and Kerr, J. (2015). "'For this I was made'. Gender and callings: the experience of being called as a woman priest." *Work, Employment and Society*, 29(5), 866–74.

Maitland, I. (1989). "Rights in the workplace: A Nozickian argument." *Journal of Business Ethics*, 8(12), 951–4.

Malka, A. and Chatman, J. (2003). "Intrinsic and extrinsic work orientations as moderators of the effect of annual income on subjective well-being." *Personality and Social Psychology Bulletin*, 29(6), 737–46.

McPherson, D. (2013). "Vocational virtue ethics: Prospects for a virtue ethics approach to business." *Journal of Business Ethics*, 116(2), 283–96.

Michaelson, C., Pratt, M. G., Grant, A. D., and Dunn, C. P. (2014). "Meaningful work: Connecting business ethics and organization studies." *Journal of Business Ethics*, 121(1), 77–90.

Moore, G. (2017). *Virtue at Work: Ethics for individuals, managers, and organizations*. Oxford: Oxford University Press.

Morse, L. and Cohen, T. R. (2017). "Virtues and Vices in Workplace Settings: The role of moral character in predicting counterproductive and Citizenship Behaviors." In A. Sison, G. Beabout, and I. Ferrero (eds.), *Handbook of Virtue Ethics in Business and Management*, pp. 761–72, Dordrecht: Springer.

Nozick, R. (1974). *Anarchy, the State, Utopia*. New York: Basic Books.

Pratt, M. G. and Ashforth, B. E. (2003). "Fostering Meaningfulness in Working and at Work." In K. Cameron, J. E. Dutton, and R. E. Quinn (eds.), *Positive Organizational Scholarship: Foundations of a new discipline*, pp. 308–27. San Francisco: Berrett-Koehler.

Pratt, M. G., Pradies, C., and Lepisto, D. A. (2013). "Doing Well, Doing Good and Doing With: Organizational Practices for Effectively Cultivating Meaningful Work." In B. J. Dik., S. Byrne, and M. F. Steger (eds.), *Purpose and Meaning in the Workplace*, pp. 173–96. Washington, DC: APA Books.

Robson, A. (2015). "Constancy and integrity: (Un)measurable virtues?" *Business Ethics: A European Review*, 24(S2), 115–29.

Rosso, B. D., Dekas, K. H., and Wrzesniewski, A. (2010). "On the meaning of work: A theoretical integration and review." *Research in Organizational Behavior*, 30, 91–127.

Ryan, R. M. and Deci, E. L. (2001). "On happiness and human potentials: A review of research on hedonic and eudaimonic well-being." *Annual Review of Psychology*, 52, 141–66.

Sayer, A. (2009). "Contributive justice and meaningful work." *Res Publica*, 15(1), 1–16.

Schwartz, A. (1982). "Meaningful work." *Ethics*, 92(4), 634–46.

von Krogh, G., Haefliger, S., Spaeth, S., and Wallin, M. W. (2012). "Carrots and rainbows: Motivation and social practice in open source software development." *MIS Quarterly*, 36(2), 649–76.

Walsh, A. (1994). "Meaningful work as a distributive Good." *The Southern Journal of Philosophy*, 32(2), 233–50.

Wrzesniewski, A. and Dutton, J. E. (2001). "Crafting a job: Revisioning employees as active crafters of their work." *Academy of Management Review*, 26(2), 179–201.

Wrzesniewski, A., McCauley, C., Rozin, P., and Schwartz, B. (1997). "Jobs, careers, and callings: People's relations to their work." *Journal of Research in Personality*, 31(1), 21–33.

Yeoman, R. (2014). "Conceptualising meaningful work as a fundamental human need." *Journal of Business Ethics*, 125(2), 235–51.

Yeoman, R. (2015). "A Philosophy of Work and a Politics of Meaningfulness." In I. Geary and A. Pabst (eds.), *Blue Labour: Forging a new politics*, pp. 179–94. London: I. B. Tauris & Co.

....

CHAPTER 5

WORK AND THE MEANING
OF BEING

....

TODD S. MEI

INTRODUCTION

....

THE phrase "meaningful work" tends to relate to the manner in which a worker finds his or her work to be personally fulfilling. Social scientific studies therefore take the occurrence of meaning in work as any instance where a person's desires concerning what it means to work meaningfully are fulfilled by his or her job, vocation, or career (Steger, Dik, and Duffy, 2012: 323–5). As relevant as this approach may be to the life and the psychology of the worker, there is, nonetheless, a problem with it. Much like forms of preference hedonism, this approach risks reducing the meaning of work to an attitude about it where one's career or vocation is merely a corollary of one's preferences, or what one finds meaningful. So if meaningfulness has associations related to subjective attitudes, what might be involved in attempting to define the meaning of work itself, as something present in any instance of work?[1]

Conventional philosophical accounts identify the universal meaning of work in terms of its *necessary* relation to being or existence. Work is that activity that fulfills necessary ends, or what is reaped in terms of one's wages, in the broadest sense of that term. Whether or not necessity is a dignified quality depends on the philosophical account one reads. But whatever the case, there are significant problems arising from this supposition

---

[1] The general distinction between meaningful work and the meaning of work can be construed respectively in terms of a subjectivist and objectivist approach to meaning. However, this general distinction may be too clumsy. A more nuanced approach might reside in seeing how the objective features or functions of work relate to subjective beliefs, attitudes, and preferences of the worker. I propose such an analysis in forthcoming research examining "the poetics of work." Suffice it to say here that I believe the account of metaphor and work in this chapter captures something objective about the way in which work generates meaning and thus relates to how we, as workers, see our lives as going best.

that will become clear when examining the two main philosophical accounts of work provided by Aristotle and Marx. In short, the consequence of defining work in terms of necessity is one where work can never really partake of an end beyond the fulfillment of physical and biological needs.

After examining the contributions and limitations of Aristotle and Marx, this chapter will argue for a more promising account. Understanding the meaning of work lies in seeing how its necessary function participates in a supra-necessary one. I refer to this supra-necessary purpose in terms of its metaphorical capacity. That is to say, work may address a necessary end, but it also discloses new possibilities for being beyond necessity by way of metaphorical reference. This way of conceiving work is decisive since it takes its most significant feature to be the transformation of understanding as opposed to the transformation of material.

ARISTOTLE AND *POIESIS*

When Aristotle identifies servile labor with slavery (*Politics* 1277a32–1277b8), he is not simply expressing a disdain for a specific class of people within the *polis*.[2] Rather, he is drawing on philosophical distinctions between different kinds of activity and how they relate to self-sufficiency (*autarkeia*) and happiness (*eudaimonia*). This relation is construed both physically and ethically. In short, Aristotle defines work as an activity that is incomplete in some physical manner and ethically incapable of partaking in happiness except as a means to providing necessaries for living. The physics and the ethics of work, as we shall see, are not unrelated.

With respect to physics, Aristotle distinguishes work, or *poiesis*, as an act whose end lies beyond its actual doing. Producing a house, for example, involves a series of actions in order to arrive at the final work (*ergon*). These actions by themselves never have the house as its actual end; rather they comprise a cumulative series that is underway to the completion of the house. This description is contrasted with action, or *praxis*, in which the doing of the action is its completion. The act of seeing, for example, achieves the end of catching sight of an object or person. *Praxis* clearly has a special sense for Aristotle, and though he recognizes that action can entail many kinds of activities, he maintains that while *poiesis* can be understood as an action, its nature is different than that of *praxis*. One way of seeing this difference is in terms of temporal constitution. Per the example of seeing, in *praxis* doing and the end are contemporaneous; it is not, on Aristotle's account, characterized by movement in time. In contrast, as we saw with house building, a series of actions are required to make progress toward the completion of the house. *Poiesis* is therefore characterized by movement in time, or *kinesis*. As Aristotle says, "movement is not complete in every portion of time, but rather that most

---

[2] For a more detailed account of what is discussed in this section, see Mei (2009: 55–73).

movements are incomplete" (*NE* 1174b3–4) and "every movement involves time…as does the movement that is building" (*NE* 1174a20–1).

This physical distinction between completion and incompletion cannot be fully appreciated unless one sees how it correlates with the ethical dimension. Accordingly, completion does not refer to achieving a final end or goal, but the enactment of a life that is most complete, a life whose hallmarks are self-sufficiency and happiness. Take for instance the following comments:

> we suppose it [happiness] to be the end of things human…as a kind of activity…for happiness is not lacking in anything, but self-sufficient…nothing about happiness is incomplete.   (Respectively, *NE* 1176a31–1177b2, *NE* 1176b5, *NE* 1177b26)

What is important to bear in mind is that happiness is not a state of mind for Aristotle but a mode of doing and practicing (*NE* 1099b27–8). Accordingly, it would seem that the activity of work might be eligible as a constituent of the happy life. However, this is not the case. Taking contemplation as the highest form of happiness,[3] what becomes quite plain is that the activity of work plays no significant or distinctive role in happiness except for providing the basis for its activities:

> the talked-about self-sufficiency will be a feature of the reflective life most of all; for both the intellectually accomplished and the just person, and everyone else, will require the things necessary for living, but given that they are adequately supplied with such things…the intellectually accomplished person will be able to engage in reflection even when by himself.   (*NE* 1177a28–35)

The necessity of work, in providing for basic needs, is not just a form of action shared by animals but also an action undertaken by someone who is not liberated from the requirements of necessity and is therefore not truly free to participate in the life of the polis (*Politics* 1254b24–36). But if Aristotle seems to take for granted that some class of people must provide the "things necessary for living," it is because he does not see them as entirely segregated from the good life. Indeed, Aristotle's well-known holistic conception of the polis suggests that servile labor is not only necessary for the self-sufficiency of the polis but participates to some degree in it. If the household (*oikos*) is the model of management, then as the household flourishes so does everyone within it, at least to some degree.[4]

But a critic would argue that while it may be possible to show how other domains of life participate in happiness i.e. not just contemplation but political activity as well— there is little in Aristotle's account of work that is substantial enough to allow it some virtuous distinction. The necessity of work is simply unflattering. Marx certainly took it upon himself to correct this view: "The most essential factor in the labour process is the

---

[3] It is debatable to what extent contemplation is really the highest. See, for example, Roche (1988). Mei (2009) argues for a different interpretation of Aristotle that is more inclusive about work.

[4] Notoriously, this argument involves a morally despicable aspect of the *Politics* when Aristotle discusses natural slavery. A natural slave can be neither self-sufficient nor happy; he or she can nonetheless benefit from the flourishing of his or her master. See Lockwood (2007).

worker himself, and in antiquity this worker was a slave. But this does not imply that the worker is a *slave* by nature (though this latter view is not entirely foreign to Aristotle)" (Marx, 1976: 997).

MARX AND *PRAXIS*

Marx's re-examination of work is not just a reaction to antiquity but to the historically prevailing view misconstruing the anthropological and economical dimensions of work. Marx argues that work is a primary, creative activity foundational for anything humanly possible. Thus instead of work providing necessaries for some putative higher activity, like contemplation, it is the highest activity. There are, of course, many ways according to which this reversal plays itself out, most famous of which is Marx's economic theories on labor value.[5] In this section, I will be concerned mainly with the anthropological dimension, or how Marx sees work as the activity defining human existence. This definition, as I will argue, is *foundationalist* about necessity since all things human have their meaning and content through work.

Marx's foundationalism can be seen in his early writings when he attempts to demonstrate how the most basic and important of human activities is labor. By prioritizing the empirically observable conditions of our existence, Marx argues that we do not, as individuals, arrive in existence with access to a universal consciousness or spirit. Rather, we arrive in an ongoing "process of development under definite conditions" (Marx, 1998: 43). These conditions are those of material necessity. So the first task of philosophy is to take heed of this relation and understand it: "It is not consciousness that determines life, but life that determines consciousness" (Marx, 1998: 42). This point becomes more cogent in the context of Marx's reaction to Feuerbach, who defined the human species' being according to its distinct form of consciousness that apprehends itself in terms of the objects of thought.

In contradistinction, for Marx material life itself, and not consciousness, defines the human species being. Humans are the "real living individuals themselves" (Marx, 1998: 43) in the struggle of having to interact with nature by use of its materials and forces. The predicate "real" denotes humans in the process of development with material and natural conditions. Marx writes,

> Man *lives* from nature, i.e., nature is his *body*, and he must maintain a continuing dialogue with it if he is not to die. To say that man's physical and mental life is linked to nature simply means that nature is linked to itself, for man is a part of nature.
>
> (Marx, 1974: 328)[6]

---

[5] For a more detailed consideration of this, especially with respect to land value, see Mei (2016: chapter 3).

[6] Elsewhere Marx (1988: 165) comments that nature "is *nothing* for man." It is nothing precisely when its conception is abstract and divorced from material necessity.

What is then key for Marx is an account of the activity by which humans use nature in a distinct way in order to exist. This mode of use, however, should not be seen as a process of development in which humans become free of work for some other end, as is the case for Aristotle. Rather, use is both an essential response to what is foundational for existence and a way of perpetuating a genuine relation to this foundation, even if this relation is constantly evolving according to the development of higher uses of material. This foundationalism is, in other words, one that complexifies over time such that it can be said that labor does not just respond to necessity but, in fact, produces life. Or to put it in terms already mentioned, labor is real life. "Objectified labour," as Marx notes, "ceases to exist in a dead state...because it is itself again posited as a moment of living labour" (Marx, 1973: 360).

Given this clarification, Marx can then distinguish labor as *praxis* as opposed to the ancient Greek *poiesis*. While the meaning of *poiesis* refers to a form of production engaging with nature, the concept's historical genesis limits its meaning since production is subservient to other non-laboring activities, e.g. contemplation. Marx's use of *praxis* is not only intended to reverse this historical understanding, but also to elucidate how the essential response to necessity is itself formative of the human species being in a way that had not been seen before. Of course, this is not to say that *praxis* does not include production as part of its activity. Rather, as already noted, its productive power requires being distinguished in such a way that we clearly see how it is formative of life and does not only meet necessary ends. *Praxis* is therefore the production of "material life," on which Marx comments:

> This mode of production must not be considered simply as being the reproduction of the physical existence of the individuals. Rather it is a definite form of activity of these individuals, a definite form of expressing their life, a definite *mode of life* on their part...What they are, therefore, coincides with their production, both with *what* they produce and with *how* they produce.   (Marx, 1998: 37)

One can say that when work merely *reproduces* the physical existence of individuals, it is an alienated activity since the worker can no longer secure the means and ends by which he or she can actualize a uniquely human life. In reproduction one is deprived of a genuine relation to material life, which is, of course, real life. Having said this, because the historical genesis of *poiesis* is really one in which laborers tend merely to reproduce, one can say that for Marx *poiesis* is reproduction whereas *praxis* is production.

It should also be noted that key to the productive aspect of *praxis* is how it effects human consciousness. *Praxis* produces real life for individuals because it objectifies the human in the object of work:

> it is only when the objective world becomes everywhere for man in society the world of man's essential powers—human reality, and for that reason the reality of his *own* essential powers—that all *objects* become for him the *objectification of himself*, become objects which confirm and realize his individuality, become *his* objects: that is, *man himself* becomes the object.   (Marx, 1988: 107–8)

As we will see in the next section, objectification is the basis for freedom, or what commentators note in terms of human self-realization.

MARX AND FREEDOM

In *Capital III*, Marx makes a distinction between two modes of work in relation to freedom. First, there is the simple fulfillment of necessity such that freedom can only be realized in terms of the collective control of nature utilizing energy efficient modes of production. Marx quickly dismisses this mode since it "always remains a realm of necessity" (Marx, 1981: 959). That is to say, work that remains confined to the continuous fulfillment of needs is impoverished since it persists as a mode of reproduction. To recall from above, it merely perpetuates physical existence. The second mode is one in which "human powers develop as an end in itself" and is not bound by the necessaries for metabolism. Marx qualifies, nonetheless, that while this is "the true realm of freedom ... it can only flourish with [the] realm of necessity as its basis" (Marx, 1981: 959). This passage is subject to much debate since some commentators allege that Marx never really works out the relation between necessity and freedom, between work and some putative higher ends.[7] A charitable reading of Marx takes it that freedom is predicated on a mode of work that recognizes in some manner that the human being is an end in itself.

Proponents in favor of a more charitable reading argue that the freedom innate to work manifests in terms of human self-realization, or what is freedom as self-determination (Gould, 1978 and Sayers, 2008: 77; cf. Sayers, 2006). Consider the following passage from *Grundrisse*:

> the external aims [of work] become stripped of the semblance of merely external urgencies, and become posited as aims which the individual himself posits—*hence as self-realization, objectification of the subject, hence real freedom, whose action is, precisely, labour.* (Marx, 1973: 611)

But a difficulty arises when considering that if work is "stripped" of its relation to necessity, then it no longer seems to be a basis for freedom. Whether Marx's comments are intended to be literal or hyperbolic, the details of how work can be both the basis for self-realization *and* the process by which it is actualized remains unclear at best. What I have termed "Marx's foundationalism about necessity" will help us to see this problem more distinctly.

Let us recall that in his early writings work is addressed to the actualization of real life—that is, a response to material necessity, which in turn shapes our consciousness (objectification). Yet, in his later thought, the role of freedom in human actualization means that consciousness develops beyond the relation to material life. If this consciousness is one of free self-determination, it cannot remain grounded in a necessary

---

[7] For a classical consideration, see Marcuse (1969). Cf. Sayers (2006).

relation to material. To be sure, material and relations to material are always involved, but the ends that humans find meaningful may not be confined to material or perpetuating relations to material. Many idealistic values are of this kind. So, for Marx, what is more substantial to self-development—material life or the values one defines in view of freedom? Answering this question is not easy. Marx's foundationalism means that human consciousness cannot have two ends. For a self-determining consciousness, there cannot be a relation in which material life continues to form consciousness, at least not if Marx also wants the relation to material life to be a mode of production that expresses a distinctly human life. In other words, his foundationalism results in a unilateral construal of the causal relation between material life and consciousness.

Another way of seeing the problem with Marx's foundationalism is in terms of an either/or dilemma. On the one hand, if we take Marx to mean that work is the basis for freedom in some strong sense, then human consciousness remains contiguous with work. This suggests that the real freedom really remains labor. As Paul Ricoeur (1965: 198) notes, this strong connection is problematic since it expresses a kind of militant attitude about work where all activities and ends, even if striving in the name of freedom, reduce to labor. *Praxis* is concerned with necessity and is in the service of necessity. This view may celebrate work, but it does so at the expense of asserting that one is at leisure in order to be at work.[8] Hannah Arendt, no doubt with this reading of Marx in mind, thus distinguishes labor as the activity that cannot transcend its own mode of exertion (Arendt, 1958: 141).

On the other hand, if we assume that self-determination is a distinct but contiguous form of consciousness, then self-determining aims and values remain inconsequential. This is because evaluative claims about what is either good or best for an individual's self-determination invoke concepts or values distinct from the original relation to material life. Indeed, they arise according to the freedom to form oneself anew. So the ends of self-realization are trivial precisely because they pertain to the development of personal preferences about one's life as they are distinct from the relation to real, material life. This view anticipates a form of preference hedonism since there is no real claim to objective values that could be said to maximize or best affirm one's self-realization (Parfit, 1984: 493–4). Freedom is nothing but the expression of personal preferences and how we might seek to fulfill them. Correcting this problem would require Marx to admit the significance of ideas, concepts, or activities as categorically distinct from the relation to material life. But this would be problematic with respect to his critical view of ideology and the history of philosophy (Dupré, 1966: 230).

WORK AS METAPHORICAL

It would seem, then, that a satisfactory conception of work would be able to accommodate the relation to both necessity and freedom. While the matter of work's necessary nature is uncontroversial, what requires clarification is how it links to something like freedom.

---

[8] Cf. Aristotle, *NE* 1177b5: "for we busy ourselves in order to have leisure."

If we choose to see freedom in terms of human actions, then it seems work can only be tangentially related since it would be an activity subject to what the human agent determines is worthy of actualization. Work may or may not be a part of this determination. But what if one were to see freedom as a discrete property of work itself in terms of what it allows us to do beyond mere metabolism?[9] In this section, I propose to see this property with regard to the metaphorical nature of work, where metaphor discloses new possibilities for being. Work therefore can be said to enlist necessary activity as part of a larger activity of disclosure. What it discloses are new forms of relations to oneself, others, and the world, or what can be broadly captured under the phrase "new possibilities for the meaning of being."

The relation between metaphor and work is not spurious. They both derive from the ancient Greek word *poiesis*. Earlier I mentioned that *poiesis* is a form of production. The limitation of this translation is its obvious economic and instrumental connotations. A more nuanced account would involve saying that *poiesis* is an event of drawing on pre-existing material in order to disclose something new (Beaufret, 2006: 100). But what does "new" mean? With respect to metaphor, there has been a tendency to see its form of predication as a kind of nonsense or confusion, much like a category mistake. Metaphorical discourse, it is alleged, employs words whose literal meanings conflict with one another. For example, consider a line from Wallace Steven's poem *The Idea of Order at Key West*, which runs: "She sang beyond the genius of the sea." This line can be said to be nonsensical since it attributes a human quality (genius) to a natural entity (the sea). This view, however, is mistaken. It is more accurate to say that what occurs in metaphorical predication is the predication of new meaning.

Paul Ricoeur's (1976, 1978, 1981) extensive investigation of metaphor, which draws on linguistics, literary theory, and philosophy, demonstrates that metaphorical discourse does not simply reduce to a clash of literal meanings but is instead a single movement of reference requiring the conflict of literal meanings in order to predicate something new. He refers to metaphor as a "semantic innovation" (Ricoeur, 1978: 98). In other words, the conflict of literal meanings prompts the listener to see through this conflict to a properly metaphorical reference. It is important to remark in anticipation of an analysis of work that the metaphorical operation is a single movement from literal to new meaning. The literal is neither transcended nor overcome since without the literal meanings remaining present in some respect, the predication of new meaning is not possible (Ricoeur, 1976: 55; 1978: 288).[10] What, then, does the metaphorical reference or new meaning disclose? Metaphor, as Ricoeur insists, has a truth function that can be described as its "power of reorganizing our perception" of the world (Ricoeur, 1978: 236). Metaphorical discourse discloses the world in a novel way by means of taking what is familiar to us in language and saying something new about it.

---

[9] Thus instead of basing work on philosophical anthropology like Marx, I am proposing a phenomenological and hermeneutical account.

[10] Cf. Ricoeur (1978: 109) where he discusses how metaphor destroys the duality of juxtaposed concepts; hence a single movement. There is some debate about whether literal meanings do in fact exist. A charitable reading of Ricoeur would suggest that what he means by literal are those meanings which are most familiar to us in a specified context.

This ability to reorganize is shared also by work, though the similarity between metaphor and work is not identical, but analogous.[11] This can be seen if one thinks of work's literal and non-literal elements in terms of its necessary and supra-necessary aims. It would be odd to say that work is involved in something like a conflict or confusion at the level of necessity, but there is nonetheless the combination of familiar yet dissimilar things to produce something distinctly and formally new. A wooden chair is no longer a living tree, and material used in its fabrication is not merely the result of an alteration of positions, as Bertrand Russell (1996: 3) would have it. In contrast to Marx's view, what is worth noting here is that material necessity is not foundational in any strong sense, but the condition according to which work operates, and is therefore part of a greater, single movement of creation. Material combines with ideas of use, design, and aesthetics to form something new. But if work produces new material forms, how might we say the reorganizing activity of work, like metaphor, results in a disclosure of new meanings?

Let us consider a response to this question in relation to necessary and supra-necessary ends. While the development of work often involves more efficient ways of fulfilling necessity, as Arendt (1958: chapter 4) points out, it is not simply that the relation to necessity is transcended or overcome. Rather, in the process of meeting necessity, something new arises. Work's power of metaphorical disclosure is the expressly human world (Arendt, 1958: 137). Debates concerning the role of technological media in postphenomenology and extended-mind cognition can be seen as alighting on the ways in which things of work both reshape the world and are already embedded in our modes of cognition, recognition, and bodily perception (Ihde, 2010; Verbeek, 2008). However, there is also another kind of supra-necessary effect of work that is important to bear in mind, especially when attempting to understand the interrelation between oneself and others.

There is a tendency to imagine that discourse between people occurs in a space emptied of things, or if things are present they are only so insignificantly. This, however, is not the case. Meaningful relations are intimately bound up with the things of work, not because they are merely necessary in constituting a human world in which discourse with others can occur, but also because as metaphorical they disclose these relations in a novel way. They are not merely instruments or vehicles for practical ends but constitute and reveal the world that is an issue for us—that is, for our understanding of what it means to be.

One might take, as an example, Odysseus's bow:

> The bow is not just a work for war or hunting but one whose use is intimately tied to the social roles set within an understanding of what is just. Thus when Odysseus strings the bow there is a moment that requires recognizing the bow itself as something that can fulfill a destiny. Odysseus, Homer tells us, turns the bow 'all up

---

[11] I leave aside the extent to which one can say work is linguistic. A hermeneutical approach to the relation would argue in view of the universality of language in the sense that work is not possible except in a world already structured by language. Work may be a physical activity, but its so-called linguistic capacity can be seen in its ability to disclose the world anew—that is, according to new meanings. To argue otherwise would uphold the reduction of work to necessity—that is, work does not participate at a higher level other than fulfilling brute necessity.

and down', testing it for worms who may have eaten the horn (XXI.394–5). More specifically, we are told that this recognition is a manner of redeeming what has gone by in "the master's absence" (XXI.395). So the bow is a work that ties together the bonds between Odysseus and Penelope, his relation to his son Telemachos who dwells in the reputation of his father, and the well-being of the kingdom while Odysseus has been far away. The symbolic meaning of distance, with respect to relations and destinies of characters, comes to a culminating point in the moment Odysseus picks up the bow. Following upon this moment is Odysseus' own recognition of divine favor, the winning of the competition, and the speaking to his son. This speaking to Telemachos extends the course of recognition, for it is his son who grasps firmly and securely his own spear which, as Homer is sure to tell us in Book I (125–44), symbolized a legacy he was not ready to assume.[12]

Without the work of the bow, the development of relations and identity would not be possible in the way that we have come to know it in the story of *The Odyssey*. The meaning of being for Odysseus and Telemachos would certainly no longer be heroic and epic, but tragic. And while such meanings are not the ones we may seek in a career or vocation, how would the meaning of being go if not for the possibilities disclosed in and by work? This is not to say that all instances of work, by virtue of being metaphorical, are meaningful. My aim here is only to give an account of how a fundamental feature of work generates meaning. It is entirely possible, as most of us know from experience, that work can be robbed of its creative and productive capacities, something that Marx notes by the term "alienation."

IMPLICATIONS AND CONCLUSION

How might this philosophical account of work have implications for the actual practices, values, and cultures of the workplace? If sociological approaches tend toward preference hedonism, their strength is one of acknowledging and attempting to appreciate how working conditions and roles correlate with how someone feels about his or her career and employment. Correcting or adjusting this feeling is a matter of coordinating the working conditions with one's desires about what it means to work meaningfully. While such sociological approaches contribute to a rehabilitation of working conditions, their focus on individual preferences means that they cannot fully rehabilitate our conception of work. It may be that, practically speaking, an employer might seek to transform its corporate culture according to its regard and care for its employees and their preferences, but without a transformation in our general attitude and conception of work itself, changes that benefit the employee may be piecemeal, short-lived, or seen as expendable.

In contrast, Aristotle and Marx are not merely offering a descriptive account of the phenomenon of work. In seeking to understand its nature, their respective philosophies

[12] A truncated version of Mei (2009: 117–18) referring to Homer (2007).

articulate a conceptual framework within which, to use Marx's phrase, we reproduce the activity of work. This chapter has attempted to trace and contextualize the Aristotelian and Marxian accounts in order to articulate a new conception. If the idea that work is metaphorical highlights how work figures into the understanding of the meaning of being, how can such a substantive account be linked to the everyday workplace? The answer lies in normative application—that is, by altering our overall conceptual attitude about what work is and should be. On the view I have presented, work is understood to include elements of necessity and supra-necessity. What would it mean if work had aims beyond necessary ends such as efficiency, profit, and growth? This is not to say such ends are abandoned, but governed by another idea that opens onto a reflective engagement with how work addresses and participates in the meaning of being.

References

Arendt, H. (1958). *The Human Condition*. Chicago: University of Chicago Press.

Aristotle. (1996). *Politics and the Athenian Constitution*, translated by Benjamin Jowett. Cambridge: Cambridge University Press.

Aristotle. (2002). *Nicomachean Ethics*, translated by Christopher Rowe. Oxford: Oxford University Press.

Beaufret, J. (2006). *Dialogues with Heidegger: Greek philosophy*, translated by Mark Sinclair. Bloomington, IN: Indiana University Press.

Dupré, L. (1966). *The Philosophical Foundations of Marxism*. New York: Hardcourt Brace & World.

Gould, C. C. (1978). *Marx's Social Ontology: Individual and community in Marx's theory of social reality*. Cambridge, MA: MIT Press.

Homer. (2007). *The Odyssey*, translated by Robert Fitzgerald. London: Vintage Books.

Ihde, D. (2010). *Heidegger's Technologies: Postphenomenological perspectives*. New York: Fordham University Press.

Lockwood, T. (2007). "Is natural slavery beneficial?" *Journal of the History of Philosophy*, 45(2): 207–21.

Marcuse, H. (1969). "The realm of freedom and the realm of necessity: A reconsideration." *Praxis*, 5(1): 20–5.

Marx, K. (1973). *Grundrisse*, translated by Martin Nicolaus. London: Penguin.

Marx, K. (1974). *Early Writings*, translated by Rodney Livingstone and Gregor Benton. London: Penguin.

Marx, K. (1976). *Capital*, Volume 1, translated by Ben Fowkes. London: Penguin.

Marx, K. (1981). *Capital*, Volume 3, translated by David Fernbach. London: Penguin.

Marx, K. (1988). *Economic and Philosophic Manuscripts of 1844*, translated by Martin Milligan. Amherst: Prometheus Books.

Marx, K. (1998). *The German Ideology*. Amherst: Prometheus Books.

Mei, T. (2009). *Heidegger, Work, and Being*. London: Continuum.

Mei, T. (2016). *Land and the Given Economy: An essay in the hermeneutics and phenomenology of dwelling*. Evanston: Northwestern University Press.

Parfit, D. (1984). *Reasons and Persons*. Oxford: Clarendon Press.

Ricoeur, P. (1965). "Work and the Word." In P. Ricoeur, *History and Truth*, translated by Charles A. Kelbley, pp. 197–219. Evanston: Northwestern University Press.

Ricoeur, P. (1976). *Interpretation Theory: Discourse and surplus of meaning*. Fort Worth: TCU Press.

Ricoeur, P. (1978). *The Rule of Metaphor: Multi-disciplinary studies of the creation of meaning in language*, translated by Robert Czerny, Kathleen McLaughlin, and John Costello. London: Routledge & Kegan Paul.

Ricoeur, P. (1981). "Metaphor and the Main Problems of Hermeneutics." In P. Ricoeur, *Hermeneutics and the Human Sciences*, edited and translated by John B. Thompson, pp. 165–81. Cambridge: Cambridge University Press.

Roche, T. (1988). "Ergon and Eudaimonia in Nicomachean Ethics I: Reconsidering the Intellectualist Interpretation." *Journal of the History of Philosophy*, 26(2): 175–94.

Russell, B. (1996). *In Praise of Idleness and Other Essays*. London: Routledge.

Sayers, S. (2006). "Freedom and the 'Realm of Necessity'." In D. Moggach (ed.), *The New Hegelians: Politics and philosophy in the Hegelian school*, pp. 261–74. Cambridge: Cambridge University Press.

Sayers, S. (2008). *Marxism and Human Nature*. Beijing: Oriental Press.

Steger, M. F., Dik, B. J., and Duffy, R. D. (2012). "Measuring meaningful work: The Work and Meaning Inventory (WAMI)." *Journal of Career Assessment*, 20(3): 322–37.

Verbeek, P.-P. (2008). "Obstetric ultrasound and the technological mediation of morality: A postphenomenological analysis." *Human Studies*, 31(1): 11–26.

CHAPTER 6

···

TO HAVE LIVED WELL

Well-being and Meaningful Work

···

NEAL CHALOFSKY AND ELIZABETH CAVALLARO

INTRODUCTION

···

To quote a famous American poet, Henry David Thoreau, "Most men lead lives of quiet desperation and go to the grave with the song still in them." That "song" is purpose. The Center for Decision Research of the Booth School of Business at the University of Chicago conducted a grant competition several years ago on the concept of a purpose-driven life. They described a purpose-driven life as "the desire and effort that individuals put forth to accomplish their goals, make significant contributions to society, and maintain a meaningful existence" (Center for Decision Research, 2013). For some people, their life purpose seems to be to just be happy. We even have rankings of countries that are the happiest.

Life happiness and satisfaction in the scholarly literature are usually referred to as well-being. Well-being is a complex construct that concerns optimal experience and functioning. Ryan and Deci (2001: 141) describe two perspectives on well-being research: "the hedonic approach, which focuses on happiness and defines well-being in terms of pleasure attainment and pain avoidance; and the eudaimonic (or psychological) approach, which focuses on meaning and self-realization, and defines well-being in terms of the degree to which a person is fully functioning." Hedonic well-being comprises an affective component (high positive affect and low negative affect) and a cognitive component (satisfaction with life). It is proposed that an individual experiences happiness when positive affect and satisfaction with life are both high (Carruthers and Hood, 2004). Eudaimonic well-being, on the other hand, is strongly reliant on Maslow's (1954) ideas of self-actualization and Rogers's (1961) concept of the fully functioning person. Happiness is therefore based on the premise that people feel happy if they experience life purpose, challenges, and growth (Deci and Ryan, 2000).

Work is a significant part of everyone's life; for most people work involves more hours in a day than any other life activity (and we include childrearing as work). Work is also a

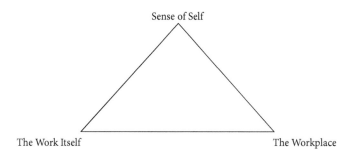

Sense of Self

The Work Itself   The Workplace

FIGURE 6.1 Construct of meaningful work

life space that forms much of our identity (the primary social question, "What do you do?"), provides motivation for learning and growth, presents challenges that build resiliency, and fosters relationship-building and interconnectedness. In 2013 (Chalofsky and Cavallaro, 2013), we described an evolving construct of meaningful work that built on an emerging construct introduced in 2003 (Chalofsky, 2003) (see Figure 6.1).

The three categories have not changed, but in light of recent research and conceptual thinking, we have modified and/or expanded on several of the components within the three categories.

Each of the three components of Chalofsky and Cavallaro's (2013) meaningful work construct relate to and contribute toward eudaimonic well-being. In particular, the idea of the "true self" is illustrated within the "sense of self" component, which involves identity, purpose, agency, self-efficacy, and "grit." The second component, the work itself, contributes to the developmental aspect of well-being. The work is about the tasks themselves and how they fit with the sense of self, the continual mastery of the competencies needed to perform the task, and the constant learning that leads to mastery. The third component, the workplace, is what provides the essential space for individual flourishing and development to take place. In our 2013 article (Chalofsky and Cavallaro, 2013), we deleted the element entitled "work–life balance" and changed it to "the workplace". The workplace is the space in which you perform your work, whether it be in an organizational setting, in a virtual setting, or as an individual practitioner. We then refer to life balance as an overall need and desire to prioritize and fit the aspects of one's life—work, family, friends, spiritual and volunteer activities, etc.—into one's day-to-day life.

THEORY OF EUDAIMONIA

Eudaimonia is translated from Aristotle as "the good life." But from the ancient Greek, the term "good" should not be simply translated as positive or pleasant, but as a life of virtue. According to Aristotle, the highest human good is "activity of the soul in accordance with virtue," which involves activities that are goal-directed and have purpose (Ryff and Singer, 2008: 16).

Eudaimonic well-being, also referred to as psychological well-being, is defined as the degree to which a person is fully functioning, or realizing his or her true potential (Waterman, 1993). According to Ryan and Deci (2001), eudaimonic well-being represents living life in accordance with a "true self," including the fulfillment of psychological needs, the experience of meaning and purpose in life, and engagement in flow experiences.

Eudaimonic well-being draws not only from Aristotle's conceptualization of the good life, but also from humanistic psychology. Carl Rogers (1961: 351) describes eudaimonia as:

> man's tendency to actualize himself, to become potentialities. By this I mean the directional trend which is evident in all organic and human life—the urge to expand, develop, mature—the tendency to express and activate all the capacities of the organism and the self... that it exists in every individual and awaits only the proper conditions to be released and expressed.

Ryan and Deci (2001) explain that eudaimonic well-being is internal to the individual's mind, personal and subjective, and within the person's control. Huppert and So (2013) presented a conceptual framework of positive well-being. Based on psychometric analysis, they claimed that the features of positive well-being, feeling, and functioning include hedonic and eudaimonic aspects. The eudaimonic aspects of positive well-being are engagement, meaning, optimism, positive emotion, positive relationships, resilience, self-esteem, and vitality (Huppert and So, 2013). The description of eudaimonia by Ryan and Deci (2001) incorporates concepts such as personal growth, fulfillment, striving toward one's potential, and finding meaning, self-realization, and purpose in one's life. There is significant overlap in the eudaimonia and meaningful work literature, particularly in relation to meaning and purpose.

EUDAIMONIA AND MEANINGFUL WORK

Eudaimonic theories involve the essential aspect of meaningfulness, as meaning-making signifies a crucial process in organizing experience and satisfies needs for purpose, value, sense of efficacy, and self-worth (Baumeister and Vohs, 2002). There is consensus in the literature that there is a significant value and benefit resulting from the experience of eudaimonia at work.

Rothausen (2014) aimed to define eudaimonic job satisfaction and explore elements of the concept in six facets. The six facets are satisfaction with the job's impact on and facilitation of: expression of the self, development of the self, role in society, financial situation, family, and life. She defined eudaimonic well-being as being well in a moral or proper manner with a focus on meaningfulness and fulfillment from met purposes. She found that eudaimonic job satisfaction is separate from job attitudes and has the potential to add to our ability to understand and predict levels of work, life, and work–life outcomes such as engagement, inclusion, retention, work–family conflict, and life satisfaction. Eudaimonic job satisfaction is defined as "the sense of contribution and purpose that comes from working" (Dik, Duffy, and Eldridge, 2009: 629).

Martin Seligman (2002) distinguished between a good life and a meaningful life in his authentic happiness model. The good life involves an individual applying his or her dominant character strengths to activities he or she enjoys doing, or pursuing a flow state, which is enjoyment of the work itself (Csikszentmihalyi, 1990). The meaningful life is about an individual using his or her strengths in the service of something greater than him/herself. The eudaimonic concept of human potential is apparent in both of these concepts. Seligman (2002) asserts that both pursuits of the good life (flow activities) and the meaningful life (service) can be considered eudaimonic. Seligman's research indicates that people who lead a more eudaimonic existence (learning, developing potential) are more satisfied with their lives than those who pursue primarily hedonia.

There is a clear overlap between the experience of meaningful work and the experience of eudaimonic well-being. Each of the three components of meaningful work, the sense of self, the work itself, and the workplace, are aligned with the concept of eudaimonic well-being.

Sense of Self

The sense of self is about purpose, identity, agency, self-efficacy, and "grit." Who am I, what is my purpose in life, where do I belong, how much personal control and autonomy do I have for me to achieve my purpose, and how well do I handle adversity so it does not derail me from pursuing my purpose? In the emerging construct, the sense of self was focused on being able to bring the whole self to the workplace. In the more recent evolving construct, one must first "know thyself." This component is about knowing the self through critical reflection on one's values, beliefs, strengths, and preferences. Similarly, the word eudaimonia from Aristotle translates to "meaningful living conditioned upon self-truth and self-responsibility" (Ryff and Singer, 2008: 18). The idea of the true self, and what Rogers referred to as the "authentic" self, is also central to meaningful work (Rogers, 1961).

There is also evidence to suggest that a strong sense of self may actually enhance the experience of eudaimonic well-being. According to research comparing measures of hedonic and eudaimonic well-being processes with well-being outcomes, eudaimonic well-being occurs when a person's life activities are congruent with his or her values and the individual is holistically or fully engaged (Bhullar, Schutte, and Malouff, 2013).

Within the sense of self, individual values are an inherent part of identifying purpose. A research study by Nelson et al. (2014) exploring how self-affirmation might lead to positive well-being outcomes found that participants who affirmed their values showed increased eudaimonic well-being, measured by need satisfaction, meaning, and flow. According to the authors, by strengthening their self-image via a values-affirmation activity, people may be less susceptible to threats in their day-to-day lives and may be able to prevent anticipated declines in well-being (Nelson et al., 2014).

Too often, we look for jobs based on the performance requirements; what we will do on the job. But what we do, according to Matthew Fox (1994), is an occupational label. It is what we tell others when they ask the proverbial question, "So what do you do?" Work is who we are; it reflects our basic values and beliefs; it is who we want to be. Studs Terkel (1974) talked about a bookbinder who loved repairing old books because "a book is a life." For him, what he did was something more than just fixing a book. He was saving something that represents the author's humanness. The waitress who proclaimed, "when I put a plate down, you don't hear a sound," was proud of her skills. Purpose for her was about the pride that comes from mastering competencies. And the gravedigger who constantly honed his skills because "a human body is going into this grave" is also contributing by perceiving the grave as not just a hole in the ground, but as a resting place that should reflect the value of what is being placed in it.

There is an old story about a man who walks up to a field where a large building is being constructed. A number of stonemasons are working, each using a hammer and chisel to carve a piece of stone. The man asks each of the masons the same question, "What are you doing?" "I'm chipping this stone" says the first. "I'm building a wall" says the second. "I'm a skilled tradesman" says another. "I'm supporting my family" says the fourth. "I'm building a church" says the last mason; "I'm worshipping God" (Pozzi and Williams, 1997: 9). So identity, in this construct, is about our authentic selves; who we really want to be. Carl Rogers (1961) believed we are inherently motivated to move toward our true self. The "fully functioning person" is in deep touch with his or her experiences and emotions, and is oriented toward meaningful work and a purposeful life.

The Self as Leader

Authenticity also has substantial implications for the meaningfulness of employees' lives, especially in the process of leadership (Ilies, Morgeson, and Nahrgang, 2005). Authenticity not only affects leaders' own well-being, but also influences their followers' well-being and self-concept. Because authentic leaders are deeply aware of their values and beliefs, are self-confident, reliable, and trustworthy, they focus on building their followers' strengths, broadening their thinking, and creating a positive and engaging organizational context.

The Self and Others

Ryff and Keyes (1995) proposed a conceptual framework of wellness that included positive relationships as an end criterion, which suggests that one's handling of interpersonal situations and relationships, including relationships at work, has great importance for one's self-realization and well-being. One benefit of authentic relationships, because of the emphasis on openness and truthfulness, is high levels of trust (Kernis, 2003). The trust between and among leaders and staff supports everyone's well-being because of the positive emotions and mutual support that ensues. Everyone in the relationship "wins."

Relationships also have to do with identity, in terms of how we fit into, or belong to, the social fabric of work and life. On the essence of belonging, May (2011: 375) noted that "one of the ways in which we experience... being in society (including in organizations) is through our sense of belonging or lack thereof." Belonging fosters an important sense of self, which allows individuals to feel rooted, having a sense of comfort with the spheres of activity in everyday life and work. Most people have a social identity, a sense of who they are based on the groups they belong to: family, peers, religion, work, and volunteer/community.

Agency

Agency is the sense of responsibility for one's life course, the belief that one is in control of one's life decisions, and is responsible for their outcomes. In addition, agency includes the confidence that one will be able to overcome obstacles that impede one's progress along the way (Côté and Schwartz, 2002). The capacities to act independently, to make choices, and to pursue interests that are self-determined are contrasted with determinism or fate, the notion that outward forces have overwhelming power (Kuchinke, 2013). When the "new employee contract" emerged in the 1990s, career development became the responsibility of the individual because one could not rely on the organization as the caretaker (Kissler, 1994). Approaches such as the Kaleidoscope Career (Sullivan and Mainiero, 2006) became more relevant for someone who wanted meaningful work because it accentuated a career created on one's own terms, defined by one's own purpose, values, life choices, and boundaries, as opposed to the more traditional predetermined succession-based career path that existed when the baby-boom generation entered the workforce. In this era of individual career development, a new focus on individual decision-making has made identity development a personal project that requires agency (Schwartz, Côté, and Arnett, 2005). The implication is that one is not locked into a career identity, such as "I am an accountant" or "I am a doctor." We just hired a hardwood floor installer who is also an electrician. A plumber we once hired was originally a therapist. We can be whoever we want to be if we have agency.

Bandura's (1977) concept of self-efficacy is related to agency. "People's level of motivation, affective states, and actions are based more on what they believe than on what is objectively true" (Bandura, 1977: 2). How people behave can often be better predicted by the beliefs they hold about their capabilities than by what they are actually capable of accomplishing. Agency and self-efficacy make for a powerful combination to finding purpose and meaning in work and in life. We can also be whoever we want to be if we believe in ourselves. We all know people, directly and indirectly, who started from an adverse childhood and went on to be successful and happy adults. They had to believe they could achieve success and happiness. Everyone deserves meaningful work, but you have to believe you are entitled to it, no matter your socio-economic environment.

Grit

The last element of the sense of self is the concept of "grit." Duckworth et al. (2007: 1087–8) define grit as:

> perseverance and passion for long-term goals. Grit entails working strenuously toward challenges, maintaining effort and interest over years despite failure, adversity, and plateaus in progress. The gritty individual approaches achievement as a marathon; his or her advantage is stamina. Whereas disappointment or boredom signals to others that it is time to change trajectory and cut losses, the gritty individual stays the course.

Michael Jordan, one of the most successful basketball players in the history of the game, once said, "I've missed more than 9,000 shots in my career. I've lost almost 300 games. Twenty six times, I've been trusted to take the game winning shot and missed. I've failed over and over and over again in my life. And that is why I succeed." There is a saying, "a can do attitude," that includes working hard, overcoming adversity, practicing, and striving to be better. The meaning is not just in the performance of the work, it is also in the effort we put into our performance. To quote a line from Marge Piercy's poem, "To Be of Use," "I love people who harness themselves, an ox to a heavy cart, who pull like water buffalo, with massive patience, who strain in the mud and the muck to pull things forward, who do what has to be done, again and again."

THE WORK ITSELF

The work we choose to perform is how we fulfill our life purpose, in terms of both paid and unpaid work. How we work, what we bring to the work of ourselves, gives meaning to the work. There is nothing like the feeling of good work, especially if the work is meaningful. Whether it is completing a challenging project on time and within budget, or crafting a cabinet with all the joints fitting perfectly, or helping a client deal with a complex problem, or even assembling your daughter's new bicycle and watching her ride it—a job worth doing is worth doing well (Chalofsky, 2010).

The work itself component of meaningful work deals with the developmental aspect of well-being. The work is about the tasks themselves and how they fit with the self, our mastery of the competencies needed to perform the task, the continual learning that leads to mastery, and the energy that we bring to bear on meaningful work (Chalofsky and Cavallaro, 2013).

The concept of energy is also a component of eudaimonic well-being. Vigor or vitality is considered a common operationalization of eudaimonic well-being (Ryan and

Deci, 2001). Vigor is an affective construct that refers to the subjective feeling of energy and aliveness, and research has shown that vigor, as a well-being indicator, predicted personal initiative, and that eudaimonic well-being is the relevant affective well-being dimension for proactive behavior (Hahn et al., 2012).

Csikszentmihalyi (1990) studied what made people happy at work and found that people in different kinds of jobs experienced a phenomenon he called "flow". He defines flow as "a state in which people are so involved in an activity that nothing else seems to matter; the experience is so enjoyable that people will continue to do it even at great cost, for the sheer sake of doing it" (Csikszentmihalyi, 1990: 4). What this research concluded was that the work itself was so meaningful that the performance of the task provided the satisfaction and fulfillment rather than the completion of the task. In fact, the completion of the task meant the work was finished and led to disappointment. The journey was far more significant in terms of meaning than reaching the destination. Csikszentmihalyi's (1990) findings echoed Maslow's (1954) theory of self-actualization. While the sense of pride and the feeling of achievement in a successfully completed piece of work is intrinsically satisfying, the work itself provides the sense of fulfillment that comes from overcoming challenges, personal mastery, creativity, and ultimately personal growth.

Learning is a critical aspect of the work itself. Susan Gayle (1997) discovered that "gold collar" workers (the top 1 percent of high-technology systems experts) were continuously honing their skills and learning new advances when they were not deeply immersed in their work. They were either improving themselves or improving the systems they were working on. Lauren Turner (2005) studied learning and meaningful work, and found two characteristics that stood out. First, learning was innately embedded in the core of each person who felt their work was meaningful. Second, all the people in her study were committed self-directed learners. The learning process was described by the study participants as experimental, continual, iterative, messy, and cumulative. A number of them used words like "sustenance" or "fuel" to describe the role that learning played in terms of their work. They described their curiosity for learning as like being a sponge and wanting to soak up as much as possible. Reflection also played a critical role in their learning. They found themselves continuously questioning, testing, challenging, trying on different perspectives, and processing how new information fitted with their present knowledge, beliefs, and values. They also tended not to accept new knowledge at face value, but wanted to dig deeper to learn more. Emotions were a part of the learning process. The awareness of the thrill of discovery, of struggling with new values and beliefs, and dealing with change, provided feedback and understanding.

This learning and growth mindset is also a fundamental element of eudaimonia, characterized by personal growth and striving to attain one's highest potential. Ryff and Singer (2008) describe eudaimonia as positive human functioning, the essence of which is the idea of striving toward excellence based on one's unique potential. According to Boniwell (2008), the actualizing tendency prompts individuals toward personal development, which involves the individual striving to grow as a person, and to become better in his or her chosen fields and domains of life.

The learning, growth, and development aspect of meaningful work may have roots not only in the philosophical conception of the human drive to actualize our highest potential (eudaimonia), or in the spiritual sense of answering a calling and serving the greater good, but also in our biological drive to grow. Findings in neuroscience support the idea that we are biologically designed to continue learning.

Neuroplasticity, or brain plasticity, is the brain's ability to change throughout life. The human brain has the ability to continually reorganize itself by forming new connections between brain cells, called neurons. Genetic factors, a person's environment, and their actions play a significant role in plasticity. Neuroplasticity occurs in the brain throughout adulthood, whenever something new is learned and memorized (Michelon, 2008). The fact that our brains do this would imply that we are designed to continue to grow and develop indefinitely throughout life.

Essentially, our brain processes are prompting us to keep pursuing meaningful work. The brain is saying to us, "I can continue to grow if you keep giving me challenges." Neuroscience research shows that certain types of actions cause neural changes that drive attitude and behavior. When a person feels they are making a contribution to a greater social good, their brain releases endorphins and dopamine which generate positive affect (Seidman, 2017).

Neuroscience research suggests that pursuit of meaningful engagement later in life can stop or reverse brain shrinkage and delay the onset of conditions such as dementia and Alzheimer's disease (Carlson et al., 2015). Results of an eighteen-year study of aging in Australia showed that having a strong sense of purpose is positively correlated with more successful aging and, according to survival analysis, to living longer (Windsor, Curtis, and Luszcz, 2015). Some researchers believe that because of the plasticity of the brain, it is possible to create work contexts that are conducive to productive development across the entire adult lifespan (Staudinger and Bowen, 2011). This type of research promotes a new approach to retirement. Instead of seeking leisure and relaxation as a reward for a life of hard work, we are better served by doing something that provides some level of challenge and meaning. In this sense, we not only desire meaning and purpose because of our philosophical or spiritual humanness; this motive is also actually a product of our biological humanness. Meaningful work may in fact be something that keeps us not only mentally and spiritually, but also physically healthy and alive.

People who have meaningful work not only continually strive, learn, and grow, they also continually strive for personal mastery. Peter Senge (1990: 142), author of *The Fifth Discipline*, describes personal mastery:

> People with a high level of personal mastery live in a continual learning mode. They never 'arrive'. Sometimes, language, such as the term 'personal mastery' creates a misleading sense of definiteness, of black and white. But personal mastery is not something you possess. It is a process. It is a lifelong discipline. People with a high level of personal mastery are acutely aware of their ignorance, their incompetence, their growth areas. And they are deeply self-confident. Paradoxical? Only for those who do not see the journey is the reward.

THE WORKPLACE

The workplace is essential to the experience of meaningful work and attainment of eudaimonic well-being. Meaningful and purpose-driven work must fit in with the larger context of our lives, and our lives must fit in with the larger context of our workplaces (Chalofsky and Cavallaro, 2013). Developing a meaningful workplace is a function of tapping into the fundamental human drive for flourishing. In particular, there are two key aspects of meaningfulness that can be created in a workplace that tap into the human experience of eudaimonia—values and development.

The good life ideal is based on the idea of a life of virtue. What constitutes human acts as virtuous is based on what is valued. An individual is able to make a contribution to the greater good when they are guided by their internal value system in a way that aligns with societal value and need. While values and contribution to the greater good can and should certainly be foundational to the mission, vision, or social responsibility of a meaningful workplace, what determines whether employees will derive meaning and purpose from their work is the alignment of those values with their internal meaning-making system. Members of the millennial generation want to work for organizations that are ethical and socially responsible, and in positions that are contributing to the social good. There is an increasing interest in social entrepreneurship, "benefit corporations," and nonprofits. The workplace can also be virtual, which allows individuals to live a more integrated life where work is woven in with other parts of their lives. The more the workplace allows for agency, the more individuals can live their values.

In a recent issue of the Society for Human Resource Management magazine (March 2017: 39–43), an article about paid leave for births, childcare, and eldercare mentioned that millennials value work–life balance more than anything except pay when evaluating job opportunities. The US is behind most developed countries in offering paid family leave at the national level, but is catching up in local and state legislation, and in organization policy. There has been an increasing consensus that government and organizational support for work–life balance contribute to both well-being and productivity.

A culture of development in the workplace enhances the individual experience of meaning. Meaningfulness will in large part emerge from the opportunity available in the organization to allow each individual to thrive and become their own greatest self, while working toward their highest purpose, in a mutually supportive and respectful community. Employees are likely to attain the actualization of their human potential if the workplace serves as an incubator for their own learning, growth, and development. Employee growth is fostered in a work environment which creates "developmental pulls" or ongoing developmental challenge and support that is deeply aligned with the strongest human motive, to grow (Kegan and Lahey, 2016). Conversely, an organization that prevents or stifles employee learning, growth, and development likely would not enable the individual to achieve meaning and eudaimonia in the workplace.

Perhaps this type of workplace would even have a negative impact. We know that employee well-being is negatively impacted by issues such as poor person–environment fit (Yang, Che, and Spector, 2008) and effort–reward imbalance (De Jonge et al., 2000). Presumably, a workplace that is not properly aligned with employee developmental needs would do the same.

The importance of lifelong learning and personal mastery are not only for the sake of the journey, but also for the contribution of these pursuits to ongoing personal development. Employees benefit from workplaces that foster learning, growth, and development, enabling them to attain well-being and eudaimonia. And, in the long run, organizations benefit from increased engagement and commitment.

Each of the three components of meaningful work, the sense of self, the work itself, and the workplace, contribute to the individual's eudaimonic well-being. The job that we do serves to ensure our attainment of hedonia by providing extrinsic rewards like pay, but the work that is who we are ensures we attain eudaimonia.

CONCLUSION

Viewing meaningful work through the lens of eudaimonia has helped clarify the construct and deepen our understanding of the three components: sense of self, work itself, and the workplace. The usefulness of this lens is that it allows us to see the bigger picture of why human beings have a desire for meaningful work. Meaningful work is not a modern concept of work deriving from recent approaches toward the study of organizations such as positive psychology or living systems. Since the time of Aristotle and likely well before, the essence of our desire for meaning has underlain our exploration of the human experience. Given our understanding of eudaimonic well-being as a fundamental, overarching aim of living, and our work as a significant and influential factor in how we live, the search for meaningful work is clearly an inherent part of our humanness—our human pursuit of the good life, the life well lived.

ACKNOWLEDGMENTS

The authors would like to acknowledge the assistance of Oliver Crocco with the literature search and Joanna Sztandur with the editing of this chapter.

REFERENCES

Bandura, A. (1977). "Self-efficacy: Toward a unifying theory of behavioral change." *Psychological Review*, 84(2), 191–215.

Baumeister, R. F. and Vohs, K. D. (2002). "The Pursuit of Meaningfulness in Life." In C. R. Synder and S. J. Lopez (eds.), *Handbook of Positive Psychology*, pp. 608–18. New York: Oxford University Press.

Bhullar, N., Schutte, N. S., and Malouff, J. M. (2013). "The nature of well-being: The roles of hedonic and eudaimonic processes and trait emotional intelligence." *Journal of Psychology*, 147(1), 1–16.

Boniwell, I. (2008). *Positive Psychology in a Nutshell: A balanced introduction to the science of optimal functioning.* London: Personal Well-Being Centre.

Carlson, M. C., Kuo, J. H., Chuang, Y., Varma, V. R., Harris, G., Albert, M. S., Erickson, K. I., Kramer, A. F., Parisi, J. M., Xue, Q., Tan, E. J., Tanner, E. K., Gross, A. L., Seeman, T. E., Gruenewald, T. L., McGill, S., Rebok, G. W., and Fried, L. P. (2015). "Impact of the Baltimore Experience Corps Trial on cortical and hippocampal volumes." *Alzheimer's & Dementia: The Journal of the Alzheimer's Association*, 11(11), 1340–8.

Carruthers, C. P. and Hood, C. D. (2004). "The power of the positive: Leisure and well-being." *Therapeutic Recreation Journal*, 38(2), 225–45.

Center for Decision Research. (2013). "Overview and Goals" [web page]. http://newpathstopurpose.org/grants/rfp/overview-and-goals [no longer live].

Chalofsky, N. E. (2003). "An emerging construct for meaningful work." *Human Resource Development International*, 6(1), 69–83.

Chalofsky, N. E. (2010). *Meaningful Workplaces: Reframing how and where we work.* New York: John Wiley & Sons.

Chalofsky, N. E. and Cavallaro, E. (2013). "A good living versus a Good Life: Meaning, purpose, and HRD." *Advances in Developing Human Resources*, 15(4), 331–40.

Côté, J. E. and Schwartz, S. J. (2002). "Comparing psychological and sociological approaches to identity: Identity status, identity capital, and the individualization process." *Journal of Adolescence*, 25(6), 571–86.

Csikszentmihalyi, M. (1990). *Flow: The psychology of optimal experience.* New York: Harper & Row.

De Jonge, J., Dollard, M. F., Dormann, C., Le Blanc, P. M., and Houtman, I. L. D. (2000). "The Demand-Control Model: Specific demands, specific control, and well-defined groups." *International Journal of Stress Management*, 7, 269–87.

Deci, E. L. and Ryan, R. M. (2000). "The 'what' and 'why' of goal pursuits: Human needs and the self-determination of behavior." *Psychological Inquiry*, 11(4), 227–68.

Dik, B. J., Duffy, R. D., and Eldridge, B. M. (2009). "Calling and vocation in career counseling: Recommendations for promoting meaningful work." *Professional Psychology: Research and Practice*, 40(6), 625–32.

Duckworth, A. L., Peterson, C., Matthews, M. D., and Kelly, D. R. (2007). "Grit: Perseverance and passion for long-term goals." *Journal of Personality and Social Psychology*, 92(6), 1087–101.

Fox, M. (1994). *The Reinvention of Work.* New York: Harper Collins.

Gayle, S. C. (1997). "Workplace Purpose and Meaning as Perceived by Information Technology Professionals: A Phenomenological Study." Doctoral dissertation, The George Washington University.

Hahn, V. C., Frese, M., Binnewies, C., and Schmitt, A. (2012). "Happy and proactive? The role of hedonic and eudaimonic well-being in business owners' personal initiative." *Entrepreneurship Theory and Practice*, 36(1), 97–114.

Huppert, F. A. and So, T. T. (2013). "Flourishing across Europe: Application of a new conceptual framework for defining well-being." *Social Indicators Research*, 110(3), 837–61.

Ilies, R., Morgeson, F. P., and Nahrgang, J. D. (2005). "Authentic leadership and eudaemonic well-being: Understanding leader–follower outcomes." *The Leadership Quarterly*, 16(3), 373–94.

Kegan, R. and Lahey, L. L. (2016). *An Everyone Culture: Becoming a deliberately developmental organization*. Cambridge, MA: Harvard Business Review Press.

Kernis, M. H. (2003). "Toward a conceptualization of optimal self-esteem." *Psychological Inquiry*, 14(1), 1–26.

Kissler, G. D. (1994). "The new employment contract." *Human Resource Management*, 33(3), 335–52.

Kuchinke, K. P. (2013). "Human agency and HRD: Returning meaning, spirituality, and purpose to HRD theory and practice." *Advances in Developing Human Resources*, 15(4), 370–81.

Maslow, A. H. (1954). *Motivation and Personality*. New York: Harper.

May, V. (2011). "Self, belonging and social change." *Sociology: The Journal of the British Sociological Association*, 45(3), 363–78.

Michelon, D. P. (2008). "Brain Plasticity: How Learning Changes Your Brain." *SharpBrains* [website], 26 February: https://sharpbrains.com/blog/2008/02/26/brain-plasticity-how-learning-changes-your-brain/ [accessed June 3, 2018].

Nelson, S. K., Fuller, J. A., Choi, I., and Lyubomirsky, S. (2014). "Beyond self-protection: Self-affirmation benefits hedonic and eudaimonic well-being." *Personality and Social Psychology Bulletin*, 40(8), 998–1011.

Pozzi, D. and Williams, S. (1997). *Success with Soul*. Melbourne: Dorian Welles.

Rogers, C. R. (1961). *On Becoming a Person: A therapist's view of psychotherapy*. Boston: Houghton Mifflin.

Rothausen, T. J. (2014). "Eudaimonic Job Satisfaction: Exploring Global and Facet Satisfaction with Fulfilled Job Purposes." Unpublished working paper. Minneapolis: University of St. Thomas.

Ryan, R. M. and Deci, E. L. (2001). "On happiness and human potentials: A review of research on hedonic and eudaimonic well-being." *Annual Review of Psychology*, 52(1), 141–66.

Ryff, C. D. and Keyes, C. L. M. (1995). "The structure of psychological well-being revisited." *Journal of Personality and Social Psychology*, 69(4), 719–27.

Ryff, C. D. and Singer, B. H. (2008). "Know thyself and become what you are: A eudaimonic approach to psychological well-being." *Journal of Happiness Studies*, 9(1), 13–39.

Schwartz, S. J., Côté, J. E., and Arnett, J. J. (2005). "Identity and agency in emerging adulthood: Two developmental routes in the individualization process." *Youth & Society*, 37(2), 201–29.

Seidman, W. (2017). "The Neuroscience of Self-directed Learning." *Chief Learning Officer* [website], 21 February: http://www.clomedia.com/2017/02/21/neuroscience-self-directed-learning/ [accessed June 3, 2018].

Seligman, M. E. (2002). *Authentic Happiness*. New York: Atria.

Senge, P. M. (1990). *The Fifth Discipline: The art and practice of the learning organization*. New York: Currency Doubleday.

Staudinger, U. M. and Bowen, C. E. (2011). "A Systemic approach to aging in the work context." *Zeitschrift für Arbeitsmarktforschung*, 44(4), 295–306.

Sullivan, S. E. and Mainiero, L. A. (2006). "Kaleidoscope careers: Benchmarking ideas for fostering family-friendly workplaces." *Organizational Dynamics*, 36(1), 45–62.

Terkel, S. (1974). *Working: People talk about what they do all day and how they feel about what they do*. New York: The New Press.

Turner, L. M. (2005). "Patterns of Learning in the Lives of People Who Experience Meaningful Work." Doctoral dissertation, The George Washington University.

Waterman, A. S. (1993). "Two conceptions of happiness: Contrasts of personal expressiveness (eudaimonia) and hedonic enjoyment." *Journal of Personality and Social Psychology*, 64(4), 678–91.

Windsor, T. D., Curtis, R. G., and Luszcz, M. A. (2015). "Sense of purpose as a psychological resource for aging well." *Developmental Psychology*, 51(7), 975–86.

Yang, L., Che, H., and Spector, P. E. (2008). "Job stress and well-being: An examination from the view of person-environment fit." *Journal of Occupational and Organizational Psychology*, 81(3), 567–87.

PART II

PROCESSES OF MEANINGFULNESS

CHAPTER 7

DO WE HAVE TO DO MEANINGFUL WORK?

CHRISTOPHER MICHAELSON

MEANINGFUL WORK AND MORAL CONCERN

Too many people in our modern economy remain stuck practicing work that has little meaning to them—for example, sweatshop laborers (Arnold and Bowie, 2003); unemployed and underemployed workers (OECD, 2015); and technologically displaced personnel (Ford, 2015). The moral responsibility for alleviating these forms of workplace alienation through the provision and protection of meaningful work has conventionally been assigned to economic and political institutions. In this vein, meaningful work has been characterized as a moral right (Bowie, 1998); a political right (Schwartz, 1982); a "fundamental human need" (Yeoman, 2014: 235, 236); and a contribution to human excellence (Beadle and Knight, 2012). Workers' pursuit of meaningful work may be protected by, among other things, engaging their participation in organizational governance (Hsieh, 2005, 2008; Moriarty, 2009, 2010) and imposing state authority to safeguard moral autonomy at work (Schwartz, 1982).

However, scarcity of meaningful work also abides among workers who have the freedom to choose it. These workers—"alienated elites," as I shall call them, in a variation on Marx's "alienated labor" (1997)—have, in theory, the choice to pursue meaningful work, yet, in practice, they experience a deficit thereof. They too may feel that their bodies are overworked and their minds are underutilized, that work detracts from their chance at a meaningful life. Unlike their less prosperous counterparts, however, they have more power to navigate out of this condition, even though they may feel stuck. If institutions have a moral obligation to provide and protect meaningful work for those who do not have the autonomy to obtain it, do individuals who have the autonomy to pursue and practice it have the moral responsibility to do so?[1] This normative question about the

---

[1] "We" includes me. It could also include you, the reader.

meaningful work obligation of individuals has been largely neglected in meaningful work scholarship.

People who have the power to choose meaningful work have a responsibility, at least to themselves and potentially also to others, to do it. This chapter provides two arguments for this conclusion. Both arguments draw on theories about the meaning of life to claim that work is a primary means by which many of us can experience meaningfulness in life. The first argues that morally autonomous individuals should pursue meaningful work as a means to the end of self-cultivation; the second argues that we should practice meaningful work to fulfill a moral obligation to others to not waste the opportunity. These arguments lead to the same conclusion: Morally autonomous individuals should pursue and practice meaningful work.

What is Meaningful Work?

In normative philosophical and political theory, meaningful work has traditionally involved moral concern for comparatively powerless workers whose work is imposed by others rather than chosen for themselves. This line of inquiry (including, among others: Arneson, 1987; Bowie, 1998; Hsieh, 2008; Moriarty, 2009; Schwartz, 1982), generally prescribes a moral obligation for institutions to provide and protect the subjective choice of individuals about what and how to work; however, it does not prescribe to individuals what they ought to do with that choice or what constitutes meaningfulness.

Social scientific research on meaningful work describes the subjective experience of meaningful work as a worthy aspiration having "positive valence" (Rosso, Dekas, and Wrzesniewski, 2010), but it does not entertain the possibility that it should be morally prescribed. This literature explores how it is associated with other features of the subjective experience, such as prosocial activity (Grant, 2007, 2008b); job satisfaction (Pratt and Ashforth, 2003; MOW, 1987); task significance (Grant, 2008a); identity formation (Pratt and Ashforth, 2003; Rosso, Dekas, and Wrzesniewski, 2010); relationship development (Grant, 2013); and others. Accordingly, meaningful work as a subjective construct considers meaningfulness to be in the eye of the beholder. Pratt and Ashforth (2003: 311) contend that "meaningfulness is *necessarily subjective*" (emphasis added), adding that they "doubt that there are any universal meanings."

For simplicity and scope, my argument considers meaningful work to be any purposeful labor, whether or not practiced for compensation, that the worker considers makes a significant contribution to one's own and/or others' eudaimonic well-being. Although we will encounter good reasons to doubt whether every subjective account of meaningful work has equal legitimacy, as a starting point this definition offers the broadest possible foundation for exploring the potential obligation to do meaningful work. My arguments contend at the very least that we have an obligation to do work that we consider to be meaningful, offering a foundation on which to add further conditions.

In the following arguments, work can be exhausting or enlivening, paid or unpaid, but it concerns workers who have *some* freedom. They may not perceive themselves to have the material wherewithal *never* to work, but they do have some choice in the matter of *which* work to do.[2] Does that choice entail a moral obligation to pursue and practice meaningful work?

Meaningful Work and the Alienated Elite

While alienated elites may not engender the moral sympathy of their comparatively powerless counterparts laboring in sweatshops and poverty, they might experience some of the same unfortunate consequences of meaningless work: unhappiness, harm to health, and a sense of entrapment. In some countries, happiness tends to be lowest during the peak working years due to a variety of factors (Branchflower and Oswald, 2011). These may include, in affluent markets, workers' tendency to trade present satisfaction for future economic well-being (Roberts, 2014). Coincidence of the low points in the U-shaped happiness curve with work years contributes to the perception that work correlates with unhappiness. Six in ten asset managers—likely to be in the upper echelons of elite earners—are bored at work (Mooney, 2017). In emerging markets, pressures outside of work brought on by career success, such as new social demands on the developing market middle class, can decrease happiness (Manulife-Sinochem, 2010), leading in the extreme to wealthy entrepreneurs who are "driven to death by success" (Yu, 2011). Since 2005, a majority of Americans have been unhappy at work (The Conference Board, 2016), and only 33 percent of Americans felt "engaged" at work in 2017 (Gallup, 2017). Stultifying or unfulfilling tasks at a cubicle desk can adversely impact health (Watson, 2012) by adding to stress (Brennan and Vinter, 2012) and discontent (Gann, 2012), sometimes contributing to incivility (Porath, 2015) and leading to tragic consequences (Moore, 2015). Technology has made it more difficult for workers to disconnect, mentally and physically, from work and feedback about work performance (Kantor and Streitfeld, 2015). This allows little time to engage in leisure or other activities as a respite.

Perhaps in reaction to the deficit of meaningful work, youth entering the workforce tend to place a higher priority on meaning than their predecessors. Park, Twenge, and Greenfield's (2014) study of millennials after the Great Recession shows the influence that this economic catastrophe had on young people to prioritize moral interests—such as concern for other people and the environment—over material ones such as concern for money. A longitudinal study of American college freshmen shows that having a meaningful philosophy of life generally increased in importance between the 9/11 terrorist attacks and the Great Recession (Eagan et al., 2016). Recent studies by the Big Four consultancies suggest greater loyalty, especially among millennial workers, to

---

[2] Questions regarding the obligation to work and fair compensation, although important, are outside the scope of my argument.

organizations where purpose is perceived to align with personal values in affluent markets (Deloitte, 2014; EY, 2016; Pfau, 2015; PwC, 2016).[3]

Notwithstanding these generational forces, among the alienated elite, conventional wisdom has long considered meaningful work to be desired, not required. Anecdotal evidence demonstrates that the population includes workers who might wish for meaningful work but do not think it is possible, as well as those who seem content not to consider meaningful work necessary. Those who accept, without resistance, the meaninglessness of work may be described as "existentially indifferent" (Schnell, 2010). If so many people who could choose meaningful work do not practice it, it stands to reason that they do not consider themselves responsible for pursuing it. This is important, because it disregards a moral duty that threatens their well-being and that of others. Why would they protect and provide meaningful work for others if pursuing and practicing it were not important to themselves?

The arguments that follow apply more readily to these workers who are not limited by external forces—economic, political, and educational, among others—to decide for themselves what work to pursue. They do not impose an obligation, for example, on the sweatshop worker struggling merely to find decent work to support material survival—although neither do they preclude the possibility that meaning may be discovered or created from such dire circumstances. The mere presence of moral autonomy guarantees only the possibility of meaningful work, not its realization.

Two Arguments for an Obligation to Pursue and Practice Meaningful Work

The first argument presents a conventional case for a duty to moral self-cultivation, based on the premise that we have an obligation to ourselves to cultivate our best selves. It contends that meaningful work is a primary means to self-cultivation. The second argument holds that we have an obligation to others not to squander our opportunity to practice meaningful work. It contends more generally that we have a parallel obligation to pursue meaningful life through the work we do.

The Self-cultivation Argument

The self-cultivation argument, simply, is as follows:

- We have a moral obligation to care for our own souls by cultivating our abilities.
- Meaningless work detracts from care for the soul (e.g. by failing to utilize our intellectual capacity and physical talents, or by overinvesting in the wrong ends),

---

[3] I worked on and was compensated for the PwC study cited here.

whereas meaningful work contributes to care for the soul (as measured by achievements, identity, and rewards, among other goods).
- Therefore, we have a moral obligation to pursue and practice meaningful work.

The argument begins with a moral duty to oneself that may fulfill obligations to others.
Morality is often supposed to be other-regarding, but this does not mean that morality
cannot also consist of responsibilities to ourselves. In Confucian thought, the identity
of the self is inseparable from the community (Kupperman, 2007), and so moral self-
cultivation is inherent in one's obligation to good citizenship (Cheng, 2007; Ivanhoe,
2000). Even in individualist traditions, the indivisibility between self and citizen has been
implied to be part of the good life. Aristotelian virtue requires the society of friends,
and it is well known that the perfect friendship involves regarding the other as another
self (Stern-Gillet, 1995). Confucius and Aristotle hold self-cultivation to be a feature of
the moral life, which in turn may be an elemental feature of meaningful life (Dahl, 1987;
Metz, 2005; Thomas, 2005).

The best known modern argument for the claim that we have a moral duty to
self-cultivation is expressed in Kant's *Groundwork for the Metaphysic of Morals* (1785).
He suggests that making ourselves better enables us to fulfill our moral duties to others. In this framing, the moral self is part of a virtuous circle that is both an end in itself
and a means to the end of serving others. Kant goes so far as to claim that it violates the
categorical imperative to allow one's "natural gifts" to corrode, that "he necessarily wills
that all his faculties should be developed" (Kant, 1964 [1785]: 423). In the "Doctrine of
Virtue," in his *Metaphysics of Morals* (1797), Kant elaborates further on the apparent
"contradiction" (1991 [1797]: 6: 417) that we can have moral duties to ourselves. Here
again, he alludes to a virtuous circle, juxtaposing a duty to one's own self-cultivation
with a duty to the happiness of others. He asserts the requirement to cultivate one's own
capacities to further other worthwhile ends (1991 [1797]: 6: 392). Kant names several
vices that would violate the duty to self-cultivation. These include suicide, lust, over-
intoxication, lying, avarice, servility, and so on. Here, his "Doctrine of Virtue" echoes
Aristotelian ethics in the enumeration of vices and implies that the good life is arranged
to maximize the exercise of our best abilities (e.g. contemplative activity) and to mini-
mize mindless activity (e.g. servile labor). While one way to justify self-cultivation is to
invoke the benefits it confers on others, Raz (1986: 12) suggests that "duties...can be of
intrinsic value to their subject...in the successful pursuit of worthwhile activities."
Indeed, Johnson (2011) examines a strand of thought in ancient Greek philosophy that
continues in Kant a veritable tradition emphasizing the importance, as Socrates put it,
of care for one's own soul.

But how do we measure self-cultivation of the human soul? According to Metz
(2005), one such marker that is a "central source of meaning" for nearly all objective
naturalist theories of meaningful life reflects that it is measured by the accumulation of
meaningful achievements. James (2005) sets forth criteria that constitute achievements
that legitimately enhance the meaningfulness of one's life, arguing that not every
achievement counts as meaningful. He enumerates the following necessary (though
perhaps not sufficient) conditions of meaningful achievements: failure would trigger a

reassessment of oneself; success provides a reason to think more highly of one's abilities (as opposed to, say, a chance lottery victory); performing the achievement is not easy but rather a challenge for an ordinary person; and performing it is also difficult for the achiever. Brogaard and Smith (2005) add that a meaningful achievement must also stand up to intersubjective measures of success beyond one's private appraisal of significance.

Another method by which we might measure self-cultivation and, for that matter, achievement, is by the rewards life confers on us, or that we confer on others. By this measure, a meaningful life is replete with meaningful rewards, and meaningful work is signified by the rewards it generates. Audi (2005) deems intrinsic reward, as well as the promotion of reward in the lives of others, as sufficient though not necessary to constitute meaning. Velleman (2005) explains that meaningfulness can also be achieved through exploring our identity, which in turn explains our character development, values, and mannerisms. Through self-understanding, we also seek the association of others who share these important elements of our worldview, or who help us discover our values as we mature.

To be clear, the self-cultivation argument offers several examples of *how* meaningful work can satisfy the obligation to moral self-cultivation. My argument asserts that meaningful work is an important and potentially indispensable means to the end of self-cultivation, but the examples are not intended to place additional restrictions on the subjective definition of meaningful work. Rather, they are examples of how work can be experienced subjectively to be meaningful. The argument gives us reason to wonder not only whether the "Monday through Friday sort of dying," reported by Studs Terkel (1974) to be endemic to the working life, is not only a failure of our economic and employment institutions but also of ourselves.

The Opportunity-cost Argument

Whereas the self-cultivation argument begins with a moral duty to oneself that may fulfill obligations to others, the opportunity-cost argument begins with a duty to others to make the most of one's own opportunities. In this case, the duty is to other people who do not share in one's opportunity to practice meaningful work.

While, for some people, meaningful life might involve minimizing or avoiding work altogether, for most of us work is unavoidable, and thus constitutes one potential means to realize a meaningful life. In the previous argument, work can detract from self-cultivation, yet it is sometimes tolerated for its beneficial contribution to non-work endeavors. The opportunity-cost argument regards time wasted practicing meaningless work as time that could have been better used. It rejects the rationalization that work is an investment in the future. Rather, meaningful life should occur in the here and now, and if that time must be spent at work, it ought to be meaningful work. The opportunity-cost argument for meaningful work accordingly goes like this:

- We have but one, non-transferable, life to live.
- It is morally better to live that life meaningfully than meaninglessly.
- Meaningful work is a significant means by which to live meaningfully.
- Therefore, we have a moral obligation to pursue and practice meaningful work.

This argument derives from Rawls's (1971) thought experiment with the veil of ignorance that generates his principles of justice. Arguably, the rights, freedoms, and protections entailed by those principles defend also the right to pursue meaningful life if one so chooses. In fact, meaningful work theorists in the tradition of Rawls say as much in their defense of the right to choose meaningful work. As discussed previously, institutions are characterized as having a negative duty to not deprive workers of the right to choose work that is meaningful (e.g. Bowie, 1998; Hsieh, 2005; Schwartz, 1982). But, in existing scholarship, that right to choose does not entail a positive duty on the part of the worker to choose meaningful work. Suppose, though, as an extension of Rawls's thought experiment, that those behind the veil—in the Audience of Life—were able to peek around it, into the Real World of Work, at uninspired, existentially indifferent office workers who together make meaningful work a topic of urgent importance today. This experience might motivate a sense that if the audience were to take the places of those workers, they would seek to make more of the opportunity than those they are observing. The cost of their not doing so is lost opportunity. Just as "your death is bad for you to the extent that you would have had a better life if you had not died" (Bradley, 2011), being stuck in the Audience of Life is unfortunate. It is even worse if you are observing someone else who occupies a spot in the Real World of Work, while wasting it when you would not have.

One purported marker of the meaningful life is morality (Dahl, 1987; Metz, 2005; Thomas, 2005). Theories suggest that the meaning in morality comes from connecting our lives to others beyond ourselves (e.g. Nozick, 1981), or that it is conferred by the universal good that necessarily extends beyond ourselves (e.g. Singer, 1997). This argument extends moral obligation beyond the realm of the living. In reality, some oppressed Real World workers have no choice but to do the work they are forced to do by sweatshop owners and ruthless managers, or out of economic necessity. If they were able to peek at those who have choices about where, how much, and what work to do, they might yearn for the opportunity to capitalize on choices that others waste. Sometimes, they regard management with such revulsion not only for oppression but also for profligacy. This argument suggests that each work opportunity is a chance at meaningful work, and a chance that is not optimized is not only a chance wasted for oneself but also a failure of one's responsibility to others who would not have wasted that chance were it their own. In other words, justice requires us to prepare for the possibility that there might be someone else, peeking from behind the veil, willing to make more of the chance at meaningful work than we are making. Our obligation to do meaningful work is an obligation to them to not waste the chance we are fortunate enough to have—that in reality we may not be able to transfer to another person. This may be a real person with the career mobility to replace us, or a hypothetical person.

For Fischer (2005), one's narrative represents evidence of one's free will in choosing endeavors and subsequently making sense of them. In concert with other theories about meaningful life, this perspective observes how stories of meaningful life reflect the challenges overcome and the effort invested, revealing markers and measures of meaning. This view does not eschew achievements, self-understanding, rewards, and morality as potentially constitutive of meaningful life. However, without narrative to make sense of them, they cannot serve their function as markers and measures of meaning. For example, when we reflect, in eulogies and obituaries, on the significance of a life well lived, nearly always the basic factual information about the deceased includes an articulation of professional and personal accomplishments: attended a certain academic institution but spent more of her time socializing; attained a particular level of excellence in a discipline; gave life to a number of offspring; cared for friends, family, pets, and plants; won awards; contributed to the community through activities; cultivated a love of adventure and activity with everyone she touched; and so on. These anecdotes convey the impression of time spent usefully and impressively and, often, socially. Narratives of meaningful life often point to work-related achievement, self-understanding, rewards, and morality as evidence, whereas narratives of meaningless life may point to how characters got work wrong.

A common fact pattern in the confessional genre involves the protagonist becoming a new person, substituting his post-confession identity for a pre-confession identity. The fact pattern, shared by Augustine, Tolstoy, and others, involves a youthful ignorance in which the protagonist believed in or worshipped the wrong things (Augustine, 1961; Tolstoy, 1988 [1882]). As the result of a particular event or maturation, the protagonist replaced those old, mistaken pursuits with religiously sanctioned or reason-sanctioned new ones; and the protagonist realized a new devotion to an ultimate, meaningful good or maturity.

As with the self-cultivation argument, the opportunity-cost argument includes descriptive examples of how work may be subjectively experienced to be meaningful, without offering them as prescriptive conditions for work to be meaningful. Together, these arguments emphasize an obligation to ourselves to do meaningful work—while granting that fulfilling that obligation may help to fulfill obligations to others. I do not claim that these arguments prove definitively that we have a moral obligation to pursue and practice meaningful work. However, I do believe that *they give enough weight* to the conclusion to shift the burden of proof to the other side.

OBJECTIONS: AUTONOMY AND UNACCEPTABLE IMPLICATIONS

There are two broad objections to the claim that we should pursue and practice work that is meaningful to ourselves. First, such an obligation infringes on the very autonomy that meaningful work is supposed to preserve. Second, accepting this claim forces us to accept some intuitively problematic implications.

The Autonomy Objection

Choice. The autonomy objection asserts that moral agency requires acting of one's free will (Kane, 2013), and that such autonomy is a precondition to moral obligation (Darwall, 2009). One version of the autonomy objection is that one cannot be held morally responsible for actions when one does not have a choice. However, my contention is not that one has an unconditional duty to practice meaningful work in the absence of choice. My formulation of the duty concerns an alienated elite population that often has choices, and therefore the duty is conditional: *If we have a choice* to pursue meaningful work, we should do so (and when we are fortunate enough to secure it, we should practice it too). Moreover, we have a choice more often than we may think we do. In a perfectly efficient labor market, individual workers are hypothetically free to seek out a fit between what they can meaningfully supply and what is meaningfully demanded. Of course, constraints on labor market elasticity temper the ability of the worker to achieve "social fit" (Muirhead, 2004). Ideally, market demand would align with legitimate needs and wants, but we can say with reasonable certainty that this is not the case. Market demands are sometimes frivolous, exaggerated, unreasonable—and non-meaningful.

Moreover, the ability to break free from non-meaningful work requires career mobility. "If we have a choice" should include the flexibility to acknowledge that acquiring the ability to make that choice sometimes takes time and credentials. Still, an enduring lesson of Frankl's (2006) experience in a death camp is that even in the depths of human desperation, we have the freedom to craft positive meaning from the seemingly absurd. There remains a modicum of choice to subjectively craft meaningfulness out of work that is objectively available (Wrzesniewski and Dutton, 2001).

Limits. If we accept that we have to do meaningful work on the grounds that it supports human self-cultivation, are there limits to how much cultivation is required? Must we then always do meaningful work at the expense of other goods in life? Often, we perceive that meaningful life ends are better pursued away from work. That may well be true in many cases, which is why the qualified restatement of the conclusion may be preferable: We should practice meaningful work if we do not satisfy the pursuit of meaningful life through our non-work endeavors. But this should not preclude the possibility that through work we might reclaim meaningfulness in our lives, that through working *better* we could live more meaningfully. In general, I do not claim to answer precisely *how much* meaningful work is enough. For example, taken to its logical conclusion, my argument could be interpreted to mean that we must be both meaningfulness maximizers and thus meaningful work maximizers. The maximization thesis may go farther than I am prepared to go. However, I am willing to assert that the optimal amount of meaningfulness in life should be greater for people who have the choice and capability to work than the amount made possible by non-work alone.

Nihilism. The most thoroughgoing objection to the meaningful work claim is nihilism, which takes autonomy to an extreme in asserting that there is no objective basis for favoring one work option over another. Nihilism is thus often associated with defense of those options often claimed to have lesser value. People who have "jobs" in the pejorative sense, who work just for a paycheck when they have the choice to do more within and outside of work, are meaningful work nihilists. Their hopelessness and lack of motivation pervades their work experience and often their lives. Management attempts to incite productivity by offering additional material rewards suggest that workers can be bought. This only adds to experienced meaninglessness, "explain[ing] man or woman in rather mechanical terms as an entity disconnected from meaning and society with no larger concerns than the satisfaction of primary, individual needs" (Sievers, 1994: 10).

Nihilism is notoriously difficult to prove or disprove (Nagel, 1986), and I shall not attempt to disprove it. The absence of choice rarely justifies nihilism, but if one chooses work (or life) nihilism, one ought to find meaningfulness in life (or work). If nihilism stood as the most serious obstacle to my argument, I would take that to be a sign of a strong argument. But, if nihilism cannot be ignored, there are weaker versions of my major premise that may be acceptable as a compromise with nihilism that do not render the primary argument uninteresting. For example, substituting the claim that we are obligated to not live meaningless lives for the major premise still supports a weaker version of the conclusion: We are obligated to not do meaningless work (if we do not engage in meaningful pursuits away from work).

Unacceptable Implications

Bad work. The moral obligation to pursue meaningful work might appear to require us to accept conclusions that are unacceptable. Whose good reasons are good enough? For example, if my definition of meaningful work were to include any work that was meaningful to the worker, then often-derided forms of work that were meaningful to someone (e.g. off-track betting and even terrorism) would be meaningful. A purely subjective definition of meaningful work enables us to rationalize any kind of work— that others might judge to be bad or even harmful—as satisfying our obligation. While I tend to agree with Wolf's formulation, that "meaning in life arises when subjective attraction meets objective attractiveness" (Wolf, 2010: 26; endorsed also in Yeoman, 2014), the argument in this chapter is intended to be a first step toward individual reclamation of meaningful work. If individuals are morally obligated to pursue work that is meaningful to them, we can build on that conclusion to explore whether they are further obligated to pursue work that is objectively meaningful. I have not sought to go further here because, as Wolf acknowledges, her requirement of objective meaningfulness opens her definition to further challenges and complications, such as elitism (Haidt, 2010).

In the present argument, asserting a moral obligation to subjectively pursue and practice meaningful work does not require us to accept that all subjects are right about the meaningfulness of the work they do. We may be able to identify some subjectively wrong answers to what meaningful work is. One kind of wrong answer may be a patently immoral answer because, while morality and meaningfulness are not synonymous, meaningfulness excludes immorality. Another kind of wrong answer involves representing what are evidently intermediate goods as final ends—for example, claiming that market value alone is a sufficient representation of meaning. A third kind of wrong account involves setting forth a meaningless objective as a final end—say, economic growth for growth's sake. While significance and meaningfulness are not synonymous, meaningfulness includes significance.

Unhelpful work. Sometimes, work that is perceived by well-intentioned workers to be meaningful to them has unintended consequences that are unhelpful or even destructive to those they are seeking to serve. Such circumstances may involve good ideas but bad execution (i.e. positive intent with unintended negative consequences). A so-called "purpose economy" (Hurst, 2014), in which everyone pursued work that was meaningful to them, could leave necessary work unfinished. Moreover, it could potentially legitimize seemingly frivolous and even harmful forms of work.

From a consequentialist standpoint, the moral impulse to do meaningful work may be less than admirable. From a deontological standpoint, the primacy of intent suggests that well-intentioned, but harmful, meaningful work should be corrected, but the bad consequences do not by themselves render the intentions bad. While my main arguments focus on the obligation to do work that is subjectively meaningful, the continuation of the argument may include exploring "market fit" (Muirhead, 2004) between meaningful work and market demand.

Market interference. Another implication of requiring meaningful work is that it may be perceived to interfere with market mechanisms that may do a better job of valuing work than meaningful work does. Broadly construed, market mechanisms compensate workers for a combination of perceived social value produced, moderated by the supply and demand curve for the type of work practiced.

The oft-cited market rationalization for why some professionals (e.g. firefighters) are paid relatively poorly despite the undeniable social value of their work (e.g. saving lives) is that they are compensated in both monetary and non-monetary terms (Sandel, 2012). That is, perceived meaningfulness of work is accounted for by efficient market mechanisms. But it is worth considering that the exact opposite could be said: The lack of consistent appreciation for the value of meaning undermines market mechanisms. If all people understood the obligation to do meaningful work and therefore pursued it, meaningful work would have greater market value and thus it might be more fairly compensated.

CONCLUSION AND UNANSWERED QUESTIONS

The alienated elite manufacture their own kind of oppression by aspiring to lifestyles and career goals that leave them with little sense of choice but to accept materially rewarding, often meaningless work. They may feel "stuck" in their jobs because of labor market efficiencies, geographic restrictions, the demands of personal finance, and other legitimate considerations that restrict perceived choice about job mobility. Perhaps less rationally, but no less salient, many among the wealthy feel similarly constrained by a moving target of higher expectations. While feelings of entrapment and lack of choice might be real, over the course of their careers such considerations can be managed away or at least improved on. Although changes may involve personal economic sacrifice, among such workers, such consequences involve choices about material preferences rather than demands for material survival. Meaningful work may be perceived to be a luxury, but even among workers who may not have the material freedom to avoid necessary work, when there remains freedom to craft meaningfulness from work that is available (Wrzesniewski and Dutton, 2001), the basic conclusion of these arguments may apply.

The meaningful work literature is replete with examples of occupations that workers have experienced as meaningful—e.g. zookeeper (Bunderson and Thompson, 2009); musician (Dobrow, 2013)—or as meaningless—e.g. accountant (Michaelson, 2015); Amway salesman (Pratt, 2000). Perhaps most pertinent to this chapter, they may have traversed a journey in previously conventional work that could be reframed or transformed as more meaningful—e.g. fundraiser (Grant et al., 2007); lifeguard (Grant, 2008a); bond trader (Michaelson, 2009); healthcare worker (Wrzesniewski et al., 1997). These examples involve workers with the resources and capacity to choose their work. In that sense, they are affluent enough to settle for alienation, to avoid it, or to emerge from it.

Few of these alienated elites are fully free of economic constraints, although some might be. Nor is there a minimum economic threshold that defines "elite." Rather, both arguments for an obligation to do meaningful work presuppose sufficient freedom to choose one's work. While they might seem somewhat paternalistic, heavy-handed, and judgmental of the alienated elites, my arguments are not overly prescriptive about what work they should do other than that it should be work that they consider personally meaningful to them.[4] The self-cultivation argument encourages them to consider the talents they supply to the labor market (i.e. what they have to give to the world), whereas the opportunity-cost argument focuses more on labor market demand (i.e. what the world needs of them). Either justification can satisfy the obligation to do meaningful work.

Meaningful work can contribute to a meaningful life, but it is not all of which a meaningful life consists. If we fail to practice meaningful work, are we unable to live a meaningful life? It seems judgmental to cast aspersions at the preponderance of workers who resign themselves to the work they have because it enables them to do meaningful things outside of work. While it may be admirable to pursue one's passion outside of work, this should not preclude or morally excuse one from pursuing meaningful work. The failure to pursue meaningful work is to some extent a moral failure to cultivate meaningfulness in our lives—for ourselves and for others, real and imagined, who would embrace meaningful work if they had the choice.

---

[4] This chapter is an exercise in self-evaluation as much as it is an exhortation to self-cultivation.

ACKNOWLEDGMENTS

The author would like to thank the editors for the invitation to include this chapter in the handbook; Pati Provinske for her editorial support; Rosemarie Monge, Katherina Pattit, and Jennifer Tosti-Kharas for their friendly reviews of paper drafts; and numerous other colleagues in the May Meaning Meeting and Society for Business Ethics for comments on earlier versions of the chapter.

REFERENCES

Arneson, R. J. (1987). "Meaningful work and market socialism." *Ethics*, 97(2), 517–45.

Arnold, D. G. and Bowie, N. E. (2003). "Sweatshops and respect for persons." *Business Ethics Quarterly*, 13(2), 221–42.

Audi, R. (2005). "Intrinsic value and meaningful life." *Philosophical Papers*, 34(3), 331–55.

Augustine. (1961). *Confessions*, translated by R. S. Pine-Coffin. New York: Penguin.

Beadle, R. and Knight, K. (2012). "Virtue and meaningful work." *Business Ethics Quarterly*, 22(2), 433–50.

Bowie, N. E. (1998). "A Kantian theory of meaningful work." *Journal of Business Ethics*, 17(9–10), 1083–92.

Bradley, B. (2011). *Well-Being and Death*. New York: Oxford University Press.

Branchflower, D. G. and Oswald, A. J. (2011). "International happiness: A new view on the measure of performance." *Academy of Management Perspectives*, 25(1), 6–22.

Brennan, L. and Vinter, P. (2012). "How work boredom is the new stress…and it affects everyone from office workers to those on the Afghan frontline." *Daily Mail*, May 3 [online]: http://www.dailymail.co.uk/news/article-2138733/The-new-stress-From-office-frontline-study-says-suffering-workplace-boredom.html [accessed November 14, 2015].

Brogaard, B. and Smith, B. (2005). "On luck, responsibility, and the meaning of life." *Philosophical Papers*, 34(3), 443–58.

Bunderson, J. S. and Thompson, J. A. (2009). "The call of the wild: Zookeepers, callings, and the dual edges of deeply meaningful work." *Administrative Science Quarterly*, 54(1), 32–57.

Cheng, C. Y. (2007). "A Theory of Confucian Selfhood: Self-Cultivation and Free Will in Confucian Philosophy." In K. L. Shun and D. B. Wong (eds.), *Confucian Ethics: A comparative study of self, autonomy, and community*, pp. 124–47. New York: Cambridge University Press.

The Conference Board. (2016). "Job Satisfaction Continues to Rise." *The Conference Board* [website blog]: https://www.conference-board.org/blog/post.cfm?post=5231&blogid=7 [accessed July 8, 2017].

Dahl, N. (1987). "Morality and the meaning of life: Some first thoughts." *Canadian Journal of Philosophy*, 17(1), 1–22.

Darwall, S. (2009). "Moral obligation: Form and substance." *Proceedings of the Aristotelian Society*, 60(1), 31–46.

Deloitte. (2014). "Culture of Purpose." https://www2.deloitte.com/us/en/pages/about-deloitte/articles/culture-of-purpose.html [accessed March 20, 2017].

Dobrow, S. R. (2013). "Dynamics of calling: A longitudinal study of musicians." *Journal of Organizational Behavior*, 34(4), 431–52.

Eagan, K., Stolzenberg, E. B., Ramirez, J. J., Aragon, M. C., Suchard, M. R., and Rios-Aguilar, C. (2016). *The American Freshman: Fifty year trends 1966–2015*. Los Angeles: Higher Education Research Institute.

EY Beacon Institute (EY). (2016). *The State of the Debate on Purpose in Business*. Global: EY. Available at: http://www.ey.com/Publication/vwLUAssets/ey-the-state-of-the-debate-on-purpose-in-business/$FILE/ey-the-state-of-the-debate-on-purpose-in-business.pdf [accessed March 20, 2017].

Fischer, J. M. (2005). "Free will, death, and immortality: The role of narrative." *Philosophical Papers*, 34(3), 379–403.

Ford, M. (2015). *The Rise of the Robots: Technology and the threat of a jobless future*. New York: Basic Books.

Frankl, V. E. (2006). *Man's Search for Meaning: An introduction to logotherapy*. Boston: Beacon Press.

Gallup. (2017). *State of the American Workplace*. Washington, DC: Gallup. Available at: http://www.gallup.com/reports/199961/state-american-workplace-report-2017.aspx [accessed July 8, 2017].

Gann, C. (2012). "Boredom, Constant Cheer, Cynicism, and Other Job Hazards." *ABC News* [blog], January 12: http://abcnews.go.com/blogs/health/2012/01/12/boredom-constant-cheer-cynicism-and-other-job-hazards/ [no longer live: accessed November 10, 2012].

Grant, A. M. (2007). "Relational job design and the motivation to make a prosocial difference." *Academy of Management Review*, 32(2), 393–417.

Grant, A. M. (2008a). "The significance of task significance: Job performance effects, relational mechanisms, and boundary conditions." *Journal of Applied Psychology*, 93(1), 108–24.

Grant, A. M. (2008b). "Employees without a cause: The motivational effects of prosocial impact in public service." *International Public Management Journal*, 11(1), 48–66.

Grant, A. M. (2013). *Give and Take: The hidden social dynamics of success*. New York: Penguin.

Grant, A. M., Campbell, E. M., Chen, G., Cottone, L., Lapedis, D., and Lee, K. (2007). "Impact and the art of motivation maintenance: The effects of contact with beneficiaries on persistence behavior." *Organizational Behavior and Human Decision Processes*, 103(1), 53–67.

Haidt, J. (2010). "Finding Meaning in Vital Engagement and Good Lives." In S. R. Wolf, *Meaning in Life and Why it Matters*, pp. 92–101. Princeton: Princeton University Press.

Hsieh, N. (2005). "Rawlsian justice and workplace Republicanism." *Social Theory and Practice*, 31(1), 115–42.

Hsieh, N. (2008). "Justice in production." *Journal of Political Philosophy*, 16(1), 72–100.

Hurst, A. (2014). *The Purpose Economy: How Your desire for impact, personal growth, and community is changing the world*. Boise: Elevate.

Ivanhoe, P. J. (2000). *Confucian Moral Self Cultivation*, 2nd edn. Indianapolis: Hackett.

James, L. (2005). "Achievement and the meaningfulness of life." *Philosophical Papers*, 34(3), 429–42.

Johnson, R. N. (2011). *Self-Improvement: An essay in Kantian ethics*. New York: Cambridge University Press.

Kane, R. (2013). "Acting 'of one's own free will': Modern reflections on an ancient philosophical problem." *Proceedings of the Aristotelian Society*, 64(1), 35–55.

Kant, I. (1964 [1785]). *Groundwork for the Metaphysic of Morals*, translated by H. J. Paton. New York: Harper Torchbooks.

Kant, I. (1991 [1797]). *The Metaphysic of Morals*, translated by M. J. Gregor. New York: Cambridge University Press.

Kantor, J. and Streitfield, D. (2015). "Inside Amazon: Wrestling big ideas in a bruising workplace." *New York Times*, August 15.

Kupperman, J. J. (2007). "Tradition and Community in the Formation of Character and Self." In K. L. Shun and D. B. Wong (eds.), *Confucian Ethics: A comparative study of self, autonomy, and community*, pp. 103–23. New York: Cambridge University Press.

Manulife-Sinochem. (2010). "China's middle class the least happy. Happiness Index." *China Daily*, March 19.

Marx, K. (1997). "Alienated Labor." In *Writings of the Young Marx on Philosophy and Society*, translated by L. D. Easton and K. H. Guddat, pp. 287–300. Indianapolis: Hackett.

Metz. (2005). "Introduction." *Philosophical Papers* (special issue on meaning in life), 34(3), 311–29.

Michaelson, C. (2009). "Meaningful work and moral worth." *Business and Professional Ethics Journal*, 28(1–4), 27–48.

Michaelson, C. (2015). "Accounting for meaning: On §22 of David Foster Wallace's *The Pale King.*" *Critical Perspectives on Accounting*, 29, 54–64.

Mooney, A. (2017). "More Than Six in Ten Asset Managers Are Bored at Work." *Financial Times* [online], February 26: https://www.ft.com/content/d6fd1a24-faa0-11e6-9516-2d969e0d3b65 [accessed March 27, 2017].

Moore, M. (2015). "Young Banker Struggled with Quitting Goldman before Death." *Bloomberg* [website], June 2: https://www.bloomberg.com/news/articles/2015-06-02/young-banker-struggled-with-quitting-goldman-weeks-before-death [accessed June 2, 2015].

Moriarty, J. (2009). "Rawls, self-respect, and the opportunity for meaningful work." *Social Theory and Practice*, 35(3), 441–59.

Moriarty, J. (2010). "Participation in the workplace: Are employees special?" *Journal of Business Ethics*, 92(3), 373–84.

MOW International Research Team (MOW). (1987). *The Meaning of Working*. New York: Academic Press.

Muirhead, R. (2004). *Just Work*. Cambridge, MA: Harvard University Press.

Nagel, T. (1986). *The View from Nowhere*. New York: Oxford University Press.

Nozick, R. (1981). *Philosophical Explanations*. Cambridge, MA: Harvard University Press.

Organisation for Economic Co-operation and Development (OECD). (2015). *OECD Employment Outlook 2015*. Paris: OECD. Available at: http://dx.doi.org/10.1787/empl_outlook-2015-en [accessed July 11, 2017].

Park, H., Twenge, J. M., and Greenfield, P. M. (2014). "The Great Recession: Implications for adolescent values and behavior." *Social Psychology and Personality Science*, 5(3), 310–18.

Pfau, B. N. (2015). "How an Accounting Firm Convinced Its Employees They Could Change the World." *Harvard Business Review* [online], October 6: https://hbr.org/2015/10/how-an-accounting-firm-convinced-its-employees-they-could-change-the-world [accessed March 20, 2017].

Porath, C. (2015). "No Time to Be Nice at Work." *New York Times* [online], June 19: https://www.nytimes.com/2015/06/21/opinion/sunday/is-your-boss-mean.html?_r=0 [accessed March 27, 2017].

Pratt, M. G. (2000). "The Good, the Bad, and the Ambivalent: Managing identification among Amway distributors." *Administrative Science Quarterly*, 45(3), 456–93.

Pratt, M. G. and Ashforth, B. E. (2003). "Fostering Meaningfulness in Working and at Work." In K. Cameron, J. E. Dutton, and R. E. Quinn (eds.), *Positive Organizational Scholarship: Foundations of a new discipline*, pp. 308–27. San Francisco: Berrett–Koehler.

PwC. (2016). *Connecting the Dots: How Purpose Can Join Up Your Business* [web page]: http://www.pwc.com/gx/en/ceo-agenda/pulse/purpose.html [accessed March 20, 2017].

Rawls, J. (1971). *A Theory of Justice*. Cambridge, MA: Harvard University Press.

Raz, J. (1986). "Liberating duties." *Law and Philosophy*, 8, 3–21.

Roberts, M. (2014). "Happiness 'Dips in midlife in the affluent West.'" *BBC News Online*, November 5: http://www.bbc.com/news/health-29899769 [accessed December 24, 2014].

Rosso, B. D., Dekas, K. H., and Wrzesniewski, A. (2010). "On the meaning of work: A theoretical integration and review." *Research in Organizational Behavior*, 30, 91–127.

Sandel, M. (2012). *What Money Can't Buy: The moral limits of markets*. New York: Farrar, Straus & Giroux.

Schnell, T. (2010). "Existential indifference: Another quality of meaning in life." *Journal of Humanistic Psychology*, 50(3), 351–73.

Schwartz, A. (1982). "Meaningful work." *Ethics*, 92(4), 634–46.

Sievers, B. (1994). *Work, Death, and Life Itself: Essays on management and organization*. New York: Walter de Gruyter.

Singer, P. (1997). *How Are We to Live? Ethics in an age of self-interest*. Oxford: Oxford University Press.

Stern-Gillet, S. (1995). *Aristotle's Philosophy of Friendship*. Albany: SUNY Press.

Terkel, S. (1974). *Working: People talk about what they do all day and how they feel about what they do*. New York: The New Press.

Thomas, L. (2005). "Morality and a meaningful life." *Philosophical Papers*, 34(3), 405–27.

Tolstoy, L. N. (1988 [1882]). *A Confession and Other Religious Writings*, translated by J. Kentish. New York: Penguin.

Velleman, J. D. (2005). "Family history." *Philosophical Papers*, 34(3), 357–78.

Watson, L. (2012). "One in Four Office Workers Is 'Chronically Bored', Putting Their Health at Risk." *Daily Mail* [online], January 12: http://www.dailymail.co.uk/health/article-2085506/Being-bored-office-bad-health-scientists-say.html [accessed November 14, 2015].

Wolf, S. (2010). *Meaning in Life and Why it Matters*. Princeton: Princeton University Press.

Wrzesniewski, A. and Dutton, J. E. (2001). "Crafting a job: Revisioning employees as active crafters of their work." *Academy of Management Review*, 26(2), 179–201.

Wrzesniewski, A., McCauley, C., Rozin, P., and Schwartz, B. (1997). "Jobs, careers, and callings: People's relations to their work." *Journal of Research in Personality*, 31(1), 21–33.

Yeoman, R. (2014). "Conceptualising meaningful work as a fundamental human need." *Journal of Business Ethics*, 125(2), 235–51.

Yu, R. (2011). "Driven to death by success." *China Daily*, September 2.

CHAPTER 8

IDENTITY AND MEANINGFUL/ MEANINGLESS WORK

NANCY HARDING

MY work for the past twenty years has been located, loosely, in a rather amorphous area of academic thought, critical management studies (CMS) (see Fournier and Grey, 2000 for a definition and discussion). CMS is in many ways adamantly opposed to the "positive organizational scholarship" in which much research on meaningful work is located (Lips-Wiersma, Wright, and Dik, 2016). CMS shares its roots with labor process theory in the seminal work of the journalist Harry Braverman (1974). Braverman argued that Taylor's instigation of what would become time-and-motion management processes heralded an era of ever tighter control over workers. Braverman's analysis, although later criticized for its failure to allow room for resistance (Meiksins, 1994), implied that the reduction of workers to automatons rendered work meaningless. In this light, the increasing advocacy of meaningful work, as reflected in the chapters in this Handbook, is a recognition of the importance of Braverman's critique of management itself. If meaningful work is understood as "concerned both with undertaking work-related activities that are pleasant, enjoyable and personally enriching, as well as contributing to something beyond pure self-interest" (Bailey et al., 2017: 417), then it becomes management's responsibility to ensure the necessary conditions are put in place.

An alternative and very different interpretation of this recent emphasis on meaningful work is that it represents another stage in management's efforts to instigate ever more subtle processes of control over staff (May, Gilson, and Harter, 2004). Through managing the meaning of work, that is, through encouraging staff to see work in a certain way, managers may use the power of discourse to persuade staff that their work is meaningful (Lips-Wiersma and Morris, 2009). This interpretation arises from the fact that CMS shares with labor process theory an intense interest in control and resistance, such that these are the fracture lines around which CMS is organized (Mumby, 2005). But CMS understands that regimes of control have expanded beyond Taylor's attempts to control bodies, and it argues that control is now sought through the manipulation of minds, psyches, and identities. This is argued, most influentially, in a seminal paper by Alvesson and Willmott (2002), which explores managerial control through the manipulation of one's very identity. Perhaps an ultimate form of control is achieved when the selves of staff members are constituted to a design defined by management, one that is to be achieved through "identity work" and that will result in staff investing in their own domination. In this interpretation, managerial attempts to persuade staff that their work is meaningful are seen as another form of manipulative control through their identities. By "identity," I mean an ongoing sense of a "self" that is maintained in interaction with others and with the social environment (Ybema et al., 2009), and that provides answers to the question: Who am I? (Alvesson, Ashcraft, and Thomas, 2008). It is understood in the poststructural tradition I draw on here as a "complex, recursive (and) reflexive" activity that is continually in process (Ybema et al., 2009: 301) and achieved through positioning of the self within competing discourses. With regard to meaningful work, then, if my identity, or my understanding of who I am, is derived through my work, then *if* I can be persuaded that I am happy and making a contribution, I will work harder.

From a critical perspective, therefore, there is little to say about meaningful work, as the paper by May, Gilson, and Harter (2004) has already said all these things. It could be possible to explore ways of resisting managerial attempts to prescribe what is meaningful work and how resistance to "meaningful work" contributes to identity formations. A vast body of literature has explored resistance against management's colonializing imperative (see Mumby et al., 2017 for a discussion), and Bailey et al. (2017) have explored "existential labor" as a form of resistance to meaningful work—that is, where "the actions, behaviors and espoused attitudes overtly adopted by individuals in response to organizational efforts to manage work-related meaningfulness" (p. 421) form a façade that disguises employees' criticisms of managerial initiatives ("surface existential labor"). On the other hand, they recognize "deep existential labor," whereby employees work on changing the self so as to conform with those initiatives. Such literature suggests the potential for developing a critical approach to meaningful work, but for the moment a discussion of meaningful work and identity seems caught in an uncomfortable binary:

- Implicit in what I will call "the managerialist approach" is an understanding that managers should and could support positive identity formation by making possible means of doing work from which one obtains pleasure and a sense of a contribution to organization and society.
- Whereas, in the more critical approaches, meaningful work is explicitly understood as another means by which managers seek to control staff by interfering in identity work through inserting persuasive but exploitative discourses of the potential self, but a sense of a "good" and "happy" self expressed in the terms offered by managerial machinations result in a "duped" self that will work harder, longer, and more profitably.

This is hugely unsatisfactory. From my critical perspective, there is a need for an understanding of meaningful/meaningless work that will form the basis for political action and a search for "meaningful" change. I suggest this cannot come from management's definitions of meaningful work, as presumed in both managerialist and critical approaches. A politics of meaningful work requires rejecting unexamined notions of both "management" and the "organization" as singular, homogeneous entities that constitute the imaginary backdrops against which the scene for meaningful work is established (see Ford and Harding, 2004 for a discussion). The organizational quotidian is beset with complexities and contradictions, something hinted at by Mitra and Buzzanell's (2017) analysis of meaningful work as dynamic and contested. Identities are constituted not only within but also outside the orbit of managerial influence or control. Indeed, individuals may move into and out of several or numerous identities as they go through their working days, in some of which they may conform with managerial initiatives, but in others of which they may act with autonomy. In some parts of the day their work may be meaningful and in others meaningless, and/or they may experience the same task in contradictory ways. There may be many definitions of meaningful/meaningless work: my understanding of what makes work meaningful or meaningless for me, as an academic, may differ from that of the porter who ensures the classrooms are in order or the administrator who makes my work possible. There is, further (as discussed below), no such thing as a homogeneous organization; organizations have within them numerous other organizations, and a single place may be the location of several or numerous "organizations" that each form contexts in which identity work is undertaken. Attempts to apply a single theory of meaningful work, whether managerialist or critical, to such fluid, unstable, dynamic, emergent "entities" is unwise.

In what follows, therefore, I develop a theory of some of the forms that "meaningful work" might take when constituted by agentive actors in organizational realms beyond managerial reach, and identities that may emerge through such staff-defined meaningful work. These identities are always fragile, subject to dissolution on the entry of managers. I am not aiming to develop an exhaustive theory but focus on those forms that emerge when one's "will to meaning" (Lips-Wiersma and Morris, 2009) or the assertion of one's egotistic needs to be an "I" (Harding, Ford, and Lee, 2017) are enabled or inhibited. In essence, although I take a detour via Marx's theory of alienation in order to provide the grounding for my arguments, the definition of meaningful work that emerges is not much different from that given above, that is, staff-instigated meaningful work is pleasurable for the self and makes a contribution to others. However, the contribution that is made is to the flourishing of both self and others, so I argue that work is *meaningless* unless it contributes to flourishing. That takes the argument back to identity: the answer to the question, "Who are you?" posed to someone at points in the day where they experience their work as meaningful may become: "I am someone who flourishes through participating in the flourishing of others." This identity will be very different from the abject identity that may be experienced when undertaking meaningless work (and work that management defines as meaningful may be regarded as meaningless by staff, as Bailey et al. (2017) have shown). The same individual may move between the proud identity made possible through meaningful work and the abject identity engendered by meaningless work. I start with Marx's theory of alienation due to its potential for arriving at definitions of meaningful/meaningless work, and then will use my own experiences (as an ethnographer before I knew there was such a thing as ethnography) and that of one person interviewed about his working life, to develop the exploration.

MEANINGFUL AND MEANINGLESS WORKPLACE IDENTITIES

There are the seeds of ideas of what meaningful work might entail in early work by the young Karl Marx (1988) who, in his twenty-sixth year, wrote the scraps that remain of the 1844 Manuscripts. He outlined a theory of a subject alienated from itself because of the conditions under which it must labor. Identity (as we call it today) emerged, for the young Marx, in the products of one's labor. One projected one's self into the products one made. Because, under capitalism, these products are taken away to be traded, one is (literally) alienated from the self who has been projected into the product. An alienated self is an abject self, one denied identity because it is unable to proclaim who it is and receive recognition of that proclamation from another (Butler, 1990). It is this early theory that offers a fertile way of conceiving of meaningful/meaningless work.

Marx did not limit his analysis to the making of a product. He argued that capitalism alienates the worker not only from her/himself, but also from their "species being" and from their fellow (wo)men. To understand "species being," think of a cow chewing the cud while grazing in a field all day. The cow exists only to exist; it labors (eats) to remain alive, but to be alive it is necessary that it eats. It has no consciousness (so far as we are aware) over and above the need to continue chewing and grazing. It has no "conscious life-activity" (Marx, 1988: 76). The human, in contrast, is a species being that is conscious of her or his own existence, who can ponder on her/himself as if she or he were an object, and so is a "Conscious Being" (Marx, 1988). Woman or man does not exist in isolation from other people; she or he is necessarily an active participant in the species that is the human animal (p. 77) and as such contributes to the sustenance of humankind as a whole (p. 77). That is, she or he goes beyond her or his own immediate physical needs so as to contribute to the greater good, producing "the whole of nature" (p. 77). She or he "forms things in accordance with the laws of beauty" (p. 77). This, then, is a theory of meaningful work. It takes the form of a social activity that produces goods and services that contribute to individual and general flourishing. Identities are constituted not in isolation but through a sociality in which one gains recognition from another of one's existence as a self. Inherent in Marx's theory is a stage on which recognition is given as part of everyday interactions between people working together.

Meaningless work is alienated work. Under capitalism a person's life activity is reduced to nothing more than a means of staying alive—she or he becomes like the cow, working only to sustain physical existence. She or he moves but does not think, create, etc., etc. The worker "must sell himself and his human identity" (Marx, 1988: 25) in order to survive. Workers thus "sink" to the level of a commodity (p. 69), a commodity that they themselves produce through their labor and which is itself sold. This commoditized self, like any other commodity produced through labor, is an object in which work is "congealed" or in which immaterial practices become material—that is, real, physical objects. So, for Marx, the conditions of capitalist organizations require that staff exist only to exist: embroiled in meaningless work, they are alienated.

This theory resonated with my own early work experience. Before I became an academic I worked on the production lines of a factory making the innards for electrical machinery. We were paid by "piece work," that is, our pay was determined by how many capacitors we made. Reflecting on that work now, I understand, on the one hand, that we existed only as extensions of machines that made meaningless products. We moved our hands, arms and feet, and disengaged our minds—the work was so menial that it did not need our brains but only our bodies as extensions of the machines at which they sat. The capacitors, sad little plastic and metal products that may have been useful in a finished product but which of themselves had no meaning, rolled down into the collecting trays and were taken away—alien objects that belonged to the employer. But this was only part of the story. Marx's arguments are that our "inner worlds" were impoverished by work that required no thought, skill, or imagination. To the observer, the women working on those machines would be seen to be busily occupied in such very mundane activity that they could not produce anything that seemed meaningful, or have the potential to contribute to the good of the community. On and on they went, one repetitive motion after another, producing 2,400 capacitors each day, 12,000 each week. The machine governed all our movements, it would seem.

But that is to describe only one part of the activities in which we were engaged. Yes, at one level management's reach was omnipotent: even the time we spent on toilet breaks was monitored. There was little scope for identity work, save as that abject identity that comes from being the appendage to a machine. But I also remember that, even while appearing to the observer as extensions of the machine, much more was going on than the mere making of capacitors. There was the making of social worlds and selves (and "species-being") within the walls of the factory, with banter between the staff, laughter, friendship-making, and care. There was lots of gossip, cakes on birthdays, tricks played on those getting married, advice about difficult life situations, and so on. In other words, it was not only capacitors that were made in that factory, but social relationships and social selves. The products—capacitors—we manufactured contained nothing of ourselves, but even while tied to the machines we constituted a social world. It was through this social world that we constituted ourselves as a member of a "species," that is, of working class women enjoying each other's company (see Young and Wilmott, 2013 [1957] for a discussion).

It is this autobiographical account that leads me to posit the possibility of being both alienated and non-alienated or, in contemporary parlance, engaged in both meaningless and meaningful work, and moving between abject, subordinated identities and social, recognition-full ones. In many ways I am not saying anything new here: the social side of work, as encapsulated in the term "unity with others" (Lips-Wiersma, Wright, and Dik, 2016), is integral to many discussions of meaningful work, and Lucas and Buzzanell (2004) and Mills (2002) have found that pink- and blue-collar staff, respectively, found "meaning" (although not necessarily meaningfulness) through working relationships even while doing work that appeared meaningless. But identity theory, as expounded by Butler (1997), contributes the understanding that positive interactions with others can prevent the slippage into abjection of the self who is undertaking meaningless work. An abjected identity is painful, replete with the pain of the abhorred. The recognition of others, gained in the agentive actions of constituting sociality, says "you are not abject; you are one of us, and we share a positive identity."

Neoliberalism and Meaningful Work

However, the shift from a manufacturing economy to a service-based one means that the types of work available today differ greatly from those of thirty or forty years ago, and neoliberalist theories' exploration of contemporary forms of work would seem to negate the possibility of there being any escape from capitalism's penetrating controls. Neoliberalism refers to an epoch in which economization spreads to spheres that previously were held to be separate and distinct from economics and markets (Harvey, 2005). It is "an order of normative reason that, when it becomes ascendant, takes shape as a governing rationality extending a specific formulation of economic values, practices, and metrics to every dimension of human life" (Brown, 2015: 30). Thus, persons and states "are expected to comport themselves in ways that maximize their capital value in the present and enhance their future value... through practices of entrepreneurialism, self-investment, and/or attracting investors" (Brown, 2015: 22). The self in neoliberal times is a project that has to be managed. No longer just someone who works for a firm, the self becomes a firm in itself, devoted to maximizing its human capital. The self is penetrated to its very psyche, to the capillaries of its body, by capitalism.

Neoliberalism is thus understood as a "culture" that provides the organizing metaphors for whole spheres of life (Couldry, 2010). Not only is it a hegemonic theory of political economy (Harvey, 2005), it is also a mobile, calculated technology for governing subjects who are constituted as self-managing, autonomous, and enterprising (Gill and Scharff, 2011: 5), and also "rational, calculating and self-motivating" (ibid.). Subjects are increasingly "exhorted to make sense of their individual biographies in terms of discourses of freedom, autonomy, and choice—no matter how constrained their lives may actually be" (ibid.: 6). Neoliberalism's tenacity is achieved, it is argued, through the production of active subjects seduced by such discourses, subjects who can best be understood as "artefacts" rather than architects of neoliberalism (Larner, 2003). If so, then there is no possibility of being both alienated and non-alienated, as I argued earlier.

But theories of neoliberalism are as totalizing as Marxist theory. Neoliberalism suggests staff are *super*-alienated because they can only approach the products of their labor from the position of the consumer. Such a deterministic and monolithic model has been challenged by, among others, Walkerdine and Bansel (2010), who coined the phrase "super-alienated." They illuminate the importance of understanding how "complex, relational and rhizomatic" responses by individuals to neoliberalist modes of governance challenge such monolithic assumptions. The workers in Walkerdine and Bansel's study were defined not only by neoliberalism, but by family, communities, socialities, and other quotidian influences, so that the notion of "a stable neoliberalism that fixes a subject totally within its orbit" unravels (p. 506).

This is important, because by definition there is no "I," no identity, available to an alienated self: the self does not exist save for the automaton (or cud-chewing cow) that sits in its place. And if there is no "I" then there is nothing in which judgments of the meaningfulness or otherwise of work can be invested. Meaningful work requires an "I," a subject, who both undertakes it and is constituted as an I through the acts of undertaking that work. Neither worker nor task pre-exist each other: they are co-constituted through its doing.

But, as Walkerdine and Bansel (2010) imply, and following Butler (1990, 1993), there appear to be not just one self that is constructed while at work, but many selves, or there are numerous subject positions and individuals move from one to another to another, constituting notions of the self in each one as they move through them. Neoliberal capitalism does not pin individuals, like butterflies, into one fixed position. It follows that someone can be constituted as an alienated, abject worker undertaking meaningless work at one moment, but can move into the position of a non-alienated, non-abjected subject undertaking meaningful work (understood in this instance as the making of the sociality of the workplace) in the next.

The argument that follows is informed, although space allows it to be only an implicit influence, by Butler's (1990, 1993, 1997, 2004) theories of the performative constitution of a subject as it moves within and through materially located subject positions that are the stage on which recognition as a subject is granted. This requires unravelling the notion that organizational space is singular and fixed. I will argue that organizations are polytopias, or scenes of multiple, overlapping places that offer subject positions in which one may be engaged (almost) simultaneously in meaningless/alienating work identities and meaningful/non-alienated work identities. As we have seen, meaninglessness and alienation are co-emergent. They are not the same as each other, but imbricated within and through each other. The same is true for meaningful and non-alienated identities. My argument is that people move between these positions, and can indeed be engaged in both meaningless and meaningful work at the same time. I am arguing that organizational space/place is multiple and fluid, and that different forms of self-, identity-, work-, and organization-making will take place within the same spaces/places. Although my focus here is on meaningful work that is undertaken in places that are out of sight of the managerial gaze, I am not precluding the possibility of managerial involvement in the processes I will describe.

MEANINGFUL WORK IN POLYTOPIC
ORGANIZATIONAL SPACE

The thesis of organizations as polytopic understands organizations as constituted within and through multiple overlapping "I/spaces" in which the same material space can afford numerous identities that in turn constitute numerous places (or emplacements) within and through that space. It was inspired by Lefebvre's *The Production of Space* (1991 [1974]) although it departs radically from Lefebvre's overall thesis. Lefebvre rejected Euclidian conceptions of space as something that exists in its own right. Think of an empty room: Euclidian space understands it as existing and awaiting occupation. Lefebvre (1991 [1974]) demurred. He reversed the concept of empty space as something existing prior to whatever ended up filling it, and argued that space is actively *produced*.

Organizational space, following Lefebvre, is understood as both the medium and the outcome of actions (Cairns, McInnes, and Roberts, 2003; Kornberger and Clegg, 2004). Familiar spatial scales bundle together different "levels" of space, such as organizational, local, regional, national, supranational, and global, and are not "natural geological foundations" (Spicer, 2006: 1470) but are socially produced, multiple scales constituted by actors engaging in political struggles. Such non-representational modes of theorizing (Beyes and Steyaert, 2012; Massey, 2005; Soja, 1996) argue that there is no pre-existing or "*a priori* organization," no "discrete and independent entity existing in one space-time framework" (Jones, McLean, and Quattrone, 2004: 734). In this "loss of cosmological innocence" (Hansen, 2004: 759) organizational space is understood through a performative perspective in which spatial orders are both constituted by and constitutive of participants. That is, organizational actors "do not simply 'find' an arena, [but] construct it interactively" (Haug, 2013: 711). Importantly for this chapter's arguments, at the same time "we do not simply occupy space, but rather become ourselves, in and through it" (Tyler and Cohen, 2010: 192), that is, material places and spaces form parts of the selves or identities of people as they, at the same time, constitute those spaces and places. It must not be forgotten that spaces and identities materialize and are materialized by power relations (Tyler and Cohen, 2010).

Just as Butler's theories argue for a processual, performative understanding of the constitution of selves/identities, such non-representational theory argues against place and space as constant, singular, and unitary. Space is, instead, conceived of as "processual and performative, open-ended and multiple, practiced and of the everyday" (Beyes and Steyaert, 2012: 47), and, indeed, encompassing a proliferation of spaces and places. Rather than space we should study "spacing" (ibid.), changing a vocabulary of "stasis, representation, reification and closure" to one of intensities, capacities and forces; rhythms, cycles, encounters, events, movements and flows; instincts, affects, atmospheres and auras; relations, knots and assemblages. There are thus multiple spaces in which organization happens, each of which may be invested with diverse, unstable, and multiple meanings (Halford and Leonard, 2006) and in which some perhaps may offer meaningful work and others will not, although all is fluid and in flux so it would be wrong to try to pin some down as "meaningful" and others as "meaningless." This is a performative concept of space, of space as "becoming." Thus, "organizations are but temporary reifications" (Czarniawaska, 2004: 780; see also Wapshott and Mallett, 2012).

To understand this more clearly, I initially turned to Foucault's thesis of heterotopias. Foucault, like Lefebvre, is specifically critical of Euclidian concepts of space: "we are not living in a homogeneous and empty space..." (Foucault, 1994: 177). Rather, Foucault understands that space is multilayered and constructed in conditions of power and ideology. In this non-Euclidian perspective, an organization's buildings are not empty spaces waiting to be filled up by staff and managers. Rather, the spaces of "the organization" are actively constructed through the interactions of participants, ideologies, power, technologies, materialities, and belief systems (Ford and Harding, 2004).

Foucault's concept of heterotopias informs this thesis. He had made a passing observation about heterotopia in the Preface to *The Order of Things* (Foucault, 1989), in which he contrasted the comfortable fantasies of utopias with heterotopias that are "disturbing, probably because they secretly undermine language" (Foucault, 1989: xix). That is, heterotopias focus on the insurrection of subjugated knowledges and provide a means of interrogating, and indeed revolting against, dominant, power-laden assumptions about space. Foucault understood heterotopias as "certain [spaces] that have the curious property of being connected to all the other emplacements, but in such a way that they suspend, neutralize, or reverse the set of relations that are designated, reflected, or represented by them" (p. 178). They may offer challenges to power, or separate the "deviant" from normative populations; they may articulate a society's unarticulated belief systems, but be connected with temporal discontinuities, and be both open and closed at the same time. They may juxtapose in the same space several incompatible emplacements, or may challenge the entire conception of space and place.

But although Foucault's is a theory that has "disruptive, transient, contradictory and transformative implications" (Genocchio, 1995: 42) it is, by reason of its name—"heterotopia"—a theory of other, or different, spaces. This does not explain how it is possible to sit at a machine that governs one's actions and at the same time be free of that machine, as I recounted earlier, so Foucault's account takes us only so far in this argument. That is, it is not a theory of polytopias, or emplacements that are not "ontologically single, and therefore inhabited by a finally limited number of objects, forces and processes that may be more or less well known... In the midst of representational singularity there is multiplicity. But this is not seen. The multiple or the fractional, the elusive, the vague, the partial and the fluid are being displaced into Otherness" (Law, 2004: 137). In what follows, I develop a theory of polytopias that accounts for how it is possible to be seated in one space but at the same time occupy several, indeed numerous, placements in which identity/self-constitution, as well as meaningful/meaningless work, goes on (Steyeart, 2010). This theory rests on six principles.

Six Principles of Polytopias

The first principle is that *the occupants of a space constitute it as emplacements in which they constitute selves/identities.* This is based on Foucault's (1994) account of emplacements as locales where speaking subjects and space are co-emergent and, importantly for a theory of polytopias, that occupants of one material space may speak from several emplacements, constituting different perspectives of the self, of identities, as they do so. Emplacements are constituted within a trialectic of power, knowledge, and space (Soja, 1996).

In these diverse, multiple, and norm-governed emplacements, occupants, albeit unknown to each other, constitute both the organizational space and the self (Harding, 2007). Different organizational actors may perceive and conceive of the same space as very different emplacements. In Ford and Harding's (2004) example of a hospital, nurses inhabited a village-like place, managers a grid that they traverse during their daily work, and chief executives a fantastic space in which complexity and size collapse into the simplicities (and manageability) of a small cottage hospital. Larner and le Heron's (2005) study of changes in New Zealand's higher education system offer a similar conclusion. They argue that "imaginaries," or the fantasies of those with power about what a sector should *be,* constitute both spaces and subjectivities through calculative practices; these constitute norms of practice that inform both the construction of material space and the occupants who occupy that space.

The second principle states that *the entrances and exits of managers transform emplacements (and thus selves) through the workings of power.* To develop this principle (and others that follow) I will draw on an empirical example from an interview with someone I will call the Worker—one of a series of ad hoc interviews that aim to explore varieties of working lives (see Harding, 2013)—who worked in a mail sorting office alongside "*up to 500 people.*"

As seen in other studies (Anthony, 1986; Stewart et al., 1994), managers are often absent from this Worker's place of work: "*his duties will take him somewhere else, you know, so now he's here, now he's not here.*" His account shows that spaces are constituted very differently according to the presence or absence of the manager. When the manager is present workers stay at their workstations, and "*you become more active, so less talking, less socializing*" in an attempt to "*keep on top of*" the work. He describes how, when managers are present, emotions are negative. There is suspicion:

> the numbers of managers have gone up in the last couple of years... the higher man-
> agement wants to recruit more managers and then if the workforce go on strike... they
> can utilise the managers to get the work through... and so [they learn how to do our
> work].

And loathing:

> [One manager's] entire body language is so full of malignancy..., he's so vicious in his
> posture. People hate him when he's stood [behind] their back, and he likes to be where

he shouldn't be...People don't feel comfortable, because why is he here, why is he looking at us, like we owe something to him?

So, when a manager enters the sorting room, staff focus on the tasks of sorting the mail. The Worker describes himself and his colleagues when in management's presence as "robots," or denigrated and abject beings, who must focus solely on getting the job done while managers are watching them.

But when there are no managers present the Worker's tasks change and the social interactions of the workplace take precedence. He talks to people *"about work and talking about management you know how cunning and how vicious they are, so I'll drip some vitriol into the conversation."* Such talk, he says, is necessary to his sense of self: *"I am not a robot...I would wilt and wither if I don't talk to people."* But also, he argues, the social side of work is vital because *"we've got all the week to go so unless everyone stays in a good mood and keeps our chins up"* then *"If you don't feel happy...[it] causes a lot of trouble at work."* So *"I find the time...to wheel round containers [and] stop by let's say for 30 seconds to say 'hello' or 'how are they doing', also sometimes [say] something funny you know and they will burst out into a fit of laughter and you know my job done, and then move on to other people...But for me it's important that people are smiling and laughing and so that's a typical day."*

It can be seen that the very same material space transmogrifies into different emplacements as managers enter and leave. The Worker thus moves between two very different spaces, albeit in the same material place and, as he moves, the self who speaks changes: a different subject with a different identity emerges. In one he speaks as the objectified, denigrated worker denied recognition of himself as anything other than the mere appendage of a machine, a machine to which he is tied, unable to move out of its orbit. In the other, he moves away from the machine and speaks as a subject who finds pleasure (and thus I suggest, meaningfulness) in a working life that allows him to constitute himself as a flourishing "species being."

The third principle is that *each emplacement is governed by different norms and regulations.* Continuing with the same example, and my own remembered experience, the norms that govern a space when managers are present are that managerial orders must be obeyed, and those orders are concerned with maximizing production. Managers must watch over staff, in the sense of ensuring they are conforming with rules and regulations. Staff, on the other hand, must conform with the norms of hierarchy and give the impression of being focused totally on the achievement of workplace objectives. As we have seen, when managers are present the Worker follows the rules: he occupies a fixed place, by the machine, and his focus is on the officially ordained task of sorting the mail. His identity is abject, no more than that of a robot. When managers are absent, the Worker has the freedom to walk around, and the focus turns to the social world of the workplace where the identities that become available are those of social beings engaged in ensuring mutual (albeit constrained) flourishing.

It follows (the fourth principle) that *what is regarded as deviant and what is regarded as normative change as the place shape-shifts.* The notion that staff can wander around, sharing a joke and engaging in conversation, so not focusing on maximizing efficiency or output, would be totally alien in manager-governed space. Similarly, the worker who focuses totally on working as hard as possible in the absence of managers would be regarded as deviant by fellow occupants of that emplacement, as numerous studies starting with the Hawthorne Studies (Mayo, 2010) have shown.

Thus, fifth, *each space has its own regime of emotions, embodiment, self- and identity-making*. In the Worker's account affect in manager-dominated space is described as negative (frustration and anger), but it switches to one of laughter and sociality in worker-dominated space. The very materiality of the body seems to change when managers enter and leave. In one space the body must adapt itself to the demands of the machine, while in another it is freer and can move away from the machine that otherwise governs its every movement.

It follows (principle 6) that *there are different conceptions of "work" in each space*. This example shows that how work is conceived shifts as different emplacements come to occupy the same place. The Worker may be situated in exactly the same position, bounded by the same walls and working with the same machinery, but when managers are present the space is management-governed, and work is defined within a managerialist frame that requires a focus on maximizing output, efficiency, production, etc. When managers are absent, the conception of work expands to incorporate the sociality of the workplace. Work here is carried out as part of a social world in which relationship-building and maintenance is included in the unwritten job description.

DISCUSSION: TOWARD A THEORY OF MEANINGFUL WORK/IDENTITIES IN THE ORGANIZATIONAL QUOTIDIAN

The examples I have used to develop this theory of organizations as polytopias, or multiple emplacements in single material spaces, have focused on only one material space with only two coexistent emplacements. Even at this simple level, it can be seen that work emplacements are labile and fissile: staff move fluidly, from moment to moment, into and out of different emplacements as if into and out of different dimensions, and as they do so their possible selves or identities shift and change.

But the major arguments derived from this theory, in relation to accounts of meaningful/meaningless work and positive/abject identities, is that identity and work are co-emergent, but the definitions of "work" shift to encompass the making of the sociality of the workplace. "Meaningful work-identities," in this account, refers to the areas of freedom that are carved out, moment to moment, in spaces and places where the rule of "the organization" may not extend, and where what is meaningful is defined by those doing the work rather than by management. This is a self-governing identity. The self may be alienated from its self when in an emplacement subject to the organizational/managerial gaze that requires the worker to become a part of a machine, say, rather than an individual, where the "I" as an extension of the machine is located in a web of formal organizational rules and norms. But when that organizational gaze is absent and the worker moves into a different emplacement, the self that is constituted is a social self that emerges through interactions with others within the physical, but not psychical, confines of "the organization." The "product" that is achieved while in that space is not so much what the employer demands, although that may be produced too, but a self as a "species being" that contributes to the flourishing of the people gathered together in that material place and through that contribution, that "meaningful work" that provides recognition itself comes into being as meaningful.

I am thus suggesting that in the conditions of neoliberal capitalism, "meaningful work" and the identities it facilitates can be something that is defined and constituted by the worker when unconstrained by the organizational gaze. It is achieved through various forms of meaning-making, defined as how the "I" perceives, understands, and thus constitutes space, place, work, and self. In my own memory of what appeared to be a totally governed workplace, and that of the Worker whose account I've given, meaning emerged through social interactions, through "species being." "Meaningful work" here then refers not to the tasks required by the organization but the other tasks of socializing with fellow workers, and achieving recognition and identity of the self as fully human rather than an appendage of a machine (Butler, 2004). To reiterate, meaningful work and meaningful (non-alienated) selves are co-emergent. In other workplaces or for other people "meaningful work" may be defined differently, but it would be something worked on outside the norms or rules that constrain the possibilities for being and becoming in that particular organization. It can coexist with meaningless, alienated work, that is, it may occur in the same material place but in a very different emplacement. It follows that because "meaningful identity constitution" is a social activity, it contributes to individual and general flourishing of the people working together. "Seeing" workplaces in this way as polytopias involves an ontological politics (Law, 2006) that strives to avoid unwittingly repressing what "fails to fit the standard package of common-sense realism" (ibid.: 10). Rather, this theory of polytopias opens up possibilities for conceiving of ontological multitudes, and understanding how meaningful work emerges despite neoliberalist capitalism's attempts to quash it.

REFERENCES

Alvesson, M., Ashcraft, K. L., and Thomas, R. (2008). "Identity matters: Reflections on the construction of identity scholarship in organization studies." *Organization*, 15(1), 5–28.

Alvesson, M. and Willmott, H. (2002). "Identity regulation as organizational control: Producing the appropriate individual." *Journal of Management Studies*, 39(5), 619–44.

Anthony, P. D. (1986). *The Foundation of Management*. London: Tavistock.

Bailey, C., Madden, A., Alfes, K., Shantz, A., and Soane, E. (2017). "The mismanaged soul: Existential labor and the erosion of meaningful work." *Human Resources Management Review*, 27, 416–30.

Beyes, T. and Steyaert, C. (2012). "Spacing organization: Non-representational theory and performing organizational space." *Organization*, 19(2), 45–61.

Braverman, H. (1974). *Labor and Monopoly Capital: The Degradation of work in the twentieth century*. New York: NYU Press.

Brown, W. (2015). *Undoing the Demos*. Cambridge, MA: MIT Press.

Butler, J. (1990). *Gender Trouble: Feminism and the subversion of identity*. New York: Routledge.

Butler, J. (1993). *Bodies That Matter*. New York: Routledge.

Butler, J. (1997). *The Psychic Life of Power*. Stanford, CA: Stanford University Press.

Butler, J. (2004). *Undoing Gender*. New York: Psychology Press.

Cairns, G., McInnes, P., and Roberts, P. (2003). "Organizational space/time: From imperfect panoptical to heterotopian understanding." *Ephemera*, 3(2), 126–39.

Couldry, N. (2010). *Why Voice Matters: Culture and politics after neoliberalism*. New York: Sage.

Czarniawska, B. (2004). "On time, space, and action nets." *Organization*, 11(6), 773–91.

Ford, J. and Harding, N. (2004). "We went looking for an organisation but could find only the metaphysics of its presence." *Sociology*, 38(4), 815–30.

Foucault, M. (1989). *The Order of Things*. London: Routledge.

Foucault, M. (1994). "Different Spaces." In M. Foucault, *Essential Works of Foucault 1954–1984: Aesthetics*, edited by J. D. Faubian, pp. 175–85. London: Penguin.

Fournier, V. and Grey, C. (2000). "At the critical moment: Conditions and prospects for critical management studies." *Human Relations*, 53(1), 7–32.

Genocchio, B. (1995). "Discourse, Discontinuity, Difference: The Question of 'Other Spaces.'" In S. Watson and K. Gibson (eds.), *Postmodern Cities and Spaces*, pp. 35–46. Oxford: Blackwell.

Gill, R. and Scharff, C. (2011). "Introduction." In R. Gill and C. Scharff (eds.), *New Femininities: Postfeminism, neoliberalism and subjectivity*, pp. 1–20. Basingstoke: Palgrave MacMillan.

Halford, S. and Leonard, P. (2006). "Place, space and time: Contextualizing workplace subjectivities." *Organization Studies*, 27(5), 657–76.

Hansen, N. V. (2004). "Where do spacing and timing happen? Two movements in the loss of cosmological innocence." *Organization*, 11(6), 759–72.

Harding, N. (2007). "On Lacan and the 'becoming-ness' of organizations/selves." *Organization Studies*, 28(11), 1761–73.

Harding, N. (2013). *On Being at Work: The social construction of the employee*. London: Routledge.

Harding, N., Ford, J., and Lee, H. (2017). "Towards a performative theory of resistance: senior managers and revolting subject(ivitie)s." *Organization Studies*, 38(9), 1209–32.

Harvey, D. (2005). *A Brief History of Neoliberalism*. Oxford: Oxford University Press.

Haug, O. (2013). "Organising spaces: Meeting arenas as a social movement infrastructure between organization, network, and institution." *Organization Studies*, 34(5–6), 705–32.

Jones, G., McLean, C., and Quattrone, P. (2004). "Spacing and timing." *Organization*, 11(6), 723–41.

Kornberger, M. and Clegg, S. R. (2004). "Bringing space back in: Organizing the generative building." *Organization Studies*, 25(7), 1095–114.

Larner, W. (2003). "Guest editorial." *Environment and Planning D: Society and Space*, 21, 509–12.

Larner, W. and le Heron, R. (2005). "Neo-liberalizing spaces and subjectivities: Reinventing New Zealand universities." *Organization*, 12(6), 843–62.

Law, J. (2004). *After Method: Mess in social science research*. London: Routledge.

Law, J. (2006). "Traduction/trahison: Notes on ANT." *Convergencia*, 13(42), 47–72.

Lefebvre, H. (1991 [1974]). *The Production of Space*. Oxford: Basil Blackwell.

Lips-Wiersma, M. and Morris, L. (2009). "Discriminating between 'meaningful work' and the 'management of meaning.'" *Journal of Business Ethics*, 88(3), 491–511.

Lips-Wiersma, M., Wright, S., and Dik, B. (2016). "Meaningful work: Differences among blue-, pink- and white-collar occupations." *Career Development International*, 21(5), 1–18.

Lucas, K. and Buzzanell, P. M. (2004). "Blue-collar work, career, and success: Occupational narratives of Sisu." *Journal of Applied Communication Research*, 32(4), 273–92.

Marx, K. (1988). *Economic and Philosophic Manuscripts of 1844*. New York: Prometheus Books.

Massey, D. (2005). *For Space*. London: Sage.

May, D. R., Gilson, R. I., and Harter, L. M. (2004). "The psychological conditions of meaningfulness, safety and availability and the engagement of the human spirit at work." *Journal of Occupational and Organizational Psychology*, 77(1), 11–37.

Mayo, E. (2010). "Hawthorne and the Western Electric Company." In R. J. Stillman II (ed.), *Public Administration: Concepts and Cases*, 9th edn., pp. 149–57. Boston, MA: Wadsworth.

Meiksins, P. (1994). "'Labor and monopoly capital' for the 1990s: A review and critique of the labor process debate." *Monthly Review*, 46(6), 45–60.

Mills, C. (2002). "The hidden dimension of blue-collar sensemaking about workplace communication." *Journal of Business Communication*, 39(3), 288–313.

Mitra, R. and Buzzanell, P. M. (2017). "Communicative tensions of meaningful work: The case of sustainability practitioners." *Human Relations*, 70(5), 594–616.

Mumby, D. K. (2005). "Theorizing resistance in organization studies: A dialectical approach." *Management Communication Quarterly*, 19(1), 19–44.

Mumby, D. K., Thomas, R., Martí, I., and Seidl, D. (2017). "Resistance Redux." *Organization Studies*, 38(9), 1157–83.

Soja, E. (1996). *Thirdspace*. Oxford: Blackwell.

Spicer, A. (2006). "Beyond the convergence–divergence debate: The role of spatial scales in transforming organizational logic." *Organization Studies*, 27(10), 1467–83.

Stewart, R., Barsoux, J.-L., Kieser, A., Ganter, H.-D., and Walgenbach, P. (1994). *Managing in Britain and Germany*. Basingstoke: St. Martin's Press.

Steyeart, C. (2010). "Queering space: Heterotopic life in Derek Jarman's garden." *Gender, Work & Organization*, 17, 45–68.

Tyler, M. and Cohen, L. (2010). "Spaces that matter: Gender performativity and organizational space." *Organization Studies*, 31(2), 175–98.

Walkerdine, V. and Bansel, P. (2010). "Neoliberalism, Work and Subjectivity: Towards a More Complex Account." In M. Wetherell and C. T. Mohanty (eds.), *The Sage Handbook of Identities*, pp. 492–507. New York: Sage.

Wapshott, R. and Mallett, O. (2012). "The spatial implications of homeworking: A Lefebvrian approach to the rewards and challenges of home-based work." *Organization*, 19(1), 63–79.

Ybema, S., Keenoy, T., Oswick, C., Beverungen, A., Ellis, N., and Sabelis, I. (2009). "Articulating identities." *Human Relations*, 62(3), 299–322.

Young, M. and Wilmott, P. (2013 [1957]). *Family and Kinship in East London*. Oxford: Routledge.

CHAPTER 9

SELF-TRANSCENDENCE AND MEANINGFUL WORK

ADRIAN MADDEN AND CATHERINE BAILEY

INTRODUCTION

THE topic of meaningful work is rightly of growing interest. Work is transformative—economically, socially, physically, and emotionally—and most people spend most of their lives doing it. Regardless of the level of skill involved, Arendt (1958) suggests that what makes work distinctive is its potential to create something of value, whose meaning goes beyond the activity of the work itself, even if that value is only transitory. However, the deeper meaning of work, beyond the activity associated with it, is not always apparent and we long for "a more humanistic work environment, increased simplicity, more meaning, and a connection to something higher" (Marques, Dhiman, and King, 2005: 81). What characterizes us as humans is our relentless pursuit or "will" for meaningfulness: we seek something more than just the "9 to 5," a search not just for daily bread but for daily meaning (Terkel, 1974). The philosopher Victor Frankl (1984) perceived the search for meaningfulness as fundamental to the human condition, defining not just "who we are" but helping us to answer the more transcendent question, "Why are we here?"

Despite the importance of meaningfulness and growing interest in the topic, we still know very little about meaningfulness, about what the experience of meaningfulness involves and how this contributes to our sense of purpose not just in work but also in life overall. Based on earlier research in which we suggested that the transcendent nature of experienced meaningfulness requires much greater attention (Bailey and Madden, 2017), in this chapter, we return to that suggestion and to the proposition that what distinguishes meaningful work from other concepts—including the meaning of work—is the centrality of *self-transcendence*, an idea most immediately associated with religious and spiritual approaches, commonly featuring in spiritual or philosophical debates about the nature of being itself. Self-transcendence is a complex concept sometimes explained as a "way in" to discover our inner spirituality, as a "way out" to escape the meaninglessness of the world, or as the destination of our transcendent journey, embodied in the idea of perfection or some "divine being." Others, however, see the *transcendent self* as a fanciful idea lacking ontological basis.

Despite this lack of consistent usage, the notion of self-transcendence is an idea that has emerged in the meaningful work literature from different disciplinary traditions, including sociology, psychology, management, and philosophy. We explore these traditions in some depth before discussing the key dimensions of self-transcendence identified in the literature and propose that the temporal and intersubjective nature of experienced self-transcendence in work does not closely match these dimensions. On this basis, we make some further recommendations for future organizational research.

APPROACHES TO MEANINGFUL WORK

There has been much debate around the precise nature of "meaningful work" and its difference from as well as its relationship—if any—with the meaning of work and ideas about work significance and purpose (Ashmos and Duchon, 2000; Spreitzer, 1995). This debate reflects multidisciplinary approaches to work meaningfulness, highlighting distinct historic emphases and interests in the topic from the fields of philosophy, sociology and psychology, and management.

Philosophical interests in meaningful work are often linked to Aristotelian virtue tradition, reflecting underlying ideals of personal fulfillment associated with eudaimonic (flourishing) or hedonic (indulgent) values (Beadle and Knight, 2012; Morgan and Farsides, 2009). Work is framed as an arena for the expression and development of virtues, through which people might find fulfillment by pursuing their quest for life meaning, and reflecting broad ideals of a "just society" or the sense of a life worth living (Frankl, 1984; Schwartz, 1992; Wong, 2012; Beadle and Knight, 2012). Sociological interests have historically been directed toward the structural and institutional processes underpinning people's experience of work, often associated with a Marxist perspective. This has stressed the subjugating and alienating effect of work relations whereby people become estranged from their essence through selling their labor in a capitalist regime (Fromm, 1955). Braverman (1974) stated that the modern process of work results in deskilling and consequently the degradation of meaningfulness. In Seeman's (1959) work on alienation, *meaninglessness* was explained as a direct result of work degradation and the rational managerialism associated with modernity, seeking ever greater efficiencies at the expense of worker choice and autonomy. Perhaps the most extensive empirical study that has been conducted in this area in the 1980s involved the Meaning of Work (MoW) international research project (England and Harpaz, 1990). This collaborative study spanned eight different countries and investigated how work meanings differed across these cultural settings, in terms of meeting basic, instrumental needs such as wages, but also in relation to expressive needs, such as social identity and status. The study identified five common patterns of meaning, including individual definitions of work, social norms about work, work goals, motivation, and work centrality. Like other cross-cultural studies of that time, the MoW research downplayed the subjective nature and content of the experience of meaningful work in the search to establish consistent, universal meanings of work across cultures.

Both the philosophical and sociological approaches have thus tended to focus on the meaning of work in terms of what work *signifies* within a broader, socio-historical system of social meanings. Budd's (2011) ten "meanings" that work possesses over time, including the idea of work as obligation or "curse," as creativity and as an expression of "freedom," as "commodity," as "citizenship" or "social relation," or even "disutility," highlights these approaches well. In a more parsimonious model of work meanings, Wrzesniewski (2003) proposed that our orientations toward work can be reduced to three fundamental motivations—career, calling, or job. While such categorizations helpfully summarize the diverse meanings that work can have over time and space, irrespective of the actual nature or context of the work itself, they have tended to focus on the functional system of meanings, in the way that things relate to one another within an integrated and cohesive reality (Heine, Proulx, and Vohs, 2006)—either in the existentialist sense associated with the thinking of Sartre (1960), where the self is the originator of all meaning, or in the more deterministic sense of Levi-Strauss (1962: 14) where human agency is "imprisoned" within systems of meaning. In seeking to explain general systems of meaning, these approaches downplay the idea of *meaningfulness* and how particular events garner *significance* over others. While everything has a meaning, not everything is meaningful.

Interest in the meaningfulness of work has been driven in the psychology and management fields from the 1960s onwards with the aim of promoting the *inner meaning* of work for workers through greater integration and "fit" of the individual with the job and the organization (Porter and Lawler, 1968; Argyris, 1964). This emerged from concern that the increasing alienation of "typical" assembly line workers caused lower productivity, because such work was "not likely to provide meaningful knowledge of the result" (Lawler, 1969: 430). It led to assertions that workers' motivation to perform better could not be explained purely by generally accepted inducements of pay and other extrinsic benefits (Turner and Lawrence, 1965; Hackman and Lawler, 1971; Hackman and Oldham, 1976). It was also about the quality of work, in terms of work variety and workplace empowerment, and also the capacity of work to enable self-realization, well-being, and happiness through the expression of the whole (physical, mental, emotional, and spiritual) self in work (Rego and Cuhna, 2008).

Hackman and Oldham's (1976) subsequent model of job characteristics became an enduringly important model of work design, in which emphasis on the experienced meaningfulness of work was identified as the most important factor in shaping the perceived significance of work. Work meaningfulness was explained as work that people *cared* about because they saw it as "generally meaningful, valuable and worthwhile" (Hackman and Oldham, 1976: 256). Although Hackman and Oldham's (1976) model did not fully explain the "interpersonal, technical or situational" factors that contributed to perceived meaningfulness (ibid.: 277), these were acknowledged to be critical to understanding people's experience of work as meaningful (Duchon and Plowman, 2005).

Hackman and Oldham's (1976) model remains influential in numerous studies of meaningful work. It contributed to a development of the concept in relation to workers' needs, initially by Kahn (1990: 704) who defined meaningfulness as "a feeling that one is receiving a return on investments of one's self in a currency of physical, cognitive or emotional energy." In the psychology and management fields, others have further refined meaningful work as something that arises from the perceived value of the content of work or its context. For example, May, Gilson, and Harter (2004) explain that this value arises when the content of work helps people meet personal goals, while Pratt and Ashforth (2003: 311) state that people can experience meaningfulness from the work content or its context when they deem it to be "purposeful and significant." Barrick et al. (2015: 116) explain that workers believe their work to be significant when they feel that what they do is "useful and valuable."

Although research in the psychology and management fields has provided refinements to our understanding of meaningful work in relation to value, purpose, and significance, this definition of meaningful work and the subjective evaluation of its significance or its context remain poorly defined and circular in nature. They provide little to help us understand what it is that makes work significant or even how much significance is needed before someone experiences their work to be meaningful. What this literature has done much more successfully however has been, through this emphasis on fulfilling workers' needs and the work context as a site for human flourishing, to link to the idea of spirituality in order to better "understand and unleash the human spirit in organizations" so people can thrive and engage in their work (May, Gilson, and Harter, 2004: 12). It is this growing interest in spirituality at work, an idea traditionally associated with philosophers, theologians, and religious commentators, that has helped to promote meaningfulness as an important research project, particularly in relation to the idea that through work people seek to go beyond the immediacy of tasks and roles in search of deeper meaning or life coherence, a sense of making a difference and a connection to something higher, beyond the self (Bailey and Madden, 2017; Lips-Wiersma and Wright, 2012; Marques, Dhiman, and King, 2005).

Spirituality is recognized as a fundamental and multidimensional aspect of human nature, whose increasing relevance and interest in the workplace spans goals of lateral connectivity through shared values with others, along with a search for higher purpose and the divine (Roof, 2015). Spirituality is defined by Neck and Milliman (1994: 10) as "a transcendent personal state which is often difficult to describe and must be experienced since it is viewed as being beyond one's physical senses, mind, and feelings." Although the experience may be difficult to describe, it is a "meaning-making construct" concerned with "breathing life into situations" (Lips-Wiersma, 2002: 500), whereby a positive connection between one's inner and outer life "can lead to a more meaningful and productive outer life" (Ashmos and Duchon, 2000: 135). It is this connection between the "inner life" (or the soul) and the "outer life" (or a sense of connection and community) that is the source of meaningfulness. Maslow (1969) saw spirituality as synonymous with self-transcendence, by which he meant a "transpersonal" state, which occurred when someone sought "a benefit beyond the purely personal ... [and comes] to identify with something greater than the purely individual self" (cited in Koltko-Rivera, 2006: 306).

The connection between meaningfulness and spirituality, or between meaningfulness and value, purpose, or significance, is clearly important but not well explained. Arguably, one may routinely have a sense of value or purpose from work without necessarily experiencing meaningfulness. The manner in which a significant connection between the inner and outer life gives rise to experienced meaningfulness in work remains similarly problematic. To makes things more complex, some suggest that because people are inherently spiritual beings, possessing an inner life that is driven by the will to meaning, this makes spirituality and meaningfulness (or significance) much the same thing (Vaill, 2000).

These ideas are clearly linked but there are reasons to seek to distinguish them. However "dispiriting" the outer life may be (Ashmos and Duchon, 2000: 136), that people can will meaningfulness from drudgery (Isaksen, 2000), suffering (Frankl, 1984), and mixed emotional states (Ersner-Hershfield et al., 2008), suggests that the significance or spirituality associated with meaningful work are distinct but interrelated things. We propose that the experience of meaningful work occurs when work events, work encounters, or work contexts gain a significance, or spiritual value that transforms the immediate meaning of the work itself or its context, allowing an individual to see their role or their contribution within a wider interpersonal, temporal or spatial context, beyond the self. This supports others who perceive meaningful work as something that transcends the traditional boundaries of the self (Palmer et al., 2010; Dik and Duffy, 2009; Lips-Wiersma and Morris, 2009; Pratt and Ashforth, 2003). It is through the mechanism of self-transcendence that people experience meaningfulness, by connecting inner, existential concerns, such as life coherence, self-fulfillment, health, and well-being (Wong and Fry, 1998), with outer concerns that go beyond self boundaries to gain a deep sense of "what matters" (Pratt and Ashforth, 2003).

If the experience of meaningfulness involves going *beyond the self*, by expanding self-boundaries in some way, this raises two important questions: the first concerns the process of transcendence and the second concerns the state of transcendence—beyond the self—and what this actually involves. In the next section we consider how self-transcendence is conceptualized in relation to the concept of meaningful work.

MEANINGFUL WORK AND SELF-TRANSCENDENCE

Ideas about self-transcendence feature in a number of meaningfulness studies but remain empirically and conceptually problematic. This includes claims about the overlapping nature of the intrapersonal, interpersonal, and transpersonal nature of self-transcendence (Reed, 2008) as well as its paradoxical nature based on its immanent or transcendent orientations (Stein, 2008). Schnell (2011) identifies self-transcendence as one source of meaningfulness which can be conceptualized on two dimensions—*vertical* self-transcendence, to denote an orientation toward a supernatural or higher power, through religion for example, and *horizontal* self-transcendence, referring to a sense of social responsibility rather than just one's own needs.

Vertical Transcendence

The idea of vertical self-transcendence emerges from a wide body of literature concerning a belief or sense of connection to the *divine* and the sacred, which lies beyond our day-to-day world (Ormerod, 2003). Ideas about the divine and the sacred are often linked in Western thought with Christian writing about the nature of God, but derive from a longer tradition of Greek thought about aesthetics and perfection, referring to self-transcendence as "a metaphysical structure grounding the contingent in the Absolute, and a practical spiritual quest of rising above changing worldly affairs to ultimate union with the Eternal" (Kalton, 2000). Based on the Aristotelian tradition, self-transcendence is explored in philosophical debates about the external nature of the divine, denoting the ineffable beyondness that lies outside our comprehension but to which we are connected through *daimon*, or our inner and "true nature" (Deci and Ryan, 2008: 2). This emerges in different conceptualizations of the relation of virtue to meaningful work, whereby *eudaimonic* values refer to the pursuit of excellence or godly perfection which brings true meaning and well-being to life (Ryff, 1989). From this perspective, work becomes inherently meaningful because it is a site for the realization of our humanity (Beadle and Knight, 2012). Aristotle never actually used the term transcendence as a virtue in itself, but it is accepted that the idea of self-transcendence was intended when

> [Aristotle] discussed the relationship of virtue and happiness...a life of perfect eudaimonia is transcendent because it indicates a "divine element" within the individual. (Peterson and Seligman, 2004: 47)

Subsequently the pursuit of eudaimonic value in religious and mystical traditions has come to denote a union with or a manifestation of the divine whereby man can "transcend his nature" (Cook, 2013: 155), and a beyondness in the sense of completeness and flawlessness (Hungerford, 2006). This is contrasted with the earthly, hedonic pursuit of well-being which, while also involving individual happiness, is often perceived as a lack of virtue through individual interests in pleasure and the satisfying of short-term, personal needs and appetites (Ryan and Deci, 2001).

This vertical expression of self-transcendence in the way that the pursuit or expression of divine perfection becomes the embodied goal of work is often associated in the meaningful work literature with religious callings. Explained by Weber (1976: 79) as "a task set by God," calling has come to connote something more secular, a "life-task, a definite field in which to work," in the form of a secular station or office in which one lives an honest life through conscious service or vocation (Elangovan, Pinder, and Mclean, 2010). This secular approach to callings has been shaped by Enlightenment debates centering on ideas of knowledge, choice, and freedom (Oates et al., 2008), as well as the redemptive promise of the Calvinist work ethic emphasizing hard work, thrift, and efficiency (Weber, 1976), and "giving work a reason that transcends our earthly predicament" (Muirhead, 2004: 104). From this perspective, the notion of calling has come to denote a secular but still inescapable moral obligation, in the form of an inner sense of duty or passion (Cardador and Caza, 2012).

Callings are intrinsically linked to meaningfulness in many studies (Berkelaar and Buzzanell, 2014; Cardador and Caza, 2012; French and Domene, 2010), and explicitly via transcendence in others. Dik and Duffy (2009: 427), for example, define callings as "a transcendent summons, experienced as originating beyond the self, to approach a particular life role in a manner oriented toward demonstrating or deriving a sense of purpose or meaningfulness and that holds other-oriented values and goals as primary sources of motivation." For Duffy and Dik, both *purpose* and *meaningfulness* emerge from the individual sense of coherence, significance, or fit that fulfilling a life role creates, although the notion and nature of the *transcendent summons experienced beyond the self* is somewhat vague yet, in our view, crucial. One way in which the "summons" associated with calling is explored in the meaningful work literature is in relation to the idea of "immanent transcendence," which Hartman and Zimberoff (2010: 3) state refers to the spiritual "other-oriented" nature of meaningfulness, arising from the experience beyond the ego and material world, of something more or greater than the self (Lips-Wiersma, Wright, and Dik, 2016; Mitroff and Denton, 1999; Rosso, Dekas, and Wrzesniewski, 2010).

Horizontal Transcendence

Kalton (2000) states that horizontal transcendence refers to a more secular orientation but which also involves a "spiritual cultivation, perfecting our relationship with the world of life around us." Unlike vertical transcendence, this denotes a connectivity with the world around us in terms of meaningful relations with others (Pavlish and Hunt, 2012), in tasks or roles that concern matters beyond one's immediate self-interest and addressing the interests of others, for example in the direct care and service for another or others (Lips-Wiersma and Wright, 2012; Lips-Wiersma and Morris, 2009).

Where the vertical dimension of self-transcendence concerns meaningfulness through fulfilling, intrapersonal connection between the inner self and a transcendent perfection that is beyond description (Reed, 2009), horizontal self-transcendence refers to concern for others in two ways. The first is in the form of shared values and diverse interpersonal connections that come through working with co-workers (Lips-Wiersma and Morris, 2009; Pavlish and Hunt, 2012; Reed, 2009) and the second, through the idea of *oneness*, in terms of a dissolution of the self and a unifying or transpersonal interconnectedness with everything (Reed, 2009; MacDonald and Holland, 2002). Horizontal self-transcendence emphasizes the idea of *beyond self* through the intersubjective relationship between self and other, whether that is with a *significant other*, such as a charge or co-worker, or indirectly as the "generalised other" in the sense of shared norms constitutive of work and society (Mead, 1934). In this context, and particularly relevant in relation to the notion of meaningful work, is the idea that the self is constituted in relation to the other (Mead, 1934; Muhe, 2010; Simmel, 1950). Mead (1934) argues that human beings construct their sense of self "in action" and interaction with others; it is through our actions in relation to others that we express and constitute our individuality.

Some explain this horizontal orientation as an individual *temperament* or character toward self-transcendence, which involves a "unitive consciousness" in which the individual sees everything as part of one totality, with "no meaningful distinction between self and other" (Cloninger, Svrakic, and Przybeck, 1993: 981). Here, the self-transcendent state is perceived as one of total absorption and concentration, experienced as a loss of self and time, highlighting the temporal displacement which Maslow (1971) associated with self-transcendent states. In it, one is able to locate the contribution of one's current work along a temporal continuum stretching from the past into a dim, infinite future, and thereby "to stand for something outside of [one's] own skin" (ibid.: 282). Further empirical research supports this temporal aspect of meaningfulness, to show that it is not a steady or sustained experience but is experienced "in transcendent moments in time" whereby the ontological separation between the past, present, and future are no longer discernible (Bailey and Madden, 2017: 16).

The vertical and horizontal dimensions of self-transcendence suggest that the experience of meaningfulness arises either through an inner summons toward the divine or an outer-orientation to the greater good, from which people gain a sense of the value, purpose, or significance of their work beyond the self and the immediate nature of the work (Yeoman, 2014). This raises a number of important issues. First, it implies that work itself is not the sole source of meaningfulness such that even if the content of work is found to be meaningless, it still has the potential for value or significance because of its orientation beyond the self. Second, the separation of the vertical and horizontal dimensions of self-transcendence is problematic, not least because certain orientations to work—such as callings—appear to involve self-transcendence both vertically in terms of summons and at the same time horizontally, in terms of personal sacrifice to a particular line of work or in service to others (Bunderson and Thompson, 2009). As Stein (2008) argues, this dichotomous approach in the literature to self-transcendence is both arbitrary and undermines the experience of "oneness" that it connotes. Third, if the experience of meaningful work emerges intersubjectively beyond the self, this raises questions about the ontological space that lies beyond the self as the source of the meaningful experience. In the next section we pursue the intersubjective turn implied by self-transcendence and consider what this means for the conceptualization of meaningful work.

Self-transcendence and the Intersubjective Nature of Meaningful Work

Psychological and management research, from which most empirical research on meaningful work is drawn, centers on the theorization of affect or behavior based on the self-concept (Madden and Bailey, 2017). Most theories of motivation, performance, and work meaning are explained to varying degrees by models of self-determination, self-efficacy, and self-esteem (Bandura, 1989), in which the self is perceived as the primary agent of all cognitions, attitudes, and beliefs. Where "others" feature in this research, in terms of co-workers, teams, supervisors, customers, organizations, community, or family, these others are framed as relevant to experienced meaningfulness through self-related mechanisms such as value congruence and self-identity.

For example, social identity theorists suggest that when individuals find their work group memberships to be valuable and distinctive, then they are likely to provide a source of meaningfulness through a process of interpersonal sense-making (Tajfel and Turner, 1985). Wrzniewski (2003) has argued that while meaningfulness arises through a concern for connection with others, the interpretation of interpersonal cues, together with "motive work," enables people to create a personal identity through others around them. Even in theories of prosocial behavior, the emphasis is on how work gives rise to the experience of meaningfulness through the activation of cognitions or affect that are perceived as meeting the needs of the self, such as purpose and coherence (Van Zyl, Deacon, and Rothmann, 2010; Lips-Wiersma, 2002). The role of the other, whether significant or generalized, is conceptualized as a resource for the "project of the self" (Clarke, Brown, and Hope Hailey, 2009: 324), where the self lacks social responsibility, obligation, or mutuality (Note, 2010). As Rosso, Dekas, and Wrzesniewski (2010: 115) assert, it is the self who is the "ultimate arbiter" of meaning. To better understand the self-transcendent dimensions of meaningfulness means problematizing the assertion that there is anything "ultimate" about the self.

The orthodox view of the self, on which most research rests, owes much to what Taylor (1989: 29) describes as the "massive subjective turn of modern culture, a new form of inwardness," echoing Durkheim's (1984) observation of the growing "cult of the individual." Marske (1985) states that this subjective turn, supported by the empirical pursuit for explanations of personality, has abstracted the self from the social world, in search of stable and measurable explanations and predictions and made "the 'preserving and/or recreating [of] a meaningful and morally coherent social life a formidable task" (ibid.: 3).

This subjective turn in social research has contributed vastly to our understanding of meaningfulness and its relationship to motivation, well-being, performance, and other work-related factors. However, it is based on assumptions about the ontological coherence of the boundaries of the self, the supposition that the self ever achieves any kind of finality or stability, and the corollary of a "self–other" dichotomy. This privileging of the self as the final arbiter of meaning has been challenged across different disciplinary traditions. In the work of Taylor (1989), for example, what is meant by the self (our consciousness) is depicted as entirely intersubjective, such that any sense of self we have is dependent on the recognition and acknowledgment we receive from others. It is a position underpinned by Heidegger's (1996) concept of "da-sein," which implies that the self cannot be understood in isolation from, or without reference to the other, and without whom the self is "no-one" alone. In da-sein, individuals are so enmeshed in their social environment and their interpersonal relationships, that distinguishing between them is illusory (Heine, Proulx, and Vohs, 2006). As Simpson (2015) states, the self is constituted relationally, continually unfolding through encounters with others, without boundary or finality (Simpson, 2015).

Religious thinkers explain self-transcendence as a way to escape the self–other dichotomy, as a "betweenness" in which the dialogic relationship between self and other provides the basis of social reality (Kramer, 2011). Betweenness, claims Polo (1986), is the "ontological ground of all relations" because the self exists and is always expressed in—or in the lack of—a relationship with the other. This idea of meaningfulness arising intersubjectively through self-transcendence raises other concerns. It suggests that our question—about the nature of meaningfulness arising in the ontological space that lies beyond self—may be the wrong question (Stein, 2008). Perhaps it is the ontological assumption of the self that is questionable, and whose persistence in theorization of meaningful work may even be a barrier to understanding the nature of experienced meaningfulness?

In contrast, although self-transcendence may contribute to meaningful outcomes as a result of its intersubjectivity, these same intersubjective relations can be deleterious to the experience of meaningfulness. For example, significant others in the form of managers, bosses, co-workers, or customers may be troublesome and significant for negative reasons, creating stress, conflict, and a lack of support (Cardador and Caza, 2012: 342). In seeking to transcend self-oriented goals or essential life roles, the pursuit of meaningfulness through callings can leave workers susceptible to manipulation through the exploitation of sacrifice (Berkelaar and Buzzanell, 2014). Just like callings or spirituality, self-transcendence may thus lead to the "dark side" of meaningfulness, whereby workers' quest for meaningfulness can leave their motivations vulnerable to misappropriation and managerial instrumentalization (Duffy and Dik, 2013; Lips-Wiersma and Morris, 2009).

TAKING SELF-TRANSCENDENCE FORWARD

Meaningful work is complex and cannot be easily described or accounted for. It is seen to be linked to a number of work orientations such as callings and spirituality but it is distinct from them. We have argued that what distinguishes it, separating it from other concepts, is the idea of self-transcendence. Self-transcendence suggests that the meaningfulness of work lies beyond what task and role signify, such that we might transcend our selfhood, expanding our self-boundaries intersubjectively, enabling us to flourish and realize our potential by gaining insight *with and through* others into the significance of our work.

One insight into this transformation, from the *signified* to the *significant*, derives from the work of Ricoeur, who states that what work signifies can be observed in its literal form, such as when a worker hammers a nail into a plank to mend a fence (Mei, 2006). All four components of this work process—worker, hammer, nail, and plank—possess literal and immediate meaning in terms of the purpose each serves. Arguably, each might serve multiple purposes and signify different things in different contexts. Importantly, each has within it the means of transformation into the significant, of *becoming* something other than itself, beyond the literal. Significance emerges from the agency of the worker in the technical, situational, and temporal context of the work. This significance may embody a summons from beyond the self to assemble a fence, perhaps as the product and the expression of a traditional skill or in the service of others. The social significance of the fence may emerge from its greater purpose in uniting (or dividing) communities, or in the symbolic capacity of the fence to create place, and the production of collective identity, a sense of belonging, or a shared history. For Arendt (1958), the work gains significance through the creation of artifacts and of institutions whose importance endures temporally beyond the act of creation and beyond its immediate use value.

In our research we reported that the self-transcendent experience of meaningful work is episodic rather than a sustained feature of work (Bailey and Madden, 2017). The conceptual roots of self-transcendence suggest that it is an irregular, unusual event rather than a routine aspect of work. It is described in terms of rich and profound moments involving an experience of connection, "oneness," or unity with the cosmic whole, either to the divine or in a more secular orientation to humanity (Hörmann, 2013), making it somewhat difficult to account for. Maslow (1971: 50) saw self-transcendence as expressed through "peak experience," in transient moments of ecstasy which "cannot be bought, cannot be guaranteed, cannot even be sought." Maslow (1971) even argued that although practically everyone has peak experiences of a self-transcendent nature, they may not even realize it, making it a difficult thing to identify, measure, and explain. It is a claim that raises important questions about the factors that might lead to an individual's realization of self-transcendence and the role of others—whether significant or generalized—in achieving this.

What the literature suggests is that however difficult self-transcendence might be to describe or realize, its association with meaningfulness links it to collective space and time, to joint venture and unity, to an intersubjective ontology that extends beyond the boundaries of the self in the search for value, purpose, and significance. Whether through rituals to mark collective achievements, paid breaks in work to reflect on a morning's travails over a cup of tea, or opportunities to interact with significant others who might provide affirmation and recognition of a job well done, it seems to us that the instrumentalized nature of much modern work denies workers the time and space to go beyond the immediate meaning of work. The temporal and spatial opportunities in work to convert the signified into the significant are being stripped away in the pursuit of ever more rationality and profit. On the other hand, there is a risk that claims about the instrumentalized nature of modern work reflect an essentialist agenda predicated on the idea of inner nature or *daimon* which is neither empirically established nor proven. So while meaningfulness is seen by some to be associated with self-transcending *daimonic* values, there has been little debate about the cultural, gender, or contextual assumptions on which such associations rest.

Consequently, work is organized in ways that disunite work from its wider social context (Seeman, 1959), from the opportunity to transcend the immediate and literal meaning of work and the potential realization of meaningfulness. There is, as Potter (2015) states, a *fracture* between our values and the capacity of modern work to fulfill them such that the technical, situational, and temporal conditions once associated with meaningfulness have themselves become despiriting rather than enriching. For example, technology now enables workplace operations to be made at speeds that are "beyond the realm of human consciousness" (Lash and Urry, 1994: 242). Work is often displaced—outsourced, off-shored, or home-based—making work situations fragmented, isolated, and lonely spaces disconnected from others. In many jobs time is either compressed in intensive jobs where workers are asked to "do more with less," or stripped away altogether in zero-hour contracts where workers are not guaranteed any work at all and usually not paid for the time spent doing anything other than the transactional minimum.

Empirical research has contributed to our knowledge of worker motivation and well-being and we know from this research that meaningfulness is linked to increased engagement, satisfaction, and commitment (Fletcher, Bailey, and Gilman, 2018; Geldenhuys, Taba, and Venter, 2014) as well as performance outcomes (Albuquerque et al., 2014). Yet the subjective turn in social science and its preoccupation with the self has the potential to be self-defeating in the longer term. By focusing on more easily operationalized concepts of self-esteem, self-efficacy, and self-determination, compared to the messy, boundary-less intersubjective space associated with self-transcendence, a lot of positivist-based social science is insensitive to the unpredictable nature of experienced meaningfulness or the dispiriting effects of modern work and its implications for our social well-being. The effect of this positivist endeavor, whether intended or not, is to represent the "everyday flow" of life and work and make it predictable, to account for work through laws of "sameness," "averageness," and "generalizability" (Luthans and Davis, 1982: 381). In so doing, research often overlooks the really meaningful stuff, seeking snapshots and cross-sectional views of workers' lived experience and thus unable to fully detect the emergent qualities of self-transcendence or describe the richness of experienced meaningfulness. Positivist social science also fails to self-reflect on the longer term implications of its preoccupation with the "self project" (Valle, 1995), characterized by a narrow focus on meaning based on immediacy, in a culture that privileges self-help over altruism, self-fulfillment over equality, and self-determination over collective responsibility, and which many argue is deleterious to the realization of meaningfulness itself. In developing this chapter we note however an increasing interest in workplace spirituality and claims for its capacity to breathe life into work situations. By exposing and exploring the deeper, spiritual meanings people can access at work we might counter the "thin" understanding of work "reflected in neoliberal economic thinking, which prioritizes rationality and the instrumental aim of work" (Dashtipour and Vidaillet, 2017: 20), and enrich the narrow, snapshot approach of positivism to gain a much more accurate and complete picture of the work experience.

Our agenda is twofold. First, we aim to develop and apply our understanding of self-transcendence in order to promote the opportunity for work to provide value, purpose, and meaningfulness in people's lives by preserving space and time for mutuality. As Conklin (2012: 307) argues, re-emphasizing intersubjectivity is important because connecting self to others "creates a meaning structure for today's actions…that provides continuity and joins them in the conversation that transcends individuals, time, and place." Without such structures, work could lose its institutional value in providing security for people, in reproducing rules about responsibility and mutuality, and creating space that engenders citizenship and participation. Our second aim is to use and develop research approaches to meaningful work that might better anticipate the precursors to—or even more directly detect the outcomes of—self-transcendence in the workplace and the wider benefits of self-transcending individuals to organizations. If meaningfulness is intersubjective, then by looking mainly at the self to understand this, we may be looking in the wrong place. By placing greater emphasis on team dynamics and group outcomes, for example, and using methods such as focused ethnography (Knoblauch, 2005), we might be better able to provide richer, contextual accounts of the emergent nature of experienced meaningfulness through self-transcendence.

References

Albuquerque, I., Cunha, R., Martins, L., and Sa, A. (2014). "Primary health care services: Workplace spirituality and organizational performance." *Journal of Organizational Change Management*, 27, 59–82.

Arendt, H. (1958). *The Human Condition*. Chicago: University of Chicago Press.

Argyris, C. (1964). *Integrating the Individual and the Organisation*. New York: John Wiley.

Ashmos, D. and Duchon, D. (2000). "Spirituality at work: A conceptualization and measure." *Journal of Management Inquiry*, 9, 134–45.

Bailey, C. and Madden, A. (2017). "Time reclaimed: temporality and the experience of meaningful work." *Work, Employment & Society*, 30(1), 3–18.

Bandura, A. (1989). "Human agency in social cognitive theory." *American Psychologist*, 44, 1175–84.

Barrick, M., Thurgood, G., Smith, T., and Courtright, S. (2015). "Collective organizational engagement: Linking motivational antecedents, strategic implementation, and firm performance." *Academy of Management Journal*, 58(1), 111–35.

Beadle, R. and Knight, K. (2012). "Virtue and meaningful work." *Business Ethics Quarterly*, 22(2), 433–50.

Berkelaar, B. and Buzzanell, P. (2014). "Bait and switch or double-edged sword? The (sometimes) failed promises of calling." *Human Relations*, 68(1), 157–78.

Braverman, H. (1974). *Labour and Monopoly Capital: The degradation of work in the twentieth century*. New York: Monthly Review Press.

Budd, J. (2011). *The Thought of Work*. Cornell: ILR Press.

Bunderson, J. and Thompson, J. (2009). "The call of the wild: Zookeepers, callings, and the dual edges of deeply meaningful work." *Administrative Science Quarterly*, 54, 32–57.

Cardador, M. T. and Caza, B. (2012). "Relational and identity perspectives on healthy versus unhealthy pursuit of callings." *Journal of Career Assessment*, 20(3), 338–53.

Clarke, C., Brown, A., and Hope Hailey, V. (2009). "Working identities? Antagonistic discursive resources and managerial identity." *Human Relations*, 63(3), 323–352, doi: 10.1177/0018726708101040.

Cloninger, C., Svrakic, D., and Przybeck, T. (1993). "A psychological model of temperament and character." *Archives of General Psychiatry*, 50, 975–90.

Conklin, R. (2012). "Work worth doing: A phenomenological study of the experience of discovering and following one's calling." *Journal of Management Inquiry*, 21(3), 298–317.

Cook, B. (2013). *Pursuing Eudaimonia: Re-appropriating the Greek philosophical foundations traditions of the Christian apophatic tradition*. Newcastle: Cambridge Scholars Publishing.

Dashtipour, P. and Vidaillet, B. (2017). "Work as affective experience: The contribution of Christophe Dejours' 'psychodynamics of work.'" *Organization*, 24(1), 18–25.

Deci, E. and Ryan, R. (2008). "Hedonia, eudaimonia, and well-being: an introduction." *Journal of Happiness Studies*, 9(1), 1–11.

Dik, B. and Duffy, R. (2009). "Calling and vocation at Work: Definitions and prospects for research and practice." *The Counseling Psychologist*, 37(3), 424–50.

Duchon, D. and Plowman, D. (2005). "Nurturing the spirit at work: Impact on work unit performance." *The Leadership Quarterly*, 16, 807–833.

Duffy, R. and Dik, B. (2013). "Research on calling: What have we learned and where are we going?" *Journal of Vocational Behavior*, 83(3), 428–36.

Durkheim, E. (1984). *The Division of Labor in Society*. New York: Free Press.

Elangovan, A., Pinder, C., and Mclean, M. (2010). "Callings and organizational behaviour." *Journal of Vocational Behavior*, 76, 428–40.

England, G. and Harpaz, I. (1990). "How working is defined: National contexts and demographic organizational role influences." *Journal of Organizational Behaviour*, 11: 253–66.

Ersner-Hershfield, H., Mikels, J., Sullivan, S., and Carstensen, L. (2008). "Poignancy: Mixed emotional experience in the face of meaningful endings." *Journal of Personality and Social Psychology*, 94(1), 158–67.

Fletcher, L., Bailey, C., and Gilman, M. (2018). "Fluctuating levels of personal role engagement within the working day: A multilevel study." *Human Resource Management Journal*, 28(1), 128–47, doi: 10.1111/1748-8583.12168.

Frankl, V. E. (1984). *Man's Search for Meaning*. New York: Washington Square Press.

French, J. R. and Domene, J. F. (2010). "Sense of 'calling': An organizing principle for the lives and values of young women in university." *Canadian Journal of Counselling*, 44(1), 1–14.

Fromm, E. (1955). *The Sane Society*. New York: Rinehart and Company.

Geldenhuys, M., Taba, K., and Venter, C. M. (2014). "Meaningful work, work engagement and organizational commitment." *SA Journal of Industrial Psychology*, 40(1), Art. #1098.

Hackman, J. R. and Lawler, E. E. (1971). "Employee reactions to job characteristics." *Journal of Applied Psychology Monograph*, 55(191), 259–86.

162   ADRIAN MADDEN AND CATHERINE BAILEY

Hackman, J. R. and Oldham, G. R. (1976). "Motivation through the design of work." *Organizational Behavior and Human Performance*, 16, 250–79.

Hartman, D. and Zimberoff, D. (2010). "Immanent Transcendence, Projection and Re-collection." *Journal of Heart-Centered Therapies*, 13(2), 3–66.

Heidegger, M. (1996). *Being and Time*. Albany: State University of New York Press.

Heine, S., Proulx, T., and Vohs, K. (2006). "The meaning maintenance model: on the coherence of social motivations." *Personality and Social Psychology Review*, 10(2), 88–110.

Hörmann, K. (2013). "Everyday experience and transcendence in music therapy." *Musik-, Tanz- und Kunsttherapie*, 24(1), 1–26.

Hungerford, A. (2006). "Don DeLillo's Latin Mass." *Contemporary Literature*, 47(3), 343–80.

Isaksen, J. (2000). "Constructing meaning despite the drudgery of repetitive work." *Journal of Humanistic Psychology*, 40, 84–107.

Kahn, W. (1990). "Psychological conditions of personal engagement and disengagement at work." *Academy of Management Journal*, 33, 692–724.

Kalton, M. (2000). "Green Spirituality: Horizontal Transcendence." In P. Young-Eisendrath and M. Miller (eds.), *The Psychology of Mature Spirituality: Integrity, wisdom, and transcendence*, pp. 148–58. New York: Routledge. Available at: https://faculty.washington.edu/mkalton/green%20spir1.htm [accessed March 14, 2017].

Knoblauch, H. (2005). "Focused ethnography." *Forum Qualitative Sozialforschung/Forum: Qualitative Social Research*, 6(3), Art. 44. Available at: http://nbn-resolving.de/urn:nbn:de:0114-fqs0503440 [accessed January 3, 2017].

Koltko-Rivera, M. (2006). "Rediscovering the later version of Maslow's hierarchy of needs: Self-transcendence and opportunities for theory, research and unification." *Review of General Psychology*, 10(4), 302–17.

Kramer, K. (2011). "Explorations and responses: Cross-reanimating Martin Buber's 'between' and Shin'ichi Hisamatsu's 'nothingness.'" *Journal of Ecumenical Studies*, 46(3), 444–56.

Lash, S. and Urry, J. (1994). *Economies of Signs and Space*. London: Sage.

Lawler, E. (1969). "Job design and employee motivation." *Personnel Psychology*, 22(4), 426–35.

Levi-Strauss, C. (1962). *The Savage Mind*. Chicago: University of Chicago Press.

Lips-Wiersma, M. (2002). "The influence of 'spiritual meaning-making' on career behavior." *The Journal of Management Development*, 21, 497–520.

Lips-Wiersma, M. and Morris, L. (2009). "Discriminating between 'meaningful work' and the 'management of meaning.'" *Journal of Business Ethics*, 88, 491–511.

Lips-Wiersma, M. and Wright, S. (2012). "Measuring the meaning of meaningful work: Development and validation of the comprehensive meaningful work scale (CMWS)." *Group and Organization Management*, 37(5), 655–85.

Lips-Wiersma, M., Wright, S., and Dik, B. (2016). "Meaningful work: Differences among blue-, pink-, and white collar occupations." *Career Development International*, 21, 534–51.

Luthans, F. and Davis, T. (1982). "An idiographic approach to organizational behavior research: The use of single case experimental designs and direct measures." *Academy Of Management Review*, 7(3), 380–91.

MacDonald, D. and Holland, D. (2002). "Examination of the psychometric properties of the Temperament and Character Inventory self-transcendence dimension." *Personality and Individual Differences*, 32(6), 1013–27.

Madden, A. and Bailey, C. (2017). "Engagement: Where has all the 'power' gone?" *Organizational Dynamics*, 46(2), 113–19.

Marques, J., Dhiman, S., and King, R. (2005). "Spirituality in the workplace: Developing an integral model and a comprehensive definition." *Journal of American Academy of Business*, 7(1), 81–91.

Marske, C. E. (1985). "Durkheim's 'Cult of the individual' and the moral reconstitution of society." *Sociological Theory*, 5(1), 1–14.

Maslow, A. (1971). *The Farther Reaches of Human Nature*. Harmondsworth: Penguin.

May, D., Gilson, R., and Harter, L. (2004). "The psychological conditions of meaningfulness, safety and availability and the engagement of the human spirit at work." *Journal of Occupational and Organizational Psychology*, 77, 11–37.

Mead, G. H. (1934) *Mind, Self and Society: From the standpoint of a social behaviorist*. Chicago: University of Chicago Press.

Mei, T. (2006). "Form and figure: Paul Ricoeur and the rehabilitation of human work." *Journal of French Philosophy*, 16(1–2), 57–70.

Mitroff, I. and Denton, E. (1999). *A Spiritual Audit of Corporate America*. San Francisco, CA: Jossey-Bass.

Morgan, J. and Farsides, T. (2009). "Measuring meaning in life." *Journal of Happiness Studies*, 10, 197–214.

Muhe, U. (2010). *Labour, Politics and Emancipation: Arendt and the historical materialist tradition*. Unpublished PhD thesis, University of Kent

Muirhead, R. (2004). *Just Work*. Cambridge, MA: Harvard University Press.

Neck, C. and Milliman, J. (1994). "Thought self-leadership: Finding spiritual fulfillment in organizational life." *Journal of Managerial Psychology*, 9(6), 9–16.

Note, N. (2010). "Reflections on meaningfulness and its social relevance." *Kritike*, 4(1), 138–49.

Oates, K., Hall, M., Anderson, T., and Willingham, M. (2008). "Pursuing multiple callings: The implications of balancing career and motherhood for women and the church." *Journal of Psychology and Christianity*, 27(3), 227–37.

Ormerod, N. (2003). "Augustine's *De Trinitate* and Lonergan's Realms of Meaning." *Theological Studies*, 64(4), 773–94.

Palmer, B., Quinn, G., Reed, P., and Fitzpatrick, J. (2010). "Self-transcendence and work engagement in acute care staff registered workers." *Critical Care Nursing Quarterly*, 3(2), 138–47.

Pavlish, C. and Hunt, R. (2012). "An exploratory study about meaningful work in acute care nursing." *Nursing Forum*, 47(2), 113–22.

Peterson, C. and Seligman, M. (2004). *Character Strengths and Virtues: A handbook and classification*. Oxford: Oxford University Press.

Polo, A. (1986). *The Realm Of The Between In Martin Buber's Writings And Its Implications For The History Of Religions*. Etd Collection For Fordham University: Aai8615689.

Porter, L. and Lawler, E. (1968). *Managerial Attitudes and Performance*. Homewood, IL: Irwin.

Potter, J. (2015). *Crisis at Work: Identity and the end of career*. London: Palgrave Macmillan.

Pratt, M. and Ashforth, B. (2003). "Fostering Meaningfulness in Working and at Work." In K. S. Cameron, J. E. Dutton, and R. E. Quinn (eds.), *Positive Organizational Scholarship*, pp. 309–27. San Francisco: Berrett-Koehler.

Reed, P. (2008). "Theory of Self-Transcendence." In M. Smith and P. Liehr (eds.), *Middle Range Theory for Nursing*, 2nd edn., pp. 105–30. New York: Springer.

Rego, A. and Cuhna, M. (2008). "Workplace spirituality and organizational commitment: An empirical study." *Journal of Organizational Change Management*, 21(1), 53–75.

Roof, R. (2015). "The Association of Individual Spirituality on employee engagement: The spirit at work." *Journal of Business Ethics*, 130(3), 585–99.

Rosso, B., Dekas, K., and Wrzesniewski, A. (2010). "On the meaning of work: A theoretical integration and review." *Research in Organizational Behavior*, 30, 91–127.

Ryan, R. and Deci, E. (2001). "On happiness and human potentials: A review of research on hedonic and eudaimonic well-being." *Annual Review of Psychology*, 52, 141–66.

Ryff, C. (1989). "Happiness is everything, or is it? Explorations on the meaning of psychological well-being." *Journal of Personality and Social Psychology*, 57(6), 1069–81.

Sartre, J. (1960). *Existentialism and Humanism*. London: Methuen.

Schnell, T. (2011). "Individual differences in meaning-making: Considering the variety of sources of meaning, their density and diversity." *Personality and Individual Differences*, 51, 667–73.

Schwartz, S. (1992). "Universals in the Content and Structure of Values: Theory and Empirical Tests in 20 Countries." In M. Zanna (ed.), *Advances in Experimental Social Psychology*, vol. 25, pp. 1–65. San Diego: Academic Press.

Seeman, M. (1959). "On the meaning of alienation." *American Sociological Review*, 24(6), 783–91.

Simmel, G. (1950). "The Field of Sociology." In G. Wolff (ed. and trans.), *The Sociology of George Simmel*, pp. 3–25. New York: Free Press.

Simpson, P. (2015). "What remains of the intersubjective: On the presencing of self and other." *Emotion, Space and Society*, 14, 65–73.

Spreitzer, G. M. (1995). "Psychological empowerment in the workplace: Dimensions, measurement and validation." *Academy of Management Journal*, 38, 1442–65.

Stein, M. (2008). "'Divinity expresses the self…' An investigation." *Journal of Analytical Psychology*, 53, 305–27.

Tajfel, H. and Turner, J. (1985). "The Social Identity Theory of Intergroup Behaviour." In S. Worchel and W. G. Auston (eds.), *Psychology of Intergroup Relations*, vol. 2, pp. 7–24. Chicago: Nelson-Hall.

Taylor, C. (1989). *Sources of the Self: The making of modern identity*. Cambridge, MA: Harvard University Press.

Terkel, S. (1974). *Working*. New York: New Press.

Turner, A. and Lawrence, P. (1965). *Industrial Jobs and the Worker*. Boston: Harvard University.

Vaill, P. (2000). "Introduction to spirituality for business leadership." *Journal of Management Inquiry*, 9(2), 115–16.

Valle, R. (1995). *Phenomenological Inquiry in Psychology: Existential and transpersonal dimensions*. New York. Plenum Press.

Van Zyl, L., Deacon, E., and Rothmann, S. (2010). "Towards happiness: experiences of work-role fit, meaningfulness and work engagement of industrial/organisational psychologists." *SAJIP. South African Journal of Industrial Psychology*, 36(1), 1–10.

Weber, M. (1976). *The Protestant Ethics and the Spirit of Capitalism*. London: Allen and Unwin.

Wong, P. and Fry, P. (eds.) (1998). *The Human Quest for Meaning: A handbook of psychological research and clinical applications*. Mahwah, NJ: Erlbaum.

Wong, W. (2012). "Meaningfulness and identities." *Ethical Theory & Moral Practice*, 11, 123–48.

Wrzesniewski, A. (2003). "Finding Positive Meaning in Work." In K. Cameron, J. Dutton, and R. Quinn (eds.), *Positive Organizational Scholarship*. San Francisco: Berrett-Koehler.

Yeoman, R. (2014). "Conceptualising meaningful work as a fundamental human need." *Journal of Business Ethics*, 125(2), 235–51.

CHAPTER 10

"BELONGING" AND ITS RELATIONSHIP TO THE EXPERIENCE OF MEANINGFUL WORK

TATJANA SCHNELL, THOMAS HÖGE,
AND WOLFGANG G. WEBER

INTRODUCTION

ARISTOTLE coined the term *zoon politikon* (social creature) to describe human beings (Aristotle, 1995). The term refers to our innate tendency to come together and form a community (Greek: *polis*). Only in this context of belonging, Aristotle suggests, can human beings fulfill their potential. Psychological research supports this assumption. A sense of belonging has been shown to impact well-being and health (Stillman and Baumeister, 2009), and to strengthen the perception of life as meaningful (Lambert et al., 2013).

While belonging is mostly understood as forming and maintaining interpersonal relationships, it is fruitful to define it more broadly. In existential terms, human beings derive meaning from the idea of being part of something larger than the self (Pierce and Jussila, 2010; Schnell, 2010). This is succinctly captured by Heidegger's (1962) concept of "dwelling," i.e. having a place in this world. Far from being an abstract impression, having a place, here, means being involved in sense-making *practices*. It is through action that we assert our position in this world, an organization, a group. The resulting objects manifest our belonging (Weber and Jeppesen, 2017). This conceptual extension takes into account another essential aspect of humanity, namely our existence as *zoon poietikon*: productive, creative, capable of making things. Bringing both defining elements together, we might presume that our productive capacities are experienced as fulfilling and meaningful when exerted with a sense of belonging. First empirical findings do point in that direction, as we will set forth in this chapter.

After introducing a general concept of meaningfulness, and *belonging* as one of its core elements, we will turn to the construct of meaningful work and the role of belonging in work contexts. Several psychological constructs tap aspects of belonging in work. Focusing on their links with meaningful work, we will deal with the following concepts: *relatedness, social support, organizational commitment, organizational identification, psychological ownership*, and *socio-moral climate*. They address workers' attitudes toward and relations with co-workers, supervisors, and social systems at higher levels (like work teams, or the organization). While belonging is typically seen as a positive construct, there is some evidence also for its "dark side." We will discuss this toward the end of the chapter, as well as potential obstructions to experiencing belonging, and one of its more topical opposites, namely *alienation*.

Meaningfulness Defined

The term "meaningfulness" denotes a fundamental sense of life being worth living. Due to its abstract and usually subconscious nature, meaningfulness has been operationalized by four more accessible elements, which are orientation/purpose, coherence, significance, and connectedness/belonging (Delle Fave and Soosai-Nathan, 2014; Schnell, 2014). These can refer to life in general, or specific life domains, like work. *Orientation* stands for a general sense of direction, guiding decision-making, goal pursuit, and personality development (Emmons, 2005; Schnell, 2009, 2010; Wong, 1998). *Coherence* concerns the intrapersonal domain, in the sense of personality integration (Schnell, 2009; Sheldon and Kasser, 1995), as well as the life world, implying non-conflicting activities, goals, and sources of meaning (Schnell, 2010). *Significance* denotes the perceived consequences of personal action on a larger scale. *Belonging* relates to a sense of being part of something larger than the self. Integration into a larger context counteracts isolation and may imbue life with meaning (Baumeister and Leary, 1995; Schnell, 2010). It is this element of meaningfulness, belonging, that will receive special emphasis in this chapter.

Of Belonging and Meaning

To belong is a basic human need. Over a long period in evolutionary history, (not only) humans depended on belonging to a group in order to survive and reproduce. Although this necessity may have decreased with the development of individualist cultures, it is still inherent in our actions and experiences. Individuals with strong social bonds report more positive emotions, satisfaction with life, and mental and physical health (Stillman and Baumeister, 2009), while loneliness, exclusion, and rejection are accompanied by severe consequences such as depression, anxiety, anger, grief, or shame (DeWall et al., 2011; MacDonald and Leary, 2005).

Meaningfulness, too, is viewed as rooted in biology, since a desire for coherent action and goal attainment is inherent to most zoological organisms (Klinger, 2012). However, human cognitive capacity to decide for or against an action elevates the instinctive drive. The employment of a meta-perspective allows for consideration of the act's coherence with personal beliefs, and its implications for others (Bandura, 1997). The social context is always present, albeit with varying levels of awareness and significance to the actor.

Baumeister and Leary (1995: 522) define belonging as a "strong desire to form and maintain enduring interpersonal attachments." In the context of meaningfulness, the facet "belonging" is defined more generally as a sense of being part of something larger than the self (Schnell, 2010). It entails perceiving oneself as having a place in this world, or "dwelling," as Heidegger (1962) called it. "Where one dwells is where one is *at home*, where one *has a place*... [By dwelling, our being] is located within a set of sense-making practices and structures with which it is familiar" (Wheeler, 2016 on Heidegger). Through activities, humans occupy their place and become part of their group. The transfer of knowledge and expertise into material form results in *collective objectification* (Weber and Jeppesen, 2017), which manifests togetherness. The social production of tools, goods, services, etc. can be a powerful sign of belonging. It makes people aware of their responsibility for something larger than the self, conveys a sense of being needed, and thus evokes personal meaningfulness.

The human tendency to favor one's own group over others (*in-group bias*) underscores the need to belong. In their striving for belonging, individuals tend to adapt to the ideology incumbent in their group. This blending of individual sphere and socio-economic structure is what Fromm (1941) called *social character*. The wish to belong causes individuals to develop those traits that make them *desire* to act, as they *have* to act (Fromm, 1976). Group norms are thus internalized; they merge with personal identity and create a *social identity* (Tajfel and Turner, 1986). A sense of place, purpose, and belonging is generated, providing an awareness of being grounded, and imbuing life with meaning (Haslam et al., 2009).

Empirical research has demonstrated close links between belonging and meaning. People from different nations mentioned *personal relationships* most frequently when asked what made their lives meaningful (Delle Fave et al., 2013; Ebersole, 1998; Little, 1998). In studies investigating sources of meaning with reference to actual behavior (Schnell, 2009, 2011), *generativity* showed the strongest relationship with meaningfulness, followed by *attentiveness* and *harmony*. All three orientations imply care and concern for others and the social environment. Lambert et al. (2013) established a *sense of belonging* as a predictor of meaningfulness in correlational, longitudinal, and experimental studies. Stavrova and Luhmann (2016) found subjective *collective connectedness* prospectively associated with meaningfulness, just as meaningfulness predicted subjective collective connectedness and the likelihood of joining voluntary associations (as behavioral measure of collective connectedness) several years later.

MEANINGFUL WORK

Because the attribution of meaning is highly subjective (Schnell, 2016), one person may perceive an occupation as meaningful, but another person may not. Nevertheless, working environments can be organized in ways that reliably correlate with the experience of work as meaningful. Such workplaces enable people to perceive coherence, orientation, significance, and belonging, the four core elements of meaningfulness (see "Meaningfulness Defined"). *Coherence* of an individual's self-concept and the role she is assigned at work is a crucial factor of work-role fit (Kristof-Brown, Zimmerman, and Johnson, 2005), which, again, is positively related to meaningful work (May, Gilson, and Harter, 2004). An organization's *orientation* is expressed in corporate values and mission statements. Providing it is exercised authentically, a prosocial, or "self-transcendent" corporate orientation has been shown to be particularly conducive to meaning in work (Duffy and Raque-Bogdan, 2010; Schnell, Höge, and Pollet, 2013). *Significance* refers to the perceived implications of one's work for others. People who assume, through their work, to contribute positively to the community, or a higher cause, report a strong sense of meaning and purpose (Grant, 2008). Finally, *belonging* to a collegial community is associated with a sense of connectedness and companionship, which has been shown to enhance the perception of work as meaningful (Bechky, 2003; Grant, Dutton, and Rosso, 2008). Affective commitment to an organization appears to be highest when organizational structures and practices are characterized by trust-based and respectful relationships, participative cooperation, openness for diversity and critique, and mutual support (Pircher Verdorfer et al., 2013), a combination of which has been termed a socio-moral climate (Weber, Unterrainer, and Höge, 2008).

BELONGING IN THE CONTEXT OF WORK

In an occupational context, belonging concerns the relational processes between a working person and an occupational group, organization, or team. We suggest construing this relationship as determined by an interaction of giving and taking. A sense of belonging motivates individuals to commit to a task, a goal, a group. In-group identification supports *self-investment* (Leach et al., 2008), which, apart from a sense of belonging, entails positive feelings about being a member of the group (group satisfaction), and salience and importance of the group for the individual's self-concept (group centrality). In turn for their attachment, working people await acknowledgment and appreciation (Siegrist, 1996). They expect to receive social support from colleagues and superiors. Moreover, they assume the organization will prove loyal to its members (Rousseau, 1995). Belonging can thus be explored from different perspectives: as a sense of belonging, as personal commitment or identification, as behavioral expression of belonging, or as a perception of supportive interpersonal and organizational processes.

So far, the term *belonging* itself is not widely used in work and organizational psychology. Explicit investigations in work contexts have only started in recent years. They have focused primarily on the relationship between the level of a sense of belonging and workers' depressive symptoms, as well as several indicators of well-being. Results in different occupational samples have established negative relations between belonging and depression, and positive relations with indicators of well-being (Cockshaw and Shochet, 2010; Cockshaw, Shochet, and Obst, 2014; Somoray, Shakespeare-Finch, and Armstrong, 2017; Shakespeare-Finch and Daley, 2017). Beyond this explicit treatment of belonging, various lines of research have explored related constructs, such as relatedness, social support, organizational commitment, organizational identification, psychological ownership, and socio-moral organizational climate. These will be dealt with in turn.

Relatedness

Relatedness is one of the three basic psychological needs proposed by self-determination theory, the other two being autonomy and competence. Relatedness refers to the extent to which a person experiences herself to be connected to and cared for by others. According to Gagné and Deci (2005), satisfaction of the need to be connected to others in a work context makes an internalization of shared values and regulatory processes of work behavior more likely. They conclude that "structuring work to allow interdependence among employees and identification with work groups, as well as being respectful and concerned about each employee, may have a positive effect on internalization of autonomous motivation and work outcomes" (Gagné and Deci, 2005: 355). Internalization, in turn, has been shown to have close links with meaningful work: Allan, Autin, and Duffy (2016) found four variables of internalized motivation—introjected regulation, identified regulation, integrated regulation, and intrinsic motivation—to be best represented by a common internal regulation factor. With more than 70 percent of shared variance, its relationship with meaningful work was substantial. It should be noted, though, that this finding unduly lumps together the different forms of internalized motivation which, according to Gagné and Deci (2005), differ with regard to the degree of autonomy involved and thus in their associations with indicators of psychological growth and well-being.

Social Support

Social support by colleagues and supervisors can be understood as behavioral and interactional expression of relatedness at work. Receiving social support may generate a sense of belonging to a caring and nurturing social system (Vaux, 1988). Although there is some evidence that under specific circumstances social support can elicit negative effects by threatening respondents' self-esteem (Deelstra et al., 2003), the generally positive impact of social support on health and well-being has been shown by an impressive body of research (Viswesvaran, Sanchez, and Fisher, 1999). In this context, existing research has predominantly focused on buffering effects of social support at work on the stressor–strain relationship to explain its positive effects. But perceiving social support should also have direct impacts. If employees receive authentic, helpful social support they may interpret such experiences as cues for the degree of belonging, thus creating or strengthening their social bonds to colleagues, supervisors, and the organization. Indeed, it has been demonstrated that perceiving social support from organizational agents is related to favorable cognitions and attitudes toward the organization in terms of stronger organizational commitment and identification (Edwards and Peccei, 2010; Meyer et al., 2002; Wiesenfeld, Raghuram, and Garud, 2001). Liden, Wayne, and Sparrowe (2000) have reported positive associations between support by superiors and co-workers and meaning.

Organizational Commitment and Identification

Organizational commitment and identification refer to individuals' experiences of their linkage with the organization as a whole (Mowday, Porter, and Steers, 1982). Allen and Meyer (1990) distinguish three components of organizational commitment: (1) continuance commitment rooted in perceived necessity, (2) normative commitment rooted in felt obligation, and (3) affective commitment rooted in positive emotions toward the organization. Affective commitment is the most extensively studied form and the one most relevant to the experience of belonging. Affective commitment is defined as "emotional attachment to, identification with, and involvement in the organization" (Allen and Meyer, 1990: 1). Although identification is an inherent part of this common definition of affective commitment, and both constructs are empirically related, affective commitment and organizational identification are distinct concepts (Ashforth, Harrison, and Corley, 2008). The construct of affective commitment is grounded in social exchange theory (e.g. Etzioni, 1961) and conceptualized as a positive attitude toward the organization, whereas the construct of organizational identification is based on a reconceptualization of social identity theory (e.g. Tajfel and Turner, 1986). Organizational identification reflects the extent to which individuals define their selves in terms of being part of the organization (Ashforth and Mael, 1989; Ashforth, Harrison, and Corley, 2008; van Knippenberg and Sleebos, 2006). Thus, organizational identification addresses the psychological merging of self and organization by an incorporation of organizational norms, values, and interests into the self (van Knippenberg and Sleebos, 2006).

Early experimental research on group identification in social psychology predominantly investigated short-term processes of social categorization and intergroup behavior resulting from the mere alignment to groups (Tajfel, 1982). In contrast, research on organizational identification in work contexts is interested in antecedents and consequences of more long term-oriented and deeper processes of social identity formation. Considering the distinction between *situated identification* and *deep structure identification* (Rousseau, 1998), it has been proposed that deep structure identification with an organization needs time and an enduring experience of *belonging* to develop (Ashforth, Harrison, and Corley, 2008; Rousseau, 1998). The same should be true for the more attitudinal construct of affective commitment.

Empirical research has demonstrated that meaningful work is an antecedent of affective commitment (e.g. Geldenhuys, Laba, and Venter, 2014; Milliman, Czaplewski, and Ferguson, 2003; Steger, Dik, and Duffy, 2012) and organizational identification (Demirtas et al., 2017). Nevertheless, we might also expect reversed causality in the sense that organizational identification and affective commitment contribute to the *creation* of meaning in everyday work and therefore serve as antecedents to meaningfulness (Ashforth, Harrison, and Corley, 2008). Both causal directions are plausible and probably mutually reinforce each other.

Psychological Ownership

Psychological ownership partly overlaps with the concept of organizational identification, albeit with a stronger focus on processes of active *appropriation* of the social environment. According to Pierce, Kostova, and Dirks's (2001: 299) definition, "the core of psychological ownership is the feeling of possessiveness and of being psychologically tied to an object. One's possessions are felt as extensions of the self." Pierce and Jussila (2010: 828) outlined collective psychological ownership as the collectively held sense that a target of ownership (or a piece of that target) is collectively "ours."

Empirical studies indicate that employees may develop psychological ownership toward ideal or material targets—their whole organization, or parts of it like jobs, projects, initiatives, work territories, tools, or ideas (for reviews see Dawkins et al., 2017; Pierce and Jussila, 2010). Collective psychological ownership represents an entire group of working persons whose interdependent members are aware of and share the same specific mindset, "a collective understanding that we are one, bound and interdependent on one another for some purpose that is larger than the self" (Pierce and Jussila, 2010: 817). Whereas previous research on belonging has focused on the development of enduring interpersonal bonds via direct interaction (e.g. Leary et al., 2013), the psychological ownership approach widens the research perspective by suggesting that tangible or intangible objects that are handled by collaborating employees may function as carriers for the gradual development of their sense of belonging. According to Pierce and Jussila's (2010) conceptual proposition, there is a shift in an employee's personal reference from the self (i.e. a personal feeling that a target belongs only to him or her) to the work group or the enterprise, which become part of the "extended self." During this process of cooperative handling of targets, the targets to which the individual employees have developed object-related bonds mediate the formation of social bonds between these employees. The interlaced unfolding of target-related and social attachments flows into a state of pronounced psychological ownership as a collective mindset. In other words, a collective sense of belonging emerges from intertwined processes of psychological acquisition and appropriation of work-related objects, and of transferring individual knowledge and experience into material or symbolic forms, namely collective objectifications (cf. activity-theoretical complements: Leontiev, 1978; Weber and Jeppesen, 2017). Referring to several theories of motivation psychology, the representatives of the approach (Avey et al., 2009; Pierce, Kostova, and Dirks, 2001; Pierce and Jussila, 2010) suppose that psychological ownership encompasses four components: efficacy or affectance (Bandura, 1997), expressing self-identity (Dittmar, 1992), having a place (Duncan, 1981) or need for belongingness (Avey et al., 2009), and social identity (Tajfel and Turner, 1986).

Pierce and Jussila (2010) consider several work-related *opportunities* for employees to develop a state of psychological ownership including a sense of belonging. These pertain to collaborating employees ...

(1) having a substantial amount of *"shared control over the target"* for a particular organizational factor, or the whole organization (as in democratically structured, employee-owned companies; see Tischer et al., 2016; Weber, Unterrainer, and Höge, 2008);

(2) acquiring and exchanging *"shared intimate knowing of the target,"* such as specific knowledge and skills when handling or reflecting the respective target to fulfill shared work tasks;

(3) achieving a substantial extent of *"shared investment of their selves into the target,"* such as energy, time, effort, and attention. Products or processes created by the employees become representations of their selves.

Research on the individual level corroborates the assumption that collective and job-related autonomy *sensu* substantial participation in decision-making, and thus sharing control over organizational targets is related to the development of organization-based psychological ownership. The latter seems to mediate effects of employee participation on affective organizational commitment and organizational citizenship behavior (Dawkins et al., 2017). Some studies show similar effects of employees' participation in collective ownership of their firm (e.g. Chiu, Hui, and Lai, 2007; Pendleton, Wilson, and Wright, 1998). However, there is still a lack of studies analyzing how participation in decision-making on group or organizational level may influence *collective* psychological ownership (including a collective sense of belonging).

To conclude, psychological ownership opens up innovative perspectives on how collaborating employees' sense of belonging might emerge, thus strengthening a sense of work as meaningful. The nomological network of psychological ownership theory is still in a developmental state, though, and problems concerning its precise conceptualization (cf. Pierce and Jussila, 2010 vs. Avey et al., 2009), measurement, and antecedents are yet to be solved (Dawkins et al., 2017).

Socio-moral Climate

At the level of the organization, socio-moral climate has been linked to meaningful work experiences. The concept encompasses conditions and practices that are assumed to foster employees' sense of belonging. Socio-moral climate (Weber, Unterrainer, and

Höge, 2008; Pircher Verdorfer et al., 2013) draws on Kohlberg's concept of "moral atmosphere" (1984). It is characterized by trust-based and respectful relationships, participative collaboration, an atmosphere open for diversity and critique, mutual support of colleagues, co-workers, and superiors, and assignment of responsibility for others' well-being. A study by Schnell, Höge, and Pollet (2013) indicated that—together with task significance and work-role fit—socio-moral climate was considerably linked with Austrian employees' perceived meaning in work.

Although, to our knowledge, it has not been investigated, we suppose that employees' sense of belonging mediates effects of socio-moral climate on those prosocial, moral, and civic orientations and behaviors that are associated with the former according to the cognitive theory of moral judgment (Kohlberg, 1984; Lind, 2016; Treviño, Weaver, and Reynolds, 2006). A few empirical studies lend evidence to this hypothesis: variance-analytical comparisons between thirty enterprises from Austria, Germany, and North Italy, varying in their level of socio-moral climate, indicated that 10 percent of the variance in employees' solidarity at work, about 2 percent in their prosocial work behavior, and about 4 percent in their democratic engagement orientation were explained by socio-moral climate (Weber, Unterrainer, and Höge, 2008). Another study with ten North Italian companies supports these findings: socio-moral climate was positively associated with prosocial work behavior, solidarity at work, and democratic engagement orientation (Pircher Verdorfer et al., 2013).

TODAY'S CHALLENGES TO BELONGING AT WORK

Various social and economic developments challenge the sense of belonging in paid labor. In recent years, organizations and employees have been confronted with increasing requirements for *flexibility* caused by aggravated global competition and necessities for structural transformation, from industrialized mass production to more customized modes of production and services (Felstead and Jewson, 1999; Oeij and Wiezer, 2002). Organizations thus make use of organizational deregulation and restructuring strategies. They include non-traditional, precarious work arrangements beyond conventional full-time and permanent contracts, with a view to reaching higher organizational flexibility (e.g. Allvin et al., 2011). Already in the 1980s, management literature propagated a distinction between a *core* workforce and a more externalized *peripheral* workforce as a key feature of the "flexible firm" (Atkinson, 1984, 1987; Hakim, 1990; Pollert, 1988). It stands to reason that developing an enduring sense of belonging should be difficult for peripheral workforce members such as temporary (agency) workers, part-time workers, and teleworkers, and nearly impossible for outsourced self-employed workers. The scarce empirical research on aspects of belonging among teleworkers, self-employed, or "nomadic" workers indeed supports the assumption of higher social isolation in these occupational groups (Taskin and Edwards, 2007; Bailey and Kurland, 2002; Vega and

Brennan, 2000). Nonetheless, results regarding the effects of temporary employment on organizational commitment are not straightforward. While some studies found lower levels of affective commitment among temporary workers compared to permanent workers (Felfe et al., 2008), most did not (De Cuyper, Notelaers, and De Witte, 2009; De Witte and Näswall, 2003; Feather and Rauter, 2004; McDonald and Makin, 2000).

Ambiguous findings are rife when it comes to the psychological consequences of temporary and other forms of contingent or flexible employment. This is partly attributable to the inhomogeneity of the concepts in use (De Cuyper et al., 2008). It has thus been suggested to focus on more fundamental psychological changes in current employment, as in psychological contract theory (Rousseau, 1995). Psychological contract theory focuses on the social and economic exchange relationships between employer and employee beyond explicit terms codified in the employment contract. Robinson, Kraatz, and Rousseau (1994) and Robinson and Rousseau (1994) have distinguished *relational* from *transactional* forms of psychological contracts. Transactional psychological contracts are primarily based on economic exchange (e.g. "high engagement" for "performance-based pay"), characterized by a short-term perspective and comparatively narrow scope. In contrast, relational contracts are primarily based on social exchange (e.g. "loyalty" and "commitment" for "job security" and "personal recognition"), are trust-based, open-ended, and feature a broader scope of perceived employee and employer obligations.

Since flexible employment relationships are often more volatile, short term-oriented, and provide less stability, they are prone to increasing the risk of breaching the psychological contract in terms of violated reciprocity and mutuality. This is particularly the case when organizations pursue a flexible strategy and offer a "new deal" transactional contract, while employees might still hold traditional work orientations and thus expect an "old deal" relational psychological contract (Cartwright and Holmes, 2006). The detrimental effects of psychological contract breaches entail a sense of loss, reduced commitment, and mistrust in the employer and the organization in general (Cartwright and Holmes, 2006; Zhao et al., 2007). Even if employees adopt the organization's transactional perspective, the problem might not be resolved. Empirical data has shown that employees who perceive their psychological contracts as more transactional than relational generally report weaker affective commitment toward the organization (Guest, 2004).

In both cases (contract breach and contract change), employees will find it hard to develop feelings of real and enduring belonging, to perceive the organization as part of their social identity or a place to "dwell." Accelerated technological and social change (Rosa, 2013) and an increased significance of individualized, short term-oriented transactions at the expense of long term-oriented, stable, and trust-based mutual relations may well result in a corrosion of meaningfulness at work (Sennett, 1998). Notably, both these authors refer to critical theory conceptualizations of social alienation to explain threats to employees' sense of belonging and meaning in work. As such, the concept of alienation is worth a renewed interest (see also Shantz, Alfes, and Truss, 2014).

ALIENATION: AN OPPOSITE OF BELONGING

The term "alienation" denotes a state of estrangement from a group or an activity to which one should theoretically belong. Originally used by Marx (1961 [1844]) to describe a lack of identification with labor products and work activity, today's use of the concept seems to shift to *social alienation*. Its sources are seen in computerized production and a strong pressure on individuals to compete, self-organize, and show extreme flexibility, justified by neoliberal reasoning (Rosa, 2013; Sennett, 1998). According to Ulrich (2008), radical economism represents the core of social alienation: a reification and dogmatic idealization of economic viewpoints and criteria contributes to the colonization of not only industrial labor, but also social service work, and even leisure activities (Habermas, 1990). This is the case when employees come to evaluate their everyday interactions and interpersonal relations pursuant to criteria of capitalistic accounting (see also Yeoman, 2014). They hereby reduce the diversity and individuality of their life-world to an extent that makes it difficult to develop and experience trusting, empathic, and understanding relationships.

The following four phenomena of social alienation, assumed to be caused by economism, may counteract the need for belonging and societal cohesiveness (in detail cf. Weber, 2006).

(a) *Instrumentalization and economistic reification of human beings* (Horkheimer, 1947; Israel, 1971; Langman, 1991; Moldaschl, 1998; Ulrich, 2008) refers to a calculating orientation toward others. People are perceived selectively and reduced to "exchange value," analogous to a commodity. Research reviews by Kasser et al. (2007) and Dittmar et al. (2014) indicate that organizational cultures reinforcing a strong desire for financial profit, self-interest, and radical competitive orientation interfere with the quality of employees' interpersonal relationships, their caring about the broader world, and thus threaten their sense of belonging.

(b) *Marketing-oriented social character and self-instrumentalization* (Fromm, 1976; Funk, 2004; Langman, 1991; Sennett, 1998) is present when a person fulfills her work role in excessively flexible, mobile, demand-driven, and adaptable ways and demonstrates social impression management to a high extent. Employees who execute permanently changing tasks, associated with different roles, will have problems developing and maintaining interpersonal attachments or practicing acts of generativity toward co-workers. Their sense of belonging at work is thus undermined. Empirical studies on emotional labor indicate that emotional dissonance as a "separation of oneself from one's emotions" (Shantz, Alfes, and Truss, 2014: 2531), resulting from marketing-oriented self-instrumentalization, corresponds to emotional exhaustion and further threats to individual well-being (Zapf, 2002).

(c) *Commodity fetishism and anthropomorphism* (Fromm, 1976; Funk, 2004; Israel, 1971; Langman, 1991) refers to the observation that marketing and commercial media project human features and capabilities like activity, love, tenderness, or youthfulness onto commodities, i.e. inanimate objects. Consequently, members of consumerist cultures (Dittmar, 2007) tend to substitute a development of close relationships with attachment to consumer goods. Moreover, vendors and customers increasingly lack experiences of non-instrumentalized, mutual, or communitarian giving and taking, which foster collective connectedness and a sense of having a place in the world. Shopping addiction and compulsory buying might be viewed as attempts to compensate for a frustrated need to belong (Dittmar, 2007).

(d) *Degeneration of community-oriented perspective-taking* (Fromm, 1976; Habermas, 1970, 1990; Ulrich, 2008) is fostered by organizational arrangements that excessively internalize global market and competition pressures. Likewise, a corporate identity characterized by social Darwinism may mislead employees either to ignore or misconstrue far-reaching social or ecological effects of their work activities, as, for example, on sweatshop workers in developing countries who are part of the supply chain. Climates of radical competition prompt organizational agents to practice forms of moral disengagement, like denying consequences or justifying their detrimental work activities for economic reasons, or displace their responsibility to extra-organizational institutions (cf. White, Bandura, and Bero, 2009). Being exposed to role models of moral disengagement through upper management may hinder employees in perspective-taking or in discovering shared interests and developing solidarity with their fellow beings suffering in supplier plants.

THE DARK SIDES OF BELONGING

There is extensive evidence that a sense of belonging at work relates to positive individual and organizational outcomes. However, these results should not give rise to an uncritical, over-optimistic view neglecting potential risks and drawbacks. In particular, the question arises of whether an excessive sense of belonging, commitment, or identification can also have negative consequences. This issue has already been addressed with respect to the concept of organizational identification. In their seminal paper, Ashforth and Mael (1989: 23) described organizational identification as "perceived oneness with the organization." Regardless of the question as to whether the "oneness" of human individuals and collectives—be it subjective or objective—is even possible in a literal sense, the risk of *over-identification pathology* (Dukerich, Kramer, and Parks, 1998) becomes apparent. In this context, over-identification means a loss of an autonomous, personal self, and a predominance of social identity derived from belonging to an organization. Over-identified individuals lose the balance between being neither too distinct nor too dependent (Kreiner, Hollensbe, and Sheep, 2006). They also tend to derive their social identity and meaning mainly from belonging to a *single* social entity, namely the organization they work for, and not from belonging to multiple social entities in different life domains (Mael and Ashforth, 2001).

Several detrimental effects of an excessive sense of belonging and over-identification in the work context have been attested. They encompass the susceptibility to unfair treatment (Bunderson and Thompson, 2009), negative effects of self-exploitation on health and social relationships (Dempsey and Sanders, 2010), an increased risk of involvement in unethical behaviors for the benefit or defense of the organization (Effelsberg and Solga, 2015), increased role-stress and an impaired work–life balance (Li, Fan, and Zhao, 2015), and difficulties with change (van Dijk and van Dick, 2009; for an overview, see Conroy et al., 2017).

Excessive belonging and over-identification are particularly risky when not grounded in authentic interpersonal relationships and participatory collaboration, but fueled by manipulative managerial strategies. From a critical management perspective, authors have argued that a targeted management of social identities via engendering feelings of belonging and a sense of community is a pathway for organizations to exercise power and control over workers (Alvesson and Willmott, 2002). This might also backfire if employees perceive managerial attempts to raise meaningfulness as inauthentic or manipulative (Bailey et al., 2017).

DISCUSSION

In this chapter, we explored the nexus of two core human qualities—the social (*zoon politikon*) and the productive (*zoon poietikon*)—in relation to the experience of meaningful work. According to the literature, affective commitment to an organization is positively related to the experience of meaningfulness at work (Geldenhuys, Laba, and Venter, 2014). The latter is also associated with support by co-workers and superiors (Liden, Wayne, and Sparrowe, 2000). People who evaluate their organizational interactions as trust-based, respectful, supportive, and participative also report high meaningfulness at work (Schnell, Höge, and Pollet, 2013). Further studies suggest that a sense of relatedness (Gagné and Deci, 2005) promotes internal motivation that, in turn, is accompanied by a perception of work as meaningful (Allan, Autin, and Duffy, 2016).

To sum up the theoretical and empirical evidence, belonging appears to be rooted in the definition and design of a person's work role (e.g. more or less participative) and evolves in line with interactive dynamics of a social (e.g. more or less support, transparency, respect, and trust) and a material kind (e.g. collaboration on shared targets). The presence of belonging is "felt" by the working person as a sense of relatedness, and expressed by affective commitment and behavioral engagement. Such personal involvement appears to encourage—and/or is encouraged by—the internalization of motivation which, again, is strongly linked to experiences of meaningfulness at work.

This wide range of potential relationships and effects illustrates the complexity of belonging. It emerges from a working person's attitudes and action, from her colleagues and superiors, and their interaction. Moreover, organizational structures play a major role, concerning the levels of transparency, participation, and democracy they adopt (Weber, Unterrainer, and Schmid, 2009). Hence, belonging can be termed a multi-perspective concept. It depends on a person's willingness to belong and a larger entity's acceptance and reciprocation. It evolves from both giving (committing, identifying) and taking (support, respect).

Future research should further explore antecedents, consequences, and risks of belonging. For meaningful experiences of belonging, related aspects of significance, orientation, and coherence are essential (Schnell, Höge, and Pollet, 2013). In order to promote perceived *significance*, processes of appropriation need to be enabled, such that personal involvement is consequential and actually makes a difference. However, organizational targets and *orientations* can be more or less *coherent* with personal capacities, goals, and values. Maintaining a sense of belonging is thus closely related to the principles guiding organizational behavior, and their affirmation by the employee. In the case of strong affirmation, risks of over-identification should not be neglected, such as self-exploitation at the expense of health and social relationships. Lastly, an absence of identification with organizational values and goals—due to either insufficient communication or conflicting values—is likely to affect the quality of belonging, which then might just be nominal instead of authentic and committed.

References

Allan, B. A., Autin, K. L., and Duffy, R. D. (2016). "Self-determination and meaningful work: Exploring socioeconomic constraints." *Frontiers in Psychology*, 7, article 71.

Allen, N. J. and Meyer, J. P. (1990). "The measurement and antecedents of affective, continuance and normative commitment to the organization." *Journal of Occupational and Organizational Psychology*, 63(1), 1–18.

Allvin, M., Aronsson, G., Hagström, T., Johansson, G., and Lundberg, U. (2011). *Work Without Boundaries: Psychological perspectives on the new working life*. Chichester: Wiley.

Alvesson, M. and Willmott, H. (2002). "Identity regulation as organizational control: Producing the appropriate individual." *Journal of Management Studies*, 39(5), 619–44.

Aristotle. (1995). *Politics: Books I and II*, translated by Trevor J. Saunders. Oxford: Clarendon Press.

Ashforth, B. E., Harrison, S. H., and Corley, K. G. (2008). "Identification in organizations: An examination of four fundamental questions." *Journal of Management*, 34(3), 325–74.

Ashforth, B. E. and Mael, F. (1989). "Social identity theory and the organization." *Academy of Management Review*, 14(1), 20–39.

Atkinson, J. (1984). "Manpower strategies for flexible organizations." *Personnel Management*, 16(8), 28–31.

Atkinson, J. (1987). "Flexibility or fragmentation? The United Kingdom labour market in the eighties." *Labour and Society*, 12, 87–105.

Avey, J. B., Avolio, B. J., Crossley, C. D., and Luthans, F. (2009). "Psychological ownership: Theoretical extensions, measurement, and relation to work outcomes." *Journal of Organizational Behavior*, 30, 173–91.

Bailey, C., Madden, A., Alfes, K., Shantz, A., and Soane, E. (2017). "The mismanaged soul: Existential labor and the erosion of meaningful work." *Human Resource Management Review*, 27, 416–30.

Bailey, D. E. and Kurland, N. B. (2002). "A review of telework research: Findings, new directions, and lessons for the study of modern work." *Journal of Organizational Behavior*, 23(4), 383–400.

Bandura, A. (1997). *Self-efficacy: The exercise of control*. London: Macmillan.

Baumeister, R. F. and Leary, M. R. (1995). "The need to belong: Desire for interpersonal attachments as a fundamental human motivation." *Psychological Bulletin*, 117(3), 497–529.

Bechky, B. A. (2003). "Sharing meaning across occupational communities: The transformation of understanding on a production floor." *Organization Science*, 14(3), 312–30.

Bunderson, J. S. and Thompson, J. A. (2009). "The call of the wild: Zookeepers, callings, and the double-edged sword of deeply meaningful work." *Administrative Science Quarterly*, 54(1), 32–57.

Cartwright, S. and Holmes, N. (2006). "The meaning of work: The challenge of regaining employee engagement and reducing cynicism." *Human Resource Management Review*, 16(2), 199–208.

Chiu, W. C. K., Hui, C. H., and Lai, G. W. F. (2007). "Psychological ownership and organizational optimism amid China's corporate transformation: Effects of an employee ownership scheme and a management-dominated board." *International Journal of Human Resource Management*, 18(2), 303–20.

Cockshaw, W. D. and Shochet, I. (2010). "The link between belongingness and depressive symptoms: An exploration in the workplace interpersonal context." *Australian Psychologist*, 45(4), 283–9.

Cockshaw, W. D., Shochet, I. M., and Obst, P. L. (2014). "Depression and belongingness in general and workplace contexts: A cross-lagged longitudinal investigation." *Journal of Social and Clinical Psychology*, 33(5), 448–62.

Conroy, S., Henle, C. A., Shore, L., and Stelman, S. (2017). "Where there is light, there is dark: A review of the detrimental outcomes of high organizational identification." *Journal of Organizational Behavior*, 38(2), 184–203.

Dawkins, S., Tian, A. W., Newman, A., and Martin, A. (2017). "Psychological ownership: A review and research agenda." *Journal of Organizational Behavior*, 38(2), 163–83.

De Cuyper, N., de Jong, J., de Witte, H., Isaksson, K., and Rigotti, T. (2008). "Literature review of theory and research on the psychological impact of temporary employment: Towards a conceptual model." *International Journal of Management Reviews*, 10(1), 25–51.

De Cuyper, N., Notelaers, G., and De Witte, H. (2009). "Job insecurity and employability in fixed-term contractors, agency workers, and permanent workers: Associations with job satisfaction and affective organizational commitment." *Journal of Occupational Health Psychology*, 14(2), 193–205.

De Witte, H. and Näswall, K. (2003). "Objective vs. subjective job insecurity: Consequences of temporary work for job satisfaction and organizational commitment in four European countries." *Economic and Industrial Democracy*, 24(2), 149–88.

Deelstra, J. T., Peeters, M. C., Schaufeli, W. B., Stroebe, W., Zijlstra, F. R., and van Doornen, L. P. (2003). "Receiving instrumental support at work: When help is not welcome." *Journal of Applied Psychology*, 88(2), 324–31.

Delle Fave, A., Brdar, I., Wissing, M. P., and Vella-Brodrick, D. A. (2013). "Sources and motives for personal meaning in adulthood." *The Journal of Positive Psychology*, 8(6), 517–29.

Delle Fave, A. and Soosai-Nathan, L. (2014). "Meaning as inter-connectedness: Theoretical perspectives and empirical evidence." *Journal of Psychology in Africa*, 24(1), 33–43.

Demirtas, O., Hannah, S. T., Gok, K., Arslan, A., and Capar, N. (2017). "The moderated influence of ethical leadership, via meaningful work, on followers' engagement, organizational identification, and envy." *Journal of Business Ethics*, 145(1), 183–99.

Dempsey, S. E. and Sanders, M. L. (2010). "Meaningful work? Nonprofit marketization and work/life imbalance in popular autobiographies of social entrepreneurship." *Organization*, 17(4), 437–59.

DeWall, C. N., Deckman, T., Pond, R. S., and Bonser, I. (2011). 'Belongingness as a core personality trait: How social exclusion influences social functioning and personality expression." *Journal of Personality*, 79(6), 979–1012.

Dittmar, H. (1992). *The Social Psychology of Material Possessions: To have is to be*. New York: St. Martin's Press.

Dittmar, H. (2007). "The costs of consumer culture and the 'cage within': The impact of the material 'good life' and 'body perfect' ideals on individuals' identity and well-being." *Psychological Inquiry*, 18(1), 23–31.

Dittmar, H., Bond, R., Hurst, M., and Kasser, T. (2014). "The relationship between materialism and personal well-being: A meta-analysis." *Journal of Personality and Social Psychology*, 107(5), 879–924.

Duffy, R. D. and Raque-Bogdan, T. L. (2010). "The motivation to serve others: Exploring relations to career development." *Journal of Career Assessment*, 18(3), 250–65.

Dukerich, J. M., Kramer, R., and Parks, J. M. (1998). "The Dark Side of Organizational Identification." In D. A. Whetten and P. C. Godfrey (eds.), *Identity in Organizations: Building theory through conversations*, pp. 245–56. Thousand Oaks, CA: Sage.

Duncan, N. G. (1981). "Home Ownership and Social Theory: Cross-cultural Perspectives." In J. S. Duncan (ed.), *Housing and identity: Cross-cultural perspectives*, pp. 98–134. London: Croom Helm.

Ebersole, P. (1998). *Types and Depth of Written Life Meanings*. Mahwah, NJ: Lawrence Erlbaum.

Edwards, M. R. and Peccei, R. (2010). "Perceived organizational support, organizational identification, and employee outcomes." *Journal of Personnel Psychology*, 9(1), 17–26.

Effelsberg, D. and Solga, M. (2015). "Transformational leaders' in-group versus out-group orientation: Testing the link between leaders' organizational identification, their willingness to engage in unethical pro-organizational behavior, and follower-perceived transformational leadership." *Journal of Business Ethics*, 126(4), 581–90.

Emmons, R. A. (2005). "Striving for the sacred: Personal goals, life meaning, and religion." *Journal of Social Issues*, 61(4), 731–45.

Etzioni, A. (1961). *A Comparative Analysis of Complex Organizations*. Glencoe, IL: Free Press.

Feather, N. T. and Rauter, K. A. (2004). "Organizational citizenship behaviours in relation to job status, job insecurity, organizational commitment and identification, job satisfaction and work values." *Journal of Occupational and Organizational Psychology*, 77(1), 81–94.

Felfe, J., Schmook, R., Schyns, B., and Six, B. (2008). "Does the form of employment make a difference? Commitment of traditional, temporary, and self-employed workers." *Journal of Vocational Behavior*, 72(1), 81–94.

Felstead, A. and Jewson, N. (eds.) (1999). *Global Trends in Flexible Labour*. Basingstoke: Macmillan.

Fromm, E. (1941). *Escape from Freedom*. New York: Farrar and Rinehart.

Fromm, E. (1976). *To Have or to Be?* New York: Harper and Row.

Funk, R. (2004). "Leitwerte marktwirtschaftlicher Praxis und ihre psychischen Folgen." In W. G. Weber, P.-P. Pasqualoni, and C. Burtscher (eds.), *Wirtschaft, Demokratie und Soziale Verantwortung*, pp. 71–102. Göttingen: Vandenhoeck & Ruprecht.

Gagné, M. and Deci, E. L. (2005). "Self-determination theory and work motivation." *Journal of Organizational Behavior*, 26(4), 331–62.

Geldenhuys, M., Laba, K., and Venter, C. M. (2014). "Meaningful work, work engagement and organisational commitment." *SA Journal of Industrial Psychology*, 40(1), 1–10.

Grant, A. M. (2008). "The significance of task significance: Job performance effects, relational mechanisms, and boundary conditions." *Journal of Applied Psychology*, 93(1), 108–24.

Grant, A. M., Dutton, J. E., and Rosso, B. D. (2008). "Giving commitment: Employee support programs and the prosocial sensemaking process." *Academy of Management Journal*, 51(5), 898–918.

Guest, D. (2004). "Flexible employment contracts, the psychological contract and employee outcomes: An analysis and review of the evidence." *International Journal of Management Reviews*, 5/6, 1–19.

Habermas, J. (1970). "Technology and Science as 'Ideology.'" In J. Habermas, *Toward a Rational Society*, pp. 81–122. Boston: Beacon Press.

Habermas, J. (1990). *Moral Consciousness and Communicative Action*. Boston: MIT Press.

Hakim, C. (1990). "Core and periphery in employers' workforce strategies: Evidence from the 1987 E.L.U.S. survey." *Work, Employment and Society*, 4(2), 157–88.

Haslam, S. A., Jetten, J., Postmes, T., and Haslam, C. (2009). "Social identity, health and well-being: An emerging agenda for applied psychology." *Applied Psychology*, 58(1), 1–23.

Heidegger, M. (1962). *Being and Time*. Oxford: Blackwell.

Horkheimer, M. (1947). *Eclipse of Reason*. Oxford: Oxford University Press.

Israel, J. (1971). *Alienation: From Marx to modern sociology*. Boston: Allyn and Bacon.

Kasser, T., Cohn, S., Kanner, A. D., and Ryan, R. M. (2007). "Some costs of American corporate capitalism: A psychological exploration of value and goal conflicts." *Psychological Inquiry*, 18(1), 1–22.

Klinger, E. (2012). "The Search for Meaning in Evolutionary Goal-theory Perspective." In P. T. P. Wong and P. S. Fry (eds.), *The Human Quest for Meaning: Theories, research, and applications*, pp. 23–55. Mahwah, NJ: Erlbaum.

Kohlberg, L. (1984). *Essays on Moral Development. Vol.2: The Psychology of Moral Development*. San Francisco: Harper & Row.

Kreiner, G. E., Hollensbe, E. C., and Sheep, M. L. (2006). "Where is the 'me' among the 'we'? Identity work and the search for optimal balance." *Academy of Management Journal*, 49(5), 1031–57.

Kristof-Brown, A. L., Zimmerman, R. D., and Johnson, E. C. (2005). "Consequences of individuals' fit at work: A meta-analysis of person-job, person-organization, person-group, and person-supervisor fit." *Personnel Psychology*, 58(2), 281–342.

Lambert, N. M., Stillman, T. F., Hicks, J. A., Kamble, S., Baumeister, R. F., and Fincham, F. D. (2013). "To belong is to matter: Sense of belonging enhances meaning in life." *Personality and Social Psychology Bulletin*, 39(11), 1418–27.

Langman, L. (1991). "Alienation and everyday life: Goffman meets Marx at the shopping mall." *International Journal of Sociology and Social Policy*, 11(6/7/8), 107–24.

Leach, C. W., van Zomeren, M., Zebel, S., Vliek, M. L., Pennekamp, S. F., Doosje, B., Ouwerkerk, J. W., and Spears, R. (2008). "Group-level self-definition and self-investment: A hierarchical (multicomponent) model of in-group identification." *Journal of Personality and Social Psychology*, 95(1), 144–65.

Leary, M. R., Kelly, C. M., Cottrell, C. A., and Schreindorfer, L. S. (2013). "Construct validity of the need to belong scale: Mapping the nomological network." *Journal of Personality Assessment*, 95(6), 610–24.

Leontiev, A. N. (1978). *Activity, Consciousness, and Personality*. Englewood Cliffs, NJ: Prentice-Hall.

Li, Y., Fan, J., and Zhao, S. (2015). "Organizational identification as a double-edged sword." *Journal of Personnel Psychology*, 14(4), 182–92.

Liden, R. C., Wayne, S. J., and Sparrowe, R. T. (2000). "An examination of the mediating role of psychological empowerment on the relations between the job, interpersonal relationships, and work outcomes." *Journal of Applied Psychology*, 85(3), 407–16.

Lind, G. (2016). *How to Teach Morality: Promoting deliberation and discussion reducing violence and deceit*. Berlin: Logos.

Little, B. R. (1998). *Personal Project Pursuit: Dimensions and dynamics of personal meaning*. Mahwah, NJ: Erlbaum.

MacDonald, G. and Leary, M. R. (2005). "Why does social exclusion hurt? The relationship between social and physical pain." *Psychological Bulletin*, 131(2), 202–23.

Mael, F. A. and Ashforth, B. E. (2001). "Identification in work, war, sports, and religion: Contrasting the benefits and risks." *Journal for the Theory of Social Behaviour*, 31(2), 197–222.

Marx, K. (1961 [1844]). *The Economic and Philosophic Manuscripts of 1844*. New York: International Publication.

May, D. R., Gilson, R. L., and Harter, L. M. (2004). "The psychological conditions of meaningfulness, safety and availability and the engagement of the human spirit at work." *Journal of Occupational and Organizational Psychology*, 77(1), 11–37.

McDonald, D. J. and Makin, P. J. (2000). "The psychological contract, organisational commitment and job satisfaction of temporary staff." *Leadership & Organization Development Journal*, 21(2), 84–91.

Meyer, J. P., Stanley, D. J., Herscovitch, L., and Topolnytsky, L. (2002). "Affective, continuance, and normative commitment to the organization: A meta-analysis of antecedents, correlates, and consequences." *Journal of Vocational Behavior*, 61(1), 20–52.

Milliman, J., Czaplewski, A. J., and Ferguson, J. (2003). "Workplace spirituality and employee work attitudes: An exploratory empirical assessment." *Journal of Organizational Change Management*, 16(4), 426–47.

Moldaschl, M. (1998). "Internalisierung des Marktes." In IfS Frankfurt a.M., INIFES Stadtbergen, ISF München and SOFI Göttingen (eds.), *Jahrbuch Sozialwissenschaftliche Technikberichterstattung—Schwerpunkt Moderne Dienstleistungswelten*, pp. 197–251. Berlin: edition sigma.

Mowday, R. T., Porter, L. W., and Steers, R. M. (1982). *Employee-organization Linkages: The psychology of commitment, absenteeism, and turnover*. New York: Academic Press.

Oeij, P. R. A. and Wiezer, N. M. (2002). *New Work Organisation, Working Conditions and Quality of Work: Towards the flexible firm?* Dublin: European Foundation for the Improvement of Living and Working Conditions.

Pendleton, A., Wilson, N., and Wright, M. (1998). "The perception and effects of share ownership: Empirical evidence from employee buy-outs." *British Journal of Industrial Relations*, 36(1), 99–123.

Pierce, J. L. and Jussila, I. (2010). "Collective psychological ownership within the work and organizational context: Construct introduction and elaboration." *Journal of Organizational Behavior*, 31(6), 810–34.

Pierce, J. L., Kostova, T., and Dirks, K. T. (2001). "Toward a theory of psychological ownership in organizations." *Academy of Management Review*, 26, 298–310.

Pircher Verdorfer, A., Weber, W. G., Unterrainer, C., and Seyr, S. (2013). "The relationship between organizational democracy and socio-moral climate: Exploring effects of the ethical context in organizations." *Economic and Industrial Democracy*, 34(3), 423–49.

Pollert, A. (1988). "The 'flexible firm': Fixation or fact?" *Work, Employment and Society*, 2(3), 281–316.

Robinson, S. L., Kraatz, M. S., and Rousseau, D. M. (1994). "Changing obligations and the psychological contract: A longitudinal study." *Academy of Management Journal*, 37(1), 137–52.

Robinson, S. L. and Rousseau, D. M. (1994). "Violating the psychological contract: Not the exception but the norm." *Journal of Organizational Behavior*, 15(3), 245–59.

Rosa, H. (2013). *Social Acceleration: A new theory of modernity*. New York: Columbia University Press.

Rousseau, D. M. (1995). *Psychological Contracts in Organizations: Understanding written and unwritten agreements*. Thousand Oaks, CA: Sage.

Rousseau, D. M. (1998). "Why workers still identify with organizations." *Journal of Organizational Behavior*, 19(3), 217–33.

Schnell, T. (2009). "The Sources of Meaning and Meaning in Life Questionnaire (SoMe): Relations to demographics and well-being." *The Journal of Positive Psychology*, 4(6), 483–99.

Schnell, T. (2010). "Existential indifference: Another quality of meaning in life." *Journal of Humanistic Psychology*, 50(3), 351–73.

Schnell, T. (2011). "Individual differences in meaning-making: Considering the variety of sources of meaning, their density and diversity." *Personality and Individual Differences*, 51(5), 667–73.

Schnell, T. (2014). "An Empirical Approach to Existential Psychology: Meaning in life operationalized." In S. Kreitler and T. Urbanek (eds.), *Conceptions of Meaning*, pp. 173–94. New York: Nova Science.

Schnell, T. (2016). *Psychologie des Lebenssinns*. Berlin/Heidelberg: Springer.

Schnell, T., Höge, T., and Pollet, E. (2013). "Predicting meaning in work: Theory, data, implications." *The Journal of Positive Psychology*, 8(6), 543–54.

Sennett, R. (1998). *The Corrosion of Character: The personal consequences of work in the new capitalism*. New York: Norton.

Shakespeare-Finch, J. and Daley, E. (2017). "Workplace belongingness, distress, and resilience in emergency service workers." *Psychological Trauma: Theory, Research, Practice, and Policy*, 9(1), 32–5.

Shantz, A., Alfes, K., and Truss, C. (2014). "Alienation from work: Marxist ideologies and twenty-first-century practice." *The International Journal of Human Resource Management*, 25(18), 2529–50.

Sheldon, K. M. and Kasser, T. (1995). "Coherence and congruence: Two aspects of personality integration." *Journal of Personality and Social Psychology*, 68(3), 531–43.

Siegrist, J. (1996). "Adverse health effects of high-effort/low-reward conditions." *Journal of Occupational Health Psychology*, 1(1), 27–41.

Somoray, K., Shakespeare-Finch, J., and Armstrong, D. (2017). "The impact of personality and workplace belongingness on mental health workers' professional quality of life." *Australian Psychologist*, 52(1), 52–60.

Stavrova, O. and Luhmann, M. (2016). "Social connectedness as a source and consequence of meaning in life." *The Journal of Positive Psychology*, 11(5), 470–9.

Steger, M. F., Dik, B. J., and Duffy, R. D. (2012). "Measuring meaningful work: The Work and Meaning Inventory (WAMI)." *Journal of Career Assessment*, 20(3), 322–37.

Stillman, T. F. and Baumeister, R. F. (2009). "Uncertainty, belongingness, and four needs for meaning." *Psychological Inquiry*, 20(4), 249–51.

Tajfel, H. (ed.) (1982). *Social Identity and Intergroup Relations*. Cambridge: Cambridge University Press.

Tajfel, H. and Turner, J. C. (1986). "The Social Identity Theory of Intergroup Behavior." In W. G. Austin and S. Worchel (eds.), *Psychology of Intergroup Relations*, 2nd edn., pp. 7–24. Chicago, IL: Nelson-Hall.

Taskin, L. and Edwards, P. (2007). "The possibilities and limits of telework in a bureaucratic environment: Lessons from the public sector." *New Technology, Work and Employment*, 22(3), 195–207.

Tischer, D., Yeoman, R., White, S., Nicholls, A., and Michie, J. (2016). "An evaluative framework for mutual and employee-owned businesses." *Journal of Social Entrepreneurship*, 7(3), 342–68.

Treviño, L. K., Weaver, G. R., and Reynolds, S. (2006). "Behavioral ethics in organizations: A review." *Journal of Management*, 32(6), 951–90.

Ulrich, P. (2008). *Integrative Economic Ethics: Foundations of a civilized market economy.* Cambridge: Cambridge University Press.

van Dijk, R. and van Dick, R. (2009). "Navigating organizational change: Change leaders, employee resistance and work-based identities." *Journal of Change Management*, 9(2), 143–63.

van Knippenberg, D. and Sleebos, E. (2006). "Organizational identification versus organizational commitment: Self-definition, social exchange, and job attitudes." *Journal of Organizational Behavior*, 27(5), 571–84.

Vaux, A. (1988). *Social Support: Theory, research, and intervention.* New York: Praeger.

Vega, G. and Brennan, L. (2000). "Isolation and technology: The human disconnect." *Journal of Organizational Change Management*, 13(5), 468–81.

Viswesvaran, C., Sanchez, J. I., and Fisher, J. (1999). "The role of social support in the process of work stress: A meta-analysis." *Journal of Vocational Behavior*, 54(2), 314–34.

Weber, W. G. (2006). "Soziale Entfremdung durch individuelle Handlungseffizienz? Probleme der gemeinwesenbezogenen Perspektivenübernahme in der Handlungsregulation." In Pierre Sachse and Wolfgang G. Weber (eds.), *Zur Psychologie der Tätigkeit*, pp. 203–33. Bern: Huber.

Weber, W. G. and Jeppesen, H. J. (2017). "Collective human agency in the context of organizational participation: Contributions from social cognitive theory and activity theory." *Zeitschrift für Arbeits- und Organisationspsychologie/German Journal of Work and Organizational Psychology*, 61(2), 51–68.

Weber, W. G., Unterrainer, C., and Höge, T. (2008). "Sociomoral atmosphere and prosocial and democratic value orientations in enterprises with different levels of structurally anchored participation." *Zeitschrift für Personalforschung/German Journal of Human Resource Research*, 22(2), 171–94.

Weber, W. G., Unterrainer, C., and Schmid, B. E. (2009). "The influence of organizational democracy on employees' socio-moral climate and prosocial behavioral orientations." *Journal of Organizational Behavior*, 30(8), 112?–49.

Wheeler, M. (2016). "Martin Heidegger." In *Stanford Encyclopedia of Philosophy* (Winter 2016 Edition). Available at: https://plato.stanford.edu/archives/win2016/entries/heidegger/ [accessed June 9, 2018].

White, J., Bandura, A., and Bero, L. A. (2009). "Moral disengagement in the corporate world." *Accountability in Research*, 16, 41–74.

Wiesenfeld, B. M., Raghuram, S., and Garud, R. (2001). "Organizational identification among virtual workers: The role of need for affiliation and perceived work-based social support." *Journal of Management*, 27(2), 213–29.

Wong, P. T. P. (1998). *Implicit Theories of Meaningful Life and the Development of the Personal Meaning Profile*. Mahwah, NJ: Erlbaum.

Yeoman, R. (2014). "Conceptualizing meaningful work as a fundamental human need." *Journal of Business Ethics*, 125(2), 235–51.

Zapf, D. (2002). "Emotion work and psychological well-being: A review of the literature and some conceptual considerations." *Human Resource Management Review*, 12(2), 237–68.

Zhao, H., Wayne, S. J., Glibkowski, B. C., and Bravo, J. (2007). "The impact of psychological contract breach on work-related outcomes: A meta-analysis." *Personnel Psychology*, 60(3), 647–80.

CHAPTER 11

....

EXPLORING WORK ORIENTATIONS AND CULTURAL ACCOUNTS OF WORK

Toward a Research Agenda for Examining the Role of Culture in Meaningful Work

....

LAURA BOOVA, MICHAEL G. PRATT, AND DOUGLAS A. LEPISTO

A fundamental question for many individuals is "what makes work worth—or not worth—doing?" In other words, what makes some kinds of work "better" or "more meaningful" than others? As organizational scholars, attempts to answer this question have taken a variety of forms, ranging from research on job satisfaction and work engagement to job design and job crafting. There are a variety of answers outside of the academic realm as well. Conventional wisdom captured in phrases like "work to live, don't live to work," "climb the corporate ladder," "do what you love," and "whatever is worth doing is worth doing well" each provide a different answer to what makes work worth doing, or in more modern academic parlance, what makes work meaningful. Such answers also appear to change over time. Gordon Gekko, a fictional corporate raider in the movie *Wall Street*, captures one way work is meaningful in the 1980s by noting that "Greed, for a lack of a better word, is good. Greed is right. Greed works." This is quite different from the sentiment expressed by Steve Jobs in his June 12, 2005 commencement address at Stanford:

> Your work is going to fill a large part of your life, and the only way to be truly satisfied is to do what you believe is great work. And the only way to do great work is to love what you do. If you haven't found it yet, keep looking. Don't settle. As with all matters of the heart, you'll know when you find it. (Jobs, 2005)

And it is not clear that either capture "other-focused" accounts of millennials who appear to be looking for work that contributes to the greater good, be it the environment (Patagonia) or helping those less fortunate (TOMS shoes[1]).

Our core claim in this chapter is that these various "accounts" of what makes work worth doing are largely cultural, and that they play a significant role in shaping or enabling what scholars refer to as "meaningful work." By meaningful work we mean an individual's positive and eudaimonic experience of one's work (Lepisto and Pratt, 2017).[2] We explore the link between cultural accounts of work (CAWs) and an individual's experience of work as meaningful via the concept of work orientation. Work orientation is a natural starting point for this investigation, because it links individuals with broader cultural meanings of work (Pratt, Pradies, and Lepisto, 2013; Pratt, 2016; Lepisto, McArdle, and Pratt, 2017). In particular, we seek to elucidate an understanding of the origin of work orientations, a particularly relevant construct in the meaningful work literature. We begin with a brief review of our starting assumptions about meaningful work. Next, we review the concept of work orientation. Although work orientations are individual-level concepts in that they are personally held, we argue they are culturally constituted. We forge this link to culture in two ways. First, we provide illustrations of the broader CAWs that work orientations tap. Second, to connect these cultural accounts to individually held work orientations, we borrow from cultural sociology and organizational theory to suggest a model with three "pathways" that link them. Finally, we draw from this model to propose new cultural mechanisms of meaningful work. We conclude by offering a program of research on the role of culture (and identity) in meaningful work.

Meaningful Work and Culture:
An Overview

Interest in the broader meanings of work is long-standing (Bellah et al., 1996 [1985]; Brief and Nord, 1990; Ciulla, 2000; Marx, 1867; Mills, 1956; Morse and Weiss, 1955; Weber, 1930). Moreover, the relationship between meaningful work and culture is central to research in the sociology of work. Indeed, from a sociological viewpoint, "[b]ecause beliefs about work do not belong to the category of innate predisposition but stem from everyday experience, they are largely determined by sociocultural factors" (Šverko and Vizek-Vidović, 1995: 3). In other words, research in this tradition explores

---

[1] TOMS initially attracted customers by offering to provide a pair of shoes to someone in need for every pair that a customer bought. They have since expanded their giving model. See https://www.toms.com/improving-lives.

[2] We also draw on Pratt and Ashforth's (2003) distinction between "meaning of work" which is a value-neutral interpretation of what work is from "meaningful work" which is a positive evaluation of work as purposeful and significant—or as we argue here, worthwhile.

cultural differences in how work is understood and has changed over time, such as how perceptions of work have changed from being a consequence of sin to work as a means of salvation (see Tausky, 1995 for a review).

Despite this research, various scholars have noted that the most recent wave of scholarship on meaningful work has largely ignored the role of societal culture in determining meaningful work (see the review in Rosso, Dekas, and Wrzesniewski, 2010).[3] To illustrate, Davis notes that recent research has been relatively unreflective about how broader forces influence how individuals evaluate work:

> A thoughtful recent review by Grant et al. (2009) implied that a variety of categories had come and gone in evaluating jobs. But why these categories? What economic and social factors lead "autonomy" to be salient, as opposed to "safety"? How do these categories change over time, and why?   (Davis, 2010: 307)

However, even when culture is not directly explicated, its role seems central to our understanding. Consider, for example, the classic "lottery studies" which asked participants if they would continue to work if they didn't need the money. These studies largely supported the notion that most people would continue to work because work provides many benefits beyond purely financial ones (Arvey, Harpaz, and Liao, 2004; Vecchio, 1980). Although perhaps not exclusive to a culture infused with a Protestant work ethic (Weber, 1930), one would expect to have found a different answer in ancient Greece where work was viewed as a curse (Arendt, 1958; Hardy, 1990).

More recently, we have argued for a closer look at the role of culture in meaningful work by delineating a Realization perspective on meaningful work from a Justification perspective (Lepisto and Pratt, 2017). Whereas the former perspective is largely about need fulfillment, the latter perspective contends that meaningful work involves the ability to account for one's work as worthy (see also Pratt and Ashforth, 2003). Specifically, a Justification perspective invites a closer look into how culture influences work meaningfulness, as it is viewed as a powerful source of accounts that individuals can draw on in answering the question, "What makes my work worth doing?" Thus, to further delimit our investigation, we adopt a Justification perspective on meaningful work, because it highlights the role of sociocultural meanings in constituting, enabling, and inhibiting individuals' account-making activity (Lepisto and Pratt, 2017). To be clear, by adopting this perspective, we are not simply arguing that culture is an important factor in determining meaningful work. Rather we use this perspective to signal our intent to explore more deeply the active relationship between cultural and individual meanings of work. To better articulate this connection, we draw on work in cultural sociology that explores the relationship between culture and individuals. Before turning to this research, we want to make our discussion of meaningful work—which spans a multitude of literatures and

---

[3] Perhaps a notable exception is the Meaning of Working study that examined attitudes toward work across 15,000 respondents and eight countries between 1981 and 1983. Yet even this research was largely focused on identifying similarities and differences of individual-level meanings across different cultures rather than examining the explicit role of culture in influencing these individual meanings (MOW International Research Team, 1987).

takes a variety of forms—more tractable by focusing on the concept of work orientations. As noted, the concept of work orientations provides a useful lens to theorize the linkages between broader cultural understandings of work and the experience of meaningful work.

WORK ORIENTATION AND CULTURE

Work orientations are "internalized evaluations about what makes work worth doing" (Pratt, Pradies, and Lepisto, 2013: 175). These evaluations provide an understanding of the primary meaning individuals associate with the activity of work as a life domain rather than meanings associated with a specific job. Put another way, work orientations are about how we view "work" alongside other institutions, such as family, church, or government. Early research on work orientations (Amabile et al., 1994) viewed them as either intrinsic (working for its own sake) or extrinsic (working for something else outside the work). Later work, however, has deviated somewhat from that initial bifurcation. Perhaps the most popular current conceptualization of work orientation builds from Bellah and colleagues' (1996 [1985]) *Habits of the Heart* to suggest a tripartite view of work orientations: jobs, careers, and callings (Wrzesniewski et al., 1997). Those with a job orientation are primarily concerned with the material benefits of work; those with a career orientation are primarily interested in achievement through advancement and the attainment of status; and those with a calling orientation seek work that is self-fulfilling, and often work that benefits society.[4]

Empirical research has suggested that work orientation is not bound to specific careers or occupations; rather, different people can approach the same type of work with a different orientation (Wrzesniewski et al., 1997). Moreover, as would be predicted by the typology, different work orientations have been associated with different work outcomes. Those with a job orientation, for example, have lower job satisfaction and well-being than those with calling orientations (Wrzesniewski et al., 1997). Career orientations have been positively associated with achievement, satisfaction with promotion, and length of employment (Lan et al., 2013). Finally, beyond job satisfaction and well-being (see also Shea-Van Fossen and Vredenburgh, 2014), those with callings have been found be more benevolent (Lan et al., 2013), tend to stay with their organizations longer (Cardador, Dane, and Pratt, 2011; Lan et al., 2013), and display higher degrees of organizational commitment (Cardador, Dane, and Pratt, 2011) and a willingness to sacrifice (Bunderson and Thompson, 2009).

Although some research in this area has focused on antecedents of work orientation (e.g. personality) rather than its outcomes (Shea-Van Fossen and Vredenburgh, 2014),

---

[4] Though the notion of a calling has religious roots such that every individual is called by God to do a particular type of work that is best suited to her/his unique talents (Calvin, 1574; Hardy, 1990), more recently scholars have conceptualized a calling as work that ties an individual to others (Bellah et al., 1985), is "socially valuable" (Wrzesniewski et al., 1997: 22), and personally fulfilling (Dobrow, 2006).

missing from these studies is the role that culture might play in determining why someone may have a specific work orientation in the first place. This is surprising given that our most prominent conceptualization of work orientations began with a cultural analysis of American society. Indeed, *Habits of the Heart* explores issues of culture as they are expressed in a variety of institutions in the US, including the institution of work. These cultural linkages were made more explicit in our own research (Pratt, Pradies, and Lepisto, 2013), where we revisited *Habits of the Heart* and noticed that what was referred to as "callings" was actually made up of several potentially discrete elements, each of which could be considered an orientation in its own right. In particular, we disassembled callings into service, craftsmanship, and kinship. A service orientation focused on working for a purpose that was broader than one's self; craftsmanship[5] centered on quality and was focused on the inherent properties of the work itself; and kinship recognized that some work is done primarily to benefit those with whom one works (i.e. one's "work family"). Although it retains some of the elements of the intrinsic–extrinsic orientation toward work, this later typology shifts emphasis toward whether one is oriented toward one's self (job and career or what we call utilitarian and expressive-status, respectively), others (kinship and service), or objects (craftsmanship). We later delineated the "other-oriented" elements of callings in a service orientation from the "self-oriented" elements of an expressive-passion orientation (Lepisto, McArdle, and Pratt, 2017; Lepisto and Pratt, 2017). The net result is six orientations whose names draw heavily from the cultural analysis in *Habits of the Heart*: utilitarian (job), expressive-status (career), expressive-passion, kinship, service, and craftsmanship.

CULTURAL ACCOUNTS OF WORK

If such orientations are indeed cultural,[6] we would expect that their existence would be evidenced in language and stories: that is, in cultural accounts of work in the media that individuals draw on to shape their evaluations of work. Thus, to provide some evidence for the existence of these various work orientations, we searched the popular press for cultural descriptions of "what made work worth doing." Various search terms were entered in a Google search engine for each of the six work orientations. For example, for craftsmanship, "high quality work" and "artisan" were used, while "friendship at work" was used for kinship. Table 11.1 provides examples of evidence—in the form of stories

[5]   A craftsmanship orientation relates to original views of a calling in that it reflects the observation that one's talents are best suited to producing high-quality work. It also harkens back to a calling orientation's link to intrinsic motivation in that the competence associated with mastering a skill can have a positive impact on self-esteem and thus be highly motivating (Bandura, 1977; Thomas and Velthouse, 1990).

[6]   At its most basic level, culture has been conceptualized as a system of meaning (Giorgi, Lockwood, and Glynn, 2015). These meanings can be expressed in a multitude of ways, from frames (Bartunek, 1984; Benford and Snow, 2000) to stories (Creed, DeJordy, and Lok, 2014; Meyer, 1995) to institutions (Glynn and Abzug, 2002; Lamont and Small, 2008; Pedersen and Dobbin, 2006). Given our focus on cultural accounts, we focus specifically on language and stories.

Table 11.1 Evidence of cultural accounts of work that support six work orientations

Work orientation	Source	Title	Representative quote
Utilitarian	*More Magazine* Author: Tracy Sestili Year: N/A	Work to Live, Don't Live to Work	A good work–life balance is one in which you work to live, not live to work. We all need to work to pay the mortgage or the rent, put food on the table, and provide for our families. But when you are working so much that you don't have time to spend with the ones you love, what good is all that money and all those lost hours with your loved ones really worth?
Utilitarian	Forbes.com Author: Rob Asghar Year: 2013	Five Reasons to Ignore the Advice to Do What You Love	You've been told that, if you do what you love, the money will follow. You've been told that, if you find your bliss, world changing success will magically come. You've been told that, if you're not changing the world in dramatic ways, it's because you're too afraid to find your passion and follow it. There are five reasons to end your personal guilt trip.
Utilitarian	*Quartz News* Author: Catherine Baab-Muguira Year: 2016	Don't do what you love for a career—do what makes you money	As Miya Tokumitsu wrote in her viral 2014 article for Jacobin, the do-what-you-love mantra can end up devaluing necessary but unglamorous labor—as well as the working-class people who perform it.
Status	*U.S. News* Author: Marcelle Yeager Date: 2016	Working Hard Isn't Enough: 4 Ways to Score a Promotion	Think of making your own progression happen as part of your day-to-day job, and there's only one person who can help you bring it to fruition: you. In order to do it effectively, you must track your work and achievements in a deliberate way, and know when and how to move your agenda forward.
Status	Forbes.com Author: David K. Williams Year: 2015	Coaching Secrets To Achieve Championship Status At Work	Brian Tracy, a success expert and one of the top trainers in the world today, says, "Those people who develop the ability to continuously acquire new and better forms of knowledge that they can apply to their work and to their lives will be the movers and shakers in our society for the indefinite future."
Passion	Forbes.com Author: Deena Varshavskaya Year: 2014	4 Practical Ways To Find Your Life's Passion And A Career You Love	If you're looking to spend your life doing something you love, the best way to start is to treat financial concerns as secondary. If the practicality of what you do and how much money you earn are your primary criteria you will instantly limit your options to what's predictable and getting to do what you love will be tough.

Table 11.1 Continued

Work orientation	Source	Title	Representative quote
Passion	Monster.com Author: Debra Davenport Year: N/A	Find Your Career Passion	Remember: Skills can be learned, but your passion is a part of who you are. The reality is you can do whatever you want to do and set your mind to do. The old adage, "Do what you love, the money will follow" is actually very good advice.
Passion	Stanford Commencement Address Author: Steve Jobs Year: 2005		Your work is going to fill a large part of your life, and the only way to be truly satisfied is to do what you believe is great work. And the only way to do great work is to love what you do. If you haven't found it yet, keep looking. Don't settle. As with all matters of the heart, you'll know when you find it.
Service	Quartz News Author: Jess Whittlestone Year: 2015	Instead of following your passion, find a career that changes people's lives	Not everyone can do what they're passionate about—we don't all have clear passions that translate easily into jobs. But almost everyone can do something valuable, something that helps others.
Service	The Atlantic Magazine Author: Adam Grant Year: 2014	How to Succeed Professionally by Helping Others	From a motivation perspective, helping others enriches the meaning and purpose of our own lives, showing us that our contributions matter and energizing us to work harder, longer, and smarter.
Service	Harvard Law Today Year: 2016	Dean Minow urges graduates to work together to change the world	Minow asked the graduates to use their influence to better their communities and the world: "Listen generously to others, dig deep into your talents, take risks, remember who you are, work on genuine solutions to hard problems, and you will make a difference, over and over again."
Craftsmanship	Fast Company Magazine Author: Sebastian Klein Year: 2014	The Secrets To Career Contentment: Don't Follow Your Passion	The craftsman's mindset acknowledges that no matter what field you're in, success is always about quality. Once you're focused on the quality of the work you're doing now rather than whether or not it's right for you, you won't hesitate to do what is necessary to improve it.

Craftsmanship	Harrison Barnes Career Blog Author: Harrison Barnes Year: 2014	You Must Produce and Do Quality Work	Incredible quality does not just change nations, it can change your life as well. The more you stress quality in your job, the better you will do in everything you attempt. You cannot avoid doing quality work and bringing improvement to your life.
Kinship	*Harvard Business Review* Author: Christine M. Riordan Year: 2013	We All Need Friends at Work	Camaraderie is more than just having fun, though. It is also about creating a common sense of purpose and the mentality that we are in–it together. Studies have shown that soldiers form strong bonds during missions in part because they…rely on each other, and share the good and the bad as a team.
Kinship	*Wall Street Journal* Author: Ben Rooney Year: 2011	Why Your Workplace Is Like Your Second Family	As the boundaries between work and home life continue to blur, as work assumes an ever greater part of our life, so too recruitment becomes a more emotional experience, more akin almost to a relationship than a job, and the workplace is becoming a second family, Ms. Higginbotham says.
Kinship	*Elite Daily* Author: Liz Rae Year: 2015	Work BFF: 10 Ways Your Coworkers Are Pretty Much Your Best Friends	Your coworkers are the best people to be around because they are what truly makes your days go by quicker. You know when they aren't there because the day isn't half as entertaining as it could be. You look forward to coming into work and spending time with them. You have moments when you wonder if work would even be worth it without them.

or news articles in the United States—of CAWs that constitute the six different work orientations in American culture.

As illustrated in Table 11.1, accounts that provide justification for Wrzesniewski and colleagues' (1997) first two orientations—jobs and careers—are prominent. People talk about the utilitarian or job-oriented accounts by emphasizing the importance of working for money to provide for one's family. This account sometimes has religious roots, with men historically carrying the burden of financial support. More recently, the emphasis on working for money and financial security frequently is communicated via the expression of "Work to live, don't live to work." Such an account emphasizes the importance of living a balanced life and not sacrificing what is "truly important" for one's work. In addition, career-oriented accounts glorify advancement and the attainment of status. In particular, these accounts praise individuals who spend significant portions of their time at work seeking recognition and the attention that comes with climbing the corporate ladder. A more recent manifestation of this account promotes working 24/7 as a status symbol in and of itself (Lebowitz, 2015).

We also found evidence for the more recent work orientations identified by Pratt, Lepisto, and colleagues (Pratt, Pradies, and Lepisto, 2013; Lepisto, McArdle, and Pratt, 2017; Lepisto and Pratt, 2017). One of the dominant accounts today is oriented around passion. This is evident in ubiquitous phrases such as "Find your passion" or "Do what you love," and is often personified by Apple's former founder and CEO, Steve Jobs. However, alongside this account is one that emphasizes service. To illustrate, Sheryl Sandberg echoed this call for a greater purpose when describing her motivation for joining Facebook as its Chief Operating Officer:

> [Y]ou watched what was going on out here, and it really felt like it was changing the world. And I always wanted to work in places that felt like they were going to have an impact on the world.   (Grossman, 2010)

This call for going beyond one's own needs to do good through one's work has been specifically tied to millennials (Benson, 2016)—a group of particular interest because they are projected to become the largest living generation in America by 2019 (Fry, 2018).

Calls for craftsmanship, perhaps evident in the seemingly endless list of products that are "craft" or "artisanal," gained voice in popular books such as *Shop Class as Soul Craft* (Crawford, 2009) and *The Craftsman* (Sennett, 2008) but harken to traditional values embodied in such phrases as "anything worth doing is worth doing well." The theme of quality, in particular, was not only "Job 1" at Ford, it was also the heart of *Zen and the Art of Motorcycle Maintenance* (Pirsig, 1974). Finally, though perhaps the least dominant of the six, a kinship orientation focuses on the importance of looking out for others at work. Indeed, having relationships with work colleagues satisfies a fundamental human need for belonging and creates a shared sense of purpose (Riordan, 2013), which allows individuals to experience meaningful work even if the work itself is not inherently meaningful to them. Although these accounts are prevalent in firefighters and other military/paramilitary organizations (e.g. Pratt, Lepisto, and Dane, 2018), recent echoes can be found in accounts about the importance of friends at work and in organizations that refer to their work colleagues as family (e.g. Pratt, 2000).

LINKING CULTURAL ACCOUNTS TO INDIVIDUAL WORK ORIENTATIONS

Up to this point, we have argued that contemporary research on meaningful work has paid little attention to the role of culture in influencing how individuals view their work. In particular, we have suggested that work orientations are, at minimum, culturally influenced and we have provided some examples of cultural accounts that would seem to justify specific work orientations. Put another way, we are suggesting that individuals' perceptions of why work is meaningful is influenced, at least in part, by the culture in which they reside. We delineate below how cultural accounts can influence how people justify their work and render it meaningful. Indeed, the bulk of our chapter discusses how a cultural account of work, which operates at the collective level, can come to be held by an individual as a work orientation. In making this link, we draw strongly on research in cultural sociology that has examined the relationship between culture and how people think, feel, and act. We illustrate these connections in Figure 11.1. This figure

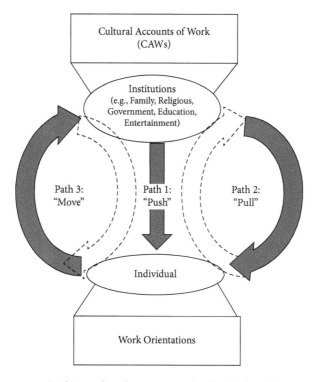

FIGURE 11.1 Linking cultural accounts and individual work orientations

not only outlines the various paths connecting cultural accounts with individually held work orientations, it also provides the foundation for a research program that explores the relationship between culture and work orientations. We discuss the latter in our next section.

Our model is anchored at the top and the bottom by cultural accounts of work, or CAWs, and work orientations, respectively. At the top, we argue that CAWs, such as those found in Table 11.1, are often expressed through institutions. In Bellah and colleagues' (1996 [1985]) cultural analysis of American society, they show that various institutions (e.g. marriage, politics) have been infiltrated with the "language of individualism" which, they contend, limits how people assess value and worth. Pratt (2016) argued that institutions such as religion (see also Weber, 1930), entertainment/media, schools, and family each are institutional reservoirs for cultural accounts of work. To illustrate with examples from the entertainment industry, the movie *LaLa Land* highlights the importance of pursuing passions in life even when it is difficult, while *The Blind Side* emphasizes helping those less fortunate.

At the bottom of our model, we have work orientations. To date, research in meaningful work has tended to assume that meanings are filtered through an individual's identity (see Pratt and Ashforth, 2003), reflecting an assumption that sense-making—more broadly—is impacted by one's self-definition. Here, we leave this question of identity more open-ended, and simply refer to "individuals" as the holders of work orientations. We return to the role of identity in meaningful work at the end of our chapter.

In linking culture and institutions to individuals, we draw on research in cultural sociology. Specifically, following Vaisey (2009), we refer to two of these general paths as "push" in Path 1 and "pull" in Path 2. We then draw on research on cultural entrepreneurship to suggest a third path which we refer to as "move." This path, we believe, may account for the presence of CAWs that become utilized in Paths 1 and 2.

Path 1: Push. The "push" pathway of culture emphasizes that various cultural values, beliefs, and motivations get deposited in individuals in the form of intuitions. Put another way, this perspective often views individuals as more passive recipients of culture, which shapes how we think and feel often without our conscious awareness. As Durkheim (1995) demonstrated long ago, evaluations of good and bad come first from embodied emotions and feelings. From this vantage, culture gets into people through "practical consciousness" (Giddens, 1984), "habitus" (Bourdieu, 1984), or moral intuitions (Haidt, 2001). D'Andrade (1995) similarly attests that certain aspects of culture are more deeply internalized than others, but those internalized at the deepest level shape our nonconscious judgments and emotions. Taken together, this path seems to suggest that work orientations can operate at the level of intuitions (Dane and Pratt, 2007) that have been passively internalized as individuals interact in a broader cultural milieu. People have a "gut feel" for what work is worthy or not, whether or not they can explain or justify it. Dekas and Baker's (2014) study of familial influence on work orientations could be viewed as taking a Path 1 perspective.

Path 2: Pull. The "pull" pathway regarding culture's role in individual evaluations offers an alternative, yet complementary approach. This path is analogous to Swidler's (1986) notion of culture as a "toolkit"[7] where individuals "pull from" the broad set of cultural resources that are available to them. This view contends that actors pick and choose from a broader cultural repertoire comprised of concepts, actions, stories, and symbols (Weber, 2005). In contrast to the push path, the pull path recognizes individual agency and the notion that individuals still have the ability to consciously draw on cultural resources to create justifications for their actions. From this vantage, work orientations are more something people "use" than something they "have." To illustrate, if someone viewed themselves as a "hard worker" and spent many long hours at the office, that individual could use different cultural accounts of work to justify this behavior and support his/her self-view. One person might resonate with cultural accounts that emphasize that "getting ahead" always involves a great investment, such as time and effort, and over time could come to adopt a career or expressive-status orientation. Another person, however, could argue that long hours in the office are needed because achieving quality takes time. As such, he/she may draw on different cultural accounts of work and eventually adopt a craftsmanship orientation. Bunderson and Thompson's (2009) discussion of zookeepers drawing on a neoclassical account of callings could be an example of work orientations from this "pull" perspective.

Path 3: Move. In both the second and third paths, the dotted and solid arrows depict an interaction between the individual and institutions. The solid arrow for the pull path in Figure 11.1, however, ultimately points toward the individual. This is because even though an individual picks and chooses from a broader cultural "menu," he/she ultimately uses these different elements for his or her own use. A third potential path between culture and individual meanings, "move," occurs when an individual or individuals create a *shift* in larger cultural meanings. Thus, the solid arrow for the move path, while traversing between individual and institutions, is ultimately "aimed" at institutions. Research on cultural entrepreneurship provides insight into how change at the individual level leads to change at the collective level. This stream of research highlights the role entrepreneurs play in bringing together existing pieces of the cultural repertoire in novel ways in order to influence the broader field. Whether acquiring resources for a new venture (Lounsbury and Glynn, 2001), establishing a new collective identity (Wry, Lounsbury, and Glynn, 2011), or ensuring the optimal categorization in order to maximize audience attention (Zhao, Ishihara, and Lounsbury, 2013), such entrepreneurs draw on existing cultural resources in order to legitimate and generate an understanding of a new cultural meaning (see also Rao, Monin, and Durand, 2003). For example, social enterprise entrepreneurs used cultural meanings from both business and philanthropy to create a new hybrid organizational form that resonated with a

---

[7] We are not encapsulating the entirety of Swidler's (1986) view of culture as "toolkits." Indeed, her ideas could probably be applied to each of our three pathways. Our point here is that "toolkits," in particular, are a potent example of our second pathway.

broad audience (Battilana and Lee, 2014). By drawing on resources across different cultural repertoires, these entrepreneurs were able to situate a new organization within existing cultural understandings to bring about change. The same logic can be applied to how cultural entrepreneurs may work to change CAWs over time.

This path, we argue, is likely to be rarer than the other two. However, one could look to the social, political, and economic events that led to the Protestant Reformation as one illustration of Path 3. Here, Martin Luther acted as a cultural entrepreneur to fundamentally change how society views what makes work worth doing by both drawing on and differentiating himself from predominant Catholic views of work (Luther, 1883; Hardy, 1990; Pratt, 2016). Indeed, his notion of callings changed how institutions talked about why one works—not as a form of punishment for original sin, but as the enactment of God's will. Moving or shifting cultural accounts is not likely the work of a sole individual, however. Luther, for example, was not the only one to articulate views of work that differed from the status quo. Similarly, Weber and colleagues' (2008) study of the grass-fed beef movement illustrates how a group of individuals, in this case family farmers, were able to change broader cultural meanings of grass-fed beef by appealing to a wider range of previously unconnected stakeholders.

CULTURAL APPROACH TO MEANINGFUL WORK: SPECULATIONS ON A NEW RESEARCH AGENDA

Our model links work orientation with culture through three pathways: pull, push, and move. In this final section, we build on these insights to argue how these various pathways may influence the experience of meaningful work and offer some provocative speculations for future research.

Meaningful Work and the Push Pathway

The first pathway focuses on the fact that work orientations may be deeply internalized. They are inscribed in our tastes, preferences, and values, often acting on a nonconscious and intuitive level (see Pratt and Crosina, 2016 for a recent review of nonconscious processes in organizations). Adopting a push pathway would suggest at least three major implications for research on work orientations and meaningful work.

First, if our evaluations of work are largely operating at a nonconscious or intuitive level, then we would expect them to be very powerful and resistant to change—at least via rational argument. Indeed, Haidt (2001) refers to these nonconscious processes as the "dog" in contrast to the rational "tail." That is, nonconscious processes control the rational. Vaisey (2009) builds on this in suggesting that nonconscious processes are the "elephant" on which rests a discursive and account-making rider. In other words, this would suggest that work orientations are very stable and that organizations would be hard pressed to effectively "manage" or change them. Rather, organizational interventions around meaningful work (e.g. job design, changes in culture) would be effective to the degree they "fit" with individuals' work orientations. Thus, certain interventions would be recognized as "attractive" or "repulsive" to the degree they resonated with deeply internalized work orientations and the sources of these work orientations: CAWs. Moreover, workers would be hard pressed to explain or justify why certain interventions succeeded or not.

Second, given that intuitive processes are infused with emotion (Dane and Pratt, 2007), then work orientations should be similarly infused with emotions. Although there is some research that suggests positive emotion is linked to meaning in life (King et al., 2006), it is perhaps striking that recent reviews (Rosso, Dekas, and Wrzesniewski, 2010), our own included (Lepisto and Pratt, 2017), largely ignore the role of emotions. This is somewhat remarkable in light of the fact that meaningfulness is often discussed in reference to morals, worthiness, and significance—all topics that conjure deep feeling. To be sure, as others note, meaningfulness is not hedonic pleasure (see Lepisto and Pratt, 2017 for a review); but it does not logically follow that meaningfulness is therefore emotionless. We know exceedingly little about when and how meaningfulness is developed and managed in organizations via emotions.

Third, to the degree that work orientations are "pushed" upon people, this raises issues of how to assess them. Could researchers extrapolate one's work orientation or work orientations from successes and failures in priming them (e.g. Bargh et al., 1996)? To illustrate, one might expect that those with craftsmanship orientations might respond more successfully to primes about quality and workmanship than those with other orientations. Alternatively, could work orientations be gleaned through evaluative assessments (e.g. good vs. bad) of different types of work via implicit attitude tests (e.g. Greenwald and Banaji, 1995)? Although there are controversies surrounding the role of these nonconscious measures, the potential of including nonconscious processes in meaningful work remains promising (see Pratt and Crosina, 2016 for a review).

Meaningful Work and the Pull Pathway

The second path focuses on the fact that work orientations provide individuals with a culturally constituted "toolkit" of resources to justify the worthiness of their work. These are the various stories, frames, myths, and other cultural materials feasibly acceptable to people (Giorgi, Lockwood, and Glynn, 2015). The metaphor of a toolkit raises intriguing theoretical questions about the nature of meaningful work and how it is created. This metaphor suggests that people have different cultural "tools" that may be more or less effective depending on the situation at hand. In terms of work orientations, it would suggest that individuals would be able to draw on different CAWs to justify their work, and that these accounts would vary in terms of how effective they were in justifying and perceiving one's work as meaningful. Moreover, a pull pathway would suggest that individuals could draw on several seemingly conflicting resources in order to justify their behavior without being aware of or concerned about such inconsistencies (Weber, 2005). Taken together, these insights would have some profound implications for research on the nature of work orientations and on how individuals find meaningfulness.

To begin, a pull pathway would suggest that individuals could draw on any number of cultural accounts to justify their work, and that what they pulled would depend on their current work situation. At its extreme, this could suggest that work orientations are not as stable as some have theorized (Pratt, Pradies, and Lepisto, 2013; Wrzesniewski, 1999). Indeed, even though work orientations are about work as a life domain, it is likely that they would also be differentially applied to one's current work situation. Thus, one's expressed work orientations could vary not only by one's job, but also by the current challenges one faces in a particular day. Thus, an academic could justify the time spent on teaching preparations with a service orientation explanation (e.g. creating knowledge with students) one day, but then justify his work following a manuscript rejection the next day with a job orientation explanation (e.g. I am glad I will continue to be paid). Taken to an extreme, this may raise questions about the nature of identity and work orientations. Work orientations are, by definition, internalized, but are all internalized accounts self-defining? If not, this would suggest that the relationship between identity and meaningful work is not as straightforward as has been theorized (e.g. Pratt and Ashforth, 2003). For example, perhaps the role of identity is largely to serve as a lens for choosing some accounts over others, rather than viewing work orientations as part of "who I am."

Further, to the degree that individuals consciously draw on multiple or even seemingly conflicting CAWs to justify their work, individuals may deploy multiple and even hybrid work orientations. Drawing parallels with hybrid organizational identities, hybrid work orientations could be comprised of orientations that are oppositional (Albert and Whetten, 1985). Thus, even though calling and job orientations should not theoretically go together, given that the former involves intrinsic motivation and the latter extrinsic, such a combination could be possible if people pull from contradictory CAWs. This also suggests greater attention needs to be spent on theorizing when and why some accounts are deployed from a toolkit and with what outcomes. Indeed, to the degree that the deployment of different cultural work accounts are situational, then observational or ethnographic methods may be more helpful, in viewing such toolkits "in use," than interviews.

Finally, the pull path suggests that whether or not one experiences meaningfulness is a function of whether or not there are CAWs available to adequately justify one's work—both to one's self and to others. Indeed, depending on the problem of justification people face, they may tap different elements of the cultural toolkit to account for worth (see Fine, 1996). By implication, the greater the repertoire in the toolkit, the more adaptive people could be to respond to various problems of justification. In turn, this suggests that breadth of a toolkit might be an important resource in fostering meaningfulness. That is, the more justifications one can bring to bear in accounting for work, the easier it may be to find meaningfulness in one's work. This would imply that rather than focusing on designing work, organizations could better foster meaningfulness by making a variety of CAWs accessible to their workers.

Meaningful Work and the Move Pathway

The move pathway highlights the notion that CAWs don't just exist but are created and transformed by cultural entrepreneurs. Indeed, it is through this path that the "raw materials" for the other paths come into being. The current literature details how entrepreneurs strategically draw on existing cultural resources to legitimate new cultural meanings but package the resources in different ways—often drawing across multiple cultural repertoires—in order to bring about change (Gehman and Soublière, 2017). This suggests that skilled cultural entrepreneurs may package existing meanings about work in different ways or combine such meanings with resonant cultural under- standings from outside the work domain to generate new CAWs. To the degree that individuals (or groups of individuals) are able to create or change CAWs through the strategic deployment of existing cultural resources, then scholars may need to examine new questions in their pursuit of understanding meaningful work, specifically work orientations.

To begin, it suggests that research should examine how CAWs come into being and how they spread (Lepisto and Pratt, 2017). For example, although we have provided evidence for the existence of six different CAWs in American society that have been identified by extant literature (Lepisto, McArdle, and Pratt, 2017; Pratt, Pradies, and Lepisto, 2013; Wrzesniewski et al., 1997) we do not know where these accounts came from in the first place or why they "catch on."

With regard to dissemination, to what degree must CAWs have cultural resonance before they are accepted, and how cognizant are entrepreneurs of this resonance? In addition, the role of cultural entrepreneurs (Gehman and Soublière, 2017) in dissemi- nating CAWs also brings to light power dynamics. It is often, but not always, the most powerful actors that are ultimately able to bring about change to existing cultural under- standings (e.g. Rao, Monin, and Durand, 2003). So who are the powerful actors with control over CAWs and how do they gain enough support from a larger collective to engender change? Such research may, by necessity, involve a historical analysis of when certain CAWs were first used and how they were disseminated.

Once identified, research may also wish to examine the types of resources entrepre- neurs draw on in crafting new or modified CAWs. As noted, Martin Luther drew on religious beliefs in crafting a calling orientation, and others may have drawn on this to develop a more secular version of callings in fostering the Industrial Revolution (Weber, 1930). Today, elements of these orientations may be part and parcel of the type of service orientation (e.g. saving the environment) that is particularly popular among millennials (Benson, 2016). Put another way, future research may explore how individuals repackage different cultural accounts and on which resources or even repertoires they draw.

Taken as a whole, our three paths suggest two other broad avenues for research. First, although this chapter has focused on the American context, there are other cultural accounts that exist in other countries across the world. The Chinese, for example, have a notion of "jingye" which represents a concept of duty and devotion that seems different from craftsmanship or service. Does the third path (or even the first two) operate similarly in other cultures? Moreover, are there cultural differences in how CAWs come into existence? And to what degree might cultural entrepreneurs draw on accounts from different cultures in recrafting work narratives?

Second, we have depicted the pathways as discrete. However, they are not likely to be independent. Cultural entrepreneurs, for example, may initially start by pulling together various stories, frames, myths, and the like for their own understanding (Path 2) before trying to influence institutions (Path 3). Moreover, Paths 1 and 2 assume that there are cultural accounts on which to draw, consciously or not. This suggests that there needs to be some action on Path 3 before Paths 1 and 2 can operate. But by the same token, even cultural entrepreneurs must initially "pull" together some existing cultural accounts— possibly from another institution. Thus, it may be that the paths are somehow linked. Research, therefore, should explore the relationships among the paths, and the mechanisms that bind them. Finally, at a more fundamental level, however, we need to better understand the conditions under which each path may be likely to operate. For example, given the relationship between routine, habits, and automaticity in influencing intuitions and other nonconscious judgments (Pratt and Crosina, 2016), it may be that Path 1 is more likely to occur in times of cultural stability, whereas other paths, such as Path 3, may occur when there is more cultural instability (see also Swidler, 1986).

Conclusion

Beyond acknowledging that culture plays a role in meaningful work, we set out to discuss more fully the relationships between individually held meanings of work and societal culture. Specifically, we draw on research in cultural sociology and work orientations to suggest that there are at least three main pathways linking cultural accounts of work (CAWs) and individuals' own "internalized evaluations about what makes work worth doing" (Pratt, Pradies, and Lepisto, 2013: 175). Moreover, we suggest that each of these pathways not only challenges how we have traditionally viewed meaningful work (e.g. the central role of identity), but also suggests new and exciting avenues for future research.[8]

References

Albert, S. and Whetten, D. A. (1985). "Organizational Identity." In L. L. Cummings and B. M. Staw (eds.), *Research in Organizational Behavior*, vol. 7, pp. 263–95. Greenwich, CT: JAI Press.
Amabile, T. M., Hill, K. G., Hennessey, B. A., and Tighe, E. M. (1994). "The Work Preference Inventory: Assessing intrinsic and extrinsic motivational orientations." *Journal of Personality and Social Psychology*, 66(5), 950–67.
Arendt, H. (1958). *The Human Condition*. Chicago: University of Chicago Press.

[8] We would like to thank Curtis Chan and Jean-François Soublière for their comments on earlier drafts of this chapter.

Arvey, R. D., Harpaz, I., and Liao, H. (2004). "Work centrality and post-award work behavior of lottery winners." *The Journal of Psychology*, 138(5), 404–20.

Asghar, R. (2013). "Five Reasons to Ignore the Advice to Do What You Love." *Forbes* [website], April 12: https://www.forbes.com/sites/robasghar/2013/04/12/five-reasons-to-ignore-the-advice-to-do-what-you-love/#552343121096 [accessed June 30, 2018].

Baab-Muguira, C. (2016). "Don't do what you love for a career—do what makes you money." *Quartz News* [website], October 26. https://qz.com/819233/do-what-you-love-is-bad-advice-work-for-money-not-for-passion/ [accessed June 30, 2018].

Bandura, A. (1977). "Self-efficacy: Toward a unifying theory of behavioral change." *Psychological Review*, 84(2), 191–215.

Bargh, J. A., Chaiken, S., Raymond, P., and Hymes, C. (1996). "The automatic evaluation effect: Unconditional automatic attitude activation with a pronunciation task." *Journal of Experimental Social Psychology*, 32(1), 104–28.

Barnes, H. (2014). "You Must Produce and Do Quality Work." *Harrison Barnes Career Blog* [online], January 13: http://www.hb.org/you-must-produce-and-do-quality-work/ [accessed June 30, 2018].

Bartunek, J. M. (1984). "Changing interpretive schemes and organizational restructuring: The example of a religious order." *Administrative Science Quarterly*, 29(3), 355–72.

Battilana, J. and Lee, M. (2014). "Advancing research on hybrid organizing: Insights from the study of social enterprises." *Academy of Management Annals*, 8(1), 397–441.

Bellah, R. N., Madsen, R., Sullivan, W. M., Swidler, A., and Tipton, S. M. (1996 [1985]). *Habits of the Heart: Individualism and commitment in American life*. Berkeley: University of California Press.

Benford, R. D. and Snow, D. A. (2000). "Framing processes and social movements: An overview and assessment." *Annual Review of Sociology*, 26(1), 611–39.

Benson, T. (2016). "Motivating Millennials Takes More than Flexible Work Policies." *Harvard Business Review* [website], February 11: https://hbr.org/2016/02/motivating-millennials-takes-more-than-flexible-work-policies [accessed June 30, 2018].

Bourdieu, P. (1984). *Distinction: A social critique of the judgement of taste*. Cambridge, MA: Harvard University Press.

Brief, A. and Nord, W. (1990). *The Meanings of Occupational Work*. Lexington, MA: Lexington Books.

Bunderson, J. S. and Thompson, J. A. (2009). "The call of the wild: Zookeepers, callings, and the double-edged sword of deeply meaningful work." *Administrative Science Quarterly*, 54(1), 32–57.

Calvin, J. (1574). *Sermons of M. John Calvin upon the Epistle of Saint Paul to the Galatians*. London: Lucas Harison and George Bishop.

Cardador, M. T., Dane, E., and Pratt, M. G. (2011). "Linking calling orientations to organizational attachment via organizational instrumentality." *Journal of Vocational Behavior*, 79(2), 367–78.

Ciulla, J. B. (2000). *The Working Life: The promise and betrayal of modern work*. New York: Three Rivers Press.

Crawford, M. B. (2009). *Shop Class as Soulcraft: An inquiry into the value of work*. New York: Penguin.

Creed, W. E. D., DeJordy, R., and Lok, J. (2014). "Myths to work by: Redemptive self-narratives and generative agency for organizational change." *Research in the Sociology of Organizations*, 41, 111–56.

D'Andrade, R. G. (1995). *The Development of Cognitive Anthropology*. New York: Oxford University Press.

Dane, E. and Pratt, M. G. (2007). "Exploring intuition and its role in managerial decision making." *Academy of Management Review*, 32(1), 33–54.

Davenport, D. (n.d.). "Find your career passion." *Monster.com* [website]: http://www.monster.com/career-advice/article/find-your-career-passion-hot-jobs [accessed March 25, 2017].

Davis, G. F. (2010). "Job design meets organizational sociology." *Journal of Organizational Behavior*, 31(2–3), 302–8.

Dekas, K. H. and Baker, W. E. (2014). "Adolescent socialization and the development of adult work orientations." In *Adolescent Experiences and Adult Work Outcomes: Connections and causes*, pp. 51–84. Bingley: Emerald Group Publishing Limited.

Dobrow, S. (2006). "Having a Calling: A Longitudinal Study of Young Musicians." Unpublished PhD dissertation, Harvard University.

Durkheim, E. (1995). *The Elementary Forms of Religious Life*. New York: Free Press.

Fine, G. A. (1996). "Justifying work: Occupational rhetorics as resources in restaurant kitchens." *Administrative Science Quarterly*, 41(1), 90–115.

Fry, R. (2018). "Millennials projected to overtake Baby Boomers as America's largest generation." *Pew Research* [website], March 1: http://www.pewresearch.org/fact-tank/2016/04/25/millennials-overtake-baby-boomers/ [accessed June 30, 2018].

Gehman, J. and Soublière, J. (2017). "Cultural entrepreneurship: From making culture to cultural making." *Innovation*, 19(1), 61–73.

Giddens, A. (1984). *The Constitution of Society: Outline of the theory of structuration*. Berkeley and Los Angeles: University of California Press.

Giorgi, S., Lockwood, C., and Glynn, M. A. (2015). "The many faces of culture: Making sense of 30 years of research on culture in organization studies." *Academy of Management Annals*, 9(1), 1–54.

Glynn, M. A. and Abzug, R. (2002). "Institutionalizing identity: Symbolic isomorphism and organizational names." *Academy of Management Journal*, 45(1), 267–80.

Grant, A. (2014). "How to Succeed Professionally by Helping Others." *The Atlantic* [website], March 17: https://www.theatlantic.com/health/archive/2014/03/how-to-succeed-professionally-by-helping-others/284429/ [accessed June 30, 2018].

Grant, A. M., Fried, Y., and Juillerat, T. (2009). "Work Matters: Job Design in Classic and Contemporary Perspectives." In S. Zedeck (ed.), *APA Handbook of Industrial and Organizational Psychology*, pp. 417–53. Washington, DC: American Psychological Association.

Greenwald, A. G. and Banaji, M. R. (1995). "Implicit social cognition: Attitudes, self-esteem, and stereotypes." *Psychological Review*, 102(1), 4–27.

Grossman, L. (2010). "Person of the Year 2010: Mark Zuckerberg." *Time* [online], December 15: http://content.time.com/time/specials/packages/article/0,28804,2036683_2037183,00.html [accessed June 30, 2018].

Haidt, J. (2001). "The emotional dog and its rational tail: A social intuitionist approach to moral judgment." *Psychological Review*, 108(4), 814–34.

Hardy, L. (1990). *The Fabric of This World: Inquiries into calling, career choice, and the design of human work*. Grand Rapids, MI: William B. Eerdmans.

Harvard Law Today. (2016). "Dean Minow urges graduates to work together to change the world." *Harvard Law Today* [website], May 26: https://today.law.harvard.edu/dean-minow-urges-graduates-work-together-change-world/ [accessed June 30, 2018].

Jobs, S. (2005). "'You've got to find what you love,' Jobs says," prepared text of Commencement address delivered by Steve Jobs on June 12, 2005. *Stanford News* [website], June 14: http://news.stanford.edu/2005/06/14/jobs-061505/ [accessed June 30, 2018].

King, L. A., Hicks, J. A., Krull, J. L., and Del Gaiso, A. K. (2006). "Positive affect and the experience of meaning in life." *Journal of Personality and Social Psychology*, 90(1), 179–96.

Klein, S. (2014). "The Secrets To Career Contentment: Don't Follow Your Passion." *Fast Company* [website], February 12: https://www.fastcompany.com/3026272/leadership-now/the-secrets-to-career-contentment-dont-follow-your-passion [accessed June 30, 2018].

Lamont, M. and Small, M. L. (2008). "How Culture Matters: Enriching our Understanding of Poverty." In A. C. Lin and D. R. Harris (eds.), *The Colors of Poverty: Why racial and ethnic disparities exist*, pp. 76–102. New York: Russell Sage.

Lan, G., Okechuku, C., Zhang, H., and Cao, J. (2013). "Impact of job satisfaction and personal values on the work orientation of Chinese accounting practitioners." *Journal of Business Ethics*, 112(4), 627–40.

Lebowitz, S. (2015). "Working around-the-clock has become a status symbol in America." *Business Insider* [website], June 3: http://www.businessinsider.com/working-all-the-time-is-a-status-symbol-2015-6 [accessed June 30, 2018].

Lepisto, D. A., McArdle, S., and Pratt, M. G. (2017). "A new measure of work orientations: Orienting toward self, others, or objects." Working paper, Western Michigan University.

Lepisto, D. A. and Pratt, M. G. (2016). "Meaningful work as realization and justification: Toward a dual conceptualization." *Organizational Psychology Review*, 7(2), 99–121.

Lounsbury, M. and Glynn, M. A. (2001). "Cultural entrepreneurship: Stories, legitimacy, and the acquisition of resources." *Strategic Management Journal*, 22(6–7), 545–64.

Luther, M. (1883). *Werke Kritische Gesamtausgabe*, vol. 44, 10I, 1: 317. Weimar: Hermann Bohlaus.

Marx, K. (1867). *Capital*, Vol. 1. New York: Penguin Books.

Meyer, J. C. (1995). "Tell me a story: Eliciting organizational values from narratives." *Communication Quarterly*, 43(2), 210–24.

Mills, C. W. (1956). *White Collar: The American middle classes*. New York: Oxford University Press.

Morse, N. and Weiss, R. (1955). "The function and meaning of work and the job." *American Sociological Review*, 20(2), 191–8.

MOW International Research Team. (1987). *The Meaning of Working*. New York: Academic Press.

Pedersen, J. S. and Dobbin, F. (2006). "In search of identity and legitimation: Bridging organizational culture and neoinstitutionalism." *American Behavioral Scientist*, 49(7), 897–907.

Pirsig, R. M. (1974). *Zen and the Art of Motorcycle Maintenance: An inquiry into values*. New York: Harper Collins.

Pratt, M. G. (2000). "The good, the bad, and the ambivalent: Managing identification among Amway distributors." *Administrative Science Quarterly*, 45(3), 456–93.

Pratt, M. G. (2016). "The power of addressing the 'why': Catholic education as a source of meaningfulness and competitive advantage." *Integritas: Advancing the Mission of Catholic Higher Education*, 7(3), 1–16.

Pratt, M. G. and Ashforth, B. E. (2003). "Fostering Meaningfulness in Working and at Work." In K. Cameron, J. Dutton, and R. Quinn (eds.), *Positive Organizational Scholarship: Foundations of a New Discipline*, pp. 309–27. San Francisco: Berrett-Koehler.

Pratt, M. G. and Crosina, E. (2016). "The nonconscious at work." *Annual Review of Organizational Psychology and Organizational Behavior*, 3, 321–47.

Pratt, M. G., Lepisto, D., and Dane, E. (2018). "The hidden side of trust: Supporting and sustaining leaps of faith among firefighters." *Administrative Science Quarterly* (online first). Available at: http://journals.sagepub.com/doi/pdf/10.1177/0001839218769252 [accessed July 16, 2018].

Pratt, M. G., Pradies, C., and Lepisto, D. A. (2013). "Doing Well, Doing Good, and Doing With: Organizational practices for effectively cultivating meaningful work." In B. Dik, Z. S. Byrne, and M. F. Steger (eds.), *Purpose and Meaning in the Workplace*, pp. 173–96. Washington, DC: American Psychological Association.

Rae, L. (2015). "Work BFF: 10 Ways Your Coworkers Are Pretty Much Your Best Friends." *Elite Daily* [website], May 22: http://elitedaily.com/life/culture/work-friends-are-best-friends/1031314/ [accessed June 30, 2018].

Rao, H., Monin, P., and Durand, R. (2003). "Institutional change in Toque Ville: Nouvelle cuisine as an identity movement in French gastronomy." *American Journal of Sociology*, 108(4), 795–843.

Riordan, C. M. (2013). "We All Need Friends at Work." *Harvard Business Review* [website], July 3: https://hbr.org/2013/07/we-all-need-friends-at-work [accessed June 30, 2018].

Rooney, B. (2011). "Why Your Workplace Is Like Your Second Family." *The Wall Street Journal* [website], July 13: http://blogs.wsj.com/tech-europe/2011/07/13/why-your-workplace-is-like-your-second-family/ [accessed June 30, 2018].

Rosso, B. D., Dekas, K. H., and Wrzesniewski, A. (2010). "On the meaning of work: A theoretical integration and review." *Research in Organizational Behavior*, 30, 91–127.

Sennett, R. (2008). *The Craftsman*. New Haven and London: Yale University Press.

Shea-Van Fossen, R. J. and Vredenburgh, D. J. (2014). "Exploring differences in work's meaning: An investigation of individual attributes associated with work orientations." *Journal of Behavioral and Applied Management*, 15(2), 101.

Šverko, B. and Vizek-Vidović, V. (1995). "Studies on the Meaning of Work: Approaches, models, and some of the findings." In D. E. Super and B. Šverko (eds.), *Life roles, Values, and Careers*, pp. 3–21. San Francisco: Jossey-Bass.

Swidler, A. (1986). "Culture in action: Symbols and strategies." *American Sociological Review*, 51(2), 273–86.

Tausky, C. (1995). "The meanings of work." *Research in the Sociology of Work*, 5, 15–27.

Thomas, K. W. and Velthouse, B. A. (1990). "Cognitive elements of empowerment: An 'interpretive' model of intrinsic task motivation." *Academy of Management Review*, 15(4), 666–81.

Vaisey, S. (2009). "Motivation and justification: A dual-process model of culture in action." *American Journal of Sociology*, 114(6), 1675–715.

Varshavskaya, D. (2014). "4 Practical Ways To Find Your Life's Passion And A Career You Love." *Forbes* [website], July 2: https://www.forbes.com/sites/forbeswomanfiles/2014/07/02/3-practical-ways-to-find-your-lifes-passion-and-a-career-you-love/#7ec2234f1413 [accessed June 30, 2018].

Vecchio, R. P. (1980). "The function and meaning of work and the job: Morse and Weiss (1955) revisited." *Academy of Management Journal*, 23(2), 361–7.

Weber, K. (2005). "A toolkit for analyzing corporate cultural toolkits." *Poetics*, 33(3–4), 227–52.

Weber, K., Heinze, K. L., and DeSoucey, M. (2008). "Forage for thought: Mobilizing codes in the movement for grass-fed meat and dairy products." *Administrative Science Quarterly*, 53(3), 529–67.

Weber, M. (1930). *The Protestant Ethic and the Spirit of Capitalism*. New York: Harper Collins.

Whittlestone, J. (2015). "Instead of following your passion, find a career that changes people's lives." *Quartz News* [website], July 9: https://qz.com/413792/instead-of-following-your-passion-find-a-career-that-changes-peoples-lives/ [accessed June 30, 2018].

Williams, D. (2015). "Coaching Secrets To Achieve Championship Status At Work." *Forbes* [website], August 10: https://www.forbes.com/sites/davidkwilliams/2015/08/10/coaching-secrets-to-achieve-championship-status-at-work/#64ce12f71538 [accessed June 30, 2018].

Wry, T., Lounsbury, M., and Glynn, M. A. (2011). "Legitimating nascent collective identities: Coordinating cultural entrepreneurship." *Organization Science*, 22(2), 449–63.

Wrzesniewski, A. (1999). "Jobs, Careers, and Callings: Work orientation and job transitions." Doctoral dissertation, University of Michigan.

Wrzesniewski, A., McCauley, C., Rozin, P., and Schwartz, B. (1997). "Jobs, careers, and callings: People's relations to their work." *Journal of Research in Personality*, 31(1), 21–33.

Yeager, M. (2016). "Working Hard Isn't Enough: 4 Ways to Score a Promotion." *U.S. News and World Report* [website], February 25: http://money.usnews.com/money/blogs/outside-voices-careers/articles/2016-02-25/working-hard-isnt-enough-4-ways-to-score-a-promotion [accessed June 30, 2018].

Zhao, E. Y., Ishihara, M., and Lounsbury, M. (2013). "Overcoming the illegitimacy discount: Cultural entrepreneurship in the US feature film industry." *Organization Studies*, 34(12), 1747–76.

CHAPTER 12

....

MEANING IN LIFE
AND IN WORK

....

MICHAEL F. STEGER

INTRODUCTION

....

To whatever degree people were able to separate work from the rest of their lives in years past, the boundaries are more blurred than ever today. Life is consumed by work, which often must be conducted on weekends, in airports, taxis, and airplanes, in the middle of vacations, over family dinners, and even during the most personal tasks. A 2015 United States survey of people's time use revealed that from Monday through Friday, the single greatest way in which employed adults spent their time was working. Whereas they spent an average of 2.6 hours each day on leisure and sports, 1.2 hours caring for others, and a single hour eating and drinking, they spent 8.8 hours working (US Bureau of Labor Statistics, 2016). In fact, the average American adult spent a full hour more working than engaged in sleep and sleep-related activities each work day. On top of these forty-four hours of working time each week, one-third of those studied also worked on weekends. Undoubtedly, people from other countries work a lot too. Some may work less, and many may work more, but in short, work may be the dominant presence in most working adults' lives.

It also is likely that such rough time use studies miss a more insidious conquest of our lives by work, the creeping expectation that we must always be available by email, text, video chat, or conference call. The global nature of business compounds the sense that eventually it will be your turn to join the international conference call or video chat at 5 a.m. on a Saturday. According to a 2012 workforce survey by Kelly Services, a global temporary workforce company, 27 percent of their 170,000 respondents felt pressured to stay connected to work during their off hours, and 32 percent said that mobile technology had contributed to feelings of burnout (Kelly Services, 2012). Work reaches us everywhere, at all times, claiming more and more of our waking (and sometimes sleeping) lives.

And yet, maybe that is not always a bad thing. As the title of this chapter indicates, work does not have to be energy-sapping drudgery. Work can be a source of excitement, fulfillment, energy, and joy. Work can be meaningful. If work gets more of our lives, then perhaps our response must be to get more out of work. This chapter focuses on the synergy meaning can create between work and life overall. To do so, I will review theory and research on meaning in life and on meaningful work. Finally, I will provide two frameworks to guide individuals on how to find meaningful work, and guide organizational leaders on how to try to create it in their workplace.

THREE MEANINGS OF MEANING

The notion of meaning as a topic of scholarly interest begins with Viktor Frankl's interest in meaning as a fundamental human drive. Frankl believed that we all have a will to meaning, a need to find purpose and meaning in our lives. Famously, Frankl (1963) wrote about the power of purpose as he witnessed it among those who survived the Nazi concentration camps of World War II. Having a purpose, a reason to live, or a destiny to fulfill kept people going despite the abuses and horrors of their imprisonment. At the end of the war, Frankl sought to inspire people around the world to seek their own purpose.

His vision spawned several decades of steady research, the pace and volume of which has accelerated dramatically over the past decade or so. Meaning in life (MIL) has grown from an obscure existential curiosity to a mainstay of health and quality of life research. Hundreds of studies have confirmed and reconfirmed that MIL is closely linked to practically every way of assessing human health and well-being. Just a small sampling reveals that those who report higher levels of MIL experience greater happiness, positive emotions, gratitude, life satisfaction, physical health, and even a longer life, while also experiencing lesser depression, anxiety, hostility, and health complications (for review, see Steger, 2009, 2012).

Originally, Frankl argued that meaning and purpose could be found through three means: acts of creativity, building relationships with others, and cultivating noble attitudes during suffering. Applications of these proposals to our working lives seem pretty straightforward. Create something new or valuable, cultivate authentic relationships, and endure suffering with dignity. More recently, other three-part theories of meaning have focused on what meaning consists of, providing different indications of meaning's origins. Martela and Steger (2016) reviewed the literature and concluded that meaning in life consists of three main dimensions. The first dimension is coherence, which refers to how people make sense of life and render it comprehensible and understandable. The second dimension is purpose, which refers to people's possession of a sense of direction and aspiration in life. The third dimension is significance, which refers to people's convictions that their lives are worthwhile and intrinsically valuable. George and Park (2014) refer to this final dimension as existential mattering and suggest that one way of feeling that one's life is worthwhile is by making a difference to other people, or otherwise demonstrating that one is relevant and important.

Thus, meaning in life may be defined as a psychological process that "necessarily involves people feeling that their lives matter, making sense of their lives, and determining a broader purpose for their lives" (Steger, 2012: 177).

MEANINGFUL WORK

A consensus definition of meaning in life took decades to evolve, and there are still some important variations and unresolved ideas. Theory and research on meaningful work is much younger, and lacks a seminal founding figure like Frankl. However, there are quite a number of efforts toward theory building occurring at the present moment. One approach sought to build a conceptual model based on the development of a new survey tool, the Work as Meaning Inventory (Steger, Dik, and Duffy, 2012). This work identified three dimensions to meaningful work: the work itself seems to have a point or is otherwise meaningful, work contributes to one's overall life purpose, and work contributes to some good beyond one's self. A similar approach is offered by Pratt, Pradies, and Lepisto (2013), who propose three orientations to gaining meaning and fulfillment through work. Depending on how they approach their work, people could find meaningfulness through a craftsmanship orientation (which values doing work well for its own sake), a serving orientation (which values work through a drive to help others), or a kinship orientation (which values work that creates bonds among people working together). A major difference between these two approaches is that Steger and colleagues suggest that their three dimensions of MW function together to create a meaningful experience, whereas Pratt and colleagues suggest that any of their three orientations could be sufficient to create a meaningful experience at work.

Other scholars have proposed dimensional approaches to MW that identify pathways to make work meaningful. Rosso, Dekas, and Wrzesniewski (2010) use the dimensions of Self ↔ Others and Agency ↔ Communion to designate four pathways. Individuation follows from the juncture of Self and Agency, and achieves MW through self-efficacy, control, competence, and self-esteem. Contribution emerges from the juncture of Agency and Other orientation and achieves MW through perceived impact, self-transcendence, and making a difference. Unification combines Other orientation with Communion and achieves MW through shared values, interpersonal connections, and developing shared social identities. Finally, Self-Connection arises from Communion and Self orientations, leading to MW through authenticity and identity affirmation.

As scholars have noted, "meaning" is made all of the time, and may be rooted in diverse aspects of both work and life (e.g. Heine, Proulx, and Vohs, 2006; Rosso, Dekas, and Wrzesniewski, 2010; Steger 2009). People may vary in how drawn they are to focusing on their selves versus others at work, or by working toward their own agency versus working together in communion with others. Organizations also may differ in the degree to which they create opportunities for—as well as reward or punish—these orientations. This highlights an important distinction that often is made between "meaning" and "meaningful" (or "meaningfulness"). Meaning essentially captures the interpretations and connections people make regarding their experiences, situations, and stimuli they encounter. Such meanings, or interpretations, can be positive (e.g. My employer is great), negative (e.g. My employers are a bunch of corrupt ghouls), or any possible blend (e.g. The company is awful but the people are good). These meanings are the conduit between the organization, its policies, procedures, people, and culture and the experience of meaningful work. The word "meaningful" also could be positive (e.g. Working here makes my life better in profound ways), negative (e.g. Being disrespected every day at work is causing me to destroy my family bonds), and every blend in between (e.g. Work takes away from time with my family but it is so important and needed in the world). However, in both the meaningful work literature and the meaning in life literature, meaning and meaningful are used interchangeably, and both are almost uniformly used to refer to work or a life that is meaningful in positive ways to people, whereas the term "meaningless" is more frequently used to refer to work that has either no meaning or is meaningful in negative ways. For this chapter, convention is followed in that meaning, MW, and meaningful work are used to refer to the positive manifestations of meaning and meaningfulness.

Because there can be such a profusion and diversity of "meanings"—in the sense of interpretations—that people generate in an organization, it is easy to imagine a mismatch between people and organizations in terms of what organizations intend to provide and what people seek and experience. The models of MW reviewed here essentially argue that these organizational factors and the meanings/interpretations people experience must align in order for MW to occur. By extension, each of these models also recognizes the potential for, and the deleterious consequences of, failures of organizations to provide opportunities for MW for its employees. People prosper if they can find a path to MW, and suffer if that path is blocked.

As noted, there is quite a bit less research on MW than there is on MIL. However, from the research that has been conducted, meaning seems every bit as important to our work as it is to the rest of our lives. People who have meaningful work are more engaged, experience greater positive emotions, feel they use their psychological strengths more often, and are less often stressed and hostile. In some cases, meaningful work is demonstrated to longitudinally predict other important metrics of work well-being, such as engagement (e.g. Johnson and Jiang, 2017). This set of characteristics likely makes them more enjoyable co-workers and employees, a supposition reflected in research showing that meaningful work is correlated with greater intrinsic motivation, more faith in management, better work team performance, higher supervisor performance ratings, and lower rates of absenteeism and intentions to leave an organization (e.g. Steger, Dik, and Duffy, 2012).

Working Together—Meaning
in Work and in Life

California's Silicon Valley has earned a reputation as a hub of innovation...and also ruthless ambition. However, according to one executive who focuses on emerging innovations in this region, even in a powerful world dominated by the digital and the virtual, there is a transcendent theme. I learned about Nina Simosko from a wonderful book on cultivating compassion at work (Worline and Dutton, 2017), in which the following startling statement is quoted: "I've come to learn that people come to work searching for purpose and meaning, *much as they do in their everyday lives*" (Simosko, 2015, emphasis added). It is at once visionary and quaint. Visionary in that even in the high-pressure world where venture capitalists joust with billionaire coders, someone understands that a critical piece sometimes goes missing; quaint in that Simosko speaks of a world in which work is separate from everyday life.

Empirical Research on Meaning in Life and at Work

Of course, one way to think about how meaning in life may connect with meaning at work is by examining research that has directly tested the link. Given the close conceptual relationship between the two variables, it should not be surprising that quite a number of studies have tested their empirical relationship as well. Research shows that meaning in life and meaningful work are positively related in a wide range of samples, including university students studied both through self-report surveys and through a workshop specifically designed to increase meaningful work (Steger and Dik, 2009), university employees (Dik et al., 2012; Steger, Dik, and Duffy, 2012), a small sample of doctors in India (Ola, 2016), a sample of professional artists in India (Vidwans and Raghvendra, 2016), and samples of general working adults obtained through internet survey panels (Allan et al., 2016; Allan, Duffy, and Douglass, 2015; Duffy et al., 2013). Research also shows that this link persists over periods of six months among students in their twenties (Praskova, Hood, and Creed, 2014). Not all of these studies employed the strongest research designs, and certainly more investigation is needed, but the consistency of results across different samples is encouraging. When people find work to be meaningful in positive ways, they also find their lives to be meaningful in positive ways. There is one exception to this body of literature, however. One study failed to find any relationship whatsoever between a single item measure of meaningful work (Delle Fave et al., 2011) and a measure of purpose in life (Ryff, 1989) among a small sample of workers for two Italian insurance companies (Bassi et al., 2013).

Despite this sole exception, meaning in life clearly is connected to meaning at work. However, current empirical research is really only able to scratch the surface of the linkages between meaning in life and at work because existing measures tend to be rather general rather than multidimensional, and existing studies tend to be snapshots rather than longitudinal investigations. For a deeper understanding, we must turn to theory.

Theoretical Connections Between Meaning in Life and at Work

At the broadest level, meaning should work together at the level of life in general and in work because similar mental processes are suspected to work in both venues. After all, if we can seek after or interpret the meaning of a word, an expression, and tragedies with similar intents, then surely we are capable of seeking after and understanding what makes life, and life's important domains (e.g. work, family, spiritual life, leisure, personal development) meaningful. Some basic meaning-creating capabilities may be applied in each case. If this is true, then an argument can be made that similar approaches should divulge meaning in life and in work.

On a more formal level, MIL theory asserts that meaning rests in part on significance, coherence, and purpose. At the most basic level, MW scholars argue that people must be able to view their work as having some fundamental point to it, or view it to be worthwhile (Hackman and Oldham, 1976; Steger, Dik, and Duffy, 2012). This clearly parallels the significance dimension of MIL theory. Some MW scholarship suggests that people use work to better understand their selves and their lives (Rosso, Dekas, and Wrzesniewski, 2010; Steger, Dik, and Duffy, 2012). Further, some work identification scholarship also suggests that people understand themselves to some degree through work and their occupational or vocational organization. For example, Ashforth, Harrison, and Corley (2008) give this process a central position in their conceptualization of organizational identification: "It is identification in this deeper, more existential sense that this article focuses on precisely because it more fully implicates the self in the experience of organizational life" (p. 332). The field of sense-making also directly addresses people's efforts to comprehend and understand their work environments (Weick, 1995). Thus there are clear links between MW and the MIL dimension of coherence. Finally, purpose is considered to enact meaning and translate it into an imperative for people to actually *do* something meaningful and impactful. MW models reserve an important spot for doing important or significant things, which could be expressed through service to some greater good or effort put toward one's own purpose. In sum, there are many reasons to suspect that MIL and MW may work together, perhaps providing reciprocal benefits.

Other themes can be drawn from the MIL and MW theories reviewed here: self-knowledge, authenticity, effective action in the world, self-transcendence, wisdom, ethics, and overarching purpose. Figure 12.1 attempts to show how both MIL and MW have links to these shared themes. It is a bit messy, but it displays convergence that could be used to inform strategies for building meaning at individual and organizational

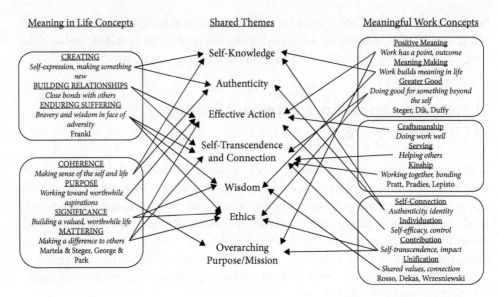

FIGURE 12.1 Model of how key concepts from meaning in life scholarship and meaningful work scholarship share several important themes

levels, whether the organization is a huge company or a small work team. For example, if a team lacks direction and seems to spin its wheels in unproductive meetings, having a clearer or more readily implemented purpose or mission should help. Figure 12.1 suggests that purpose might be enhanced by coaching individual members of the work team to discern their own life purposes and seek ways to service those purposes through work responsibilities and tasks. Alternatively, from the meaningful work side, a leader could help team members determine ways to facilitate working toward some greater good or creating paths toward contribution, which in turn ought to infuse a more salient sense of purpose to the team.

Certainly, this is a preliminary effort to draw direct links between meaning in life and meaningful work, and in addition to being aesthetically iffy, several key iterative processes are neglected. For example, one of the insights generated in MIL theory is that understanding ourselves provides us with the basis for understanding how we are different from other people, enabling us to relate to them more deeply while still engaging empathically (and hopefully nonjudgmentally). For example, if I understand that I work best under tight deadlines with high-pressure motivational tactics, it makes it easier for me to realize that this preference is specific to me, rather than "people," preparing me for better developed motivational strategies for those I am leading. In Figure 12.1, there should be some indication of how particular concepts interact with, support, or lead to each other. It may be important to understand how these interactions unfold both within MIL or MW, and also across MIL to MW and vice versa. Using this same example, the feedforward of self-understanding to empathic understanding of others is particularly applicable in the workplace, where the most effective people are able to identify how they can apply their strengths and also work to bring out the strengths of others as well as of teams and groups.

SPIRE and CARMA

Perhaps in no other domain does meaning confront the necessity of being practical more than in the work domain. Work is about applying effort to specific tasks and contexts. To make it easier to apply meaning to work, I proposed two mnemonic models: SPIRE and CARMA (Steger, 2017). Both of these models draw on psychological research to identify high-value levers for encouraging and enacting meaningful work. SPIRE is intended to provide individuals with some direction on finding their own paths to meaningful work, and CARMA is intended to provide leadership and management with some guidelines for creating an occupational ecosystem that can nurture meaningful work. Figure 12.2 provides a summary of these two models.

SPIRE stands for Strengths, Personalization, Integration, Resonance, and Expansion. Strengths emphasizes that people who are able to use their character strengths at work report higher levels of meaning and engagement (e.g. Littman-Ovadia and Steger, 2010). Personalization highlights the role of finding work that expresses important parts of ourselves (e.g. Dobrow and Tosti-Kharas, 2011). Integration refers to the relationship that exists between meaning in work and meaning in life, suggesting that people are best

Creating Meaningful Work at the LEADERSHIP Level				
C Clarity Setting, sharing, and teaching vision and mission throughout the organization	**A** Authenticity Act ethically and honestly, pursue the organization's mission with integrity	**R** Respect Model, support, and guide interactions based on respect to foster positive connections among personnel	**M** Mattering Convey to each worker the vital importance of the contribution she or he makes to the success and mission of the organization	**A** Autonomy Provide employees responsible and responsive opportunities for self-direction, trial-and-error, interchange of ideas
S Strengths Identify your strengths and use them at work, even if it means doing a bit extra	**P** Personalization Foster an ownership mentality at work by aligning work with your values and taking responsibility within your area	**I** Integration Ensure that your work benefits other areas of your life and helps you achieve meaning and purpose in your life	**R** Resonance Find out about your company's mission and discover ways in which it resonates with your own values and meaning	**E** Expansion Transcend your self-interests and expand your perspective on work to see how it can benefit something beyond yourself
Creating Meaningful Work at the INDIVIDUAL Level				

FIGURE 12.2 SPIRE and CARMA models of fostering meaningful work from the individual bottom-up level (SPIRE) and the leadership/management top-down level (CARMA).

able to find meaningful work when it harmonizes with their values and meaning outside of work (e.g. Hoffman et al., 2011). Resonance points to the important role that leadership and organizational mission play in supporting the perception of workers that their effort is valuable and supports a worthwhile cause (e.g. Nielsen and Randall, 2009; Steger, Dik, and Duffy, 2012). Research demonstrating that people's nostalgia for their employing organization fosters meaningful work (Leunissen et al., 2018) supports SPIRE in general, but in particular the middle elements of Personalization, Integration, and Resonance, because these capture the degree to which people embrace their workplace and link it to durably important matters in their lives as a whole. Expansion captures people's desires for their work to make a positive difference to some cause or entity beyond their selves. Aside from the large amount of research on prosocial behavior and the need to belong to positive relationships, more work-specific sources of evidence for Expansion include positive relations between perceived societal appreciation for and benefit from one's work and measures of meaningful work (Jung and Heppner, 2017).

The CARMA model was developed to provide leaders with a loose blueprint for creating an organization that can better create meaningful work. CARMA is intended to remind leaders that you reap what you sow. CARMA stands for Clarity, Authenticity, Respect, Mattering, and Autonomy. Clarity stresses the importance to employee meaningful work of setting a clear expression of mission, purpose, and direction for an organization. Visionary leaders, such as those referred to as transformational leaders, foster meaningful work among those inspired to follow them (e.g. Judge and Piccolo, 2004). Authenticity refers to the necessity for leaders to behave in an authentic, ethical manner to avoid cynicism. The path from Authenticity to meaningful work is supported by several studies on leadership, but most closely by research linking beneficial work outcomes to the capacity for ethical leadership to create meaningful work (Demirtas et al., 2017). Respect is the basic foundation for positive relationships at work, supporting people in feeling connected and valued at their organization (e.g. Tummers and Knies, 2013). Putting these first three elements together gives the impression that leaders must value those who follow them, demonstrate that important things are being pursued at the organization, and show that it is not just empty talk. One line of research that supports this claim focuses on corporate social responsibility campaigns. Such campaigns appear to create meaningful work for employees, which in turn boosts their levels of well-being (Leal, Rego, and Cunha, 2015). Mattering targets the most basic notion of what makes work meaningful, that a worker can see how her or his labor leads to an outcome that is noticed and useful in the organization. In support of mattering, employees who feel more central to an organization's functions report greater levels of meaningful work (Jiang, Tripp, and Probst, 2017). Finally, Autonomy reflects the central importance to meaningful work of being able to exercise volition and judgment in one's work and life (e.g. Ryan and Deci, 2001; Rodell, 2013).

In an ideal setting, SPIRE and CARMA work together. Individual workers strive to maximize attention to the elements of SPIRE while keeping note of how well their organization, leaders, and managers are providing the elements of CARMA. Leaders and managers may use the elements of CARMA to maintain consistent nourishment of meaningful work in their organizations and the elements of SPIRE to assess how well they are doing. Of course, leaders and managers also benefit from meaningful work, so the two models together remind them to tend to meaningful work both for their followers and also for themselves.

MEANING AND THE FUTURE OF WORK

Currently, work seems to be described as a battle. Workers of one country have their jobs taken by those of another, humans fight algorithms and robots for their jobs, sectors disappear, small companies are swallowed up by bigger ones, and online sellers rob everyone of local jobs and tax revenue. When work is primarily about acquiring wealth, economic security, or material possessions, then all of the incentives line up to create, move, and destroy work, workers, and workers' rights whenever there is an advantage to be had. However, there is an alternative future out there, one in which work is not only there to capture economic leverage, but instead work is there to provide psychological and social goods, well-being, and lives worth living. Work can be the way in which people feel they fulfill their purpose in life.

It is possible that, to some extent, parts of this future are inevitable. Our organizations will want or need to do more to offer meaningful work. Doing so provides competitive advantages (through employer of choice status) and cost advantages (through lower healthcare and replacement costs). Organizations increasingly are expected to reflect social values in order to attract and keep talent. One example is the uproar in the United States over how companies should or should not have responded to a 2017 Executive Order by the President that banned travel to the US by citizens of a small number of countries. Customers and advertisers were joined by employees in pressing companies to generate a response. To some degree, this may reflect frustrated people's tendencies to work with whatever tool is at hand, but I think it is more likely that people want to feel that their employer is worth investing their very best effort in.

The SPIRE and CARMA models help support this idea. People seem to experience work to be meaningful when they are able to Personalize their work, Integrate it into their overall life meaning, and Resonate with their organization's mission ("sPIRe"). Employees therefore might be expected to look to their organization's public behavior as signals of what it stands for and how warmly employees' values, meaning, and purpose are likely to be respected and nurtured. Likewise, the public behavior of companies can be seen as demonstrating corporate values and vision, which might contradict the Clarity leaders have provided their workforce, calling into question the Authenticity of leadership overall, and raising doubts about whether employees' effort Matters in a company that fails to project itself into the broader public sphere ("CArMa"). For today's workers, the way in which organizations rise to the challenge—or bungle the opportunity—of political, social, and environmental issues may strengthen, or perhaps sever, pathways to meaningful work.

Meaningful work is work that people gladly, gratefully, and energetically give their best selves and effort to. Meaningful work creates a workforce of brand ambassadors, living symbols of how great working for a company can be. It has been exciting watching meaningful work grow from being an interesting idea to being a viable and vigorous area of research. As this research increasingly supplies organizations with paths to meaningful work, we will reap the benefits of greater meaning. In life and in work.

References

Allan, B. A., Douglass, R. P., Duffy, R. D., and McCarty, R. J. (2016). "Meaningful work as a moderator of the relation between work stress and meaning in life." *Journal of Career Assessment*, 24(3), 429–40.

Allan, B. A., Duffy, R. D., and Douglass, R. (2015). "Meaning in life and work: A developmental perspective." *The Journal of Positive Psychology*, 10(4), 323–31.

Ashforth, B. E., Harrison, S. H., and Corley, K. G. (2008). "Identification in organizations: An examination of four fundamental questions." *Journal of Management*, 34, 325–74.

Bassi, M., Bacher, G., Negri, L., and Delle Fave, A. (2013). "The contribution of job happiness and job meaning to the well-being of workers from thriving and failing companies." *Applied Research in Quality of Life*, 8(4), 427–48.

Delle Fave, A., Brdar, I., Friere, T., Vella-Brodrick, D., and Wissing, M. P. (2011). "The eudaimonic and hedonic components of happiness: Qualitative and quantitative findings." *Social Indicators Research*, 100, 185–207.

Demirtas, O., Hannah, S. T., Gok, K., Arslan, A., and Capar, N. (2017). "The moderated influence of ethical leadership, via meaningful work, on followers' engagement, organizational identification, and envy." *Journal of Business Ethics*, 145(1), 183–99.

Dik, B. J., Eldridge, B. M., Steger, M. F., and Duffy, R. D. (2012). "Development and validation of the Calling and Vocation Questionnaire (CVQ)." *Journal of Career Assessment*, 20(3), 242–63.

Dobrow, S. R. and Tosti-Kharas, J. (2011). "Calling: The development of a scale measure." *Personnel Psychology*, 64, 1001–49.

Duffy, R. D., Allan, B. A., Autin, K. L., and Bott, E. M. (2013). "Calling and life satisfaction: It's not about having it, it's about living it." *Journal of Counseling Psychology*, 60(1), 42–52.

Frankl, V. E. (1963). *Man's Search for Meaning: An introduction to logotherapy*. New York: Washington Square Press.

George, L. S. and Park, C. L. (2014). "Existential Mattering: Bringing Attention to a Neglected but Central Aspect of Meaning?" In A. Batthany and P. Russo-Netzer (eds.), *Meaning in Positive and Existential Psychology*, pp. 39–51. New York: Springer.

Hackman, J. R. and Oldham, G. R. (1976). "Motivation through the design of work. Test of a theory." *Organization Behavior and Human Decision Processes*, 16, 250–79.

Heine, S. J., Proulx, T., and Vohs, K. D. (2006). "The meaning maintenance model: On the coherence of social motivations." *Personality and Social Psychology Review*, 10, 88–110.

Hoffman, B. J., Bynum, B. H., Piccolo, R. F., and Sutton, A. W. (2011). "Person–organization value congruence: How transformational leaders influence work group effectiveness." *Academy of Management Journal*, 54, 779–96.

Jiang, L., Tripp, T. M., and Probst, T. M. (2017). "Being an organizational 'lynchpin': Development and validation of the core-versus-peripheral position scale." *Journal of Occupational and Organizational Psychology*, 90(3), 329–53.

Johnson, M. J. and Jiang, L. (2017). "Reaping the benefits of meaningful work: The mediating versus moderating role of work engagement." *Stress and Health*, 33(3), 288–97.

Judge, T. A. and Piccolo, R. F. (2004). "Transformational and transactional leadership: A meta-analytic test of their relative validity." *Journal of Applied Psychology*, 89, 755–68.

Jung, A. K. and Heppner, M. J. (2017). "Development and validation of a Work Mattering Scale (WMS)." *Journal of Career Assessment*, 25(3), 467–83.

Kelly Services (2012). *New wave of virtual employees working smarter but risking burnout, according to workplace survey by Kelly Services®* [web page]: http://ir.kellyservices.com/releasedetail.cfm?ReleaseID=723297 [no longer live: accessed February 1, 2017].

Leal, S., Rego, A., and Cunha, M. P. (2015). "How the employees' perceptions of corporate social responsibility make them happier and psychologically stronger." *International Journal of Sustainable Development*, 8, 113–26.

Leunissen, J. M., Sedikides, C., Wildschut, T., and Cohen, T. R. (2018). "Organizational nostalgia lowers turnover intentions by increasing work meaning: The moderating role of burnout." *Journal of Occupational Health Psychology*, 23(1), 44–57.

Littman-Ovadia, H. and Steger, M. F. (2010). "Character strengths and well-being among volunteers and employees: Towards an integrative model." *The Journal of Positive Psychology*, 5, 419–30.

Martela, F. and Steger, M. F. (2016). "The three meanings of meaning in life: Distinguishing coherence, purpose and significance." *The Journal of Positive Psychology*, 11, 531–45.

Nielsen, K. and Randall, R. (2009). "Managers' active support when implementing teams: The impact on employee well-being." *Applied Psychology: Health and Well-Being*, 1, 374–90.

Ola, M. (2016). "Impact of eudaimonic well being on depression, anxiety, stress and meaning at work in male and female doctors." *Indian Journal of Health and Wellbeing*, 7(6), 639–41.

Praskova, A., Hood, M., and Creed, P. A. (2014). "Testing a calling model of psychological career success in Australian young adults: A longitudinal study." *Journal of Vocational Behavior*, 85(1), 125–35.

Pratt, M. G., Pradies, C., and Lepisto, D. A. (2013). "Doing Well, Doing Good, and Doing With: Organizational Practices for Effectively Cultivating Meaningful Work." In B. J. Dik, Z. S. Byrne, and M. F. Steger (eds.), *Purpose and Meaning in the Workplace*, pp. 173–96. Washington, DC: American Psychological Association.

Rodell, J. B. (2013). "Finding meaning through volunteering: Why do employees volunteer and what does it mean for their jobs?" *Academy of Management Journal*, 56, 1274–94.

Rosso, B. D., Dekas, K. H., and Wrzesniewski, A. (2010). "On the meaning of work: A theoretical integration and review." *Research in Organizational Behavior*, 30, 91–127.

Ryan, R. M. and Deci, E. L. (2001). "On happiness and human potentials: A review of research on hedonic and eudaimonic well-being." *Annual Review of Psychology*, 52(1), 141–66.

Ryff, C. D. (1989). "Happiness is everything, or is it? Explorations of the meaning of psychological wellbeing." *Journal of Personality and Social Psychology*, 57, 1069–81.

Simosko, N. (October 6, 2015). *Leading innovation in the workplace. First step: Cultivate compassion* [web page]: http://www.ntti3.com/blog/leading-innovation-in-the-workplace-first-step-cultivate-compassion/ [accessed June 20, 2018].

Steger, M. F. (2009). "Meaning in Life." In S. J. Lopez (ed.), *Oxford Handbook of Positive Psychology*, 2nd edn., pp. 679–87. Oxford: Oxford University Press.

Steger, M. F. (2012). "Experiencing Meaning in Life: Optimal Functioning at the Nexus of Spirituality, Psychopathology, and Well-being." In P. T. P. Wong (ed.), *The Human Quest for Meaning*, 2nd edn., pp. 165–84. New York: Routledge.

Steger, M. F. (2017). "Creating Meaning and Purpose in Work." In L. Oades, M. F. Steger, A. Della Fave, and J. Passmore, (eds.), *The Wiley-Blackwell Handbook of Psychology of Positivity and Strengths-based Approaches at Work*, pp. 60–81. London: Wiley-Blackwell.

Steger, M. F. and Dik, B. J. (2009). "If one is searching for meaning in life, does meaning in work help?" *Applied Psychology: Health and Well-Being*, 1, 303–20.

Steger, M. F., Dik, B. J., and Duffy, R. D. (2012). "Measuring meaningful work: The Work and Meaning Inventory (WAMI)." *Journal of Career Assessment*, 20, 322–37.

Tummers, L. G. and Knies, E. (2013). "Leadership and meaningful work in the public sector." *Public Administrative Review*, 73, 859–66.

US Bureau of Labor Statistics. (2016). *American Time Use Survey: 2015 results* [online]: https://www.bls.gov/tus/ [accessed February 1, 2017].

Vidwans, S. S. and Raghvendra, P. (2016). "A study of meaningful work, hope and meaning in life in young professional artists." *Indian Journal of Positive Psychology*, 7(4), 469–71.

Weick, K. E. (1995). *Sensemaking in Organizations*. Thousand Oaks, CA: Sage.

Worline, M. C. and Dutton, J. E. (2017). *Awakening Compassion at Work*. Oakland, CA: Barrett-Koehler.

PART III

THE EXPERIENCE OF MEANINGFUL WORK

···

CHAPTER 13

MEANINGS AND DIRTY WORK

A Study of Refuse Collectors and Street Cleaners

···

RUTH SIMPSON, NATASHA SLUTSKAYA, AND JASON HUGHES

INTRODUCTION

···

DRAWING on a recent study of street cleaners and refuse collectors, this chapter explores some of the meanings created around "dirty work," i.e. work that is generally seen as disgusting or undesirable (Ashforth and Kreiner, 1999). Such work has been seen to offer particular challenges in terms of how and what meanings are drawn—in a context where both the work and the worker may suffer stigmatization through the close proximity to dirt (waste, debris) as well as through the devalued nature of the work. Drawing on Ashforth and Kreiner's (1999) conceptualization of dirty work, we focus here on "physically tainted" work, i.e. occupations associated with dirt or danger, into which our two occupational groups of street cleaning and refuse collection might be seen to fit. However, we also acknowledge potential overlaps with Ashforth and Kreiner's other identified forms of taint, namely social taint (where the job is seen as servile to others) and moral taint (occupations that might be seen as having a dubious moral nature). As they argue, occupations may be tainted on multiple dimensions—thus street cleaners and refuse collectors deal with physical dirt in the form of debris, litter, and waste (physical taint); the work entails serving the public through collecting waste in ways that can be seen as demeaning (social taint); at the same time, work with physical dirt can involve some moral taint in so far as society equates "clean with good and dirt with bad" (Ashforth and Kreiner, 2014: 86).

Our aim here is to draw out the meanings that members of our two occupational groups, as "dirty workers" involved in mundane and messy practices and routines, attach to their work. Our sample comprised white working-class men as broadly representative of those working in these occupations (migrant workers were excluded on the grounds that they are likely to have a different experience, and hence create different meanings around the work). We draw on Bourdieu's (1984) notion of habitus as a lens to further our aim. Habitus is conceptualized as a set of embodied dispositions which relate to the contextual conditions of the "field," enabling a focus on meaning-making as "dispositions" and how these might be generated from particular contexts. In so doing, we expose aspects of a (classed and gendered) "dirty work" habitus characterized by particular meanings, i.e. those that relate to work opportunities and occupational choice; to aspirations and futurity; and to traditionalism—which we position within neoliberalism and the specific conditions and relations of the dirty work "field." We highlight the fragility of meanings and argue that meanings are not just a "reaction" or response to specific contextual conditions but, in a Bourdieusian sense, are generative in that they reproduce particular social relations and conditions of power.

MEANINGFULNESS: EMERGING PERSPECTIVES

Arrayed across different fields, the literature on work-based meanings has focused on two main concerns: why meaningful work matters in an organizational context, and what conditions need to be cultivated for work to be and remain meaningful (Michaelson et al., 2014). Here, meaningfulness can be seen in general terms as arising when an individual "perceives an authentic connection between their work and a broader transcendent life purpose beyond the self" (Bailey and Madden, 2017: 4) which goes beyond personal ability to create and manage to encompass, for example, the influence of institutional and normative settings (Wrzesniewski, 2003). As such, meaningful work has been named as a central characteristic that individuals pursue in their jobs, ahead of income, job security, and promotion (Cascio, 2003). Such scholars as Kuhn et al. (2008) note that as work is a key source of self-identification, meaningfulness should be pursued at work purely as an important condition for human development and self-realization. Studies in support of Kuhn's argument have looked at how individuals experience meaningfulness and what the personal outcomes of these experiences might be. However, most empirical studies have coupled meaningfulness with sought-after organizational goals (Michaelson et al., 2014). This research has confirmed that enhanced job performance, job satisfaction, and organizational identification are regular consequences of meaningful work.

Although scholars have noted that non-material aspects of meaningfulness arguably apply more to "good" rather than "bad" jobs, an abundance of literature indicates that individuals seek meaningfulness no matter what kinds of conditions they endure (Isaksen, 2000; Bailey and Madden, 2017). For example, in his discussion of repetitive work, Isaksen (2000) stresses that the sheer status of being employed evokes feelings of belonging in those who have experienced unemployment, leading to increased confidence and self-esteem. Other studies show how, in the face of stigma such as that experienced by many "dirty workers," individuals reframe the work in positive terms (Ashforth and Kreiner, 1999), often drawing on wider discourses about what is socially valuable (e.g. hospital cleaners may introduce notions of patient care as integral to the work). Drawing on their comparative study of stigmatized, craft, and professional work, Bailey and Madden (2017) demonstrate how moments of meaningfulness could be captured and preserved in any job. The majority of studies in this stream of literature draw attention to the emancipatory nature of meaningfulness as an integral part of autonomous self-determination and personal fulfillment and as a way of enhancing individual agentic capabilities (Rosso, Dekas, and Wrzesniewski, 2010).

Another group of scholars has highlighted the role of intersubjectivity in the construction of meaningfulness (Wrzesniewski, 2003; Rosso, Dekas, and Wrzesniewski, 2010). In contrast to the more utilitarian reliance on individual self-interest as a drive for human development, this is a perspective of agency that recognizes an individual's desire for merited recognition as a key mechanism underpinning the individual's relation to the self and the surrounding world. In other words, the integrity and possibilities of individual self-realization depend on approval and recognition being forthcoming from others. Patterns of recognition function as a "steering wheel" in individual self-realization through the formulation of normative standards and aspirations. Fundamentally, since work remains central to the functioning of the market economy, work achievement serves as an evaluative standard for the judgment of structures of social distribution and reward. In this stream of literature, recognition is rendered a driving force to achieve both self-realization and normative progress. Human dependency on the promise of recognition from others highlights the role of social processes in the production and institutionalization of what is deemed meaningful.

BOURDIEU, MEANINGS, AND DIRTY WORK

Relatively few studies have considered the ways in which individual dispositions might be implicated in the perception and production of meaningfulness. As Bourdieu (1996) suggests, meanings and values (e.g. around work or biographical events) are not generated solely by the subject, neither are they produced by emerging normative systems. Instead, they are conditioned in a historically shaped social space that frames individuals' perceptions of what discursive resources are available to them. While taking into account individuals' capacities to act as agents, Bourdieu acknowledges that these actions take place within a field that molds them whereby a specific habitus associated with a particular field—its history, opportunity structures, and cultural constraints— becomes internalized, entering bodies to become part of identity. Referred to as "bodily hexis," the body is seen as a "repository" of historically informed cultural and symbolic value—a physical expression of all the factors that make up one's habitus: postures, movement, speech styles, comportment, and ways of thinking and feeling ("doxa") that come to be seen as "natural." There is therefore a dialectical interrelationship between action and structure, i.e. between the field and the "structured" disposition and predisposition of actors, where the field delineates a dynamic set of potentialities while the habitus gives rise to the possible "position taking" within the field, mobilizing cultural distinction from other individuals and groups.

For example, Slutskaya et al. (2016) explored how masculinity and class intersect to shape what could be adopted as meaningful in terms of attitudes and practices, and strengths and vulnerabilities, with working-class men giving primacy to the physicality of work and mobilizing personal capacities of endurance, effort, and fortitude to give value and purpose to work-based experiences (Sennett and Cobb, 1972; Connell, 2000; Ashforth and Kreiner, 1999). As they show, social conditions dictate the availability, credibility, and legitimacy of sources of meaningfulness, according to lived traditions, class- and gender-shaped embodied practices. The habitus can accordingly be seen to embody potential meanings assigned to work and to reflect how these are constituted in a set of social relations, thus helping to place, in the manner suggested by Jahoda (1982) and others, such meanings within a wider social context.

Although scholars have increasingly recognized that meaningfulness goes beyond personal ability to attach, maintain, and manage meanings (Wrzesniewski, 2003), and that it involves a complex system of interactions between psychological processes, institutionalized meanings, embodied practices, and normative judgment, they have been less successful in developing effective frameworks or understandings that incorporate these different aspects (Hitlin and Vaisey, 2013). In this respect, as we have pointed out elsewhere (R. Simpson et al., 2014), Bourdieu's approach affords an analytical frame in which individual and broader contextual processes of meaning-making in relation to work can be incorporated into a unified scheme. The perspective therefore offers potential to examine the "field" of physically tainted work as a system of relations—with its specific constraints and opportunity structures—and how this shapes dispositions and meanings.

In this respect, physically tainted work has been characterized by several factors, including limited opportunities for progression, poor prospects and pay, and restricted autonomy (Bolton and Houlihan, 2009; Simpson, Hughes, and Slutskaya, 2016) where there are few options for action and where maintaining employment (keeping one's job) is a key challenge. As Atkinson, Roberts, and Savage (2012) and the authors in their edited volume have shown, neoliberalism and its doctrine of individualism and unfettered markets have had a profound impact on the lives of working-class men, many of whom may be undertaking work that could be identified as "dirty" or undesirable in some way. Neoliberalism has not only established compelling norms, based on a moral discourse of individualism oriented toward free choosing, responsible agents unfettered by structural constraints, but has had long-lasting and pervasive material, structural, and social consequences through demands for greater flexibility, free movement of labor, contracting out and the erosion of trade union power. Deindustrialization, for example, has led to a decline in traditionally "masculine" work and a growth in service sector jobs where there is little place for the masculine "hard graft" valued by working-class men

(Nixon, 2009; McDowell, 2003). Deregulation, inward migration, and demands for greater flexibility have meant that low-level work is increasingly "disposable" and insecure. Thus, exacerbated by austerity measures, public sector manual workers now face reduced employment prospects, lower wages and pension entitlements, less job security, downward pressure on wages, and greater work intensification through a singular focus on performance (Simpson, Hughes, and Slutskaya, 2016). Together with a neoliberalist ideology that locates the source of inequality in the poor choices or low aspirations of the individual (overlooking class-based structural constraints), these changing contextual conditions are likely to shape, from a Bourdieusian perspective, the meanings given to the work. Following this discussion, a key aim of the chapter therefore is to develop a more integrated understanding of individual and contextual influences on meaningfulness in dirty work.

THE RESEARCH CONTEXT AND METHOD

The contextual factors outlined earlier were particularly evident in the context of our London-based ethnographic study of street cleaning and refuse collection. Expenditure cuts and contracting out have reduced the number of workers employed directly by the council while private contractors routinely draw on agency workers who receive lower wages and have fewer employment rights than permanent employees (Aguiar and Herod, 2006). Workers have faced work intensification and reduced employment/pension conditions—and experience, as a matter of routine, problematic encounters with members of the public who were seen to devalue the work (discussed further later in the chapter). Here, team-based work practices of refuse collectors help to engender a strong occupational culture based on camaraderie and a valued and pleasurable humor, providing resources to withstand potential assaults on identity. Such subcultural resources are less available to street cleaners, who typically work on their own, and who appear more vulnerable to negative effects (from the grim nature of the work and from negative attitudes on the part of the public).

The research, funded by the British Academy, followed institutional ethical guidelines to explore work-based experiences through participant and non-participant observation. The observational fieldwork involved two members of the research team spending several days working alongside refuse collectors "on the dust," taking full part in the day-to-day activities. This allowed a direct experience of the physicality of dirt (the smell on a hot day; the touch of waste matter; the feelings of aversion) as well as the physical demands of collecting refuse from, routinely, 1,600 houses in a day. One member of the research team then accompanied the street cleaners on their rounds, observing work practices and relations with the public, and talking informally and more formally in an interview situation about the work. Field note "jottings" were taken during breaks in work routines and full field notes were written up at the end of each working day. Twenty-one semi-structured interviews were conducted (thirteen with street cleaners, and eight with refuse collectors/recycling workers). All participants were male, white, and had been born in the UK. Most had left school at 16—some older workers as young as 14—with no formal qualifications or only a few GCSEs. Work histories were diverse, with all the men picking up a variety of jobs within their locality (e.g. in the council, in haulage, warehouse work, and factory work). In this respect, participants typically had a narrow history of geographical mobility, working and living close to where they grew up.

Interviews from both projects as well as field notes were subject to detailed thematic analysis involving searches across the data set to find repeated configurations of meaning or "patterns of experience" (Braun and Clarke, 2006). Interviewer reflexivity and awareness of power dynamics were important in, for example, acknowledging that occupational distance (e.g. from the manual/non-manual divide inherent in our respective positions) may have influenced data collection and analysis. Through "active listening" and an acute awareness of the potential influence of our own privileged occupational position, we sought a sympathetic dialogue where, in a more general context, male working-class voices are rarely heard. For a full articulation of the challenges faced in researching marginalized groups (e.g. working-class men) and how these might be overcome, see Slutskaya et al. (2016) and A. Simpson et al. (2014).

WORK-BASED MEANINGS: A "DIRTY WORK" HABITUS

The physicality of the work became evident from our first day working with the refuse team. It was pleasantly hot and dry, with a light early morning breeze as we set off with our crew. It was not long, however, before the dust kicked up and became almost unbearable as we followed the truck. The smell was particularly invasive and the need to deal with disgusting matter (cat litter, rotting food, dirty nappies) was routine. Few participants wore protective clothing as this provided little defence against the smell that penetrated nevertheless. Further, the practices of dirt's removal placed a considerable stress on the body. Not surprisingly given our novice status, the effort of lifting hundreds of bags and the monotony of the work exhausted us. It was with great relief that we left the team in the early afternoon so as not to slow down their work. Our aching muscles got considerably worse by the end of the second day.

Field notes, refuse collection

For Bourdieu, action becomes meaningful within the dynamics of particular fields, molding a habitus as an embodied scheme of perceptions and meanings that represents a mark of social position and social difference. These in turn generate action that is both reflective of the structural relations of the field and generative of its power effects. Social conditions and dominant power relations of the field—including the physical dimension of work as outlined in the field notes just quoted—produce traditions, practices, and values which adhere to individuals through understandings of potential or constraint, e.g. in terms of what individuals see as meaningful and possible. These opportunity structures are perpetuated as chances of success or failure and are internalized in meanings and action in that a specific habitus associated with a particular field "enters bodies" to become part of identity. Drawing on our study, we highlight three schemata that we suggest make up a classed "dirty work" habitus in this context: meanings and practices around hard work and traditionalism; around choice and security; and around aspirations and futurity.

Hard Work and Traditionalism

As has been charted elsewhere (Sennett and Cobb, 1972; R. Simpson et al., 2014), capacities for hard work and for endurance, captured in notions of physical capital, are given value in the context of physically tainted work, underpinning a traditionally oriented working-class masculine identity. Across the two occupational groups, we identified traditional notions of hard work, discipline, and continuous effort as intrinsic to meanings that men gave to the work. Here, toughness and effort can be seen to be part of a male working-class habitus based historically on a culture of necessity, a physical body, and attributes of endurance and bodily strength. As captured in the field notes at the start of this section, the work is physically draining and all participants complained of feeling exhausted by the end of the day. One street cleaner commented, highlighting the repetitive, physical nature of the work:

> When all the leaves are coming down and it's been raining and you're shoveling, it makes your arms ache 'cause you're shoveling and shoveling all the time

Traditional notions of working-class endurance could be the source of masculine pride, helping workers to position themselves favorably as "hard grafters"—taking satisfaction from providing an essential service and from doing a job that others would struggle to undertake. One street cleaner commented with explicit criticism of the limited capacities of white-collar workers:

> Not everyone is able to actually do road sweeping because it's a bit more difficult than they think... Physically, physically it's very demanding... We've had businessmen that have fallen out of work, very well educated... and decided that if they can't get another job they would just go and be a road sweeper, and they come here and I'll take them out and I'll explain to them "This is what we have to do." And more likely than not they will last about two hours because they're unable to do it.

In this quote, "*very well educated*" is positioned in detrimental terms against a strong practical sense, seen as part of a working-class habitus, and the extreme physical rigors of the work, and creating a valued distinction through the possession of specialist skills. Normally valued middle-class backgrounds and privileges are, in these spaces, resisted and diminished—carrying little worth in a context where meaning is placed on embodied strength and fortitude.

Changed understandings of the value of physical work, however, were widely acknowledged—understandings which undermined the potential for men to gain pride and respect. Observing the declining appeal of the physical work (where work is seemingly defined in terms of physical effort), one of the refuse collectors tersely noted:

> *They [people] are looking for a job where they don't have to do any work, any manual work.*

Similarly, one of the refuse collectors referred to how the occupation is seen by others as demeaning (*"they think you're low-life"*) and how manual work is often dismissed as less challenging and less deserving of esteem. Pride in work was further undermined by day-to-day encounters with members of the public that were often based on attitudes of disrespect—felt to have intensified over the years: *"A lot of people do take it for granted when you sweep the roads or a dustman, they don't appreciate you no more, not like in the old days."* Physical labor, a source of masculine pride, could therefore at the same time attract feelings of devaluation, destabilizing traditional meanings attached to the work. These meanings nevertheless continue to form part of male, working-class habitus that, in Bourdieu's terms, is historically informed, integrating past experiences through current perceptions, values, and actions—a bodily hexis or "incorporated history" that has been undermined by wider changes in the "field." Thus, from our study, attachment to traditional values and work-based meanings is accompanied by an acknowledgment that these meanings are under threat through a widespread devaluation of physical, manual work.

Choice, Security, and Utility

As Roberts and Evans (2012) contends, the new "politics of aspiration" within neoliberalism encourages the belief that we can choose, where choice is often presented as "disinterested" and disconnected from relations of power. On this basis, whatever our circumstances, we are encouraged to think of ourselves as the agents of our own destiny with the ability to shape and coordinate our lives through the uptake of opportunities and commitment to mobility. For Bourdieu, not only can material circumstances preclude full participation in the aspiration agenda, but the limited complicity between dispositions and opportunities can also constrain the perception and production of meanings. In short, meanings are partly derived from an individual's place in a social order where Bourdieu's concept of "doxa" captures ways of thinking and feeling about our everyday world. For example, in this study, parental influence had often steered men toward continuous uninterrupted traditional forms of employment, taken for granted by family as the "best" option available, rather than remaining in education. In the context of limited opportunities, finding and retaining secure employment was a key aspiration, with a permanent job with the council seen as their ultimate goal.

> *I'm not the sort of person to sit around, sponging off the dole, I found it all the time I was out of work I was just tired out all the time, it's just the boredom and I kept going*

to the Job Centre signing on, hated it, so I see this agency, the money was low but I thought, I've got to take it and I did, and I'm glad I did in the end 'cos it led on to a permanent job with the council which is, you know, quite amazing really.

A strong desire for security and aspirations for stable, continuous employment often fashioned workers' decisions. One of the participants reflected on his original motive to become a road sweeper in terms of greater personal security—though this was couched in terms of a passing age:

The road sweepers, refuse collectors...there used to be job security, you would come and join the Local Authority and think you'd got a job for life etc., it was low paid but we had that security.

Working for local authorities, particularly in what could be seen as an essential service, was also seen by participants as *useful to communities*, therefore providing workers with traditional sources of meaningfulness. Here, pride was taken in "doing a job well." Workers insisted that all jobs should be treated with respect—undertaken to the best of one's ability—with priority given to the usefulness and utility of the work:

It is important you're doing a good job and we've had paper come in, like emails and that, say "thanks for doing a good job" which that also gives us satisfaction because they [the public] know we're doing a good job.

However, these sources of meaning were being weakened by recent changes in the sector. Here, cuts to public funds as a result of austerity measures were perceived by participants as undermining the meaningfulness of their work. Participants saw funding cuts as being detrimental in two vital ways. First, the introduction of neoliberal "market discipline" through commercialization and privatization undermined the security of public sector jobs. One refuse collector commented:

You know, you've got all the councils doing different cut backs and all this sort of thing now...I've been made redundant twice thinking, you know, you're sound [i.e. secure] enough

The waste management industry has been, over time, pushed to extend the role of private companies, which resulted in competitive tendering or contracting out—with private companies and agencies offering less favorable pay and conditions. Over half of participants in the study were employed by agencies, adding further instability to already uncertain job prospects, and with recent work histories characterized by instability and turmoil through job losses. Nearly all participants referred to the detrimental effects of these changes, with lack of job security undermining their ability to rely on continuous employment as a source of meaning:

A lot of Local Authorities...dealt with waste and other areas but it went out private and many Authorities paid the price over many years, once you get rid of, some got rid of the depots, got rid of your vehicles, got rid of your vehicle workshops to maintain the vehicles, outsource all the labour, it's gone...

Second, changes in employment conditions were linked directly to increased workloads and quality deterioration, compromising their satisfaction from doing a good job. Both refuse collectors and street cleaners gave detailed accounts of job losses, work intensification, "corner cutting," and falling standards of equipment. This is captured in the following quote, where a street cleaner expresses with great clarity some of the frustration experienced and how hard it has become to "*do a satisfying job*":

> It used to be five people would go out...they would go out with scrapers, brooms, shovels, loppers, they would scrape the back lines, they would scrape the channels, they would cut overhanging branches, because they had a crew of five people, and they had more crews. Now everything's been made so small...that they go out with like two to four people, less crews, so rather than doing all the scraping they're going out with litter-pickers, brooms when needed, all the back lines are being left, the channels are being left, purely because of cuts and under staff.

We can see from this section how participants found meanings through continuous employment and the sense of security and self-reliance that continuous work brings (Connell, 2000; Simpson, Hughes, and Slutskaya, 2016)—comprising a "doxa" of taken-for-granted assumptions that can establish limits to what is seen as possible or feasible. Pride is taken from undertaking an essential service, though repeated redundancies and the vulnerability of "replaceability" has destabilized workers' reliance on uninterrupted employment as a source of pride and self-worth and limited resources have diluted intrinsic meanings they attach to each task in terms of "doing a good job." Individualism and agency, as hallmarks of the neoliberal regime, appear to have little relevance to the men in our study—where decisions about life course, in the form of job trajectories, are presented as "in the hands of others." As one street cleaner commented prosaically, "*they [the agency] decide when it's time for you to go*."

Habitus and Futurity

While partly historically determined, habitus is also oriented toward future potentiality not only through the accrual processes of different forms of capital but also through its social location, which has implications for how individuals perceive their future chances. This perception may depend on relative positioning within a set of hierarchical relations. Through his concept of "symbolic violence" and resonant with our data, Bourdieu highlights how those with power impose their "worldview" as legitimate so that the dominant and the dominated accept, through taken-for-granted assumptions, their own condition and what is seen as achievable. Here, men in our study engaged in very tentative terms with future possibilities, often foreclosing the likelihood of change. This is captured evocatively in the following brief exchange with a street cleaner below:

How do you see yourself in the future?
Well, don't know what I think about that, um, what you mean on this job or...?

You can do that, yeah. And in two or three years' time, where do you see yourself?
Two or three years' time, oh I don't know. Don't know what to say about that. As I say unless something else came along in that time I would be doing this still.

A highly uncertain engagement with the future ("*don't know what to say about that*") based on narrow expectations of change ("*I would be doing this still*") was offset to some extent by aspirations for children's careers, with meaning found in the ability for continuous employment on their part, however menial in nature, to offer children security and financial support. Notions of personal sacrifice as voluntarily offered to family helped to provide a rationale and meaning for work that required endurance and fortitude, and where there was little hope of progression. Here, men drew on "breadwinner" discourses to highlight how they were able, through their employment, to provide financial resources for family and the chance to offer them a "better" future—i.e. one which is more promising than their own:

I just want better for them...I'm having to work hard to do it but I want to do it, for them to have a better life than I'm having

However, there were clear limits to the financial and material support that could be afforded on the back of manual work. Perceived inability to adequately perform the breadwinner role could translate into a feeling of personal failure, becoming a source of embarrassment and shame. In the following quote, this shame is focused—in embodied and material ways—around the uniform of the manual worker (signifying a devalued status) and the ownership of a secondhand car, emblematic of lack of consumer power:

I shouldn't be, right, but I'm embarrassed, you know...it's like, you know, I go home wearing me [sic] Council gear and, you know, you can tell by the car that I drive, you know...I'd like to be able to afford a car, a nice safe newish car to take my kids in, instead I've got an old car...with dents and scratches here and there, I can't afford to buy another...and when your kids ask you for like...and I have to buy things from like Primark and stuff...and I think well I've never claimed any money, I've worked since I've left school, you know, and you just, you feel bad

As we have argued elsewhere (R. Simpson et al., 2014), while the future may hold little meaning given poor prospects of improvement or change, working hard to give a better life to partners and children can be a key priority that helps to give hard, mundane work a positive value. Participants accordingly adhered to traditional meanings of "sacrifice for children." These meanings, however, were fractured by limited material circumstances associated with manual work. While hard physical work and continuous employment can be a source of pride for the autonomy and feeling of self-reliance they may bring, such work also positions men in a devalued economic sphere with limited access to material resources to support themselves and their families—undermining traditional meanings associated with a breadwinner role.

CONCLUSION

Through a study of refuse collectors and street cleaners, we have explored in this chapter the meanings that working-class men attach to "dirty work." As Collinson (1992) notes, looking at the more general context of blue-collar occupations, while such work has traditionally been excluded from theories of work trajectories on the grounds that it does not portray the upward mobility on which the "normative" model of career experiences depends, blue-collar workers accumulate skills over time, are subject to organizational arrangements and opportunity structures, and are concerned about the meanings of work. As our chapter demonstrates, these meanings go beyond a narrow, instrumental orientation toward financial rewards that have been seen to be the dominant value system of manual workers. While the men in our study display a "functional reality" in terms of particular meanings rooted in necessity and the "now," we also highlight more complex meanings around choice, security, and constraint; around the physicality of work and "doing a good job"; and around future aspirations for children—meanings that are both produced and constrained by the conditions of the field.

In particular, we can identify a specific classed and gendered embodied habitus associated with the forms of physically tainted work that made up our study. This incorporates understandings of and practices relating to: choice and constraint where options become naturalized as "inevitable" in terms of what is perceived to be appropriate and which generate particular practices in terms of, for example, job trajectories; an uncertain and unconfident investment in the future where hopes and aspirations are attached, through hard work and notions of sacrifice, to children's potential and choice of careers; and, relatedly, hard work and discipline as part of a culture of necessity and affective attachment to the past. At the same time, the study demonstrates that although those involved in dirty work adhere to traditional meanings and envision their possibilities only within what is designated by the social field, these meanings are at the same time fragile and insecure—limited, destabilized, and weakening as a result of changes in economic and normative demands.

Here we can highlight the interplay between habitus and field—where the field offers "spaces of possibilities" and options for certain action (Bourdieu, 1996). Thus, we can trace these meanings, in part, to the "vulnerability of replaceability" that results from neoliberal policies and practices that have weighed heavily on the public sector working class, as well as to neoliberal agendas with their emphasis on credentialism, self-development, and mobility that affords little value to manual work. Here, we can see in Bourdieusian terms a struggle for distinction as men in our study seek to distinguish themselves from others (e.g. white-collar workers) through the possession of particular physical aptitudes and skills, deriving significance from difference. At the same time, limited options from the field and "repressed dispositions" of the habitus can create conditions for "radical emptiness" (Skeggs, 2004), namely a fatalistic realism and an acceptance of life's conditions based on a habitus of non-belonging and non-caring. This can be seen as a form of resistance to the dominant "symbolic game," in our case neoliberalist-inspired ideologies of individualistic aspiration and self-improvement.

These meanings may accordingly be read as a response to normative understandings of middle-class careers based on "non-physical" principles of variety, mobility, and self-development. Further, as Sayer (2005) suggests, temporal uncertainty and low self-regard from forms of disrespectful treatment by others, as commonly experienced by the men in our study, may interfere with their vision of the future, further constraining the sense of potential. Meanings therefore are profoundly contextual and only "make sense" within the conditions and social relations of the field.

Finally, Bourdieu points to how the habitus not only reflects but also reinforces the power relations of the field—both constitutive of and constituted by a broader set of (class- and gender-based) social relations, helping to reproduce the social order. Here we can see how work-based meanings mobilized and articulated by working-class men, as part of the dispositions of the habitus and of symbolically meaningful "position taking," both reflect and reinforce the subordinating conditions of dirty work: how continual reference to "anchors" in a working-class past can serve to reinforce men's entrapment in subjugated occupational fields; how a primacy placed on physical capital and on hard work and endurance reinforce capacities and a fixed subject position that hold little value in a neoliberal labor market; how attitudes and meanings given to choice that presume low personal entitlement based on a minimal sense of "deservingness" create a worldview or "sense of one's place" that leads "one to exclude oneself from the goods, persons, place and so forth from which one is excluded" (Bourdieu, 1984: 471). Street cleaners and refuse collectors may construct distinctions between manual and non-manual work and reify the former through attachment to values of hard work, but they are subject, largely, to the latter's disciplinary power—with little autonomy in their working lives. The meanings that working-class men create around their work as a response to their particular circumstances, social relations, and conditions accordingly reinforce those conditions and the power relations they face—contributing to the reproduction of the social order in which they are embedded. Taken together, this consolidates dirty work and class as markers of devalued identity. Meanings matter in this sense because they not only reflect but serve to reproduce hierarchical social relations and existing systems of power.

REFERENCES

Aguiar, L. and Herod, A. (2006). *The Dirty Work of Neo-Liberalism: Cleaners in the global economy*. Oxford: Blackwell.

Ashforth, B. and Kreiner, G. (1999). "'How can you do it?' Dirty work and the challenge of constructing a positive identity." *Academy of Management Review*, 24(3), 413–34.

Ashforth, B. and Kreiner, G. (2014). "Dirty work and dirtier work: Differences in countering physical, social and moral taint." *Management and Organization Review*, 10(1), 81–108.

Atkinson, W., Roberts, S., and Savage, M. (eds.) (2012). *Class Inequality in Austerity Britain: Power, difference and suffering*. Basingstoke: Palgrave MacMillan.

Bailey, C. and Madden, A. (2017). "Time reclaimed: Temporality and the experience of meaningful work." *Work, Employment and Society*, 31(1), 3–18.

Bolton, S. and Houlihan, M. (2009). *Work Matters: Critical reflections on contemporary work*. Basingstoke: Palgrave Macmillan.

Bourdieu, P. (1984). *Distinction: A social critique of the judgement of taste*. Cambridge, MA: Harvard University Press.

Bourdieu, P. (1996). "Understanding." *Theory Culture and Society*, 13(2), 17–37.

Braun, V. and Clarke, V. (2006). "Using thematic analysis in psychology." *Qualitative Research in Psychology*, 3(2), 77–101.

Cascio, W. F. (2003). "Changes in Workers, Work and Organization." In W. Borman, R. Klimoski, and D. Ilgen (eds.), *Handbook of Psychology: Industrial and organizational psychology*, pp. 401–52. New York: Wiley.

Collinson, D. (1992). *Managing the Shop Floor*. Berlin: Walter de Gruyter.

Connell, R. (2000). *The Men and the Boys*. Cambridge: Polity Press.

Hitlin, S. and Vaisey, S. (2013). "The new sociology of morality." *Annual Review of Sociology*, 39(1), 51–68.

Isaksen, J. (2000). "Constructing meaning despite the drudgery of repetitive work." *Journal of Humanistic Psychology*, 40(3), 84–107.

Jahoda, M. (1982). *Employment and Unemployment: A social psychological analysis*. Cambridge: Cambridge University Press.

Kuhn, T., Golden, A., Jorgenson, J., Buzzanell, P., Kerkelaar, B., Kisselburgh, L., Kleiman, S., and Cruz, D. (2008). "Cultural discourses and discursive resources for meaning/ful work." *Management Communication Quarterly*, 22(1), 162–71.

McDowell, L. (2003). *Redundant Masculinities: Employment change and white working class youth*. Oxford: Blackwell.

Michaelson, C., Pratt, M., Grant, A., and Dunn, C. (2014). "Meaningful work: Connecting business ethics and organizational studies." *Journal of Business Ethics*, 121(1), 77–90.

Nixon, D. (2009). "'I can't put a smiley face on': Working class masculinity, emotional labour and service work in the 'New Economy.'" *Gender, Work & Organization*, 16(3), 302–22.

Roberts, S. and Evans, S. (2012). "'Aspirations' and imagined futures: The im/possibilities for Britain's young working class." In W. Atkinson, S. Roberts, and M. Savage (eds.), *Class Inequality in Austerity Britain: Power, difference and suffering*, pp. 70–89. Basingstoke: Palgrave Macmillan.

Rosso, B. D., Dekas, K. H., and Wrzesniewski, A. (2010). "On the meaning of work: A theoretical integration and review". *Research in Organizational Behavior*, 30, 91–127.

Sayer, A. (2005). *The Moral Significance of Class*. Cambridge: Cambridge University Press.

Sennett, R. and Cobb, J. (1972). *The Hidden Injuries of Class*. New York: Norton.

Simpson, A., Slutskaya, N., Hughes, J., and Simpson, R. (2014). "The use of ethnography to explore meanings that refuse collectors attach to their work." *Qualitative Research in Organizations and Management*, 3(9), 183–200.

Simpson, R., Hughes, J., and Slutskaya, N. (2016). *Gender, Class and Occupation: Working class men doing dirty work*. Basingstoke: Palgrave MacMillan.

Simpson, R., Slutskaya, N., Hughes, J., and Balta, M. (2014). "Sacrifice and distinction in dirty work: Men's construction of meanings in the butcher trade." *Work, Employment and Society*, 28(5), 754–70.

Skeggs, B. (2004). *Class, Self and Culture*. London: Routledge.

Slutskaya, N., Simpson, R., Hughes, J., and Simpson, A. (2016). "Masculinity and class in the context of dirty work." *Gender, Work & Organization*, 23(2), 165–82.

Wrzesniewski, A. (2003). "Finding Positive Meaning in Work". In K. Cameron, J. Dutton, and R. Quinn (eds.), *Positive Organizational Scholarship*. San Francisco: Berrett-Koehler.

CHAPTER 14

··

FINDING MEANING IN THE WORK OF CARING

··

CAROL L. PAVLISH, ROBERTA J. HUNT,
HUI-WEN SATO, AND
KATHERINE BROWN-SALTZMAN

INTRODUCTION

Hui-wen's reflection: Once we earned a license to practice medicine, nursing, respiratory care, pharmacy, social work, physical or occupational therapy, we were not only entrusted to write orders, administer medications, or give breathing treatments. We were granted a trust that goes far beyond a technical practice. Of course, honing our technical skills is vital. Good intention and a kind disposition can never replace safe, technical practice. But while we bear the weightiness of our practice on our shoulders, it is the weightiness of that trust that we bear most on our hearts.

I came in for my shift, and saw on paper that my patient would be fairly light in terms of technical nursing practice. Not many meds to give. Provide the basic essentials of nursing care. But one hour into the shift, the physician came in to ever so gently break the news to the family and the patient that this once healthy individual was going to have significant medical needs for a lifetime. It was going to affect **every single thing** about this patient's future. I was filled with such awe and gratitude for her straightforwardness balanced with the most delicate sensitivity as she explained the prognosis. What respect she showed for **the trust** that has been given to her to have that kind of conversation. She was not rushed by any means, but she did not stay for long after she delivered the news. As she quietly exited, I felt the weight of **the trust** fall very, very heavily on my shoulders. I still had eleven hours as the most consistent person at the bedside with a patient and family whose world had just been completely, irreversibly turned upside down. They were reeling. I didn't know them before this shift, but it was **the trust** given to me to **care-fully,** full-of-care, read their emotional cues and navigate those cues with compassion and grace every step of the next eleven hours. Do they want a lot of privacy, or a strong nursing presence? Do they want to jump into all the practical questions about what their future might look like, or do they need me to talk very minimally at this raw stage about the reality that awaits them? Will they trust me enough to share a little bit about their grief and fears? Will they trust me to go to that hard place with them and not let them down? I felt it. The weight. The trust. It intimidates me and it shapes me. I fear it but I embrace it. Oh let me always be a faithful, ever-teachable, humble steward of this trust.

Caring work is a human activity that can occur at any point in time, in any context, and by anyone who is called to respond in a considered (and considerate) manner. Many health professions adopt caring as a foundation for professional practice. For example, social workers operationalize care through the principles of social justice, and physicians provide care primarily based on the ethics of non-maleficence ("Do no harm"). The nursing profession centralizes the noun and verb of "**care**" in all actions performed with and for patients, families, and communities. Nurses are entrusted—and trusted—to care. The International Council of Nurses (ICN, 2002) defines nursing as "autonomous and collaborative *care* of individuals of all ages, families, groups and communities, sick or well and in all settings." The World Health Organization (WHO) acknowledges,

> Nurses and midwives are critical in the delivery of essential health services and are core in strengthening the health system. Acting both as individuals and as members and coordinators of interprofessional teams, nurses and midwives bring people-centred care closer to the communities where they are needed most, thereby helping improve health outcomes and the overall cost-effectiveness of services (WHO, 2016: 6).

The American Nurses Association (ANA, 2016) states that nursing is the "protection, promotion, and optimization of health and abilities, prevention of illness and injury, facilitation of healing, alleviation of suffering through the diagnosis and treatment of human response, and advocacy in the *care* of individuals, families, groups, communities, and populations." ANA outlines these responsibilities in six essential features—all of which involve *care* of individuals, groups, and entire populations (Box 14.1).

Caring work is central to the identity of the nursing profession and a core value as noted in the ICN Code of Ethics and the ANA Code of Ethics (ANA, 2015; ICN, 2012). In fact, nurses around the world often like to say, "We put the 'care' in healthcare." This chapter examines the meaning of caring work and what makes caring work meaningful. Based on our narratives about nurses' caring practices and on research, including our own research, on meaningful moments in nursing, we explore conditions conducive to caring and creating meaning in caring work. We also describe the occasional struggle to find meaning in caring. Finally, we consider the intersections between caring encounters and meaningful moments. We hope this chapter inspires readers to further study the reciprocal relationship between human caring and meaningfulness—in life and work.

Box 14.1 Six Essential Features of Nursing (American Nurses Association)

Provision of a caring relationship that facilitates health and healing.

Attention to the range of human experiences and responses to health and illness within the physical and social environments.

Integration of objective data with knowledge gained from an appreciation of the patient or group's subjective experience.

Application of scientific knowledge to the processes of diagnosis and treatment through the use of judgment and critical thinking.

Advancement of professional nursing knowledge through scholarly inquiry.

Influence on social and public policy to promote social justice.

Although this chapter highlights caring exemplars and research from nursing, we recognize that caring moments may occur in any workplace. Investigating the value of creating work environments that allow and promote meaningful encounters in caring relationships has broad application that extends beyond nursing and healthcare.

CARING THEORY AND RESEARCH

Carol's reflection: As a critical care nurse and nurse educator, I remember sitting alongside my father's ICU bed during one of his hospitalizations for congestive heart failure. My dad was a retired professor who lived with fairly severe dementia although he could usually make sense of his surroundings and understand people's roles in that context. He was hospitalized because of a recurring lung infection that required oxygen and frequent medication. He had been resting when the evening nurse entered his ICU room to assess his current status, change some required equipment, and administer some medications. I remember watching the nurse carefully, and I noted that her actions were accurate and efficient. She asked several questions that seemed relevant to his care, although she rarely looked at him while he responded to her queries. When she was done, she left the room with a promise to be back later. Dad looked over at me and quietly said, "She doesn't care about me." I looked at dad to see if he understood where he was, and he said again, "That nurse does not care about me." I remember reaching for his hand and starting to reassure him that she does care and that she would be back periodically through the evening to check on him... but I stopped and instead asked what he meant... and why he thought she did not care. He answered quite simply, "It was the look on her face when she did not see me. I just don't matter. I can always tell which ones care about me." Technically, the nurse was competent and efficient during her assessment and safety checks. But something of utmost importance was missing... a caring attitude.

Theorists and researchers have explored the concept of care. Political theorist, Joan Tronto (1993: 103) proposed that an ethic of care "includes everything we do to maintain, continue and repair our 'world' so that we may live in it as well as possible. That world includes our bodies, our selves and our environment, all of which we seek to interweave in a complex, life-sustaining web." Four elements of care include: attentiveness, responsibility, competence, and responsiveness of the care receiver. Tronto argued that care relationships are an integral part of being human, and form the foundation of our mutual interdependence. In contrast to obligation-based ethics derived from ethical theories such as deontology, utilitarianism, and principalism, an ethic of care calls for responsibility-based ethics in which caring relationships are the starting point for determining what needs to be done.

Perhaps the nursing profession's best known care perspective is Watson's Theory of Human Caring/Caring Science (Watson, 2012), which proposes three major care elements: a) caritas processes such as being authentically present and creating healing environments, b) transpersonal caring relationship between nurse and patient, and c) the caring occasion/caring moment. Relational care is the heart of nursing deliberation and caritas action.

An integrative review of the nursing literature on the concept of care found five major categories: caring as a human trait, a moral imperative, an affect, an interpersonal interaction, and an intervention. These researchers defined caring as "a set of behaviors (knowledge, skills, and attitudes) exhibited in the process and context of the nurse–patient interaction" (Leyva et al., 2015: 23). This review indicates that care is not only affective but is also action-oriented. Caring comes from the intention and capacity to do good for patients such as relieve suffering and address needs, and therefore must include competence and expert practice, i.e. having the knowledge, attitudes, and skills to provide safe, high-quality nursing care (Finfgeld-Connett, 2008). However, the relational aspects of nursing cannot be separated from the intellectual, physical, and spiritual work of nurses as they intentionally intervene (during "caring moments") to improve patient situations and health outcomes for individuals, families, and communities (Wolf, King, and France, 2015). Caring, therefore, involves responsive and intentional actions to improve health-related situations in the context of relational responsibilities.

Personal characteristics, culture, and the general environment that surrounds the patient–nurse encounter influences caring practices. Jarrin (2012: 17) proposed that nursing care "is situated in space, place, and time, shaped by the internal and external environments of both the nurse and patient/client." The internal environment refers to individuals' beliefs about nursing work, their moral and psychological development and propensities, and their level of skill and experience. These individual attributes interact with the context in which work occurs, including societal and professional norms and values as well as the practice environment where caring moments are rendered (or not rendered). In other words, caring depends on both internal and external conditions that are more or less conducive to creating caring opportunities. For example, if inadequate resources limit staffing, time compresses, which impinges caring moments.

Alternatively, if nurses lack sensitivity to patient distress, caring opportunities do not develop. Furthermore, if hierarchical power restricts nurses' autonomy to create relational space with patients, caring moments, such as patient–nurse dialogue regarding end-of-life preferences, are less likely to occur. Likewise, nurses benefit from having relationship space with colleagues to support one another in creating meaning from caring encounters.

Patients' perspectives on caring not only involve competence but also include connectedness, compassion, effective communication, advocacy, and support (Canzan et al., 2014; Griffiths et al., 2012; Harrowing, 2011; Joolaee et al., 2010; Sinclair et al., 2016). In a qualitative study, Griffiths and colleagues (2012) found that while patients and health services users valued technical competence, the humanizing, caring aspects of nursing actions were particularly valued. Minor gestures that may be considered insignificant in any other setting may be perceived as caring when one is having a significant life event such as surgery, hospitalization, or a visit to the emergency department. For example, Roberta describes her partner's hospitalization for extensive surgery to repair his spine ravaged by a deformity:

> He had been in chronic pain for several years, barely able to walk. After the 12-hour surgery and a night spent in ICU he was transferred to another unit. When his cart arrived, the nurse greeted us warmly, carefully looked at all his tubes, checked him over, explained the self-administered medication, the bed and lights, and quickly scanned the room. She quietly paused, looked at him and asked if he had any questions or needed anything. Then she looked directly at me asking me the same thing. After hearing that I did not, she told us she would be back in an hour but to use the call light if we needed her and [she] left the room. She **saw** us both. I felt seen and knew she was attentive. She took care of him a few days later. She came in the room, greeted us both and then went around the bed so she was close to the head of the bed. She quietly checked him out, looking and listening carefully to him. Her whole approach was filled with care: care filled. It was almost spiritual how she tended to him.

Caring has been shown to improve outcomes such as physical and mental well-being (Finfgeld-Connett, 2008; Leyva et al., 2015; Wolf, King, and France, 2015), patient satisfaction (Desmond et al., 2014; Leyva et al., 2015; Palese et al., 2011; Tejero, 2012), treatment adherence (Owens, 2006), and work satisfaction for nurses (Hines and Gaughan, 2014; Leyva et al., 2015). Nurses' recognition of these beneficial effects deepens an appreciation for the complexity and significance of caring moments, which are viewed by some nurses as "peak or best nursing experiences" (Wolf, King, and France, 2015: 19). For example, in a qualitative study, pediatric nurses defined caring in terms of creating a sacred space where compassion and nursing presence can lead to caring moments from which trust often develops. In these caring moments, nurses deepen their appreciation for nursing and frequently become inspired to create more caring moments in the future (Hines and Gaughan, 2014). Reflecting on these treasured moments usually increases nurses' awareness of their shared humanness and their contributions to patients' well-being from which many derive meaning in their life and work.

MEANINGFUL WORK

Hui-wen's reflection: "How is work?" It's an entirely ordinary question, part of an entirely ordinary conversation, which is why it can be so hard for nurses to answer. Most of the time, I give the simple answer, for my ease and perhaps more so for the ease of my listener. "Work is busy. It gets a little crazy sometimes. Hard? Yes, sometimes it can be hard. But it's rewarding." It's a palatable, expected response from a nurse. The person inquiring about my work is usually satisfied, and the ordinary conversation moves on. But as a nurse, I am left uncomfortably unsatisfied, as that simple question has triggered a quiet but loaded myriad of thoughts, memories and emotions regarding my patients, their families, their stories, their implications, and my role, all so profound and complex and significant. What we see, what we hear, what we do every day we come to work, it is extraordinary. The real response to that ordinary question would only just begin to tell the listener how nurses go above and beyond, every single day.

Recently, I spent an afternoon with a child who was not well. He got really sick, and then he got a little better, and then he got a lot worse. The doctors and I looked at the monitor, and they told me I should probably go get more help, in that calm, sober voice that PICU doctors use when they recognize what is starting to happen. You should probably go get more help. I went to get the crash cart and I had to pass by the parents. I could feel their searching eyes on me. I could not look at them. I always thought that would be my strength, reaching out and bravely giving the parents the respect of eye contact, acknowledging their fear, giving them some kind of expression that would tell them I see their fear, I'm going to help, I hope I can help. I could not look at them because I was afraid my eyes would tell them I'm sorry for your loss, before it was time to say I'm sorry. The numbers on the monitor were not good. It was my first time doing compressions. It was just like all those CPR classes, but it wasn't, really. It mattered now. The two longest minutes of compressions finally were up and we looked for the rhythm. It wasn't good. Two more minutes. No. Two more. No. Two more. No. Two more. No. Two more. No. Two more. No. Two more. No. Two more. No. No. No more. I turned off the pain medicine, the heart medicines. The parents had been at the doorway the entire time. The nurses and doctors quietly stepped away from the bedside to let the family come say goodbye. "No me dejes!!! Tu eres mi bebe!! No me dejes, mi amor…!!" There is no sound that exists in the world like that of a mother's cry for her baby to please, don't leave me. I barely kept my composure long enough to take off my mask, gown, and gloves before leaving the room. A coworker found me and I rested in her arms for a long while. We carried each other's heaviness. The team met to debrief about the medical situation and the code. We ended with a moment of silence for the patient, the family, and for ourselves. A moment to acknowledge a life, a mother's heartache, and our own humanness as healthcare workers who do so much, but can only do so much.

According to Viktor Frankl (2000), finding meaning is a complex process that is driven by a deep human longing but can be achieved in three simple ways. Meaning might be discovered through "creating a work or doing a deed" or by "experiencing something or encountering someone" (p. 143). Last, meaning may be realized "by facing a fate we cannot change... by rising above ourselves and growing beyond ourselves" (p. 144). In other words, "meaning may be squeezed out from even suffering, and that is the very reason that life remains potentially meaningful in spite of everything" (p. 114). Frankl posits that meaning occurs through one's inner dialogue in response to the events that are happening in the immediate environment. This process may be enhanced by others who are present in the experience. Finally, the meaning of life differs from one time and place to another, so meaning is not experienced as life in general but rather in a given moment.

In the context of a caring practice such as nursing, meaningful work is viewed as a "positive psychological state whereby people feel they make positive, important, and useful contributions to a worthwhile purpose" (Albrecht, 2013: 239). This includes deriving meaning *in* work, which refers to job attributes, and deriving meaning *at* work, which refers to a sense of belonging (Pratt and Ashforth, 2003). In nursing, caring tasks and caring relationships intersect to create an overall sense of value, significance, and purpose.

It may be tempting to parallel meaningful work with happiness at work. Both concepts are interrelated and generally rooted in a paradigm of positive psychology. For example, feeling connected to others and feeling productive are common elements of both experiences (Baumeister et al., 2013). However, key differences exist. As noted in the nurse's reflection at the beginning of this section, caring work can be meaningful and rewarding even though this work does not always produce outcomes that result in happiness. One key difference between meaningfulness and happiness is that happiness comes from "getting what one wants and needs" (Baumeister et al., 2013: 515). In contrast, meaningfulness emerges from actions that reflect the self and particularly from actions that aim to do good for others. However, being associated with figuring out how to benefit others, meaningfulness can actually accentuate one's stress and worries, which in turn can reduce happiness. Another key difference is that happiness tends to be linked to feeling good in the present moment. When people assess meaningfulness, they tend to take account of past, present, and future experiences and describe those events in terms of making contributions or surmounting challenges (Baumeister et al., 2013).

Based on these differences, a few conclusions about caring work can be drawn. First, clinicians involved in caring work can certainly find meaning and happiness in their work—but caring work is not necessarily dependent on happiness, whereas it does seem to benefit from a sense of meaning. In fact, intentionally finding meaning in work often provides the energy and motivation to continue being committed and invested in the goals and aims of caring, thereby avoiding compassion fatigue and burnout (Bjarnadottir, 2011; Hines and Gaughin, 2014; Rushton et al., 2015; Santos, Chambel, and Castanheira, 2016; Traudt, Liaschenko, and Peden-McAlpine, 2016; Vogt et al., 2016) and promoting patient safety (Collier et al., 2016). Second, even though caring theory often alludes to caring events or moments, it appears that the accumulation of these moments over time to the point of "becoming caring" is what actually contributes to meaningfulness in caring work.

RESEARCH ON MEANINGFUL MOMENTS
IN NURSES' CARING WORK

We conducted a qualitative, descriptive study on meaningful moments in nursing (Pavlish and Hunt, 2012). Participants included thirteen hospital nurses and thirteen public health nurses, who provided twenty-four acute care stories and thirteen public health stories that detailed meaningful moments enacted in the ordinary days of work. Nurses who work in hospitals frequently experienced a sense of worthiness and value in the connections they made during their caring work with patients and families. Nurses also described feelings of pleasure and satisfaction when making positive contributions to patient situations through individual or team effort. The feeling of worth hit a crescendo when caring work was recognized in a meaningful manner by others. The consequences of meaningfulness were profound and often described as "never forgotten" moments. These moments seemed to make the daily stress of nurses' work easier to endure and resulted in positive feelings about their work and the organization. These consequences also nurtured nurses' abilities to contribute to an environment where meaningfulness was more likely to occur.

Public health nurses also defined caring work as meaningful. These nurses described relational activities of connecting and being with clients, having an impact on people's lives, and being valued and appreciated by others. Building relationships as central to meaningful work is seen in the following narrative as a public health nurse described a meaningful moment during the research study:

> I remember a visit to a new mom. She had other school-age and preschool children who were there when I came. They didn't have any furniture except a table. [Whenever I visited,] we would go in the living room, and I would sit on the floor to check the baby. The time that I remember was when I came and they had gotten a camping chair. I came in with my scale, adult blood pressure cuff, and they [children in the family] just surrounded me... and guided me from the kitchen into the living room and sat me down in this chair. It touched my heart because here I was sitting, and mom comes in with the baby and it was just like, a cool moment. I didn't realize that it meant something to the children, but to greet me at the door and guide me in to sit in this important chair—I really felt important. It validated that what I was doing here was important to the family. When I talked to mom, I remember telling her that I was really impressed with the children—that it really made me happy. They only had one chair and this was where I was supposed to sit and to be for the visit... it really touched my heart and stands out [as a special moment].

Using a phenomenological approach, Raingruber and Wolf (2015) explored meaningfulness in oncology nursing practice and found very similar themes. Being in the moment and "opening the nurses' heart" to patients and their situations is a way of connecting with patients (p. 294). These researchers also found that when nurses recognized and responded to patients' vulnerabilities, they found work meaningful, which is very similar to our finding of making significant contributions to patients' well-being. Finally, meaningfulness was reinforced when patients expressed their gratitude to nurses, which also mirrored our findings.

CONDITIONS ESSENTIAL TO CARING AND MEANINGFUL MOMENTS

Nurses in our study also described conditions that are most conducive to nurses' opportunities to find meaning in their caring work. Recognizing both personal and structural components to work conditions, nurses alluded to shared responsibility for creating these conditions (Figure 14.1). For example, nurses highlighted personal attributes and skills such as respectful communication, openness to experiences, and learning from others. Autonomy to make decisions about client and family care along with the nurses' personal attitudes and openness to "walk side by side with that person and be there for them" were also important to public health nurses. Structural components included an organizational culture that provided both the time and space for co-workers to consult and support one another. Working with colleagues who were respectful and caring contributed to cohesive teamwork and meaningfulness. Public health nurses mentioned

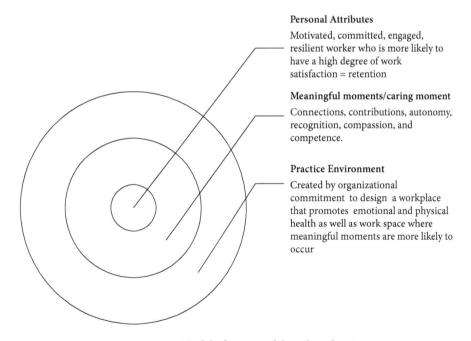

Personal Attributes
Motivated, committed, engaged, resilient worker who is more likely to have a high degree of work satisfaction = retention

Meaningful moments/caring moment
Connections, contributions, autonomy, recognition, compassion, and competence.

Practice Environment
Created by organizational commitment to design a workplace that promotes emotional and physical health as well as work space where meaningful moments are more likely to occur

FIGURE 14.1 Model of meaningful work and caring

that being part of a team effort and a valued part of the whole, as well as having opportunities to measure outcomes, contributed to making work meaningful. Similarly, Miller (2006) examined variables that impacted good work in nursing and found that cohesive teamwork was a strong contributor. In our study, a learning-focused environment and adequate time spent with patients promoted opportunities to find meaning in work. Nurses also identified constructive management (i.e. positive, approachable, supportive, respectful, empowering, and fair) as an essential condition for meaningful work.

Participants also recognized barriers to finding meaning and value in their work. These circumstances included an environment that is task-focused rather than relationship-focused. For example, a nurse stated, "Treating patients like numbers and depending on gadgets...it's like a current that flows...you get caught up in the little things and have to step away from patients. It's hard to find meaning in that." Work stress often stemmed from relational conflict and inadequate resources. For example, an acute care nurse stated, "I have no meaningful moments if I don't have time with my patients." Public health nurses need a work environment where interactions between colleagues can take place. Work in the community often allows ample access to the patient and their family but lacks opportunities to consult other nurses about care situations. Following a difficult encounter, nurses in the community do not have instant access to colleagues to confidentially discuss the case. Public health nurses expressed moral distress when working under conditions that limited healthcare access or resulted in substandard care. For example, a nurse explained, "We have lost our way to do prevention... [by the time I see patients] the damage has been done. I have cases where babies' brains have already been damaged. They lacked access to prenatal care...I get cases after the baby is born with huge problems. That's what I am seeing lately, [and] that really hurts."

Similarities with hospital and public health nurses' viewpoints about working conditions could indicate that a common set of circumstances or "opportunity structure" supports finding meaning in the work of caring (Yeoman, 2014: 39). Positive practice environments (Global Health Workforce Alliance, 2012; ICN, 2007; Roche et al., 2016) and healthy work environments for nurses (American Association of Critical-Care Nurses, 2016) seem to increase the opportunity to find meaning in caring about others. Researchers have related work environment to quality of care, healthcare outcomes, and patient safety (Aiken et al., 2011a, 2011b, 2012; Press Ganey, 2015; Purdy et al., 2010; Ulrich, 2014; Van Bogaert et al., 2013). As a result, work environments have become an important topic for research, nursing standards, and magnet credentialing (American Association of Critical-Care Nurses, 2016; Leiter and Laschinger, 2006; Stimpfel, Rosen, and McHugh, 2014; Van Bogaert et al., 2013). Workplace factors, such as the opportunity to find meaning and support during daily work, often mediate employees' work engagement, productivity, caring, and commitment (Andersson et al., 2015; Bargagliotti, 2012; Burtson and Stichler, 2010; Laschinger, Finegan, and Wilk, 2009; May, Gilson, and Harter 2004; McClelland and Vogus, 2014; Schmalenberg and Kramer, 2008). Meaningfulness has also been linked to work satisfaction, employee retention (Spence Laschinger, Zhu, and Read, 2016), quality job performance, and organization commitment

(Chalofsky, 2003; May, Gilson, and Harter, 2004; Ritter, 2011), and may act as a buffer against work stress (Allan et al., 2016) and moral distress (Rushton et al., 2015).

THE STRUGGLE TO FIND MEANING IN CARING WORK

Because nursing is recognized as a caring profession, an assumption can be made that caring work is inherently meaningful. Evidence has long revealed steady turnover and nurse burnout (Epp, 2012; Freeney and Tiernan, 2009; McConnell, 1979) and much research already exists on the topics of nursing burnout and compassion fatigue (Moss et al., 2016; Whitehead et al., 2015), which may lead to disengagement and loss of meaning at work (May et al., 2014). This section looks at other factors worth considering that can contribute to the struggle to find meaning in caring work.

The availability of life-sustaining medicines, therapies, and interventions continues to escalate, and many nurses feel trapped in this trajectory, particularly in high-acuity care. A common story is that of a patient with a chronic illness such as cancer who becomes septic and decompensates. His overall prognosis is poor and he is now waxing and waning on life support. The daily work of the nurse in this scenario, and many like it, often includes sustaining care with treatment escalation, but the end goal is unclear, or at times outright unattainable. One medical resident expressed frustration about the constant "medicalization of the dying process." It is as though *the actual caring process itself* has been upended when the caregiver feels moral distress about being trapped as a key player in the endless application of medical technology to keep patients alive. The tenets of nursing to comfort, help, and care are challenged by job responsibilities that feel as if they are contributing to suffering, medical futility, and insensitive care. Given enough of these scenarios without other options on how to compassionately approach the topic of death and dying, the nurse experiences a profound incongruence between the caring role to which he/she once felt drawn and his/her actual role. The result can be moral distress leading to loss of meaning in his/her work.

Another obstacle to finding meaning in caring work is the effect of the electronic medical record (EMR) in suppressing the narrative and its inherent power to create meaning. Consider the case of the morbidly obese teenage boy in respiratory failure who also had an underlying syndrome, which, some would say, compromised his overall quality of life. The implication is that some may perceive this patient as less worthy of extraordinary life-saving measures. At one point in his hospitalization, he had severe diarrhea requiring at least four nurses to keep him clean multiple times a shift. Many nurses found it challenging to find motivation, much less meaning, in doing this work. While documenting patient hygiene in the EMR, the bedside nurse commented, "It feels like such a disservice to us to just click those boxes: "Perineal Care" and "Linen Change." It doesn't even begin to describe all our work in caring for this patient." In its checklist form, the EMR simply fails to depict heart-wrenching details of the patient story. The narrative that matters—the one about the father calling this patient his best friend and bringing his son to various work sites where clients greet them both so fondly—is lost in the EMR. This missing narrative about the tenderness between father and son positively transformed the feelings nurses had about washing and caring for the soiled body of a young, intubated, obese patient. Only nurses can tell these important stories to each other. However, in this electronic era, they do not always tell the stories that matter—that bring meaning to their care.

For the demand and burden placed on nurses, there is rarely enough recognition or gratitude to replenish and sustain a robust sense of meaning in nurses' caring work. It is worth taking a moment to consider why this is, because in many situations, meaning-making cannot depend on external recognition or gratitude. Nurses give to and care for people who are unable to reciprocate gratitude of equal measure. Patients may be incapacitated and family members emotionally depleted. The nurse must then find his/her own ways to identify meaning in these situations, which can be challenging, but if meaning is to be found in nurses' caring work, an avenue must be discovered. Perhaps the nurse can find deeper significance in the beauty of caring for others *especially* when the care goes unrecognized, as it can highlight the caregiver's generosity of spirit all the more in a world often marked by profound self-centeredness.

Nurses are also restricted in what they can publicly share about their work, their burdens, and their heartbreaking encounters. In the United States, the Health Insurance Portability and Accountability Act of 1996 (HIPAA) places sweeping and often confusing limits on what nurses can share with people who know and care about them most. To come home from an intense shift swollen with critical moments and overwhelming emotion, but only be allowed to say "I had a hard day at work" minimizes the tremendous work of caring, silences the story of both patient and nurse, and leaves the nurse stuffing the weight of the day into an internal pocket that may or may not be adequately addressed in any meaningful way. Thus, some meaning is lost because the nurse cannot fully tell the story. Furthermore, not all friends and family members welcome talk of death, dying, and life-altering illnesses, even under the best HIPAA screening. This contributes to an additional obstacle for nurses when their loved ones struggle to hear the nurse's story because of such discomfort with these heavy topics.

By identifying means of adhering to the core tenets of nursing even in the midst of morally distressing cases, nurses preserve a sense of significance in their caring work. In looking beyond their patients and patients' families for a more intrinsic sense of appreciation for the nurse's contribution, nurses can find the work rewarding because it is humble and sacrificial, rather than in spite of these characteristics. As nurses struggle to discover ways to uphold HIPAA standards, and yet also tell their stories and the stories of their patients, they can help not only themselves but also others find and celebrate the rich meaning behind these deeply significant moments of care.

The Interaction between
Caring and Meaning

Hui-wen's reflection: I could picture the 10-month old baby girl as my own child, and the emotional connection was hard to hold at bay. These were always the hardest for me as a mother and nurse. Previously healthy, the story the family initially told providers in the ED was that she had been eating and playing like normal in the morning, but was then found purple and pulseless by her father when he checked on her during her afternoon nap. By the time they reached our hospital, she had no response to any stimulation and her EEG showed no brain activity. There was no clear physiological explanation as of yet. The family was stunned beyond tears, grief and shock sitting like a heavy cloud through which no one could see clearly. My heart ached for the entire family, and all I wanted to do as their nurse was care for them the way I would want to be cared for. But then... the ophthalmology exam revealed new findings: extensive bilateral retinal hemorrhages. Someone had abused this child, and now it was a homicide case. There was a tremendous shift in my heart from compassion to anger. WHO did this? WHY did you bring this child here for care as she died, if you had no regard for her when she lived? What do you expect me as the nurse to do for her since you have already killed her? What do you expect me to do for you as one of you pretends to grieve? I had no idea who to direct these thoughts to. Where I once sought out meaningful, compassionate eye contact, I now struggled to look at any family member or visitor at all.

There was a new level of wrestling within my heart. What meaning remained in the care I was to provide to this brain-dead child? In the care I was to provide for this family when someone amongst them was potentially the abuser, the killer? Self-awareness, self-control, and self-care were vital. I was angry and rightfully so. I was struggling to care for this family, and understandably so. I had to find the meaning, the redemption. I was committed to giving them my best, for the sake of this child, for the sake of those who did not hurt her and grieved, even for the sake of the one who did hurt her and may still have been grieving nonetheless. It may not have been within my right to know the details but I was committed to giving them my best, because this is what makes me a wholehearted caregiver, in the worst of circumstances.

I made a conscious decision despite the anger and disgust: I will care for this child because even in brain death, she has a right to compassion, to tenderness, to justice, to excellence, and to the opportunity to donate her organs if her family chooses to do so. I will care for this family because I do not know the story and I am not their ultimate judge. I am a caregiver who sees genuine grief, and I will respond with gracious compassion. Withholding this from people whose story I do not know will make my work less

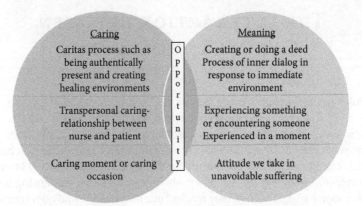

Caring		Meaning
Caritas process such as being authentically present and creating healing environments	O p p o r t u n i t y	Creating or doing a deed Process of inner dialog in response to immediate environment
Transpersonal caring-relationship between nurse and patient		Experiencing something or encountering someone Experienced in a moment
Caring moment or caring occasion		Attitude we take in unavoidable suffering

FIGURE 14.2 Parallels in caring (Watson) and meaning (Frankl)

powerful, less meaningful. I will tell the larger story of all those children who have come through our doors due to abuse, to empower others to speak up when they suspect abuse, to support parents on the edge of abuse. I will extend compassion to the grieving mother who may very well soon discover that she has not only lost her child to death, but will soon be losing her partner to jail time as well. If I do not know the facts, I cannot withhold compassion from someone who may need it in overwhelming measure to survive the upcoming days, weeks, months, years. Even in this scenario, there is tremendous meaning behind my caring work.

Frankl's ways of creating meaning are evident in the nurse's narrative of providing care to the injured child (Figure 14.2). When attending to the needs of the child and family, the nurse both experiences something, the devastating condition of the child, and encounters someone, the severely injured child but also realizes that the parents or someone close to the child may be responsible. The nurse's attitude toward the situation evolves as she struggles to focus on the caritas process while continuing to care for the child. Through her moment-to-moment quest to create meaning, she takes the opportunity to step back and mindfully transform the experience of caring for a child suffering from a blatant, avoidable injury to discover meaning in the pledge to care—not only for this child and family but also for a larger community where child abuse quietly resides.

CONCLUSION

The very nature of illness and injury brings together many people in search of meaning. Each individual—the patient, their family, the housekeeper washing the floor, the translator repeating bad news, and the clinicians—struggling as they witness suffering, challenges beyond measure, as well as heroic interventions with good outcomes just down the hall. For the nurse, close proximity, which creates intimacy, and the extensive time engaged with the patient and family may be the crucible of finding meaning in work. The very nature of that position places meaning and care at the core of the nursing profession. Caring responses are not the clichés so frequently heard after tragedy. In fact, caring is often conveyed without a single word or with a few simple words. Caring gestures that signal "we are in this together" can create the gateway to a journey that is filled with meaning-making and often becomes the stories that sustain generations of families, clinicians, and entire communities.

> **Katherine's reflection:** I am reminded of a role-playing session with a group of medical students in which the actor portrayed a patient receiving a new diagnosis with a poor prognosis, and after some discussion and coaching one of the medical students took on the role of informing the patient. Clinging to his clipboard he struggled valiantly, attempting to use statistics to soften the blow, to make sense of the unbearable. I motioned for a timeout and said quietly to the student to put down the papers, to take the patient's hand, to look him in the eye, to face both his own fears as well as the patient's, allowing for the awful news to sit in silence and then slowly conveying the most important message—we will be with you as you go through this journey. The student in that moment understood the role and it terrified him to appreciate what it might mean. Despite careful modeling, he decided to forgo a career in clinical work as he had planned and become a researcher. He felt he did not have the capability to face the responsibility of making meaning in the midst of existential free fall.
>
> Many years later, I ran into him on a hospital unit; he revealed that despite the excitement of the lab it was not enough. He said he often went back to that moment of mentoring, when he felt so helpless, but also began to appreciate the moments where the transformation of caring could happen. He sought work in the clinic because he now understood the power of meaningful work as he learned to move beyond his fear and enter into the seeming abyss where, with heartfelt intention and service, his vocation could be realized.

The potentiality and actuality of finding meaning not only in work but in life itself quickly becomes apparent. Nursing provides many layers of meaningful presence, their magnitude often unseen or unknown. Sometimes the story comes back to us, as it did in this chance encounter, and we come to realize how one small intentional encounter ripples out into the world. Searching for and reflecting on meaning becomes the wellspring that helps balance the draining aspects of caring work, and perhaps even more importantly, is a constant reminder of the richness of a life well lived.

Final Thoughts
Parted by Love
You believe your love of biology
and your heart's desire of helping others
will be more than enough.
Until these first few patients become yours.
Pure innocence,
they are so young and untarnished yet
ravaged by trauma and disease

your heart falls a million miles
and you are only twenty-two,
so young yourself
perfectly perched with your university degree
that taught you the periodic table and thankfully ethics
but not how to hold a dying child,
not how to make meaning of all that should not be.
Little by little you are broken down
witnessing, not willing to give in
you go in search of
explanations, creating order
a soothing balm
and find it is the responding,
that changes everything.
Meaning,
the many threads have been woven
into a tapestry of caring.
The toddler
finally sleeps in your arms,
death will come
gently
as the night is parted by love.

Katherine Brown-Saltzman

References

Aiken, L. H., Cimiotti, J. P., Sloane, D. M., Smith, H. L., Flynn, L., and Neff, D. F. (2011). "The effects of nurse staffing and nurse education on patient deaths in hospitals with different nurse work environments." *Medical Care*, 49(12), 1047–53.

Aiken, L. H., Sermeus, W., Van den Heede, K., Sloane, D. M., Busse, R., McKee, M., Bruyneel, L., Rafferty, A. M., Griffiths, P., Moreno-Casbas, M. T. and Tishelman, C. (2012). "Patient safety, satisfaction, and quality of hospital care: Cross sectional surveys of nurses and patients in 12 countries in Europe and the United States." *BMJ*, 344, e1717.

Aiken, L. H., Sloane, D. M., Clarke, S., Poghosyan, L., Cho, E., You, L., Finlayson, M., Kanai-Pak, M., and Aungsuroch, Y. (2011). "Importance of work environments on hospital outcomes in nine countries." *International Journal for Quality in Health Care*, 23(4), 357–64.

Albrecht, S. L. (2013). "Work Engagement and the Positive Power of Meaningful Work." In A. B. Bakker (ed.), *Advances in Positive Organizational Psychology*, vol. 1, pp. 237–60. Bingley: Emerald Group Publishing Limited.

Allan, B. A., Douglass, R. P., Duffy, R. D., and McCarty, R. J. (2016). "Meaningful work as a moderator of the relation between work stress and meaning in life." *Journal of Career Assessment*, 24(3), 429–40.

American Association of Critical-Care Nurses. (2016). *AACN Standards for Establishing and Sustaining Healthy Work Environments* [web page]: https://www.aacn.org/nursing-excellence/standards/aacn-standards-for-establishing-and-sustaining-healthy-work-environments [accessed June 28, 2018].

American Nurses Association. (2015). *Code of Ethics for Nurses with interpretive statements* [web page]: http://nursingworld.org/DocumentVault/Ethics-1/Code-of-Ethics-for-Nurses. html [accessed June 28, 2018].

American Nurses Association. (2016). *ANA FAQs* [web page]: http://www.nursingworld.org/ FunctionalMenuCategories/FAQs#def [accessed June 28, 2018].

Andersson, E. K., Willman, A., Sjöström-Strand, A., and Borglin, G. (2015). "Registered nurses' descriptions of caring: A phenomenographic interview study." *BMC Nursing*, 14(1), 16.

Bargagliotti, L. A. (2012). "Work engagement in nursing: A concept analysis." *Journal of Advanced Nursing*, 68(6), 1414–28.

Baumeister, R. F., Vohs, K. D., Aaker, J. L., and Garbinsky, E. N. (2013). "Some key differences between a happy life and a meaningful life." *The Journal of Positive Psychology*, 8(6), 505–16.

Bjarnadottir, A. (2011). "Work engagement among nurses in relationally demanding jobs in the hospital sector." *Nordic Journal of Nursing Research*, 31(3), 30–4.

Burtson, P. L. and Stichler, J. F. (2010). "Nursing work environment and nurse caring: Relationship among motivational factors." *Journal of Advanced Nursing*, 66(8), 1819–31.

Canzan, F., Heilemann, M. V., Saiani, L., Mortari, L., and Ambrosi, E. (2014). "Visible and invisible caring in nursing from the perspectives of patients and nurses in the gerontological context." *Scandinavian Journal of Caring Sciences*, 28(4), 732–40.

Chalofsky, N. (2003). "An emerging construct for meaningful work." *Human Resource Development International*, 6(1), 69–83.

Collier, S. L., Fitzpatrick, J. J., Siedlecki, S. L., and Dolansky, M. A. (2016). "Employee engagement and a culture of safety in the intensive care unit." *Journal of Nursing Administration*, 46(1), 49–54.

Desmond, M. E., Horn, S., Keith, K., Kelby, S., Ryan, L., and Smith, J. (2014). "Incorporating caring theory into personal and professional nursing practice to improve perception of care." *International Journal for Human Caring*, 18(1), 35–44.

Epp, K. (2012). "Burnout in critical care nurses: A literature review." *Dynamics*, 23(4), 25–31.

Finfgeld-Connett, D. (2008). "Meta-synthesis of caring in nursing." *Journal of Clinical Nursing*, 17(2), 196–204.

Frankl, V. E. (2000). *Man's Search for Ultimate Meaning*. Cambridge, MA: Perseus.

Freeney, Y. M. and Tiernan, J. (2009). "Exploration of the facilitators of and barriers to work engagement in nursing." *International Journal of Nursing Studies*, 46, 1557–65.

Global Health Workforce Alliance. (2012). *Positive Practice Environments Campaign* [web page]: http://www.who.int/workforcealliance/about/initiatives/ppe/en/ [accessed June 28, 2018].

Griffiths, J., Speed, S., Horne, M., and Keeley, P. (2012). "'A caring professional attitude': What service users and carers seek in graduate nurses and the challenge for educators." *Nurse Education Today*, 32(2), 121–7.

Harrowing, J. N. (2011). "Compassion practice by Ugandan nurses who provide HIV care." *OJIN: The Online Journal of Issues in Nursing*, 16(1), 5. Available at: http://www.nursingworld. org/MainMenuCategories/ANAMarketplace/ANAPeriodicals/OJIN/Tableof Contents/Vol-16-2011/No1-Jan-2011/Compassion-Practice-and-HIV-Care-.html [accessed June 28, 2018].

Hines, M. E. and Gaughan, J. (2014). "Pediatric nurses acknowledging praxis: Recognizing caring in reflective narratives." *International Journal for Human Caring*, 18(3), 26–35.

International Council of Nurses. (2002). *Definition of Nursing* [web page]: http://www.icn.ch/ who-we-are/icn-definition-of-nursing/ [accessed June 28, 2018].

International Council of Nurses. (2007). *Positive Practice Environments: Quality workplaces = quality care* [online]: http://www.icn.ch/publications/2007-positive-practice-environments-quality-workplaces-quality-patient-care/ [accessed June 28, 2018].

International Council of Nurses. (2012). *The ICN Code of Ethics for Nurses.* Geneva: International Council of Nurses. Available at: http://www.icn.ch/images/stories/documents/about/icncode_english.pdf [accessed June 28, 2018].

Jarrin, O. F. (2012). "The integrality of situated caring in nursing and the environment." *ANS. Advances in Nursing Science*, 35(1), 14–24.

Joolaee, S., Joolaei, A., Tschudin, V., Bahrani, N., and Nikbakht-Nasrabadi, A. (2010). "Caring relationship: The core component of patients' rights practice as experienced by patients and their companions." *Journal of Medical Ethics and History of Medicine*, 3, 4.

Laschinger, H. K. S., Finegan, J., and Wilk, P. (2009). "Context matters: The impact of unit leadership and empowerment on nurses' organizational commitment." *Journal of Nursing Administration*, 39(5), 228–35.

Leiter, M. P. and Laschinger, H. (2006). "Relationships of work and practice environment to professional burnout." *Nursing Research*, 55, 137–46.

Leyva, E. W. A., Peralta, A. B., Tejero, L. M. S., and Santos, M. A. (2015). "Global perspectives of caring: An integrative review." *International Journal for Human Caring*, 19(4), 7–29.

May, D. R., Gilson, R. L., and Harter, L. M. (2004). "The psychological conditions of meaningfulness, safety and availability and the engagement of the human spirit at work." *Journal of Occupational and Organizational Psychology*, 77(1), 11–37.

May, D. R., Li, C., Mencl, J., and Huang, C. C. (2014). "The ethics of meaningful work: Types and magnitude of job-related harm and the ethical decision-making process." *Journal of Business Ethics*, 121(4), 651–69.

McClelland, L. E. and Vogus, T. J. (2014). "Compassion practices and HCAHPS: Does rewarding and supporting workplace compassion influence patient perceptions?" *Health Services Research*, 49(5), 1670–83.

McConnell, E. (1979). "Burnout and the critical care nurse." *Critical Care Update*, 6, 5–14.

Miller, J. F. (2006). "Opportunities and obstacles for good work in nursing." *Nursing Ethics*, 13(5), 471–87.

Moss, M., Good, V. S., Gozal, D., Kleinpell, R., and Sessler, C. N. (2016). "An official critical care societies collaborative statement—burnout syndrome in critical care health-care professionals: A call for action." *CHEST Journal*, 150(1), 17–26.

Owens, R. A. (2006). "The caring behaviors of the home health nurse and influence on medication adherence." *Home Healthcare Now*, 24(8), 517–26.

Palese, A., Tomietto, M., Suhonen, R., Efstathiou, G., Tsangari, H., Merkouris, A., Jarosova, D., Leino-Kilpi, H., Patiraki, E., Karlou, C., and Balogh, Z. (2011). "Surgical patient satisfaction as an outcome of nurses' caring behaviors: A descriptive and correlational study in six European countries." *Journal of Nursing Scholarship*, 43(4), 341–50.

Pavlish, C. and Hunt, R. (2012). "An exploratory study about meaningful work in acute care nursing." *Nursing Forum*, 47(2), 113–22.

Pratt, M. G. and Ashforth, B. E. (2003). "Fostering Meaningfulness in Working and at Work." In K. Cameron, J. Dutton, and R. Quinn (eds.), *Positive Organizational Scholarship: Foundations of a new discipline*, pp. 309–27. San Francisco: Berrett-Koehler.

Press Ganey Associates (2015). *Nursing Special Report: The influence of nurse work environment on patient, payment and nurse outcomes in acute care settings.* South Bend: IN: Press

Ganey. Available at: http://healthcare.pressganey.com/2015-Nursing-SR_Influence_Work_ Environment [accessed July 16, 2018].

Purdy, N., Spence Laschinger, H. K., Finegan, J., Kerr, M., and Olivera, F. (2010). "Effects of work environments on nurse and patient outcomes." *Journal of Nursing Management*, 18(8), 901–13.

Raingruber, B. and Wolf, T. (2015). "Nurse perspectives regarding the meaningfulness of oncology nursing practice." *Clinical Journal of Oncology Nursing*, 19(3), 292–6.

Ritter, D. (2011). "The relationship between healthy work environments and retention of nurses in a hospital setting." *Journal of Nursing Management*, 19(1), 27–32.

Roche, M., Duffield, C., Friedman, S., Twigg, D., Dimitrelis, S., and Rowbotham, S. (2016). "Changes to nurses' practice environment over time." *Journal of Nursing Management*, 24(5), 666–75.

Rushton, C. H., Batcheller, J., Schroeder, K., and Donohue, P. (2015). "Burnout and resilience among nurses practicing in high-intensity settings." *American Journal of Critical Care*, 24(5), 412–20.

Santos, A., Chambel, M. J., and Castanheira, F. (2016). "Relational job characteristics and nurses' affective organizational commitment: The mediating role of work engagement." *Journal of Advanced Nursing*, 72(2), 294–305.

Schmalenberg, C. and Kramer, M. (2008). "Essentials of a productive nurse work environment." *Nursing Research*, 57(1), 2–13.

Sinclair, S., McClement, S., Raffin-Bouchal, S., Hack, T. F., Hagen, N. A., McConnell, S., and Chochinov, H. M. (2016). "Compassion in health care: An empirical model." *Journal of Pain and Symptom Management*, 51(2), 193–203.

Spence Laschinger, H. K., Zhu, J., and Read, E. (2016). "New nurses' perceptions of professional practice behaviours, quality of care, job satisfaction and career retention." *Journal of Nursing Management*, 24(5), 656–65.

Stimpfel, A. W., Rosen, J. E., and McHugh, M. D. (2014). "Understanding the role of the professional practice environment on quality of care in Magnet® and non-Magnet hospitals." *The Journal of Nursing Administration*, 44(1), 10–16.

Tejero, L. (2012). "The mediating role of the nurse–patient dyad bonding in bringing about patient satisfaction." *Journal of Advanced Nursing*, 68, 994–1002.

Traudt, T., Liaschenko, J., and Peden-McAlpine, C. (2016). "Moral agency, moral imagination, and moral community: Antidotes to moral distress." *The Journal of Clinical Ethics*, 27(3), 201–13.

Tronto, J. (1993). *Moral Boundaries: A political argument for an ethic of care*. New York: Routledge.

Ulrich, B. T., Lavandero, R., Woods, D., and Early, S. (2014). "Critical care nurse work environments 2013: A status report." *Critical Care Nurse*, 34(4), 64–79.

Van Bogaert, P., Kowalski, C., Weeks, S. M., Van heusden, D., and Clarke, S. P. (2013). "The relationship between nurse practice environment, nurse work characteristics, burnout and job outcome and quality of nursing care: A cross-sectional survey." *International Journal of Nursing Studies*, 50, 1667–77.

Vogt, K., Hakanen, J. J., Jenny, G. J., and Bauer, G. F. (2016). "Sense of coherence and the motivational process of the job-demands-resources model." *Journal of Occupational Health Psychology*, 21(2), 194–207.

Watson, J. (2012). *Human Caring Science: A theory of nursing*. Sudbury, MA: Jones & Bartlett.

Whitehead, P. B., Herbertson, R. K., Hamric, A. B., Epstein, E. G., and Fisher, J. M. (2015). "Moral distress among healthcare professionals: Report of an institution-wide survey." *Journal of Nursing Scholarship*, 47(2), 117–25.

Wolf, Z., King, B., and France, N. (2015). "Antecedent context and structure of communication during a caring moment: Scoping review and analysis." *International Journal for Human Caring*, 19(2), 7–21.

World Health Organization (WHO). (2016). *Global Strategic Directions for Strengthening Nursing and Midwifery, 2016–2020.* Geneva: WHO. Available at: http://www.who.int/hrh/ nursing_midwifery/global-strategy-midwifery-2016-2020/en/ [accessed June 28, 2018].

Yeoman, R. (2014). *Meaningful Work and Workplace Democracy: A philosophy of work and a politics of meaningfulness.* New York: Palgrave Macmillan.

CHAPTER 15

EXPLORING MEANINGFUL WORK IN THE THIRD SECTOR

REBECCA TAYLOR AND SILKE ROTH

INTRODUCTION

THERE has been a surge of interest in the notion of and possibilities for meaningful work—i.e. work that is experienced as holding positive meaning and significance for individuals (Bailey and Madden, 2017; Rosso, Dekas, and Wrzesniewski, 2010). These debates have arisen alongside and partly in relation to wider concerns about an increasingly polarized labor market in which intensification, outsourcing, and declining representation have created the context for a proliferation of poor-quality, precarious, and undervalued work (Standing, 2011). The notion of meaningful work, offering an alternative vision, contributes to a broader project to identify and define "good jobs" and "good work" (Kalleberg, 2011; Taylor, 2017). However, meaningful work itself is not clearly defined. Scholars in diverse disciplines, from psychology and management studies to career guidance, have identified various sources and locations of meaningful work such as tasks, roles, interactions, and organizations or focal constructs such as "the self" and "the other" (Bailey et al., 2017; Lips-Wiersma and Morris, 2009; Rosso, Dekas, and Wrzesniewski, 2010).

In sociology, discussions draw on classically informed ideas about meaningfulness in work—autonomy and freedom, vocation and calling, dignity, and self-realization. These suggest meaningful work has both intrinsic subjective dimensions and more extrinsic, objective dimensions. Work can be inherently meaningful because it is useful or expressive or serves a common good or "transcendent life purpose" (Duffy and Dik, 2013), and it can be meaningful because the conditions mean the worker is afforded autonomy, dignity, and respect (Sennett, 1998; Simpson et al., 2014; Sayer, 2007). Yet there is no single definition which resolves how these dimensions and factors intersect or constitute meaningfulness. If we are to understand how work can be meaningful and the possibilities for the promotion of meaningful work as a "fundamental human need" (Yeoman, 2014) then it seems important to explore empirical knowledge on how work is subjectively experienced "on the ground" by workers in different social contexts, in particular occupations, sectors, and fields, and to keep a critical eye on the social and cultural constructions of what is defined as meaningful.

In this chapter we explore work in one particular arena—the third sector (also called the voluntary or nonprofit sector)—and examine the way this work might be experienced as meaningful or not by those working there. This is not a straightforward undertaking. Not only is meaningful work a rather nebulous idea, but the third sector is itself a diverse and contested terrain that evades generalization (Salamon and Sokolowski, 2016; Kendall, 2003). It is constituted by an array of organizations that differ in their form, function, and legal status, and include charities, community associations, non-governmental organizations (NGOs), activist groups, unions, and social enterprises (Kendall, 2003; Salamon, 2015). These operate at global, national, or local levels, providing a spectrum of functions and services, in a range of fields from health and social service to recreation, political activism, and humanitarian aid. Third sector organizations (TSOs) have various relations with the state and the private sector and their workers may or may not be paid. Some have multimillion pound budgets, smart premises, and are highly professionalized; others have tiny budgets, no formal office space, and rely solely on volunteers (Salamon and Sokolowski, 2016; NCVO, 2016). However, TSOs share some key features. Most are self-governing, exercise limits on profit distribution, and operate with some notion of serving the common good. In other words they have social, political, or environmental aims and are values-driven rather than primarily profit-driven (Salamon and Sokolowski, 2016; Evers and Laville, 2004).

These broad characteristics make the sector a pertinent context for exploring meaningful work and may partly explain why meaningful work is a recurring, albeit largely unexamined, trope in studies of the sector. First, the sector's workforce are seen to reflect their organizations' aims to serve a greater good and to be interested in social values rather than economic reward (Wuthnow, 2004; Evers and Laville, 2004; Dempsey and Saunders, 2010). This is particularly the case for volunteers, who in the absence of material recompense are seen to be motivated by symbolic rewards associated with altruism and prosocial behavior (Taylor, 2015; Musick and Wilson, 2008). Work in the sector tends to be regarded, at least discursively, as vocational, and as intrinsically meaningful to the worker (Dempsey and Saunders, 2010; Kuhn et al., 2008; Duffy and Dik, 2013). Second, the sector's "independence" from, or intermediate position between, the state and the market implies that it has the potential to offer its workers freedom from both state bureaucracy and regulation and the financial imperatives of the market (Smith, 2011; Evers and Laville, 2004) and in turn worker autonomy and self-determination provide meaningful work (Dempsey and Saunders, 2010).

However, other factors would appear to challenge the assumption that work in the sector must be meaningful. Employment is often low paid and insecure with poor terms and conditions and higher levels of underemployment than the other two sectors (Leete, 2006). The independence of the sector is, in reality, patchy and contingent with processes of professionalization and marketization reducing the scope for autonomy and self-determination in some areas (Smith, 2011; Salamon and Sokolowski, 2016). There is a fundamental paradox at the heart of these debates (Bunderson and Thompson, 2009; Berkelaar and Buzzanell, 2015). Work in the sector can simultaneously be meaningful for workers, while at the same time undervalued, exploitative, and stressful, resulting in those same workers experiencing "burnout" or disillusionment (Cox, 2009; Chen and Gorski, 2015; Rosso, Dekas, and Wrzesniewski, 2010; Dempsey and Saunders, 2010).

In this chapter we look first at the concept of meaningful work and, drawing on classical debates in sociology, explore the various dimensions that might be seen to constitute it. We then outline what is known about the sector's paid and unpaid work-force and focus on three different fields within the sector: social service, political activism, and humanitarian aid. Drawing on empirical studies of workers' subjective experiences and motivations, we explore what, if anything, makes this work meaningful. In doing so we highlight the different ways meaningfulness is experienced, how understandings are shaped by social identity and life course, and the paradox that meaningful work in the sector can also be the source of stress and burnout.

WHAT IS MEANINGFUL WORK?

The origins of the concept of meaningful work can be located in classical social theory where scholars, documenting the shift to industrial capitalism, mourned the loss of meaning they saw in the dwindling craft skills and workmanship of a pre-industrial era (Veblen, 1914; Wright Mills, 1956; Sennett, 2009). Marx's account of the alienated worker, for whom routinized manual work meant separation of the self from the product of labor, implied a loss of autonomy and dignity (Marx, 1988). Alienation, freighted with notions of powerlessness, normlessness, and isolation (Seeman, 1959), came to capture the plight of the modern worker (Blauner, 1964; Braverman, 1998 [1974]). Yet Weber, approaching the problem of the modern worker from a different angle, saw Calvinist teaching on working for the greater good and fulfilling talents given by God, as providing the possibility for work to be inherently virtuous—a calling (Weber, 1958 [1930]). As such these classical debates contain an underlying distinction between the intrinsic meaningfulness of work, captured by Weber's notion of a calling, and the extrinsic meaningfulness afforded when the conditions of work respect human dignity and autonomy rather than exploit it.

In contemporary debates about meaningful work the idea of a "calling" or vocation has been secularized. It refers to work or a career driven by a personal need, passion, or an external summons (which may or may not be religious) to contribute to the greater good that echoes its Weberian origins (Cuilla, 2000; Duffy and Dik, 2013; Madden, Bailey, and Kerr, 2015). While a vocation or calling can be a summons to creative or expressive or indeed any kind of work, it tends to be associated with ideas of altruistic and selfless commitment to others (Hunter, Dik, and Banning, 2010). Reviewing the debates, Duffy and Dik (2013: 429) note that "calling is most often defined as a highly meaningful career that is used to help others in some fashion." Certain professions such as a medicine, social work, nursing, and teaching are seen to embody these motivations, as do the third sector or the public sector with their focus on social service and care (Dik and Duffy, 2009).

A second strand in contemporary debates about meaningful work invokes the notion of dignity, being treated as worthy of honor and respect (Yeoman, 2014), and rests on an understanding of industrial capitalism's denial of the humanity of the worker (Hodgkiss, 2015; Bolton, 2007). Multiple challenges to workers' dignity (echoing early accounts of the alienated worker) include abuse, poor management, overwork, and lack of participation and involvement (Hodson, 2001). A further distinction between "dignity in work" and "dignity at work" (Bolton, 2007) reflects intrinsic/extrinsic dimensions of meaningful work. In the former, the act of working brings dignity and meaning to individuals' lives. In the latter, meaningful work is an issue of ethical work practices; workers have rights, a voice, and are not bullied and harassed. It is employers' responsibility, even duty, to ensure work is meaningful (Michaelson, 2011) and, more than that, dignity at work is achieved by respecting workers, treating them as people, and trusting them to act autonomously (Sayer, 2007). Workers' autonomy, their capacity to dictate the terms of their labor, what they do and how they do it, constitutes an important articulation of meaningful work.

A third strand in the meaningful work debates draws on ideas of self-realization or personal development: processes through which individuals fulfill their possibilities and potentials and in doing so find meaningfulness in their work. The origins of these ideas lie partly in the emergence of humanistic psychology in the mid-twentieth century, and in particular the work of Maslow (1943) who sought to conceptualize a hierarchy of human needs in which he positioned self-actualization at the pinnacle of the pyramid. The search for meaningfulness through self-realization means securing work that aligns with personal values, develops skills, and fulfills individual potentials (Bandura, 1977). While much of this discussion draws on work psychology and various notions of self-concept and work redesign (Hackman and Oldham, 1980; Rosso, Dekas, and Wrzesniewski, 2010; Grant, 2007), narratives of personal growth have also been explored in sociological debates about reflexive modernity and the processes of individualization in which self-identity becomes an organized endeavor in a reflexive project of the self (Beck, 1992; Giddens, 1991).

These ideas of autonomy, vocation, dignity, and self-realization that populate contemporary debates are not definitive but capture the complexity of the issues at stake in attempting to conceptualize and explore meaningful work empirically. How these ideas are articulated in individuals' experiences of meaningful work in particular contexts is an important question. Below we focus in on one particular context, the third sector, and outline the contours and parameters of work in the sector.

PAID AND UNPAID WORK
IN THE THIRD SECTOR

Work in the sector is as diverse as the types of organization that constitute it. Its workers occupy a range of occupations and roles from formal professional positions such as fundraiser, human resources manager, nurse, or accountant, to jobs such as befriender, driver, or administrative assistant (NCVO, 2015). While a swathe of the work is unpaid, the distinction between paid and unpaid workers is not always clear. Some paid staff also "donate work" by undertaking voluntary work for the same organization (Baines, 2004; Almond and Kendall, 2000) and some volunteers receive a nominal fee or stipend and might more accurately be described as very low-paid workers (Taylor, 2015; Musick and Wilson, 2008). Many of those providing aid in disaster zones for organizations like Oxfam, for example, are low-paid or unpaid "volunteering professionals" such as doctors, engineers, logisticians, and nurses (Shutt, 2012; Eltanani, 2016). Either way, whether a worker is paid or unpaid in the sector does not define their understanding and experiences of meaningfulness in work.

Across the sector employees experience a broad range of working conditions. Pay is generally lower than in the public and particularly the private sector. What is termed the "third sector wage discount" means workers earn less than those in other sectors operating in that particular industry or field, although the gap has been closing (Leete, 2001; Rutherford, 2015). Yet not all staff are poorly paid and a small number of executive salaries in international NGOs are comparable with the for-profit sector (Stroup, 2012). The insecure funding arrangements for many organizations in the sector are reflected in a higher prevalence of non-standard contracts such as part-time and fixed term arrangements (Almond and Kendall, 2000; Leete, 2006)—what could be defined as precarious or poor-quality jobs (Standing, 2011; Kalleberg, 2011). In the UK as many as 40 percent of employed staff are on part-time contracts and around 10 percent on some form of temporary contract. And compared to the other two sectors, workers also tend to be overqualified and underemployed, i.e. working fewer hours than they would like or in jobs that do not match their qualifications (Almond and Kendall, 2000; NCVO, 2016; Clark and Wilding, 2011; Mirvis, 1992). However, within the sector there is significant variation and an ever shifting landscape in those parts of the sector that maintain a relationship with the state and its various policy agendas. Employees of TSOs contracted to deliver public services are likely to have experienced the intensification and under-resourcing of work as effects of outsourcing and austerity (Baines, 2011). Low-paid domestic care roles in particular are likely to be zero hours or "on call" arrangements (Rubery and Urwin, 2011). Yet others, working, or more likely volunteering, for small community or activist groups operating largely outside state governance and funding structures, may have seen little change to their working conditions and pay.

Studies of the motivations for working in the sector, particularly subjective accounts, illuminate some of what individuals find meaningful about the work. Staff report higher levels of job satisfaction than in other sectors despite lower wages (Donegani, McKay, and Moro, 2012; Benz, 2005; Borzaga and Depedri, 2005). Low remuneration is argued to be offset by various symbolic rewards that come from working for a greater good, helping those in need or promoting social justice (Grant, 2007: Cunningham, 2011; Baines, 2011; Borzaga and Tortia, 2006; Onyx and Maclean, 1996). Studies suggest workers seek out workplaces that reflect their core values or beliefs (Rosso, Dekas, and Wrzesniewski, 2010) whether those are in faith-based organizations (Wuthnow, 2004), political activist groups (Andrews, 2007), humanitarian organizations (Roth, 2015), or those that provide social justice through social care (Baines, 2004, 2011). Research on the motivations of unpaid volunteers highlight a similar set of values-based motivations for doing the work and which shape how it is framed as meaningful (Dempsey and Saunders, 2010; Musick and Wilson, 2008). However, not everyone who works in the sector does so because it reflects their values or beliefs. Some sector workers are there by accident and have little affinity for the cause or the values of their organization (Taylor, 2005; Harrow and Mole, 2005), and instrumental motivations for volunteering such as getting work experience are well documented (Taylor, 2015; Eliasoph, 2011; Lyons et al., 2012; Musick and Wilson, 2008).

EXPLORING MEANINGFUL WORK IN THREE THIRD SECTOR FIELDS

We explore meaningful work by looking in more detail at three fields of work within the third sector—social service, political activism, and humanitarian aid work. Few studies directly address the question of what makes the work meaningful for the workers themselves, so instead we review research that explored the experience and subjective motivations of workers. Although this involves a certain amount of interpretation, these qualitative studies provide useful insights into how workers articulate what they find meaningful and an opportunity to test out whether notions of autonomy, freedom, calling, vocation, dignity, and self-realization are reflected in their narratives.

Social Service

A significant proportion of paid and unpaid work in the third sector is carried out in organizations providing some form of social service (Salamon and Sokolowski, 2016; NCVO, 2014). The work involves diverse activities and services that range from befriending older people or running a youth club to providing advocacy for refugees (NCVO, 2014). While some of this will be supported by donations and legacies, a large proportion involves delivering services in partnership with the state, supported by grants and contracts, meaning work in the field is shaped by shifting policy priorities and outsourcing arrangements (Salamon, 2015; Alcock and Kendall, 2011; Cunningham and James, 2011). Care work is a central component of work in the field and this is work that is often gendered and undervalued (Baines, 2011; McDonald and Charlesworth, 2011).

In studies of the subjective experiences and motivations of those in social service roles, workers reflected the values of their organization and articulated the importance of its social value (social inclusion, participation, and social justice) and contributing to the greater good (Baines, 2010; Nickson et al., 2008). Phrases such as "wanting to make a difference to people's lives," and "giving something back" were expressed as part of a vocational narrative which framed the cause, the work itself, as the source of meaning (Hardill and Baines, 2011; Harrow and Mole, 2005). In a study of third sector CEOs, for example, Harrow and Mole (2005) identified one group—"the paid philanthropists"—whose career narratives emphasized a lifelong commitment to the cause and their prioritizing of working "for love not money" (p. 93). But other narratives were also visible. Young graduates undertaking paid and unpaid work for refugee organizations wanted to work in the sector and to "make a difference," but couched this work not as a calling but as a skilled professional career with social value (Taylor, 2004, 2005). Careerist CEOs identified by Harrow and Mole (2005) were interested in the possibility work in the sector gave them for skilled and interesting work, and drew on notions of autonomy and self-development in their accounts of what motivated them to work in the sector.

What workers in these studies understood and articulated as meaningful or at least important and motivating about their work was shaped by social position (gender, class, ethnicity) and where they were in their career and life course. Several studies of social service work located in deindustrialized towns in England revealed a different way of understanding and articulating what individuals found meaningful about their work (see for example Hardill and Baines, 2009, 2011; Parry, 2005; Taylor, 2005). For these staff and volunteers, what made their work meaningful—its social value—was the role it played in sustaining their local community in the face of endemic unemployment and high levels of poverty. Many of the workers in Halford, Leonard, and Bruce's (2015) study of a small community support center for people with learning and physical disabilities in a deprived area of the UK had worked in local fishing and food processing industries, before being made redundant as these industries contracted. One participant in his 50s had become a trustee of several local charities and found personal reward in giving something back to the area in which he was born and had lived his life (Halford, Leonard, and Bruce, 2015). In these studies meaningfulness was embedded in working-class narratives of community self-help rather than a more middle-class narrative around calling or vocation. Parry's (2003) study highlighted how in the context of high unemployment in post-mining communities some individuals strategically embraced unpaid community work, seeing it as a "fulfilling" and "socially useful" alternative to unemployment. While the social value of the work was important, its meaningfulness for individuals was shaped by the context in which they were undertaking the work.

Political Activism

The third sector also includes activists who are engaged in trade unions, citizen groups, political parties, and social movement organizations connected to various causes such as the environment, gender equality, the rights of lesbian, gay, bisexual, trans, or queer (LGBTQ) people, rights of ethnic minorities and migrants, social justice, and human rights (NCVO, 2016). Non-governmental human rights organizations like Amnesty International, or the Occupy movement engage in a wide range of more or less polite or disruptive strategies to bring about or prevent social change (Saunders and Roth, 2019 forthcoming). Some activists are employed in formal non-governmental organizations—Amnesty International, for example, employs human rights activists (Hopgood, 2006; Rodgers, 2010)—but some are freelance and undertake insecure work for various organizations (Eltanani, 2016). Many activists are unpaid and this work may vary substantially from informal part-time campaigning work to full-time formal volunteering (Roth, 2016). The latter, formalized in large NGOs, has been described as "bureaucratic activism" because it is tightly defined and controlled (Hensby, Sibthorpe, and Driver, 2012). As such, activist work is often conducted alongside or juggled with other forms of occupation or paid work. Examining the narratives of four generations of activists, Newman (2012) revealed how voluntary participation in grassroots organizations was supported by paid positions in trade unions, political parties, and academia.

Studies of workers' experiences of social movement organizations and other forms of activism provide useful insights into the way in which this work relates to the wider debates on meaningful work. Studies of activists' narratives reveal the risks and costs that are involved (high-risk, high-cost, low-risk, low-cost) (McAdam, 1986) and the tension between altruism and sacrifice which underpin the notion of activism as a vocation or calling. Full-time staff working for organizations addressing environmental, human rights, and humanitarian issues revealed their vocational pursuit of a political career in NGOs underpinned by the desire to contribute to social and political change (Frantz, 2005). Nepstad and Smith (2001) described the moral outrage about human rights abuses and atrocities that motivated Central American peace activists focused on preventing human rights violations and rejecting complicity in the circle of violence. Activists' narratives not only articulated meaningfulness in the vocational pursuit of social change but also in ideas of self-realization, autonomy, and freedom. Jasper's (1997) life-history interviews and participant observation with anti-nuclear and animal rights activists documented motivations and orientations to the work that were not only about a calling, but also about the autonomy and freedom activism offered them. Similarly, Andrews's (1991) biographical interviews with socialist activists revealed how their lifelong social justice activism was motivated by vocational concerns with pursuing political conviction and also drew on notions of self-development and self-realization.

However, other accounts reveal a paradox: that the high expectations that activists have of themselves and each other can be associated with burnout (Roth, 2016). Bobel's (2007) interviews with menstrual activists engaged in raising awareness and challenging the status quo found that some felt being activist required being "super-active," engaged in "tireless commitment and unparalleled devotion," but these stringent requirements meant they felt that they did not meet the "perfect standard" (Bobel, 2007: 154). These activists felt that only those who "live the issue," working very hard and at great personal cost over a long period of time deserved the label "activist" (Bobel, 2007: 153). Other studies have noted the macho heroism articulated by men and women in activist roles which glorifies long hours and self-sacrificing devotion to the cause even at the expense of personal relationships and health (Brown and Pickerill, 2009; Hopgood, 2006). Although the work is experienced as intrinsically meaningful, this brings with it pressure to demonstrate commitment and instigate change. A study of the Swiss solidarity movement found that those who experienced a dissonance between the spheres of activism, work, and family tended to leave the movement (Passy and Giugni, 2000). One study of social justice activists revealed a "culture of martyrdom" in which they failed to take advantage of high-quality healthcare or take time out because they believed that this would undermine their activism (Gorski and Chen, 2015: 397). Activists suffered mental health problems including anxiety, depression and loss of self-esteem, disillusionment and hopelessness, and others experienced racism within the movement (Gorski, 2018).

Humanitarianism and Development

Humanitarian relief and development cooperation are carried out by local, national, and international organizations which offer opportunities for paid and unpaid work. International non-governmental organizations (INGOs) engage in fundraising, service provision, and advocacy and are active in long-term development (including education) and in short-term emergency relief (providing medical support, food, and shelter in man-made and natural disasters) across the globe (Roth, 2019 forthcoming). Some of the biggest and most prominent organizations like Oxfam and Save the Children have a head office in a global city, regional offices, and field offices in the countries where they are carrying out projects (Krause, 2014; Roth, 2015). Their workforce consists of a wide range of professionals trained in various disciplines –medicine, law, engineering, economics, and management—but many are low-paid or unpaid. Some work for long time periods as "volunteering professionals" or "professional volunteers" (Roth, 2015). While data on workers in INGOs are poor (Walker and Russ, 2010), studies suggest that the field is feminized and characterized by high-turnover and fixed-term contracts (Damman, Heyse, and Mills, 2014; Korff et al., 2015). International aid has been subject to professionalization pressure and the budget cuts to governmental bilateral organizations as a consequence of neoliberalism (Watkins, Swidler, and Hannan, 2012). The sector has seen the recruitment of staff from the private sector and some salaries that are comparable to the private sector, consistent occupational standards, and the adoption of core humanitarian competencies as a way to ensure professional practice and further financial support (Roth, 2012).

Aid workers' narratives provide evidence of their motivations and priorities and many draw on the idea of a calling to help those in need and make a difference Roth (2015). Studies of volunteers and staff in INGOs highlight the way in which direct or vicarious experience of critical events such as the 9/11 terrorist attacks, the Asian Tsunami of 2004, or Hurricane Katrina trigger a sense of calling which can lead to temporary or permanent career change as individuals set out to help those affected (Eidelson, D'Alessio, and Eidelson, 2003). The tension between altruism and self-interest is a key theme in the aid work literature (de Jong, 2011; Fechter, 2012). Studies have revealed how workers found meaning not only in the vocational aspects but in what they saw as the opportunities aid work offered for self-realization and self-actualization (Roth, 2015; de Jong, 2011, 2017). Studies of women from high-income countries involved in NGOs suggested the sector was seen to provide a context where the social values of altruistic support could be combined with a challenging and fulfilling career (de Jong, 2011, 2017). Aid work can be experienced as deeply meaningful by national and international staff, but it is also shaped by and perpetuates North–South inequalities (Roth, 2015; Swidler and Watkins, 2017). Studies have found that working conditions in humanitarian organizations are characterized by long working days, conflict, and lack of resources and recognition (Roth, 2015). Burnout, a combination of exhaustion, cynicism, and inefficacy, is caused by high workload, lack of support, feedback, information, and control, and is particularly prevalent in the caring professions such as medicine, social work, and teaching (Maslach and Gomes, 2006). Rodgers (2010), analyzing the work culture at Amnesty International, found it to be characterized by high levels of organizational commitment but also sacrifice and guilt. What made the work meaningful in the abstract, the expectations of selflessness, resulted in a high turnover of paid staff.

Alongside professional humanitarian work, the field is also a site of volunteer tourism which sees young people, often gap year students, visiting developing countries for short periods to work on projects that purport to support local development (Simpson, 2004; Tiessen, 2012). Studies of young people undertaking these initiatives suggests they found the social value of the work, the "helping imperative" (Heron, 2007), meaningful but they also articulated instrumental motivations such as travelling and adventure and gaining useful skills for future careers (Lyons et al., 2012), the desire for personal growth (Simpson, 2004; Tiessen, 2012), and valued opportunities for self-realization (Vrasti, 2013). An ethnographic study of German volunteers in Uganda explored the mixed motives of doing something "worthwhile" and the desire for self-development and fun. It addresses the ambivalence that the volunteers experienced in their privileged position vis-à-vis the local population (Mangold, 2012).

Meaningful Work in the Third Sector: Context, Paradox, and Critical Questions

We began this chapter by arguing that at first glance the third sector appears to offer an ideal space for meaningful work. The social, political, and environmental aims of its diverse organizations and their partial independence from state and market provide opportunities for work that is socially useful, vocational, and autonomous. Despite this "fit," there are few empirical studies of meaningful work in the sector and indeed the concept of meaningful work is itself nebulous. Reviewing sociological debates rooted in classical texts identified a broad set of ideas about what makes work meaningful—it might be a calling or vocation linked to its social utility, it might offer the worker autonomy over their tasks, or enable self-development and self-realization, it might offer dignity and respect—this list is not exhaustive. Drawing on these ideas and focusing on three particular fields (social service, political activism, and humanitarianism), our chapter has explored how we might understand meaningful work in the third sector and revealed the many challenges of this exercise.

Our review of empirical research and conceptual debates on meaningful work in the third sector raised some critical questions and tensions. Exploring the subjective motivations of paid and unpaid workers provided some insights into how meaningfulness was experienced and how understandings were shaped by social identity and life course. What was experienced and understood as important in individuals' working lives was defined by social and cultural narratives. While the vocational importance of working for a social cause or a greater good underpinned many individual narratives in all three fields, those aims were framed differently in each and related not only to the specific focus of the field but were shaped by the social identity of the workers. In the social services field, for example, some articulated their values as working to help people, making the world better, while others drew on notions of solidarity and community self-help. Meaningful work was discursively framed by its social context and wider cultural norms.

Subjective accounts from all three fields also touched on the opportunities the work offered for autonomy over tasks and roles, and highlighted the different experiences of meaningful work in the context of, on the one hand, outsourced government service delivery where meaningfulness was constrained by poor working conditions and, on the other, campaigning for social change where meaningful work was experienced via collective action and mediated by the pressures this created for individuals. Narratives of self-realization and personal development were visible in accounts of middle-class young people working for short periods in the global South, for whom volunteer tourism provided work that was socially valued alongside opportunities for career development. This same example also highlights how life stage played a part in how meaningfulness was understood and articulated. There are implications here for a project to establish meaningful work as a fundamental human need. These studies suggest that the challenges of defining what constitutes meaningful work involve a critical approach to framings which serve to reproduce class-based symbolic notions of what is or should be considered meaningful.

A further challenge was revealed by the paradox that even where the sector appears to offer work that is vocational and meaningful, that has social value or serves a greater good, the work is often low-paid and insecure, and demands long hours and commitment. At its worst it may be very far from offering employees dignity and respect. The various studies across all three fields suggest that meaningfulness is not an inexhaustible well if the other dimensions (respect or autonomy or self-development) are lacking or absent, and that the conditions for stress and burnout are embedded in these fields. The challenge is in understanding how these positive and negative experiences coexist and at what point the work is no longer meaningful for individual workers.

Perhaps the clearest conclusion to draw from the chapter is the need for more research that focuses explicitly on what is meaningful to individuals rather than simply interpreting motivation studies (Rosso, Dekas, and Wrzesniewski, 2010) as we have mostly done here. Future research would need to go beyond simply rehearsing normative narratives of motive that characterize third sector research, to explore the way in which social identity and symbolic meanings shape how individuals understand their work as meaningful not only in terms of social class but also gender and race. It might also focus on the paradox of meaningful work in the sector that is also a source of burnout, or examine more closely how meaningfulness might shift in relation to the blurred boundaries between paid and unpaid work, or examine the way in which understandings and experiences of meaningful work shift in relation to restructuring of the sector and its workforce. And these research ideas demand methodologies that will enable the collection of rich work history narratives, set in the context of equally rich accounts of the sector, its fields, its organizations, and its groups.

REFERENCES

Alcock, P. and Kendall, J. (2011). "Constituting the third sector: Processes of decontestation and contention under the UK Labour governments in England." *Voluntas: International Journal of Voluntary and Nonprofit Organizations*, 22(3), 450–69.

Almond, S. and Kendall, J. (2000). "Taking the employees' perspective seriously: An initial United Kingdom cross-sectoral comparison." *Nonprofit and Voluntary Sector Quarterly*, 29(2), 205–31.

Andrews, M. (1991). *Lifetimes of Commitment: Aging, politics, psychology*. Cambridge: Cambridge University Press.

Andrews, M. (2007). *Shaping History. Narratives of political change*. Cambridge: Cambridge University Press.

Bailey, C. and Madden, A. (2017). "Time reclaimed: Temporality and the experience of meaningful work." *Work, Employment and Society*, 31(1), 3–18.

Bailey, C., Madden, A., Alfes, K., Shantz, A., and Soane, E. (2017). "The mismanaged soul: Existential labor and the erosion of meaningful work." *Human Resource Management Review*, 27(3), 416–30.

Baines, D. (2004). "Caring for nothing: Work, organization and unwaged labour in social services." *Work, Employment and Society*, 18(2), 267–95.

Baines, D. (2010). "'If We Don't Get Back to Where We Were Before': Working in the restructured non-profit social services." *British Journal of Social Work*, 40(3), 928–45.

Baines, D. (2011). "Restructuring and Labour Processes under Marketisation: A Canadian Perspective." In I. Cunningham and P. James (eds.), *Voluntary Organisations and Public Service Delivery*, pp. 168–84. New York and Abingdon: Routledge.

Bandura, A. (1977). "Self-efficacy: Toward a unifying theory of behavioral change." *Psychological Review*, 84, 191–215.

Beck, U. (1992). *Risk Society: Towards a new modernity*. London and New York: Sage.

Benz, M. (2005). "Not for the profit, but for the satisfaction? Evidence on worker well-being in non-profit firms." *Kyklos*, 58(2), 155–76.

Berkelaar, B. L. and Buzzanell, P. M. (2015). "Bait and switch or double-edged sword? The (sometimes) failed promises of calling." *Human Relations*, 68(1), 157–78.

Blauner, R. (1964). *Alienation and Freedom: The factory worker and his industry*. Chicago: University of Chicago Press.

Bobel, C. (2007). "'I'm not an activist, though I've done a lot of it': Doing activism, being activist and the 'Perfect Standard' in a contemporary movement." *Social Movement Studies: Journal of Social, Cultural and Political Protest*, 6(2), 147–59.

Bolton, S. (ed.) (2007). *Dimensions of Dignity at Work*. Oxford: Elsevier.

Borzaga, C. and Depedri, S. (2005). "Interpersonal Relations and Job Satisfaction: Some Empirical Results in Social and Community Care Services." In B. Gui and R. Sugden (eds.), *Economics and Social Interaction: Accounting for interpersonal relations*, pp. 132–53. Cambridge: Cambridge University Press.

Borzaga, C. and Tortia, E. (2006). "Worker motivations, job satisfaction, and loyalty in public and nonprofit social services." *Nonprofit and Voluntary Sector Quarterly*, 35(2), 225–48.

Braverman, H. (1998 [1974]). *Labor and Monopoly Capital: The degradation of work in the twentieth century*. New York: NYU Press.

Brown, G. and Pickerill, J. (2009). "Space for emotion in the spaces of activism." *Emotion, Space and Society*, 2(1), 24–35.

Bunderson, J. and Thompson, J. (2009). "The call of the wild: Zookeepers, callings, and the double-edged sword of deeply meaningful work." *Administrative Science Quarterly*, 54(1), 32–57.

Chen, C. W. and Gorski P. C. (2015). "Burnout in social justice and human rights activists: Symptoms, causes and implications." *Journal of Human Rights Practice*, 7(3), 366–90.

Ciulla, J. (2000). *The Working Life: The promise and betrayal of modern work*. New York: Three Rivers Press.

Clark, J. and Wilding, K. (2011). "Trends in Voluntary Sector Employment." In I. Cunningham and P. James (eds.), *Voluntary Organisations and Public Service Delivery*, pp. 37–53. Abingdon: Routledge.

Cox, L. (2009). "'Hearts with one purpose alone'? Thinking personal sustainability in social movements." *Emotion, Space and Society*, 2(1), 52–61.

Cunningham, I. (2011) "Taking the Strain? The Psychological Contract of Voluntary Sector Employees Following Transfers of Employment." In I. Cunningham and P. James (eds.), *Voluntary Organisations and Public Service Delivery*, pp. 136–52. Abingdon: Routledge.

Cunningham, I. and James, P. (eds.) (2011). *Voluntary Organisations and Public Service Delivery*. Abingdon: Routledge.

Damman, M., Heyse L., and Mills, M. (2014). "Gender, occupation, and promotion to management in the nonprofit sector." *Nonprofit Management and Leadership*, 25(2), 97–111.

de Jong, S. (2011). "False Binaries: Altruism and Egoism in NGO Work." In A.-M. Fechter and H. Hindman (eds.), *Inside the Everyday Lives of Development Workers: The challenges and futures of Aidland*, pp. 21–40. Bloomfield: Kumarian.

de Jong, S. (2017). *Complicit Sisters: Gender and women's issues across North–South divides*. New York: Oxford University Press.

Dempsey, S. E. and Saunders, M. L. (2010). "Meaningful work? Nonprofit marketization and work/life imbalance in popular autobiographies of social entrepreneurship." *Organization*, 17(4), 437–59.

Dik, B. J. and Duffy, R. D. (2009). "Calling and vocation at work: Definitions and prospects for research and practice." *The Counselling Psychologist*, 37(3), 424–50.

Donegani, C. P., McKay, S., and Moro, D. (2012). "A Dimming of the 'Warm Glow'? Are Non-profit Workers in the UK still more Satisfied with their Jobs than other Workers?" In A. Bryson (ed.), *Advances in the Economic Analysis of Participatory and Labor-Managed Firms*, vol. 13, pp. 313–42. Bingley: Emerald Group Publishing Limited.

Duffy, R. D. and Dik, B. J. (2013). "Research on calling: What have we learned and where are we going?" *Journal of Vocational Behavior*, 83(3), 428–36.

Eidelson, R. J., D'Alessio, G. R., and Eidelson, J. I. (2003). "The impact of September 11 on psychologists." *Professional Psychology: Research and Practice*, 34(2), 144–50.

Eliasoph, N. (2011). *Making Volunteers: Civic life after welfare's end*. Princeton, NJ: Princeton University Press.

Eltanani, M. (2016). "But it Comes with a Price": Employment in Social Movement Organizations. PhD, University of Edinburgh.

Evers, A. and Laville, J. L. (eds.) (2004). *The Third Sector in Europe*. Cheltenham: Edward Elgar Publishing.

Fechter, A.-M. (2012). "'Living Well' while 'Doing Good'? (Missing) debates on altruism and professionalism in aid work." *Third World Quarterly*, 33(8), 1475–91.

Frantz, C. (2005). *Karriere in NGOs: Politik als Beruf jenseits der Parteien*. Wiesbaden: VS Verlag fuer Sozialwissenschaften.

Giddens, A. (1991). *Modernity and Self-identity: Self and society in the late modern age*. Stanford, CA: Stanford University Press.

Gorski, P. C. (2018). "Fighting racism, battling burnout: Causes of activist burnout in US racial justice activists." *Ethnic and Racial Studies* [online], 1–21.

Gorski, P. C. and Chen, C. (2015). "'Frayed All Over': The causes and consequences of activist burnout among social justice education activists." *Educational Studies*, 51(5), 385–405.

Grant, A. M. (2007). "Relational job design and the motivation to make a prosocial difference." *Academy of Management Review*, 32, 393–417.

Hackman, J. R. and Oldham, G. R. (1980). *Work Redesign*. Reading, MA: Addison-Wesley.

Halford, S., Leonard, P., and Bruce, K. (2015). "Geographies of labour in the third sector: Making hybrid workforces in place." *Environment and Planning A*, 47(11), 2355–72.

Hardill, I. and Baines, S. (2009). "Active citizenship in later life: Older volunteers in a deprived community in England." *The Professional Geographer*, 61(1), 36–45.

Hardill, I. and Baines, S. (2011). *Enterprising Care? Unpaid voluntary action in the 21st century*. Bristol: Policy Press.

Harrow, J. and Mole, V. (2005). "'I want to move once I have got things straight': Voluntary sector chief executives' career accounts." *Nonprofit Management and Leadership*, 16(1), 79–100.

Heneby, A., Sibthorpe, J., and Driver, S. (2012). "Resisting the 'protest business': Bureaucracy, post-bureaucracy and active membership in social movement organizations." *Organization*, 19(6), 809–23.

Heron, B. (2007). *Desire for Development: Whiteness, gender, and the helping imperative*. Waterloo, Ontario: Wilfrid Laurier University Press.

Hodgkiss, P. (2015). "The Origins of the Idea and Ideal of Dignity in the Sociology of Work and Employment." In S. Edgell, H. Gottfried, and E. Granter (eds.), *The SAGE Handbook of the Sociology of Work and Employment*, pp. 129–47. London: Sage.

Hodson, R. (2001). *Dignity at Work*. Cambridge: Cambridge University Press.

Hopgood, S. (2006). *Keepers of the Flame: Understanding Amnesty International*. Ithaca, NY: Cornell University Press.

Hunter, I., Dik, B. J., and Banning, J. H. (2010). "College students' perceptions of calling in work and life: A qualitative analysis." *Journal of Vocational Behavior*, 76(2), 178–86.

Jasper, J. M. (1997). *The Art of Moral Protest: Culture, biography and creativity in social movements*. Chicago: University of Chicago Press.

Kalleberg, A. L. (2011). *Good Jobs, Bad Jobs: The rise of polarized and precarious employment systems in the United States, 1970s–2000s*. New York: Russell Sage Foundation.

Kendall, J. (2003). *The Voluntary Sector: Comparative perspectives in the UK*. London: Routledge.

Korff, V. P., Balbo, N., Mills, M., Heyse, L., and Wittek, R. (2015). "The impact of humanitarian context conditions and individual characteristics on aid worker retention." *Disasters*, 39(3), 522–45.

Krause, M. (2014). *The Good Project: Humanitarian relief NGOs and the fragmentation of reason*. Chicago: University of Chicago Press.

Kuhn, T., Golden, A. G., Jorgenson, J., Buzzanell, P. M., Berkelaar, B. L., Kisselburgh, L. G., Kleinman, S., and Cruz, D. (2008). "Cultural discourses and discursive resources for meaning/ful work: Constructing and disrupting identities in contemporary capitalism." *Management Communication Quarterly*, 22(1), 162–71.

Leete, L. (2001). "Whither the non-profit wage differential? Estimates from the 1990 census." *Journal of Labour Economics*, 19(1), 136–70

Leete, L. (2006). "Work in the Nonprofit Sector." In W. Powell and R. Steinberg (eds.), *The Nonprofit Sector: A research handbook*, pp. 159–79. New Haven and London: Yale University Press.

Lips-Wiersma, M. and Morris, L. (2009). "Discriminating between 'meaningful work' and the 'management of meaning.'" *Journal of Business Ethics*, 88(3), 491–511.

Lyons, K., Hanley, J., Wearing, S., and Neil, J. (2012). "Gap year volunteer tourism: Myths of global citizenship?" *Annals of Tourism Research*, 39(1), 361–78.

Madden, A., Bailey, C., and Kerr, R. (2015). "'For this I was made': Conflict and calling in the role of a woman priest." *Work, Employment and Society*, 29(5), 866–74.

Mangold, K. (2012). "'Struggling to do the right thing': Challenges during international volunteering." *Third World Quarterly*, 33(8), 1493–509.

Marx, K. (1988). *Economic and Philosophic Manuscripts of 1844*, translated by M. Millington. New York: Prometheus Books.

Maslach, C. and Gomes M. E. (2006)." Overcoming Burnout." In R. M. MacNair (ed.), *Working for Peace: A handbook of practical psychology and other tools*, pp. 43–9. Atascadero: Impact Publishers.

Maslow, A. (1943). "A theory of human motivation." *Psychological Review*, 50(4), 370.

McAdam, D. (1986). "Recruitment to high risk activism." *American Journal of Sociology*, 92, 64–90.

McDonald, C. and Charlesworth, S. (2011). "Outsourcing and the Australian Nonprofit sector." In I. Cunningham and P. James (eds.), *Voluntary Organisations and Public Service Delivery*, pp. 185–201. Abingdon: Routledge.

Michaelson, C. (2011). "Whose responsibility is meaningful work?" *Journal of Management Development*, 30(6), 548–57.

Mirvis, P. H. (1992). "The quality of employment in the nonprofit sector: An update on employee attitudes in nonprofits versus business and government." *Nonprofit Management and Leadership*, 3(1), 23–41.

Musick, M. and Wilson, J. (2008). *Volunteers: A social profile*. Bloomington, IN: Indiana University Press.

NCVO. (2014). *UK Civil Society Almanac 2014* [website]: https://data.ncvo.org.uk/almanac14/ [accessed August 5, 2017].

NCVO. (2015). *UK Civil Society Almanac 2015* [website]: https://data.ncvo.org.uk/almanac15/ [accessed August 5, 2017].

NCVO. (2016). *UK Civil Society Almanac 2016* [website]: https://data.ncvo.org.uk/category/almanac16/ [accessed August 5, 2017].

Nepstad, S. and Smith, C. (2001). "The Social Structure of Moral Outrage in Recruitment to the U.S. Central America Peace Movement." In J. Goodwin, J. M. Jasper, and F. Polletta (eds.), *Passionate Politics: Emotions and social movements*, pp. 158–74. Chicago: University of Chicago Press.

Newman, J. (2012). *Working the Spaces of Power: Activism, neoliberalism and gendered labour.* London: A&C Black.

Nickson, D., Warhurst, C., Dutton, E., and Hurrell, S. (2008). "A job to believe in: Recruitment in the Scottish voluntary sector." *Human Resource Management Journal*, 18(1), 20–35.

Onyx, J. and Maclean, M. (1996). "Careers in the third sector." *Nonprofit Management and Leadership*, 6(4), 331–45.

Parry, J. (2003). "The changing meaning of work: restructuring in the former coalmining communities of the South Wales Valleys." *Work, Employment & Society*, 17(2), 227–46.

Parry, J. (2005). "Care in the Community? Gender and the reconfiguration of community work in a post-mining neighbourhood." *Sociological Review*, 53, 149–66.

Passy, F. and Giugni, M. (2000). "Life-spheres, networks, and sustained participation in social movements: A phenomenological approach to political commitment." *Sociological Forum*, 15(1), 117–44.

Rodgers, K. (2010). "'Anger is why we're all here': Mobilizing and managing emotions in a professional activist organization." *Social Movement Studies*, 9(3), 273–91.

Rosso, B. D., Dekas, K. H., and Wrzesniewski, A. (2010). "On the meaning of work: A theoretical integration and review." *Research in Organizational Behavior*, 30, 91–127.

Roth, S. (2012). "Professionalisation trends and inequality: Experiences and practices in aid relationships." *Third World Quarterly*, 33(8), 1459–74.

Roth, S. (2015). *The Paradoxes of Aid Work: Passionate professionals.* Abingdon: Routledge.

Roth, S. (2016). "Professionalisation and precariousness: Perspectives on the sustainability of activism in everyday life." *Interface: A Journal For and About Social Movements*, 8(2), 29–58.

Roth, S. (2019 forthcoming). "Humanitarian NGOs." In T. Davies (ed.), *Routledge Handbook of NGOs and International Relations*. Abingdon: Routledge.

Rubery, J. and Urwin, P. (2011). "Bringing the employer back in: Why social care needs a standard employment relationship." *Human Resource Management Journal*, 21(2), 122–37.

Rutherford, A. C. (2015). "Rising wages in the expanding UK nonprofit sector from 1997 to 2007." *Nonprofit and Voluntary Sector Quarterly*, 44(1), 123–45.

Salamon, L. M. (2015). *The Resilient Sector revisited: The new challenge to nonprofit America.* Washington, DC: Brookings Institution Press.

Salamon, L. M. and Sokolowski, S. W. (2016). "Beyond nonprofits: Re-conceptualizing the third sector." *VOLUNTAS: International Journal of Voluntary and Nonprofit Organizations*, 27(4), 1515–45.

Saunders, C. and Roth, S. (2019 forthcoming). "NGOs and Social Movement Theory." In T. Davies (ed.), *Routledge Handbook of NGOs and International Relations*. Abingdon: Routledge.

Sayer, A. (2007). "Dignity at work: Broadening the agenda." *Organization*, 14(4), 565–81.

Seeman, M. (1959). "On the meaning of alienation." *American Sociological Review*, 24(6), 783–91.

Sennett, R. (1998). *The Corrosion of Character: The personal consequences of work in the new capitalism*. New York: WW Norton & Company.

Sennett, R. (2009). *The Craftsman*. New Haven, CT: Yale University Press.

Shutt, C. (2012). "A moral economy? Social interpretations of money in Aidland." *Third World Quarterly*, 33(8), 1527–43.

Simpson, K. (2004). " 'Doing development': The gap year, volunteer-tourists and a popular practice of development." *Journal of International Development*, 16, 681–92.

Simpson, R., Hughes, J., Slutskaya, N., and Balta, M. (2014). "Sacrifice and distinction in dirty work: Men's construction of meaning in the butcher trade." *Work, Employment & Society*, 28(5), 754–70.

Smith, S. R. (2011). "Contracting with Voluntary Sector Agencies in the USA: Implications for Employment and Professionalisation." In I. Cunningham and P. James (eds.), *Voluntary Organisations and Public Service Delivery*, pp. 202–22. Abingdon: Routledge.

Standing, G. (2011). *The Precariat: The new dangerous class*. London/NewYork: Bloomsbury.

Stroup, S. (2012). *Borders Among Activists: International NGOs, in the United States, Britain, and France*. Ithaca, NY: Cornell University Press.

Swidler, A. and Watkins, S. C. (2017). *A Fraught Embrace: The romance and reality of AIDS altruism in Africa*. Princeton, NJ: Princeton University Press.

Taylor, M. (2017). *Good Work: The Taylor review of modern working practices*. London: Department for Business, Energy and Industrial Strategy.

Taylor, R. (2004). "Extending conceptual boundaries: Work, voluntary work and employment." *Work, Employment & Society*, 18(1), 29–49.

Taylor, R. (2005). "Rethinking voluntary work." *Sociological Review*, 53(2), 117–35.

Taylor, R. (2015). "Volunteering and Unpaid Work." In S. Edgell, H. Gottfried, and E. Granter (eds.), *The SAGE Handbook of the Sociology of Work and Employment*, pp. 485–501. London: SAGE.

Tiessen, R. (2012). "Motivations for learn/volunteer abroad programs: Research with Canadian youth." *Journal of Global Citizenship and Equity Education*, 2(1).

Veblen, T. (1914). *The Instinct of Workmanship and the State of the Industrial Arts*. New York: Macmillan.

Vrasti, W. (2013). *Volunteer Tourism in the Global South: Giving back in neoliberal times*. London/New York: Routledge.

Walker, P. and Russ, C. (2010). *Professionalising the Humanitarian Sector: A scoping study*. Cardiff: Enhancing Learning and Research for Humanitarian Assistance.

Watkins, S. C., Swidler, A., and Hannan, T. (2012). "Outsourcing social transformation: Development NGOs as organizations." *Annual Review of Sociology*, 38(1), 285–315.

Weber, M. (1958 [1930]). *The Protestant Ethic and the Spirit of Capitalism*. London: Allen and Unwin.

Wright Mills, C. (1956). *The Power Elite*. New York: Oxford University Press.

Wuthnow, R. (2004). *Saving America? Faith-based services and the future of civil society*. Princeton, NJ: Princeton University Press.

Yeoman, R. (2014). *Meaningful Work and Workplace Democracy: A philosophy of work and a politics of meaningfulness*. New York: Springer.

CHAPTER 16

....

CALLINGS

....

RYAN D. DUFFY, JESSICA W. ENGLAND, AND BRYAN J. DIK

THE term "calling," as it applies to the work role, usually refers to a sense of purpose (internally or externally prompted) that draws an individual toward a personally and/or socially meaningful engagement with work. The importance of discerning and living a calling in one's career has been demonstrated through an abundance of research conducted on the effects that a sense of calling can have on career-related and overall well-being. Research has consistently found that those who approach their work as a calling are happier and experience both increased meaning and satisfaction at work and subsequently in life (e.g. Dik et al., 2012; Duffy and Dik, 2013; Hirschi and Hermann, 2012; Peterson et al., 2009; Wrzesniewski et al., 1997). Recent research also has revealed that perceiving a calling is necessary but not always sufficient for experiencing such benefits; actively living out one's calling is the key (e.g. Duffy et al., 2012a; Gazica and Spector, 2015). In addition to the positive outcomes associated with living a calling, evidence of some vulnerabilities and negative outcomes under some conditions has begun to emerge, suggesting a potential dark side to the pursuit of a calling (e.g. Bunderson and Thompson, 2009; Dobrow and Tosti-Kharas, 2012; Duffy et al., 2016b). The ongoing research on discerning and living a calling in one's work and how it relates to well-being offers an important pathway for reaching a more comprehensive and nuanced understanding of meaning, purpose, and well-being in the world of work.

Perceiving one's work as a calling has been shown to fall within the larger construct of meaningful work. According to Steger, Dik, and Duffy (2012), the concept of meaningful work includes the experience of personal significance in one's work, meaning-making in life through one's work, and contribution to the greater good of others. Experiencing meaning and purpose through one's work is necessary for an individual to feel they are living a calling (Dik and Duffy, 2009), but meaning can be discovered at the workplace without an individual actually living out his or her calling. The constructs are not mutually exclusive. In fact, through adjusting aspects of one's current job, such as changing work tasks, developing more or deeper relationships at work, and/or changing thoughts about work, individuals can make their current jobs more meaningful

(Wrzesniewski and Dutton, 2001). In this chapter, calling and meaningful work overlap but are considered separate constructs.

The aim of this chapter is to provide an overview of research on a sense of calling in individuals' career development and work experience. First, we explore the conceptualization of calling and highlight the difference between perceiving a calling and living a calling. Second, we review constructs that have been examined as antecedents and correlates of a calling. Third, we explore the positive work and individual outcomes of enacting a calling as well as the potentially harmful outcomes. Finally, implications and future directions are suggested for the continued investigation of work as a calling.

DEFINITION AND MULTIDIMENSIONAL NATURE

One of the more interesting and in some ways troublesome aspects of the literature on calling concerns the diverse ways in which the construct is conceptualized. In their 2013 review, Duffy and Dik noted a spectrum of different definitions ranging from simply a consuming passion (Dobrow and Tosti-Kharas, 2011) to more complex, multidimensional definitions with upwards of three different components, all needing to be satisfied in order for work to be considered a calling (e.g. Dik and Duffy, 2009; Hagmaier and Abele, 2012). Most scholars frame calling as multidimensional in nature, and propose dimensions for which there is substantial overlap. For example, when applied to the work role, most definitions include a sense of work as personally meaningful or purpose-laden. Many also convey a sense that work is carried out with prosocial motives, as a pathway for making a positive difference (e.g. Dik, Duffy, and Steger, 2012). Finally, some definitions (e.g. Dik and Duffy, 2009; Hagmaier and Abele, 2012) suggest that a summons toward a particular line of work, whether external or internal, is a required component of the construct.

Most studies which have examined how calling links to criterion variables have found relatively consistent relations regardless of how calling is conceptualized (Duffy and Dik, 2013). Given the evolving nature of how the term "calling" is used in modern English, it is likely the case that no one definition is the "right" one. Nevertheless, a series of qualitative studies suggest that calling is best viewed as multidimensional, given how frequently participants define the construct this way (e.g. Hernandez, Foley, and Beitin, 2011; Hunter, Dik, and Banning, 2010; Oates, Hall, and Anderson, 2005; Zhang et al., 2015). A multidimensional perspective also assists in distinguishing calling from related variables such as passion, meaning, or prosocial work attitudes. The "transcendent summons" component of calling is perhaps most distinct of all, clearly separating this construct from others that may be considered overlapping (Brown and Lent, 2016). Additional research using typological approaches such as taxometric analysis (Dik and Shimizu, 2018) may shed new light on how calling is defined (and by whom). For the purposes of this review, we conceptualize calling as an approach to work in which one seeks to demonstrate or derive a sense of meaning driven by prosocial motives, often arising out of an internal or external summons (Duffy and Dik, 2013). Importantly, although people can feel summoned to a particular career, even one that provides meaning, we contend that if that career is not approached with prosocial motives it would not constitute a calling according to our conceptualization.

Perceiving a Calling and Living a Calling

Having a sense of calling does not necessarily imply that one is actively living out that calling in one's work life. For example, just because someone has a calling (e.g. a desire to have their work be a source of meaning), this person may not actually be able to find a work environment where this meaning can be experienced. This simple, but important, distinction is one that several researchers have noted over the last five years (e.g. Duffy and Autin, 2013; Gazica and Spector, 2015). Studies have consistently demonstrated that perceiving and living a calling are correlated, but at levels far from suggesting they are redundant constructs (Duffy and Dik, 2013). Indeed, several studies have demonstrated that the positive outcomes that result from a calling occur primarily when people are able to live it out (Duffy et al., 2013; Duffy et al., 2016b). Put another way, perceiving a calling may only have a positive impact when individuals can actually enact that calling. Recent efforts to develop a theoretical framework around calling (Duffy et al., 2018) that incorporates these studies have positioned perceiving a calling as predictive of living a calling, which in turn predicts positive work and well-being outcomes. In the following sections we review research on variables that may facilitate the development of a sense of calling, and also variables that may assist in helping people live out their callings.

Predictors of Perceiving a Calling

Most research on calling has been conducted with working adults, with fewer studies specifically examining what leads to the development of this approach to work in the first place (mainly with college student samples). For example, several longitudinal studies completed with undergraduate students found that those more likely to endorse a calling over time had greater vocational self-clarity or identity, were more likely to have meaning in life or to be searching for meaning, and were more oriented toward personal growth (Bott and Duffy, 2015; Duffy et al., 2014; Hirschi and Herrmann, 2013). Other cross-sectional research has found moderate to strong positive correlations between perceiving a calling and career maturity as measured by variables such as career self-efficacy, adaptability, and decidedness (Duffy and Dik, 2013). In totality, these studies suggest that a calling may best develop when one has a strong sense of one's vocational interests and abilities, is oriented to grow as a person, and is committed to making life meaningful. These quantitative results mirror data from qualitative studies on individuals who have reflected on their journeys to finding their calling (Ahn, Dik, and Hornback, 2017; Bott et al., 2017; Duffy et al., 2012c).

PREDICTORS OF LIVING A CALLING

Naturally, to live out a calling an individual must perceive a calling in the first place. Estimates suggest that approximately half of all working adults (in the US and the other economically developed nations studied to date) perceive a calling, but that only a fraction of these are currently working in jobs where they are living out that calling (Duffy et al., 2015). Thus, although perceiving a calling and living a calling are highly correlated, simply having a calling is not the only requirement for being able to live it out. Other variables that facilitate living a calling are reviewed below.

Access to opportunity. One key predictor of living a calling is access to opportunity. In their theoretical model, Duffy, Dik, Douglass, England, and Velez (2018) positioned access to opportunity as one of two direct predictors to living out a calling (along with perceiving a calling). Access to opportunity refers to an individual's ability to pursue tangible pathways that align with their calling, and scholarship has consistently demonstrated that only relatively privileged individuals have an unconstrained ability to follow their career dreams (Duffy, Autin, and Douglass, 2016). Markers of access to opportunity include objective indicators such as income, education, and social class as well as subjective indicators such as work volition, defined as the perceived ability to make career decisions despite constraints (Duffy et al., 2012b).

Studies have consistently demonstrated that greater access to opportunity is associated with a greater likelihood of living out a calling. Objective indicators of income, education, and social class demonstrate weak to moderate correlations with living out a calling among working adult populations, and these relations are mediated by work volition (Duffy and Autin, 2013; Duffy et al., 2016b; Duffy et al., 2017a). This is likely due to work volition capturing a broader array of perceived supports or barriers to opportunity that may not be completely captured by traditional objective indicators. Overall, results demonstrate that to live one's calling, it is important that an individual has the actual and perceived opportunity to enact that calling in available jobs.

Linking perceiving and living a calling. Even for individuals who have a calling and also have high access to opportunity, there often remain some barriers to living their calling. This is because there are important individual and workplace factors that explain how a perceived sense of calling turns into a lived calling. At the workplace level, Duffy, Autin, and Douglass's (2018) model suggests that there are two sets of variables that explain the link between perceiving and living a calling. The first set consists of work meaning and career commitment. A number of studies have found both perceiving and living a calling to correlate moderately to strongly with scores on these variables (Duffy and Dik, 2013; Duffy et al., 2016b), with commitment and meaning most often positioned as outcomes of calling. However, in the first study to test these relations longitudinally, Duffy et al. (2014) found that work meaning and career commitment were best positioned as predictors of living a calling. For this reason, work meaning and career commitment are positioned as the primary mediators that explain why experiencing a calling is associated with living a calling. Individuals feel their calling is enacted when they are deriving meaning from their work and feel committed to their career. A more recent study empirically supported the connections among these variables (Duffy et al., 2018).

If meaning and commitment are the key ingredients for living out a calling, the question then becomes: How do employees build meaning and commitment in the job to which they feel called? According to Duffy et al.'s (2018) theoretical model, person–environment fit (P–E Fit) is a central variable linking one's sense of calling to meaning and commitment. Specifically, building from the classic idea that positive work experiences result from a match between a person's characteristics (P) and the work environment (E) they are in (Pervin, 1968), when a person's work environment matches her or his calling, that person is believed to grow high levels of meaning and commitment. Conversely, when individuals with a calling are working in environments that are a poor match, this will promote a lack of meaning and commitment, which will eventually lead to dissatisfaction and withdrawal (Berkelaar and Buzzanell, 2015).

To summarize, living a calling is proposed to be the result of perceiving a calling and having access to opportunity to pursue that calling. People who perceive a calling are especially likely to actively live their callings when they experience high levels of work meaning and exhibit a high level of career commitment, characteristics that flow from working in an environment that is a good fit with one's calling.

Maximizing a Calling at Work

Finding a work environment that fits one's calling is an early link in the chain that begins with perceiving a calling, proceeds to living a calling, and ends with the associated work and well-being benefits. However, identifying and entering a best-fitting environment is often very difficult. Arguably, landing a job in an environment that perfectly aligns with one's calling is the exception rather than the rule, and for most people a variety of factors probably shape their ability to align their calling with their job. In this section we focus on three potentially malleable factors that are proposed to help individuals maximize their calling at work: calling motivation, job crafting, and organizational support.

Calling motivation. A calling reflects the manner in which a person views her or his work, but enacting that calling requires a sufficient level of motivation (Duffy et al., 2017a). It is certainly possible that some individuals with a calling could be in a place where their motivation is low and as a result they are unlikely to seek out work environments that would enable them to live their calling. For example, Duffy et al. (2015) found that among unemployed adults, a lower level of calling motivation was significantly related with less proactive job search behaviors. Conversely, other research by Duffy et al. (2017a) found calling motivation to significantly moderate the links of perceiving a calling to living a calling and life meaning, such that these relations were stronger for individuals with higher motivation. Based on these studies, it is reasonable to propose that calling motivation functions as a moderator linking perceiving a calling to P–E fit (Duffy et al., 2016c). Specifically, individuals who are more motivated to pursue their calling may be more likely to actually find work environments that fit their calling.

Job crafting. Once in a work environment, most individuals will need to actively adapt this environment to maintain a strong fit with their calling. Job crafting refers to relational, task-oriented, or cognitive adaptations that individuals can make regarding their work (Wrzesniewski and Dutton, 2001). A study by Berg, Grant, and Johnson (2010) explored techniques used by employees seeking to turn a perceived calling into an enacted calling in the workplace. These included emphasizing some work tasks over others, adding new work tasks, or making stronger cognitive links regarding how one's job helps others. More recent research has found that being able to take on more work-related challenges increased the likelihood of viewing one's job as a calling (Esteves and Lopes, 2017). Like calling motivation, job crafting is viewed as an adaptable construct that can foster a stronger connection between a perceived calling and P–E fit. Specifically, individuals who are willing to adapt how they work will likely experience their environment as a stronger fit with their sense of calling.

Organizational support. The final variable discussed here—organizational support—is also viewed as malleable, but is likely more malleable on the organization side than the individual side. Specifically, working in an organization that is supportive of an individual's calling likely helps individuals with a calling feel that this work environment is a good fit. Several studies have found aspects of organizational support to relate to perceiving and living a calling (Duffy and Autin, 2013; Lee, 2016). Although it is likely that individuals with a calling seek out organizations that support the calling, it is just as likely (if not more so) that organizational support is something that is modified once a person enters the environment. Toward this end, it is incumbent on organizations to acknowledge and support employees' callings where possible. Specifically, individuals with a calling who are more supported by their organization will experience a stronger fit between that calling and the work environment.

Summary. The three variables described here—calling motivation, job crafting, and organizational support—are malleable and viewed as constructs that, when increased, may strengthen the relation between a perceived calling and P–E fit. To maximize the positive effects of a felt calling, individuals should be encouraged to harness their motivation to pursue their calling and, once employed, commit to adjusting their work environments where needed. In parallel, organizational leaders are encouraged to support employees' efforts to live out their calling in their current work environment. Calling motivation, job crafting, and organizational support are discussed above as factors that may be manipulated by the employee or by the organization. It is important to note that there is a distinction in the literature between the constructs of meaningful work, where meaning is understood as an intrinsic human will, and the management of meaning, where organizations work to provide and manage meaning at the workplace (Lips-Wiersma and Morris, 2009). This may have impacts on how these variables are manipulated at an individual and organizational level.

Outcomes of Living a Calling

Research has consistently shown that individuals who are able to live out their callings are more likely to experience beneficial outcomes, both at work and personally. On the other hand, individuals may also experience a dark side to living a calling, in which their motivation to work in their callings may be associated with overwork (e.g. workaholism and burnout) and/or organizational exploitation through their workplace. The following sections explore the positive and potentially negative outcomes associated with living a calling.

Vocational Outcomes

Individuals who report that they are living their callings also report experiencing more favorable vocational outcomes associated with their jobs. To begin with, employed adults who are living out their callings tend to be more satisfied with their jobs (Chen et al., 2016; Douglass, Duffy, and Autin, 2016; Duffy et al., 2014; Kim, Praskova, and Lee, 2017; Lazar, Davidovitch, and Coren, 2016; Xie et al., 2016), more engaged in their work (Hirschi, 2012), and more committed to the careers and organizations in which they work (Cardador, Dane, and Pratt, 2011; Duffy and Autin, 2013; Duffy et al., 2012a). Employees who are more committed to their work experience lower withdrawal intentions, and thus are less likely to leave their jobs (Duffy, Allan, and Dik, 2011). Furthermore, qualitative research has suggested an association between living a calling and higher performance at work (Bunderson and Thompson, 2009; Duffy et al., 2012c). This relation has been further supported in recent research with teachers (Lobene and Meade, 2013), salespersons (Park, Sohn, and Ha, 2016), and employees representing twenty-four organizations (Lee, Chen, and Chang, 2018). Thus, those who are able to live out their callings are more likely to be happy, engaged, committed, and perform well at their workplace.

Well-being Outcomes

In addition to positive work outcomes, individuals who live out their callings are also more likely to experience increased well-being in general. For example, finding meaning in life and life satisfaction (Allan et al., 2015; Douglass, Duffy, and Autin, 2016;

Duffy et al., 2013; Duffy and Autin, 2013; Duffy et al., 2012c; Duffy et al., 2017b; Wrzesniewski et al., 1997) are often associated with the ability to live one's calling. However, along with increased well-being in work and life, some employees may experience potentially harmful outcomes associated with a calling.

Dark Side to Living a Calling

Not only can individuals be adversely impacted by unanswered callings (Berg, Grant, and Johnson, 2010; Gazica and Spector, 2015), but some individuals may live out their calling in an unhealthy fashion (Berkelaar and Buzzanell, 2015; Cardador and Caza, 2012; Duffy et al., 2015). For example, some individuals may foreclose on a career path for which they may not be best suited due to a sense of calling, to the point where they may ignore helpful feedback from trusted mentors that challenges their goals (Dobrow and Tosti-Kharas, 2012). Also, greater energy, involvement, and motivation toward the work in one's career is often involved in living a calling, which may be associated with increased workaholism and/or burnout (Dik and Duffy, 2012). Workaholism is defined as an addiction to work, including the commitment of personal time and long hours to work (Berkelaar and Buzzanell, 2015; Ng, Sorensen, and Feldman, 2007). Previous research has indicated that living a calling and calling intensity are associated with employees devoting greater personal time and putting in longer hours at work (Bunderson and Thompson, 2009; Clinton, Conway, and Sturges, 2017), as well as employees making substantial personal sacrifices for their work (Duffy et al., 2012c; Levoy, 1997; Serow, 1994). Furthermore, Keller et al. (2016) have found evidence supporting the association between calling and workaholism. In addition to workaholism, burnout—or the sustained response to chronic stress at work (i.e. relational and emotional stressors)—has also been discussed as a potential outcome related to a calling (Cardador and Caza, 2012). In samples of employed adults living out their callings, nurses and junior doctors have been found to experience greater burnout (Creed et al., 2014; Sherman, 2004; Vinje and Mittelmark, 2007), and teachers who perceive a calling to teach were more likely to leave their jobs early in their careers (Hartnett and Kline, 2005). Indeed, it seems that when working in very meaningful and impactful professions, unhealthy overinvestment in work may be easy to rationalize, and individuals who are overworked may be more likely to experience burnout.

Finally, organizational exploitation is another potentially harmful outcome that individuals may experience as a result of living a calling (Berkelaar and Buzzanell, 2015). Bunderson and Thompson (2009) found among a sample of zookeepers that they were more likely to experience exploitation at work because of their strong motivation to work hard without additional rewards. A sample of animal shelter employees reported similar experiences, with employers being more likely to ask participants to complete very demanding tasks because of their high willingness to work (Schabram and Maitlis, 2017). Individuals working in their callings may be vulnerable to being taken advantage of by employers because of their increased intrinsic motivation to work hard in their careers.

Summary

Past research investigating the outcomes of living a calling have demonstrated that a sense of calling is associated with overwhelmingly positive vocational and individual results. However, research and theory have both illustrated the possible negative outcomes that may be associated with securing work in one's calling, including career "tunnel vision," workaholism, burnout, and organizational exploitation by employers. Future research is needed to shed more light on how these outcomes may occur across different situations.

IMPLICATIONS

Considering the substantial research on callings and the (usually) positive impact that living a calling has on well-being, there are a number of implications to consider that may improve individuals' experiences of their work. In this section, we explore promising future directions for this area of research, including aspects of potentially helpful psychological interventions, as well as multicultural considerations that may impact applications of the calling construct.

Increasing Motivation

Calling motivation is associated with the ability to live out a calling (Duffy et al., 2017a); thus, increasing motivation should in turn increase one's ability to pursue a calling. Engaging in motivational interviewing has been suggested as an intervention that may help people explore and increase their autonomy, competence, and relatedness needs (Markland et al., 2005), which are outlined in Self-determination Theory (Deci and Ryan, 2000). Also, interventions aimed at increasing critical consciousness (i.e. critical reflection, political efficacy, and critical action; Freire, 1993; Watts, Diemer, and Voight, 2011) may also increase individuals' abilities to overcome barriers and constraints, increasing their motivation toward pursuing their callings.

Crafting Techniques

As discussed earlier in the chapter, job crafting techniques are very useful in modifying work experiences to increase fit and match, increasing the alignment with one's calling (Dik and Duffy, 2015; Esteves and Lopes, 2017; Wrzesniewski and Dutton, 2001). This can be achieved through making more enjoyable choices at work, such as by choosing or adding more fitting work tasks to one's agenda or changing specific roles at work (Berg, Grant, and Johnson, 2010). Cognitive crafting techniques are also useful in working to reframe thoughts about work, connecting work tasks or decisions with a global sense of meaning or purpose (Park, 2012). Thus, any change or reframe that individuals can make in order to find a better fit in the workplace may help them to pursue their callings in life.

Multicultural Considerations

Although the vast majority of early research on calling occurred in an American context, research on calling has become a global phenomenon in recent years, with approximately twenty countries now represented in the research literature. Nevertheless, much of this research has used samples of participants who may hold individualistic worldviews, and the concept of living one's calling in life seems to be associated with higher levels of privilege. It is likely that most people across the globe lack the economic resources and access to opportunity that would allow them to pursue their callings in life (Dik and Duffy, 2012), and many pursue work solely to support themselves and their families financially. Further research, such as in testing the tenets of the Psychology of Working Theory (Duffy et al., 2016a) within the calling domain, must be dedicated to sampling more diverse populations.

CONCLUSION

Living a calling in one's career has consistently been shown to play a significant role in the attainment of work-related and general well-being. Access to opportunity is often predictive of the ability to live out a calling, such that less opportunity may act as a barrier in this pursuit. Furthermore, increasing calling motivation, engaging in job crafting, and gaining more organizational support have all been shown to maximize one's ability to live out a calling. When individuals are able to live out their callings, they often experience increased satisfaction, performance, engagement, and commitment associated with their jobs. Through these experiences in their calling, individuals often report greater life meaning and satisfaction. It is important to note, however, that in some situations living a calling may be associated with vulnerabilities, such as poor receptivity to challenging career advice, workaholism, burnout, and exploitation. Through increasing one's calling motivation and employing job crafting techniques, individuals can work toward living out their callings.

REFERENCES

Ahn, J., Dik, B. J., and Hornback, R. (2017). "The experience of a career change driven by a sense of calling: An interpretative phenomenological approach." *Journal of Vocational Behavior*, 102, 48–62.

Allan, B. A., Tebbe, E. A., Duffy, R. D., and Autin, K. L. (2015). "Living a calling, life satisfaction, and workplace climate among a lesbian, gay, and bisexual population." *Career Development Quarterly*, 63, 306–19.

Berg, J. M., Grant, A. M., and Johnson, V. (2010). "When callings are calling: Crafting work and leisure in pursuit of unanswered occupational callings." *Organization Science*, 21, 973–94.

Berkelaar, B. L. and Buzzanell, P. M. (2015). "Bait and switch or double-edged sword? The (sometimes) failed promises of calling." *Human Relations*, 68, 157–78.

Bott, E. M. and Duffy, R. D. (2015). "A two-wave longitudinal study of career calling among undergraduates: Testing for predictors." *Journal of Career Assessment*, 23, 250–65.

Bott, E. M., Duffy, R. D., Borges, N. J., Braun, T. L., Jordan, K., and Marino, J. F. (2017). "Called to medicine. Physicians' experiences of a career calling." *The Career Development Quarterly*, 65, 113–30.

Brown, S. D. and Lent, R. W. (2016). "Vocational psychology: Agency, equity, and well-being." *Annual Review of Psychology*, 67, 541–65.

Bunderson, J. S. and Thompson, J. A. (2009). "The call of the wild: Zookeepers, callings, and the double-edged sword of deeply meaningful work." *Administrative Science Quarterly*, 54(1), 32–57.

Cardador, M. T. and Caza, B. B. (2012). "Relational and identity perspectives on healthy versus unhealthy pursuit of callings." *Journal of Career Assessment*, 20, 338–53.

Cardador, M. T., Dane, E. I., and Pratt, M. G. (2011). "Linking calling orientations to organizational attachment via organizational instrumentality." *Journal of Vocational Behavior*, 79, 367–78.

Chen, J., May, D. R., Schwoerer, C. E., and Augelli, B. (2016). "Exploring the boundaries of career calling: The moderating roles of procedural justice and psychological safety." *Journal of Career Development*, 45(2), 103–16.

Clinton, M. E., Conway, N., and Sturges, J. (2017). "'It's Tough Hanging-Up a Call'": The relationships between calling and work hours, psychological detachment, sleep quality, and morning vigor." *Journal of Occupational Health Psychology*, 22, 28–39.

Creed, P. A., Rogers, M. E., Praskova, A., and Searle, J. (2014). "Career calling as a personal resource moderator between environmental demands and burnout in Australian junior doctors." *Journal of Career Development*, 41, 546–61.

Deci, E. L. and Ryan, R. M. (2000). "The 'what' and 'why' of goal pursuits: Human needs and the self-determination of behavior." *Psychological Inquiry*, 11(4), 227–68.

Dik, B. J. and Duffy, R. D. (2009). "Calling and vocation at work: Definitions and prospects for research and practice." *The Counseling Psychologist*, 37, 424–50.

Dik, B. J. and Duffy, R. D. (2012). *Make Your Job a Calling: How the psychology of vocation can change your life at work.* West Conshohocken, PA: Templeton Press.

Dik, B. J. and Duffy, R. D. (2015). "Strategies for Discerning and Living a Calling." In P. Hartung, M. Savickas, and B. Walsh (eds.), *APA Handbook of Career Intervention*, pp. 305–17. Washington, DC: APA.

Dik, B. J., Duffy, R. D., and Steger, M. F. (2012). "Enhancing social justice by promoting prosocial values in career development interventions." *Counseling and Values*, 57, 31–7.

Dik, B. J., Eldridge, B. M., Steger, M. F., and Duffy, R. D. (2012). "Development and validation of the calling and vocation questionnaire (CVQ) and brief calling scale (BCS)." *Journal of Career Assessment*, 20, 242–63.

Dik, B. J. and Shimizu, Z. (2018). "Multiple meanings of calling: Next steps for studying an evolving construct." *Journal of Career Assessment* [advance online publication].

Dobrow, S. R. and Tosti-Kharas, J. (2011). "Calling: The development of a scale measure." *Personnel Psychology*, 64, 1001–49.

Dobrow, S. R. and Tosti-Kharas, J. (2012). "Listen to your heart? Calling and receptivity to career advice." *Journal of Career Assessment*, 20, 264–80.

Douglass, R. P., Duffy, R. D., and Autin, K. L. (2016). "Living a calling, nationality, and life satisfaction: A moderated, multiple mediator model." *Journal of Career Assessment*, 24, 253–69.

Duffy, R. D., Allan, B. A., Autin, K. L., and Bott, E. M. (2013). "Calling and life satisfaction: It's not about having it, it's about living it." *Journal of Counseling Psychology*, 60, 42–52.

Duffy, R. D., Allan, B. A., Bott, E. M., and Dik, B. J. (2014). "Does the source of a calling matter? External summons, destiny, and perfect fit." *Journal of Career Assessment*, 22, 562–74.

Duffy, R. D., Allan, B. A., and Dik, B. J. (2011). "The presence of a calling and academic satisfaction: Exploring potential mediators." *Journal of Vocational Behavior*, 79, 74–80.

Duffy, R. D. and Autin, K. L. (2013). "Disentangling the link between perceiving a calling and living a calling." *Journal of Counseling Psychology*, 60, 219–27.

Duffy, R. D., Autin, K. L., and Douglass, R. P. (2016). "Examining how aspects of vocational privilege relate to living a calling." *The Journal of Positive Psychology*, 11, 416–27.

Duffy, R. D., Blustein, D. L., Diemer, M. A., and Autin, K. L. (2016a). "The psychology of working theory." *Journal of Counseling Psychology*, 63(2), 127–48.

Duffy, R. D., Bott, E. M., Allan, B. A., and Autin, K. L. (2015). "Calling among the unemployed: Examining prevalence and links to coping with job loss." *The Journal of Positive Psychology*, 10, 332–45.

Duffy, R. D., Bott, E. M., Allan, B. A., Torrey, C. L., and Dik, B. J. (2012a). "Perceiving a calling, living a calling, and job satisfaction: Testing a moderated, multiple mediator model." *Journal of Counseling Psychology*, 59, 50–9.

Duffy, R. D., Diemer, M. A., Perry, J. C., Laurenzi, C., and Torrey, C. L. (2012b). "The construction and initial validation of the Work Volition Scale." *Journal of Vocational Behavior*, 80, 400–11.

Duffy, R. D. and Dik, B. J. (2013). "Research on calling: What have we learned and where are we going?" *Journal of Vocational Behavior*, 83, 428–36.

Duffy, R. D., Douglass, R. P., Autin, K. L., England, J., and Dik, B. J. (2016b). "Does the dark side of a calling exist? Examining potential negative effects." *The Journal of Positive Psychology*, 11, 634–46.

Duffy, R. D., Dik, B. J., Douglass, R. P., England, J. W., and Velez, B. L. (2018). "Work as a calling: A theoretical model." *Journal of Counseling Psychology*, 65, 423–39.

Duffy, R. D., England, J. W., Douglass, R. P., Autin, K. A., and Allan, B. A. (2017a). "Perceiving a calling and well-being: Motivation and access to opportunity as moderators." *Journal of Vocational Behavior*, 98, 127–37.

Duffy, R. D., Foley, P. F., Raque-Bogdan, T. L., Reid, L., Dik, B. J., Castano, M. C., and Adams, C. (2012c). "Counseling psychologists who view their careers as a calling: A qualitative study." *Journal of Career Assessment*, 20, 293–308.

Duffy, R. D., Torrey, C. L., England, J. W., and Tebbe, E. A. (2017b). "Calling in retirement: A mixed methods study." *The Journal of Positive Psychology*, 12, 399–413.

Esteves, T. and Lopes, M. P. (2017). "Crafting a calling: The mediating role of calling between challenging job demands and turnover intention." *Journal of Career Development*, 44, 34–48.

Freire, P. (1993). *Pedagogy of the Oppressed*. New York: Continuum.

Gazica, M. W. and Spector, P. E. (2015). "A comparison of individuals with unanswered callings to those with no calling at all." *Journal of Vocational Behavior*, 91, 1–10.

Hagmaier, T. and Abele, A. E. (2012). "The multidimensionality of calling: Conceptualization, measurement and a bicultural perspective." *Journal of Vocational Behavior*, 81(1), 39–51.

Hartnett, S. and Kline, F. (2005). "Preventing the fall from the 'Call to Teach': Rethinking vocation." *Journal of Education and Christian Belief*, 9(1), 9–20.

Hernandez, E. F., Foley, P. F., and Beitin, B. K. (2011). "Hearing the call: A phenomenological study of religion in career choice." *Journal of Career Development*, 38, 62–88.

Hirschi, A. (2012). "Callings and work engagement: Moderated mediation model of work meaningfulness, occupational identity, and occupational self-efficacy." *Journal of Counseling Psychology*, 59, 479–85.

Hirschi, A. and Herrmann, A. (2012). "Vocational identity achievement as a mediator of presence of a calling and life satisfaction." *Journal of Career Assessment*, 20(3), 309–21.

Hunter, I., Dik, B. J., and Banning, J. H. (2010). "College students' perceptions of calling in work and life: A qualitative analysis." *Journal of Vocational Behavior*, 76, 178–86.

Keller, A. C., Spurk, D., Baumeler, F., and Hirschi, A. (2016). "Competitive climate and workaholism: Negative sides of future orientation and calling." *Personality and Individual Differences*, 96, 122–6.

Kim, H. J., Praskova, A., and Lee, K. H. (2017). "Cross-cultural validation of the Career Calling Scale for Korean emerging adults." *Journal of Career Assessment*, 25(3), 434–49.

Lazar, A., Davidovitch, N., and Coren, G. (2016). "Gender differences in calling and work spirituality among Israeli academic faculty." *Journal of International Education Research*, 12(3), 87–98.

Lee, K. J. (2016). "Sense of calling and career satisfaction of hotel frontline employees." *International Journal of Contemporary Hospitality Management*, 28, 346–65.

Lee, A. Y. P., Chen, I. H., and Chang, P. C. (2018). "Sense of calling in the workplace: The moderating effect of supportive organizational climate in Taiwanese organizations." *Journal of Management & Organization*, 24(1), 129–44.

Levoy, G. (1997). *Callings: Finding and following an authentic life*. New York: Crown.

Lips-Wiersma, M. and Morris, L. (2009). "Discriminating between 'meaningful work' and the 'management of meaning.'" *Journal of Business Ethics*, 88, 491–511.

Lobene, E. V. and Meade, A. W. (2013). "The effects of career calling and perceived overqualification on work outcomes for primary and secondary school teachers." *Journal of Career Development*, 40, 508–30.

Markland, D., Ryan, R. M., Tobin, V. J., and Rollnick, S. (2005). "Motivational interviewing and self-determination theory." *Journal of Social and Clinical Psychology*, 24, 811–31.

Ng, T. W. H., Sorensen, K. L., and Feldman, D. C. (2007). "Dimensions, antecedents, and consequences of workaholism: A conceptual integration and extension." *Journal of Organizational Behavior*, 28(1), 111–36.

Oates, K. L. M., Hall, M. E. L., and Anderson, T. L. (2005). "Calling and conflict: A qualitative exploration of interrole conflict and the sanctification of work in Christian mothers." *Journal of Psychology and Theology*, 33, 210–23.

Park, C. L. (2012). "Religious and Spiritual Aspects of Meaning in the Context of Work Life." In P. Hill and B. Dik (eds.), *Psychology of Religion and Workplace Spirituality*, pp. 25–42. Charlotte, NC: Information Age Publishing.

Park, J., Sohn, Y. W., and Ha, Y. J. (2016). "South Korean salespersons' calling, job performance, and organizational citizenship behavior: The mediating role of occupational self-efficacy." *Journal of Career Assessment*, 24, 415–28.

Pervin, L. A. (1968). "Performance and satisfaction as a function of individual–environment fit." *Psychological Bulletin*, 69, 56–8.

Peterson, C., Park, N., Hall, N., and Seligman, M. E. P. (2009). "Zest and work." *Journal of Organizational Behavior*, 30, 161–72.

Schabram, K. and Maitlis, S. (2017). "Negotiating the challenges of a calling: Emotion and enacted sensemaking in animal shelter work." *Academy of Management Journal*, 60(2), 584–609.

Serow, R. C. (1994). "Called to teach: A study of highly motivated preservice teachers." *Journal of Research and Development in Education*, 27, 65–72.

Sherman, D. (2004). "Nurses' stress and burnout: How to care for yourself when caring for patients and their families experiencing life-threatening illness." *American Journal of Nursing*, 104, 48–56.

Steger, M. F., Dik, B. J., and Duffy, R. D. (2012). "Measuring meaningful work: The Work and Meaning Inventory (WAMI)." *Journal of Career Assessment*, 20, 322–37.

Vinje, H. F. and Mittelmark, M. B. (2007). "Job engagement's paradoxical role in nurse burnout." *Nursing & Health Sciences*, 9, 107–11.

Watts, R. J., Diemer, M. A., and Voight, A. M. (2011). "Critical consciousness: Current status and future directions." *New Directions for Child and Adolescent Development*, 134, 43–57.

Wrzesniewski, A. and Dutton, J. E. (2001). "Crafting a job: Revisioning employees as active crafters of their work." *Academy of Management Review*, 26, 179–201.

Wrzesniewski, A., McCauley, C. R., Rozin, P., and Schwartz, B. (1997). "Jobs, careers, and callings: People's relations to their work." *Journal of Research in Personality*, 31, 21–33.

Xie, B., Xia, M., Xin, X., and Zhou, W. (2016). "Linking calling to work engagement and subjective career success: The perspective of career construction theory." *Journal of Vocational Behavior*, 94, 70–8.

Zhang, C., Dik, B. J., Wei, J., and Zhang, J. (2015). "Work as a calling in China: A qualitative study of Chinese college students." *Journal of Career Assessment*, 23, 236–49.

CHAPTER 17

DOES MY ENGAGEMENT MATTER?

*Exploring the Relationship Between Employee
Engagement and Meaningful Work
in Theory and Practice*

BRAD SHUCK

SCHOLARS have reasoned that experiences of meaningful work are central to the development of employee engagement (Bailey et al., 2017; Fletcher, Bailey, and Gilman, 2017; Kahn, 1990; Shuck and Rose, 2013). Being enveloped in truly purposeful, meaningful work points to the core of what it means to be engaged (Bunderson and Thompson, 2009; Chalofsky, 2010; May, Gilson, and Harter, 2004). Notwithstanding, undignified work, coercive practices, and the decay of meaning in the psychology and practice of work threaten the very centrality and humanness of the working experience (Yeoman, 2014). The question of how and where employees place their energy and attention may be best understood in a simple question posed by Kahn (2010): "*does my engagement matter?*" If experiences of employee engagement are to matter, scholars and practitioners must understand how to best approach employee engagement as a practice and also as a consequence of the engagement they seek. Infusing employee engagement within the experience of meaningful work starts with a re-evaluation of what employee engagement is as a psychological state, rather than as an outcome we take from, or that takes from an employee as a normative, exploitative product.

This chapter explores the relationship between meaningful work and employee engagement as well as emerging implications for research and practice in the context of the principles that drive our understanding of both these constructs. First, the chapter details the positioning of employee engagement, exploring engagement's political roots alongside its conceptualization as a psychological state. Second, the ideals of employee engagement are considered through the tenets of meaningful work. Finally, the chapter concludes by looking forward to the future of meaningful work as a condition for employee engagement and proposes brief implications for research and practice.

Positioning Employee Engagement from Political Roots to Psychological State

At this time, there is no unified definition, framework, or understanding of the engagement phenomenon—employee engagement, or otherwise (c.f. work engagement, job engagement, etc.; Schaufeli, 2013; Shuck et al., 2017b). There is, however, a growing clarity about engagement linked-states, as well as distinctions regarding the positionality of employee engagement (c.f. Saks and Gruman, 2014; Shuck, Nimon, and Zigarmi, 2016b). While *work* engagement is focused toward an employee's energy at work (Schaufeli, 2013), and *job* engagement is concerned with the energy directed toward a specific job task (Rich, Lepine, and Crawford, 2010), *employee* engagement has been defined as a *positive, active, work-related psychological state* (Nimon, Shuck, and Zigarmi, 2016; Shuck et al., 2016a, 2017b) operationalized *by the maintenance, intensity,* and *direction of cognitive, emotional,* and *behavioral energy* (Shuck and Wollard, 2010). Despite growing definitional clarity among constructs, the idea of employee engagement remains a highly politicized and potentially exploitive construct (Keenoy, 2013).

For example, situated in the more established motivation literature, much of the research on employee engagement remains focused on those variables shown to influence a heightened state of performance, yet scholars provide little to ground this claim in solid, evidence-based practice (Briner, 2015). Consequently, much of the employee engagement research is focused on engagement (as a general term) and the immediate work task (i.e. performance). Generally speaking, research around employee engagement has been about harnessing the power of engagement to do things faster, better, and more profitably (Harter et al., 2010; Hoon Song et al., 2012). The ambition toward driving performance has inextricably positioned employee engagement as benefiting the organization at the expense of the employee and, consequently, as an organizationally political ideal (Guest, 2014; Purcell, 2014; Shuck et al., 2016a). From this perspective, employee engagement is a privilege, benefiting a handful of the powerful but failing to take account of the employee (Shuck et al., 2016a). For example, when employee engagement is positioned as an outcome only, the *employee* in *employee engagement* becomes irrelevant and the construct anchored in an insatiable appetite for more, with little concern about cost or causality. Unfortunately, within this outcome focus, there exists a wealth of documented undignified and coercive practices directed at increasing levels of engagement by way of objectification, meager leadership, and dysfunction (Brown and Starkey, 2000; Rose et al., 2015; Sutton, 2010). For example, as detailed in Shuck et al. (2017a), some of those coercive practices include, in one instance, the development of a winning-at-all-cost culture where employees "who suffered from cancer, miscarriages, and other personal crises" (Kantor and Streitfeld, 2015: B1) were evaluated unfairly, fired, or forced to resign, all in the pursuit of higher levels of performance. Such objectified practices are clearly undignified, and lead to extreme dysfunction in the workplace (Goh, Pfeffer, and

Zenios, 2015). In this vein, engagement has been seemingly dominated by studies exploring linkages between engagement and performance-centric outcomes such as turnover
intention (Bal, De Cooman, and Mol, 2011), discretionary effort (Lloyd, 2008; Shuck,
Reio, and Rocco, 2011), and profitability (Harter et al., 2010; Xanthopoulou et al., 2009).

Notwithstanding, a handful of scholars have begun evaluating the available evidence
between employee engagement and performance. For example, in their narrative
synthesis, Bailey et al. (2017) noted the important empirical linkages between employee
engagement and variables such as job satisfaction, organizational commitment, and
intention to turnover, as well as in-role, extra-role, and counter-role behaviors. While
these results were promising, Bailey et al. (2017) contended that much of the existing
research included in their study was limited, often grounded in cross-sectional, self-report
data, potentially confounded by common methods bias, and with almost no evidence of
replication. They further stated that, "Given the scarcity of studies, their individualistic
nature, methodological limitations and the range of interventions studied, it is difficult
to draw any robust conclusions" (2017: 44). Taking a more extreme perspective, Briner
(2014) has suggested that research on employee engagement is contaminated with over-
hyped claims, widespread misunderstanding, and inaccurate measurement.

In defense of engagement as an outcome, this positioning is understandable, given that
new variables in the fields of management and human resources need to demonstrate
instantaneous practical utility (Barrick, Mount, and Li, 2013), or risk being disregarded
altogether. Any other focus would not translate quickly to adoption and use; consequently, without a clear path to practical application, employee engagement would
likely have already faded into irrelevancy. Nonetheless, such a narrow assessment of
the employee engagement construct has resulted in a disjointed understanding and the
development of only one perspective on engagement, regularly valuing the outcome
(e.g. performance) over the individual experience. However, the individual experience
of engagement is rooted in the person, and does not take for granted that engagement
can also be connected to performance, i.e. that there is an immediate link between how
people both experience their work and perform at their work (Chalofsky and Krishna,
2009; Chalofsky, 2010; Fairlie, 2011; Fletcher, Bailey, and Gilman, 2017; Kahn, 2010;
Shuck and Rose, 2013; Yeoman, 2014). The individual experience of engagement denotes
personally perceived significance (Barrick, Mount, and Li, 2013); it is unique to the
person and their interpretation of a context, not to the overt or objective significance of
an event in isolation (i.e. performance). As suggested earlier, the question of how and
where employees engage is best understood in a question posed by Kahn (2010): *"Does
my engagement matter?"*—which, by extension, also begs questions such as *does my
performance matter, do the outcomes I am involved with matter,* and *does my presence
matter?* Such questions are asked from an individual perspective, interpreted through
an individual lens, and grounded in an individual's unique experience (Kahn, 1990).

Parker and Griffin (2011) cautioned that an inordinate amount of attention in the
research literature has been focused toward the measurement of engagement. This
disproportionate focus has neglected an understanding of the state of engagement and
accelerated the outcome perspective, valuing objectification over formation. In many

cases, for example, the measurement of engagement has come to broadly define the theoretical domain (e.g. the Utrecht Work Engagement Scale [UWES]; Schaufeli et al., 2002)—that is, the measurement and theoretical structure have become conjoined. This conjoining occurred as the measurement of engagement became synonymous with what engagement was believed to be: the measurement of how *vigorous*, *dedicated*, and/or *absorbed* a person was in their work. Yet, "a measure should tap important aspects of a construct, but it should not define the domain of research" (Parker and Griffin, 2011: 61). Employee engagement has, however, become very much entangled with its measurement at the peril of ignoring the processes and context from which it forms as an experience—consequently robbing it of meaning (Jenkins and Delbridge, 2013). Defining any one construct, engagement or otherwise, by its measurement with little regard to the processes that influence the phenomenon being measured leaves the theoretical structure inadequately developed, and consequently increasingly politicized. This has presented a major challenge for understanding the full range and applicability of employee engagement as "context can affect what types of behavior are possible and/or important" (Parker and Griffin, 2011: 65).

Unfortunately, the process of politicizing engagement has resulted in a disconnect from the tenets of meaningful work. In most cases, the objectification of employee engagement—the degrading of engagement to an object of performance—is devoid of meaning and/or meaningful work. Examples of this objectification are most obvious in a practical context, for instance through the recommendation to classify groups of employees with arbitrary labels (e.g. engaged, disengaged, and/or actively disengaged), by referring to employees as "prisoners" (Hewitt, 2015), and by way of an increasing focus on "easy steps" to raise levels of employee engagement (Lockwood, 2007), "top ten" lists for building engagement (Potgieter, 2016), and books with titles such as *Employee Engagement for Dummies* (Kelleher, 2013).

From a scholarly perspective, the objectification of engagement can be linked to early versions of the Utrecht perspective on engagement (Schaufeli, Bakker, and Salanova, 2006), where the definition of work engagement is concerned only with an employee's levels of absorption, vigor, and dedication, at the expense of Kahn's early perspective on personal role engagement, which clearly situated meaningful work at the very core of personal engagement (Kahn, 1990).

Employee engagement is not easy, and there are no quick steps. Employee engagement is also not for dummies, and employees are not prisoners; instead, employees are people who have context, meaning, and a voice. Moreover, employee engagement is not only about vigor and absorption, but we must also consider why an employee might be dedicated in the first place, not just how dedicated they are and what can easily be measured. Suggesting that employee engagement is any of those things in isolation devalues what it means to be engaged with work that is deeply personal and meaningful, and positions engagement as a tangible outcome to be manipulated and moved at the whim of organizational need and profitability. The overarching challenge with this performance-centric perspective is that, through this lens, when employees are defined as prisoners, or when employee engagement is reduced to its lowest common denominator (i.e. engagement for dummies), employees are treated as resources to be manipulated and controlled, in the same way that lumber, coffee beans, and cattle are resources to be organized and measured (Wagner, 2015). Under the guise of objectification, employees are pawns, shifted to satisfy the corporate structure of a neo-political capitalist agenda to generate as much revenue as possible and to do what they are told: to be more engaged (i.e. work faster and harder). In this space, employee engagement is an outcome and not a meaningful experience.

Employee engagement as an outcome is, however, a myth—a murmuration of objects (Keenoy, 2013). Leaders have very little power to demand engagement, and can do little to fabricate its existence. From this politicized perspective, Guest (2014) and Keenoy (2013) were right. When employee engagement is objectified, it is nothing more than the normative, overt exploitation of workers and a keen source of cunning corporate propaganda. As such, and when politicized, employee engagement comes with the baggage of privilege and power (Shuck et al., 2016a). Because employee engagement is an unbalanced state of being (e.g. an employee cannot be engaged in two places at the same time), when politicized, employee engagement is something that takes from the employee, and employee engagement becomes transactional (e.g. exchange; c.f. Saks, 2006). In the most extreme form, the outcome perspective on employee engagement is a cleverly devised social system designed to perpetuate a state of corporate/employee aggression.

On the other hand, employee engagement is much more than an objectified, politicized outcome. Exploitation and objectification were not the original intent of the employee engagement idea; this is especially true as we connect employee engagement to experiences of meaningful work (Bunderson and Thompson, 2009; Chalofsky and Krishna, 2009; Chalofsky, 2010; Yeoman, 2014). Kahn (1990), one of the very first scholars to focus toward the ideals of being engaged, was clear that personal engagement was a deeply meaningful and motivating momentary psychological state. Being engaged meant being fulfilled and accomplished (i.e. transformed by work), not controlled and exploited. The bastardization of the general engagement construct occurred as it became increasingly professionalized and coupled with business outcomes that defined the relevancy of being engaged and offered the alluring promise of performance and profit (Harter et al., 2010; Xanthopoulou et al., 2009).

As the literature on employee engagement has started a deepening development, it is also coming full circle: from an objectified, political focus, to an emphasis on meaning and meaningful work. As an artifact of this meaningful work emphasis, the employee engagement construct continues to transform. What scholars interact with—the term "engagement" itself—has changed little, yet our understanding of what employee engagement is continues to shift from one driven by objectified connections to performance and profitability to one of personal significance and intense meaning. To depoliticize employee engagement, researchers have begun the process of detaching the psychological roots of the construct from organizational exploitation and re-establishing the boundaries of engagement within the personal influence of the employee (c.f. Bailey et al., 2017; Fletcher, Bailey, and Gilman, 2017; Soane et al., 2013; Truss et al., 2013), shifting the power back to the employee and giving voice and psychological empowerment to each individual (Yukl and Becker, 2006).

Apart from the political positioning, the emerging understanding of employee engagement is that the construct, and how we experience it, is an individual, psychological experience that unfolds in three interrelated dimensions: *cognitively, emotionally,* and *behaviorally*. Each interrelated dimension is understood as an appraisal connected to both lived and future-expected experiences, used in the development of beliefs that inform decision-making about in-the-moment and future behavior. Grounded in earlier psychological models (e.g. Kahn, 1990; Rich, Lepine, and Crawford, 2010; Soane et al., 2012; Truss et al., 2013), this positioning captures salient, contextually sensitive cues regarding an employee's interpretation of their organizational environment and informs an *intention* to act, not the observable outcome. It is impossible, for example, for engagement to be simultaneously both a latent state and an observable outcome. Consequently, as an individual, psychological experience, employee engagement is wholly about the employee and the interpretation of information used to make decisions that influence action within that experience.

This emerging positioning (c.f. Shuck et al., 2017b) provides voice to the way an employee experiences their work, how they understand messages regarding their value, as well as detail about the processing and integration of clear messages regarding personal contribution. Remarkably, positioning engagement as an individual, psychological experience takes nothing from the outcomes. Employee engagement can be, and still is, linked to performance; this repositioning, from an objectified outcome to an individual, psychological experience, however, shifts the power of engagement back to the employee as a transformational experience that builds from the employee and is defined by the employee, rather than takes from them, and is defined by someone else (Shuck et al., 2016a). This repositioning infuses the tenets of meaningful work as a core experience of employee engagement, and offers substantive power to the employee to define, interpret, and inform decision-making about what is meaningful and what is not, and to engage accordingly.

Repositioning Employee Engagement as a Psychological State Through Meaningful Work

Scholars have long suggested that how employees experience degrees of meaningfulness in their work remains an important antecedent condition to building sustainable cultures of employee engagement. That is, without meaning, engagement is an unlikely experience. Numerous scholars have gone on to suggest that experienced meaningfulness—the degree to which an employee sees their involvement as contributory and toward a purpose—is central to the formation of employee engagement (Bailey et al., 2017; Chalofsky and

Krishna, 2009; Chalofsky, 2010; Fairlie, 2011; Fletcher, Bailey, and Gilman, 2017; Shuck and Rose, 2013).

Individual and personal experience are often linked to significance, and experienced meaningfulness denotes personally perceived significance (Barrick, Mount, and Li, 2013). Such significance is unique to the person and to their interpretation of a context, not to the objective significance of an event (i.e. what is interpreted as meaningful to one person may not be interpreted as meaningful to another). Positioning engagement in this light removes its political and exploitative nature. When someone defines the value of engagement for an employee, it is political and devoid of meaning, but when the employee defines the value about a context they are in (however they may see it), meaning and engagement become symbiotically linked. It would follow that employees would give very little energy, intensity, and direction to those contexts deemed meaningless.

The meaningfulness of work is a transitory, comprehensive evaluation where an employee weighs whether or not they trust that their participation adds some degree of value or significance and whether this significance is received and reciprocated (i.e. degree of meaningfulness; Kahn, 1990; Maslow, 1968). More, the reciprocation of the value in participation is continuously monitored, as an employee ebbs and flows in each moment, constantly monitoring and judging how they are being received in the present and whether continued participation is a meaningful activity. Maintenance, intensity, and direction follow (Shuck et al., 2017b). The cognitive interpretation of whether a situation, interaction, or some request for action is meaningful is a moment-to-moment decision, in constant flux, and emerging from the interpretation and perspective of the employee.

Ultimately, when an employee believes their participation is meaningful, and that their engagement matters, they take action toward a target (however a target or action is defined). In consequence, those who fail to interpret their personal contributions as meaningful, or when an employee makes the interpretation that an overall context is not meaningful (there is nothing for me to gain here; this is a waste of my time; or, I cannot do this), they pull away, redirect their energy, and engage someplace else. Engagement must be a choice, not an objectified mandate, and this choice is centered in an appraisal connected to lived and future-expected experiences, that drive intention and, from a working perspective, connect directly to the ideals of meaningful work.

In summary, meaningful work goes hand in hand with the experienced state of employee engagement. The two are linked in reciprocal fashion. It seems plausible that employees rarely place energy into a context where they find little meaning or where they believe their efforts will ultimately result in a fruitless, empty endeavor. Thus, work devoid of meaning would be work that is both politicized and objectified, and perhaps damaging and unhealthy, physically, emotionally, and socially. In such contexts, the psychological state of employee engagement seems unlikely to flourish, and it would be absurd to expect anything different. On the other hand, when employees perceive their work as deeply meaningful, and their contributions as adding value, increased levels of employee engagement are a potentially transformative and fulfilling experience.

Connecting Meaningful Work and Employee Engagement: Looking Forward without Objectifying the Experience

There are several fruitful opportunities for future work to be highlighted within this narrative. First, employee engagement should be positioned, and continue to be developed, as a psychological state, and not an outcome. One of the connected challenges that researchers continually face revolves around accurate measurement of the state itself, not just the antecedents. There are many scales that purport to measure some aspect of employee engagement. On closer inspection, however, what such scales actually measure are the conditions that precede a state of engagement, with one of those conditions being meaningful work. As discussed at length throughout this chapter, research on employee engagement has been reliably linked to meaningful work as a critical condition for development. Meaningful work is, however, not the same as the state of employee engagement, and we must be careful to not confuse the two constructs (or experiences). Should employee engagement and meaningful work become conflated, scholars could easily fall back into objectifying both constructs, and then miss important nuances that might help researchers and practitioners better understand how both operate in practice.

Second, while the focus of this chapter is on the intersection of meaningful work and employee engagement, there remains a lack of focused research connecting the two constructs. Only a small grouping of research has empirically explored this specific connection (e.g. Chalofsky and Krishna, 2009; Fairlie, 2011; Fletcher, Bailey, and Gilman, 2017; Kahn, 1990; May, Gilson, and Harter, 2004; Shuck, Reio, and Rocco, 2011; Soane et al., 2013; Steger, Dik, and Duffy, 2012), and there is yet to be replication of findings across most studies. Notwithstanding, emerging support is growing (c.f. Fletcher, Bailey, and Gilman, 2017) and the evidence we do have suggests that experiences of meaningful work can influence the psychological state of employee engagement to a great extent. There is more to uncover and this should be a focus of promising future research and theorizing.

In this vein, focus should be placed on how meaningful work is operationalized, the theoretical structure from which it is derived, and what measures best capture the salient experience of meaning. One of the growing challenges will be to find ways of measurement that do not extinguish meaning and/or meaningful work when operationalized in practice. One way scholars could accomplish this would be to focus on the experience of meaningful work, and not the outcomes of having meaningful work, until the phenomenon is accurately captured. Similar to the positioning of the employee engagement construct, meaningful work has an adaptable positionality, yet without careful attention to that locus (e.g. as an outcome, as an antecedent, or as a state), researchers could inadvertently muddle the meaning and interpretation of what it signifies to have a work experience that is meaningful, or what it means to be engaged in meaningful work. Qualitative inquiry, or mixed methods approaches could be exciting avenues from which to explore the ideas of meaningful work, as highlighted in the rigorous diary study by Fletcher, Bailey, and Gilman (2017).

DEVELOPING CULTURES OF EMPLOYEE ENGAGEMENT THROUGH MEANINGFUL WORK: GUIDELINES FOR PRACTICE

What seem most salient to connections between employee engagement and meaningful work are those specifics of practice that can aid practitioners in positively nudging forward their places of work.

Scholars have recommended several important implications for practice around the development of engagement-related meaningful work, such as reconceptualizing meaningful work as a right, and lowering financial constraints through livable wages (Allan, Autin, and Duffy, 2014; Roessler, 2012), focusing on employees' psychological well-being (Arnold et al., 2007), continual opportunity for work-related learning, competency mastery, stimulating and energizing work, and cohesive fit (Chalofsky and Cavallaro, 2013), as well as implementing mentoring programs (Kennett and Lomas, 2015) and emotional intelligence training (Thory, 2016). Notwithstanding these exceptional suggestions for practice-focused work, the temptation to focus toward explicit practices that look enticing without regard to the principles that drive such practice often derail meaning, and consequently levels of employee engagement. Mentoring programs often fall short because they feel forced. Emotional intelligence training is mandated, and learning becomes regulated, and consequently extrinsically motivated. While any one practice may be inherently meaningful, when focused on as a practice only, leaders can unintentionally, yet easily, squash the practice of creating meaningful work. Free food in a cafeteria, a relaxed dress code on Friday, or after hours get-togethers are popular practices that appear in books that espouse "top ten" lists (Kelleher, 2013). It is important to point out, however, that mentoring programs and relaxed dress codes do not build engagement (this is an example of objectification). What is far more important than any one practice is an understanding of the principles that drive engagement (i.e. that employees engage when they experience work that is meaningful; Kahn, 1990). When engagement is limited to implementation at the surface level only, the experience is devoid of principle and becomes politicized. Engagement on the surface is inauthentic, exploitative, and objectified and we must go beyond practices by connecting our practice to fundamental principles that drive the experience.

A second important implication for practice is in understanding that employee engagement is the long game. That is, employee engagement builds over time, and is connected to cumulative experiences of meaningful work. What feels sudden in the moment (e.g. an employee finds themselves engaged in tremendously fulfilling work) has been building in ethos, purpose, and meaning over a long period of time. We might assume from reading the research that employee engagement operates like a light switch. An employee is either engaged, or not engaged/disengaged. They are on or off. This is not, however, an accurate depiction of how employee engagement operates in the real world.

Organizations launch engagement movements, or events, in hopes that engagement-focused campaigns will provide much needed momentum to inspire employees toward higher levels of engagement. Often spending excessive capital, expectations are understandably high. Unfortunately, for many leaders, their hope of a more engaged, meaningful future has been placed in weak promises that execute poorly. The mystique of employee engagement is not in movements and launch parties, or an annual survey. Rather, proven strategies for building higher levels of employee engagement are exceptionally easy to do: help people see and connect to the meaning in their work; capitalize on opportunities to recognize employees; deeply consider and talk about the development and career path of individuals; treat people with dignity; among others. Such strategies are low-risk and low-cost. In fact, these strategies are so easy to undertake, they often get overlooked as strategies at all. The hard work is in operationalizing what it means to treat people with dignity, or to connect meaning to work. On paper this sounds dismissively easy, yet many organizations do these things so very poorly.

Last, knowing that meaningful work is likely connected to employee engagement is not enough. Practitioners must go further in defining those practices that operationalize what it means to have meaningful work driven by autonomy, freedom, and dignity (Yeoman, 2014). More, May, Gilson, and Harter (2004) operationalized Kahn's (1990) notion of meaningful work as that work that has value, is important, and is experienced as worthwhile. But, as practitioners, we should go further in naming and applying what that means. It would behoove leaders to derive practices that are well grounded, and that have deep roots in a recognized theoretical framework (c.f. Yeoman, 2014), but also that can be implemented and taught. This is, unfortunately, not the current state of the meaningful work–employee engagement linkage, and will be admittedly hard work to complete. Notwithstanding, taking on this hard work will ensure that those practices of meaningful work connected to the development of employee engagement will not only be theoretically sound, but also sensitive to the context of their own work and organization, and most importantly, usable. Creating communities of purposeful, meaningful work where employees are authentically engaged is a worthy effort, indeed.

REFERENCES

Allan, B. A., Autin, K. L., and Duffy, R. D. (2014). "Examining social class and work meaning within the psychology of working framework." *Journal of Career Assessment*, 22(4), 543–61.

Arnold, K. A., Turner, N., Barling, J., Kelloway, E. K., and McKee, M. C. (2007). "Transformational leadership and psychological well-being: The mediating role of meaningful work." *Journal of Occupational Health Psychology*, 12(3), 193–203.

Bailey, C., Madden, A., Alfes, K., and Fletcher, L. (2017). "The meaning, antecedents and outcomes of employee engagement: A narrative synthesis." *International Journal of Management Reviews*, 19, 31–53.

Bal, P. M., De Cooman, R., and Mol, S. T. (2011). "Dynamics of psychological contracts with work engagement and turnover intention: The influence of organizational tenure." *European Journal of Work and Organizational Psychology*, 22(1), 107–22.

Barrick, M. R., Mount, M. K., and Li, N. (2013). "The theory of purposeful work behavior: The role of personality, higher-order goals, and job characteristics." *Academy of Management Review*, 38(1), 132–53.

Briner, R. B. (2014). "What is employee engagement and does it matter? An evidence-based approach." *The Future of Engagement Thought Piece Collection*, pp. 51–71. London: CIPD.

Briner, R. (2015). "What's the evidence for . . . evidence-based HR?" *HR Magazine*, January 14.

Brown, A. D. and Starkey, K. (2000). "Organizational identity and learning: A psychodynamic perspective." *Academy of Management Review*, 25(1), 102–20.

Bunderson, J. S. and Thompson, J. A. (2009). "The call of the wild: Zookeepers, callings, and the double-edged sword of deeply meaningful work." *Administrative Science Quarterly*, 54, 32–57.

Chalofsky, N. E. (2010). *Meaningful Workplaces: Reframing how and where we work*. San Francisco: Jossey-Bass.

Chalofsky, N. and Cavallaro, L. (2013). "A good living versus a good life: Meaning, purpose, and HRD." *Advances in Developing Human Resources*, 15(4), 331–40.

Chalofsky, N. and Krishna, V. (2009). "Meaningfulness, commitment, and engagement: The intersection of a deeper level of intrinsic motivation." *Advances in Developing Human Resources*, 11(2), 189–203.

Fairlie, P. (2011). "Meaningful work, employee engagement, and other key employee outcomes: Implications for human resource development." *Advances in Developing Human Resources*, 13(4), 508–25.

Fletcher, L., Bailey, C., and Gilman, M. (2017). "Fluctuating levels of personal role engagement within the working day: A multilevel study." *Human Resource Management Journal*, 28(1), 128–47.

Goh, J., Pfeffer, J., and Zenios, S. (2015). "Exposure to harmful workplace practices could account for inequality in life spans across different demographic groups." *Health Affairs*, 34(10), 1761–8.

Guest, D. (2014). "Employee engagement: A sceptical analysis." *Journal of Organizational Effectiveness: People and Performance*, 1(2), 141–56.

Harter, J. K., Schmidt, F. L., Asplund, J. W., Killham, E. A. and Agrawal, S. (2010) "Causal impact of employee work perceptions on the bottom line of organizations." *Perspectives on Psychological Science*, 5(4), 378–89.

Hewitt, A. (2015). *Actively Disengaged and Staying: Dealing with "prisoners" in the workplace*. Minneapolis, MN: Modern Survey. Available at: http://www.modernsurvey.com/wp-content/uploads/2016/10/Actively-Disengaged-Staying.pdf [accessed June 9, 2018].

Hoon Song, J., Kolb, J. A., Hee Lee, U., and Kyoung Kim, H. (2012). "Role of transformational leadership in effective organizational knowledge creation practices: Mediating effects of employees' work engagement." *Human Resource Development Quarterly*, 23(1), 65–101.

Jenkins, S. and Delbridge, R. (2013). "Context matters: examining 'soft' and 'hard' approaches to employee engagement in two workplaces." *International Journal of Human Resource Management*, 24(14), 2670–91.

Kahn, W. A. (1990). "Psychological conditions of personal engagement and disengagement at work." *Academy of Management Journal*, 33(4), 692–724.

Kahn, W. A. (2010). "The Essence of Engagement: Lessons from the Field." In S. L. Albrecht (ed.), *Handbook of Employee Engagement: Perspectives, issues, research and practice*, pp. 20–30. Cheltenham, UK: Edward Elgar.

Kantor, J. and Streitfeld, D. (2015). "Inside Amazon: Wrestling big ideas in a bruising workplace." *New York Times*, August 15.

Keenoy, T. (2013). "Engagement: A Murmuration of Objects?" In C. Truss, R. Delbridge, K. Alfes, A. Shantz, and E. Soane (eds.), *Employee Engagement in Theory and Practice*, pp. 197–220. New York: Routledge.

Kelleher, B. (2013). *Employee Engagement for Dummies*. Hoboken, NJ: John Wiley & Sons.

Kennett, P. and Lomas, T. (2015). "Making meaning through mentoring: Mentors finding fulfilment at work through self-determination and self-reflection." *International Journal of Evidence Based Coaching and Mentoring*, 13(2), 29–44.

Lloyd, R. (2008). "Discretionary effort and the performance domain." *Australasian Journal of Organisational Psychology*, 1, 22–34.

Lockwood, N. R. (2007). "Leveraging employee engagement for competitive advantage." *Society for Human Resource Management*, 1, 1–12.

Maslow, A. H. (1968). *Toward a Psychology of Being*. New York: Van Nostrand.

May, D. R., Gilson, R. L., and Harter, L. M. (2004). "The psychological conditions of meaningfulness, safety and availability and the engagement of the human spirit at work." *Journal of Occupational and Organizational Psychology*, 77(1), 11–37.

Nimon, K., Shuck, B., and Zigarmi, D. (2016). "The tie that binds employee engagement and job attitudes: Harmonious passion and work affect?" *Proceedings of the Academy of Human Resource Development Conference, Academy of Human Resource Development International Conference in the Americas, Jacksonville, FL*. St. Paul, MN: AHRD.

Parker, S. K. and Griffin, M. A. (2011). "Understanding active psychological states: Embedding engagement in a wider nomological net and closer attention to performance." *European Journal of Work and Organizational Psychology*, 20(1), 60–7.

Potgieter, L. (2016). *10 steps that ensure employee engagement success* [web page]. Engagement Strategies Media. Available at: http://enterpriseengagement.org/articles/content/8289281/10-steps-that-ensure-employee-engagement-success/ [accessed July 16, 2018].

Purcell, J. (2014). "Disengaging from engagement." *Human Resource Management Journal*, 24(3), 241–54.

Rich, B. L., Lepine, J. A., and Crawford, E. R. (2010). "Job engagement: Antecedents and effects on job performance." *Academy of Management Journal*, 53(3), 617–35.

Roessler, B. (2012). "Meaningful work: Arguments from autonomy." *Journal of Political Philosophy*, 20(1), 71–93.

Rose, K., Shuck, B., Twyford, D., and Bergman, M. (2015). "Skunked: An integrative review exploring the consequences of the dysfunctional leader and implications for those employees who work for them." *Human Resource Development Review*, 14(1), 64–90.

Saks, A. M. (2006). "Antecedents and consequences of employee engagement." *Journal of Managerial Psychology*, 21(7), 600–19.

Saks, A. M. and Gruman, J. A. (2014). "What do we really know about employee engagement?" *Human Resource Development Quarterly*, 25(2), 155–82.

Schaufeli, W. B. (2013). "What is Engagement?" In C. Truss, R. Delbridge, K. Alfes, A. Shantz, and E. Soane (eds.), *Employee Engagement in Theory and Practice*, pp. 15–35. New York: Routledge.

Schaufeli, W. B., Bakker, A. B., and Salanova, M. (2006). "The measurement of work engagement with a short questionnaire." *Educational and Psychological Measurement*, 66(4), 701.

Schaufeli, W. B., Salanova, M., González-Romá, V., and Bakker, A. B. (2002). "The measurement of engagement and burnout: A two sample confirmatory factor analytic approach." *Journal of Happiness Studies*, 3(1), 71–92.

Shuck, B., Alagaraja, M., Rose, K., Owen, J., Osam, K., and Bergman, M. (2017a). "The health-related upside of employee engagement: Exploratory evidence and implications for theory and practice." *Performance Improvement Quarterly*, 30(3), 165–78.

Shuck, B., Collins, J. C., Rocco, T. S., and Diaz, R. (2016a). "Deconstructing the privilege and power of employee engagement issues of inequality for management and Human Resource Development." *Human Resource Development Review*, 15(2), 208–29.

Shuck, B., Nimon, K., and Zigarmi, D. (2016b). "Untangling the predictive nomological validity of employee engagement: Decomposing variance in employee engagement using job attitude measures." *Group & Organization Management*, 42(1), 79–112.

Shuck, B., Osam, K., Zigarmi, D., and Nimon, K. (2017b). "Definitional and conceptual muddling: Identifying the positionality of employee engagement and defining the construct." *Human Resource Development Review*, 16(3), 263–93.

Shuck, B., Reio, T. G., and Rocco, T. S. (2011). "Employee engagement: An examination of antecedent and outcome variables." *Human Resource Development International*, 14(4), 427–45.

Shuck, B. and Rose, K. (2013). "Reframing employee engagement within the context of meaning and purpose: implications for HRD." *Advances in Developing Human Resources*, 15(4), 341–55.

Shuck, B. and Wollard, K. (2010). "Employee engagement and HRD: A seminal review of the foundations." *Human Resource Development Review*, 9(1), 89–110.

Soane, E., Shantz, A., Alfes, K., Truss, C., Rees, C., and Gatenby, M. (2013). "The association of meaningfulness, well-being, and engagement with absenteeism: A moderated mediation model." *Human Resource Management*, 52(3), 441–56.

Soane, E., Truss, C., Alfes, K., Shantz, A., Rees, C., and Gatenby, M. (2012). "Development and application of a new measure of employee engagement: The ISA Engagement Scale." *Human Resource Development International*, 15(5), 529–47.

Steger, M. F., Dik, B. J., and Duffy, R. D. (2012). "Measuring meaningful work: The work and meaning inventory (WAMI)." *Journal of Career Assessment*, 20(3), 322–37.

Sutton, R. (2010). *Good Boss, Bad Boss: How to be the best and learn from the worst*. New York: Hachette Book Group.

Thory, K. (2016). "Developing meaningfulness at work through emotional intelligence training." *International Journal of Training and Development*, 20(1), 58–77.

Truss, C., Shantz, A., Soane, E., Alfes, K., and Delbridge, R. (2013). "Employee engagement, organisational performance and individual well-being: Exploring the evidence, developing the theory." *International Journal of Human Resource Management*, 24(14), 2657–69.

Wagner, R. (2015). *Widgets: The 12 new rules for managing your employees as if they're real people*. New York: McGraw-Hill Professional.

Xanthopoulou, D., Bakker, A. B., Demerouti, E., and Schaufeli, W. B. (2009). "Work engagement and financial returns: A diary study on the role of job and personal resources." *Journal of Occupational and Organizational Psychology*, 82(1), 183–200.

Yeoman, R. (2014). "Conceptualising meaningful work as a fundamental human need." *Journal of Business Ethics*, 125(2), 235–51.

Yukl, G. A. and Becker, W. S. (2006). "Effective empowerment in organizations." *Organization Management Journal*, 3(3), 210–31.

CHAPTER 18

WORK THROUGH A GENDER LENS

More Work and More Sources of Meaningfulness

HEATHER HOFMEISTER

INTRODUCTION

LOOKING for a gender dimension of meaningful work in the existing literature has been a needle-in-the-haystack endeavor. The gender scholars have not looked explicitly at meaningful work, and the meaningful work scholars, with rare exceptions, have either not looked for, or not found and reported, gender dimensions (but see Yeoman, 2014 and Broadfoot et al., 2008). My search for "meaning," no pun intended, in the indexes of classic research on gender and women and men's lives was fruitless. Although Hannah Arendt (1958) comes closest to distinctions I am engaged with in this chapter— between work and labor, and public and private spheres—her writing uses an andro-centric lens.

A thesis could be put forth that there is little or no "there" there, no gender dimension to meaningful work. That's not my thesis. I think we haven't looked at meaningful work in a gender-sensitive way. Given the different life courses and socialization pressures that men and women have, I find it unlikely that men and women experience meaning-ful work and meaning in work at exactly the same average amount, rate, and from the same sources. Even if there are no measurable or identifiable differences between men and women in meaningfulness when the type of work considered is just paid work, an expansion of the definition of work to include the kinds of work that women tend to do more of than men, such as care work and household work, would likely indicate massive gender differences in the experience of meaningful work. Not just gender differences are likely: meaningful work may be defined and experienced differently along social distinctions, interacting with gender, such as age, social class, education level, ethnicity, nationality, amount and types of work experiences, and parents' attitudes toward work. Most of these distinctions will intersect. In this chapter I outline what a "there" might look like in the intersection of gender and meaningful work.

A gender perspective necessarily dissolves and reconstitutes the concept of "work," which prisms "meaningful work" into an abundance of new research questions. Even just with a binary concept of gender (reducing gender to socially identified categories of "men" and "women") and a view of work as paid activity, the "gender and meaningful work" prism has multiple facets:

- Subject-centered: Do men and women assign different *meanings* or *levels of meaningfulness to their own work?* Does meaningfulness of work depend on whether the observed worker is male or female? If so, how?
- Work-centered: How and why does the gendered nature of jobs, tasks, or subject fields impact the meaningfulness men and women experience in their work or the meaningfulness that others assign to their work?
- Meaning-centered: Gender identities are drawn from, or hurt by, particular aspects of paid work. How does the match between type of paid work and the gender of the worker influence the sense of meaningfulness?

The moment we stop assuming that work is only paid work, we get even more richness of research questions along the overlap of meaningfulness and work and the gendering taking place there.

My position on gender is that biological functional differences become socially interpreted and put into a value hierarchy. Society inherits and perpetuates the idea of two categories of biological functional difference and then assigns behaviors, feelings, and life course pathways to each. Individuals conform to or contest these two social assignments, but most internalize these social positions, thus reinforcing and ultimately reifying the social construction of difference. Those who contest these assignments experience, depending on the society, tremendous social pressure to conform and may face ostracism or even death for their non-conformity. Gender is omnirelevant "as a sociocultural construction in virtually all human collectivities, past and present" (Chafetz, 2006: vii).

Gender distinction and inequality are fertile terrain for meaningful work research (Broadfoot et al., 2008). For reasons exceeding this chapter's scope, the socially constructed gender hierarchy worldwide places men on top. More power and prestige reside in masculine concepts, persons, occupations, and forms of self-expression (Friedl, 1996), with resulting political, social, and physical oppression of women, to different degrees across historical time, societies, social classes, ethnicities, ages, parenting statuses, and other social group memberships. Even women's worthiness in the eyes of the law draws on narrow stereotypes, and pigeonholes women in race, age, and family categories (Brown, Williams, and Baumann, 1996). These factors deserve consideration for meaningful work.

ANDROCENTRISM IN
THE DEFINITION OF WORK AND IN
MEANINGFUL WORK RESEARCH

Because gender differences are attached to behavioral expectations, and because work, whether paid or unpaid, is a key activity of human beings, work is fundamentally gendered. Women, and women's work, are socially constructed to carry lower prestige than men or men's work (Rich, 1986; de Beauvoir, 2011 [1949]). Women's work is often not even paid or considered "work." When it is paid, it is often paid less (England, Budig, and Folbre, 2002). Lower pay and lower prestige is part of what keeps certain occupations female-dominated: male breadwinners avoid low pay and diminished status if they can (England, Hermsen, and Cotter, 2000; England, Allison, and Wu, 2007). The same activity or task may or may not even be considered work depending on whether the observer or the worker is male or female (Martin, Hess, and Siegel, 1995). That value hierarchy is a social construction.

Legal and cultural exclusion have created gender segregation in access to all kinds of paid work activities (Hofmeister, 2016; Kanter, 1993; de Beauvoir, 2011 [1949]). A legacy of the Industrial Revolution in the nineteenth century that continues to this day is the separation and gendering of human activity into "public" and "private" spheres (Cowan, 1983; Degler, 1980; Hall, 1992; Taylor, 2004). In this schema, paid work in an office or factory was defined as a male domain, and unpaid work took place at home, was feminized, devalued, and defined as "not work," playing no role in gross domestic product calculations (Bock and Duden, 1977).

Disciplinary boundaries in academia mirror industrial capital's interests and specializations. In academic fields like sociology and economics, "work" has meant paid employment (Feldberg and Glenn, 1979; Taylor, 2004). Economists measure work only as wage labor (Glucksmann, 1995; Taylor, 2004) and have spent decades framing research on work around *job models* for men and *gender models* if researching women (Feldberg and Glenn, 1979). The strict separation of work and non-work creates challenges for studying processes as they are lived by people moving fluidly across and between various kinds of work (Taylor, 2004) and may help explain why meaningful work research has so far focused primarily on paid work.

These conceptual limits aren't just academic. They infiltrate commonplace work understandings: "Do you work?" means "Do you have a paid job?" For one or two centuries, middle-class women answered the question with, "No, I am a housewife" (Bock and Duden, 1977), an answer that reveals the work/non-work sphere internalization and points to the "political economy of love, sexuality, and housework" (Ostner, 1993). Unpaid homekeeping and care work under dependence on a male breadwinner signaled arrival in the middle class in nineteenth- and twentieth-century Western industrializing societies. Women in this new class were expected to create "havens in a heartless world" for their men and children (Degler, 1980; Glazer, 1984; Lasch, 1989). New mass-produced technologies, like washing machines and vacuum cleaners, changed laborious tasks (like laundry or rug-beating) that formerly required multiple people to one-person chores. The result was the demotion of the housewife from a household manager who directed the work of several assistants to proletarian status as an invisible laborer. Advertisers tried to elevate the role emotionally by implying that laboring away in the home was feminine, an act of love and care, and should be a source of deep meaning and pleasure (Cowan, 1999, 1976).

Women's non-wage labor devaluation is not new or exclusive to the nineteenth and twentieth centuries, however. The very real work of meeting human needs, giving care, and reproducing the species are gendered female, are unpaid or low paid, take place outside of the public sphere, and have been deemed "necessary, but inferior, activity from Aristotle through to Marx" (Yeoman, 2014: 73, see also de Beauvoir, 2011 [1949]). Correspondingly, women's work in the home remains mainly invisible in research on meaningful work (for exceptions, see Yeoman, 2014 and Broadfoot et al., 2008).

Devaluing women's work stigmatizes reproductive home and care work generally (Yeoman, 2014), and it squeezes unpaid care work around the edges of paid work, even though care work, and not the production of things, is essential for sustaining life on earth (Arendt, 1958). Devaluation of work done by women occurs in paid work fields, too. Among formerly male-dominated paid occupations, like education and psychology, as the proportion of women in a field rises, the salary decreases, and so does men and women's interest in joining that field (England et al., 2007).

Several demographic trends are likely to impact the sources of meaningfulness of paid work differently for men and women, possibly not *because of* gender, but with gender as one of several proxies for social position and job and family possibilities (Baldry et al., 2007). The social construction of difference—which often becomes domination and subordination—occurs along multiple dimensions at the same time (Broadfoot et al., 2008: 3). Race, class, gender, and age are experienced as sets of difference that together can influence experiences of meaningful work. Broadfoot and colleagues emphasize that all scholars are responsible for the biases they reproduce in their analysis and thus must consider intersectionalities in reflexive and nuanced ways in research on meaningful work (Broadfoot et al., 2008: 3).

Meaningful work research may also contain a Western industrialized bias, recognizable by the individualized focus on whether the *worker* experiences the work as meaningful. What about whether the family experiences the work as meaningful? Or society? May these be equally, or even more, relevant for assessing meaningful work (Broadfoot et al., 2008: 3)?

Reducing Androcentrism by Expanding the Definition of Work

Second wave feminism from the late 1960s challenged the work–non-work and public–private dichotomies. First, arguments served male paid work domains: housework is work because it is essential to the successful operation of factories, offices, and commerce

male	female
culture	nature
productive	reproductive
activity	passivity
mind	matter
reason	instinct
human	subhuman
needs-creating	needs-meeting
work	non-work
paid	unpaid

FIGURE 18.1 Dichotomous gendered value assignments deeply embedded in cultures and thus unconscious associations, observed by Yeoman (2014: 74)

generally, because if workers are not born, raised, fed, clothed, healthy, and rested, nothing else can happen (Bock and Duden, 1977; Gilman, 1997 [1898]; Glazer, 1984; Oakley, 1974; Primeau, 1992). Women scholars (for example, Gilman, 1997 [1898]) had been advocating for recognition of the economic contribution of housework nearly a hundred years before, but it took, not coincidentally, a man and labor economist, Gary Becker, to finally legitimate the study of non-market behavior (housework) (Taylor, 2004), who even won a Nobel Prize for it (Nobelprize.org, 2014).

Unpaid spheres have started to get recognition as work (Feldberg and Glenn, 1979; Primeau, 1992). The 2008 International Conference of Labor Statisticians admitted that the definition of work should include domestic work and volunteer work (Bollé, 2009). Conceptual umbrellas like *provisioning, prosuming, the universal carer model,* and *work timespaces* capture the interplay of the social and material world and give much-needed attention to formerly invisible and gendered dimensions of work (Bock and Duden, 1977; Cameron and Gibson-Graham, 2003; Neysmith and Reitsma-Street, 2005; Pascall and Lewis, 2004; Ritzer, 2017; Toffler, 1980; Yeoman, 2014). Nonetheless, broadening the concept of work to include "activities required to reproduce society," like care work, emotional work, volunteering, and other acts of creative endeavor, may not eliminate the gendered value hierarchy, because the kinds of paid wage work that replace unpaid care work are also lower paid and, not coincidentally, most often done by women (Yeoman, 2014: 73). Indeed, the line-up of gender associations is deeply cultural, binary, and disadvantageous to women (see Figure 18.1 for a summary of associations identified by Yeoman, 2014).

But if work concepts become more multifaceted, various kinds of work may become more evenly distributed between men and women. Taylor (2004) offers a "total social organization of labor" to look at connections among different kinds of work that move away from dichotomies and recognize that individuals' labor is connected within and across settings. Her categories seem inspired by Arendt's (1958) work. I develop the categories further and apply a gender lens to the varieties of work to arrive at nineteen types of work, within five categories of social organization, summarized in Figure 18.2.

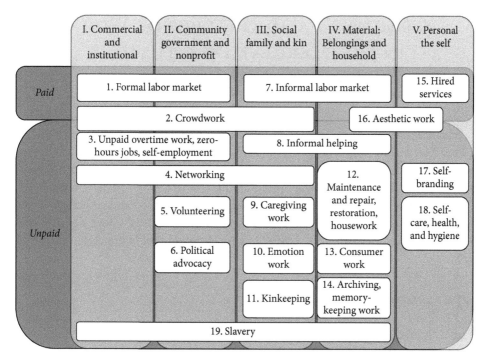

FIGURE 18.2 Nineteen types of work across paid and unpaid domains and along five organizational dimensions: commercial/institutional, community, social, material, and personal

The gender lens creates the multiplicity of work types by considering *what* women and men do to create and sustain life and society and *where* they do it. How are human activities organized? What matters for the continuation of individual lives, family, and community? What keeps societies going? My "working definition" of work has been created to include the array of invisible and disregarded work performed overwhelmingly by women: *activities or thoughts that affirm life and growth, imagine or create the future, or that abate or delay death and decay*. Abating or delaying death and decay has to be seen broadly: it includes slowing or abating the decay or death of our own and others' bodies, minds, spirits, and relationships; our built and natural environment; our societies; our institutions; and our moral foundations. There is more to explore with this definition of work, but let me turn first to some concrete types of work that come to light when using this definition.

The varieties of work can be grouped into five columns: I) Commercial and institutional; II) Community, including government and nonprofit work; III) Social, which includes family and kin; IV) Material, including belongings and household; and V) Personal, meaning work around the self. The first three categories were identified by Taylor (2004), the latter two are my extensions. Within each column, I categorize different types of work by whether they are paid or unpaid.

Next, I describe the sections of Figure 18.2 and discuss how meaningful work research could advance the field by exploring these with gender sensitivity.

Columns I and II: Types of Work in Commercial Institutions and Communities

The meaningful work literature focuses on paid work, and often in formal work organizations (Hardering, Will-Zocholl, and Hofmeister, 2016). I highlight the possibility for difference in commercial institutional work settings (column I), and nonprofit or governmental community settings (column II). Formal labor market, crowdwork, unpaid overtime work and related on-call or zero-hours contracts and self-employment, and networking activities could happen in either of these settings. Other kinds of work like volunteering and political advocacy tend not to occur in the commercial sector.

Type 1: Formal Labor Market

The only kind of "work" in Figure 18.2 that is typically considered work and researched extensively by scholars of meaningful work is formal labor market work at the institutional or community level (Type 1). This dimension of work can and should be considered in meaningful work scholarship with gender sensitivity. Constructing the gendered self is often done through paid work, and even choosing a field of study is a gendered act (Charles and Bradley, 2009). The meaning of paid work for women may be very different than that for men. Men's status and earnings are associated with safety, security, providership, required of the good breadwinner, and part of being a good father (Hofmeister and Baur, 2015). A woman with paid work may be seen as a bad mother because the meanings of mother and earner are culturally constructed to be far apart (Garey, 1999; Hays, 1996). Paid work can have a source of personal meaning as freedom (Budd, 2011), including freedom to leave an abusive partner.

Individuals' own perceptions of meaningfulness and the societal ascription of meaningfulness can be different (Baldry et al., 2007). Gender categories separate occupations and may influence the societal views of the meaningfulness of the work and the individual experience of meaningfulness. Gender-atypical occupations, in particular, may offer new or different sources of meaning compared to gender-typical work. A male nurse, like a male librarian, teacher, or social worker, may find his work extremely meaningful. But if his work does not conform to gender norms, others may react negatively. His devotion to his work in the face of social pressure may take effort or outright resistance. Or he may experience a "glass escalator" to leadership and higher pay, being exalted due to his exceptional status (Williams, 1998).

Women also experience tension when working in a gender-non-conforming job, or, depending on the national context, even any paid job. Her paid work may draw skepticism or ridicule from the community if she's seen as abandoning the caregiver role or other markers of femininity. Girls have to overcome gendered socialization and stigma from parents, teachers, peers, media, and, later, from work organizations and professional communities to be able to join and continue in fields like natural science and engineering (Hofmeister, 2016; Kisselburgh, Berkelaar, and Buzzanell, 2009).

Social identity theory describes a mechanism by which others influence an individual's sense of meaningful work. Individuals take on as their own identity the social groups of which they are members (Hogg and Reid, 2006). Categories give identity, and this identity gives meaning to certain kinds of work (Rosso, Dekas, and Wrzesniewski, 2010). When social identities are inconsistent (male nurse, female engineer), which identity becomes more salient, and how does perceived inconsistency affect meaningfulness? Future research can examine how gender non-conformity in paid or unpaid work affects the sense of meaningfulness of the work.

Gender-atypical paid work may lead to compensatory actions, especially in intimate relationships. Individuals may implement the "gender display model"—a high-earning woman may do more housework than her male partner to help construct herself as a woman and compensate for success in the paid labor market that calls her femininity and his masculinity into question (Shelton, 2006: 385). Men may define themselves as men in part by doing less or no housework or childcare, especially if their masculine identity receives a hit through unemployment (Brines, 1994).

Industries expand and contract along gender-segregated lines. Factories and construction sites—male-dominated fields—were big employers in the 1960s and 1970s. Professional care services in hospitals and schools, with high proportions of employed women, have grown dramatically. These services replace unpaid care work and provide paid work opportunities for a demographically broad population (Folbre and Nelson, 2000), a process that has enormous gender implications, also around the societal value put on social services and political debates around the size of government. Meaningful work scholarship looking at gender dimensions of industry types, their dynamics, and those working in those industries is rich uncharted territory.

Type 2: Crowdwork

Crowdwork arises from digitalization, straddles the border of paid and unpaid work, and disintegrates boundaries between public and private, work and non-work, and physical and virtual spaces. This type of work may be paid by unit of time or task; it may be unpaid activities like contributing content to shared public resources such as online evaluations, open source programming, and databases (Margaryan and Hofmeister, 2017). Crowdwork can be done in the context of any of the first three categories of social organization (see Figure 18.2). The gender dimensions of crowdwork further include questions around which workers perform which kinds of crowdwork and why, who contributes which kinds of content in open-source platforms, whether gender bias exists in evaluations and pay for crowdwork, and how gendered avatars represent online identities. Little is known about meaningfulness in crowdwork, but it could vary by workers' gender, crowdwork type, or the interaction of crowdwork with other types of work in individuals' life courses.

Type 3: Unpaid Overtime Work, On-call Work, Zero-hours Jobs, Self-employment

How is unpaid overtime, or the work that goes unpaid but "should" be paid, as in self-employment, on-call work, or zero-hours contracts, experienced as meaningful? Does this kind of work detract from, or enhance, the meaningfulness of regular guaranteed paid hours? Unpaid occupational work, unpaid overtime work, or the work of waiting for a call to go to work as needed, may represent work commitment or engagement, which may enhance the subjective experience of meaningfulness. Or the unpaid time may create feelings of resentment as "lost time" that cannot be used for other parts of life. How might these experiences and reactions differ for men and women, or for those with and without primary care responsibilities, or along other dimensions (like volunteering)? Who is caring for children or pets when unpaid or short-notice occupational work is required? Consider that men still tend to be seen as good fathers not only, but also, for being breadwinners (Hofmeister and Baur, 2015), and women are more likely to be seen as neglecting their families if working overhours, or responding to on-call work, so there may be gender differences in the experiences of meaningfulness in these kinds of work.

Type 4: Networking

Research on networking is vast, including its usefulness for paid work and job-searching (Granovetter, 1995 [1974]) and the gender dimensions of networking (Smith-Lovin and McPherson, 1993). Although the word network contains the word "work," the practice is rarely recognized as a type of (typically unpaid) work. The experienced meaningfulness of networking as work, and the gender dimensions of this meaningfulness, have not been explored.

Type 5: Volunteering

The reasons for engaging in volunteering and its meaningfulness may be experienced differently by the type of work and by the gender of the volunteer. Men are overrepresented in formal volunteering, "giving time or skills during a planned activity for a volunteer group or organization" (Rodell, 2013: 1274), and women are overrepresented in informal helping (Type 8, below) (Hofmeister and Edgell, 2014). The meaning and type of volunteering can be gendered (Felt and Sinclair, 1992; Hofmeister and Edgell, 2014; Messner and Bozada-Deas, 2009) as well as its relationship to the broader economy, welfare state, and individuals' identities (Neysmith and Reitsma-Street, 2000). Leadership in formal volunteer organizations is also likely gendered and connected to paid work opportunities, or a lack thereof. Meaningfulness would be relevant to understanding willingness to volunteer, also for leadership positions, in both paid and volunteer settings. What are the connections among meaningfulness of paid work, overhours, and volunteering (Rodell, 2013; Schnell and Hoof, 2012)? How may these connections be gendered?

Type 6: Political Advocacy

Citizen involvement in volunteer political advocacy could be seen as a part of volunteer work, but it deserves extra consideration. Reasons for involvement, topics, and degree of meaningfulness may all show gendered dimensions. Advocates for hunting rights, labor rights, early childhood well-being, or domestic violence relief are likely skewed to male or female. The experienced meaningfulness may be gendered accordingly. Political involvement historically was male-dominated in Western societies. What are the contemporary impacts of that history for the meaningfulness of this work for men and women?

COLUMNS III AND IV: TYPES OF WORK IN SOCIAL AND MATERIAL CONTEXTS

Informal labor market work and informal helping span the relational and material dimensions of social organization. I present some types of work within and bridging these two columns next.

Type 7: Informal Labor Market: Paid Work in the Social and Material Dimensions

Informal labor markets are those where cash is exchanged for work but the work is done "off the books," without any contracts, legal protections, visibility, or measurability. Changes in gender norms, and the corresponding increase in women's opportunities for paid work and decline in women's incentives to offer unpaid care, mean that the things housewives used to do at home are being outsourced for pay: "paid child care, nursing homes for the elderly, talk therapy and phone sex are just a few examples" (Folbre and Nelson, 2000: 123). As a result, less advantaged workers, male and female—often from elsewhere in the world and often paid off the books—take over some of this work, leaving their own loved ones to be cared for by the next level of disadvantaged worker, family, or in self-care, creating global care chains (Ehrenreich and Hochschild, 2004; Lutz, 2016).

Further research could easily expand our understandings of meaningfulness by looking at this informal labor market and the kinds of precarious work done for low wages to care for people, animals, and belongings, or in sex work. How is informal paid work experienced differently whether the objects are inanimate, such as the work of cleaning or gardening, versus caring for or servicing animate beings? Is meaningfulness experienced differently by a man or a woman doing the work, depending on the work? And is the meaningfulness assigned differently by men and women?

Type 8: Informal Helping: Unpaid and Along Social and Material Dimensions

Women help informally at higher rates than men do, and have a long legacy of doing so (Hook, 2004; Kaminer, 1984). Women also experience higher demands with the "second shift" of combining informal helping and paid employment (Hochschild, 1989). Men are called on more often to help with large, visible projects like construction and repair. Changes in amounts, kinds, and meaningfulness of informal helping over time for men and women are areas that meaningful work research could address. Also relevant is others' assignment of meaningfulness: is a man's informal helping more visible and given more credit and accolades than a woman's? Does it depend on the type of help?

COLUMN III: SOCIAL RELATIONS

Three types of work fit squarely in the social dimension of work: caregiving, emotion work, and kinkeeping work. All are highly gender-typed female.

Type 9: Caregiving or Care Work

Viewing caregiving as *work* is not new (Gilman, 1997 [1898]; Hochschild, 2004; Hofmeister and Blossfeld, 2006), although care work is among the most privatized work (Bielby, 2006). But if care work is not done by unpaid volunteers like family, in most cases it must be hired out. Care work includes caring for children, people with disabilities, those facing temporary or chronic illness, and the elderly. Such labor is essential for the survival of the species and planet. But providing care for others is highly gendered. Women "produce themselves appropriately as women" by attending to children (Shelton, 2006: 385). Maternal gatekeeping, whereby mothers protect their identities as mothers by setting rigid standards and emphasizing separate roles for men and women, contributes to the gendering of caregiving (Allen and Hawkins, 1999). Cultural contexts are relevant. Nordic countries have normalized men's caregiving more than other regions, whereas in other contexts men call caregiving for their own children "babysitting," implying it is temporary, voluntary, and therefore worthy of praise or rewards (Shelton, 2006; Wilson and Prior, 2010). In countries from Japan to rural China to the United States, daughters and daughters-in-law are expected to step in for caregiving of elders before sons or strangers would (Stone, Cafferata, and Sangl, 1987; Tokunaga,

Hashimoto, and Tamiya, 2015). Beliefs that caregiving is exclusively a woman's duty puts women at risk of overexertion (Toepfer, Foster, and Wilz, 2014). Care work can be experienced as deeply meaningful, but also as repetitive and frustrating: this kind of work is laden with ambivalence (Luescher and Pillemer, 1998). Its importance, its ambivalence, and the extreme gender differences among caregivers suggest research should ask how and why the meaningfulness of care work is experienced differently for men and women in various cultural contexts. How are these activities gendered? How are they experienced as meaningful? Caring for animals or the planet can also be seen as care work, opening up new avenues for research on gender and meaningfulness.

Type 10: Emotion Work

Emotion work is related to care work, but it focuses on managing feeling, or "intentional activities done to promote another's emotional well-being" (Thomeer, Reczek, and Umberson, 2015: 12). Emotion work done for pay is called emotional labor and has been researched for decades (Heaphy, 2017; Hochschild, 1983). An example of emotional labor is the Japanese occupation of young women "hostesses" who listen empathetically to the "salarymen" at bars in the evenings (van Wolferen, 1990). Unpaid emotion work helps manage relationships with family, friends, neighbors, acquaintances, and even colleagues, because it focuses on helping others feel good (Hochschild, 1983), noticing how the setting affects people, being warm and cheerful, and including everyone (Bielby, 2006).

A recent comprehensive review of the work–family interface recognizes the blurring of boundaries between paid work and home, or "work and family," but does not report gender differences as part of the review except briefly in this one area: emotion work, which is assumed to be "natural" for women but not men (Grandey and Krannitz, 2016). Other research indicates some husbands avoid emotion work because they don't consider it manly enough, even when their wives are ill and need support (Thomeer, Reczek, and Umberson, 2015). Emotion work is undervalued and literally unseen, highly gendered, and yet central to human interconnectivity (Bielby, 2006). Emotion work is ripe for research on gender dimensions of meaningfulness.

Type 11: Kinkeeping Work

Women are not only typical emotion workers, they're also typically the primary kinkeepers (Gallagher and Gerstel, 1993) and thereby "the unsung heroines of social integration" (Bielby, 2006: 399). Sending birthday cards, making social phone calls, arranging holiday gatherings, purchasing and wrapping gifts, and organizing visits are examples of aspects of kinkeeping (di Leonardo, 1987) and, "in *all* of the countries studied, women contact kin more frequently than men" (Bielby, 2006: 398). Kinkeeping operates as a reciprocal process and thus creates and maintains networks vital for health and social cohesion. Kinkeeping is a key source of social integration, and social integration is a leading contribution to longevity (Holt-Lunstad, Robles, and Sbarra, 2017). But men delegate kinkeeping to their wives, and that has consequences for men's loneliness and mortality in old age or after divorce. Kinkeeping also creates stress and can be oppressive. Kinkeeping work is a prime topic for further research regarding its meaningfulness.

Column IV: Material Spheres of Unpaid Work

Three types of work fit in the material category: maintenance and household work, consumer work, and archival work. All these manage material artifacts; housework has often been studied with care work, but research on meaningfulness would benefit from keeping them distinct.

Type 12: Maintenance, Repair, Restoration, and Housework

Housework is a "resource for the reproduction of gender or a way to display gender" (Shelton, 2006: 384; West and Fenstermaker, 1995). A clean and tidy house is associated with being a good woman (Boydston, 2009). Different kinds of housework are strongly gendered. Men do more repair work and outdoor chores that can be conveniently scheduled and whose results are long-lasting and can be admired by all. Women do daily routine housework like cooking, tidying, and laundry whose results must be repeated regularly, if not daily, and mainly go unnoticed unless they are not done at all (Hochschild, 1989; Shelton, 2006). The meaningfulness assigned to each task, subjectively and from the outside, is likely to vary by task and doer.

Type 13: Consumer Work

Purchasing resources for the household, part of "provisioning," is another invisible but time-consuming type of work that is highly gendered (Cowan, 1983; Glazer, 1984; Neysmith and Reitsma-Street, 2005). Consumption is essential for converting wages into useful goods; it drives most economies and also contributes to environmental destruction. Consumer work also has a class dimension that interacts with gender, identity, and experiences of meaning in paid work and in private life (Du Gay, 1996). For example, men working on the assembly line of a beef-processing plant purchased motorcycles, cars, and stereos to compensate for the dehumanizing, backbreaking work, which generated peer admiration during breaks but also debt that made leaving the bad jobs impossible—creating a "financial trap" (Thompson, 2003: 328). Women are often responsible for household purchases, and family prestige is drawn in large part from these visible decisions (Segal and Podoshen, 2013; McIntosh and Zey, 1989). Research on meaningful work can consider myriad gender dimensions of consumer work.

Type 14: Archival and Memory-keeping Work

Family genealogy research and archiving family memories through song, storytelling, writing, scrapbook-keeping, and archiving provide identity-building for self and kin and represent ways of honoring the past, passing on legacies and memories, as well as creating culture. Little research has explicitly articulated these practices as work and researched their meaningfulness (but see Downs, 2006; Hof, 2006). This work is highly feminized, often experienced privately as deeply meaningful, and viewed primarily as leisure. Yet it is work.

COLUMN V: PERSONAL SPHERES OF PAID AND UNPAID WORK

This category of social organization includes ways of working on the self: body, mind, or soul. Types of work I cover here include hired services, self-branding, and self-care. Some may contest whether personal spheres are work or rather leisure, but extensive focus on "the body project," captured in abundant social science literature on themes like self-objectification, dieting, exercising, cosmetic surgery, weight-lifting, body modification, and self-presentation online suggest that the meaningfulness of this work and the gender dimensions of the meaningfulness would be important areas of future research.

Type 15: Hired Services for the Self

Hired services are a special category of paid work. How is paid work that addresses the body, mind, or soul experienced as meaningful by the receiver, the client? How is that experience gendered? Many hired services require the client to put in work. When we hire someone to help us with our education or personal care, for example a teacher, coach, therapist, masseuse, hairdresser, cosmetologist, or dentist, we are deeply involved in the work ourselves. Anyone immediately after a medical procedure or a therapeutic session would agree that their participation involved some work investment of their own, processing learning, practicing, bearing pain or holding still, wrestling with deep topics, or remembering and sharing. The experience of meaningfulness for the clients may vary based on clients' and providers' gender identities and the gender-typing of the work. Self-work that involves professional assistance has fluid boundaries and invites scholarly attention on the relationships between, for example, 1) the self (client) and the professional, 2) the self-work and the formal and informal labor markets, and 3) self-work that is outsourced (where others are paid to perform it) and unpaid self-care (Type 18, below).

Type 16: Aesthetic Work

A discussion of types of work needs to mention aesthetic work (Nickson et al., 2003). Producing art, arranging objects, managing the appearances of body and home, designing things not only for their function but also for their form, are types of work. Artists perform aesthetic work, and the art community is heavily gendered: art schools are full of women, but art galleries are full of the artwork of men (Provansal, 2016). Home and seasonal decoration is aesthetic work, done more often by women than men (Boydston, 2009). Research on gender dimensions of aesthetic labor, particularly in the retail service sector, modeling, and public performance, abound (Entwistle and Wissinger, 2006). Aesthetic labor is an ongoing production of the body, incorporating both appearance and performance, and having the body used for the brand or image of the employer. Like emotional labor, aesthetic labor is paid, and "foregrounds embodiment, revealing how the corporeality, not just the feelings of employees, are organizationally appropriated and transmuted for commercial benefit" (Warhurst and Nickson, 2009: 386). Aesthetic work bridges material and personal dimensions and paid and unpaid spheres; it includes all kinds of work that has visual pleasure or communication at its core. Gender dimensions in the meaningfulness of aesthetic work have yet to be explored.

Type 17: Self-branding

Self-branding is a visible phenomenon in the age of social media, online dating, and frequent job changes that is relatively invisible and largely unpaid work. Individuals are expected to develop their own unique brand identity, deliverable in a small, digestible "elevator pitch" that can be presented symbolically and repeated in various social media channels (Vallas and Cummins, 2015). The idea behind self-branding is to increase visibility and attractiveness on the job market, the dating market, or in the broader network generally. Curating and consuming social media posts to develop and enhance the self-presentation or brand, whether or not it's articulated as such, consumes unpaid time but is serious work, with job prospects and marriage prospects potentially at stake: branding is not leisure. Some people's personal brand turns into a business due to its popularity on social media, drawing advertising revenue. Others start with blogs and become recognized authors and experts. The work of helping others with their personal branding has become a cottage industry. I present self-branding here as a type of unpaid work in the domain of the self, another example of the fluidity of boundaries between paid and unpaid work, between hired services and self-care, between networking and cultivating an image. The gendered components of branding have received far too little scholarly attention (but see Lair, Sullivan, and Cheney, 2005 for a brief discussion).

Type 18: Self-care, Health and Hygiene

Self-care is a type of work that may be likely seen very differently for men and women due to social stereotypes about appropriateness of various kinds of self care (Dean, 1989). Massages, meditation, manicures, facials, regular exercise, healthy dietary choices, regular hydration, sleep, and routine medical and dental visits, even drinking herbal tea, show strongly gendered patterns and have consequences for health and longevity. Researchers in the sociologies of sport, food, and leisure are actively studying some of these features, but we have yet to scratch the surface on self-care as a dimension of work, the feminine stigma, and consequences for meaningfulness.

An additional dimension of self-care is related to emotion work, but it is done for the self. Processing feelings of loss and grief or adjusting to new circumstances such as a job change, status change, or family transition is intensive work. Whether conducted with the support of a paid professional (Type 15) or alone (Type 18), the nature of this work and the gender dimensions could be examined in meaningful work research.

Type 19: Slavery

Researching slavery is incredibly difficult, much less the meaning or meaningfulness attached to the work while enslaved. Slavery is illegal, so access to the population is challenging, though studying prison populations or archival historical evidence are options. A true examination of meaningfulness and sources of meaning for those enslaved could give them and their situations visibility and voice. Boundaries among some forms of paid and unpaid work and slavery are more fluid than one might like to believe, and so studies in one area can help us extend knowledge about experiences in the other. The gender identities of the enslaved and the enslaving, their relationship to each other, and the gendered nature of the work done in slavery (agriculture, mining, textile work, housework, care work, sex work) would be important gender components of research. Recognizing that hope is a crucial aspect of surviving difficult circumstances, how do hope, and meaningfulness, relate to each other in conditions of slavery? Can work still be found meaningful, even if it is not freely entered into (Bailey and Madden, 2017)?

INTEGRATING THE MODEL

The nineteen types of work provide a framework through which we can unpack and understand better the relationships among meaningfulness dimensions and gender dimensions of work. The framework can be especially useful as workers move among types, or as the work itself moves among types.

Looking at Figure 18.2, most types of work are unpaid. The formal and informal labor market (Types 1 and 7), hired services (Type 15), and some parts of crowdwork (Type 2) would be the paid exceptions. But overlaps and similarities abound. Consumer work (Type 13) is sometimes paid, as with mystery shoppers or bloggers promoting products. Self-branding (Type 17) can become a source of income, but it never starts that way. Emotion work (Type 10) is typically unpaid, but within it is a category of paid emotional labor. People with chronic illnesses or medically necessary healthcare rituals (Type 18) can feel sometimes like slaves to their bodies and medical regimes. Some people who think they are joining a formal labor market (Type 1), recruited as fashion models or restaurant servers, for example, discover that they're in an informal labor market without a work contract or job protections (Type 7), and they may even be tricked into slavery (Type 19).

CHANGES OVER TIME AND MOVEMENT AMONG WORK TYPES

How does meaningfulness change as work transforms across paid and unpaid spheres or among columns or types of work? How do shifts across types occur over time? The server whose formal employment dream turns into an arrangement off the books may not have chosen that change. But other times an individual is an active agent in shifts among types. Someone bringing canned goods to a food pantry (Type 8, informal helping) is so impressed with the food pantry that she takes on a regular shift at that food pantry as a volunteer (Type 5), and, through her devotion and enthusiasm, she's offered formal labor market work in that nonprofit agency (Type 1). Unpaid internships (Type 3) may become formal or informal labor market work (Type 1 or 7).

Over historical time, macro-level trends may create changes in the social assignment of specific tasks and work types over time. Meaningfulness is likely concurrently impacted. For example, caring for elderly relatives is, or was, part of the expectation for daughters and daughters-in-law in many places (Type 9). As women's formal paid labor market participation increased, families became less able to assume there would be an adult woman at home to care for elderly relatives or young children. And men on average are unlikely to fill the gap, even when they are unemployed or underemployed. Thus, instead of men or women helping informally and caregiving in their own kinship networks (Types 8 and 9), there has been a rise in labor market positions in caregiving, be they in the government or private sector (Type 1) or in informal labor market care (Type 7). Some paid caregivers may be on-call (Type 3), coming in only if the staff is short-handed, but not really free in their unpaid time. The formal and informal labor markets for caregivers often reflect global inequalities. Imported care workers are far from their original homes and families. Some may be in slavery. How is the work experienced as meaningful in these contexts? Who is caring for the family members back home? How does the absence from home of origin affect meaningfulness? Where might gender differences lie?

Bloggers and vloggers also move among types of work over time. As they maintain, repair, decorate things, or teach skills (Type 12), they may perform consumer work, if there are product placements and trials (Type 13), and they are definitely doing self-branding (Type 17). They are archiving projects, images, and thoughts (Type 14) as they record and post their perspectives. Bloggers and vloggers may turn their work into a paying job (Type 1 or 3). There are huge gender dimensions to the type of topics they cover and the level of visibility that they receive. Are there gender differences in the meaningfulness of this type of work? Does meaningfulness, and the gendered nature of meaningfulness, depend on the stage at which the work is measured? The boundary negotiation or fluidity among types of work and the meanings that emerge within each type of work and along their interfaces will be fruitful places for research on meaningfulness.

Conclusions

Our research questions can become more beautiful and interesting when we nuance them by looking through a gender lens. That lens does two things: it expands the idea of work, and it invites us to ask whether men and women are equally likely to partake of the phenomenon we're interested in and whether they experience that activity the same way. Are access to, and costs and benefits of, work different for men and women? Does the meaning of the activity vary for men and women? How are the spiritual dimensions of the self, influences from others, and broader societal values enhancing or detracting from meaningfulness of an activity for men and women differently? How is meaningfulness of a task reduced or enhanced by the way work is gendered and bodies are gendered? How might gender socialization encourage, for example, more men than women to see their role as provider—of both material resources and social status—as a source of meaning, and more women than men to feel that home and family, caregiving, and social justice are meaningful? How do gendered paid work experiences affect perceived meaningfulness? Meaningfulness is socially constructed: it helps make sense of activities that feel relevant for others and in the context of broader life experiences, affirming or aiding toward the way things are supposed to be or what is considered important (Bailey and Madden, 2016; Pratt and Ashforth, 2003). A person's gender identity, intersecting with age, life course stage, ethnicity, race, class, and other social markers, may affect an individual's sense of meaningfulness in and among types of work (Baldry et al., 2007, Rosso, Dekas, and Wrzesniewski, 2010).

My argument is that exactly when we take a gender perspective to work, and to meaningful work, we have to expand the definition of work to include *thoughts and activities that affirm life and growth, imagine or create the future, and abate death, discomfort, and decay of minds, bodies, relationships, objects, memories, societal institutions, social life, and the natural world.* That definition can certainly be tightened up, but if we leave it broad and loose, and map these various components with the nineteen types of work, two generalizations emerge. First, the five columns reveal a division: the first two columns, commercial and governmental/community aspects, generally reflect the *way* work is done or paid. The last three columns, social and material and personal, generally reflect what *kind* of work is done. These five columns themselves are not as distinct from each other as they may appear. Second, most types of work accomplish multiple goals or intentions. Emotion work and kinkeeping, for example, abate decay of relationships and at the same time create the future. Archival work abates decay of objects and memories and also affirms life. Networking creates the future and abates decay of relationships and societal institutions. Much work is used to maintain the status quo against the inevitable pull of atrophy, chaos, and disintegration. Other work is used to advance an agenda of comfort, expansion, creation, connection, or learning. I believe it is a moral obligation to recognize the effort that goes in every day to create and recreate the world and the population and to improve relationships, efficiencies, or the built or natural environment. Many of these actions are not paid. They are still work.

My definition of *work* includes value-laden aspects: affirming life and maintaining relationships, institutions, or objects that matter. My definition of *meaningful work is activities that are consciously experienced as aligned with deeply held values.* The values can be held by societies, families, or individuals: meaningful work is not just an individual phenomenon to be measured by psychological scales. Values stem from, and are affirmed by, cultural systems. Our cultural systems are deeply gendered. Thus our deeply held values, and our assessment of meaningfulness of different kinds of work, are at least partly gendered. For example, paid work has been typified as meaningful for men, as part of being a good man and a good father and husband, by supporting the values of protection, providing, being productive, contributing to a greater whole. Emotion work and caregiving are seen as part of the role of a good mother, good wife, good woman, good sister, good daughter, or good friend, and these types of work support the values of caring, nurturing, and helping. But the masculine and the feminine, yang and yin, doing and being, are vital parts of all human beings. Recognizing and encouraging full expression of all parts of our humanity would go a long way toward improving the gendered distribution in work activities and allow more people subjectively to experience all kinds of their work as meaningful. Health, longevity, and social connectedness are likely to improve for men who care for themselves and others, for example.

During the writing of this chapter, one of my parents passed away unexpectedly and the other's health took a life-threatening turn for the worse. Death experiences and illnesses are times that highlight meaningfulness, filled with poignancy (Bailey and Madden, 2016). Gender differences abounded in the types of work that happened next. Who takes responsibility for clearing out the lifetime possessions of a deceased family member or friend (Type 8)? Who preserves the family history when the oldest members of the family pass on (Type 14)? Who spends time in the hospital with an ailing family member (Types 9, 10, 11)? Who are the aides, the nurses, the ones on site round the clock, tending to physical needs (Type 1)? Who invites the caregiver to dinner or brings over a meal (Types 8, 11)? Who helps haul donations to charity (Types 5, 8)? I saw only women at all of this work, except for husbands who were dragged along, or one male nursing aide from Haiti. What are the men missing out on? What is the meaningfulness, to them and to society, of the activities that keep them away from the meaningfulness of managing death, loss, illness, and grief?

Work, in all its variety, deserves to be valued. Everyone deserves his or her work to connect to his or her values, to be meaningful. The gender lens allows us to see work, workers, and the values that connect them to meaningfulness, in new ways. These new links can open the door for more justice, equality, validation, and access to broader fulfillment for men and women in all the activities we need to do to affirm life, abate death, and grow and maintain our selves, homes, families, relationships, and societies.

REFERENCES

Allen, S. M. and Hawkins, A. J. (1999). "Maternal gatekeeping: Mothers' belief and behaviors that inhibit greater father involvement in family work." *Journal of Marriage and the Family*, 61(1), 199–212.

Arendt, H. (1958). *The Human Condition*, 2nd edn. Chicago: University of Chicago Press.

Bailey, C. and Madden, A. (2016). "What makes work meaningful—or meaningless?" *MIT Sloan Management Review*, 57(4), 1–9.

Bailey, C. and Madden, A. (2017). "Why meaningful work matters." *Industrial Management*, 59(3), 10–13.

Baldry, C., Bain, P., Taylor, P., Hyman, J., Scholarios, D., Marks, A., Watson, A., Gilbert, K., Gall, G., and Bunzel, D. (2007). *The Meaning of Work in the New Economy*, foreword by P. Nolan. Houndsmills, Basingstoke and New York: Palgrave Macmillan.

Bielby, D. D. (2006). "Gender and Family Relations." In J. S. Chafetz (ed.), *Handbook of the Sociology of Gender*, pp. 391–406. New York: Springer Science+Business Media.

Bock, G. and Duden, B. (1977). "Arbeit aus Liebe—Liebe als Arbeit: Zur Entstehung der Hausarbeit im Kapitalismus." In Gruppe Berliner Dozentinnen (eds.), *Frauen und Wissenschaft. Beiträge Zur Berliner Sommeruniversität Für Frauen, Juli 1976*, pp. 118–99. Berlin: Courage Verlag.

Bollé, P. (2009). "Labor statistics: The boundaries and diversity of work." *International Labor Review*, 148(1–2), 183–93.

Boydston, J. (2009). *Home and Work: Housework, wages, and the ideology of labor in the early republic*. Oxford: Oxford University Press.

Brines, J. (1994). "Economic dependency, gender, and the division of labor at home." *American Journal of Sociology*, 100(3), 652–88.

Broadfoot, K. J., Carlone, D., Medved, C. E., Aakhus, M., Gabor, E., and Taylor, K. (2008). "Meaningful work and organizational communications: Questioning boundaries, positionalities, engagements." *Management Communication Quarterly*, 22, 152–61.

Brown, J. O., Williams, L. A., and Baumann, P. T. (1996). "The mythogenesis of gender: judicial images of women in paid and unpaid work." *UCLA Women's Law Journal*, 6(2), 457–539.

Budd, J. W. (2011). *The Thought of Work*. Ithaca, NY: Cornell University Press.

Cameron, J. and Gibson-Graham, J. K. (2003). "Feminising the economy: Metaphors, strategies, politics." *Gender, Place and Culture*, 10(2), 145–57.

Chafetz, J. S. (2006). *Handbook of the Sociology of Gender*. New York: Springer Science+Business Media.

Charles, M. and Bradley, K. (2009). "Indulging our gendered selves? Sex segregation by field of study in 44 countries." *American Journal of Sociology*, 114(4), 924–76.

Cowan, R. S. (1976). "The 'industrial revolution' in the home: Household technology and social change in the 20th century." *Technology and Culture*, 17(1), 1–23.

Cowan, R. S. (1983). *More Work for Mother: The ironies of household technology from the open hearth to the microwave*. New York: Basic Books.

Cowan, R. S. (1999). "The Industrial Revolution in the Home." In D. MacKenzie and J. Wajcman (eds.), *The Social Shaping of Technology*, pp. 281–300. Buckingham: Open University Press.

de Beauvoir, S. (2011 [1949]). *The Second Sex*, translated by C. Borde and S. Malovany-Chevallier. London: Vintage Books.

Dean, K. (1989). "Self-care components of lifestyles: The importance of gender, attitudes and the social situation." *Social Science & Medicine*, 29(2), 137–52.

Degler, C. N. (1980). *At Odds: Women and the family in America from the revolution to the present*. Oxford: Oxford University Press.

di Leonardo, M. (1987). "The female world of cards and holidays: Women, families, and the work of kinship." *Signs*, 12(3), 440–53.

Downs, H. A. (2006). "Crafting Culture: Scrapbooking and the Lives of Women." Dissertation, Sociology, University of Illinois at Urbana-Champaign. Available at: https://www.ideals.illinois.edu/handle/2142/86217 [accessed June 30, 2018].

Du Gay, P. (1996). *Consumption and Identity at Work*. London: Sage Publications.

Ehrenreich, B. and Hochschild, A. (2004). *Global Woman: Nannies, maids, and sex workers in the new economy*. New York: Owl Books/Henry Holt.

England, P., Allison, P., Li, S., Mark, N., Thompson, J., Budig, M. J., and Sun, H. (2007). "Why are some academic fields tipping toward female? The sex composition of U.S. fields of Doctoral degree receipt, 1971–2002." *Sociology of Education*, 80, 23–42.

England, P., Allison, P., and Wu, Y. (2007). "Does bad pay cause occupations to feminize, Does feminization reduce pay, and How can we tell with longitudinal data?" *Social Science Research*, 36(3), 1237–56.

England, P., Budig, M., and Folbre, N. (2002). "Wages of virtue: The relative pay of care work." *Social Problems*, 49(4), 455–73.

England, P., Hermsen, J. M., and Cotter, D. A. (2000). "The devaluation of women's work: A comment on Tam." *American Journal of Sociology*, 105(6), 1741–51.

Entwistle, J. and Wissinger, E. (2006). "Keeping up appearances: Aesthetic labour in the fashion modelling industries of London and New York." *The Sociological Review*, 54(4), 774–94.

Feldberg, R. L. and Glenn, E. N. (1979). "Male and female: Job versus gender models in the sociology of work." *Social Problems*, 26(5), 524–38.

Felt, L. F. and Sinclair, P. R. (1992). "'Everyone does it': Unpaid work in a rural peripheral region." *Work, Employment & Society*, 6(1), 43–64.

Folbre, N. and Nelson, J. A. (2000). "For love or money—or both?" *The Journal of Economic Perspectives*, 14(4), 123–40.

Friedl, E. (1996). "Society and Sex Roles." in K. B. Costello (ed.), *Gendered Voices: Readings from the American experience*, pp. 50–8. Boston: Heinle and Heinle.

Gallagher, S. K. and Gerstel, N. (1993). "Kinkeeping and friend keeping among older women: The effect of marriage." *Gerontologist*, 33(5), 675–81.

Garey, A. I. (1999). *Weaving Work and Motherhood*. Philadelphia: Temple University Press.

Gilman, C. P. (1997 [1898]). *Women and Economics*. Mineola, NY: Courier Dover Publications.

Glazer, N. Y. (1984). "Servants to capital: Unpaid domestic labor and paid work." *Review of Radical Political Economics*, 16(1), 61–87.

Glucksmann, M. A. (1995). "Why 'work'? Gender and the 'total social organization of labour.'" *Gender, Work & Organization*, 2(2), 63–75.

Grandey, A. A. and Krannitz, M. A. (2016). "Emotion Regulation at Work and at Home." In T. D. Allen and L. T. Eby (eds.), *The Oxford Handbook of Work and Family*, pp. 81–94. Oxford and New York: Oxford University Press.

Granovetter, M. (1995 [1974]). *Getting a Job: A study of contacts and careers*. Chicago: University of Chicago Press.

Hall, S. (1992). "The West and the Rest: Discourse and power." In S. Hall and B. Gieben (eds.), *Formations of Modernity*, pp. 275–332. Cambridge: Polity Press.

Hardering, F., Will-Zocholl, M., and Hofmeister, H. (2016). "Sinn der Arbeit und Sinnvolle Arbeit: Zur Einführung." *Arbeit*, 24(1–2), 3–12.

Hays, S. (1996). *The Cultural Contradictions of Motherhood*. New Haven, CT: Yale University Press.

Heaphy, E. D. (2017). "'Dancing on hot coals': How emotion work facilitates collective sensemaking." *Academy of Management Journal*, 60(2), 642–70.

Hochschild, A. (1983). *The Managed Heart: The commercialization of human feeling*. Berkley and Los Angeles: University of California Press.

Hochschild, A. (1989). *The Second Shift*. New York: Avon Books.

Hochschild, A. (2004). "Love and Gold." In B. Ehrenreich and A. R. Hochschild (eds.), *Global Woman: Nannies, maids, and sex workers in the new economy*, pp. 15–30. New York: Owl Books/Henry Holt.

Hof, K. (2006). "'Something you can actually pick up': Scrapbooking as a form and forum of cultural citizenship." *European Journal of Cultural Studies*, 9(3), 363–84.

Hofmeister, H. (2016). "Gender and Science: A Trial. Women Versus 16 Other Suspects Guilty for Causing Women's Underrepresentation in Science Careers." In N. Baur, C. Besio, M. Norkus, and G. Petschik (eds.), *Wissen—Organisation—Forschungspraxis: Der Makro-Meso-Mikro-Link in der Wissenschaft*, pp. 626–70. Weinheim: Beltz-Juventa.

Hofmeister, H. and Baur, N. (2015). "The idealization of the 'New Father' and 'Reversed Roles Father' in Germany." *Family Science*, 6(1), 1–16.

Hofmeister, H. and Blossfeld, H.-P. (2006). "Women's Careers in an Era of Uncertainty: Conclusions from a 13-Country International Comparison." In H.-P. Blossfeld and H. Hofmeister (eds.), *Globalization, Uncertainty and Women's Careers: An international comparison*, pp. 433–50. Cheltenham, UK and Northampton, MA: Edward Elgar.

Hofmeister, H. and Edgell, P. (2014). "The relevance of place and family stage for styles of community involvement." *Community, Work & Family*, 18(1), 58–78.

Hogg, M. A. and Reid, S. A. (2006). "Social identity, self-categorization, and the communication of group norms." *Communication Theory*, 16, 7–30.

Holt-Lunstad, J., Robles, T. F., and Sbarra, D. A. (2017). "Advancing social connection as a public health priority in the United States." *American Psychologist*, 72(6), 517–30.

Hook, J. L. (2004). "Reconsidering the division of household labor: Incorporating volunteer work and informal support." *Journal of Marriage and Family*, 66(1), 101–17.

Kaminer, W. (1984). *Women Volunteering: The pleasure, pain, and politics of unpaid work from 1830 to the present*. Garden City, NY: Doubleday.

Kanter, R. M. (1993). *Men and Women of the Corporation*. New York: Basic Books.

Kisselburgh, L., Berkelaar, B. L., and Buzzanell, P. M. (2009). "Discourse, gender, and the meaning of work: Rearticulating science, technology, and engineering careers through communicative lenses." *Communication Yearbook*, 33(1), 384–414.

Lair, D. J., Sullivan, K., and Cheney, G. (2005). "Marketization and the recasting of the professional self: The rhetoric and ethics of personal branding." *Management Communication Quarterly*, 18(3), 307–43.

Lasch, C. (1989). "The Family as a Haven in a Heartless World." In A. S. Skolnick and J. H. Skolnick (eds.), *Family in Transition*, pp. 561–72. Glenview, IL: Scott, Foresman and Company.

Luescher, K. and Pillemer, K. (1998). "Intergenerational ambivalence: A new approach to the study of parent–child relations in later life." *Journal of Marriage and the Family*, 60(2), 413–25.

Lutz, H. (2016). *Migration and Domestic Work: A European perspective on a global theme*. Abingdon and New York: Routledge.

Margaryan, A. and Hofmeister, H. (2017). "Using Life Course Perspective to Understand Learning Practices Within Crowdwork." Paper presented at the Research methods for digital work: innovative methods for studying distributed and multi-modal working practices conference, May 25–6, 2017, University of Surrey, Guildford, UK.

Martin, E. A., Hess, J., and Siegel, P. M. (1995). "Some Effects of Gender on the Meaning of 'Work': An Empirical Examination." Working paper. Washington, DC: Bureau of the Census, Center for Survey Methods Research.

McIntosh, W. A. and Zey, M. (1989). "Women as gatekeepers of food consumption: A sociological critique." *Food and Foodways*, 3(4), 317–32.

Messner, M. A. and Bozada-Deas, S. (2009). "Separating the men from the moms: The making of adult gender segregation in youth sports." *Gender & Society*, 23(1), 49–71.

Neysmith, S. and Reitsma-Street, M. (2000). "Valuing unpaid work in the third sector: The case of community resource centres." *Canadian Public Policy*, 26(3), 331–46.

Neysmith, S. and Reitsma-Street, M. (2005). "'Provisioning': Conceptualizing the work of women for 21st century social policy." *Women's Studies International Forum*, 28, 381–91.

Nickson, D., Warhurst, C., Cullen, A. M., and Watt, A. (2003). "Bringing in the excluded? Aesthetic labour, skills and training in the 'new' economy." *Journal of Education and Work*, 16(2), 185–203.

Nobelprize.org. (2014). "Gary S. Becker—Facts." *Nobel Media AB* [website]: http://www.nobelprize.org/nobel_prizes/economic-sciences/laureates/1992/becker-facts.html [accessed September 19, 2017].

Oakley, A. (1974). *The Sociology of Housework*. New York: Pantheon Books.

Ostner, I. (1993). "Slow Motion: Women, Work and the Family in Germany." In J. Lewis (ed.), *Women and Social Policies in Europe: Work, family, and the state*, pp. 92–115. Aldershot: Edward Elgar

Pascall, G. and Lewis, J. (2004). "Emerging gender regimes and policies for gender equality in a wider Europe." *Journal of Social Policy*, 33(3), 373–94.

Pratt, M. G. and Ashforth, B. E. (2003). "Fostering Meaningfulness in Working and at Work." In K. S. Cameron, J. E. Dutton, and R. E. Quinn (eds.), *Positive Organizational Scholarship: Foundations of a new discipline*, pp. 309–27. San Francisco: Berrett-Koehler.

Primeau, L. A. (1992). "A woman's place: Unpaid work in the home." *The American Journal of Occupational Therapy*, 46(11), 981–8.

Provansal, M. (2016). "Au-delà de la vocation artistique: Un recrutement sexuellement différencié des candidat-e-s à une carrière de plasticien-ne?" *Éducation et socialization*, 42. doi: 10.4000/edso.1821.

Rich, A. (1986). *Of Woman Born: Motherhood as experience and institution*. New York: W. W. Norton & Company.

Ritzer, G. (2017). "From Production and Consumption to Prosumption: A Personal Journey and its Larger Context." In M. Keller, B. Halkier, T.-A. Wilska, and M. Truninger (eds.), *Routledge Handbook on Consumption*, pp. 83–93. Abingdon and Oxford: Routledge.

Rodell, J. B. (2013). "Finding meaning through volunteering: Why do Employees volunteer and what does it mean for their jobs?" *Academy of Management Journal*, 56(5), 1274–94.

Rosso, B. D., Dekas, K. H., and Wrzesniewski, A. (2010). "On the meaning of work: A theoretical integration and review." *Research in Organizational Behavior*, 30, 91–127.

Schnell, T. and Hoof, M. (2012). "Meaningful commitment: Finding meaning in volunteer work." *Journal of Beliefs and Values*, 33(1), 35–53.

Segal, B. and Podoshen, J. S. (2013). "An examination of materialism, conspicuous consumption and gender differences." *International Journal of Consumer Studies*, 37(2), 189–98.

Shelton, B. A. (2006). "Gender and Unpaid Work." In J. S. Chafetz (ed.), *Handbook of the Sociology of Gender*, pp. 375–90. New York: Springer Science+Business Media.

Smith-Lovin, L. and McPherson, M. (1993). "You Are Who You Know: A Network Approach to Gender." In P. England (ed.), *Theory on Gender/Feminism on Theory*, pp. 223–52. New York: Aldine de Gruyter.

Stone, R. I., Cafferata, L., and Sangl, J. (1987). "Caregivers of the frail elderly: A national profile." *The Gerontologist*, 27, 616–26.

Taylor, R. F. (2004). "Extending conceptual boundaries: Work, voluntary work and employment." *Work, Employment and Society*, 18(1), 29–49.

Thomeer, M. B., Reczek, C., and Umberson, D. (2015). "Gendered emotion work around physical health problems in mid- and later-life marriages." *Journal of Aging Studies*, 32, 12–22.

Thompson, W. E. (2003). "Hanging Tongues: A Sociological Encounter with the Assembly Line." In D. Harper and H. M. Lawson (eds.), *The Cultural Study of Work*, pp. 313–34. Lanham, MD: Rowman & Littlefield.

Toepfer, N. F., Foster, J. L. H., and Wilz, G. (2014). "'The Good Mother and Her Clinging Child': Patterns of anchoring in social representations of dementia caregiving." *Journal of Community and Applied Social Psychology*, 24, 234–48.

Toffler, A. (1980). *The Third Wave*. New York: William Morrow and Company.

Tokunaga, M., Hashimoto, H., and Tamiya, N. (2015). "A gap in formal long-term care use related to characteristics of caregivers and households, under the Public Universal System in Japan: 2001–2010." *Health Policy*, 119(6), 840–9.

Vallas, S. P. and Cummins, E. R. (2015). "Personal branding and identity norms in the popular business press: Enterprise culture in an age of precarity." *Organization Studies*, 36(3), 293–319.

van Wolferen, K. (1990). *The Enigma of Japanese Power*. New York: Vintage Books.

Warhurst, C. and Nickson, D. (2009). "'Who's got the look?' Emotional, aesthetic and sexualized labour in interactive services." *Gender, Work & Organization*, 16(3), 385–404.

West, C. and Fenstermaker, S. (1995). "Doing difference." *Gender and Society*, 9(1), 8–37.

Williams, C. L. (1998). "The Glass Escalator: Hidden Advantages for Men in the 'Female' Professions." In M. S. Kimmel and M. A. Messner (eds.), *Men's Lives*, 4th edn., pp. 285–99. Boston: Allyn and Bacon.

Wilson, K. R. and Prior, M. R. (2010). "Father involvement: The importance of paternal solo care." *Early Childhood Development and Care*, 180(10), 1391–1405.

Yeoman, R. (2014). "Meaningful Work and Workplace Democracy." Doctor of Philosophy, Department of Politics and International Relations, Royal Holloway College, University of London.

....

CHAPTER 19

LEADERSHIP AND MEANINGFUL WORK

....

DENNIS TOURISH

INTRODUCTION

....

THE search for meaning is fundamental to human existence. Yet it is hard to find. There is no divine plan, our existence has no intrinsic purpose, and each of us is ultimately fated to eternal oblivion. *Homo sapiens* is an accidental species, emerging from a long chain of evolutionary episodes that were not predetermined to produce a biped species equipped with language, some form of consciousness, and a belief that the universe owes us an explanation as well as an existence (Gee, 2013). Harari (2011) argues that any sense of meaning we intuit is built on myths created partly to shield ourselves from this realization but also to sustain cooperation between people, including in business organizations. Ultimately, life and work may be meaningless. This does not prevent us from craving a sense of meaningfulness in our lives, including at work, or leaders from seeking to provide it. Without this, any form of social organization might be impossible.

This idea has become commonplace. Thus, there has been a proliferation of mission statements, vison statements, creed statements, statements of purpose, statements of philosophy, values statements, and more, often couched in quasi-religious terms. They are intended to suggest that there is more to work than the prosaic need to earn a living, and that a greater end is in sight than the promotion of shareholder value (Khurana, 2002). In line with this, theories of leadership have increasingly suggested that a sense of meaningful work can be created (or fabricated) by leaders, ostensibly to the benefit of leaders themselves, organizations, and employees. Summarizing research in this area, Rosso, Dekas, and Wrzesniewski (2010: 101) conclude that "leaders can imbue work with meaningfulness by prompting employees to transcend their personal needs or goals in favour of those tied to a broader mission or purpose."

In this chapter, I subject these arguments to critical scrutiny. This means looking at how some dominant theories of leadership address the issue of meaningful work, and questioning whether it is desirable for leaders to see themselves as the architects of purpose for others in the way that is being suggested. A core problem is that leadership theory is often insensitive to issues of power, control, and resistance (Tourish, 2013). It tends to be assumed that powerful people have a right and even an obligation to craft values for others, and that they will do so in the imagined unitarist interest of all concerned. This means that, paradoxically, attempts by leaders to provide a sense of meaningfulness at work for followers can be regarded as an unwelcome intrusion, threatening whatever meanings they may have already attached to their work.

It is worth noting that, despite the many invocations of the role of leaders and leadership in the creation of meaningful work, it remains elusive. Paulsen's (2014) study of "empty labor" discusses the extent to which people are underemployed at work, and while away their time in pretended obedience, fake commitment, straightforward soldiering, and non-work tasks such as surfing pornography websites. He pointedly asks: "what if work is no more than a bad joke for many employees?" (p. 9). A Gallup Survey (2013) concluded that only 13 percent of employees worldwide liked going to work. This is a snapshot measure, but one that is consistent with long-term trends. Typically, most employees have little opportunity to feed ideas to those in positions of authority: their voices are largely muted and their agency atomized (Tourish and Robson, 2006). Fleming (2017: 692) refers to the "ongoing individualization of the workforce" with a growth in zero-hours work, individual contracts, and full-time employees who are nevertheless deemed to be "self-employed," and thereby responsible for their own training, uniforms, and often left without such basics as sick pay. Rather than promote a sense of meaningful work, Fleming (2017) suggests that burnout, hypertension, and low productivity are key features of the modern workplace.

Little of this finds reflection in most of the leadership literature. Rather, as Podolny, Khurana, and Besharov (2010: 65) note, the dominant assumption remains that "Leaders are the source of institutionalized values which, in turn, condition the actions of organizational members." It is assumed that the values in question will generate a sense of meaningful work that may even be strong enough to compensate for the deterioration of material conditions. Such assumptions are, of course, grossly simplistic. They take it for granted that there actually are such things as organization-wide values, and that leaders can successfully determine what these should be on behalf of compliant others. One unsettling conclusion may be that leadership as practiced in the context of contemporary business organizations is incapable of creating meaningful work. It follows that urging leaders to do so is misplaced, theoretically unsustainable, and may do more harm than good. It is these issues that form the central focus of this chapter.

THE CLAIMS OF LEADERSHIP

It is not difficult to find claims for the significance of leadership in terms of providing meaningful work. Thus, we read that leadership helps employees to form "high-quality" relationships with the organization (Kurtessis et al., 2017). This, it is suggested, offers them a sense of purpose and so enhances meaningfulness (Barrick, Mount, and Li, 2013).

One of the most long-standing leadership approaches is leader–member exchange (LMX) theory. In essence, this focuses on the quality of relationships between individual leaders and followers. Many studies purport to show that high-quality relationships between leaders and individual followers foster organizational commitment and job satisfaction, among much else (Epitropaki and Martin, 2016). In short, the emotional ties that develop between employees and their immediate supervisor are central to how much meaning is attributed to work. How so? Graen (1976) argued that LMX is positively related to commitment because leaders encourage this during the role-making process. They also assign challenging tasks to those employees who they value. This, it is said, is combined with appropriate feedback, thereby leading to greater commitment. Committed employees, of course, are more likely to invest their work with desirable meanings, and perhaps quell challenging questions about its value.

While not directly drawing on LMX, Finkelstein's (2016) book on those he called "Superbosses" (defined as people who can motivate exceptional people to do the impossible) also stresses the importance of relationships between leaders and followers. When this "works," he writes approvingly of the outcome as being

> akin to a Stockholm syndrome of leadership: employees push themselves to their limits for their superbosses, but rather than resent the superboss for it, they feel even greater loyalty. They'll do anything to keep from disappointing this larger-than-life figure and they yearn to please him [sic], not only because they've completely bought into the boss's vision but also because they want to feel that their boss was correct in selecting then for the job.   (Finkelstein, 2016: 63)

This is a terrifyingly cult-like vision of the workplace, and indeed Finkelstein goes on to say that superbosses also "drive their people exceptionally hard" (p. 65).

Other approaches are equally explicit in depicting leaders as powerful actors who deservedly have most if not all authority over meaning-making, and to whose vision employees should uncritically subscribe. Banks (2008: 11) observes that: "Conventionally, leaders show the way, are positioned in the vanguard, guide and direct, innovate, and have a vision for change and make it come to actuality. Followers on the other hand conventionally track the leader from behind, obey and report, implement innovations and accept leaders' vision for change." As Collinson (2012) has critically observed, most leadership scholarship tends to assume that visionary leadership is powerful, exciting, and necessary, with leaders acting as a force for good whose efforts almost invariably produce positive outcomes. This includes the development of positive values, norms, and meanings (or beliefs) that others should internalize more or less uncritically. The consistent expectation is that "leaders do special, significant things... turning everyday activities into something remarkable" (Alvesson and Sveningsson, 2003: 1452). Meaningful work is among the results.

In line with this, Sashkin (2004: 175) asserts that "Leaders transform followers. That is, followers are changed from being self-centered individuals to being committed members of a group." The implication is that while followers are "self-centered," leaders are less so. Sashkin, incidentally, offers not a shred of evidence to show that this is the case. The appeal of such an approach is largely ideological in nature, since it supports the unitarist view of organizations that is characteristic of functionalist approaches in management and organization studies (Alvesson and Karreman, 2016). Meaningful work is to be found through identification with the leader, the organization, and its goals, rather than in challenging them and in developing one's own goals and values. Whatever values actors might attribute to an oppositional stance are, by definition, illegitimate, since they could be considered subversive of efficiency and effectiveness. Yet, when employees are asked about what makes their work meaningful they typically do not respond in terms of how much they identify with the goals of their leaders. Rather, they highlight such issues as personal growth, their sense of unity and belonging with others, and how well they can express their full potential (Lips-Wiersma and Morris, 2009).

Of course, there is a growing number of studies that explore "toxic" leader behavior (Pelletier, 2010), "bad" leadership (Kellerman, 2004), "narcissistic" leadership (Kets de Vries and Miller, 1985), "destructive leadership behavior" (Aasland et al., 2010), "leadership derailment" (Furnham, 2010), "the dark side of personality and extreme leader behaviour" (Kaiser, LeBreton, and Hogan, 2015), and "destructive leadership" (including abusive supervision and petty tyranny) (Krasikova, Green, and LeBreton, 2013). "Negative" leadership has been variously conceived as behavior that is insincere, despotic, exploitative, restrictive, failed, laissez-faire, and involving the active and passive avoidance of leadership responsibilities (Schilling, 2009). There has also been a recognition of "exploitative" leadership where leaders prioritize egotistical and self-interested goals above those of the wider organization (Schmid, Verdorfer, and Peus, 2017). Such leaders are often depicted as "pseudo-transformational leaders," who pursue absolute power and personal gain (Barling, Christie, and Turner, 2008). But in the field of leadership studies every study pointing to the dark side is met by a chorus of voices that presents leaders as saints (articulating, living, and promoting compelling core values), commanders (making tough decisions), architects (redesigning society), pedagogues (teaching appropriate behaviors), and physicians (healing stricken organizations). Such metaphors are widely employed by leaders, determined to present themselves as indispensable purveyors of meaning at work (Amernic, Craig, and Tourish, 2007).

Authentic Leadership?

Some mainstream scholars are aware of these issues, and are even troubled by them. In response, it has been suggested that "bad" leadership is not really leadership at all. Rather, leadership is by definition positive since it is oriented to achieving ends that are in line with the real needs of followers. One of the most popular expressions of this is the idea of "authentic leadership." An authentic leader, we are told, "is confident, hopeful, optimistic, resilient, moral/ethical, future oriented, and gives priority to developing associates to be leaders" (Luthans and Avolio, 2003: 43). They are, in effect, paragons of virtue, whose positive example inspires others to live lives suffused with meaning, purpose, and commitment. As with LMX, the key is an excellent relationship between authentic leaders and their followers.

The problem lies in the presumption that the leader actually knows and cares about what the real needs of followers are. Thus, we read that "Authentic leaders... retain their distinctiveness as individuals, yet they know how to win acceptance in strong corporate and social cultures and how to use elements of those cultures as a basis for radical change" (Goffee and Jones, 2006: 88). "Strong" corporate and social cultures are presented as unproblematic since they articulate an incontestable public good. The problem is that business organizations are not churches, whose members may readily cohere around common values and an overarching sense of purpose that give their lives meaning. Rather, they are mostly unwieldy coalitions of differentiated individuals, pursuing instrumentalist and usually short-term ends through transactional means. For this reason, Kunda's (1992) study is one of many that show how a strong organizational culture often comes up against people's existing values and identities, thereby undermining their pursuit of meaningful work. They have to negate their own values to identify with those of the organization, a singularly alienating experience. This presents a paradox. Leaders who pursue the creation of shared meanings may inadvertently undermine whatever meanings people have already attached to their work. They may even threaten "any sense of natural community—for example, by imposing uniformity that is actually more aligned with the beliefs of one subgroup in the organization than others" (Podolny, Khurana, and Besharov, 2010: 91).

More problematic still, it is also assumed that the imagined "authenticity" of the leader and their inner values are consistent with the needs of the organization and of the managerial role (Avolio, Luthans, and Walumbwa, 2004). Authentic leaders express values that are inherently positive and to which everyone can subscribe (Algera and Lips-Wiersma, 2012). In this way, they will be "relatively immune to situational pressures" (Gardner, Fischer, and Hunt, 2009: 468). In turn, followers are expected to discover no conflict between their inner values and those of the organization. This is a view of the employment relationship that many would struggle to reconcile with their actual experiences. Meaning is derived from conformity, the suppression of doubt, and the internalization of belief systems determined by powerful others. As Ford and Harding (2011: 476) put it, there is "little possibility of freedom of speech or thought: if the model was successfully implemented then to demand such things would result in being seen as inauthentic and thus unsuitable for the organization... Only the leader, and thus the follower... who mimics the organization and its demands will be acceptable." This standpoint is nowhere more apparent than in theories of "transformational leadership," to which I now turn.

TRANSFORMATIONAL LEADERSHIP AND MEANINGFUL WORK

Transformational leadership (henceforth, TFL) is widely recognized as the dominant leadership theory of recent decades (van Knippenberg and Sitkin, 2013). Its origins can be traced to Burns (1978), who proposed that leadership could be viewed as either transactional or transformational. His work is considered seminal in the field. Transactional leadership recognizes that leaders and followers have different goals (Flauto, 1999). But they exchange goods, services, and other rewards to achieve their independent goals. Burns (1978: 425) observed that the object of this transactional approach "is not a joint effort for persons with common aims acting for the collective interests of followers but a bargain to aid the individual interests of persons or groups going their separate ways." He viewed this in negative terms, since it implies that we may always have conflict and dissent. A shared sense of values, purpose, goals, and meaningful work is likely to be absent. The result is reduced organizational cohesion. This outcome is anathema to conventional leadership scholarship.

In contrast, TFL argues that effective leaders seek to change the goals and values of followers rather than let them be. It is assumed that the new goals represent the "collective good or pooled interests of leaders and followers" (Burns, 1978: 426). Free of the burdens produced by conflict, all parties will find the meaning of work in a higher sense of purpose devoted to the achievement of common organizational goals. It is assumed that the visionary goals proposed by a transformational leader speak to some ultimate purpose that animates greater effort. Yet this approach often backfires. As Carton (2017: 3) notes: "the very properties that make ultimate aspirations meaningful are those that leave employees unable to sense how their daily responsibilities are associated with them. Employees are likely to perceive the organization's ultimate aspirations as more significant than the time-constrained goals they work toward each day—yet also severely disconnected from them." Paradoxically, work may end up feeling less meaningful rather than more so.

What if, also, a leader develops goals, visions, and an ultimate purpose that reflect only their own selfish interests? In a period when the maximization of shareholder value is often presented as the main purpose of business, the fear that those at the top might pursue self-interested goals is not an idle fancy (Bower and Paine, 2017). Having power does not generally encourage empathy or concern for the well-being of dependent others. Accordingly, the model proposed by Burns (1978) is a highly idealized version of an inherently problematic process. This is evident in the following depiction: "In contrast to the transactional leader who practices contingent reinforcement of followers, the transformational leader inspires, intellectually stimulates, and is individually considerate of them...The transformational leader emphasizes what you can do for your country; the transactional leader, on what your country can do for you" (Bass, 1999: 9). This greater goal is presumed to provide meaning through work for followers, from which they will become more committed to the leader and the leader's goals.

Thus, TFL theorists suggest that leaders must satisfy followers' needs, values, and goals and confirm their identities as part of a process of shaping attitudes to make them conform to a common, unitary interest (Chemers, 2003). Personal and organizational goals are aligned, heightening employee commitment (Bass, 1999). An organization's "vision" is "shared" by employees and leaders (Conger, Kanungo, and Menon, 2000). Empirical studies also suggest that transformational leadership fosters much closer identification with both the leader and the designated work unit—an outcome generally viewed by its advocates as desirable (Kark, Shamir, and Chen, 2003).

Consistent with much corporate practice, a transformational leader is assumed to possess and energetically communicate "a vision" (Diaz-Saenz, 2011). The vision portrays an idealized future to which all can commit, and provides a shared sense of meaning that legitimizes the prevailing organization of work (Conger, 1989; Awamleh and Gardner, 1999). This is consistent with the movement toward "corporate culturism" that was unleashed in large part through the work of Peters and Waterman (1982). They argued that "Improvements in productivity…flow from corporate cultures that *system-atically* recognise and reward individuals, symbolically and materially, for identifying their sense of purpose with the values that are designed into the organization" (p. 516). As Willmott (1993, 2013) argued, employees are encouraged to become devoted to their work. Rival ends are assumed to be illegitimate, while other interests and relationships are squeezed by the all-consuming imperatives of work. He suggests that this can be viewed as "*a totalitarian remedy for the resolution of indeterminacy and ambiguity: thought control through the uniform definition of meaning*" (Willmott, 1993: 527, original emphasis). It may make work feel very meaningful, at least for a time. But whether this is a positive thing is increasingly questionable.

In addition, it is suggested that transformational leaders should communicate high performance expectations (Podsakoff et al., 1990), provide inspirational communication (Rafferty and Griffin, 2004), display unconventional behavior and sensitivity to members' needs (Conger and Kanungo, 1994), and demonstrate an ideological emphasis focused on building a collective identity (Shamir et al., 1998). There is seemingly no end to the good things that ostensibly flow from this, including greater individual creativity (Gong, Huang, and Farh, 2009), increased job satisfaction and commitment (Bono and Judge, 2003), and improved follower self-esteem, self-efficacy, and loyalty (Bass and Riggio, 2006). Consistent with LMX theory, the assumption is that people find meaningful work through their relationships with one or more leaders. Of course, this requires them to identify with the visions, goals, and values that the leader articulates. If these conflict with pre-existing follower beliefs, a simple choice exists. The follower must update their values, much as they would the virus protection software on their computer—or leave.

As Delaney and Spoelstra (2015) have noted, the stress here is on followers identifying with goals articulated by leaders emphasizes self-actualization and satisfaction rather than the pursuit of material rewards. These authors also go on to argue that: "Casting transformational leaders in the image of a Great Man is thus dangerous because of the fundamentally unequal power relationship between the leader and the follower, which makes us question what (and whose) interest this power serves" (p. 73). For TFL theorists, these questions do not arise, since a common interest between leaders and followers is simply assumed. A leader's job is to bring this interest to the fore, getting rid of any ideological clutter that impedes a realization of the obvious.

Transformational leaders must therefore cultivate the impression of charisma. But here also there are challenges. As Weber argued in his seminal work on charisma (1948), followers may gain a sense of meaning from following a charismatic leader. However, this is conditional on the leader's success. As he eloquently put it: "If [the charismatic leader] wants to be a prophet, he must perform miracles; if he wants to be a warlord, he must perform heroic deeds. Above all, however, his divine mission must 'prove' itself in that those who faithfully surrender to him must fare well. If they do not fare well, he is obviously not the master sent by the gods" (p. 249). The prospect of disillusionment and the loss of meaning is thereby rooted in such relationships, as many once revered leaders and disappointed followers have found to their cost.

Despite these concerns, the impact of TFL has gone beyond its core theory. I turn briefly to one example—that of spiritual leadership theory. This is even more overtly concerned with meaningful work than its parent theory, and is thus worthy of some attention. Spirituality at work is discussed in detail elsewhere in this volume. Here, consistent with my critical intention, I focus on its leadership implications, arguing that it shares the flaws of TFL while adding some fresh ones of its own.

SPIRITUAL LEADERSHIP IN THE WORKPLACE

Advocates of Spirituality at Work (henceforth, SAW) argue that since people now spend most of their waking hours at work they increasingly look to their organizations "as a communal centre" (Mirvis, 1997: 702), thereby legitimating the concern of leaders with the private belief systems of employees. People, allegedly, now expect their leaders to offer meaning in both their work and wider lives (Ashmos and Duchon, 2000). The management of meaning and the creation of meaningful work are therefore held to be crucial activities for leaders (Singhal and Chatterjee, 2006). Fry (2003: 702) bizarrely suggests that "Companies as diverse as Taco Bell, Pizza Hut, BioGenenex, Aetna International, Big Six accounting's Deloitte and Touche, and Law firms such as New York's Kaye, Scholer, Fierman, Hayes and Haroller are extolling lessons usually doled out in churches, temples and mosques."

In general, SAW has been described in terms of a deep relationship with the core of what it means to be a human being (Wong, 1998), the promotion of a relationship with a higher power that affects how one conducts oneself in the world (Armstrong, 1995), and as an animating force that inspires one toward purposes beyond oneself and which in turn gives work a sense of meaning (McKnight, 1984). In straightforward religious terms, spiritual well-being on the part of both leaders and followers has also been posited as requiring an affirmation of life in a relationship with God and the celebration and nurturing of wholeness (Ellison, 1983). One inescapable irony is that leaders are often encouraged to promote spirituality of one kind or another on the decidedly unspiritual basis that, since people will find their work more meaningful, performance and productivity will improve (e.g. Fry and Cohen, 2009; Fry et al., 2017).

It seems evident that this approach encourages corporate leaders to exercise a dominating influence over the private values and belief systems of employees (Tourish and Tourish, 2010). The paradox is clear. On the one hand, since it is asserted that employees bring spiritual values with them to work, it follows that "the organization is cast neutrally as the provider of opportunities for individual spiritual expression" (Bell and Taylor, 2003: 343). But, simultaneously, spiritual values are to be defined, shaped, and introduced by managers. Thus, spiritual leadership involves "creating a vision wherein organization members experience a sense of calling in that their life has meaning and makes a difference" (Fry, 2003: 711). As with TFL, this means that leaders should promote a common vision and achieve value congruence at all organizational levels (Maghroori and Rolland, 1997).

A key proposition is that workplace spirituality is related to the leader's ability to "enable" the worker's inner life, sense of meaningful work, and community (Duchon and Plowman, 2005). Accordingly, a leader who embraces SAW will have a heightened ability to define for others what is meant by living a meaningful life, and incidentally to transform their inner life so that it is more consistent with corporate purposes. It is an agenda built on the familiar assumption that organizations have a unitarist nature, thereby ensuring that the extension of leaders' power in ever wider and more intrusive directions will have a benign effect.

The problem is that this fails to address the issue of power. The prerogatives of leaders are presented in an unassailable light. Wagner-Marsh and Conley (1999: 107) argue that:

> The president or CEO is usually the key person to initiate a process defining an organization's mission and vision, and, as stated, this should be part of his or her job description, but a governing board should be deeply involved in the process, especially in the case of religious and other non-profit institutions...staff must be consulted throughout the process in meaningful ways that take seriously their input but don't place inappropriate expectations on them to ultimately control the outcome.

Thus, leaders have a legitimate right, and even a duty, to determine values and beliefs for employees, who have the consolation that they have been "consulted" about what these might be. Little thought has been given to the potentially negative effects of breaching boundaries between the personal and professional domains of people's lives in this manner. Since people want "soul enriching fulfilment at work" (Dean and Safranski, 2008: 359), it is assumed that those in charge of organizations have an obligation to provide it. Admittedly, it is sometimes suggested that when this is genuinely based on the teachings of Jesus or other important religious figures it can be said to imply "a radical independence" which includes "a willingness to critique wrong-doing and wrong-thinking" (Mabey et al., 2017: 3). In practice, the preservation of individual autonomy and voice may not be so straightforward. For example, Chick-fil-A is a private franchise chain in the USA with 1,300 stores that specializes in chicken sandwiches. The company says that its primary purpose is to "glorify God." Its stores close on Sunday to facilitate church attendance, and their managers are encouraged to host Bible study groups (Fry and Slocum, 2007). In the context of asymmetrical power relations in the workplace, it is difficult to see how such an agenda could genuinely serve an emancipatory purpose. The centrality of power in leadership scholarship needs far greater attention.

THE ROLE OF POWER AND THE PARADOXES OF MEANINGFUL WORK

Keltner (2016) has identified what he terms "the power paradox." As he puts it, the problem is that:

> the very practices that enable us to rise in power vanish in our experience of power. We gain and maintain power through empathy, but in our experience of power we lose our focus on others. We gain and maintain power through giving, but when we are feeling powerful, we act in self-gratifying and often greedy ways. Dignifying others with expressions of gratitude is essential to achieving enduring power, but once we are feeling powerful, we become rude and offensive.   (Keltner, 2016: 100)

Of course, there are always exceptions. But the more power we have the more likely it seems to be that these negative traits will come to the fore. The general tendency is for leaders to covet ever greater levels of power rather than aspire to less. The dysfunctional dynamics of possessing power over others are thus reinforced. In such a context, it is challenging to see leaders as the purveyors of meaningful work for others.

In contrast, there are accounts of workplaces where employees are radically empowered, freed from tyrannical oversight and given a great deal of control over company decision-making. Semler's (1993) account of Semco in Brazil, where he was CEO and principal shareholder at the time of his book's publication, typifies this. Employees, he reports, are responsible for selecting managers and evaluate their performance frequently. They set their own hours, are directly involved in the selection of senior managers, and determine their own levels of pay. Leader/follower relations appear to be upended, and are certainly different from what we mostly find in corporate hierarchies. The job of leaders, if they can be so called, is to stand aside and do what they can to prevent an accumulation of bureaucratic regulations and practices that stifle creativity. But, rather surprisingly, there are no independent accounts of Semco that can either verify or contradict Semler's account, while the voices of the supposedly uber-empowered people who work there are strangely absent from his book. As Grey (2017) has noted, we are required to take the author's account on trust.

Moreover, as Barker (1993) argues, there is a downside to systems that rely on employees becoming so committed that they exert team-based pressure on each other to perform. Power relationships still exist. But they may be covert, and therefore more rather than less insidious. Rules are now strengthened by informal forms of peer pressure that create a new iron cage which constrains autonomy. From this perspective, participation and involvement can become a new tyranny (Cooke and Kothari, 2001). What do you do if you work in a putatively autonomous team but are in a minority of one? What if you secretly doubt the value of the organization's goals, or even think that they are nonsense? Concertive control is likely to ensure that you keep such heretical thoughts to yourself, while maintaining a public facade of enthusiastic conformity. On the other hand, if you genuinely feel the zeal of a convert then the organization has successfully colonized your inner world, and extended its influence ever further into your life. Bailey et al. (2017: 416) describe this as "existential labour" and discuss it in the context of what they term "the mis-managed soul," whereby people's belief systems are manipulated to mislead them about the nature of their work. Likewise, Fleming (2014) refers to what he calls "the new corporate enclosure movement," in which the difference between work and non-work life is eroded, to the detriment of any attempt people might make to find purpose and meaning in life beyond their paid occupations.

These views are consistent with the work of Stohl and Cheney (2001: 357), who highlight numerous paradoxes associated with participation and involvement. They say that "worker participation comprises organizational structures and processes designed to empower and enable employees to identify with organizational goals and to collaborate as control agents in activities that exceed minimum coordination efforts normally expected at work." Identification with organizational goals is generally assumed as a given and a prerequisite for participation. As they say: "participation is also a perceptual and political matter: Its very meaning can be controlled by a dominant group, its prevailing interpretation can change over time, and it may be understood quite differently in various quarters of the organization" (Stohl and Cheney, 2001: 358). This generates a paradox of autonomy, in which individual rights are handed over to group decision-making processes. It also produces a paradox of commitment whereby one commits to a group's values and beliefs but can be excluded from the group if this commitment is not expressed with enough fervor. Ultimately, Stohl and Cheney (2001) argue that we may find leaders defaulting to what they more or less have always done—demanding compliance from those in less powerful positions.

The leadership literature tends to define meaningful work in terms of identification with organizational goals, and accords leaders a privileged voice in determining what these might be. Where dissent is acknowledged, it is viewed as resistance to be overcome rather than, say, useful feedback. It is rarely acknowledged that, for many people, a sense of meaning at work is derived from resistance. Generations of trade union activists can testify to this (Fleming and Spicer, 2007). Even when work itself is perceived as meaningless, this does not always mean that people feel no sense of meaning while they are at work. However, resistance, and other non-managed sources of meaning, does not sit well in the conventional leadership landscape. Insufficient acknowledgment of resistance reduces leadership to simplistic formulae for success that prove elusive in practice, ignores the fractured context in which many leaders and followers actually work, and disregards the intensification of distance between leaders and others in organizations (Petriglieri and Petriglieri, 2015). This distance itself inhibits the development of meaningful work, since it suggests divergent rather than unitarist goals between organizational actors.

Ignoring this, and possibly ignorant of it, Porter and Nohria (2010: 464) argue that: "Most people in an organization don't begrudge the fact that the CEO is paid manifold more than them or enjoys privileges that they can only dream of. People accept that those who reach the top are rare achievers and must be compensated accordingly. What galls people is when the CEO appears to put self-interest above the company's interests." This reflects the increasingly unwarranted assumption that leaders and others share a same page agenda: the unselfish pursuit of "the company's interests," viewed as the same thing for everyone. Were it true, we would be hard pushed to explain the levels of disenchantment with work that I noted at the outset of this chapter. Rather than find meaningful work, more and more people seem to find it meaningless. Bland assurances of a unitarist interest are unlikely to solve the problem. Frantic attempts by leaders to promote evangelical visions divorced from the lived experiences of their employees are also unlikely to be successful.

CONCLUSION

We have a natural fascination with leadership, tending to attribute all responsibility for success or failure to those at the top (March, 2010). This has been memorably described as "the romance of leadership" (Meindl, Ehrlich, and Dukerich, 1985). We look to leaders for inspiration, guidance, and salvation to a far greater extent than most of them can deliver (Newark, 2018). I contend that the limitations of leader agency are perhaps especially pronounced when it comes to providing a sense of meaningful work.

It is useful to recall the words of Marcel Proust (1992: 513): "We do not receive wisdom, we must discover it for ourselves, after a journey through the wilderness which no one else can make for us, which no one can spare us, for our wisdom is the point of view from which we come at last to regard the world." An individual's journey to a meaningful life, including at work, does not depend on finding a guru, identifying with a powerful leader, or making work the fulcrum of their existence. The more leaders attempt to provide meaning for others, the more they may constrain the ability of people to embark on their own voyage of self-discovery. This is all the more true when the leader is pursuing their own self-interest, even if it is couched in unitarist language: "We are all in this together." There may be no meaningful work other than whatever meanings we invest in it ourselves. Consistent with this, Bailey and Madden (2016: 55) describe the results of interviews with 135 people on meaningful work as follows: "our research showed that the quality of leadership received virtually no mention when people described meaningful moments at work, but poor management was the top destroyer of meaningfulness."

More recent leadership theories may offer the glimmer of an alternative. Notions of relational leadership (Uhl-Bien and Ospina, 2012), discursive leadership (Fairhurst, 2007), processual/communication leadership (Tourish, 2014), and collective leadership (Friedrich, Griffith, and Mumford, 2016) all put more stress on how leaders and followers influence each other. They explore the processes whereby leadership is socially constructed for finite amounts of time—for example, through talk—and how it is often shared among individuals in social groups. Will these help to ensure that the terms "meaningful work" and "leadership" can coexist in the same sentence without provoking hoots of derision? Much depends on the macro-environment in which ideas are applied.

Hierarchy, intolerance, disrespect, and powerlessness have been resilient features of human existence for thousands of years. They are difficult to banish. But adopting an uncritical view of leadership which ensures that power remains tightly held by a few individuals will certainly do nothing to move us forward.

Let us recall the useful injunction: "First, do no harm." Perhaps leaders would be best advised to recognize their own limitations and the relative insignificance of the organizations they lead. Pink Floyd's song *Another Brick in The Wall* contains the line: "Hey! Teachers! Leave them kids alone." In terms of creating a sense of meaning at work, it is a line that could usefully be adapted for business leaders: "Hey, leaders: leave us all alone."

References

Aasland, M., Skogstad, A., Notelaers, G., Nielsen, B., and Einarsen, S. (2010). "The prevalence of destructive leadership behavior." *British Journal of Management*, 21, 438–52.

Algera, P. and Lips-Wiersma, M. (2012). "Radical authentic leadership: Co-creating the conditions under which all members of the organization can be authentic." *Leadership Quarterly*, 23, 118–31.

Alvesson, M. and Karreman, D. (2016). "Intellectual failure and ideological success in organization studies: The case of transformational leadership." *Journal of Management Inquiry*, 25, 139–52.

Alvesson, M. and Sveningsson, S. (2003). "Managers doing leadership: The extra-ordinarization of the mundane." *Human Relations*, 56, 1435–59.

Amernic, J., Craig, R., and Tourish, D. (2007). "The charismatic leader as pedagogue, physician, architect, commander, and saint: Five root metaphors in Jack Welch's letters to stockholders of General Electric." *Human Relations*, 60, 1839–72.

Armstrong, T. D. (1995). *Exploring Spirituality: The development of the Armstrong measure of spirituality*, Paper presented at the annual convention of the American Psychological Association, New York, NY.

Ashmos, D. and Duchon, D. (2000). "Spirituality at work: A reconceptualisation and measure." *Journal of Management Inquiry*, 9, 134–45.

Avolio, B., Luthans, F., and Walumbwa, F. O. (2004). *Authentic Leadership: Theory-building for veritable sustained performance*. Working paper. Lincoln, NE: Gallup Leadership Institute, University of Nebraska, Lincoln.

Awamleh, R. and Gardner, W. (1999). "Perceptions of leader charisma and effectiveness: The effects of vision content, delivery, and organizational performance." *Leadership Quarterly*, 10, 345–73.

Bailey, C. and Madden, A. (2016). "What makes work meaningful—Or meaningless?" *MIT Sloan Management Review*, 57, 53–61.

Bailey, C., Madden, A., Alfes, K., Shantz, A., and Soane, E. (2017). "The mis-managed soul: Existential labor and the erosion of meaningful work." *Human Resource Management Review*, 27(3), 416–30.

Banks, S. (2008). "The Problems with Leadership." In S. Banks (ed.), *Dissent and the Failure of Leadership*, pp. 1–21. London: Edward Elgar.

Barker, J. (1993). "Tightening the iron cage: Concertive control in self-managing teams." *Administrative Science Quarterly*, 38, 408–37.

Barling, J., Christie, A., and Turner, N. (2008). "Pseudo-transformational leadership: Towards the development and test of a model." *Journal of Business Ethics*, 81, 851–61.

Barrick, M., Mount, M., and Li, N. (2013). "The theory of purposeful work behaviour: The role of personality, higher-order goals, and job characteristics." *Academy of Management Review*, 38, 132–53.

Bass, B. (1999). "Two decades of research and development in transformational leadership." *European Journal of Work and Organizational Psychology*, 8, 9–26.

Bass, B. and Riggio, R. (2006). *Transformational Leadership*, 2nd edn. London: Lawrence Erlbaum.

Bell, E. and Taylor, S. (2003). "The elevation of work: Pastoral power and the new age work ethic." *Organization*, 10, 329–49.

Bono, J. and Judge, T. (2003). "Self-concordance at work: Toward understanding the motivational effects of transformational leadership." *Academy of Management Journal*, 46, 554–71.

Bower, J. and Paine, L. (2017). "The error at the heart of corporate leadership." *Harvard Business Review*, 95(3), 50–60.

Burns, J. (1978). *Leadership*. New York: Harper and Row.

Carton, A. (2017). "'I'm not mopping floors, I'm putting a man on the moon': How NASA leaders enhanced the meaningfulness of work by changing the meaning of work." *Administrative Science Quarterly*, 63(2), 323–69.

Chemers, M. (2003). "Leadership Effectiveness: Functional, Constructivist and Empirical Perspectives." In D. van Knippenberg and M. Hogg (eds.), *Leadership and Power: Identity processes in groups and organizations*, pp. 5–17. London: Sage.

Collinson, D. (2012). "Prozac leadership and the limits of positive thinking." *Leadership*, 8, 87–108.

Conger, J. (1989). *The Charismatic Leader: Behind the mystique of exceptional leadership*. San Francisco, CA: Jossey-Bass.

Conger, J. and Kanungo, R. (1994). "Charismatic leadership in organizations: Perceived behavioural attributes and their measurement." *Journal of Organizational Behavior*, 15, 439–52.

Conger, J., Kanungo, R., and Menon, S. (2000). "Charismatic leadership and follower effects." *Journal of Organizational Behaviour*, 21, 747–67.

Cooke, B. and Kothari, U. (eds.) (2001). *Participation: The new tyranny?* London: Zed Books.

Dean, K. and Safranski, S. (2008). "No harm, no foul? Organizational intervention in workplace spirituality." *International Journal of Public Administration*, 31, 359–71.

Delaney, H. and Spoelstra, S. (2015). "Transformational Leadership: Secularised Theology?" In B. Carroll, J. Ford, and S. Taylor (eds.), *Leadership: Contemporary critical perspectives*, pp. 69–86. London: Sage.

Diaz-Saenz, H. (2011). "Transformational Leadership." In A. Bryman, D. Collinson, K. Grint, B. Jackson, and M. Uhl-Bien (eds.), *The SAGE Handbook of Leadership*, pp. 299–310. London: Sage.

Duchon, D. and Plowman, D. (2005). "Nurturing the spirit at work: Impact on work unit performance." *Leadership Quarterly*, 16, 807–33.

Ellison, C. (1983). "Spiritual well-being: Conceptualisation and measurement." *Journal of Psychology and Theology*, 11, 330–40.

Epitropaki, O. and Martin, R. (2016). "LMX and Work Attitudes: Is There Anything Left Unsaid or Unexamined?" In T. Bauer and B. Erdogan (eds.), *The Oxford Handbook of Leader–Member Exchange*, pp. 139–56. Oxford: Oxford University Press.

Fairhurst, G. (2007). *Discursive Leadership*. London: Sage.

Finkelstein, S. (2016). *Superbosses: How exceptional leaders master the flow of talent*. London: Penguin.

Flauto, F. (1999). "Walking the talk: The relationship between leadership and communication competence." *The Journal of Leadership Studies*, 6, 86–97.

Fleming, P. (2014). *Resisting Work: The corporatization of life and its discontents*. Philadelphia: Temple University Press.

Fleming, P. (2017). "The human capital hoax: Work, debt and insecurity in the age of Uberization." *Organization Studies*, 38, 691–709.

Fleming, P. and Spicer, A. (2007). *Contesting the Corporation: Struggle, power and resistance in organizations*. Cambridge: Cambridge University Press.

Ford, J. and Harding, N. (2011). "The impossibility of the 'true self' of authentic leadership." *Leadership*, 7, 463–79.

Friedrich, T., Griffith, J., and Mumford, M. (2016). "Collective leadership behaviours: Evaluating the leader, team network, and problem situation characteristics that influence their use." *Leadership Quarterly*, 27, 312–33.

Fry, L. (2003). "Toward a theory of spiritual leadership." *Leadership Quarterly*, 14, 693–727.

Fry, L. and Cohen, M. (2009). "Spiritual leadership as a paradigm for organizational transformation and recovery from extended work hours cultures." *Journal of Business Ethics*, 84, Supplement 2, 265–78.

Fry, L., Latham, J., Clinebell, S., and Krahnke, K. (2017). "Spiritual leadership as a model for performance excellence: A study of Baldridge award recipients." *Journal of Management, Spirituality & Religion*, 14, 22–47.

Fry, L. and Slocum, J. (2007). "Maximising the triple bottom line through spiritual leadership." *Organizational Dynamics*, 37, 86–96.

Furnham, A. (2010). *The Elephant in the Boardroom: The causes of leadership derailment*. London: Palgrave MacMillan.

Gallup (2013). *State of the Global Workplace*. Washington, DC: Gallup.

Gardner, W. L., Fischer, D., and Hunt, J. G. J. (2009). " Emotional labor and leadership: A threat to authenticity?" *Leadership Quarterly*, 20, 466–82.

Gee, H. (2013). *The Accidental Species: Misunderstandings of human evolution*. Chicago: University of Chicago Press.

Goffee, R. and Jones, G. (2006). *Why Should Anyone Be Led By You? What it takes to be an authentic leader*. Boston, MA: Harvard Business School Press.

Gong, Y., Huang, J., and Farh, J. (2009). "Employee learning orientation, transformational leadership, and employee creativity: The mediating role of employee creative self-efficacy." *Academy of Management Journal*, 52, 765–78.

Graen, G. (1976). "Role-making Processes Within Complex Organizations." In M. Dunnette (ed.), *Handbook of Industrial and Organizational Psychology*, pp. 1201–45. Chicago, IL: Rand McNally.

Grey, C. (2017). *A Very Short, Fairly Interesting and Reasonably Cheap Book About Studying Organizations*, 4th edn. London: Sage.

Harari, Y. (2011). *Sapiens: A brief history of humankind*. London: Vintage Books.

Kaiser, R., LeBreton, J., and Hogan, J. (2015). "The dark side of personality and extreme leader behavior." *Applied Psychology: An International Review*, 64, 55–92.

Kark, R., Shamir, B., and Chen, G. (2003). "The two faces of transformational leadership: Empowerment and dependency." *Journal of Applied Psychology*, 88, 246–55.

Kellerman, B. (2004). *Bad Leadership*. Boston, MA: Harvard Business School Press.

Keltner, D. (2016). *The Power Paradox: How we gain and lose influence*. London: Allen Lane.

Kets de Vries, M. and Miller, D. (1985). "Narcissism and leadership: An object relations perspective." *Human Relations*, 38, 583–601.

Khurana, R. (2002). *Searching for a Corporate Savior: The irrational quest for charismatic CEOs*. Princeton, NJ: Princeton University Press.

Krasikova, D., Green, S., and LeBreton, J. (2013). "Destructive leadership: A theoretical review, integration, and future research agenda." *Journal of Management*, 39, 1308–38.

Kunda, G. (1992). *Engineering Culture: Control and commitment in a high-tech corporation*. Philadelphia: Temple University Press.

Kurtessis, J., Eisenberger, R., Ford, M., Buffardi, L., Steward, K., and Adis, C. (2017). "Perceived organizational support: A meta-analytic evaluation of organizational support theory." *Journal of Management Inquiry*, 43(6), 1854–84.

Lips-Wiersma, M. and Morris, L. (2009). "Discriminating between 'meaningful work' and the 'management of meaning.'" *Journal of Business Ethics*, 88, 491–511.

Luthans, F. and Avolio, B. (2003). "Authentic Leadership: A Positive Developmental Approach." In K. Cameron, J. Dutton, and R. Quinn (eds.), *Positive Organizational Scholarship*, pp. 241–61. San Francisco: Barrett-Koehler.

Mabey, C., Conroy, M., Blakeley, K., and de Marco, S. (2017). "Having burned the straw man of Christian spiritual leadership, what can we learn from Jesus about leading ethically?" *Journal of Business Ethics*, 145(4), 757–69.

Maghroori, R. and Rolland, E. (1997). "Strategic leadership: The art of balancing organizational mission with policy, procedures, and external environment." *Journal of Leadership Studies*, 2, 62–81.

March, J. (2010). *The Ambiguities of Experience*. Ithaca, NY: Cornell University Press.

McKnight, R. (1984). "Spirituality in the Workplace." In J. Adams (ed.), *Transforming work: A collection of organizational transformation readings*, pp. 138–53. Alexandria, VA: Miles River.

Meindl, J., Ehrlich, S., and Dukerich, J. (1985). "The romance of leadership." *Administrative Science Quarterly*, 30, 78–102.

Mirvis, P. H. (1997). "'Soul work' in organizations." *Organization Science*, 8(2), 193–206.

Newark, D. (2018). "Leadership and the logic of absurdity." *Academy of Management Review*, 43(2), 198–216.

Paulsen, R. (2014). *Empty Labor: Idleness and workplace resistance*. Cambridge: Cambridge University Press.

Pelletier, K. (2010). "Leader toxicity: An empirical investigation of toxic behaviour and rhetoric." *Leadership*, 6, 373–89.

Peters, T. and Waterman, R. (1982). *In Search of Excellence*. London: MacMillan.

Petriglieri, G., and Petriglieri, J. (2015). "Can business schools humanize leadership?" *Academy of Management Learning & Education*, 14, 625–47.

Podolny, J., Khurana, R., and Besharov, M. (2010). "Revising the Meaning of Leadership." In N. Nohria and R. Khurana (eds.), *Handbook of Leadership Theory and Practice*, pp. 65–105. Booton, MA: Harvard Business School Press

Podsakoff, P., MacKenzie, S., Moorman, R., and Fetter, R. (1990). "Transformational leader behaviors and their effects on followers' trust in leader, satisfaction, and organizational citizenship behaviors." *Leadership Quarterly*, 1, 107–42.

Porter, M. and Nohria, N. (2010). "What is Leadership? The CEO's Role in Large, Complex Organizations." In N. Nohria and R. Khurana (eds.), *Handbook of Leadership Theory and Practice*, pp. 433–73. Boston, MA: Harvard Business School Press.

Proust, M. (1992). *In Search of Lost Time*, Vol. 2, *Within A Budding Grove*, translated by C. Moncreiff and T. Kilmartin. London: Chatto and Windus.

Rafferty, A. and Griffin, M. (2004). "Dimensions of transformational leadership: Conceptual and empirical extensions." *Leadership Quarterly*, 15, 329–54.

Rosso, B., Dekas, K., and Wrzesniewski, A. (2010). "On the meaning of work: A theoretical integration and review." *Research in Organizational Behavior*, 30, 91–127.

Sashkin, M. (2004). "Transformational Leadership Approaches: A Review and Synthesis." In J. Antonakis, A. Cianciolo, and R. Sternberg (eds.), *The Nature of Leadership*, pp. 179–96. London: Sage.

Schilling, J. (2009). "From ineffectiveness to destruction: A qualitative study on the meaning of negative leadership." *Leadership*, 5, 102–28.

Schmid, E., Verdorfer, A., and Peus, C. (2017). "Shedding light on leaders' self-interest: Theory and measurement of exploitative leadership." *Journal of Management*, [advance online publication] doi: 10.1177/0149206317707810.

Semler, R. (1993). *Maverick*. New York: Random House.

Shamir, B., Zakay, E., Breinin, E., and Popper, M. (1998). "Correlates of charismatic leader-behavior in military units: Subordinates' attitudes, unit characteristics, and superiors' appraisals of leader performance." *Academy of Management Journal*, 41, 387–409.

Singhal, M. and Chatterjee, L. (2006). "A person–organization fit-based approach for spirituality at work: Development of a conceptual framework." *Journal of Human Values*, 12, 161–78.

Stohl, C. and Cheney, G. (2001). "Participatory processes/paradoxical practices." *Management Communication Quarterly*, 14, 349–407.

Tourish, D. (2013). *The Dark Side of Transformational Leadership*. London: Routledge.

Tourish, D. (2014). "Leadership, more or less? A processual, communication perspective on the role of agency in leadership theory." *Leadership*, 10, 79–98.

Tourish, D. and Robson, P. (2006). "Sensemaking and the distortion of critical upward communication in organizations." *Journal of Management Studies*, 43, 711–30.

Tourish, D. and Tourish, N. (2010). "Spirituality at work, and its implications for leadership and followership: A post-structuralist perspective." *Leadership*, 5, 207–24.

Uhl-Bien, M. and Ospina, S. (eds.) (2012). *Advancing Relational Leadership Research: A dialogue among perspectives*. Charlotte, NC: Information Age Publishing.

Van Knippenberg, D. and Sitkin, S. (2013). "A critical assessment of charismatic-transformational leadership research: Back to the drawing board?" *Academy of Management Annals*, 7, 1–60.

Wagner-Marsh, F. and Conley, J. (1999). "The fourth wave: The spiritually based firm." *Journal of Organizational Change Management*, 12, 292–301.

Weber, M. (1948). "The Sociology of Charismatic Authority." In H. G. Gerth and C. W. Mills (eds.), *From Max Weber: Essays in sociology*, pp. 245–52. London: Routledge.

Willmott, H. (1993). "Strength is ignorance; slavery is freedom: Managing culture in modern organizations." *Journal of Management Studies*, 30, 515–52.

Willmott, H. (2013). "'The substitution of one piece of nonsense for another': Reflections on resistance, gaming, and subjugation." *Journal of Management Studies*, 50, 443–73.

Wong, P. (1998). "Implicit Theories of Meaningful Life and the Development of the Personal Meaning Profile (PMP)." In P. Wong and P. Fry (eds.), *Handbook of Personal Meaning: Theory, research and practice*, pp. 111–40. Mahwah, NJ: Lawrence Erlbaum.

PART IV

....

CONTEXTS AND BOUNDARIES OF MEANINGFUL WORK

CHAPTER 20

FOSTERING THE HUMAN SPIRIT

A Positive Ethical Framework for Experiencing Meaningfulness at Work

DOUGLAS R. MAY, JIATIAN (JT) CHEN,
CATHERINE E. SCHWOERER,
AND MATTHEW D. DEEG

THIS chapter brings together the literatures of behavioral ethics, positive organizational scholarship, and meaningful work to develop a positive ethical framework for understanding how virtuous actions may foster employee meaningfulness and, ultimately, an organizational culture that supports and enhances the likelihood of positive ethical behaviors at work. Scholars in positive psychology, positive organizational scholarship, and ethics have called for such a positive approach to ethics (Moore, 2017; Handelsman, Knapp, and Gottlieb, 2009; Sekerka, Comer, and Godwin, 2014; Stansbury and Sonenshein, 2012). Positive ethics focuses research and practice on morally praiseworthy behaviors rather than ethical misconduct and sanctions.

Our framework contributes to the interdisciplinary scholarship on meaningful work found in normative philosophy (Bowie, 1998; Beadle and Knight, 2012; Moore and Beadle, 2006), political theory (Yeoman, 2014), qualitative sociological perspectives (Bailey and Madden, 2015), psychological and motivational approaches (Chalofsky and Krishna, 2009; May, Gilson, and Harter, 2004; May et al., 2014; Pratt and Ashforth, 2003), and the exploration of a holistic quantitative methods approach for measurement (Lips-Wiersma and Wright, 2012). The model advances the paradigm of "positive organizational ethics" (Sekerka, Comer, and Godwin, 2014) in answer to a call from Michaelson et al., (2014), and extends recent research on ethical decision-making in the context of meaningful work (May et al., 2014) with its focus on the positive ethical determinants and outcomes surrounding meaningful work.

We discuss how the influence of virtues and character strengths (as defined by Peterson and Seligman, 2004) on work-related behaviors, perceptions of career callings,

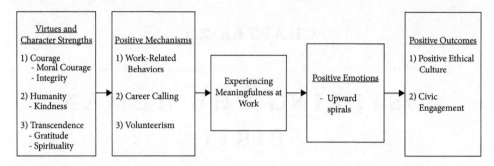

FIGURE 20.1 A positive ethical framework for experiencing meaningfulness at work

and volunteerism contribute to experienced meaningfulness, positive ethics organizational cultures, and civic engagement. We argue that these outcomes are facilitated by the positive emotions experienced by employees during meaningful events at work. See Figure 20.1 for an overview of this positive ethical framework for experiencing meaningfulness at work. This theoretical framework is offered as initial guidance for future empirical research in this area (Whetten, 1989).

EXPERIENCING MEANINGFULNESS AND IDENTITY

Scholarly attention to meaningful work has accelerated in recent years with the positive psychology and positive organizational scholarship movements. These focus on optimal psychological states and fostering flourishing and engagement of the human spirit at work (May, Gilson, and Harter, 2004). The human spirit refers to "that part of the human being which seeks fulfillment through self-expression at work" (p. 12). Work in this area has recognized that meaningfulness in life is a fundamental human need (Baumeister and Vohs, 2002; Frankl, 1959; King and Napa, 1998; Yeoman, 2014) in both non-work and work domains. Formal recognition of the psychological state of experienced meaningfulness in the work domain dates to the origins of the job characteristics research by Hackman and Oldham (Oldham and Fried, 2016). Experienced meaningfulness is defined here as the *valuing of a work activity judged in relation to an individual's own ideals or standards* (May, Gilson, and Harter, 2004). Meta-analyses of work on job design demonstrate the importance of meaningfulness as a mediating psychological state for a variety of positive work outcomes (Humphrey, Nahrgang, and Morgeson, 2007). Indeed, research has found meaningfulness to be the most significant psychological state associated with the cognitive, emotional, and physical means by which we are engaged at work (May, Gilson, and Harter, 2004).

To develop the positive organizational ethics framework, we contemplated how character strengths may influence employees' experienced meaningfulness in the workplace.

We first considered the primary sources of the construct suggested by extant research. Rosso, Dekas, and Wrzesniewski (2010) maintain that the *self-concept or identity* is a fundamental source of meaning (Shamir, 1991). An individual's values, motivations, and beliefs are all elements of one's identity. One's character strengths are illustrative of key elements of one's identity, including deeply held moral values. Morality is central to the self (Blasi, 1999). To the extent that the moral self is easily accessible to an individual, it can be expected to influence behaviors (Shao, Aquino, and Freeman, 2008). Shamir (1991) argues that actions will be perceived as meaningful if they are tied to the self-concept. Indeed, past research has shown that a good fit between one's work role and one's identity results in meaningfulness (May, Gilson, and Harter, 2004). Thus, it is likely that character strengths will lead to meaningful actions for individuals to the extent that they provide a means to display underlying moral values incorporated in the self.

This research contributes to past work in the area of the self and meaningful behaviors. We explore how positive emotions are linked to the meaningfulness associated with individuals' character strengths, as called for by Rosso, Dekas, and Wrzesniewski (2010). Finally, we explore relations between character strengths and work orientations such as calling and volunteerism. These two orientations were explored because of their positive orientation toward employee and societal well-being, their potential relevance to meaningfulness based on recent research (e.g. Hirschi, 2012; Rodell, 2013), and because Rosso, Dekas, and Wrzesniewski (2010) noted in their review that *other persons* (e.g. co-workers, leaders, groups, communities, and families), the *work context* (e.g. the design of job tasks, organizational mission, financial circumstances, non-work domains, national culture), and *spiritual life* (spirituality, sacred callings) are related to meaningfulness. Calling and volunteerism can both help individuals express deeply held values close to their identities and experience meaningfulness. Character strengths may also foster work-related behaviors that influence each of these sources. We explore these connections below as we develop our discussion of character strengths, callings, volunteerism, and experienced meaningfulness.

POSITIVE ORGANIZATIONAL SCHOLARSHIP, VIRTUES, AND CHARACTER STRENGTHS

Recent reviews of the literature on positive psychology and positive organizational scholarship have noted the relevance of both strengths and positive emotions for organizations (Green, Evans, and Williams, 2017). For example, Peterson et al.'s (2010) research suggests that the character strengths of gratitude and spirituality have been linked to job satisfaction in a number of occupations. Furthermore, virtuousness (i.e. integrity) at an organizational level has been linked to improved organization profit margins (Cameron, Bright, and Caza, 2004). Although research on character strengths is directly relevant to organizations, authors have noted a lack of studies in this area

(Kong and Ho, 2016). Our research attempts to fill this important void with a conceptual framework that can guide future work.

In the field of positive psychology, Peterson and Seligman (2004) focus on six broad categories of virtues valued by moral philosophers: wisdom, courage, humanity, justice, temperance, and transcendence. They argue that these are universal in nature across cultures. From these, Peterson and Seligman chose character strengths that fit ten criteria. Two of the criteria were the strength's contribution to fulfillment in a good life and whether it was morally valued in its own right. For illustrative purposes, we have chosen to focus on the three virtues of courage, humanity, and transcendence. These general virtue categories encompass the character strengths that we examine in our framework: *courage* (e.g. moral courage, integrity/honesty), *humanity* (e.g. kindness, caring), and *transcendence* (e.g. gratitude, spirituality).

Research on issues of character strengths and virtues in the management literature is limited, but growing (Wright and Goodstein, 2007). Bright, Winn, and Kanov (2014) outlined how the positive social science perspective on virtues and character strengths adopted here assumes an empirical lens that emphasizes virtuous behaviors, rather than a normative character lens that philosophers take to examine virtue ethics (e.g. see Beadle and Knight, 2012; Moore and Beadle, 2006). In Weaver's (2006) view, virtues, moral agency, and moral identity play key roles in organizational ethics; this perspective places the focus on the *self-concept* of the individual and its interaction with organizational factors as a driver of ethical actions. We contribute to this literature by examining the role that character strengths play in determining work activities, perceptions of career calling, and volunteering activities, and that they subsequently lead to meaningful experiences and positive outcomes for the individual and organization. Identity plays a central role in these linkages since character strengths are closely tied to one's moral identity, and meaningfulness is derived from the evaluation of work activities relative to values tied to one's identity. In the following sections, we outline key definitions of the virtues and character strengths explored here, and then discuss extant research on their linkages to work-related behaviors and attitudes, career callings, and volunteerism.

Courage

According to Peterson and Seligman (2004: 29), *courage* includes "the emotional strengths that involve the exercise of will to accomplish goals in the face of opposition, external or internal." Courage in the workplace has received a great deal of recent attention from researchers in the organizational sciences (see Detert and Bruno, 2017 for a review); these authors offer a similar definition: "a work domain-relevant act done for a worthy cause despite significant risks perceivable in the moment to the actor" (p. 100). We will use the term "moral courage" here when such actions involve the individual's moral intentions, principles, or greater good (May, Luth, and Schwoerer, 2014; Sekerka, Bagozzi, and Charnigo, 2009).

Integrity is defined as "speaking the truth, but more broadly presenting oneself in a genuine way and acting in a sincere way; being without pretense; taking responsibility for one's feelings and actions" (Peterson and Seligman, 2004: 29). Thus, individuals with integrity tend to believe and act in accordance with their self-identities.

Humanity

Humanity encompasses "interpersonal strengths that involve tending and befriending others" and the character strength of *kindness* entails "doing favors and good deeds for others; helping them; taking care of them" (Peterson and Seligman, 2004: 29). Thus, all actions of kindness reflect a shift from the individual to others and a shared humanity. Kindness includes such characteristics as generosity, nurturance, care, and compassion. Care and compassion have received significant attention in the organizational sciences in recent years (Dutton, Workman, and Hardin, 2014; Rynes et al., 2012). Generosity has received less attention.

Transcendence

Peterson and Seligman (2004: 30) defined the virtue of transcendence as involving character strengths that "forge connections to the larger universe and provide meaning." Consistent with Frankl (1959), such a broader sense of self-transcendence entails forgetting oneself by giving oneself to a cause, to another human being, or something larger than oneself. Thus, character strengths here include *gratitude*—"being aware of and thankful for the good things that happen; taking time to express thanks"—and *spirituality* (religiousness, faith, purpose)—"having coherent beliefs about the higher purpose and meaning of the universe; knowing where one fits within the larger scheme; having beliefs about the meaning of life that shape conduct and provide comfort" (Peterson and Seligman, 2004: 30). Since spirituality in some form is a part of many people's lives and linked to meaning in life overall, we have included it here.

CHARACTER STRENGTHS, WORK BEHAVIORS, AND MEANINGFULNESS

While relatively little research has investigated links between character strengths and work behaviors and their contributions to meaningfulness experienced by employees, research in positive psychology argues that individuals who regularly use the handful of "signature" strengths most characteristic of their identities may experience more *fulfillment* or *meaning* (Peterson and Seligman, 2004). As noted earlier, the strengths were selected, in part, for this potential and for their moral worth. Most character strengths and signature strengths have been shown to be associated with perceptions of meaning in life, particularly in the US (Peterson et al., 2007; Peterson and Park, 2012).

Of the strengths discussed in the current framework, bravery, kindness, gratitude, and religiousness tended to be associated most strongly with meaning in life in this empirical research. Thus, we expect these virtuous strengths to be associated with experienced meaningfulness in the workplace. Preliminary evidence linking the endorsement of strengths and work meaningfulness by adult volunteers and paid workers has been gathered by Littman-Ovadia and Steger (2010). Harzer and Ruch (2012) similarly found that signature strengths were related to job meaning and callings.

Little research has linked *morally courageous* acts with meaningfulness. Woodard (2004) argues that meaningfulness is a part of the courageous action itself. Given the potential sacrifice to one's self or career represented by such principled acts (Detert and Bruno, 2017), we would expect them to be deeply meaningful. Second, *integrity* in one's actions and words has been associated with being seen as trustworthy (Whitener et al., 1998), and leaders' behavioral integrity was linked to employees' job satisfaction, affect toward the organization, and intentions to engage in organizational citizenship behaviors (Simons, Tomlinson, and Leroy, 2011). Thus, *authentic* and *honest* actions consistent with the "true" self-identity are likely to lead to enhanced meaningfulness at work (Markus, 1977; Shamir, 1991).

Next, the broad virtue of humanity encompasses the character strength of *kindness*, which involves helping, caring, and doing good deeds for others (Peterson and Seligman, 2004). Social relations and meeting the basic need of belongingness have been shown to be central to a meaningful life (e.g. Baumeister and Leary, 1995). Caring for others and making the world better for others are powerful social motivators and means of fulfillment (Grant and Berg, 2012). Thus, to the extent that opportunities for helping and caring for others exist in work activities, individuals should value such social relations and experience more meaningfulness at work.

Finally, the character strengths of gratitude and spirituality are both related to how individuals look beyond themselves to make broader connections. Specifically, research on *gratitude* suggests that the process of becoming aware of, and thankful for, positive things received from others enhances individuals' subjective well-being and social relationships (Emmons, 2003; Mills, Fleck, and Kozikowski, 2013). Such thankful acts are likely to deepen the fulfillment and meaning obtained from relationships. Individuals with high levels of *spirituality* often reflect transcendence and supererogation, a recognition of themselves in the "bigger picture," and subsequent actions that provide meaning as individuals act in accordance with their beliefs.

CHARACTER STRENGTHS, CAREER CALLINGS, AND MEANINGFULNESS

The term *calling* is deeply rooted in Western culture and religious traditions. Once narrowly defined and literally understood as being summoned by a deity to choose and pursue a particular line of work, callings have been widely accepted to have secular meaning as occupational pursuits for individuals who seek work that is not only necessary but intrinsically worthwhile (Bellah et al., 1985). A secular sense of calling refers to an intense beckoning or being drawn to pursue work that is socially significant and personally meaningful (Bunderson and Thompson, 2009; Dik, Duffy, and Eldridge, 2009; Dobrow and Tosti-Kharas, 2011; Wrzesniewski, 2003; Wrzesniewski, Dekas, and Rosso, 2012). Research on callings has identified their conceptual and empirical relationship with work meaningfulness.

Character Strengths and Callings

One key question in the positive organizational scholarship literature is: "What predicts callings?" Research has suggested that the virtues of *courage, humanity*, and *transcendence* are closely related to callings. First, consistent with character strengths categorized under *courage*, authors argue that callings embody a burning sense of *passion* or *vitality* (Dobrow and Tosti-Kharas, 2011); Peterson et al. (2009) found that dispositional *zest* was a contributor to callings. In terms of the character strength of *integrity, honesty* has also been found to be associated with callings (Smith, 2010). This makes sense theoretically because to identify or recognize callings individuals need to be true to their identities, particularly with respect to their career passions at work. Second, research has also revealed that the virtue of *humanity*, especially *capacity to love and to be loved*, predicted callings (Smith, 2010).

Finally, the character strengths represented by the virtue of *transcendence* have demonstrated the closest relations with callings. For example, in a study focusing on hospital nurses and child protective service workers, Gorjian (2006) revealed that the character strengths of *hope, humor, gratitude*, and *spirituality* all positively predicted callings. Similarly, Smith (2010) found that among all twenty-four strengths, dispositional *hope* was the best predictor of callings.

Other researchers have examined the use of "signature" strengths at work. Consistent with Peterson and Seligman (2004), Harzer and Ruch (2012) found that individuals who were able to employ more than four of their character strengths at work have stronger callings compared to those who could apply fewer than four. Recently, employing a quasi-experimental design, Harzer and Ruch (2016) found that individuals instructed to use their highest four character strengths for four weeks increased their level of callings. Others who did not receive the intervention instructions saw no increase. Overall, findings from studies provide initial evidence that character strengths can be particularly instrumental as influences on career callings.

Callings and Meaningfulness

While callings and work meaningfulness are related concepts, researchers such as Hirschi (2012) have argued that they are distinct because one may experience meaningfulness at work without claiming a calling to the work role. However, some researchers incorporate meaningfulness within the definition of the construct of calling. Dobrow and Tosti-Kharas (2011: 1005) defined calling as "a consuming, meaningful passion people experience toward a domain." These authors explained that by "meaningful" they meant having personal or social significance, implying that one will experience meaningfulness through the pursuit of one's calling. Dik and Duffy's (2009) definition more explicitly outlined this causal relationship. They defined calling as "a transcendent summons ... to approach a particular life role in a manner oriented toward demonstrating or deriving a sense of purpose or meaningfulness" (p. 427). In their view, the life role one is propelled to take will inevitably generate the experience of meaningfulness. Taken as a whole, the different approaches to callings all seem to suggest that calling is an antecedent to evaluating actual work activities as significant or meaningful.

The theoretical connection of calling and work meaningfulness has been empirically supported. Bunderson and Thompson (2009) examined callings in a sample of 982 US zookeepers. Those who endorsed stronger callings considered their jobs to be more meaningful. A study by Duffy et al. (2012), with a sample of 201 working adults in a variety of occupations, found that both *perceiving* and *living* one's calling significantly predicted work meaningfulness, a distinction not made by past researchers. Thus, the actual fulfillment of one's calling is necessary for individuals to judge the value of such activities relative to their core values and to experience meaningfulness at work.

Character Strengths, Volunteering, and Meaningfulness

In their review, Rosso, Dekas, and Wrzesniewski (2010) called for research that investigates how others *outside* of the workplace influence individuals' experienced meaningfulness in work. Here we respond by exploring how volunteering may create an opportunity for individuals to act on their character strengths and find meaning through interactions with others outside of work. Consistent with Rodell (2013: 1274), volunteering is defined as "giving time or skills during a planned activity for a volunteer group or organization (e.g., charitable groups, non-profit groups)." Through the volunteering experience, individuals are likely to develop new skills, gain a sense of belongingness, and experience prosocial impact, all of which should positively impact their felt meaningfulness as individuals' self-identities value these needs (Deeg and May, 2017).

Character Strengths and Volunteering

Omoto, Snyder, and Hackett (2010) argue that individual differences can affect volunteers' motivations and decisions. Based on the discussion earlier, it is likely a number of the character strengths under the three virtues of *courage*, *humanity*, and *transcendence* noted by Peterson and Seligman (2004) will influence an individual's volunteering intentions and choices. We focus on three character strengths here that the literature suggests may be related to these.

First, falling under the virtue of *courage*, *integrity* is composed of *authenticity* and *honesty* (Peterson and Seligman, 2004). As suggested earlier, individuals with high levels of integrity and authenticity seek congruence between their beliefs and actions (Shamir, 1991). Thus, individuals with high levels of integrity *and* kindness or spirituality may have an enhanced motivation to act on their identity-related strengths and volunteer in the community.

Second, falling under the virtue of *humanity*, *kindness* is composed of a range of variants—"generosity, nurturance, care, compassion, and altruistic love" (Peterson and Seligman, 2004: 326). Individuals with this strength feel a connection to others because of shared humanity and appreciation for others. We maintain that individuals who act on these aspects of kindness will naturally be disposed to help and serve others—core components of volunteering (Rodell, 2013). The focus of volunteering will likely differ between individuals, given the aspect of kindness most frequently accessed. For example, individuals with high *compassion* (a focus on people who are suffering or in need) may be more likely to volunteer in a caregiving capacity (e.g. hospice work, women's shelters, etc.). For other, more generalized, aspects of kindness, individuals will rely on personal interests to find ways to give to others.

Third, falling under the virtue of *transcendence*, individuals with high levels of *spirituality* are driven by faith and purpose (Peterson and Seligman, 2004). In their daily lives, they are guided and motivated to act by principles of their faith. Indeed, most faith traditions inspire some form of giving to or serving of others (Fischer and Schaffer, 1993); thus spirituality is likely to prompt volunteering. Furthermore, spirituality (religion-based or otherwise) (Liu and Robertson, 2011) elicits feelings of transcendence in individuals, causing them to look beyond themselves and see their connection with the larger universe.

Volunteering and Meaningfulness

Volunteering has generally been assumed to be meaningful. Rodell (2013) noted that individual perceptions of volunteering as a meaningful activity drive volunteering behaviors. Further, qualitative work has highlighted the meaningfulness volunteers experience as a result of engaging in volunteer activities (Geroy, Wright, and Jacoby, 2000). Nevertheless, the theoretical underpinnings of meaningfulness in volunteering are underexplored. As noted above, meaningfulness derives from the valuing of a work activity in relation to one's own values. Grant's (2012) conceptualization of volunteering characteristics is helpful in making connections between volunteering activities and how they lead to meaningfulness. He notes three aspects of volunteering that may contribute to meaningfulness: enriched roles (task characteristics), enhanced interpersonal relationships (social characteristics), and the development and utilization of knowledge and skills (knowledge characteristics).

First, volunteers experience enriched roles because they are often able to see the outcomes of their work or are informed of the effect of their work on beneficiaries. Further, volunteers have the ability to create enriched roles for themselves through their own job crafting; they can find the best opportunities for self-expression and utilization of their skills outside of work (Berg, Dutton, and Wrzesniewski, 2013; Oldham and Hackman, 2010). Second, volunteering is rarely a solo activity (Prouteau and Wolff, 2008) and humans value social relations (Rosso, Dekas, and Wrzesniewski, 2010); volunteers typically interact with fellow volunteers or with beneficiaries. Finally, volunteering allows individuals to use or develop their skills. Using held skills connects an individual's sense of self with the surrounding world, enhancing the experience of meaning (Heine, Proulx, and Vohs, 2006). The development of skills enhances an individual's potential (Pratt and Ashforth, 2003). Thus, volunteering should enhance meaningfulness through the valuing of enriched roles, relationships, and utilization and development of knowledge and skills.

Experiencing Meaningfulness and Positive Emotions

In earlier sections, we have discussed virtues and character strengths as contributors to the mechanisms and actions inherent in work-related behaviors, career calling, and volunteerism, which are predictors of experiencing meaningfulness at work. Figure 20.1 proposes that experiencing meaningfulness results in the experience of positive emotions. Here we review research that supports this link.

The role of emotions at work and in work organizations has received significantly increased attention since Weiss and Cropanzano (1996) proposed their affective events theory (AET). They intended AET to be a framework to encourage the investigation of emotions at work that arise from employees' experiences, and that moods and emotions be more directly considered, and viewed as processes, in the organization sciences. Research has been consistent with a view of individual differences (such as, although not specifically, virtues and character strengths) as influences on behaviors and outcomes. Reactions to events or experiences, such as those that lead to experienced meaningfulness, were also proposed as key to emotional processes in work organizations (Weiss and Beal, 2005).

Research has examined dispositional and situational antecedents of emotional experiences and consequences (Donaldson, Dollwet, and Rao, 2015). Exploring the range and intensity of human emotion, along with beginning to investigate the distinctions and interdependence between cognition and emotion, has resulted in a more dynamic view of emotions at work, one that is consistent with Figure 20.1. Indeed, Barsade and Gibson (2007: 36) have characterized affect as "permeating" organizations.

The beginnings of positive psychology (Seligman and Csikszentmihalyi, 2000) also stimulated attention to emotions and their role in the workplace. Frederickson's "broaden-and-build" theory of positive emotions (Fredrickson, 2001) was proposed initially to distinguish the unique benefits of positive emotions compared to negative emotions. It has become axiomatic in positive psychology for investigating the function and benefit of positive affect or emotions and its relevance to emotional experiences in organizations is clear (Conway et al., 2013). The developing field of positive psychology has emphasized the role and benefit of positive emotions, and the ratio of positive to negative evaluative judgments, as predictors of flourishing, or the building of positive mental health (Fredrickson and Losada, 2005). Positive mental health assumes frequent experience of positive emotions.

Positive emotions broaden one's attention and awareness. They can arise from seemingly inconsequential or more substantial experiences at work. Work activities or events that are valued by individuals are likely to trigger positive emotional reactions, particularly because they are central to the individual's identity. Enhanced attention resulting from positive emotions can include cognitive adaptability and more accepting, social views of others. Positive emotions also, over time, build durable personal resources. These key tenets of the framework have been supported by a growing body of data (Vacharkulksemsuk and Fredrickson, 2013). The durable resources that develop due to experiences of positive emotion, such as those frequently associated with experiences of meaning, are relevant at multiple levels of analysis.

Ashkanasy and Dorris (2017) conceptualize emotions in the workplace as best understood by employing a multilevel framework in theorizing and conducting empirical research. They specify a five-level model of emotions in organizations, ranging from within-person to organization-wide. This perspective is consistent with the view that positive emotion is a necessary precondition for positive organizational behavior (Ashkanasy and Ashton-James, 2007) and that its benefits include upward spirals that can be both individual and collective in nature, ultimately leading to positive organizational outcomes.

Organizational theory and research have supported the benefits of experiencing positive affect at work and begun to explore the nuances of optimal levels of such experiences (Lam, Spreitzer, and Fritz, 2014). Theory and research have also begun to investigate the ways in which affect or emotional experience spreads beyond individuals to others (Barsade, 2002) and the need to conceptualize and investigate affective phenomena at multiple levels in order to detect cross-level effects (Ashkanasy and Dorris, 2017) such as upward spirals.

Up to this point, we have discussed Figure 20.1 as a framework that depicts the process of key virtues and character strengths influencing work behaviors, career callings, and volunteerism. These in turn influence the experience of meaningfulness in human pursuits, at work and outside of work. Meaningfulness as an experience, by its nature as a positive evaluation of the worthwhile nature of work activities, is generative of positive emotions. And these positive emotions are in turn proposed, through upward spirals, to affect individuals, ethical organizational cultures, and increase civic engagement.

Ashkanasy, Humphrey, and Huy (2017) affirmed the rich accumulation of knowledge of emotions and affect in organizations over the past twenty years and the need to integrate emotions and affect in cross-level theories of management. A recent example of such an approach is Parke and Seo's (2017) theory of affect climate. This posits that affect climates, created by sources such as company practices, leadership, and the meaningful activities we discuss here, in turn create environments that promote different types of affective experiences and uses of affect. These then contribute to organization outcomes. One example of the prototypes discussed, an affect climate characterized by high authenticity and encouragement of positive affect, would seem to fit well with helping to establish a positive ethical culture; it would offer the benefit of support for employees' moral courage and commitment to ethical decision-making.

Positive Ethical Culture and Civic Engagement Outcomes

In this section we explore how positive emotions from meaningful experiences at work and volunteer activities, and associated upward spirals, may lead to the development of positive ethical cultures in organizations and broader civic engagement.

Positive Ethical Culture

As part of our positive ethical framework, we are interested in how positive emotions may help to create positive ethical cultures. These are defined as cultures in which employees flourish, team members work synergistically together, leaders act with integrity and inspire employees, and organizational goals are achieved. Consistent with other authors (Verbos et al., 2007), we argue for an organization in which positive actions occur regularly and a positive ethical identity emerges for the organization as a whole. For such an organization, our hope is that individuals are attracted to, retained by, and identify with such positive ethical organizations (May, Chang, and Shao, 2015).

Building on discussions above, we envision a positive ethical culture in which the use of character strengths creates a virtuous upward spiral of positive actions fueled by fulfilling meaningfulness and positive emotions. This perspective is based, in part, on Staw, Sutton, and Pellod (1994), who found that employees with positive emotions experienced greater support from both their supervisors and co-workers (i.e. a supportive social climate overall). Other benefits associated with positive emotions included more favorable evaluations and greater pay. This finding suggests that positive emotions and actions are rewarded directly or indirectly in the workplace. The character strengths that foster the meaningfulness and positive emotions thus should be reinforced and subsequent use of one's strengths should build further employee well-being outcomes. Green, Evans, and Williams (2017) reviewed research that also suggests that positive emotions are related to helpfulness to customers and respectful behaviors. Thus, positive emotions facilitate positive social relationships both inside and outside of the organization.

Positive emotions derived from the character strength of compassion have also been linked with subsequent affective organizational commitment (Lilius et al., 2008). Indeed, narrative analysis illustrated that "employees who receive, witness, participate in the delivery of compassion reshape understandings of their co-workers, themselves, and their organizations" (p. 193). Thus, practicing character strengths can dramatically impact the organizational cultural values for caring and compassion and encourage others to act in a similarly positive way.

Positive ethical cultures should also foster a constructive ethical problem-solving approach in which individuals feel confident in their abilities to deal with ethical issues that arise, that is, they have a high degree of moral efficacy (May, Luth, and Schwoerer, 2014; Hannah, Avolio, and May, 2011). In such cultures, it is expected that from time to time employees will feel the need to act courageously to bring up ethical issues that are not being addressed. Thus, we expect such cultures to foster moral courage in employees (May, Luth, and Schwoerer, 2014; Sekerka, Bagozzi, and Charnigo, 2009).

At an organizational level, virtuousness (i.e. integrity) has been linked to profit (Cameron, Bright, and Caza, 2004). Researchers maintain that virtuousness can amplify such behaviors and serve as a buffering for poor organizational conditions (Caza, Barker, and Cameron, 2004). Here we are focused on how individual virtuous actions by individuals may help promote similar actions in others and sustain such actions over time. The mechanisms of vicarious learning from the social cognitive model of behavior (Bandura, 1986) help explain such organizational processes in a positive ethical culture. Leaders may also further encourage and reward individuals who practice their character strengths at work, but we fundamentally see this as a cultural system that is self-sustaining. Normative perspectives on virtues in organizations argue similarly for organizations with these characteristics (Moore, 2017; Moore and Beadle, 2006).

Finally, individual employees may help foster such a positive culture by actively investing in the process of job crafting (Berg, Dutton, and Wrzesniewski, 2013) to create conditions in which they can engage in virtuous actions consistent with their identities, and experience meaningfulness from their actions and subsequent associated positive emotions. For example, based on Berg, Dutton, and Wrzesniewski's (2013) research, workers may add, emphasize, or even redesign particular tasks that allow them to exercise their signature character strengths; they may build, reframe, or adapt particular relationships at work that facilitate opportunities for them to practice their strengths or otherwise experience deep meaningful relations and positive emotions at work; or, finally, employees may choose to cognitively broaden their perceptions of the impact or purpose of their positions, focus on particular aspects of their positions that create meaning, or make cognitive connections with particular aspects of their positions from which they gain meaning and fulfillment. Preliminary research using a jobs demands and resources perspective suggests that job crafting may positively influence person–job fit and meaningfulness at work (Tims, Derks, and Bakker, 2016). Next, we explore how the crafting of one's roles at work to include some form of volunteerism may lead to broader positive civic engagement.

Civic Engagement

As individuals experience meaningfulness through positive experiences, specifically volunteering, several mechanisms are activated that will foster further civic engagement. First, individuals may feel a sense of increased passion for their work (Perttula and Cardon, 2012) as they engage more of their core selves. Because of the choice inherent in volunteering, individuals will find themselves in roles and organizations about which they are passionate. If this passion is activated in a harmonious way (Vallerand, 2008), individuals experience positive outcomes both during and after volunteer activity. Ryan and Deci (2000) note that these positive experiences will foster further meaningfulness and motivation to engage in similar activities, because individuals see the value in the activity for themselves and the organization.

The felt positive outcomes of volunteering will also likely enhance an individual's feeling of self-efficacy, enhancing their self-concept and lowering barriers to engaging in similar activities (Gist, 1987). Thus, we believe that passion during and after a positive experience will foster deeper motivation to engage further in that experience or similar activities, increasing civic engagement as an extension of the volunteering experience.

Further, meaningful positive experiences gained through volunteering foster further civic engagement through an enhanced sense of community. First, volunteering connects individuals with other, like-minded, individuals who share a commitment to a cause. As their relationships form and deepen, individuals feel additional motivation to foster even closer relationships and to integrate qualities of others into their own self-concepts (Gable and Gosnell, 2011). Beyond the individual relationships, volunteering connects individuals to a higher *purpose* in the community. Because volunteering can have an impact on an entire community, individuals experience self-transcendence as they see themselves as a part of a greater whole. Thus, they recognize the contributions of their work and service and begin to notice other opportunities for service in the community.

Finally, volunteering may help individuals enhance or acquire new skills. Individuals may be drawn to the organizations or experiences that provided these skill development opportunities and become motivated to further engage in community volunteer opportunities.

FUTURE DIRECTIONS

This positive ethical framework for experienced meaningfulness suggests many fruitful future directions for encouraging positive behaviors in the workplace that ultimately lead to positive individual and organizational outcomes. We outline a few of these in this section.

Character Strengths

Character strengths provide the most promising psychological basis for enhancing positive ethical behaviors and employee well-being in organizations. Given that the character strengths are fulfilling and meaningful for individuals as well as morally praiseworthy, they provide a sound foundation for developing sustainable positive ethical cultures. Future research should continue to explore the general role of specific character strengths in the workplace as they relate to employee well-being, work meaningfulness, and ethical cultures. It should also examine the influence of employees' top signature strengths and how character strengths that may be in conflict with one another are balanced (Allan, 2015; Littman-Ovadia and Steger, 2010). Research should examine whether characteristics of the organizational context influence the use and outcomes of such character strengths. The characteristics of the job itself may determine whether or not individuals are able to use particular character strengths.

Because much of the character strengths literature is grounded in the meaning in life and satisfaction with life literatures, future research would benefit from teasing out the distinctions between these constructs and their associated measures. Longitudinal research should also examine the impact of work-related meaningfulness on life meaning and satisfaction over time. In addition, research should continue to seek evidence regarding whether to focus measures on the different potential sources of meaningfulness (Lips-Wiersma and Wright, 2012) or be more general in nature and measure the characteristics of the sources separately to determine their influence on work meaningfulness (May, Gilson, and Harter, 2004).

Future research should also explore relations of the character strengths to work-related meaningfulness across cultures. Research by Peterson et al. (2007) suggests that differences exist in the relation between strengths and life meaning across countries. Similar research should be conducted in organizational contexts to examine the influence of such strengths on work-related meaningfulness in different countries. While the fundamental virtues and strengths may be universal in nature, cultural norms may either foster or inhibit the expression of specific character strengths in particular contexts.

Perhaps one of the most promising directions for future research is determining the efficacy of interventions in organizations to build character strengths, employee well-being, and positive ethical cultures. Positive psychology researchers have been working in recent years on ways to foster awareness and use of individuals' strengths to enhance well-being (Meyers, van Woerkom, and Bakker, 2013; Quinlan, Swain, and Vella-Brodrick, 2012). These researchers suggest that the relational environment and facilitator attitudes in organizational contexts need exploration. Indeed the group reinforcement or praising of morally worthwhile strengths-related behavior may influence the effectiveness of any strengths intervention. Thus, questions remain regarding whether such reinforcement helps build and sustain feelings of meaningfulness and positive emotions or fosters positive emotional contagion in organizational contexts.

Future research should focus systematically on the strengths explored here, and go on to examine the extent to which positive emotions occur and subsequent organizational improvements ensue. Strengths of moral efficacy and moral courage are underrepresented in the positive psychology literature but are starting to be used as outcome measures of training (May, Luth, and Schwoerer, 2014) and need to be examined in future organizational interventions.

Given its powerful effects (Donaldson, Dollwet, and Rao, 2015), gratitude is another promising area for exploration in organizations. Wood, Froh, and Geraghty (2010) have noted that there are three major types of gratitude interventions: daily diaries, contemplation, and behavioral actions. Mills, Fleck, and Kozikowski (2013) suggest that such strategies, as well as more contextually based approaches, may hold promise for future research on gratitude in organizations. Future research may also wish to pursue collective gratitude, an idea proposed recently by Müceldili et al. (2015). This may extend our knowledge about positive outcomes at a team and organizational level for a character strength of such import.

Furthermore, consistent with research reviewed by Green, Evans, and Williams (2017), we believe managers should attempt to foster these character strengths to build a flourishing workforce that experiences meaning at work. Indeed, Mroz and Quinn (2009) outline a clear process for implementing positive organizational scholarship principles in organizations. It involves creating a common understanding, selecting early adopters, creating pockets of success, sharing stories across boundaries, and adjusting across boundaries. While this is more inductive in nature, Wright and Goodstein (2007) suggest that organizations that have a strong purpose may influence individual character through transcendence, and subsequently influence employees' personal fulfillment.

Finally, future research should work on developing an integration of the philosophical virtue ethics approach to meaningful work (e.g. Beadle and Knight, 2012; Moore, 2017; Moore and Beadle, 2006) with the positive social science approach for virtues and character strengths outlined here. Bright, Winn, and Kanov (2014) have provided an initial exploration of the ideas for how virtue ethics may serve as the theoretical foundation for positive organizational ethics. Any integration should include the Aristotelian tradition of virtue (e.g. Beadle and Knight, 2012) that is not fully realized in the positive organizational sciences approach.

Callings

Our understanding of callings, their antecedents, and consequences has been improved notably through the research conducted in the past decade. Literature has clearly shown that through the conviction that work is particularly meaningful, callings increase individuals' levels of satisfaction and engagement at work (Hirschi, 2012; Duffy et al., 2012). Less clear is the understanding of the conditions under which callings can be fostered. Exploration in this area is hindered by a lack of consensus among scholars regarding a core question about callings: are callings malleable? Some scholars believe that callings are discovered rather than developed and therefore hardly malleable. In their views, a calling is a destined occupational niche that is preordained by a deity, a particular need of society, or personal talent (Bunderson and Thompson, 2009). Other scholars believe not only that individuals develop their own callings (Dobrow, 2013), but that they can also have multiple callings (Berg, Grant, and Johnson, 2010). This disagreement perhaps can be reconciled using research findings on value change. Callings reflect work values integral to one's identity, which convey what is important in work. Values are generally believed to be stable yet malleable (Bardi et al., 2009). Opportunity for value change occurs when people experience a high level of inconsistency between what they believe is right and desirable and new information obtained from their environment that counters what they believe (Rokeach, 1972). Future research may wish to explore the degree to which an individual feels called to a particular profession. Even the choice of profession may change to reflect changes in the work experiences an individual finds to be meaningful in an organization.

Another potentially fruitful research area is attention to callings, character strengths, and upward spirals of positive emotions. Although character strengths have been linked to callings, we know little about whether or how callings lead to the type of positive individual outcomes that can in turn reinforce character strengths. Chen et al. (2018) surveyed 526 law enforcement employees and found that individuals with stronger callings better endure suboptimal justice and psychological safety organizational conditions than those with weaker callings. It is possible that those with stronger callings, through successfully persevering in undesirable organizational justice conditions, gained satisfaction that subsequently fortified their character strength of *persistence*. Research is needed to formally examine the types of upward spirals that spring from character strengths and rise through callings.

Volunteering

At this point, the best understood outcomes of volunteering are individual quality of life and well-being (see Binder and Freytag, 2013; Thoits and Hewitt, 2001). While volunteering is hypothesized to enhance skills, this outcome still needs to be investigated from a work context perspective—i.e. how do individuals use the skills they gain or maintain in volunteer roles in their jobs? In the context of work, past research has noted how volunteering may serve in a compensatory role for absent work meaningfulness or as an extension of felt work meaningfulness (Rodell, 2013). Research is still relatively silent, however, on how volunteering influences individual work outcomes beyond meaningfulness and engagement. Specifically, further investigation is needed on mediating factors related to one's identity that result from volunteering and lead to increased work meaningfulness. Lastly, Mojza et al. (2010) have noted the renewing role of volunteer work in creating new resources to draw from in the workplace and community; this relationship should be explored further with a focus on how volunteering generates and sustains upward spirals of prosocial behavior (Fredrickson, 1998).

Positive Emotions, Upward Spirals, and Cross-level Effects

In reviewing research on the broaden-and-build theory of positive emotions in organizational scholarship, Vacharkulksemsuk and Fredrickson (2013) concluded that while the benefits of positive emotions are evident, there is a need to demonstrate broader workplace benefits and to investigate process variables and moderators such as organization climate. They also noted the need for field studies that are longitudinal in design. Such studies could provide understanding of the dynamics of individual and collective upward spirals that can result in more positive outcomes, including a positive ethical culture. Future research should also explore the dynamic relation between experiencing meaningfulness in the workplace and such positive emotion spirals. There may be reciprocal relations between these two.

The Potential of Paradox and Experiencing Meaningfulness at Work

The process of experiencing meaningfulness through dynamic interrelations among virtues and character strengths, positive mechanisms, and emotions, and a positive ethical culture and civic engagement, has synergistic links to research on ambiguity and paradox in organizations. Thus, adopting a "paradox lens" to examine how individuals experience meaningfulness and organization ethical climates could be fruitful. Process characteristics of particular relevance are the interdependence of the model's elements, the focus on individual cognition and emotion, and the implicit emphasis on change rather than stasis.

Interest in tensions that underlie organizational systems has led to growth in research on paradox. Smith and Lewis (2011: 386) defined paradox as "contradictory yet interrelated elements that exist simultaneously and persist over time," and built an integrative, dynamic model of organizing as a foundation for a theory of paradox. This highlights conflicting forces and purposeful responses over time that enable sustainability that is not static but rather is characterized by dynamic equilibrium (Fairhurst et al., 2016). Schad et al. (2016: 6) have defined paradox as a "persistent contradiction between interdependent elements," and stated that "paradox and related phenomena form in and through dynamic actions and . . . emerge as cyclical relationships. Reviewers of the paradox literature have called for research that emphasizes ongoing paradoxical interactions.

Experiencing meaning is inherently less than stable or constant and can be seen to involve natural tensions. Allan (2015) noted that different character strengths, such as kindness and honesty, can be in conflict. More of a character strength is not always "better." Context can affect the dynamic equilibrium building toward positive outcomes in inconsistent ways. Virtues and strengths may not be consistently linked to positive mechanisms and experienced meaningfulness. Unanticipated developments or shocks at work may call into question an experience of meaningfulness. An upward spiral due to experienced meaningfulness may be attenuated by a lack of support or a conflicting experience. Culture change can be seen as ongoing, and some organization cultures may be inherently resistant to change (Bate, 1984; Meyerson and Martin, 1987).

Smith and Lewis's (2011) theory of paradox suggests that conflicting and paradoxical roles, competing strategies and goals, and differing and conflicting stakeholder demands can make paradox salient. These authors characterize potential reactions to paradox as varied. In addition to acceptance and separation, Smith and Lewis suggest that paradoxical roles can create "virtuous cycles" of embracing paradox through the experience of meaningfulness. Future research should investigate this possibility by asking how organizational paradoxes may lead to positive emotional reactions rather than anxiety and defensiveness. Nevertheless, Cameron (2008) maintains that both the positive and negative tendencies and experiences are necessarily, although paradoxically, essential for the perpetuation of positive change in organizations. Finally, our hope is that positive change not only occurs within organizations, but also in broader social contexts as individuals create and foster deeply meaningful work that can drive positive social change (Stephan et al., 2016).

CONCLUSION

In summary, the purpose of this chapter was to bring together literatures on behavioral ethics, positive organizational scholarship, and meaningful work to propose a framework for studying positive organizational ethics that builds experienced meaningfulness, positive emotions, and positive organizational and civic outcomes. Our hope is that we will inspire much research and practice that adopts a similar paradigm, as we believe it is fundamental to creating moral organizations that encourage individuals to flourish at work!

ACKNOWLEDGMENTS

The authors would like to thank Ruth Yeoman, Katie Bailey, Adrian Madden, and Marc Thompson for their gracious invitation to contribute this chapter to the *Oxford Handbook of Meaningful Work*. The authors thank Adrian Madden for his thoughtful comments on an earlier draft of this chapter.

REFERENCES

Allan, B. A. (2015). "Balance among character strengths and meaning in life." *Journal of Happiness Studies*, 16(5), 1247–61.

Ashkanasy, N. and Ashton-James, C. E. (2007). "Positive Emotion in Organizations: A Multi-level framework." In C. L. Cooper and D. Nelson (eds.), *Positive Organizational Behavior*, pp. 57–73. Chichester: John Wiley & Sons.

Ashkanasy, N. and Dorris, A. (2017). "Emotions in the workplace." *Annual Review of Organizational Psychology and Organizational Behavior*, 4(1), 67–90.

Ashkanasy, N., Humphrey, R., and Huy, Q. (2017). "Integrating emotions and affect in theories of management." *Academy of Management Review*, 42, 175–89.

Bailey, C. and Madden, A. (2015). "Time reclaimed: Temporality and the experience of meaningful work." *Work, Employment & Society*, 31, 3–18.

Bandura, A. (1986). *Social Foundations of Thought and Action: A social cognitive perspective.* Englewood Cliffs, NJ: Princeton-Hall.

Bardi, A., Lee, J. A., Hofmann-Towfigh, N., and Soutar, G. (2009). "The structure of intraindividual value change." *Journal of Personality and Social Psychology*, 97(5), 913–29.

Barsade, S. G. (2002). "The ripple effect: Emotional contagion and its influence on group behavior." *Administrative Science Quarterly*, 47(4), 644–75.

Barsade, S. G. and Gibson, D. E. (2007). "Why does affect matter in organizations?" *The Academy of Management Perspectives*, 21(1), 36–59.

Bate, P. (1984). "The impact of organizational culture on approaches to organizational problem-solving." *Organization Studies*, 5(1), 43–66.

Baumeister, R. F. and Leary, M. R. (1995). "The need to belong: desire for interpersonal attachments as a fundamental human motivation." *Psychological Bulletin*, 117, 497–529.

Baumeister, R. F. and Vohs, K. D. (2002). "The Pursuit of Meaningfulness in Life." In C. R. Snyder and S. J. Lopez (eds.), *Handbook of Positive Psychology*, pp. 608–18. New York: Oxford University Press.

Beadle, R. and Knight, K. (2012). "Virtue and meaningful work." *Business Ethics Quarterly*, 22(2), 433–50.

Bellah, R., Madsen, R., Sullivan, W. M., Swidler, A., and Tipton, S. M. (1985). *Habits of the Heart.* Berkeley: University of California Press.

Berg, J. M., Dutton, J. E., and Wrzesniewski, A. (2013). "Job Crafting and Meaningful Work." In B. J. Dik, Z. S. Byrne, and M. F. Steger (eds.), *Purpose and Meaning in the Workplace*, pp. 81–104. Washington, DC: American Psychological Association.

Berg, J. M., Grant, A. M., and Johnson, V. (2010). "When callings are calling: Crafting work and leisure in pursuit of unanswered occupational callings." *Organization Science*, 21(5), 973–94.

Binder, M. and Freytag, A. (2013). "Volunteering, subjective well-being and public policy." *Journal of Economic Psychology*, 34, 97–119.

Blasi, A. (1999). "Emotions and moral motivation." *Journal for the Theory of Social Behaviour*, 29(1), 1–19.

Bowie, N. E. (1998). "A Kantian theory of meaningful work." *Journal of Business Ethics*, 17, 1083–92.

Bright, D. S., Winn, B. A., and Kanov, J. (2014). "Reconsidering virtue: Differences of perspective in virtue ethics and the positive social sciences." *Journal of Business Ethics*, 119(4), 445–60.

Bunderson, J. S. and Thompson, J. A. (2009). "The call of the wild: Zookeepers, callings, and the double-edged sword of deeply meaningful work." *Administrative Science Quarterly*, 54(1), 32–57.

Cameron, K. S. (2008). "Paradox in positive organizational change." *The Journal of Applied Behavioral Science*, 44(1), 7–24.

Cameron, K. S., Bright, D., and Caza, A. (2004). "Exploring the relationships between organizational virtuousness and performance." *American Behavioral Scientist*, 47(6), 766–90.

Caza, A., Barker, B. A., and Cameron, K. S. (2004). "Ethics and ethos: The buffering and amplifying effects of ethical behavior and virtuousness." *Journal of Business Ethics*, 52(2), 169–78.

Chalofsky, N. and Krishna, V. (2009). "Meaningfulness, commitment, and engagement: The intersection of a deeper level of intrinsic motivation." *Advances in Developing Human Resources*, 11, 189–203.

Chen, J., May, D. R., Schwoerer, C. E., and Augelli, B. (2018). "Exploring the boundaries of career calling: The moderating roles of procedural justice and psychological safety." *Journal of Career Development*, 45(2), 103–16.

Conway, A. M., Tugade, M. M., Catalino, L. I., and Fredrickson, B. L. (2013). "The Broaden-and-build Theory of Positive Emotions: Form, Function, and Mechanisms." In S. David, I. Boniwell, and A. Conley Ayers (eds.), *The Oxford Handbook of Happiness*, 17–34. Oxford: Oxford University Press.

Deeg, M. D. and May, D. R. (2017). "The volunteer experience: Influences on work meaningfulness, passion and civic engagement." Paper accepted for presentation at the 2017 Fifth World Congress on Positive Psychology, Montreal.

Detert, J. and Bruno, E. (2017). "Workplace courage: Review, synthesis, and future agenda for a complex construct." *Academy of Management Annals*, 11(2), Advance online publication available at: https://doi.org/10.5465/annals.2015.0155 [accessed July 1, 2018].

Dik, B. J. and Duffy, R. D. (2009). "Calling and vocation at work definitions and prospects for research and practice." *The Counseling Psychologist*, 37(3), 424–50.

Dik, B. J., Duffy, R. D., and Eldridge, B. M. (2009). "Calling and vocation in career counseling: Recommendations for promoting meaningful work." *Professional Psychology: Research and Practice*, 40(6), 625–32.

Dobrow, S. R. (2013). "Dynamics of calling: A longitudinal study of musicians." *Journal of Organizational Behavior*, 34(4), 431–52.

Dobrow, S. R. and Tosti-Kharas, J. (2011). "Calling: The development of a scale measure." *Personnel Psychology*, 64(4), 1001–49.

Donaldson, S. I., Dollwet, M., and Rao, M. A. (2015). "Happiness, excellence, and optimal human functioning revisited: Examining the peer-reviewed literature linked to positive psychology." *The Journal of Positive Psychology*, 10(3), 185–95.

Duffy, R. D., Bott, E. M., Allan, B. A., Torrey, C. L., and Dik, B. J. (2012). "Perceiving a calling, living a calling, and job satisfaction: Testing a moderated, multiple mediator model." *Journal of Counseling Psychology*, 59(1), 50–9.

Dutton, J. E., Workman, K. M., and Hardin, A. E. (2014). "Compassion at work." *Annual Review of Organizational Psychology and Organizational Behavior*, 1(1), 277–304.

Emmons, R. (2003). "Acts of Gratitude in Organizations." In K. Cameron, J. Dutton, and R. Quinn (eds.), *Positive Organizational Scholarship: Foundations of a new discipline*, pp. 81–93. San Francisco: Berrett-Koehler.

Fairhurst, G. T., Smith, W. K., Banghart, S. G., Lewis, M. W., Putnam, L. L., Raisch, S., and Schad, J. (2016). "Diverging and converging: Integrative insights on a paradox meta-perspective." *Academy of Management Annals*, 10(1), 173–82.

Fischer, L. and Schaffer, K. B. (1993). *Older Volunteers*. Newbury Park, CA: Sage Publications.

Frankl, V. E. (1959). *Man's Search for Meaning: An introduction to logotherapy*. New York: Simon & Schuster.

Fredrickson, B. L. (1998). "What good are positive emotions?" *Review of General Psychology*, 2(3), 300–19.

Fredrickson, B. L. (2001). "The role of positive emotions in positive psychology." *American Psychologist*, 56(3), 218–26.

Fredrickson, B. L. and Losada, M. F. (2005). "Positive affect and the complex dynamics of human flourishing." *American Psychologist*, 60(7), 678–86.

Gable, S. L. and Gosnell, C. L. (2011). "The Positive Side of Close Relationships." In K. M. Sheldon, T. B. Kashdan, and M. F. Steger (eds.), *Designing Positive Psychology: Taking stock and moving forward*, pp. 265–79. New York: Oxford University Press.

Geroy, G. D., Wright, P. C., and Jacoby, L. (2000). "Toward a conceptual framework of employee volunteerism: An aid for the human resource manager." *Management Decision*, 38, 280–6.

Gist, M. (1987). "Self-efficacy: Implications for organizational behavior and human resource management." *Academy of Management Review*, 12(3), 472–85.

Gorjian, N. (2006). "Virtue of transcendence in relation to work orientation, job satisfaction and turnover cognitions." Unpublished doctoral dissertation Alliant International University, San Diego, CA. Retrieved from ProQuestDissertations Publishing (2006.3208703).

Grant, A. M. (2012). "Giving time, time after time: Work design and sustained employee participation in corporate volunteering." *Academy of Management Review*, 37(4), 589–615.

Grant, A. M. and Berg, J. (2012). "Prosocial Motivation at Work: When, Why, and How Making a Difference Makes a Difference." In K. S. Cameron and G. M. Spreitzer (eds.), *The Oxford Handbook of Positive Organizational Scholarship*, pp. 28–44. New York: Oxford University Press.

Green, S., Evans, O., and Williams, B. (2017). "Positive Psychology at Work: Research and Practice." In C. Proctor (ed.), *Positive Psychology Interventions in Practice*, pp. 185–206. New York: Springer International Publishing.

Handelsman, M. M., Knapp, S., and Gottlieb, M. C. (2009). "Positive Ethics: Themes and Variations." In C. R. Snyder and S. J. Lopez (eds.), *Oxford Handbook of Positive Psychology*, pp. 105–13. New York: Oxford University Press.

Hannah, S. T., Avolio, B. J., and May, D. R. (2011). "Moral maturation and moral conation: A capacity approach to explaining moral thought and action." *Academy of Management Review*, 36(4), 663–85.

Harzer, C. and Ruch, W. (2012). "When the job is a calling: The role of applying one's signature strengths at work." *The Journal of Positive Psychology*, 7(5), 362–71.

Harzer, C. and Ruch, W. (2016). "Your strengths are calling: Preliminary results of a web-based strengths intervention to increase calling." *Journal of Happiness Studies*, 17(6), 2237–56.

Heine, S. J., Proulx, T., and Vohs, K. D. (2006). "The meaning maintenance model: On the coherence of social motivations." *Personality and Social Psychology Review*, 10, 88–110.

Hirschi, A. (2012). "Callings and work engagement: Moderated mediation model of work meaningfulness, occupational identity, and occupational self-efficacy." *Journal of Counseling Psychology*, 59(3), 479–85.

Humphrey, S. E., Nahrgang, J. D., and Morgeson, F. P. (2007). "Integrating motivational, social, and contextual work design features: A meta-analytic summary and theoretical extension of the work design literature." *Journal of Applied Psychology*, 92(5), 1332–56.

King, L. A. and Napa, C. K. (1998). "What makes a life good?" *Journal of Personality and Social Psychology*, 75(1), 156–65.

Kong, D. T. and Ho, V. T. (2016). "A self-determination perspective of strengths use at work: Examining its determinant and performance implications." *The Journal of Positive Psychology*, 11(1), 15–25.

Lam, C. F., Spreitzer, G., and Fritz, C. (2014). "Too much of a good thing: Curvilinear effect of positive affect on proactive behaviors." *Journal of Organizational Behavior*, 35(4), 530–46.

Lilius, J., Worline, M., Maitlis, S., Kanov, J., Dutton, J., and Frost, P. (2008). "The contours and consequences of compassion at work." *Journal of Organizational Behavior*, 29(2), 193–218.

Lips-Wiersma, M. and Wright, S. (2012). "Measuring the meaning of meaningful work: Development and validation of the Comprehensive Meaningful Work Scale (CMWS)." *Group & Organization Management*, 37, 655–85.

Littman-Ovadia, H. and Steger, M. (2010). "Character strengths and well-being among volunteers and employees: Toward an integrative model." *The Journal of Positive Psychology*, 5(6), 419–30.

Liu, C. H. and Robertson, P. J. (2011). "Spirituality in the workplace: Theory and measurement." *Journal of Management Inquiry*, 20(1), 35–50.

Markus, H. (1977). "Self-schemata and processing information about the self." *Journal of Personality and Social Psychology*, 35(2), 63–78.

May, D. R., Chang, Y. K., and Shao, R. (2015). "Does ethical membership matter? Moral identification and its organizational implications." *Journal of Applied Psychology*, 100(3), 681–94.

May, D. R., Gilson, R. L., and Harter, L. M. (2004). "The psychological conditions of meaningfulness, safety and availability and the engagement of the human spirit at work." *Journal of Occupational and Organizational Psychology*, 77, 11–37.

May, D. R., Luth, M. T., and Schwoerer, C. E. (2014). "The influence of business ethics education on moral efficacy, moral meaningfulness, and moral courage: A quasi-experimental study." *Journal of Business Ethics*, 124(1), 67–80.

May, D. R., Mencl, J., Li, C., and Huang, C. C. (2014). "The ethics of meaningful work: Types and magnitude of job-related harm and the ethical decision-making process." *Journal of Business Ethics*, 121(4), 651–69.

Meyers, M. C., van Woerkom, M., and Bakker, A. B. (2013). "The added value of the positive: A literature review of positive psychology interventions in organizations." *European Journal of Work and Organizational Psychology*, 22(5), 618–32.

Meyerson, D. and Martin, J. (1987). "Cultural change: An integration of three different views [1]." *Journal of Management Studies*, 24(6), 623–47.

Michaelson, C., Pratt, M. G., Grant, A. M., and Dunn, C. P. (2014). "Meaningful work: Connecting business ethics and organization studies." *Journal of Business Ethics*, 121, 77–90.

Mills, M. J., Fleck, C. R., and Kozikowski, A. (2013). "Positive psychology at work: A conceptual review, state-of-practice assessment, and a look ahead." *The Journal of Positive Psychology*, 8(2), 153–64.

Mojza, E. J., Lorenz, C., Sonnentag, S., and Binnewies, C. (2010). "Daily recovery experiences: The role of volunteer work during leisure time." *Journal of Occupational Health Psychology*, 15(1), 60–74.

Moore, G. (2017). *Virtue at Work: Ethics for individuals, managers, and organizations.* Oxford: Oxford University Press.

Moore, G. and Beadle, R. (2006). "In search of organizational virtue in business: Agents, goods, practices, institutions and environments." *Organization Studies*, 27(3), 369–89.

Mroz, D. and Quinn, S. (2009). "Positive Organizational Scholarship Leaps into the World of Work." In N. Garcea, S. Harrington, and P. A. Linley (eds.), *Oxford Handbook of Positive Psychology and Work*, pp. 251–64. New York: Oxford University Press.

Müceldili, B., Erdil, O., Akgün, A. E., and Keskin, H. (2015). "Collective gratitude: Positive organizational scholarship perspective." *International Business Research*, 8(8), 92–102.

Oldham, G. R. and Fried, Y. (2016). "Job design research and theory: Past, present and future." *Organizational Behavior and Human Decision Processes*, 136, 20–35.

Oldham, G. R. and Hackman, J. (2010). "Not what it was and not what it will be: The future of job design research." *Journal of Organizational Behavior*, 31(2–3), 463–79.

Omoto, A. M., Snyder, M., and Hackett, J. D. (2010). "Personality and motivational antecedents of activism and civic engagement." *Journal of Personality*, 78(6), 1703–34.

Parke, M. and Seo, M. G. (2017). "The role of affect climate in organizational effectiveness." *Academy of Management Review*, 42(2), 334–60.

Perttula, K. H. and Cardon, M. S. (2012). "Passion." In K. S. Cameron and G. M. Spreitzer (eds.), *The Oxford Handbook of Positive Organizational Scholarship*, pp. 190–200. New York: Oxford University Press.

Peterson, C. and Park, N. (2012). "Character Strengths and the Life of Meaning." In P. T. P. Wong (ed.), *The Human Quest for Meaning: Theories, research, and applications*, 2nd edn., pp. 277–95. New York: Routledge.

Peterson, C., Park, N., Hall, N., and Seligman, M. E. P. (2009). "Zest and work." *Journal of Organizational Behavior*, 30(2), 161–72.

Peterson, C., Ruch, W., Beermann, U., Park, N., and Seligman, M. E. P. (2007). "Strengths of character, orientations to happiness, and life satisfaction." *The Journal of Positive Psychology*, 2(3), 149–56.

Peterson, C. and Seligman, M. E. P. (2004). *Character Strengths and Virtues: A handbook and classification*. New York: Oxford University Press.

Peterson, C., Stephens, J. P., Park, N., Lee, F., and Seligman, M. E. P. (2010). "Strengths of Character and Work." In P. A. Linley, S. Harrington, and N. Garcea (eds.), *Oxford Handbook of Positive Psychology and Work*, pp. 221–31. New York: Oxford University Press.

Pratt, M. G. and Ashforth, B. E. (2003). "Fostering Meaningfulness in Working and at Work." In K. S. Cameron, J. E. Dutton, and R. E. Quinn (eds.), *Positive Organizational Scholarship: Foundations of a new discipline*, pp. 309–27. San Francisco, CA: Berrett-Koehler.

Prouteau, L. and Wolff, F.-C. (2008). "On the relational motive for volunteer work." *Journal of Economic Psychology*, 29, 314–35.

Quinlan, D., Swain, N., and Vella-Brodrick, D. A. (2012). "Character strengths interventions: Building on what we know for improved outcomes." *Journal of Happiness Studies*, 13(6), 1145–63.

Rodell, J. B. (2013). "Finding meaning through volunteering: Why do employees volunteer and what does it mean for their jobs?" *Academy of Management Journal*, 56(5), 1274–94.

Rokeach, M. (1972). *Beliefs, Attitudes and Values: A theory of organization and change*. San Francisco: Jossey-Bass.

Rosso, B. D., Dekas, K. H., and Wrzesniewski, A. (2010). "On the meaning of work: A theoretical integration and review." *Research in Organizational Behavior*, 30, 91–127.

Ryan, R. M. and Deci, E. L. (2000). "Self-determination theory and the facilitation of intrinsic motivation, social development, and well-being." *American Psychologist*, 55(1), 68–78.

Rynes, S. L., Bartunek, J. M., Dutton, J. E., and Margolis, J. D. (2012). "Care and compassion through an organizational lens: Opening up new possibilities." *Academy of Management Review*, 37(4), 503–23.

Schad, J., Lewis, M., Raisch, S., and Smith, W. (2016). "Paradox research in management science: Looking back to move forward." *Academy of Management Annals*, 10, 1–60.

Sekerka, L. E., Bagozzi, R. P., and Charnigo, R. (2009). "Facing ethical challenges in the workplace: Conceptualizing and measuring professional moral courage." *Journal of Business Ethics*, 89(4), 565–79.

Sekerka, L. E., Comer, D. R., and Godwin, L. N. (2014). "Positive organizational ethics: Cultivating and sustaining moral performance." *Journal of Business Ethics*, 119(4), 435–44.

Seligman, M. E. P. and Csikszentmihalyi, M. (2000). "Positive psychology: An introduction." *American Psychologist*, special issue, 55(1), 5–14.

Shamir, B. (1991). "Meaning, self and motivation in organizations." *Organization Studies*, 12(3), 405–24.

Shao, R., Aquino, K., and Freeman, D. (2008). "Beyond moral reasoning: A review of moral identity research and its implications for business ethics." *Business Ethics Quarterly*, 18(4), 513–40.

Simons, T., Tomlinson, E., and Leroy, H. (2011). "Research on Behavioral Integrity: A Promising Construct for Positive Organizational Scholarship." In K. S. Cameron and G. M. Spreitzer (eds.), *The Oxford Handbook of Positive Organizational Scholarship*, pp. 325–39. Oxford: Oxford University Press.

Smith, M. (2010). "The relationship between character strengths and work satisfaction." Unpublished doctoral dissertation, Massachusetts School of Professional Psychology, Newton, MA. Retrieved from ProQuest Dissertations Publishing (2010.3415719).

Smith, W. K. and Lewis, M. W. (2011). "Toward a theory of paradox: A dynamic equilibrium model of organizing." *Academy of Management Review*, 36(2), 381–403.

Stansbury, J. M. and Sonenshein, S. (2012). "Positive Business Ethics: Grounding and Elaborating a Theory of Good Works." In K. S. Cameron and G. M. Spreitzer (eds.), *The Oxford Handbook of Positive Organizational Scholarship*, pp. 340–52. New York: Oxford University Press.

Staw, B. M., Sutton, R. I., and Pellod, L. H. (1994). "Employee positive emotion and favorable outcomes at the work place." *Organizational Science*, 5(1), 51–71.

Stephan, U., Patterson, M., Kelly, C., and Mair, J. (2016). "Organizations driving positive social change: A review and an integrative framework of change processes." *Journal of Management*, 42(5), 1250–81.

Thoits, P. A. and Hewitt, L. N. (2001). "Volunteer work and well-being." *Journal of Health and Social Behavior*, 42(2), 115–31.

Tims, M., Derks, D., and Bakker, A. B. (2016). "Job crafting and its relationships with person–job fit and meaningfulness: A three-wave study." *Journal of Vocational Behavior*, 92, 44–53.

Vacharkulksemsuk, T. and Fredrickson, B. L. (2013). "Looking Back and Glimpsing Forward: The Broaden-and-build Theory of Positive Emotions as Applied to Organizations." In A. B. Bakker (ed.), *Advances in Positive Organizational Psychology*, pp. 45–60. Bingley: Emerald.

Vallerand, R. J. (2008). "On the psychology of passion: In search of what makes people's lives most worth living." *Canadian Psychology/Psychologie Canadienne*, 49(1), 1–13.

Verbos, A. K., Gerard, J. A., Forshey, P. R., Harding, C. S., and Miller, J. S. (2007). "The positive ethical organization: Enacting a living code of ethics and ethical organizational identity." *Journal of Business Ethics*, 76(1), 17–33.

Weaver, G. R. (2006). "Virtue in organizations: Moral identity as a foundation for moral agency." *Organization Studies*, 27, 341–68.

Weiss, H. M. and Beal, D. J. (2005). "Reflections on Affective Events Theory." In N. Ashkanasy, W. Zerbe, and C. Härtel (eds.), *The Effect of Affect in Organizational Settings*, pp. 1–21. Bingley: Emerald Group Publishing.

Weiss, H. M. and Cropanzano, R. (1996). "Affective events theory: A theoretical discussion of the structure, causes and consequences of affective experiences at work." *Research in Organizational Behavior*, 18, 1–74.

Whetten, D. (1989). "What constitutes a theoretical contribution?" *Academy of Management Review*, 14, 490–5.

Whitener, E. M., Brodt, S. E., Korsgaard, M. A., and Werner, J. M. (1998). "Managers as initiators of trust: An exchange relationship framework for understanding managerial trustworthy behavior." *Academy of Management Review*, 23(3), 513–30.

Wood, A. M., Froh, J. J., and Geraghty, A. W. (2010). "Gratitude and well-being: A review and theoretical integration." *Clinical Psychology Review*, 30(7), 890–905.

Woodard, C. R. (2004). "Hardiness and the concept of courage." *Consulting Psychology Journal: Practice and Research*, 56(3), 173–85.

Wright, T. A. and Goodstein, J. (2007). "Character is not 'dead' in management research: A review of individual character and organizational-level virtue." *Journal of Management*, 33(6), 928–58.

Wrzesniewski, A. (2003). "Finding Positive Meaning in Work." In K. S. Cameron, J. E. Dutton, and R. E. Quinn (eds.), *Positive Organizational Scholarship: Foundations of a New Discipline*, pp. 296–308. San Francisco, CA: Berrett-Koehler.

Wrzesniewski, A., Dekas, K., and Rosso, B. (2012). "Callings." In K. S. Cameron and G. M. Spreitzer (eds.), *The Oxford Handbook of Positive Organizational Scholarship*, pp. 45–55. New York: Oxford University Press.

Yeoman, R. (2014). "Conceptualising meaningful work as a fundamental human need." *Journal of Business Ethics*, 125(2), 235–51.

....

CHAPTER 21

DIRECT PARTICIPATION AND MEANINGFUL WORK

The Implications of Task Discretion and Organizational Participation

....

DUNCAN GALLIE

INTRODUCTION

CONCERN with the meaningfulness of work is rooted in a eudaimonistic conception of well-being that has become increasingly influential inter alia in the fields of psychiatry (Frankl, 2004) and positive psychology (Baumeister et al., 2013). Although there have been diverse approaches to the conceptualization of "meaningful work" (Rosso, Dekas, and Wrzesniewski, 2010), an important feature of the term is that it highlights the importance to people of pursuing activities that they view as worthwhile in terms of their values. As Rokeach (1973) has argued, it is values that give meaning to action.

Values can be conceived as relatively enduring culturally derived ideals that provide personal goals, motivate behavior, and give standards for judging the desirability of situations and actions (Hitlin and Piliavin, 2004). While in principle there may be a multiplicity of values, it has been argued that there is a much more limited range of "basic values" that are recognized very widely (although with varying degrees of priority) across different cultures (Schwartz, 1992, 2012). The extent to which such values reflect underlying "needs" is controversial, but there is broad agreement that the values of principal interest are those which are relatively widely held and which promote, or at least are consistent with, longer term well-being. While research is still relatively underdeveloped, there is a growing body of evidence that participation at work affects opportunities for the fulfillment of several values that are central for a sense of work as meaningful.

Very broadly, two arguments about the importance of participation for meaningful work can be distinguished. The first underlines its intrinsic importance: participative decision-making at work allows people to pursue working lives that concord with the importance they attach to the value of self-determination. The second emphasizes the instrumental importance of participation for helping to establish a work environment conducive to the realization of other valued aspects of the working environment. In this respect, research has focused primarily on the implications of participation for opportunities for learning and for a working environment conducive to health.

Direct participation refers to the influence that employees can exercise through consultation or delegated decision-making with respect to their immediate work task, work organization, and working conditions (Geary and Sisson, 1994). Two principal levels of decision-making are usually distinguished: decisions with respect to the immediate job task (task discretion or autonomy) and decisions relating to broader organizational issues (organizational participation or voice) (Heller et al., 1998). This distinction is important because they may have different implications for the meaningfulness of work. In particular, while there has been relatively high agreement about the positive implications of task discretion, employer policies to extend voice have sometimes been viewed as detrimental to employees' experience of work.

THE INTRINSIC IMPORTANCE OF DIRECT PARTICIPATION

Direct Participation and Self-determination

Initially informed by Marxian analyses of alienation in work, theories premised on the importance of self-determination in work for personal fulfillment have become prevalent in quite diverse traditions of thought. A recent approach, that seeks to ground its arguments in empirical research, has argued for the intrinsic importance of decision-making autonomy drawing on theories of basic needs. "Self-determination Theory" postulates three basic psychological needs—competence, autonomy, and relatedness (Ryan and Deci, 2000).[1] Needs are a distinctive category of motive in that they are innate, universal, and essential for psychological health and well-being, equivalent to the need for nutrients for bodily health. Autonomy is the basic need that relates most directly to the importance of participation at work. Managerial support for autonomy is held to relate directly to employees' psychological adjustment (Deci, Connell, and Ryan, 1989; Deci et al., 2001; Baard, Deci, and Ryan, 2004; Ilardi et al., 1993).

Theories of needs make demanding assumptions about universality. An argument allowing for greater variation between individuals and societies attributes the importance of self-determination at work to the way institutions—in particular the family,

---

[1] These also feature in Warr's (1987) "vitamin model" of essential requirements for psychological health, although Warr introduces the notion that oversupply may also be damaging. They also appear in Schwartz's (1992) typology of ten motivational values under the terms of "self-direction," "achievement," and "security."

education, work structures, and religion—affect value formation. For instance, Argyris (1964) suggests that the importance attached to self-determination and growth is partly an outcome of socialization in the educational systems of advanced societies. Kohn and Schooler (1982) have argued that jobs that involve more complex work and greater autonomy increase the importance people attach to self-direction. At the macro-societal level it has been suggested that progressive conquest of legal and political citizenship rights, with their explicit emphasis on equality between citizens, has a contagious effect with respect to the expectation of rights of participation in decision-making at work (Marshall, 1964).

While there is now substantial cross-cultural evidence about the importance of self-direction as a general value (Schwartz and Bardi, 2001), the extent to which it is regarded as relevant to the work situation has been controversial. As Pateman (1970) recognized despite her strong advocacy of the benefits of participative democracy, case studies of forms of participatory management which allowed workers a measure of control over higher level policies (for instance choice of technologies and investment strategy) did not reveal widespread interest or high levels of uptake of the opportunities for involvement. She argued that there is stronger evidence that workers value participation in decisions that affect their immediate job.

Research in recent decades provides confirmation that workers do attach considerable importance to the control they can exercise over their immediate task activities. For instance, the British Skills and Employment Surveys showed that, in 1992, 75 percent of employees reported that "being able to use their initiative" in work was either an essential or very important factor in what they looked for in a job (Gallie, Felstead, and Green, 2012). Moreover, the trend over time was for its salience to increase—by 2006 the proportion citing the importance of use of initiative had risen to 83 percent. It is notable that, in both years, the ability to use initiative at work was considered more important than the level of pay (which was ranked as essential or very important by 72 percent in 1992 and 76 percent in 2006).

Cross-national surveys in the European Union also confirm the widespread importance of discretion over the job task, as indicated by the importance attached to the use of initiative in the job. As can be seen in Table 21.1, the European Social Survey carried out in 2004 showed that three-quarters or more of employees in all of the major European regions thought that, in the choice of a job, it was important that it should be "a job that enabled you to use your own initiative." Even in the wake of the most severe post-war economic crisis this was still the case for all of the regions, with the exception of Eastern Europe where the proportion fell to two-thirds (67.5 percent).

Despite its prevalence as a work value, it can be seen from Table 21.1 that there were at the same time significant differences in the importance attached to use of initiative in different parts of Europe. Employees in the Nordic countries were the most likely to consider it important, while those in the East European countries were the least likely (with the proportions ranging from 90 percent to 68 percent). Moreover, whereas in the Nordic, Liberal, and Continental countries, use of initiative was more likely to be regarded as important in the choice of a job than high pay, this was reversed in the Southern and East European countries.

Table 21.1 Percentage who thought initiative and high income "Very important or Important" in choosing a job

	Nordic	Liberal	Continental	Southern	East Europe
Initiative					
2004	90.0	87.6	83.6	84.3	75.5
2010	88.9	85.0	85.2	80.5	67.5
High income					
2004	68.5	76.3	71.9	94.6	89.8
2010	72.3	76.0	77.3	92.3	89.8
	7,999	3,908	7,976	5,953	11,853

Note: Data from ESS 2004 and 2010 (author's analyses). Nordic = Denmark, Finland, Norway, Sweden; Liberal = Great Britain and Ireland; Continental = Belgium, France, Germany, Netherlands; Southern = Greece, Spain, Portugal; East Europe = Czech, Estonia, Hungary, Poland, Slovakia, Slovenia.

There was also an expansion from the 1970s onwards of research into the importance employees attached to organizational participation. A representative national survey of 1,725 British employees was conducted in the late 1970s to assess their perceived level of influence over decision-making and the extent of their aspirations for influence (Heller et al., 1979). The results showed that employees' existing influence over organizational decisions was generally rather low. Only 23 percent could even give an opinion with respect to investment decisions and less than a quarter thought that decisions about work conditions or internal transfers were jointly regulated (Heller et al., 1979).

However, the study also revealed that aspirations for control over strategic areas of decision-making such as capital investment decisions were relatively modest. While nearly 90 percent wanted some involvement in decisions about working conditions and 80 percent in decisions about personnel transfers, less than half (47 percent) wanted influence over major capital investments. Moreover, even with respect to working conditions and transfers, influence was largely conceived in terms of being able to give an opinion: only around a third thought that such decisions should be jointly regulated or controlled by employees. Aspirations for influence were higher than current opportunities to take part in decisions, but this was true for only for a minority. Slightly over a quarter of employees wanted more involvement in organizational decisions than they currently had, while nearly three-quarters were satisfied with their current level of involvement.

Later research broadly confirms this picture, although there is some indication that the gap between actual and desired influence may have grown greater. The British Skills and Employment Surveys show that, overall, 42 percent of British employees felt that they should have more influence over organizational decisions. However, the desire for more influence depends on the degree of influence people have currently in their jobs. As can be seen in Table 21.2, consistent with the view that people value influence, dissatisfaction increases sharply the lower the existing level of participation. Whereas less than 20 percent of those with a great deal or quite a lot of influence over organizational

Table 21.2 British employees' level of and satisfaction with their participation in organizational decisions

Organizational participation (influence over wider organizational decisions)	% want more influence
None	57.4
A little	44.3
Quite a lot	19.8
A great deal	12.0

Note: Pooled data from British Skills and Employment Surveys 1992, 2001, 2006 and 2012.

decisions felt they should have more influence, the proportions that were dissatisfied were as high as 57 percent among those with low organizational participation.

This suggests that there is no general process of self-selection into, or accommodation to, limited opportunities for organizational participation, but rather that organizational voice was valued and that its absence led to a sense of deprivation. Moreover, although procedural differences in the way estimates were constructed mean that comparisons should be treated as very approximate, it is notable that the overall proportion expressing dissatisfaction with the level of organizational participation in the more recent period (43 percent) is considerably higher than was found in the 1970s (25 percent).

Overall, the evidence points to the importance workers attached to self-determination and hence to the intrinsic importance of direct participation in making work meaningful. This was particularly the case with respect to task discretion or control over the immediate job task. But consultative participation in wider organizational decisions was also valued and it is possible that its importance has been increasing.

The Instrumental Importance of Direct Participation

The instrumental argument for the importance of direct participation in affecting the meaningfulness of work has focused on its benefits for other valued aspects of the working environment. In his classic discussion, Hirschman (1970) pointed to the importance of voice as a lever for improving organizational deficiencies, in particular when it is difficult for people to express dissatisfaction through leaving their job. There is certainly empirical support for the view that employees see participation as valuable for improving the quality of the working environment. Indeed, an international study (International Democracy in Europe, 1981) found that people were more likely to cite the wider advantages of participation in terms of the protection of their interests than the intrinsic benefit of having greater say. Bryson and Freeman (2007) found, in a survey conducted in 2001, that both collective and non-union channels for voice were thought to be effective in reducing the number of reported problems at work. More detailed empirical research on the implications of participation for the broader working environment has focused particularly on its implications for employees' learning opportunities and for health risks.

Direct Participation and Learning

Learning is central to the realization of values of competence, personal development, and achievement, which have been found to be very widely prevalent across the economically advanced societies.[2] A cross-national study of eleven countries found that personal development, ability utilization, and achievement generally occupied the highest position in people's hierarchy of values (Sverko, 2001). One measure of the value employees attach to workplace learning opportunities is the importance they attribute to good training provision in their choice of a job. A survey carried out across the EU-15 countries in 2001 showed that in all but one country 70 percent or more of employees thought that good training provision was important for the choice of job. The proportions ranged from 68 percent in Belgium to 86 percent in Portugal (see Table 21.3).

A core proposition of the advocates of "high involvement" systems of management, which gives a central place to direct participation, is that it provides an environment conducive to the development of workers' skills (Lawler, 1986; Lawler, Mohrman, and Ledford, 1995; Appelbaum et al., 2000). These learning benefits have been seen as coming both from task discretion and from organizational participation. Task discretion, it is argued, allows employees to learn through carrying out their daily work activities (Felstead et al., 2010). Where they have greater influence over how their job tasks are done, they will be able to experiment with different methods of work and enhance their skills through trial and error. Organizational participation, by providing greater involvement in decisions about work organization, the adoption of new technologies, and human resource policies, also has the potential to increase employee learning by increasing knowledge of the overall work environment and awareness of the benefits and costs of potential options. At the same time it helps employees to influence decisions—such as investment in skills training—that tend to be taken at a higher level of management since they require significant deployment of organizational resources.

The evidence that direct participation improves opportunities for learning at work is now substantial. It has been shown that both task discretion and organizational participation are associated with greater informal learning through the task activity itself and through knowledge sharing between colleagues (Felstead et al., 2010; Inanc et al., 2015; Leach, Wall, and Jackson, 2003). However, the effects of the two forms of

---

[2] The very general importance attached to feelings of competence has been underlined by the work of Ryan and Deci (2000). For the cross-national importance of the fulfillment of personal potential or "self-realization," see Super and Sverko (1995). Similarly, a study of ten developed countries in 1989 found that in nine of the ten countries 75 percent or more of workers thought that good opportunities for advancement were important in a job (Luettel, Mueller, and Uher, 1991).

Table 21.3 The importance of good training
provision in the choice of a job (2001)

	% Very important or Important	Ns
Austria	79.9	557
Belgium	67.7	511
Denmark	75.8	623
France	72.5	539
Germany (West)	71.8	554
Germany (East)	71.3	508
Great Britain	82.3	587
Greece	77.4	446
Ireland	84.1	565
Italy	84.1	428
Luxembourg	84.9	292
Netherlands	75.5	613
Portugal	85.8	515
Spain	84.1	434
Sweden	69.9	491

Data from Eurobarometer 56, 2001 (author's analyses). For details
on the survey, see Gallie and Paugam, 2003.

direct participation differ with respect to training provision. Inanc et al. (2015) have
shown that task discretion does not affect either the chances of being trained or the
chances of receiving longer spells of training. In contrast, organizational participation
has a significant effect on both aspects of training, possibly reflecting the more centralized
nature of training decisions.

Potentially more crucial than training incidence for learning and skills development
is the quality of training (Felstead et al., 2010). In some cases, training provision may be
primarily designed to raise employee commitment or to reinforce knowledge of the
rules, which may just reinforce prescribed ways of working and restrict self-development
(Felstead et al., 2009). Inanc et al. (2015) found in cross-sectional analysis that, even with
a very wide range of controls, both task discretion and organizational participation were
associated with a higher quality of training—training that helped employees to improve
the way they did their job, improved their skills, led to a qualification, and provided skills
that were useful for another employer. The importance of organizational participation for
training quality has been confirmed by longitudinal analysis that found significant
within-individual effects over time, although there is conflicting evidence about whether
this is also the case for task discretion (Felstead et al., 2016; Gallie et al., 2017b).

A notable finding is that the benefits for learning opportunities of both types of direct
participation are particularly strong for employees in relatively low skilled categories
(Gallie, 2013; Inanc et al., 2015). This fits well with the argument that voice has a particularly
important function for employees with limited opportunities for exit (Hirschman, 1970).
For higher skilled employees, jobs are likely to be inherently more open to individual

on-the-job learning due to their greater complexity and their closer association with technical innovation, while higher skill also means greater market power to influence decisions about job discretion and training. This is reflected in the very consistent finding of a strong class gradient with respect to training (Dieckhoff, Jungblut, and O'Connell, 2007). Job redesign and provisions for organizational participation are then an important way in which disadvantaged groups can counter the inequalities in opportunities for self-development usually associated with class position.

Direct Participation and Health

Perhaps because good health is regarded as self-evidently important, it is rarely to be found as a specific item in value studies—whether they are concerned with general or work-specific values. However, with respect to work values, a proxy of its importance can be found in the priority people attach in their choice of a job to the nature of physical working conditions—a key factor in workplace health and safety. In Britain in the early 2000s around 70 percent of employees regarded good physical working conditions as an important feature in their choice of job (Gallie, Felstead, and Green, 2012).

Although traditionally physical health risks have been at the center of concern about the effects of the work environment on health, the focus of research has increasingly turned to the prevalence of psychosocial health risks (Karasek and Theorell, 1990; Siegrist and Wahrendorf, 2016). There is now substantial longitudinal evidence that task discretion at work is a significant determinant of mental health (Bentley et al., 2015; Theorell et al., 2015; Gallie et al., 2017b). The role of participation in moderating the effects of two key features of the work environment—work intensity and job insecurity—is likely to be important in accounting for this.

Work Intensity

The implications of direct participation for work intensity have been the most controversial issue with respect to workers' health. For some analysts, direct participation has been an important factor in work intensification, undermining employee well-being and health. Others, in contrast, have argued that control at work is a powerful moderator of the effects of work intensity, not only reducing its negative effects but also making it a source of creativity and self-development.

The critical perspective, largely embodied in labor process theory, has emphasized the potential of direct participation to lead to increased work intensity (Barker, 1993; Legge, 1995; Ramsay, 1977; Ramsay, Scholarios, and Harley, 2000; Willmott, 1993). Higher task discretion contributes to this through the internalized pressures it introduces for greater discretionary effort. At the same time, organizational participation allows management to heighten its control of employees by inculcating a vision of the employment relationship that gives priority to the objectives of the organization. Employees are led to internalize the importance of meeting, and improving on, performance objectives, which increases voluntary work effort and gives management greater scope to intensify work pressure.

The empirical evidence for an effect of direct participation on work intensity has been mixed. Some studies confirm that high involvement practices raise levels of work effort, while others have found no relationship with measures of work intensity (Boxall and Macky, 2014; Macky and Boxall, 2008; White et al., 2003). There have been few studies that have adopted a longitudinal methodology to assess the causal assumptions underlying the argument and to control for the effects of prior individual differences. However, two recent British analyses using longitudinal data find no effect of either task discretion or organizational participation in increasing work demands (Gallie et al., 2017b) or work exhaustion (Felstead et al., 2016).

The alternative view that the effects of work demands depend on the extent of control at work has been developed in the "demand–control" model of work strain (Karasek and Theorell, 1990). The negative effects of work demands are to be found primarily in work settings that combine high work demands with low levels of job control. There is now impressive longitudinal evidence that such conditions do lead to significantly higher risks of psychological distress, cardiac illness, and indeed cardiac-related mortality (Theorell et al., 2015, 2016; Kivimaki et al., 2012; Slopen et al., 2012; Stansfeld et al., 2012).

However, the proponents of demand–control theory (Karasek and Theorell, 1990) contend that the implications of high work demands are quite different in conditions where employees have a high level of control over task decisions. These are "active" jobs where job demands are a source of new learning experiences and stimulate greater creativity in finding improved ways to do the work. In conditions of high job control, work demands can contribute to self-development and a sense of fulfillment in the job. There has been much less research on the "active job" hypothesis than on the consequences of high demand and low job control. While, given the number of studies available, conclusions must be regarded as tentative, there is some support for the view that high control–high demand jobs are conducive to innovative work behavior. In particular, in a study involving some 3,000 Belgian employees from seventy-six companies across a range of industries, De Spiegelaere et al. (2015) found that such jobs were associated with the highest level of innovative work.

Direct Participation and Job Security

There has been growing evidence of the severe implications of job insecurity for employees' psychological and physical health—indeed its effects would appear to comparable to those of unemployment (Ferrie et al., 2002; Probst, 2009; Burchell, 2011; De Witte, Pienaar, and De Cuyper, 2016; Griep et al., 2016). An important cause of this is attributable to the negative effects of prolonged uncertainty (Probst, 2009; Schweiger and DeNisi, 1991). But job insecurity also implies a severe loss of control over the individual's work life and, as has been seen earlier, control has been found to be an important factor for health outcomes (Bordia et al., 2004).

Organizational change has long been found to be a major proximate source of job insecurity. It may make positions entirely redundant or affect the quality of employees' experiences at work. These two sources of insecurity are now increasingly recognized as distinct (Hellgren, Sverke, and Isaksson, 1999; Sverke, Hellgren, and Näswall, 2006; De Witte et al., 2010; Gallie et al., 2017a). Whereas traditionally job insecurity was equated with worry about loss of employment (job tenure or quantitative insecurity), there has been a growing awareness that organizational changes also may increase insecurity by threatening employees' status in the organization, their ability to exercise skills, and their scope for decision-making in their jobs (job status or qualitative insecurity). Evidence from Britain suggests that job status insecurity is more widely prevalent than job tenure insecurity (Gallie et al., 2017a). De Witte et al. (2010) have shown that the two types of job insecurity have independent, but equally strong, negative effects on well-being.

There is now growing evidence that participative decision-making may significantly reduce the prevalence of job insecurity (Gallie et al., 2017a). Moreover, this is the case for both job tenure insecurity and for job status insecurity. It also has been shown to reduce both the negative effects of job insecurity for job satisfaction, worker withdrawal, and turnover intentions (Probst, 2005) and the negative effects of organizational change for employee well-being (Bordia et al., 2004; De Witte, Vander Elst, and De Cuyper, 2015).

There are several possible reasons for these beneficial effects. Participation is conducive to better communications about the extent, phasing, and implications of change, thereby reducing the contagious effects of anxieties that accompany the spread of rumor (Schweiger and DeNisi, 1991; Smet et al., 2016). It is likely to lead to greater acceptance of the fairness of new arrangements as a result of the legitimacy of the procedures involved. Research on organizational justice theory (Greenberg, 1987, 1990) has shown that procedures tend to be considered fair to the extent that those subject to them have a degree of "process control," whereby they are able to present their own arguments on the merits of a case and feel that their opinions are taken into account (Colquitt et al., 2001; Clay-Warner, Reynolds, and Roman, 2005). Finally, involvement in decisions about the way in which reorganizations are handled restores some of the control that is eroded by job insecurity (Bordia et al., 2004; Probst, 2005). This could be seen as an extension of the demand–control model, whereby high levels of psychological demand (in this case arising from job insecurity) can be attenuated by greater employee control (Probst, 2005).

Conclusion

Taking as a point of departure the idea that to be meaningful work has to provide opportunities for people to pursue activities that they regard as worthwhile in terms of widely shared salient values, it has been seen that direct participation contributes to meaningful work in at least three ways: it allows for higher levels of self-determination, it increases opportunities for learning and skill development, and finally it helps to sustain good health.

The work value that is perhaps most consistently emphasized in the literature on meaningful work is that of self-determination. Empirical research has indeed shown this to be very widely important to people in economically developed societies. Direct participation intrinsically involves higher self-determination. People's principal concern relates to the immediate control that they have over their job tasks. It is the ability to exercise initiative in work through control over the choice of tasks, the methods of work, the effort that they have to expend, and the quality of the products or services that they are producing. But exercising influence over wider organizational decisions is also regarded as important by a substantial section of the workforce, even if it is envisaged more in terms of a right to consultation than of joint regulation.

While the intrinsic benefits of self-determination are very important, direct participation also enhances the meaningfulness of work by improving the opportunities for realizing other valued objectives. Of central importance in this respect is its effect on opportunities for learning at work. This is true both for relatively informal learning through the everyday activities of work and for more formal learning through the provision of training. The two types of direct participation are complementary: task discretion is particularly important for increasing the scope for informal learning, while organizational participation is a stronger lever for securing higher levels of training provision. Moreover, there are two findings in recent research that are particularly noteworthy. The first is that both forms of direct participation are associated with significantly higher quality of training in terms of its benefits for skill development. The second is that the benefits of direct participation are particularly strong for those in lower occupational categories, who have much more limited opportunities to express their discontent through leaving their jobs.

The most controversial issue with respect to direct participation has been whether it promotes or undermines good health. The involvement of workers in decision-making has been seen by some to be a technique by which management increases its demands on its employees and ratchets up the level of work intensity. While there has been conflicting evidence on this, the most rigorous longitudinal studies, which focus on change over time, and take account of prior differences between individuals, have not found this effect. There is moreover substantial evidence that participative decision-making, particularly in the form of control over the work tasks, moderates the impact of work pressure and reduces its negative effects on health. There is also growing evidence that it plays a protective role with respect to job insecurity, which has been found to be a major threat to mental and physical health. Participation both reduces the likelihood of experiencing job insecurity and reduces the negative effects of job insecurity when it occurs.

There is then substantial evidence that participation in decision-making, both at the level of the work task and in wider organizational decisions, is an essential precondition of meaningful work. It allows people to lead work lives that are congruent with values that are widely prevalent in the advanced societies—values of self-determination, self-development, and competence, and the preservation of health. Further, there is some evidence that it is particularly vital to those who are in positions of disadvantage, such as the low-skilled, for whom the exercise of influence through market power (or the threat of exit) are highly constrained.

References

Appelbaum, E., Bailey, T., Berg, P., and Kalleberg, A. L. (2000). *Manufacturing Advantage: Why high performance work systems pay off*. Ithaca, NY: Cornell University Press.

Argyris, C. (1964). *Integrating the Individual and the Organisation*. New York: Wiley.

Baard, P. P., Deci, E. L., and Ryan, R. M. (2004). "Intrinsic need satisfaction: A motivational basis of performance and well-being in two work settings." *Journal of Applied Social Psychology*, 34(10), 2045–68.

Barker, J. R. (1993). "Tightening the iron cage—concertive control in self-managing teams." *Administrative Science Quarterly*, 38(3), 408–37.

Baumeister, R. F., Vohs, K. D., Aaker, J. L., and Garbinsky, E. N. (2013). "Some key differences between a happy life and a meaningful life." *The Journal of Positive Psychology*, 8(6), 505–16.

Bentley, R., Kavanagh, A., Krnjacki, L., and Lamontagne, A. D. (2015). "A longitudinal analysis of changes in job control and mental health." *American Journal of Epidemiology*, 182(4), 328–34.

Bordia, P., Hunt, E., Paulsen, N., Tourish, D., and Di Fonzo, N. (2004). "Uncertainty during organizational change: Is it all about control?" *European Journal of Work and Organizational Psychology*, 13(3), 345–65.

Boxall, P. and Macky, K. (2014). "High-involvement work processes, work intensification and employee well-being." *Work, Employment & Society*, 28(6), 963–84.

Bryson, A. and Freeman, R. B. (2007). "What Voice Do British Workers Want?" In R. B. Freeman, P. Boxall, and P. Haynes (eds.), *What Workers Say: Employee Voice in the Anglo-American Workplace*, pp. 72–96. Ithaca, NY: Cornell University Press.

Burchell, B. (2011). "A Temporal Comparison of the Effects of Unemployment and Job Insecurity on Wellbeing." *Sociological Research Online*, 16(9), 1–20. Available at:http://www.socresonline.org.uk/16/1/9.html [accessed June 25, 2018].

Clay-Warner, J., Reynolds, J., and Roman, P. (2005). "Organizational justice and job satisfaction: A test of three competing models." *Social Justice Research*, 18(4), 391–409.

Colquitt, J. A., Conlon, D. E., Wesson, M. J., Porter, C. O. L. H., and Ng, K. Y. (2001). "Justice at the millennium: A meta-analytic review of 25 years of organizational justice research." *Journal of Applied Psychology*, 86(3), 425–45.

De Spiegelaere, S., Van Gyes, G., De Witte, H., and Van Hootegem, G. (2015). "Job design, work engagement and innovative work behavior: A multi-level study on Karasek's learning hypothesis." *Management Review*, 26(2), 123–37.

De Witte, H., De Cuyper, N., Handaja, Y., Sverke, M., Näswall, K., and Hellgren, J. (2010). "Associations between quantitative and qualitative job insecurity and well-being." *International Studies of Management and Organization*, 40(1), 40–56.

De Witte, H., Pienaar, J., and De Cuyper, N. (2016). "Review of 30 years of longitudinal studies on the association between job insecurity and health and well-being: Is there causal evidence?" *Australian Psychologist*, 51(1), 18–31.

De Witte, H., Vander Elst, T., and De Cuyper, N. (2015). "Job Insecurity, Health and Well-Being." In J. Vuori, R. Blonk, and R. Price (eds.), *Sustainable Working Lives: Managing Work Transitions and Health through the Life Course*, pp. 109–28. Dordrecht: Springer.

Deci, E. L., Connell, J. P., and Ryan, R. M. (1989). "Self-determination in a work organization." *Journal of Applied Psychology*, 74(4), 580–90.

Deci, E. L., Ryan, R. M., Gagne, M., Leone, D. R., Usunov, J., and Kornazheva, B. P. (2001). "Need satisfaction, motivation, and well-being in the work organizations of a former

Eastern Bloc country: A cross-cultural study of self-determination." *Personality and Social Psychology Bulletin*, 27(8), 930–42.

Dieckhoff, M., Jungblut, J. M., and O'Connell, P. J. (2007). "Job-Related Training in Europe: Do Institutions Matter?" In D. Gallie (ed.), *Employment Regimes and the Quality of Work*, pp. 77–104. Oxford: Oxford University Press.

Felstead, A., Fuller, A., Jewson, N., and Unwin, L. (2009). *Improving Working as Learning*. New York: Routledge.

Felstead, A., Gallie, D., Green, F., and Henseke, G. (2016). "The determinants of skills use and work pressure: A longitudinal analysis." *Economic and Industrial Democracy* [online]. Available at: https://doi.org/10.1177/0143831X16656412 [accessed June 25, 2018].

Felstead, A., Gallie, D., Green, F., and Zhou, Y. (2010). "Employee Involvement, the quality of training and the learning environment: An individual level analysis." *The International Journal of Human Resource Management*, 21(10), 1667–88.

Ferrie, J. E., Shipley, M. J., Stansfeld, S. A., and Marmot, M. (2002). "Effects of chronic job insecurity and change in job security on self-reported health, minor psychiatric morbidity, physiological measures, and health related behaviours in British civil servants: The Whitehall II study." *Journal of Epidemiology and Community Health*, 56(6), 450–4.

Frankl, V. (2004). *Man's Search for Meaning*. London: Rider.

Gallie, D. (2013). "Direct participation and the quality of work." *Human Relations*, 66(4), 453–73.

Gallie, D., Felstead, A., and Green, F. (2012). "Job preferences and the intrinsic quality of work: The changing attitudes of British employees 1992–2006." *Work, Employment and Society*, 26(5), 806–21.

Gallie, D., Felstead, A., Green, F., and Inanc, H. (2017a). "The hidden face of job insecurity." *Work, Employment and Society*, 31(1), 36–53.

Gallie, D. and Paugam, S. (2003). *Social Precarity and Social Integration*. Luxembourg: Office for Official Publications of the European Communities.

Gallie, D., Zhou, Y., Felstead, A., Green, F., and Henseke, G. (2017b). "The implications of direct participation for organisational commitment, job satisfaction and affective psychological well-being: A longitudinal analysis." *Industrial Relations Journal*, 48(2), 174–91.

Geary, J. and Sisson, K. (1994). *Europe: Direct Participation in Organisational Change. Introducing the EPOC Project*. European Foundation for the Improvement of Living and Working Conditions Working Paper No: WP/94/18/EN. Dublin: European Foundation for the Improvement of Living and Working Conditions.

Greenberg, J. (1987). "A taxonomy of organizational justice theories." *Academy of Management Review*, 12(1), 9–22.

Greenberg, J. (1990). "Looking fair vs being fair: Managing impressions of organizational justice." *Research in Organizational Behavior*, 12, 111–57.

Griep, Y., Kinnunen, U., Natti, J., De Cuyper, N., Mauno, S., Makikangas, A., and De Witte, H. (2016). "The effects of unemployment and perceived job insecurity: A comparison of their association with psychological and somatic complaints, self-rated health and life satisfaction." *International Archives of Occupational and Environmental Health*, 89(1), 147–62.

Heller, F., Pusic, E., Strauss, G., and Wilpert, B. (1998). *Organizational Participation: Myth and reality*. Oxford: Oxford University Press.

Heller, F., Wilders, M., Abell, P., and Warner, M. (1979). *What Do the British Want From Participation and Industrial Democracy?* London: Anglo-German Foundation.

Hellgren, J., Sverke, M., and Isaksson, K. (1999). "A two-dimensional approach to job insecurity: Consequences for employee attitudes and well-being." *European Journal of Work and Organizational Psychology*, 8(2), 179–95.

Hirschman, A. O. (1970). *Exit, Voice and Loyalty: Responses to decline in firms, organizations and states*. Cambridge, MA: Harvard University Press.

Hitlin, S. and Piliavin, J. A. (2004). "Values: Reviving a dormant concept." *Annual Review of Sociology 2004*, 30, 359–93.

Ilardi, B. C., Leone, D., Kasser, T., and Ryan, R. M. (1993). "Employee and supervisor ratings of motivation: Main effects and discrepancies associated with job satisfaction and adjustment in a factory setting." *Journal of Applied Psychology*, 23(21), 1789–805.

Inanc, H., Zhou, Y., Gallie, D., Felstead, A., and Green, F. (2015). "Direct participation and employee learning at work." *Work and Occupations*, 42(4), 447–75.

Industrial Democracy in Europe (IDE) International Research Group. (1981). *Industrial Democracy in Europe*. Oxford: Clarendon Press.

Karasek, R. and Theorell, T. (1990). *Healthy Work: Stress, Productivity and the Reconstruction of Work Life*. New York: Basic Books.

Kivimaki, M., Nyberg, S. T., Batty, G. D., Fransson, E. I., Heikkila, K., Alfredsson, L. et al. (2012). "Job strain as a risk factor for coronary heart disease: A collaborative meta-analysis of individual participant data." *Lancet*, 380(9852), 1491–7.

Kohn, M. L. and Schooler, C. (1982). "Job conditions and personality: A longitudinal assessment of their reciprocal effects." *American Journal of Sociology*, 87, 1257–86.

Lawler, E. (1986). *High Involvement Management*. San Francisco: Jossey-Bass.

Lawler, E., Mohrman, S. A., and Ledford, G. E. (1995). *Creating High Performance Organizations*. San Francisco: Jossey-Bass.

Leach, D. J., Wall, T. D., and Jackson, P. R. (2003). "The effect of empowerment on job knowledge: An empirical test involving operators of complex technology." *Journal of Occupational and Organizational Psychology*, 76, 27–52.

Legge, K. (1995). *Human Resource Management: Rhetorics and realities*. Basingstoke: Macmillan.

Luettel, A., Mueller, I., and Uher, R. (1991). *International Social Survey Programme—ISSP 1989 Work Orientations 1989 Codebook*. Koeln: Zentralarhiv fuer empirische Sozialforschung.

Macky, K. and Boxall, P. (2008). "High Involvement work processes, work intensification and employee well-being: A study of New Zealand worker experiences." *Asia Pacific Journal of Human Resources*, 46(1), 38–55.

Marshall, T. H. (1964). "Citizenship and Social Class." In T. H. Marshall, *Class, Citizenship and Social Development*, pp. 71–134. Chicago: University of Chicago Press.

Pateman, C. (1970). *Participation and Democratic Theory*. Cambridge: Cambridge University Press.

Probst, T. M. (2005). "Countering the negative effects of job insecurity through participative decision making; Lessons from the Demand–Control Model." *Journal of Occupational Health Psychology*, 10(4), 320–9.

Probst, T. M. (2009). "Job Insecurity, Unemployment and Organizational Well-Being. Oxymoron or Possibility?" In S. Cartwright and C. L. Cooper (eds.), *The Oxford Handbook of Organizational Well-Being*, pp. 387–410. Oxford: Oxford University Press.

Ramsay, H. (1977). "Cycles of control." *Sociology*, 11(3), 481–506.

Ramsay, H., Scholarios, D., and Harley, B. (2000). "Employees and high performance work systems: Testing inside the Black Box." *British Journal of Industrial Relations*, 38(4), 501–31.

Rokeach, M. (1973). *The Nature of Human Values*. New York: Free Press.

Rosso, B. D., Dekas, K. H., and Wrzesniewski, A. (2010). "On the meaning of work: A theoretical integration and review." *Research in Organizational Behavior*, 30, 91–127.

Ryan, R. and Deci, E. L. (2000). "Self-determination theory and the facilitation of intrinsic motivation, social development and well-being." *American Psychologist*, 55(1), 66–78.

Schwartz, S. H. (1992). "Universals in the content and structure of values: Theoretical advances and empirical tests in 20 countries." In M. Zanna (ed.), *Advances in Experimental Psychology* Vol. 25, pp. 1–65. New York: Academic Press.

Schwartz, S. H. (2012). "An Overview of the Schwartz Theory of Basic Values." *Online Readings in Psychology and Culture*, 2(1). Available at: https://doi.org/10.9707/2307-0919.1116 [accessed June 25, 2018].

Schwartz, S. H. and Bardi, A. (2001). "Value hierarchies across cultures: Taking a similarities perspective." *Journal of Cross-Cultural Psychology*, 32(3), 268–90.

Schweiger, D. M. and DeNisi, A. S. (1991). "Communication with employees following a merger: A longitudinal field experiment." *Academy of Management Journal*, 34(1), 110–35.

Siegrist, J. and Wahrendorf, M. (eds.) (2016). *Work Stress and Health in a Globalized Economy: The Model of Effort–Reward Imbalance*. AG Switzerland: Springer International Publishing.

Slopen, N., Glynn, R. J., Buring, J. E., Lewis, T. T., Williams, D. R., and Albert, M. A. (2012). "Job strain, job insecurity, and incident cardiovascular disease in the Women's Health Study: Results from a 10-year prospective study." *PLoS One*, 7(7). Available at: https://doi.org/10.1371/journal.pone.0040512 [accessed June 25, 2018].

Smet, K., Vander Elst, T., Griep, Y., and De Witte, H. (2016). "The explanatory role of rumours in the reciprocal relationship between organizational change communication and job insecurity: A within-person approach." *European Journal of Work and Organizational Psychology*, 25(5), 631–44.

Stansfeld, S. A., Shipley, M. J., Head, J., and Fuhrer, R. (2012). "Repeated job strain and the risk of depression: Longitudinal analyses from the Whitehall II Study." *American Journal of Public Health*, 102(12), 2360–6.

Super, D. E. and Sverko, B. (eds.) (1995). *Life Roles, Values, and Careers: International Findings of the Work Importance Study*. San Francisco: Jossey-Bass.

Sverke, M., Hellgren, J., and Näswall, K. (2006). *Job Insecurity: A literature review*. SALTSA—Joint Programme for Working Life Research in Europe Report No 1:2006. Stockholm: National Institute for Working Life.

Sverko, B. (2001). "Life roles and values in international perspective: Super's contribution through the Work Importance Study." *International Journal for Educational and Vocational Guidance*, 1(1–2), 121–30.

Theorell, T., Hammarstrom, A., Aronsson, G., Bendz, L. T., Grape, T., Hogstedt, C., Marteinsdottir, I., Skoog, I., and Hall, C. (2015). "A systematic review including meta-analysis of work environment and depressive symptoms." *BMC Public Health*, 15(738), 1–14.

Theorell, T., Jood, K., Jarvhom, L. S., Vingaard, E., Perk, J., Ostergren, P. O., and Hall, C. (2016). "A systematic review of studies in the contributions of the work environment to ischaemic heart disease development." *The European Journal of Public Health*, 26(3), 470–7.

Warr, P. (1987). *Work, Unemployment and Mental Health*. Oxford: Clarendon Press.

White, M., Hill, S., Mcgovern, P., Mills, C., and Smeaton, D. (2003). "'High-performance' management practices, working hours and work–life balance." *British Journal of Industrial Relations*, 41(2), 175–95.

Willmott, H. (1993). "Strength is ignorance; slavery is freedom: Managing culture in modern organizations." *Journal of Management Studies*, 30(4), 515–52.

CHAPTER 22

ACCOUNTING FOR MEANINGFUL WORK

MATTHEW HALL

INTRODUCTION

ALTHOUGH meaningful work as a concept has not featured in accounting research, accounting scholars and practitioners have considered how to account for work and human capital in organizational accounting systems. Drawing on these discussions, it is possible to examine how the basic features of an accounting system would likely impact the way in which meaningful work could be accounted for and managed in organizations. Basic features of an accounting system include recording and reporting on the financial performance and financial position of an entity, such as an organization, primarily through the recording of financial transactions between the entity and other parties. For example, a transaction may be a sale of goods between an organization and a customer (e.g. selling an iPhone), or the purchase of inventory by an organization from a supplier (e.g. raw materials). In the context of accounting for work, an accounting system will record and report on transactions involving the organization and individuals providing paid labor, for example the payment of wages to individuals engaged in work for an organization.[1]

In the following discussion, I will focus on how these features of an accounting system would likely have important implications for accounting for meaningful work. I will analyze how much of what counts as meaningful work would likely not be accounted for and recognized in an accounting system; and, even where it could be recognized, the accounting system will only account for meaningful work in a very particular and thus

[1] This is necessarily a simplification of the accounting process. For example, basic cash accounting records revenues when cash is received and records expenses when cash is paid out. In contrast, accrual accounting recognizes revenues when they are earned and recognizes expenses when they occur, which may or may not correspond to the receipt and payment of cash.

partial way. I will then critically analyze claims that a particular object like meaningful work is too subjective to be included in an accounting system, as well as consider whether it is productive to attempt to quantify and represent meaningful work in monetary terms. Moving from the sphere of financial accounting and reporting, I then examine how predominant perspectives on internal control and management accounting tend to neglect meaningful work and/or focus solely on its instrumental contribution toward organizational ends. In the final section I examine ways in which accounting and control practices could be mobilized to express values and beliefs, fulfill personal needs, and generate and sustain meaning at work, but at the same time also create more subtle forms of control that harness employee engagement for the sole purpose of enhancing organizational productivity.

MEANINGFUL WORK—DOES IT COUNT?

For financial accounting purposes, employees are typically not considered as part of the accounting entity (such as an organization), even though they form an important part of the organization's functioning.[2] As such, to be recognized in the organizational accounts, a person needs to perform work involving a transaction with the entity in question, such as the payment of a wage. Another feature is that transactions are recorded in the accounting system according to the monetary value at which the work was exchanged, such as the financial amount of a wage or salary. And, finally, from the organization's perspective, financial payments to individuals for work are typically recognized in the accounts as an expense rather than being recognized as an asset.

The basic features of an accounting system mean that only a very particular type of work is recognized and accounted for—that is, paid work. As such, where an individual provides labor for an organization without financial compensation, such as volunteering time, this is typically not recognized in the accounting system except in vary particular circumstances (Mook et al., 2005). Yet scholars of meaningful work argue that restricting the conception of work as relating to only paid activity is unsatisfactory on both historical and conceptual grounds. For example, packaging tasks into paid jobs is a very recent phenomenon in human history (Veltman, 2016). Furthermore, work includes all the activities which contribute to producing and reproducing a complex system of social cooperation, not only those emanating from a formal employment relationship (Yeoman, 2014). Indeed, much of what intuitively counts as work is not paid, such as rearing children, caring for sick family and friends, work around the house, homework, subsistence farming, and volunteer work (Veltman, 2016). If we accept the

---

[2] The entity concept in accounting relates to specifying the object or activity to be accounted for, which includes assumptions about the relationship between that entity and other parties (such as that between an organization as an accounting entity and other parties, such as employees). The implications of the entity concept for accounting for (meaningful) work are significant but well beyond the scope of this chapter—for further discussion, see, for example, Meyer (1973).

very reasonable idea that what counts as work can be in the form of both paid and unpaid work, and that meaningful work can be found in both the paid and unpaid varieties, then the accounting system as currently formulated would exclude all meaningful work that is not paid.

The exclusion of meaningful work that is unpaid is fundamentally important because whether meaningful work is recognized in an accounting system will influence its level of visibility and thus its importance. This is because, far from being engaged in an objective, value-free, technical enterprise, accountants are subjective constructors of reality, presenting and representing situations in limited and thus partial ways (Morgan, 1988; Hines, 1988). For example, discussions about the "value" of a nonprofit organization based on financial accounts that exclude the value of volunteer time will undoubtedly tend to downplay or render invisible the value of such volunteer work. This also resonates with criticisms of how mainstream economics renders invisible and thus valueless caring or reproductive work (e.g. Spencer, 2015; Waring, 1999). As such, the focus on accounting for transactions means that organizational accounts, as currently prepared and reported, would not recognize forms of meaningful work that are unpaid, thus reducing their level of visibility and potential value. As discussed in the next section, an accounting system's focus on the financial dimension of transactions also places limits on the ways in which meaningful work could be accounted for.

MEANINGFUL WORK—HOW TO ACCOUNT?

From the organization's perspective, financial payments to individuals for paid work are typically recognized as an expense. This expensing of paid work has the effect of reducing the net income of the organization, in contrast to viewing work as investments providing future benefits to the organization and reported as assets on the organization's balance sheet (Flamholtz, Bullen, and Hua, 2002). The typical approach of accounting for paid work as an expense has important implications for how the accounting system is likely to shape views on the value of meaningful work. For example, if an organization's stated objective is to generate a profit, then any increase in paid work (meaningful or otherwise) translates into an increase in expenses and thus a reduction in the reported profit of the organization. In this context, meaningful work may struggle to be seen as valuable because the accounting system would treat it not as an asset but as an expense to be minimized.

Work is also typically accounted for according to the monetary value of a transaction, such as the financial amount of a wage or salary. This means work is typically accounted for according to its exchange value, that is, the value at which labor is exchanged in a market transaction, such as a formal employment relationship between an employer and employee. As such, an organizational accounting system would only capture and recognize the meaningfulness of work to the extent that meaningfulness is reflected in the monetary value of a wage or other financial payment.

Whether the monetary value of a wage is reflective of the meaningfulness of work is complicated by the fact that meaningful work has objective and subjective dimensions. Objective accounts of meaningful work focus on providing a normative basis for what makes work meaningful. This can include work that enables autonomy, freedom, and social recognition (Yeoman, 2014), as well as exercising workers' human capabilities, supporting virtues like self-respect and dignity, and work that produces something of enduring value and seeks to integrate different elements of a worker's life (Veltman, 2016). The subjective dimension of meaningful work relates to a worker's personal experience of and feelings about the meaningfulness of her/his work. The objective and subjective dimensions may differ, as not everyone will experience work characterized by autonomy, freedom, or dignity as personally meaningful or fulfilling for them (Yeoman, 2014).

Although an open question, on first inspection it appears somewhat unlikely that the monetary value of a wage would necessarily correspond to or be reflective of the meaningfulness of work. For example, jobs that are objectively meaningful are often considered to be those in which people directly help others, alleviate suffering, make people happier or healthy, improve the environment, or create products making life better for people (Yeoman, 2014). Although not excluding the potential for all types of work to include these dimensions, in this context we can readily envisage particular types of jobs, such as healthcare, teaching, early childhood education, elderly care, and many other vocations, as well as work producing essential and helpful products. While some of this work may be associated with relatively high wages, such as doctors, much work involving caring for and helping others seems to be associated with relatively low wages.[3] Thus, although necessarily preliminary, the monetary value of wages may bear little correspondence to or reflection of the objective meaningfulness of particular jobs. This is even more problematic in the context of the subjective dimension of meaningful work. As an accounting system focuses on recording verified financial transactions between the organization and other parties, in its current formulation it is not equipped to incorporate subjective accounts of how much meaning individual employees personally experience in their work.

The focus on monetary transactions further highlights the way in which the partiality of accounting systems would likely impact the recognition of meaningful work. In particular, as accounting systems tend to focus on those aspects of organizational reality that are quantifiable, particularly in monetary terms, they ignore those aspects that are not quantifiable in this way (Morgan, 1988). Again, there are parallels with economics. As Spencer (2015) notes, the formalism of mainstream economics, which is analogous to standard financial accounting practices, only permits the treatment of work in units of time and money because these are easily inserted into formal models. In the process, representations of the value of work that cannot be reflected in wages typically do not

[3] For example, see recent debates over low pay for early childhood educators (http://theconversation.com/early-childhood-educators-rely-on-families-to-prop-up-low-income-research-finds-69283), nurses (http://theconversation.com/soon-nurses-will-pay-for-their-education-they-should-demand-higher-wages-63011), or aged care workers (http://www.smh.com.au/federal-politics/political-news/12b-pay-rise-incentive-for-aged-care-workers-20130304-2fh9o.html) [all accessed April 7, 2017].

find a place in such formal modeling (Spencer, 2015), just as the value of work beyond that reflected in the financial amount of a wage typically has no place in the financial accounts as conventionally prepared and reported. Given the limitations associated with accounting for only the wages paid to employees, the next section examines efforts by accountants to estimate the value of work using financial models or other valuation methods to account for the worth of employees.

ESTIMATING THE VALUE
OF MEANINGFUL WORK

Accounting for employees as assets has spurred much debate in the area of "human resource accounting," particularly in modern post-industrial economies where organizations increasingly view intellectual property, and specifically so-called "human capital," as core assets (Flamholtz and Main, 1999). A stated challenge in estimating the value of employees as assets is that it involves more subjectivity than measuring physical assets. This subjectivity could potentially result in reduced comparability between organizations (Flamholtz, Bullen, and Hua, 2002; Steen, Welch, and McCormack, 2011) and the potential for manipulation through certain measurement choices, reflecting debate over whether a satisfactory valuation methodology can be provided to reflect employees as assets (Morrow, 1996; Steen, Welch, and McCormack, 2011).[4] Indeed, the problem of producing credible financial valuations of human capital has been linked to the lack of uptake and development of human capital reporting (Scraggs et al., 2013). Given the likely subjectivity involved in estimating the value of meaningful work, the concerns documented in relation to estimating the value of employees as assets would also likely be key impediments to any efforts to estimate the value of meaningful work in organizations.

Although concerns over subjectivity are no doubt legitimate, they tend to ignore or downplay several important issues. One is that the subjectivity of an accounting or valuation method is connected to the extent of investment in the systems, experts, standards, and procedures typically required to generate information that is considered sufficiently objective. Put simply, methods to estimate the value of meaningful work could easily be considered too subjective if little investment has been made in testing and then agreeing on valuation methods that are potentially more robust. In this vein, some companies have invested the time and resources to produce credible estimates of human resources as intangible assets on the balance sheet. For example, Infosys reports a human resource valuation in its balance sheet based on a complex valuation model. This model takes into account both the increase in future earnings of employees during their employment, as well as any benefits derived by society once employees leave the company owing to their

---

[4] Interestingly, one type of employee, the football player, is regularly recognized as an asset on the balance sheet of football clubs (e.g. Morrow, 1996).

potentially enhanced human capital from training and employee development.[5] Estimating the value of unpaid work can involve developing systems to impute the monetary value of volunteer hours contributed toward the efforts of organizations (Mook et al., 2005). This is also the approach pursued by the World Bank, which imputes the monetary value of factors typically not accounted for in standard measures of GDP, such as the value of unpaid work or elements of human capital (Waring, 1999).

More broadly, there is ample evidence that developing systems for producing accounting measures can take significant time and effort. For example, during the 1854 Mercantile Laws Commission in the UK, Lord Curriehill and others seriously questioned "the impracticability of ascertaining correctly, at any time, the amount or even the existence of profits" (Ruff, 2013). In contrast, today the reporting of profit is a routine occurrence, built on the substantial efforts of accountants and auditors and a vast array of accounting and auditing standards. More recently, many debates have ensued about the (im)possibility of measuring assets using the "fair value" basis (e.g. Laux and Leuz, 2009), yet organizations now regularly produce fair value estimates and recognize them on balance sheets notwithstanding evidence that estimates of the fair value of certain categories of assets are seemingly very subjective (Barker and Schulte, 2017). As such, the production of more objective information about a new accounting object like meaningful work is perhaps better thought of as a process requiring significant effort rather than ruling out its measurement altogether because of a claim that subjectivity is somehow intrinsic to the object itself.

Beyond investments in systems and procedures, it is also important to consider the extent to which the subjectivity of estimates should be prioritized. For example, in the context of measuring social value, practitioners who had epistemic beliefs oriented toward prioritizing the use of only standardized and objective data tended to exclude certain types of benefits from their social value calculations. In contrast, practitioners in other settings who had epistemic beliefs prioritizing the use of data obtained directly from stakeholders tended to include those very same benefits in their calculations of social value (Hall, Millo, and Barman, 2015). This shows how the choice to prioritize subjectivity in an accounting system will, as a consequence, exclude many objects, such as meaningful work, that cannot (or cannot yet) meet the current standards. Yet an accounting system could also prioritize other characteristics such as inclusivity or representativeness, thus potentially accepting more subjective estimates of objects like meaningful work as part of efforts to ensure they are not excluded from the accounting process. The prioritization of certain characteristics in the process of representation further serves to highlight how practices of accounting and evaluation reflect different normative underpinnings and assumptions regarding the "right" way to go about measuring and accounting for the performance and contributions of organizations (e.g. Hall, 2014; Neesham, McCormick, and Greenwood, 2017).

Beyond issues of investment and the feasibility of producing estimates lies the question of whether it is productive to actually try and quantify meaningful work in

---

[5] See https://www.infosys.com/investors/reports-filings/Documents/additional-information-2011-12.pdf for more detail [accessed March 7, 2018].

monetary terms at all. In particular, choices over whether to develop methods to monetize the value of meaningful work provide an exemplary illustration of a broader dilemma of quantification, eloquently explained by the twentieth-century British philosopher Bernard Williams. In reflecting on those who advocate for values such as social justice, welfare, sustainability, and conservation (and, by extension, meaningful work), Williams (1972: 88–9) stated that,

> Again and again defenders of such values are faced with the dilemma, of either refusing to quantify the value in question, in which case it disappears from the sum altogether, or else of trying to attach some quantity to it, in which case they misrepresent what they are about and also usually lose the argument, since the quantified value is not enough to tip the scale.

Monetizing the value of meaningful work poses the same dilemma. On the one hand, attempts to monetize meaningful work could be abandoned, but this could create difficulties in trying to demonstrate the value of meaningful work in contexts where showing quantified, and particularly monetized, value is becoming the new norm. On the other hand, monetizing the meaningfulness of work runs the risk of not only underestimating its value, but, critically, of appearing to represent the value of meaningful work such that the generation of a monetary return was its actual aim, rather than only one (among many) possible representations of its value.

Given the likely problematic nature of quantifying meaningful work using monetary estimates, other developments have focused on alternative forms of representation such as non-financial metrics and narrative accounts. For example, there has been a focus on developing employee well-being indexes to measure and report on the health of the workplace.[6] This is similar to the UN's focus on moving away from imputing monetary values and trying to represent human development using measures such as the human development index (Waring, 1999).[7] Well-being indexes aim to establish common measures that can be used across organizations and could potentially be included in senior management bonuses (Hannan, 2016). Given the recency of these developments, it is an open question as to whether and how well such indexes can really capture "well-being." Perhaps more importantly, it is not clear whether indexes of this type are focused on trying to measure objective characteristics of the workplace (such as whether work is arranged and organized in ways to enable expression of capabilities, autonomy, freedom, and dignity, for example) or the subjective experience of employees, such as whether employees feel engaged and satisfied at work. As workers can over value or undervalue their work (Veltman, 2016), this distinction is important because an index showing that workers feel satisfied or engaged does not necessarily mean that an organization is providing opportunities for objectively meaningful work. As such, a focus on measuring

---

[6] See, for example, https://www2.deloitte.com/au/en/pages/about-deloitte/solutions/wellbeing-work-index-2017.html [accessed July 11, 2018].

[7] This is not to downplay the potentially problematic nature of *any* efforts (monetary or otherwise) to quantify and develop standardized measures (see, for example, Espeland and Sauder, 2007; Espeland and Stevens, 2009).

objective characteristics of the workplace is potentially more powerful because it could address whether and how workplaces as a whole can provide opportunities for objectively meaningful work.

Other policy options have eschewed efforts to account for work in quantified terms and focused on the production of narrative reports. Here suggestions include reporting on worker health and safety, retention, training, morale, and workforce performance (Scraggs et al., 2013). While potentially promising and part of wider moves to supplement financial accounts with social and environmental accounts (e.g. Global Reporting Initiative), evidence suggests that because of the voluntary and more unstructured nature of such disclosures, companies tend to disclose only the bare minimum (Scraggs et al., 2013). More fundamentally, narrative accounts of this kind, even if they are rigorous and comprehensive, are somewhat limited because they have no direct impact on a firm's balance sheet or bottom line, typically the prime focus of senior executives and boards of directors.

In summary, a typical accounting system would likely exclude unpaid forms of meaningful work and only record the value of paid meaningful work with reference to the monetary value of a transaction, such as the financial amount of a wage or salary. Efforts to estimate (rather than just record) the value of meaningful work would likely face concerns over its subjectivity, which has prompted reflection on moving away from efforts to monetize meaningful work toward other means of accounting including non-financial metrics and narrative accounts. The next section moves from the sphere of financial accounting and reporting to examine the treatment of meaningful work in the internal accounting and control practices of organizations.

ACCOUNTING AND CONTROL PRACTICES AND MEANINGFUL WORK

Organizations have a variety of accounting and control practices designed to direct attention, incentivize particular behaviors, provide information for building knowledge and decision-making processes, and allocate responsibility and accountability for resource allocation and performance. Although it is not explicitly addressed, existing research on the design and operation of accounting and control practices seemingly treats meaningful work in two ways: it assumes the absence of meaningful work in the workplace, and/or it considers meaningful work from an instrumental perspective.

An Absence of Meaningful Work

Drawing from predominately economic-driven approaches, much analysis of the operation of accounting and control practices is premised on an absence of meaningful work. From this viewpoint, work is seen as an activity having merely instrumental or extrinsic value (Veltman, 2016). This relates to classic ideas in mainstream economics where it is assumed work is a disutility whereby individuals suffer some personal loss through the act of work, thus requiring some form of compensation for the time lost (Spencer, 2015). Analysis of accounting and control practices premised on these ideas focuses on how to provide incentives to promote and direct effort toward organizationally productive tasks, and to provide information to individuals in order to make decisions in ways that seek to improve organizational performance (e.g. Bonner and Sprinkle, 2002). For example, agency theory assumes individuals will shirk (i.e. exert no effort) on a task unless it can contribute to their economic well-being (Bonner and Sprinkle, 2002). Under this perspective, practices such as performance-contingent incentives, typified through bonus payments linked to specified levels of performance, have become commonplace in for-profit organizations as well as the public and non-profit sectors (e.g. Gibbons, 1998; Speckbacher, 2011). In fact, pay-for-performance systems can be viewed as the uncontested instrument of choice for eliciting higher performance from employees (Frey and Jegen, 2001).

Such accounting and control practices are focused on the economic dimensions of work and tend to exclude the possibility that work can and does serve other purposes. There is little consideration of the social and moral dimensions of work where people can value work for its own sake and perform work for non-economic reasons (Spencer, 2015). For example, over the past three decades, Americans have consistently identified meaningful work as the most important feature they seek out in a job, ahead of income, job security, promotions, and hours (Michaelson et al., 2013). In this context, the strong focus on the potential for "shirking" in economic approaches is somewhat at odds with the non-economic motivations for carrying out work. Scholars have shown how in such contexts the provision of monetary incentives can "crowd out" non-economic motivations for work such as intrinsic motivation (see Frey and Jegen, 2001). More critical views point to the way in which the picture of workers as incorrigible "shirkers" provides employers with a ready-made excuse to blame them for work resistance, and can function to support more traditional, top-down governance and control systems that seek to curtail the discretionary power and freedom of workers (Spencer, 2015).

Meaningful Work and Organizational Performance

Where existing research does acknowledge the presence and possibility of meaningful work, it does so from an instrumental perspective premised on enhancing organizational performance. In this perspective, management's concern for meaningful work is instrumentally attentive to organizational aims and addresses the needs of employees only so far as their satisfaction is likely to promote improved financial outcomes (Yeoman, 2014). Management's concern is not surprising given the considerable evidence that employees' subjective experience of meaningful work is associated with a range of desirable consequences for organizations, including increased employee job performance, organizational citizenship behaviors, organizational commitment, occupational identification, and customer satisfaction (Michaelson et al., 2013). Indeed, as noted earlier, there has been increased focus on employee engagement and well-being surveys and using the resulting scores in firms' accounting and control systems. Importantly, however, employee engagement is not typically considered as an end in itself, but as a means to encourage improved outcomes for the organization, such as higher productivity, customer service, and employee retention (e.g. Mone and London, 2014).

Research also shows how accounting and control practices can direct employee effort and engagement using subtler forms of control. For example, managers can use ideological control to focus workers' attention on seemingly shared values as a way to reduce resistance to a newly implemented financially oriented control system (Kraus, Kennergren, and von Unge, 2017). This can form part of efforts to engage employees with positive values and ideals that managers believe the company would benefit most from employees believing in (Alvesson and Karreman, 2004). Indeed, a long line of accounting research has shown the power of seemingly mundane metrics and other accounting practices to reorganize and reshape organizations to better achieve commercial, financial, or other shareholder-focused ends, often under the guise of seemingly beneficial programs (e.g. Dent, 1991; Ezzamel, Lilley, and Wilmott, 2004; Ezzamel, Wilmott, and Worthington, 2008). In these ways, efforts to measure and focus on employee engagement, well-being, or satisfaction can be viewed as a subtler way in which to enroll employees into managerial change initiatives, premised on employee engagement but typically aimed at shifting employees' focus toward organizationally productive ends.

Mobilizing Accounting and Control Practices for Meaningful Work

Empirical work focused on linking management practices, such as accounting and control systems, to organizational members' experienced meaningfulness of work is relatively rare (Michaelson et al., 2013). But there has been related research on how accounting and control practices can affect the subjective experience of work, primarily focused on links with employees' self-reported job satisfaction, psychological empowerment, or intrinsic motivation (e.g. Chenhall and Brownell, 1988; Hall, 2008; Wong-On-Wing, Guo, and Lui, 2010; Kunz, 2015). For example, providing adequate performance information to employees can improve the subjective meaningfulness of work by providing feedback about task behavior and performance (Luckett and Eggleton, 1991; Hall, 2008). In contrast, where a performance measurement system is inadequate in measuring the individual's contribution to the organization and the outcomes achieved, the individual will be demotivated and disengaged in their work, leading to job dissatisfaction and likely reducing the subjective meaningfulness of the work undertaken (Luckett and Eggleton, 1991).

Other research has focused on links between incentives, whether in the form of cash bonuses, salary increases, stock options, shares, or even non-monetary rewards like praise and recognition, and employee motivation and performance. It is clear from prior research that tangible rewards for task performance have a negative effect on intrinsic motivation for interesting tasks (Frey and Jegen, 2001). As meaningful work is also likely to be interesting work, it would be expected that tangible rewards for task performance could also crowd out the experienced meaningfulness of work. But this does not necessarily mean that incentives per se will impact negatively on meaningful work. For example, verbal rewards can enhance intrinsic motivation, and tangible rewards do not necessarily crowd out intrinsic motivation when they are unexpected or not related to task behavior (Frey and Jegen, 2001). Furthermore, organizational incentive practices are likely to crowd in intrinsic motivation if the individuals affected perceive them to be supportive of their work. For example, in a university research context, performance evaluation and incentive structures providing rewards in the form of increased opportunities to do more research were seen to facilitate researchers' autonomous motivation to engage in research that was a source of passion and meaning in their lives (Sutton and Brown, 2016). In these cases, self-esteem can be fostered, and individuals can feel they are given more freedom to act, thus enlarging self-determination (Frey and Jegen, 2001) and potentially the experienced meaningfulness of work.

Research has also analyzed important distinctions between the nature of formalization evident in organizations and how this interacts with employees' experience of work. For example, Adler and Borys (1996) distinguish between two types of bureaucracy, coercive and enabling, and argue that whether the impact of formalization on employee attitudes is positive or negative depends on whether and how it enables employees to master their work or is a means by which management tries to coerce employees' effort and compliance. Subsequent research in accounting shows how control systems can be designed to draw on employees' skills and intelligence by enabling workers to repair control practices through discussing practical problems in existing procedures, by making the design of control practices accessible and transparent to all employees, by situating work within a broader organizational context, and through flexibility and discretion in how employees use control practices (Ahrens and Chapman, 2004; Jordan and Messner, 2012; Wouters and Wilderom, 2008; Wouters and Roijmans, 2011). While this research has not been linked with meaningful work per se, it is reasonable to expect that the development and mobilization of enabling rather than coercive control practices may facilitate meaningful work. For example, Yeoman (2014) discusses how meaningful work requires a mode of thought and action where workers can develop principles, adapt rules, and respond to the variety of problems at hand, which resonates with the characteristics of a more enabling approach to control practices.

Research is also suggestive of how performance measurement systems can be deployed in ways to enhance the experienced meaningfulness of work, particularly through providing a context whereby employees can express their beliefs and the value and meaning of their work. Chenhall, Hall, and Smith (2017) show how this expressive role is facilitated through performance measurement systems that are easily understandable and accessible to employees, operate in more playful ways emphasizing jokes, laughter, and trial and error, and include measures directly addressing the important values and beliefs identified by employees. This resonates with the way in which employees experience the prosocial impact of their work more vividly when they are directly connected to the beneficiaries of their work, such as clients, customers, patients, and other end users (Michaelson et al., 2013). In this way, performance measurement systems containing measures illustrating the end impact of employees' work could play an important role in reinforcing employees' connections with beneficiaries and thus potentially enhance the experienced meaningfulness of their work.

In summary, dominant perspectives on accounting and control tend to assume meaningful work does not exist, or that it can be usefully mobilized to enhance organizational productivity. These perspectives notwithstanding, some research focuses more directly on how accounting and control practices could play a stronger role in expressing employee values and generating meaning at work. Yet this research is also limited in its focus on the subjective experiences of employees in the workplace. As such, it is unclear whether and how the operation of accounting, incentives, and performance measurement systems impacts the objective dimensions of meaningful work, that is, the opportunities for employees to engage in work that genuinely exercises capabilities, expresses virtues, and enables freedom and autonomy.

CONCLUSION

Given its recent conceptualization (Yeoman, 2014; Veltman, 2016), meaningful work has not been addressed explicitly in existing accounting research. By drawing on longer standing debates concerning accounting for work and estimating the value of employees, I have focused on examining how features of a typical accounting system would impact the treatment of meaningful work in organizational accounts. This served to illustrate how the focus on accounting for transactions means that organizational accounts would not recognize forms of meaningful work that are unpaid. Where meaningful work takes form in paid work, it would likely be accounted for in particular and thus partial ways, such as being treated as an expense and only accounting for its financial value as evidenced by a monetary transaction. Efforts to move beyond transactions and estimate the value of meaningful work would likely face concerns over the subjectivity of estimates and the lack of comparability of valuation methods between organizations. But rather than rule out the measurement of meaningful work altogether, developing more robust methods of valuation can be thought of as a process requiring significant effort and investment, as is the case in other domains of accounting, such as estimating the fair values of assets using valuation models. The discussion also reflected on whether it is productive to attempt to quantify and represent meaningful work in monetary terms at all, particularly where casting meaningful work in such ways may reinforce the idea of work as a purely economic exchange rather than as a fundamental human need (Yeoman, 2014).

The analysis also focused on how the design and operation of accounting and control practices is embedded in perspectives either assuming the absence of meaningful work in the workplace, or examining it as a means to enhance organizational performance. Yet even in these dominant perspectives there has been some consideration of how accounting and control practices could potentially be mobilized to enhance the experienced meaningfulness of work, such as the use of incentive practices employees perceive to be supportive of their work, the operation of control practices enabling employees to master their work by drawing on their skills and intelligence, and the use of performance measurement systems to enable employees to express their beliefs and the value and meaning of their work. Yet the contribution of this research to the context of meaningful work is limited by its focus on employees' subjective experiences of work, with little analysis of how the objective dimensions of meaningful work might be shaped or influenced by the operation of accounting and control practices.

It has long been recognized that accountants and accounting systems are not mere recorders of objective facts about an organization's financial dealings, but provide a particular representation of activities and events. In this way, whether and how meaningful work could be accounted for is fundamentally important because it will shape the way it can become more visible and thus valuable, or remain hidden and thereby rendered irrelevant. As Waring (1999) notes, the reproduction of the human species is left out of the economic equation, for all the models would collapse with its sheer magnitude if its value were imputed. Similarly, we can speculate how the balance sheet of many organizations might collapse under the weight of the value of meaningful work carried out and contributed by employees, or, conversely, how the balance sheets of other organizations might shrink drastically in response to a lack of opportunities for meaningful work. With these new balance sheets in mind, we could imagine a future where the most "profitable" organizations are those providing opportunities for meaningful work as a central and integral part of organizational life. And, in this future, it might be organizations like Barnardos, rather than British American Tobacco, sitting atop a list of the most valuable companies.

But the development of these new balance sheets would require fundamental changes to conceptual frameworks, accounting standards, and organizational accounting systems premised on broader changes regarding the purpose of work and organizations. For example, there are ongoing debates about whether the purpose of organizations is to focus on profit maximization for shareholders or to enable a variety of organizational stakeholders to flourish (e.g. Freeman et al., 2010; Friedman, 1962; Jensen, 2001). In this context, it is difficult to envisage how opportunities for meaningful work could be repositioned as an organizational asset in an accounting system unless the purpose of a firm is seen to include the interests of a wider variety of stakeholders rather than simply maximizing returns to shareholders. Furthermore, the possibility of conceiving of accounting and control practices as being primarily oriented toward enhancing opportunities for meaningful work would depend on it being recognized as a fundamental human need rather than only an instrumental activity geared toward enhanced organizational productivity (Yeoman, 2014; Veltman, 2016). As accounting systems provide a partial representation of activities and events, whether these fundamental changes can come to fruition will impact how meaningful work is made visible and potentially valuable in organizations and society more generally.

ACKNOWLEDGMENTS

Thanks to Marc Thompson and Richard Pucci for feedback on earlier drafts.

REFERENCES

Adler, P. S. and Borys, B. (1996). "Two types of bureaucracy: Enabling and coercive." *Administrative Science Quarterly*, 41(1), 61–89.

Ahrens, T. and Chapman, C. S. (2004). "Accounting for flexibility and efficiency: A field study of management control systems in a restaurant chain." *Contemporary Accounting Research*, 21(2), 271–301.

Alvesson, M. and Kärreman, D. (2004). "Interfaces of control: Technocratic and socio-ideological control in a global management consultancy firm." *Accounting, Organizations and Society*, 29(3–4), 423–44.

Barker, R. and Schulte, S. (2017). "Representing the market perspective: Fair value measurement for non-financial assets." *Accounting, Organizations and Society*, 56, 55–67.

Bonner, S. E. and Sprinkle, G. B. (2002). "The effects of monetary incentives on effort and task performance: Theories, evidence, and a framework for research." *Accounting, Organizations and Society*, 27, 303–45.

Chenhall, R. and Brownell, P. (1988). "The effect of participative budgeting on job satisfaction and performance: Role ambiguity as an intervening variable." *Accounting, Organizations and Society*, 13(3), 225–33.

Chenhall, R., Hall, M., and Smith, D. (2017). "The expressive role of performance measurement systems: A field study of a mental health development project." *Accounting, Organizations and Society*, 63, 60–75.

Dent, J. F. (1991). "Accounting and organizational cultures: A field study of the emergence of a new organizational reality." *Accounting, Organizations and Society*, 16(8), 705–32.

Espeland, W. N. and Sauder, M. (2007). "Rankings and reactivity: How public measures recreate social worlds." *American Journal of Sociology*, 113(1), 1–40.

Espeland, W. N. and Stevens, M. L. (2009). "A sociology of quantification." *European Journal of Sociology*, 49, 401–36.

Ezzamel, M., Lilley, S., and Willmott, H. (2004). "Accounting representation and the road to commercial salvation." *Accounting, Organizations and Society*, 29(8), 783–813.

Ezzamel, M., Willmott, H., and Worthington, F. (2008). "Manufacturing shareholder value: The role of accounting in organizational transformation." *Accounting, Organizations and Society*, 33(2–3), 107–40.

Flamholtz, E. G., Bullen, M. L., and Hua, W. (2002). "Human resource accounting: A historical perspective and future implications." *Management Decision*, 40, 947–54.

Flamholtz, E. G. and Main, E. D. (1999). "Current issues, recent advancements, and future directions in human resource accounting." *Journal of Human Resource Costing & Accounting*, 4, 11–20.

Freeman, R. E., Harrison, J. S., Wicks, A. C., Parmar, B. L., and De Colle, S. (2010). *Stakeholder Theory: The state of the art*. Cambridge: Cambridge University Press.

Frey, B. and Jegen, R. (2001). "Motivation crowding theory." *Journal of Economic Surveys*, 15(5), 589–611.

Friedman, M. (1962). *Capitalism and Freedom*. Chicago: University of Chicago Press and Phoenix Books.

Gibbons, R. (1998). "Incentives in organizations." *The Journal of Economic Perspectives*, 12, 115–32.

Hall, M. (2008). "The effect of comprehensive performance measurement systems on role clarity, psychological empowerment and managerial performance." *Accounting, Organizations and Society*, 33(2–3), 141–63.

Hall, M. (2014). "Evaluation logics in the third sector." *Voluntas: International Journal of Voluntary and Nonprofit Organizations*, 25, 307–36.

Hall, M., Millo, Y., and Barman, E. (2015). "Who and what really counts? Stakeholder prioritisation and accounting for social value." *Journal of Management Studies*, 52, 907–34.

Hannan, W. (2016). "Wellbeing survey tied to CEO pay." The Australian, November 23.

Hines, R. D. (1988). "Financial accounting: in communicating reality, we construct reality." *Accounting, Organizations and Society*, 13, 251–61.

Jensen, M. C. (2001). "Value maximization, stakeholder theory, and the corporate objective function." *European Financial Management*, 7(3), 297–317.

Jordan, S. and Messner, M. (2012). "Enabling control and the problem of incomplete performance indicators." *Accounting, Organizations and Society*, 37(8), 544–64.

Kraus, K., Kennergren, C., and von Unge, A. (2017). "The interplay between ideological control and formal management control systems: A case study of a non-governmental organization." *Accounting, Organizations and Society*, 63, 42–59.

Kunz, J. (2015). "Objectivity and subjectivity in performance evaluation and autonomous motivation: An exploratory study." *Management Accounting Research*, 27, 27–46.

Laux, C. and Leuz, C. (2009). "The crisis of fair value accounting: Making sense of the recent debate." *Accounting, Organizations and Society*, 34, 826–34.

Luckett, P. F. and Eggleton, I. R. C. (1991). "Feedback and management accounting: A review of research into behavioural consequences." *Accounting, Organizations and Society*, 16, 371–94.

Meyer, P. E. (1973). "The accounting entity." *Abacus*, 9(2), 116–26.

Michaelson, C., Pratt, M. G., Grant, A. M., and Dunn, C. P. (2013). "Meaningful work: Connecting business ethics and organization studies." *Journal of Business Ethics*, 121, 77–90.

Mone, E. M. and London, M. (2014). *Employee Engagement through Effective Performance Management: A practical guide for managers*. Abingdon: Routledge.

Mook, L., Sousa, J., Elgie, S., and Quarter, J. (2005). "Accounting for the value of volunteer contributions." *Nonprofit Management and Leadership*, 15, 401–15.

Morgan, G. (1988). "Accounting as reality construction: Towards a new epistemology for accounting practice." *Accounting, Organizations and Society*, 13, 477–85.

Morrow, S. (1996). "Football players as human assets. Measurement as the critical factor in asset recognition: A case study investigation." *Journal of Human Resource Costing & Accounting*, 1, 75–97.

Neesham, C., McCormick, L., and Greenwood, M. (2017). "When paradigms meet: Interacting perspectives on evaluation in the non-profit sector." *Financial Accountability & Management*, 33, 192–219.

Ruff, K. (2013). "The Role of Intermediaries in Social Accounting: Insights from Effective Transparency Systems." In L. Mook (ed.), *Accounting for Social Value*, pp. 230–48. Toronto: University of Toronto Press.

Scraggs, E., van Stolk, C., Janta, B., Celia, C., Goshev, S., van Welsum, D., Patil, S., and Villalba-van-Dijk, L. (2013). *Encouraging Employers to use Human Capital Reporting: A literature review of implementation options*. Briefing paper, February. London: UK Commission for Employment and Skills.

Speckbacher, G. (2011). "The use of incentives in non-profit organizations." *Non-profit and Voluntary Sector Quarterly*, 45, 1006–25.

Spencer, D. A. (2015). "Developing an understanding of meaningful work in economics: The case for a heterodox economics of work." *Cambridge Journal of Economics*, 39, 675–88.

Steen, A., Welch, D., and McCormack, D. (2011). "Conflicting conceptualizations of human resource accounting." *Journal of Human Resource Costing & Accounting*, 15, 299–312.

Sutton, N. C. and Brown, D. A. (2016). "The illusion of no control: Management control systems facilitating autonomous motivation in university." *Accounting and Finance*, 56, 577–604.

Veltman, A. (2016). *Meaningful Work*. Oxford: Oxford University Press.

Waring, M. (1999). *Counting for Nothing: What men value and what women are worth*, 2nd edn. Toronto: University of Toronto Press.

Williams, B. (1972). *Morality: An introduction to ethics*. Cambridge: Cambridge University Press.

Wong-On-Wing, B., Guo, L., and Lui, G. (2010). "Intrinsic and extrinsic motivation and participation in budgeting: Antecedents and consequences." *Behavioral Research in Accounting*, 22, 133–53.

Wouters, M. and Roijmans, D. (2011). "Using prototypes to induce experimentation and knowledge integration in the development of enabling accounting information." *Contemporary Accounting Research*, 28(2), 708–36.

Wouters, M. and Wilderom, C. (2008). "Developing performance-measurement systems as enabling formalization: A longitudinal field study of a logistics department." *Accounting, Organizations and Society*, 33(4–5), 488–516.

Yeoman, R. (2014). *Meaningful Work and Workplace Democracy: A philosophy of work and a politics of meaningfulness*. Basingstoke: Palgrave MacMillan.

CHAPTER 23

......

MEANINGFUL WORK
AND FAMILY

How does the Pursuit of Meaningful Work Impact one's Family?

......

EVGENIA I. LYSOVA

C: How could you do this to us? How could you walk away from the operation?

J: I was not walking away from anything. I was walking towards... some kind of resolution for two little girls whose lives were stolen from them. I was walking towards something I thought was bigger than myself.

C: You are a brilliant, loving man and amazing detective... but right now you are a selfish child. You know, you will storm into a building, armed with a loaded gun, risking your life to make an arrest but you would not take the same risk for people who love you. This job, this obsession, this addiction [...] It has to end. You have to come home.

(TV series *The Missing*, Season 2, Episode 7, New Pictures)

THIS short dialogue has been taken from a conversation between detective Julien Baptiste and his wife Celie in the TV series *The Missing*. Julien has spent years trying to solve a case involving the disappearance of two young girls, while neglecting his wife and daughter at home. Even though he has been diagnosed with cancer, he still cannot distance himself from the case, pursuing any possible clue to the fate of the missing girls, while irresponsibly postponing potentially life-saving treatment. This dialogue dramatically reveals how an individual deliberately sacrifices his family, relationships with significant others, and even his own health to pursue his work, in which he finds meaning through making a difference in the lives of other people.

Reflecting on this episode, it becomes clear that Julien perceives his work as being of great importance to himself and to others. This perception embodies the concept of work meaningfulness or meaningful work, which could be generally understood as work that is significant, worthwhile, or valuable to oneself and/or others[1] (Pratt and Ashforth, 2003; Rosso, Dekas, and Wrzesniewski, 2010). However, it could be argued that in the case of Julien, these meaningful experiences of work resemble a career-related calling, that is a "purposeful, meaningful, and passion-driven engagement in a career that one feels drawn to pursue"[2] (Lysova et al., 2018: 261). Meaningful work and career calling are related yet distinct concepts. A calling represents a form of meaningful work, but experiencing one's work as meaningful is not enough for someone to be described as having a calling. Being called to a career implies that an individual has a sense of urge, feels compelled or "called" to engage in a particular type of work, which can arise either from an external caller (Dik and Duffy, 2009), a sense of destiny (Bunderson and Thompson, 2009), or an inner drive (Dobrow and Tosti-Kharas, 2011). Despite these conceptual differences between meaningful work and calling concepts, this chapter does not make a distinction between the two, and instead broadly explores meaningful work experiences and how they influence family life.

The dialogue between Julien and his wife reveals the dark side of meaningful work in relation to the non-work domain, which in this case is Julien's family. However, this is in contrast to prevailing positive perspectives in the literature on the outcomes of meaningful work. Indeed, the literature extensively shows that meaningful work contributes to greater job satisfaction, work engagement, and well-being, among other outcomes (e.g. May, Gilson, and Harter, 2004; Steger, Dik, and Duffy, 2012; Wrzesniewski et al., 1997). However, this dialogue resonates with a scant but growing body of research that acknowledges that the pursuit of meaningful work is associated with various challenges (e.g. Lips-Wiersma and Morris, 2009; Mitra and Buzzanell, 2017) and negative outcomes (i.e. sacrifice in pay and personal time; e.g. Bunderson and Thompson, 2009; Dempsey and Sanders, 2010). While great efforts have been made by scholars to understand the outcomes of meaningful work in the work domain, it is important to acknowledge that an individual is a "whole person" and not just the person working in an organization (Friedlander, 1994). Thus, the impact of meaningful work on other domains that an individual is involved in outside work should also be studied. This chapter aims to enrich understanding of how meaningful work impacts one's family domain.

To get a better understanding of whether meaningful work positively or negatively impacts one's family, this chapter provides an overview of existing research on the topic. Given the scarcity of research that explicitly studies meaningful work and family, relevant research in the domains of meaningful work, calling, and work–family interplay is

---

[1] Given its focus on the relationship between meaningful work and family, this chapter concentrates on this broad definition of meaningful work. However, it is important to acknowledge that prior research argues for the importance of treating meaningful work as a multidimensional construct in empirical studies (Lips-Wiersma and Morris, 2009; Steger, Dik, and Duffy, 2012).

[2] This definition reflects and builds on the prominent definitions suggested by prior research (Bunderson and Thompson, 2009; Dik and Duffy, 2009; Dobrow and Tosti-Kharas, 2011).

reviewed. The chapter continues by first discussing theoretical perspectives and prior research proposing that meaningful work contributes to one's family. Second, it provides a review of research that argues for negative implications of meaningful work for one's family. Third, it discusses potential conditions that may influence the way meaningful work impacts one's family. Finally, the chapter finishes with the discussion of implications and possible future research directions to foster more research on the interplay between meaningful work and the family domain.

MEANINGFUL WORK AND FAMILY: A WIN-WIN PERSPECTIVE

Theoretical arguments for the beneficial role of meaningful work in relation to family take an enriching perspective to the relationship between work and family (work–family enrichment), i.e. "the extent to which experiences in one role improve the quality of life in the other role" (Greenhaus and Powell, 2006: 73; Rothbard, 2001). Greenhaus and Powell's (2006) model of work–family enrichment proposes that resources derived from a work role may be transferred to a non-work role (e.g. family role), contributing to a higher quality of one's personal life. The authors suggest that resources obtained from a work role can be either directly transferred to a family role, or indirectly, through an increased positive effect resulting from these resources. Since scholars suggest that meaningful work is a resource which functions similarly to other job resources (Lee, Idris, and Delfabbro, 2017), experiences of meaningful work as a positive resource may boost positive effects, facilitating the transition of resources obtained at work to the family. The focus on meaningful work as a positive resource in the interplay between work and family has been explicitly examined in the studies of Voydanoff (2004, 2005). In particular, Voydanoff showed that meaningful work should be treated as an important psychological reward. This within-domain work resource is transmitted into the family domain via the psychological spillover of positive emotions, and energy expansion contributes to work-to-family facilitation.

Besides more conceptual work that relies on the work-to-family enrichment perspective, there have been some empirical studies that examine the positive impact of work meaningfulness on one's family. For example, Tummers and colleagues (Tummers and Bronkhorst, 2014; Tummers and Knies, 2013) found that midwives who reported greater work meaningfulness experienced high work–family enrichment. Nomaguchi (2009) found that parents with greater meaningfulness in their jobs reported lower work–family conflict. What is more, meaningful work has been associated with greater work-to-life enrichment (Johnson and Jiang, 2017), work–life balance (Chalofsky, 2003), and lower work-to-life interference (McCrea, Boreham, and Ferguson, 2011). What is more, Ilies et al. (2017) show that meaningfulness can be seen as a contextual resource of work engagement that produces a desire in individuals to share work events or experiences at home (i.e. engage in work–family interpersonal capitalization), which in turn contributes to family satisfaction and an increase in work–family balance. This study adds to prior research that argues for the positive influence of work engagement on families (e.g. Culbertson, Mills, and Fullagar, 2012; Rodríguez-Muñoz et al., 2014). Thus, since meaningful work is associated with greater work engagement (e.g. May, Gilson, and Harter, 2004), the abovementioned research provides support for the positive impact of meaningful work on one's family. In addition, Ba' (2014) suggests that meaningful work narratives foster an emotional culture that favors the processes of positive integration between meaningful work and the family domain, as it enables individuals to be emotionally involved in their life as a whole.

Additional support for the positive influence of meaningful work on one's family is provided by the literature on callings. For example, Cardador and Caza (2012) suggest that when individuals pursue their calling in a healthy and flexible manner, it can lead to greater experiences of balance in their non-work relationships. Indeed, Oates, Hall, and Anderson (2005) found that having a sense of calling helps women to effectively cope with the tension between mothering and career duties, and positively contributes to non-work relationships. Similarly, Duffy et al. (2012) showed that for some of the interviewed participants, a sense of calling enables them to feel more centered and fulfilled, leading to more positive personal relationships.

MEANINGFUL WORK AND FAMILY: A WIN-LOSE PERSPECTIVE

The argument that meaningful work might be detrimental to family life is given theoretical support by a depleting perspective that incorporates research on resource depletion and work–family conflict, i.e. a "form of inter-role conflict in which the role pressures from the work and family domains are mutually incompatible in some respect" (Greenhaus and Beutell, 1985: 77; Rothbard, 2001). Depletion of resources with regard to work–family interaction may happen because people have fixed amounts of psychological and physiological resources to spend, and they make trade-offs to accommodate these fixed resources (Edwards and Rothbard, 2000; Rothbard, 2001). Work-to-family conflict literature further explains that the work domain can interfere with the family domain in three different ways: *time-based* (a person's greater time involvement in a work role takes away time in a family role), *strain-based* (experiences of strain in a work role carry over to the family role or make it difficult to fulfill obligations of the family role), and *behavior-based* (certain expectations of behaviors in a work role make it difficult to fulfill obligations of the family role) (Greenhaus and Beutell, 1985).

Although the empirical research that studies the negative influence of meaningful work on the family domain does not always explicitly use resource depletion and work-to-family literature to support the negative relationship, it pursues a line of argument relevant to these perspectives. For example, in their qualitative study, Dempsey and Sanders (2010) found that the pursuit of meaningful work by social entrepreneurs jeopardizes their personal relationships, reflected in the complete dissolution of a work–life boundary, and privileging of work over family. Similarly, Bailey and Madden (2017) showed how academics found it hard to make enough time to work on their research during work hours, and chose to work on their academic projects during the weekend, which thus involved a trade-off with family time. What is more, some scholars suggest that work engagement, which is considered an important outcome of meaningful work (e.g. May, Gilson, and Harter, 2004), can also be regarded as a depleting resource and result in greater work-to-family conflict (e.g. George, 2011; Halbesleben, Harvey, and Bolino, 2009).

Support for the potentially negative influences of experiences of meaningful work on one's family have been also provided by the relevant literature on calling. In particular, it was suggested that an unhealthy pursuit of a calling could reduce work–life balance and decrease one's satisfaction with social relationships (Bakker, Demerouti, and Burke, 2009; Piotrowski and Vodanovich, 2006; as cited in Cardador and Caza, 2012). Similarly, other studies showed that individuals with a calling make personal time sacrifices (Bunderson and Thompson, 2009), devote extra time to their job, blurring work and non-work domains (Serow, 1994), sacrifice family and social life (Fraher and Gabriel, 2014), and experience greater tensions between work and family (Kreiner, Hollensbe, and Sheep, 2009). The overinvestment in doing work that is one's calling was found to be associated with greater workaholism, work overload, stress, and burnout (Duffy et al, 2012, 2016; Keller et al., 2016; Madden, Bailey, and Kerr, 2015), which was found to be positively associated with work-to-life interference (e.g. Ilies et al., 2007). Thus, these negative consequences might limit the time that individuals spend in a family role (time-based work-to-family conflict), while perhaps transferring the strain from work to a family role (strain-based work-to-family conflict).

CONDITIONS SHAPING THE INFLUENCE OF MEANINGFUL WORK ON ONE'S FAMILY

The prior sections provide a review of existing conceptual and empirical work that supports both the contributing and damaging influences of meaningful work on family life. While the literature emphasizes the importance and relevance of studying the interaction between meaningful work and family, it also sheds light on the scarcity of empirical research on the topic. It might be fruitful to propose research directions which would enable a richer understanding of how meaningful work influences the family domain. Therefore, the focus of this section is to explore the condition(s) under which meaningful work is likely to contribute to, rather than detract from, family life.

Recent meta-analyses on the antecedents of work–family enrichment (Lapierre et al., 2018) and work-to-family conflict (Michel et al., 2011) highlight diverse factors that could serve as conditions influencing how meaningful work impacts family life. For example, Lapierre et al. (2018) examined the influence of resource-providing characteristics (e.g. social support at work, family-friendly policies, etc.), resource-depleting characteristics (e.g. work role overload, family role overload, etc.), and personal characteristics associated with work and family in relation to work-to-family enrichment. In turn, Michel et al. (2011) discussed the influence of personality and other factors in the work and family domains on the emergence of work-to-family conflict. While some of the factors mentioned by the two groups of scholars could be relevant to understanding the interplay of meaningful work and family, they concern mainly how family influences work (family-to-work conflict and enrichment), which is not the focus of this chapter and is therefore not discussed here. For example, social support from family could be regarded as a relevant and important variable when studying the interplay between meaningful work and family. However, because it was found to be an antecedent of how family can contribute to or interfere with work rather than how work contributes to or interferes with family (e.g. Lapierre et al., 2018; Michel et al., 2011; Van Daalen, Willemsen, and Sanders, 2006), this chapter does not elaborate on this factor as a potential condition influencing how meaningful work impacts one's family.

The experiences of meaningful work are likely to already imply the presence of important supportive and resource-providing contextual characteristics that exist in the work domain to sustain these meaningful work experiences (Rosso, Dekas, and Wrzesniewski, 2010) and therefore to potentially facilitate work–family interaction. Thus, this chapter draws attention to person-related factors that could influence how meaningful work impacts on the family domain. Drawing on prior research in related fields, the following conditions are likely to explain the potential of meaningful work to contribute to, rather than damage, family life: *family role salience* and *identification*, and *harmonious passion* rather than *obsessive passion*.

Family Role Salience and Identification Shaping how Meaningful Work Impacts one's Family

Family role salience concerns the psychological or subjective importance of a family role to an individual (Thoits, 1991; Powell and Greenhaus, 2010). The salience of a particular role in one's identity suggests that this role is more likely to be invoked in a variety of situations when making a decision (Stryker, 1968). Thus, role salience can be influential in individual decision-making when it involves the expectations and responsibilities of two or more roles that are not compatible, such as in the case of work and family roles (Carlson and Kacmar, 2000; Powell and Greenhaus, 2010). Indeed, conceptual work on the topic (Greenhaus and Powell, 2012; Powell and Greenhaus, 2012) suggests that the salience of the family role identity to an individual's overall self-concept is likely to determine whether they would evoke their family identity when making a work decision, resulting in their decision being more family-oriented—i.e. the decision is "influenced by a family situation and aimed to foster a positive outcome for the family" (Powell and

Greenhaus, 2012: 247). For example, prior empirical research revealed the influential role of family role salience in shaping the involvement of family considerations in an individual's career sense-making (Lysova et al., 2015). Thus, meaningful work is more likely to contribute to rather than damage one's family for those individuals who perceive their family role as being salient.

Proposition 1.   Meaningful work may contribute to the family of those individuals who have a high, as opposed to low, level of family role salience.

Family role identification refers to the extent to which one defines oneself in terms of a family role (Sluss and Ashforth, 2007; Greenhaus and Powell, 2012). Being theoretically grounded in the relational identity theory (Sluss and Ashforth, 2007), family role identification reflects one's role-related relationship with another person (e.g. parent–child, spouse–spouse, etc.). The focus on identification at the level of a particular relationship distinguishes family role identification from the closely related concept of family role salience. According to Sluss and Ashforth (2007), greater identification with a particular role-related relationship (such as in the family domain) would suggest that individuals are more connected to this relationship, find it important that this relationship thrives, and thus enjoy contributing to the well-being of this relationship. Conceptual work on family-related work decisions (Greenhaus and Powell, 2012; Powell and Greenhaus, 2012) further suggests that a strong identification with family role relationships strengthens the impact of the family situation on a work-domain decision. This is because individuals care about meeting the needs of family members and contributing to their well-being, which results in more work decisions which are beneficial to the family. Thus, similarly to family role salience, greater family role identification is likely to shape the relationship between meaningful work and the family domain into a more positive one.

Proposition 2.   Meaningful work may contribute to the family of those individuals who have a high, as opposed to low, level of family role identification.

Harmonious versus Obsessive Passion Shaping how Meaningful Work Impacts one's Family

Whether meaningful work contributes to or detracts from family life is likely to also be influenced by the nature of passion that the experiences of meaningful work are associated with. Drawing on the research by Vallerand et al. (2003), passion refers to "a strong inclination towards an activity that people like, that they find important, and in which they invest time and energy" (p. 757), with particular focus on activities in the work domain. The authors suggest that it is important to distinguish between *harmonious* and *obsessive* passion in terms of how the work activity is internalized by one's identity. Harmonious passion emerges from an autonomous internalization of the activity by the person's identity, meaning that individuals freely choose to pursue their passion activity because of the importance they attach to it and their love of doing it. By contrast, obsessive passion emerges from a controlled internalization of the activity into one's identity, meaning that individuals are not free but rather compelled to engage in the activity that they love and find important in order to feel good about themselves (Vallerand et al., 2003).

Individuals experiencing both types of (work) passion feel good about investing time and energy in their passionate work activity. However, in the case of harmonious passion, individuals approach it in a manner that protects other aspects of their life, and thus they take time for their non-work (family) activities (Vallerand et al., 2003). In the case of obsessive passion, individuals feel a sense of guilt if they do not engage in their passionate work activity to the maximum, which prevents them from making time for non-work (family) activities (Vallerand et al., 2003). Indeed, prior research has shown that harmonious passion contributes to decreases in work–family conflicts, while obsessive passion results in greater work–family conflict (Caudroit et al., 2011; Houlfort et al., 2017; Thorgren, Wincent, and Sirén, 2013; Vallerand et al., 2010). A recent study by Houlfort et al. (2017) showed that harmonious passion negatively (and obsessive passion positively) predicts both time-based and strain-based work-to-family conflicts.

Drawing on the abovementioned literature, it is likely that harmonious passion and obsessive passion would be important conditions that shape how meaningful work impacts one's family. For example, a harmonious passionate worker who experiences his or her work as meaningful may attempt to actively engage in the work that he or she loves during the weekdays only, leaving time during weekends for his or her family activities, thus minimizing the conflict between work and other life domains. By contrast, an obsessive passionate worker who experiences his or her work as meaningful would not be able to stop working on a project even during the weekends, neglecting the importance of spending time with family and thus leading to greater conflict between work and other life domains. Thus, for individuals whose experiences of meaningful work are associated with harmonious passion, there would be a positive spillover from work to family, suggesting that meaningful work will contribute to one's family. In turn, for individuals whose experiences of meaningful work are associated with obsessive passion there would be a negative spillover from work to family, suggesting that meaningful work will damage one's family.

Proposition 3a.   Meaningful work may contribute to one's family when an individual's experiences of meaningful work are associated with harmonious passion.

Proposition 3b.   Meaningful work may damage one's family when an individual's experiences of meaningful work are associated with obsessive passion.

Conclusions and Future Directions

The aim of this chapter is to draw attention to the need for a better understanding of how meaningful work influences individuals beyond their work- and career-related outcomes, namely their family. The review of literature on meaningful work, career calling, and work–family interplay suggests theoretical explanations exist for why experiences of meaningful work can both contribute to and damage one's family domain. Nevertheless, the review reveals that the empirical evidence on the impact of meaningful work on the family is growing but limited, and thus requires further research attention of scholars. Conducting research on the intersection between meaningful work and the family domain is of importance if we are to study an individual as a "whole person" and not just as the person working in an organization (Friedlander, 1994).

Not only are scholars encouraged to pursue research that provides additional empirical support for positive and negative implications of meaningful work for one's family, they are also encouraged to investigate conditions that could facilitate this spillover, whether positive or negative, from the work to the family domain. This chapter specifically discusses the role of such person-related conditions as family role salience and identification, and harmonious passion and obsessive passion, in shaping the relationship between meaningful work and family as a more positive or negative one. However, conditional factors that can influence whether meaningful work contributes to or damages family life are not limited to those discussed. More research is needed to incorporate other family-related factors that may shape how meaningful work influences the family domain. Investigating the role of resources provided by organizations (e.g. family-friendly policies, family-supportive supervision, etc.; e.g. Hammer et al., 2009; Lapierre et al., 2018) appears to be especially promising. Prior research on family-relatedness of work decisions (Greenhaus and Powell, 2012; Powell and Greenhaus, 2012) suggests that organizations with a family-supportive environment send cues that they respect employees' lives outside of work, and that employees are not expected to prioritize work demands over family responsibilities. In workplaces with a more family-supportive environment, individuals who experience their work as meaningful could receive more opportunities to plan their work time in such a way that it does not conflict with their family life. Investigating conditions affecting how the work and family domains interact will allow the development of concrete suggestions for organizations willing to facilitate the ability of their employees to flourish in both work and non-work domains.

Besides highlighting diverse future research opportunities through the review of existing conceptual and empirical work on the interplay between meaningful work and family, it is important to challenge the current literature and discourse around meaningful work for its exclusive promotion of and striving for meaningful work, without considering the implications this may have for family life. Indeed, contemporary discourse on meaningful work often portrays it as a tool for organizations to keep their employees engaged, and thus to secure their high individual performance and productivity (Deloitte, 2017). This discourse does not acknowledge that meaningfulness for the "whole person" may be shaped by factors that are outside the work domain, such as family (Brief and Nord, 1990; Rosso, Dekas, and Wrzesniewski, 2010). In their essay on the dark side of the workplace spirituality movement, Lips-Wiersma, Lund Dean, and Fornaciari (2009) suggest that the contemporary discourse on meaningful work in organizations is presented as a substitute for family and community life "while real families and communities recede in prominence" (pp. 290–1). What is more, by limiting any references to family in organizational discourse on meaningful work, it is implied that the significant others of those pursuing meaningful work are available to take care of children and the family as a whole. In so doing, an increasing disconnection between individuals pursuing meaningful work and their families can occur, such as in the example of Julien and his family. This disconnection limits the possibilities for individuals to experience the sense of wholeness or coherence in one's life, which Martela (2010) suggests is important to experience a meaningful life. Therefore, both scholars and organizations are encouraged to understand and examine meaningful work as a concept that incorporates other aspects of a person's life beyond their work.

References

Ba', S. (2014). "'A great job and a family': Work narratives and the work and family interaction." *Community, Work and Family*, 17(1), 43–59.

Bailey, C. and Madden, A. (2017). "Time reclaimed: Temporality and the experience of meaningful work." *Work, Employment and Society*, 31(1), 3–18.

Bakker, A. B., Demerouti, E., and Burke, R. (2009). "Workaholism and relationship quality: A spillover-crossover perspective." *Journal of Occupational Health Psychology*, 14(1), 23–33.

Brief, A. P. and Nord, W. R. (1990). "Work and the Family." In A. P. Brief and W. R. Nord, (eds.), *Meanings of Occupational Work*, pp. 203–32. Lexington: Lexington Books.

Bunderson, J. S. and Thompson, J. A. (2009). "The call of the wild: Zookeepers, callings, and the double-edged sword of deeply meaningful work." *Administrative Science Quarterly*, 54(1), 32–57.

Cardador, M. T. and Caza, B. B. (2012). "Relational and identity perspectives on healthy versus unhealthy pursuit of callings." *Journal of Career Assessment*, 20(3), 338–53.

Carlson, D. S. and Kacmar, K. M. (2000). "Work–family conflict in the organization: Do life role values make a difference?" *Journal of Management*, 26, 1031–54.

Caudroit, J., Boiche, J., Stephan, Y., Le Scanff, C., and Trouilloud, D. (2011). "Predictors of work/family interference and leisure-time physical activity among teachers: The role of passion towards work." *European Journal of Work and Organizational Psychology*, 20(3), 326–44.

Chalofsky, N. (2003). "An emerging construct for meaningful work." *Human Resource Development International*, 6(1), 69–83.

Culbertson, S. S., Mills, M. J., and Fullagar, C. J. (2012). "Work engagement and work–family facilitation: Making homes happier through positive affective spillover." *Human Relations*, 65, 1155–77.

Deloitte. (2017). *Deloitte Global Human Capital Trends: Rewriting the rules for the digital age*. No place: Deloitte University Press. Available at: https://www2.deloitte.com/content/dam/Deloitte/global/Documents/HumanCapital/hc-2017-global-human-capital-trends-gx.pdf [accessed February 6, 2018].

Dempsey, S. E. and Sanders, M. L. (2010). "Meaningful work? Nonprofit marketization and work/life imbalance in popular autobiographies of social entrepreneurship." *Organization*, 17(4), 437–59.

Dik, B. J. and Duffy, R. D. (2009). "Calling and vocation at work: Definitions and prospects for research and practice." *The Counseling Psychologist*, 37(3), 424–50.

Dobrow, S. R. and Tosti-Kharas, J. (2011). "Calling: The development of a scale measure." *Personnel Psychology*, 64(4), 1001–49.

Duffy, R. D., Douglass, R. P., Autin, K. L., England, J., and Dik, B. J. (2016). "Does the dark side of a calling exist? Examining potential negative effects." *The Journal of Positive Psychology*, 11(6), 634–46.

Duffy, R. D., Foley, P. F., Raque-Bodgan, T. L., Reid-Marks, L., Dik, B. J., Castano, M. C., and Adams, C. M. (2012). "Counseling psychologists who view their careers as a calling: A qualitative study." *Journal of Career Assessment*, 20(3), 293–308.

Edwards, J. R. and Rothbard, N. P. (2000). "Mechanisms linking work and family: Clarifying the relationship between work and family constructs." *Academy of Management Review*, 25(1), 178–99.

Fraher, A. L. and Gabriel, Y. (2014). "Dreaming of flying when grounded: Occupational identity and occupational fantasies of furloughed airline pilots." *Journal of Management Studies*, 51(6), 926–51.

Friedlander, F. (1994). "Toward whole systems and whole people." *Organization*, 1(1), 59–64.

George, J. M. (2011). "The wider context, costs, and benefits of work engagement." *European Journal of Work and Organizational Psychology*, 20, 53–9.

Greenhaus, J. H. and Beutell, N. J. (1985). "Sources of conflict between work and family roles." *Academy of Management Review*, 10(1), 76–88.

Greenhaus, J. H. and Powell, G. N. (2006). "When work and family are allies: A theory of work–family enrichment." *Academy of Management Review*, 31(1), 72–92.

Greenhaus, J. H. and Powell, G. N. (2012). "The family-relatedness of work decisions: A framework and agenda for theory and research." *Journal of Vocational Behavior*, 80(2), 246–55.

Halbesleben, J. R., Harvey, J., and Bolino, M. C. (2009). "Too engaged? A conservation of resources view of the relationship between work engagement and work interference with family." *Journal of Applied Psychology*, 94, 1452–65.

Hammer, L. B., Kossek, E. E., Yragui, N. L., Bodner, T. E., and Hanson, G. C. (2009). "Development and validation of a multidimensional measure of family supportive supervisor behaviors (FSSB)." *Journal of Management*, 35(4), 837–56.

Houlfort, N., Philippe, F. L., Bourdeau, S., and Leduc, C. (2017). "A comprehensive understanding of the relationships between passion for work and work–family conflict and the consequences for psychological distress." *International Journal of Stress Management*. [Advance online publication], available at: http://dx.doi.org/10.1037/str0000068 [accessed June 9, 2018].

Ilies, R., Liu, X. Y., Liu, Y., and Zheng, X. (2017). "Why do employees have better family lives when they are highly engaged at work?" *Journal of Applied Psychology*, 102(6), 956–70.

Ilies, R., Schwind, K. M., Wagner, D. T., and Johnson, M. D. (2007). "When can employees have a family life? The effects of daily workload and affect on work–family conflict and social behaviors at home." *Journal of Applied Psychology*, 92(5), 1368–79.

Johnson, M. J. and Jiang, L. (2017). "Reaping the benefits of meaningful work: The mediating versus moderating role of work engagement." *Stress and Health*, 33(3), 288–97.

Keller, A. C., Spurk, D., Baumeler, F., and Hirschi, A. (2016). "Competitive climate and workaholism: Negative sides of future orientation and calling." *Personality and Individual Differences*, 96, 122–6.

Kreiner, G. E., Hollensbe, E. C., and Sheep, M. L. (2009). "Balancing borders and bridges: Negotiating the work–home interface via boundary work tactics." *Academy of Management Journal*, 52(4), 704–30.

Lapierre, L. M., Li, Y., Kwan, H. K., Greenhaus, J. H., DiRenzo, M. S., and Shao, P. (2018). "A meta-analysis of the antecedents of work–family enrichment." *Journal of Organizational Behavior*, 39(4), 385–401.

Lee, M. C. C., Idris, M. A., and Delfabbro, P. H. (2017). "The linkages between hierarchical culture and empowering leadership and their effects on employees' work engagement: Work meaningfulness as a mediator." *International Journal of Stress Management*, 24(4), 392–415.

Lips-Wiersma, M., Lund Dean, K., and Fornaciari, C. J. (2009). "Theorizing the dark side of the workplace spirituality movement." *Journal of Management Inquiry*, 18(4), 288–300.

Lips-Wiersma, M. and Morris, L. (2009). "Discriminating between 'meaningful work' and the 'management of meaning.'" *Journal of Business Ethics*, 88, 491–511.

Lysova, E. I., Jansen, P. G., Khapova, S. N., Plomp, J., and Tims, M. (2018). "Examining calling as a double-edged sword for employability." *Journal of Vocational Behavior*, 104, 261–72.

Lysova, E. I., Korotov, K., Khapova, S. N., and Jansen, P. G. (2015). "The role of the spouse in managers' family-related career sensemaking." *Career Development International*, 20(5), 503–24.

Madden, A., Bailey, C., and Kerr, R. C. J. (2015). "'For this I was made': Conflict and calling in the role of a woman priest." *Work, Employment and Society*, 29(5), 866–74.

Martela, F. (2010). "Meaningful work: An integrative model based on the human need for meaningfulness." Paper presented at the Academy of Management, Montreal, Quebec.

May, D. R., Gilson, L., and Harter, L. M. (2004). "The psychological conditions of meaningfulness, safety and availability and the engagement of the human spirit at work." *Journal of Occupational and Organizational Psychology*, 77, 11–37.

McCrea, R., Boreham, P., and Ferguson, M. (2011). "Reducing work-to-life interference in the public service: The importance of participative management as mediated by other work attributes." *Journal of Sociology*, 47(3), 313–32.

Michel, J. S., Kotrba, L. M., Mitchelson, J. K., Clark, M. A., and Baltes, B. B. (2011). "Antecedents of work–family conflict: A meta-analytic review." *Journal of Organizational Behavior*, 32(5), 689–725.

Mitra, R. and Buzzanell, P. M. (2017). "Communicative tensions of meaningful work: The case of sustainability practitioners." *Human Relations*, 70(5), 594–616.

Nomaguchi, K. M. (2009). "Change in work–family conflict among employed parents between 1977 and 1997." *Journal of Marriage and Family*, 71(1), 15–32.

Oates, K. L. M., Hall, M. E. L., and Anderson, T. L. (2005). "Calling and conflict: A qualitative exploration of interrole conflict and the sanctification of work in Christian mothers in academia." *Journal of Psychology and Theology*, 33, 210–23.

Piotrowski, C. and Vodanovich, S. J. (2006). "The interface between workaholism and work–family conflict: A review and conceptual framework." *Organization Development Journal*, 24, 84–92.

Powell, G. N. and Greenhaus, J. H. (2010). "Sex, gender, and the work-to-family interface: Exploring negative and positive interdependencies." *Academy of Management Journal*, 53(3), 513–34.

Powell, G. N. and Greenhaus, J. H. (2012). "When family considerations influence work decisions: Decision-making processes." *Journal of Vocational Behavior*, 81(3), 322–9.

Pratt, M. G. and Ashforth, B. E. (2003). "Fostering Meaningfulness in Working and at Work." In K. S. Cameron, J. E. Dutton, and R. E. Quinn, (eds.), *Positive Organizational Scholarship*, pp. 309–27. San Francisco: Berrett-Koehler Publishers.

Rodríguez-Muñoz, A., Sanz-Vergel, A. I., Demerouti, E., and Bakker, A. B. (2014). "Engaged at work and happy at home: A spillover-crossover model." *Journal of Happiness Studies*, 15, 271–83.

Rosso, B. D., Dekas, K. H., and Wrzesniewski, A. (2010). "On the meaning of work: A theoretical integration and review." *Research in Organizational Behavior*, 30, 91–127.

Rothbard, N. P. (2001). "Enriching or depleting? The dynamics of engagement in work and family roles." *Administrative Science Quarterly*, 46(4), 655–84.

Serow, R. C. (1994). "Called to teach: A study of highly motivated preservice teachers." *Journal of Research and Development in Education*, 27, 65–72.

Sluss, D. M. and Ashforth, B. E. (2007). "Relational identity and identification: Defining ourselves through work relationships." *Academy of Management Review*, 32, 9–32.

Steger, M. F., Dik, B. J., and Duffy, R. D. (2012). "Measuring meaningful work: The Work and Meaning Inventory (WAMI)." *Journal of Career Assessment*, 20, 322–37.

Stryker, S. (1968). "Identity salience and role performance: The relevance of symbolic interaction theory for family research." *Journal of Marriage and the Family*, 30(4), 558–64.

Thoits, P. A. (1991). "On merging identity theory and stress research." *Social Psychology Quarterly*, 54, 101–12.

Thorgren, S., Wincent, J., and Sirén, C. (2013). "The influence of passion and work–life thoughts on work satisfaction." *Human Resource Development Quarterly*, 24(4), 469–92.

Tummers, L. G. and Bronkhorst, B. A. C. (2014). "The impact of leader-member exchange (LMX) on work–family interference and work–family facilitation." *Personnel Review*, 43, 573–91.

Tummers, L. G. and Knies, E. (2013). "Leadership and meaningful work in the public sector." *Public Administration Review*, 73(6), 859–68.

Vallerand, R. J., Blanchard, C., Mageau, G. A., Koestner, R., Ratelle, C., Léonard, M. et al. (2003). "Les passions de l'ame: On obsessive and harmonious passion." *Journal of Personality and Social Psychology*, 85(4), 756–67.

Vallerand, R. J., van Paquet, Y., Philippe, F. L., and Charest, J. (2010). "On the role of passion for work in burnout: A process model." *Journal of Personality*, 78(1), 289–312.

Van Daalen, G., Willemsen, T. M., and Sanders, K. (2006). "Reducing work–family conflict through different sources of social support." *Journal of Vocational Behavior*, 69(3), 462–76.

Voydanoff, P. (2004). "The effects of work demands and resources on work-to-family conflict and facilitation." *Journal of Marriage and Family*, 66(2), 398–412.

Voydanoff, P. (2005). "Toward a conceptualization of perceived work–family fit and balance: A demands and resources approach." *Journal of Marriage and Family*, 67(4), 822–36.

Wrzesniewski, A., McCauley, C., Rozin, P., and Schwartz, B. (1997). "Jobs, careers, and callings: People's relations to their work." *Journal of Research in Personality*, 31, 21–33.

CHAPTER 24

DOES CORPORATE SOCIAL RESPONSIBILITY ENHANCE MEANINGFUL WORK?

A Multi-perspective Theoretical Framework

MARJOLEIN LIPS-WIERSMA

INTRODUCTION

THIS chapter attempts to answer the question: "Does corporate social responsibility cultivate meaningful work?" The premise that underpins meaningful work theory is that it is a fundamental need (Frankl, 1959; Yeoman, 2014). From this perspective, humanity's yearning for meaningful work is not a resource, nor a problem to be fixed, but a reality to be worked with. A healthy human being evaluates actions and outcomes as to whether or not these are meaningful and accordingly gives them attention, energy, and effort. Subsequently, a healthy human being also withdraws engagement and discretionary effort when their need for meaningful work is not being met.

In this context, the relationship between corporate social responsibility (CSR) and meaningful work (MW) has been posited as follows: "because CSR expands the notion of work to go outside of one's particular job and organization, and beyond an exclusive profit-focused perspective, it is an ideal conduit for individuals to make sense of and find meaningfulness through work" (Aguinis and Glavas, 2017: 2). While it is generally assumed that CSR promotes MW, CSR is also a confused, diverse, and contradictory set of initiatives, practices, values, and ideals (Hahn et al., 2015). It can therefore be anticipated that under certain circumstances CSR leads to MW and under others it does not. In this chapter, I differentiate five different theoretical MW perspectives from which to explore the CSR–MW relationship. Collectively these cover individual, organizational, and societal levels. However, MW is a complex concept and each theoretical perspective does not neatly fit into one particular level.

CSR is commonly understood to include ethical, social, and environmental issues and is described as voluntarily (above legal requirements) increasing the positive impact and mitigating the harmful impact of the organization on a range of stakeholders (Dahlsrud, 2008). When the organization engages in CSR practices, this leads to employee pride in their organization (Bhattacharya, Sen, and Korschun, 2008; Zhu et al., 2015), increased organizational identification (Berger, Cunningham, and Drumwright, 2006; Glavas and Godwin, 2013; Houghton, Gabel, and Williams, 2009), greater employee commitment (Peterson, 2004), energy and motivation (Wang et al., 2016), and stronger engagement (Benn, Teo, and Martin, 2015). While there has been ample research looking at the influence of CSR on desirable employee outcomes from the perspective of the corporation, the question of whether, and under which circumstances, CSR leads to meaningful work is undertheorized (Bolton, Kim, and O'Gorman, 2011; Aguinis and Glavas, 2017; Michaelson et al., 2014; Lepisto and Pratt, 2017).

Both CSR and MW are complex concepts. Therefore I attempt to ground the discussion in an (extreme) case of Volkswagen (VW) which, in spite of having an impressive range of CSR practices, intentionally programmed diesel engines[1] to deceive emissions testing.[2]

VOLKSWAGEN

Volkswagen has a stated purpose beyond profit and has won multiple awards for its CSR practices. It presented itself as the most sustainable car maker in the world (Siano et al., 2017). It also had top scores in the Down Jones Sustainability Index on codes of conduct, compliance, climate strategy, and life cycle assessment. More than 74,000 of its 600,000 employees were trained in its code of conduct in 2014 alone, and in total 185,000 employees received training on compliance issues. The company also contributes to dozens of causes in various parts of the world and has an extensive sustainable supply chain practice (Ewing, 2017). At the same time, 500,000 diesel cars, sold in the US between 2009 and 2015, were emitting oxides thirty-five times higher than permissible legal levels. On January 11, 2017, the US Justice Department announced that Volkswagen had pleaded guilty to three criminal felony counts and had to pay US \$4.3 billion in penalties. It has subsequently become apparent that VW's fraud was not just a case of a few "rotten apples," but rather of systemic unethical behavior. Does all of this mean that in the case of VW, CSR did not lead to MW? I will attempt to answer this question from the perspective of five MW theories, depicted in Figure 24.1.

---

[1] https://en.wikipedia.org/wiki/Diesel_engine
[2] https://en.wikipedia.org/wiki/Emissions_testing

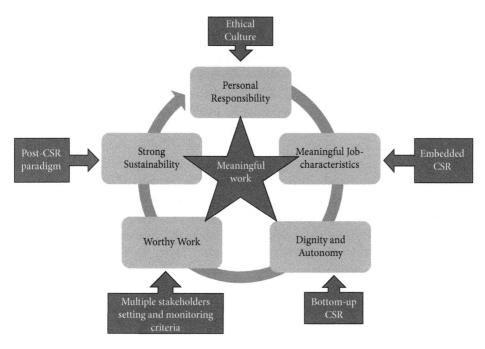

FIGURE 24.1 Five theoretical perspectives on the MW–CSR relationship with associated conditions for meaningful work

FIVE THEORETICAL PERSPECTIVES
ON THE MW–CSR RELATIONSHIP

Personal Responsibility

MW theory recognizes the importance of taking personal responsibility for meaningful living. In this context, for example, Yeoman (2014) quotes Frankl: 'Life ultimately means taking the responsibility to find the right answer to its problems and to fulfil the tasks which it constantly sets for each individual '(Frankl, 1994, cited in Yeoman, 2014: 240). Yeoman (2014: 240) states,

> Frankl acknowledges that there is a givenness to everyday problems, which appears to undermine our personal autonomy, but this does not mean that we are not choosers, since it is incumbent upon us to take responsibility for resolving the struggles of everyday living, demanding that we make reflective judgements when choosing the modes of acting and being appropriate to the situations in which we find ourselves.

Yeoman (2014) also suggests that the individual does not bear all the responsibility for finding her life to be meaningful, since social structures influence the extent to which a person takes responsibility.

It seems fair to say that for those directly involved in the cheating at VW, CSR policy did not translate into taking personal responsibility for MW. These managers and software engineers spent their time finding clever ways to circumvent CSR commitments rather than choosing what Yeoman refers to as "appropriate actions." In VW social structures also seem to have influenced the extent to which the engineers in particular could take responsibility. There was collective cheating, with increasing numbers involved. At the same time that many formal practices, such as codes of conduct and compliance, were put in place to prevent unethical behavior, VW is said to have maintained a culture of silence (Coffee, 2016). In the direct work environment of the software engineers, social structures influenced the extent to which they could take responsibility: the defeat device was authorized by managers (Castille and Fultz, 2018). VW engineers who found out about the cheating, and took responsibility by making a presentation to a superior, were instructed to destroy the presentation and refine the software (Ewing, 2017; Monzani, Braun, and Dick, 2016). In fact, while there had been some concerns over the propriety of the defeat software, all those involved in the discussions were instructed not to get caught and to destroy related documents (Leggett, 2017). As increasing numbers of people were enveloped in the scandal, speaking up would not just threaten one's own livelihood but also that of fellow workers (Castille and Fultz, 2018).

At least on the part of the managers, denial of wrongdoing continued when the cheating finally came to light: VW at first offered false explanations such as "irregularities." While several employees can be directly identified as not taking responsibility, employees throughout VW were affected. Strauss (2017) reports that before the scandal VW's staff morale was rated the best (among other companies such as Mercedes and BMW) on almost every dimension of workplace satisfaction, whereas when the scandal became public it was rated the worst. In the end, to live meaningfully one has to take responsibility for choosing right over wrong, and in the case of VW, it was not so hard to discern the right choice. At the same time, the organizational culture can thwart a person from acting on what would be the responsible thing to do, ultimately destroying both meaning and CSR. Creating and maintaining an ethical culture - which encourages each employee to act on their ethical responsibility - is therefore a primary condition for individuals to be responsible and for " CSR to lead to MW".

CSR Job Characteristics: Opportunities for MW

Job characteristics theory is central to MW. To understand the impact of CSR on MW it is therefore also important to understand how CSR influences the characteristics of the day-to-day job. The job characteristics model (JCM) posits that MW is "enhanced primarily by three of the core dimensions: skill variety, task identity, and task significance" (Hackman and Oldham, 1975: 160). Aguinis and Glavas (2017) suggest these three dimensions can be enhanced through CSR, as CSR practices often go beyond traditional job and organizational boundaries.

Those who participate in CSR activities often gain concrete skills that can be carried over to other aspects of their job (Bhattacharya, Sen, and Korschun, 2008). VW's E-Up is a small electric car that has been designed to achieve a zero operational carbon footprint and can cover 150 km on a single charge. VW is also putting significant effort into designing new vehicles so they can be taken back and materials can be reused. Such CSR initiatives lead to greater skill variety for those directly involved. For example, an employee at VW who is put in charge of a volunteer program learns valuable managerial skills (Boiral and Paillé, 2012), whereas an employee who is asked to rethink the currently unsustainable transport system acquires systems thinking and future scenario planning skills. Such tacit employee skills and process knowledge can be harnessed by the organization to achieve CSR goals (Renwick, Redman, and Maquire, 2013). Overall, time invested in skills training for the 626,000 VW Group employees is high at an average of 21.5 hours per employee in 2016. Whereas in some companies CSR is peripheral and, as a result, only a few individuals may be involved in CSR initiatives, at VW sustainability is embedded in a diverse range of jobs in design, production, and supply chain management. Consequently, for many workers there are opportunities for CSR initiatives to enrich jobs. Embedded, rather than peripheral CSR is a condition for CSR to lead to meaningful job characteristics for large numbers of employees (Sun, Stewart, and Pollard, 2010; Aguinis and Glavas, 2013).

Dignity and Autonomy

Dignity and freedom are core concepts in MW literature (Bowie, 1998). In the MW literature, dignity refers to whether work is basically degrading or enabling (Wolfe, 1997). Dignified work refers to the right to work and the freedom to make choices, as well as being fairly compensated. Freedom is enhanced by just rewards (Phelps, 1997), the ability to resist and oppose (Ciulla, 2012; Lamont, 2002), and the capacity to balance paid work and other commitments (Lips-Wiersma and Morris, 2017). The trades unions have a relatively strong presence in VW, employees enjoy good working conditions, including generous leave provisions, and (also under the pressure of the unions and local government) VW provides local, secure, and well-paid employment.

Dignity also rests on the opportunity to exercise agency (Hodson, 2001), and for work to be meaningful, it needs to allow workers to exercise their autonomy and independence, enabling them to develop rational capacities (Bowie, 1998). Managerialism and excessive control negatively affect the extent to which a person can exercise agency and hence can experience MW (Bailey and Madden, 2016; Pauchant, 1995; Sievers, 1994).

From the outside, it is very hard to discern how much agency a person can exercise, nor is it clear how much autonomy a person needs to exercise in order to experience MW and it is currently not know whether this is mediated by individual traits. However, in the context of the VW scandal, several reports (Lindebaum, Geddes, and Gabriel, 2017) emerged of the top-down hierarchy and heroic leadership style: "the leeway for anyone inside Volkswagen to resist the demands of top management had, if anything, grown narrower" and "Winterkorn was treated like a regent when he travelled the far-flung Volkswagen empire" (Ewing, 2017: 156). Some suggest Volkswagen was an autocratic company in which dissent and discussion was avoided (Mansouri, 2016). Thus, where one aspect of dignity, that of the right to good employment, is met by VW, another aspect, that of exercising agency, might have been curtailed through a combination of both fear and unrealistic expectations (Ewing, 2017).

In principle, CSR can enhance the opportunity for employee freedom, but paradoxically, the feeling of belonging that can come from working for a company that regularly asserts its sustainability credentials can also be a form of normative control (Costas and Kärreman, 2013). To take responsibility for CSR, the individual employee needs to have the freedom to identify, advocate for, and implement CSR initiatives (Garavan and McGuire, 2010; Hahn et al., 2015; Ulus and Hatipoglu, 2016). This also means that procedures are in place for workers to speak up safely. At the extreme end of speaking up, it means employees can grab power by whistle-blowing on non-ethical and environmentally degrading practices. A company that was truly interested in becoming sustainable would put in place a strong system of employee voice practices and employee protection processes, whereas employees in VW were clearly not encouraged to speak up. Employee participation is critical to CSR success (Godkin, 2015; Markey, McIvor, and Wright, 2016).

Aguinis and Glavas (2017) found that at present most approaches to CSR are top-down, with the senior management team and CEO being responsible for creating the CSR strategy, through their own vision and values and guidelines. In such cases, the senior management team might well believe CSR practices are being implemented whereas the experience of the workers (at least in some units) is completely different due to lack of guidance, resources, or commitment of middle management. With regard to dignity and autonomy, a strong system of employee voice practices and processes through bottom-up CSR is a primary condition for CSR to lead to MW.

Worthy Work

A worthy organizational purpose is seen to be foundational to creating meaningful work (Carbo et al., 2014; Yeoman, 2014). It has been found that worthy purpose has a more dominant relationship to MW than other antecedents such as responsible leadership and fairness (Lips-Wiersma, Haar, and Wright, 2018). Therefore, VW's stated purpose was to be the most sustainable car manufacturer, which conflicted with its prioritized purpose to be the biggest car manufacturer in the world. Where MW concerns itself with purpose, it is important to make a distinction between stated purpose and the purpose that is actually enacted. Lips-Wiersma and Morris (2009) suggest that "meaning is distinguished from meaninglessness in that such a cause [for which one works] does not only transcend self, but also transcends the organization to a more universally beneficial legacy." Ciulla (2011: 127) suggests a set of criteria to objectively discern that work is worthy:

> Work is worthy because there is some real or potential good in doing it. The most worthy jobs are those that have worthy purposes. They are jobs in which people help others, alleviate suffering, eliminate difficult, dangerous or tedious toil, make someone healthier and happier, aesthetically or intellectually enrich people, or improve the environment in which we live. All work that is worthy does at least one of these things in some big or small way.

CSR does not automatically meet these criteria as it can be normative or instrumental (Aguinis and Glavas, 2013). However, applying such criteria is by no means straightforward.

VW was poisoning the planet and showing blatant disregard for human health and well-being. The nitrogen oxide emitted by the 11 million cars worldwide that were fitted with the defeat device causes smog, acid rain, reduced growth in vegetation, and negatively affects health through lung inflammation, asthma, bronchitis, and emphysema (Ewing, 2017). VW was clearly not meeting the criteria of "improving the environment," nor the CSR criteria of mitigating harmful impact (Dahlsrud, 2008). However, most corporations will meet each of the criteria set for worthy work some of the time. VW also helps millions of people to meet a basic need of transporting themselves and their families, and supports numerous charities, and this might meet the criteria of "helping people," but it ignored the needs of other stakeholders such as the general public. For CSR to lead to MW, it is important to ask whether multiple affected stakeholders agree the work is worthy. This requires involving affected stakeholders in setting, monitoring, and living up to the criteria and ensuring the best long-term outcome for all in spite of what are usually complex and divergent needs.

Strong Sustainability

VW is still an economic success story and became the largest car manufacturer in the world in 2018. However, meaningful work entails safeguarding the planet for future generations (Lips-Wiersma and Morris, 2017). This ultimately means that companies need to be able to source, produce, and distribute their products within the planetary boundaries. To better understand this aspect of MW it is relevant for MW scholars to pay attention to the political and economic context in which businesses currently operate.

Some CSR scholars make the distinction between weak sustainability (the paradigm from which much CSR literature still operates) and strong sustainability (Neumayer, 2012). Weak sustainability indicates that manufactured capital is of equal value to, and can take the place of, natural capital. For example, this would mean that it is reasonable to pollute rivers in order to support a strong agricultural industry, contributing to jobs and GDP growth. In strong sustainability, the existing stock of natural capital must be maintained because the functions it performs cannot be duplicated by manufactured capital. Some key concepts in weak sustainability are substitution, zero sum, eco-efficiency, corporate-centric management, incremental and technology-driven change. Some key concepts in strong sustainability are planetary boundaries, critical natural capital, scientific input for public deliberation, intergenerational equity, equal distribution of wealth, radical change, and whole systems approaches.

In the case of VW it could be argued that it practiced weak sustainability in that it substituted natural capital (clean air) for human capital (quality jobs, transport). But it would also be fair to say that the car industry as a whole does not yet manufacture cars in ways that enable humanity to stay within the boundaries of the planet, and all operate in a socio-political context that encourages weak over strong sustainability. For example, while VW has to pay $billions in fines in the US, it sold twenty times as many faulty diesel cars in Europe, yet the European Commission (EC) imposed no fines. The EC has been very protective of Germany, its largest manufacturer (Teffer, 2017), and at the time of writing was struggling to agree on some form of European emission control regulation. The Porsche and Piech families controlled 31 percent of shares and Ferdinand Piech was CEO of VW before becoming chair of the board. This may well have led to seriously conflicted incentives (Elson, Ferrere, and Goossen, 2015), but at present membership across company boards throughout the world is not exactly representative of community interests. Another example of a socio-political context that does not support strong sustainability is that there had been a lot of pressure on VW by both the unions and local government (which has a 20 percent voting interest) "to provide stable employment". The current economic growth model puts pressure on the planet (Elson, Ferrere, and Goossen, 2015). Strong sustainability requires strong democracy, yet even in a strong democratic country such as the Netherlands, the largest VW car importer had input into the minister's brief to parliament (Teffer, 2017). Strong sustainability also requires transition finance. If government subsidies had gone into more alternative energy rather than fossil fuels, would the car industry have been incentivized much earlier to consider electric or hydro-cars?

In summary, a combination of technological failure, limited board oversight, corporate lobbying, divergent national interests, corporations being too big to fail, and misdirected subsidies/lack of transition finance created incentives for VW to enact weak sustainability. And in this VW is not alone; while there are some examples of corporations exploring a different type of economy, at present most CSR efforts are at best doing less harm while unjust outcomes for people and planet continue (Tregidga, Milne, and Kearins, 2014). This raises significant questions about what the meaning of our work is, and what type of work and organizations bring hope at this particular time.

To create meaningful work, the organization would not necessarily be in a place where every person could currently enact strong sustainability through their daily work, but it would have identified a trajectory toward this and be transparent about where it is on this trajectory. Interface is an interesting example here. Quite early on in the process of becoming an environmentally responsible organization, they created a graph of "mount sustainability." While the first steps up the mountain were about eco-efficiency, such as eliminating waste, the next steps were about zero carbon, which requires significantly more investment in building clean factories. The next step, closing the loop, requires the redesign of products. The final step of mount sustainability they identified was "redesigning commerce." Clearly, Interface cannot redesign commerce by itself, but it shows an acute awareness that a modified form of business as usual is not enough to live within the boundaries of the planet, nor is it enough to truly satisfy the quest for meaning. The human need for meaning inevitably leads to questions of "what more can we do?" and "how do we know we do enough?" This means an ongoing process of transparently narrowing the gap between symbolic and substantive actions. At the time of writing, Interface is well on its way to creating a completely closed loop production system, being carbon free, and even identifying some manufacturing processes that restore the environment.

The current economic, political, ecological, and social system, while having done much good for many, has also led to large discrepancies between the rich and the poor, too much work for many as well as too little (secure work) for many others, as well as environmental degradation. In this context a MW agenda needs to address two questions: 1) how to create an experience of living in an ecologically sustainable society that is conducive to the experience of meaningful life, and 2) what are the kind of behaviors that promote ecological sustainability and also satisfy the need for meaning? Strong sustainability is a post-CSR paradigm. It goes far beyond largely PR-led, niche-oriented, self-regulated CSR (Siano et al., 2017) and asks how, through meaningful paid and non-paid work, we rebuild economic, social, and political systems to support the good life for all. It is therefore an important condition for CSR to lead to MW.

CONCLUSION

In deliberating if and how corporate social responsibility cultivates meaningful work, it has to be recognized that CSR is fraught with apparently irreconcilable tensions, and consequently the relationship between CSR and meaningful work is anything but straightforward. Using the example of Volkswagen, this chapter shows that, at present, it is reasonable to conclude that an employee may simultaneously experience more and less MW as a result of CSR implementation.

This is not necessarily a problem, as meaningful living and working will always take place between gravity and grace (Lips-Wiersma and Morris, 2017). MW does not require CSR to be perfect but meaning is lost when reality is not faced. As researchers, too, we need to face the whole of the complexity that the CSR–MW relationship entails, including the meaning of working at a time when inequalities are increasing and we are rapidly reaching the limits of planetary boundaries.

References

Aguinis, H. and Glavas, A. (2013). "Embedded versus peripheral corporate social responsibility: Psychological foundations." *Industrial and Organizational Psychology*, 6(4), 314–32.

Aguinis, H. and Glavas, A. (2017). "On Corporate Social Responsibility, Sensemaking, and the Search for Meaningfulness Through Work." *Journal of Management*, doi: 10.1177/0149206317691575. Available at: http://journals.sagepub.com/doi/pdf/10.1177/0149206317691575 [accessed July 16, 2018].

Bailey, C. and Madden, A. (2016). "What makes work meaningful—or meaningless." *MIT Sloan Management Review*, 57(4), 53–61.

Benn, S., Teo, S. T. T., and Martin, A. (2015). "Employee participation and engagement in working for the environment." *Personnel Review*, 44(4), 492–510.

Berger, I. E., Cunningham, P. H., and Drumwright, M. E. (2006). "Identity, identification, and relationship through social alliances." *Journal of the Academy of Marketing Science*, 34(2), 128–37.

Bhattacharya, C.B., Sen, S., and Korschun, D. (2008). "Using corporate social responsibility to win the war for talent." *MITSloan Review*, 49(2), 37–48.

Boiral, O. and Paillé, P. (2012). "Organizational citizenship behaviour for the environment: Measurement and validation." *Journal of Business Ethics*, 109, 431–45.

Bolton, S. C., Kim, R. C., and O'Gorman, K. (2011). "Corporate Social Responsibility as a dynamic internal organizational process: A case study." *Journal of Business Ethics*, 101(1), 61–74.

Bowie, N. E. (1998). "A Kantian theory of meaningful work." *Journal of Business Ethics*, 17(9), 1083–92.

Carbo, J., Langella, I. M., Dao, V. T., and Haase, S. J. (2014). "Breaking the ties that bind: From corporate sustainability to socially sustainable systems." *Business and Society Review*, 119(2), 175–206.

Castille, C. M. and Fultz, A. (2018). "How does collaborative cheating emerge? A case study of the Volkswagen emissions scandal." *Proceedings of the 51st Hawaii International Conference on Systems Science*, pp. 94–103. Manoa, Hawaii: Hawaii International Conference on System Sciences. Available at: https://scholarspace.manoa.hawaii.edu/handle/10125/49901 [accessed June 21, 2018].

Ciulla, J. B. (2011). *The Working Life: The promise and betrayal of modern work*. London: Random House.

Ciulla, J. B. (2012). "Worthy work and Bowie's Kantian theory of meaningful work." In D. G. Arnold and J. D. Harris (eds.), *Kantian Business Ethics: Critical perspectives*, pp. 115–31. Cheltenham: Edward Elgar Publishing.

Coffee, J. (2016). *Volkswagen and the culture of silence* [web page]. http://clsbluesky.law.columbia.edu/2016/05/23/volkswagen-and-the-culture-of-silence/ [accessed June 21, 2018].

Costas, J. and Kärreman, D. (2013). "Conscience as control: Managing employees through CSR." *Organization*, 20(3), 394–415.

Dahlsrud, A. (2008). "How corporate social responsibility is defined: An analysis of 37 definitions." *Corporate Responsibility and Environmental Management*, 15(1), 1–13.

Elson, C. M., Ferrere, C. K., and Goossen, N. J. (2015). "The bug at Volkswagen: Lessons in co-determination, ownership and board structure." *Journal of Applied Corporate Finance*, 27(4), 36–43.

Ewing, J. (2017). *Faster, Higher, Farther: The inside story of the Volkswagen scandal*. London: Random House.

Frankl, V. E. (1959). *Man's Search for Meaning*. New York: Pocket Books.

Garavan, T. N. and McGuire, D. (2010). "Human resource development and society: Human resource development's role in embedding corporate social responsibility, sustainability, and ethics in organizations." *Advances in Developing Human Resources*, 12(5), 487–507.

Glavas, A. and Godwin, L. N. (2013). "Is the perception of 'Goodness' good enough? Exploring the relationship between perceived Corporate Social Responsibility and employee organizational identification." *Journal of Business Ethics*, 114(1), 15–27.

Godkin, L. (2015). "Mid-management, employee engagement, and the generation of reliable sustainable Corporate Social Responsibility." *Journal of Business Ethics*, 130(1), 15.

Hackman, J. R. and Oldham, G. R. (1975). "Development of the Job Diagnostic Survey." *Journal of Applied Psychology*, 60(2), 159–70.

Hahn, T., Pinkse, J., Preuss, L., and Figge, F. (2015). "Tensions in Corporate Sustainability: Towards an integrative framework." *Journal of Business Ethics*, 127(2), 297–316.

Hodson, R. (2001). *Dignity at Work*. Cambridge: Cambridge University Press.

Houghton, S. M., Gabel, J. T., and Williams, D. W. (2009). "Connecting the two faces of CSR: Does employee volunteerism improve compliance?" *Journal of Business Ethics*, 87(4), 477–94.

Lamont, G. (2002). *The Spirited Business: Success stories of soul-friendly companies*. London: Hodder & Stoughton.

Leggett, T. (2017). "VW papers shed light on emissions scandal." *BBC News* [online], January 12. http://www.bbc.com/news/business-38603723 [accessed June 21, 2018].

Lepisto, D. and Pratt, M. (2017). "Meaningful work as realization and justification: Toward a dual conceptualization." *Organizational Psychology Review*, 7(2), 99–121.

Lindebaum, D., Geddes, D., and Gabriel, Y. (2017). "Moral emotions and ethics in organisations: Introduction to the special issue." *Journal of Business Ethics*, 141(4), 645–56.

Lips-Wiersma, M. S, Haar, J., and Wright, S. (2018 forthcoming). "The effect of fairness, responsible leadership and worthy work on multiple dimensions of meaningful work." *Journal of Business Ethics*.

Lips-Wiersma, M. and Morris, L. (2009). "Discriminating between 'meaningful work' and the 'management of meaning.' " *Journal of Business Ethics*, 88(3), 491–511.

Lips-Wiersma, M. S. and Morris, L. (2017). *The Map of Meaningful Work: A practical guide to sustaining our humanity*, 2nd edn. London: Routledge

Mansouri, N. (2016). "A case study of Volkswagen unethical practice in diesel emission test." *International Journal of Science and Engineering Applications*, 5(4), 211–16.

Markey, R., McIvor, J., and Wright, C. F. (2016). "Employee participation and carbon emissions reduction in Australian workplaces." *The International Journal of Human Resource Management*, 27(2), 173–91.

Michaelson, C., Pratt, M., Grant, A., and Dunn, C. (2014). "Meaningful work: Connecting Business Ethics and Organization Studies." *Journal of Business Ethics*, 121(1), 77–90.

Monzani, L., Braun, S., and Dick, R. V. (2016). "It takes two to tango: The interactive effect of authentic leadership and organizational identification on employee silence intentions." *German Journal of Human Resource Management*, 30(3–4), 246–66.

Neumayer, E. (2012). "Human development and sustainability." *Journal of Human Development and Capabilities*, 13(4), 561–79.

Pauchant, T. C. (ed.) (1995). *In Search of Meaning: Managing for the health of our organizations, our communities, and the natural world*. San Francisco: Jossey- Bass.

Peterson, D. K. (2004). "The relationship between perceptions of corporate citizenship and organizational commitment." *Business & Society*, 43(3), 296–319.

Phelps, E. S. (1997). *Rewarding Work*. Cambridge, MA: Harvard University Press.

Renwick, D. W. S., Redman, T., and Maquire, S. (2013). "Green human resource management: A review and research agenda." *International Journal of Management Reviews*, 15(1), 1–14.

Siano, A., Vollero, A., Conte, F., and Amabile, S. (2017). "'More than words': Expanding the taxonomy of greenwashing after the Volkswagen scandal." *Journal of Business Research*. 71: 27–37.

Sievers, B. (1994). *Work, Death and Life Itself: Essays on management and organization*. Berlin: Walter de Gruyter.

Strauss, K. (2017). "How Volkswagen rallied its employees after its emissions scandal (at least for now)." *Forbes* [website], July 26: https://www.forbes.com/sites/karstenstrauss/2017/07/26/how-volkswagen-rallied-its-employees-after-its-emissions-scandal-at-least-for-now/#69ed4c4a181b [accessed July 16, 2018].

Sun, W., Stewart, J., and Pollard, D. (2010). *Reframing Corporate Social Responsibility: Lessons from the global financial crisis*. Critical Studies on Corporate Responsibility, Governance and Sustainability, volume 1. Bingley: Emerald.

Teffer, P. (2017). *Dieselgate: Hoe de industrie sjoemelde en Europa faalde*. Amsterdam: Uitgeverij Q.

Tregidga, H., Milne, M., and Kearins, K. (2014). "(Re)presenting 'sustainable organisations.'" *Accounting, Organizations and Society*, 39(6), 477–94.

Ulus, M. and Hatipoglu, B. (2016). "Human aspect as a critical factor for organization sustainability in the tourism industry." *Sustainability*, 8(3), 232.

Wang, H., Tong, L., Takeuchi, R., and George, G. (2016). "Corporate Social Responsibility: An overview and new research directions: Thematic issue on Corporate Social Responsibility." *Academy of Management Journal*, 59(2), 534–44.

Wolfe, A. (1997). "The moral meaning of work." *Journal of Socio-Economics*, 26(6), 559–70.

Yeoman, R. (2014). "Conceptualising meaningful work as a fundamental human need." *Journal of Business Ethics*, 125: 235–51.

Zhu, Y., Xie, Y., Warner, M., and Guo, Y. (2015). "Employee participation and the influence on job satisfaction of the 'new generation' of Chinese employees." *The International Journal of Human Resource Management*, 26(19), 2395–411.

CHAPTER 25

CULTURAL, NATIONAL, AND INDIVIDUAL DIVERSITY AND THEIR RELATIONSHIP TO THE EXPERIENCE OF MEANINGFUL WORK

SEBASTIAAN ROTHMANN, LAURA ANNE WEISS, AND JOHANNES JACOBUS REDELINGHUYS

INTRODUCTION

MEANINGFUL work appears to be critical to individual and organizational outcomes for different countries and diverse individuals and cultures. Steger (2017) suggests that it is necessary to move beyond engagement and commitment to focus on meaningful work as an essential lever to improve individual functioning and organizational performance. Yeoman (2014) argues that meaningful work is a human need, which all people require to satisfy their interest in autonomy, freedom, and dignity.

Western psychology primarily focuses on the subjective dimension of meaning-making and on the level of autonomy individuals experience in determining which goals, values, and meanings individuals want to endorse in their lives (Delle Fave et al., 2013b). However, it neglects contextual factors such as culture. The presence of meaningful work is linked to how people view themselves (Baumeister, 1991), and cultural influences on the self may influence experienced meaning (Steger et al., 2008). Therefore, culture shapes the experiences individuals regard as meaningful (Kitayama and Markus, 2000). It affects the values and norms of its members (Erez and Gati, 2004). Values and norms are transmitted from one generation to another via social learning (e.g. modeling and observation).

This chapter starts with the definition of terms, followed by an overview of the cultural context of meaningful work. Next, individual diversity and meaningful work are discussed. Diversity on a national level will then be reviewed. Finally, conclusions and recommendations for future research about meaningful work are discussed.

DEFINITION OF TERMS

According to Rosso, Dekas, and Wrzesniewski (2010), two concepts are often used in relation to meaningful work, namely meaning and meaningfulness. Meaning is defined as the result of having made sense of something—for instance, the role that work plays in the context of an individual's life. Meaningful work occurs when individuals regard work as significant and high in positive meaning. There is a significant difference between the two concepts: meaning refers to what work signifies, while meaningfulness refers to the amount of significance attached to the work (Rosso, Dekas, and Wrzesniewski, 2010).

Steger, Dik, and Duffy (2012) integrate different dimensions in their definition of meaningful work. According to Steger, Dik, and Duffy (2012), meaningful work consists of three dimensions, namely psychological meaningfulness, meaning-making, and greater good motivations. Psychological meaningfulness in work is defined as a subjective experience that one's work matters and is significant. Meaning-making through work refers to the idea that work is a primary source of meaning in one's life, i.e. to help people to understand their selves and the world around them. Greater good motivations capture the desire to make a difference and to help others.

THE CULTURAL CONTEXT
OF MEANINGFUL WORK

Few studies have addressed the relationship between culture and meaningful work. One cross-cultural study by Claes and Ruiz-Quintanilla (1993) focused on work meaning patterns. The researchers found that cultures vary regarding work centrality, the importance of work goals, and orientation toward societal norms about working. They reported that individuals' age, country, work environment, work socialization, and behaviors had an impact on work meanings two years later. A poor work environment, poor person–environment fit, poor psychological well-being, poor career-enhancing strategies, and low effort level were characteristic of people whose work meaning patterns reflect low work centrality, high economic and expressive work goals, and low to moderate duty orientation on societal norms.

It is necessary to consider the themes that have characterized empirical research in cross-cultural psychology over time to understand the cultural context of meaningful work (Poortinga, 2011). First, it focused on differences in perception and cognition between countries. Research showed that different cultures understand cognitive tasks in the same way, and that differences in exposure to specific stimuli and tasks will lead to quantitative differences in performance levels. Van de Vijver and Leung (1997) showed that cultural factors (bias) might lead to a systematic representation of cultural differences. Therefore, it is crucial to assess the equivalence and bias (i.e. measurement invariance) of measures before scores of different cultures can be compared.

Van de Vijver (2011) distinguished between four types of equivalence, namely construct equivalence, structural equivalence, metric equivalence, and scalar (full score) equivalence. *Construct inequivalence* occurs when constructs lack a shared meaning (e.g. when a construct is tied up to its natural context and cannot be studied outside this context). *Structural equivalence* exists if an instrument measures the same construct in all cultural groups. *Metric equivalence* exists when the measurement scales have the same measurement units but a different origin. *Scalar equivalence* refers to identical scale across groups. However, full equivalence of measures is often out of reach (Poortinga, 2011). Applied to meaningful work, construct inequivalence occurs when meaningful work has different meanings in different cultures. Therefore, it is not possible to compare different cultures regarding meaningful work. Furthermore, meaningful work and its antecedents and outcomes can be compared when structural, metric, and scalar equivalence are confirmed. Measures developed in one culture cannot be used in another culture without assessing equivalence.

Second, social psychological variables became more prominent over time. Value dimensions according to the models of Hofstede (1980) and Schwartz (2011) became the backbone of cross-cultural comparative research. Since the seminal book by Hofstede (1980) on the consequences of culture, research has focused on identifying cultural values that distinguish between cultures and their implications for work behavior (Poortinga, 2011; Schwartz, 1999). Hofstede's (1980) recognition of the need to differentiate levels of analysis played a significant role in cross-cultural psychology. According to Schwartz (1999), culture-level dimensions of values rather than individual-level dimensions are appropriate to understand the meanings that members of different societies attach to work. Therefore, the culture of societies rather than the individual person is the unit of analysis. Cultural values refer to the implicitly or explicitly shared abstract ideas about what is good, right, and desirable in a society (Schwartz, 1999). Such cultural values are in contrast with individual values, which are relevant when individual differences are studied.

Hofstede et al. (1990) stated that organizational cultures have a different basis from national cultures: values differ between countries and practices differ between organizations. However, the research of House et al. (2004) on national and organizational culture in sixty-one nations showed different findings. House et al. studied nine dimensions of cultural variation on four measures (perceived nation-level values, nation-level practices, organization-level values, and organization-level practices). Their results showed that nation-level practices were a significant predictor of organization-level practices (Brodbeck et al., 2004). Nation-level values were also positively associated with organization-level values. Hofstede's view that organizations differ regarding practices and not values was only confirmed for four of the nine dimensions. Organizational researchers and cross-cultural researchers differ on the way in which scores of constructs are aggregated to understand culture. Organizational researchers use procedures that imply that individual viewpoints define a culture. In contrast, cross-cultural researchers employ a perspective that implies that individual viewpoints cluster together (Smith, 2011).

Van Hemert (2011) found that researchers overestimate the size of cross-cultural differences compared to similarities. She argued that score differences are often taken as an indication of cross-cultural differences (compared to similarities). Poortinga (2011) pointed out that differences between cultures were overpredicted in previous research, while the absence of differences was underpredicted. Culture should incorporate both cultural invariance and variations in theories.

Cultural and organizational values and practices might affect perceptions of meaningful work. However, researchers from different disciplines differ regarding how such variables should be measured, aggregated, and analyzed: on the individual, organizational, and country level.

Third, cultural psychology has emerged as a separate perspective, especially after publications by Markus and Kitayama (1991) and Shweder (1990). Markus and Kitayama (1991) distinguished between an independent and interdependent construal of the self.

Fourth, two perspectives—etic and emic—are relevant to understanding variables in different cultures. The etic approach addresses the comparability of variables across cultures and requires the equivalence of measuring instruments (Cheung, Van de Vijver, and Leong, 2011). An emic construct is defined differently across cultures and requires that a specific construct be studied in a specific culture. In the emic approach sensitivity to the family, social, cultural, and ecological contexts are incorporated. Cultural variables, such as the worldview of participants, acculturation level, and racial identity, might influence the assessment of a construct. When imported measurement instruments are used, emic aspects of a construct will be hidden. An emic analysis focuses on a single culture and employs descriptive and qualitative methods to study the behavior of interest.

INDIVIDUAL DIVERSITY AND MEANINGFUL WORK

Individuals have different backgrounds, values, motivations, and beliefs about work. Those individual differences play a role in the experience of meaningful work (Rosso, Dekas, and Wrzesniewski, 2010).

The Nature of the Task

How employees deal with the same tasks can differ widely, depending if and how much they use job *crafting*. Employees can craft or (re)design their work tasks and social work environment to better fit their competencies, values, and aims, thereby creating better circumstances to experience work as meaningful (Wrzesniewski and Dutton, 2001). Similar to crafting a task, meaningfulness can also be increased through relational crafting: by controlling with whom, how, and when to interact. A third way is cognitive crafting, which entails changing the perception of tasks and relationships, e.g. by focusing on the larger purpose and the value of the person's role rather than on the specific tasks the job requires (Berg, Dutton, and Wrzesniewski, 2013). A job can be crafted to lead to a better person–environment fit. Work is meaningful when individuals' values and mission fit those of the organization (Steger and Dik, 2010) and the values of the culture they live in (Suh and Choi, 2018).

Meaningful work is associated with work beliefs (e.g. whether work is believed to be a job, a career, or a calling), resulting in a serving orientation (Wrzesniewski et al., 1997). Rothmann and Hamukangandu (2013) confirmed this finding in a study of educators in Zambia. Berg, Dutton, and Wrzesniewski (2013) describe how another personal characteristic that decides if an employee can experience more meaning at work through job crafting is a specific mindset. That depends on how people see change and who is allowed to initiate change (themselves or their managers), as well as if they see their job as fixed or malleable, the extent of feeling agency, and the desirability of agency and job crafting. Also, the extent of seeing opportunities to job craft and the willingness to experiment with tasks, relationships, and perceptions of the job decides if someone establishes a job crafting mindset.

Many personal variables influence how likely an employee is to engage in job crafting: cognitive ability, knowledge, self-efficacy, self-image, trust, readiness to change, performance, and perceived level of control and competence (Clegg and Spencer, 2007). Berg, Wrzesniewski, and Dutton (2010) showed that how well employees see and use opportunities to craft their jobs is also dependent on their rank (high- vs. low-ranking jobs). While employees with high-ranking jobs felt constrained from crafting their job because of their time management, their low-ranking colleagues saw the challenges in job crafting in limits others impose on them and the expectations of others. They coped autonomously with these challenges by actively seeking others' support, thereby creating new job crafting opportunities. Felt autonomy, rather than formal autonomy in a job might be impaired with high-power jobs, which affects whether someone feels free to craft their job. Job crafting can be seen as a sense-making tool that helps individuals to make sense of the internal environment of their organization and can be enabled by empowerment (Asik-Dizdar and Esen, 2016).

Motivation for doing work tasks can differ widely between employees, from extrinsic motivation with external regulation to intrinsic motivation. When employees experience intrinsic motivation, they are more likely to interpret that as a sign of congruence between what they are doing at work and their self-concept. This process, in turn, leads to increased experiences of meaningfulness (Cardador, Pratt, and Dane, 2006). When work tasks are connected to one's self-concept, they will be experienced as meaningful and intrinsically motivating. This is even the case when they are not inherently enjoyable.

Workplace Relationships

Significance (the feeling of mattering to the social world) in the form of social relationships and generativity (contributing to the world and future generations) and the satisfaction of the need for relatedness is essential for work to be regarded as meaningful (Ward and King, 2017). Positive social relationships at work have been shown to improve perceived meaningful work (Ragins and Dutton, 2007). Therefore, having a job that offers little opportunity for social interaction, such as being a truck driver, can be derogative for experiencing meaning (Stillman et al., 2009). Organizations could specifically focus on employees who have fewer social interactions with their colleagues because of the nature of their task, for instance using telecommunication, to enable them to connect to others.

Having work that promotes *generativity* by contributing to the world gives people purpose (De St. Aubin, 2013). Schnell (2011) looked at individual differences in meaning-making and found that generativity is a strong predictor of meaningfulness. However, her study looked at general differences in meaning-making, not specifically related to work. Work can, however, give opportunities for generativity. Acting as a mentor for others can have a positive impact on the experience of generativity and meaningfulness, even after retirement (Miranda-Chan and Nakamura, 2015). Age also impacts generativity: as older people perceive their future time as limited, they value generativity goals that provide meaningful outcomes concerning the greater good, rather than individualistic goals (Lang and Carstensen, 2002). How much individuals prioritize could also impact what kind of careers they seek, with higher generativity levels maybe leading to the pursuit of more social jobs (Ward and King, 2017).

Work Beliefs

Ward and King (2017) found that there is also an individual diversity when it comes to attitudes about meaning and work. Work beliefs can relate to job involvement and work orientations (Rosso, Dekas, and Wrzesniewski, 2010). First, the *job involvement*, defined as the extent to which people see their job as a central part of their lives, is related to the experience of meaningfulness. The more job involvement someone has, the harder it gets to dissociate him or herself from the job, making their self-esteem also depend on the job. This makes the job more meaningful.

Second, individuals differ in their *work orientation*. As Rosso, Dekas, and Wrzesniewski (2010) describe, people either see their work as a calling, a career, or a job. The way they view their work shapes how they interpret the meaning of their work and how meaningful they find their work. A calling orientation is positively associated with meaningful work (Fouché, Rothmann, and van der Vyver, 2017), as work that allows someone to act on his or her calling is fulfilling and has an impact on others. Similar to beliefs, work values vary across individuals (Rosso, Dekas, and Wrzesniewski, 2010). People tend to select an occupation that is in line with their values (Lan et al., 2013).

Other Antecedents

Happiness. People who feel happy and satisfied with their life have been shown to tend also to be happy with their job and experience their work to be meaningful (Tenney, Poole, and Diener, 2016). If work is perceived as meaningful, it does not matter for their work engagement if people are more prone to experience positive emotion or not. But when work is seen as having little meaningfulness, employees with a more positive affective disposition show higher work engagement than employees with a low positive affective disposition (Steger et al., 2013).

Coherence and structure. Being in a (work) environment that makes sense to someone and that is regular, coherent, stable, and in line with their expectations enhances a feeling of meaningfulness. Work can be a way to provide structure and routine, thereby bolstering the sense of meaning, in itself and by offering opportunities for goal progress (Ward and King, 2017). However, if the given structure is increased externally, autonomy can suffer. Also, too much predictability can lead to the experience of boredom. Both reduced autonomy and feeling bored are threats to experiencing work to be meaningful. The need for structure, boredom-proneness, and being able to flourish in a chaotic and unstructured work environment will differ from person to person (Ward and King, 2017). So, the level of how organized a work environment should be for optimal meaningfulness is different for different employees.

Financial resources. Individuals' financial circumstances influence their experience of the meaning of work. Income and other indices of economic success, e.g. education, have been shown to be related to experiencing meaningfulness (Kobau et al., 2010). Reasons for this relationship could be the control it gives you on how to live your life, pursue goals, and help your family and others, which are all factors that in turn can foster meaning (Ward and King, 2016). A higher level of meaningful work is predictive of a gain in income across time (Hill et al., 2016). However, the impact of monetary rewards on work motivation and meaning-making remains highly controversial. The relationship between income and meaning in life is curvilinear, showing a decrease in the benefits of income when income is very high. Once a comfortable life is assured, meaningful work is not affected by more financial means. While an increase in income or offering educational possibilities likely improves meaning in employees with a low income, this will not affect the level of experienced meaningfulness in high-earning employees, who would instead profit from more flexibility (Costa et al., 2004). Interestingly, the negative effects of earning little money can be buffered by a good mood (Ward and King, 2016). Poverty constrains people from focusing on the meaning aspect of work, as the focus lies on the monetary value (Leana, Mittal, and Stiehl, 2012).

Spirituality, religion, and self-transcendent sources. There seems to be a relationship between spirituality and meaning of work (Giacalone, Jurkiewicz, and Fry, 2005). Studies have indicated that spiritual employees perceive their work differently than non-spiritual employees (Rosso, Dekas, and Wrzesniewski, 2010). Employees who aspire to connect to something sacred, such as a guiding power, have been shown to also interpret their work tasks as related to something greater than themselves. This, in turn, is related to a greater feeling of meaningfulness and purpose (Lips-Wiersma, 2002; Sullivan, 2006). They see their work activities more often in a spiritual context of transcendence, caring, and service (Curlin et al., 2007). Perceiving one's work in spiritual terms can lead to a deeper sense of meaningfulness and the experience of a purpose at work. Religious people also more often see their work as a calling (Ward and King, 2017).

Personal life. Family and personal life have been found to be the most important source of meaning (Delle Fave et al., 2013a). Sometimes, personal life can interfere with work life. For example, having children could lead to a conflict between work and personal goals. Long work hours are related to work interference with family and work–family conflict (Major, Klein, and Ehrhart, 2002). If people must spend long hours at work while feeling reluctant to do so, they experience lower purpose in life (Bonebright, Clay, and Ankenmann, 2000). Therefore, employers should consider offering family support and a flexible work schedule if they want to improve meaningfulness at work.

Generational differences. Being born in the same generational cohort means that people share particular life stages and experiences during the same historical time frame, such as starting school and work during roughly the same period. Shared experiences, such as being exposed to historical events and certain time-specific cultural phenomena, influence how they think and behave, so it is possible that there would be generational differences in how generations seek meaningful work. Some studies provide evidence that generation does indeed matter to some extent (Hoole and Bonnema, 2015; Kompier, 2005; Wong, Wan, and Gao, 2017).

Hoole and Bonnema (2015) looked at meaningful work across the generational cohorts of the baby boom generation (born between 1946 and 1964), Generation X (1965–1980) and Generation Y/Millennials (1981–1999). They found significant differences in the experience of meaningful work between the generational cohorts, including a significant difference between Generation Y and the baby boomers, with the latter experiencing the highest levels of meaningfulness and engagement at work. For employers, it means that they should consider using different strategies for meaningfulness for their oldest and youngest employees.

Several studies have taken a closer look at Generation Y employees. Allen (2004) found that performing meaningful work matters to this generation. Kompier (2005) proposed that employees from Generation Y tend to question the nature of the meaningfulness of their work at a higher level than people from older generations. According to Baruch (2004), people from Generation Y are not so much interested in getting a permanent job. Instead, they want to have meaningful and challenging work tasks, which also support them in reaching their career goals.

Wong, Wan, and Gao (2017) found a relationship between Generation Y's experience of meaningful work and their career choices. Three different categories of meanings were found: work-as-self, work-as-community, and work-as work. Work-as-self relates to the employee him or herself, to develop and grow, achieve goals, promotion, and move upward on the career ladder. Employees in this category pursue their career for achievement and self-attainment. Work-as-community is about the perception of the organization as a community, where workers can find recognition, acceptance, and relatedness. People in this category often pursue their career for communal benefits. Work-as-work means that work is seen as pure means to financial gain. People who only work to earn money view their job as tiring and unpleasant. This shows that on top of looking at different generations, organizations should also be aware of different meaning motives within a generational cohort.

   Occupation. When it comes to meaningful work, occupations seem to play a role. Lips-Wiersma, Wright, and Dik (2016) looked at the differences of meaningful work between white-collar (e.g. managers, business owners), pink-collar (e.g. waitresses, care workers), and blue-collar (e.g. laborer) occupations. They studied four factors: unity with others, developing the inner self, expressing full potential, and serving others. The development of the inner self, as well as the feeling of unity with others, were seen as equally necessary for all occupations. Serving others and expressing one's full potential were seen as more important by white-collar workers. How frequently work was experienced as meaningful also differed between the occupations. White-collar workers experienced higher levels of unity with others, expressing full potential, and serving others. The factors of unity with others and serving others can be seen as part of the relationship-antecedent in the framework for antecedents of meaningful work by Pratt and Ashforth (2003).

Mechanisms of Meaning

Rosso, Dekas, and Wrzesniewski (2010) have reviewed the processes through which the sources of meaning play a role in meaningful work. They summarized seven mechanisms. First, work can become meaningful through *authenticity*, manifested via experiencing self-concordance, identity affirmation, or personal engagement in work. *Self-efficacy* is the second mechanism, that works by experiencing autonomy and competence in your work, through overcoming work challenges or experiencing perceived impact by being able to make a difference for others. The third mechanism is *self-esteem*. The fourth process identified by Rosso, Dekas, and Wrzesniewski (2010) is *purpose*, by perceiving your work as being significant for the world around you or acting in accordance with the value systems of your organization. Fifth, they found *belongingness* to act as a mechanism toward meaningful work, via social identification with others at work or interpersonal connectedness. Sixth, *transcendence* can act as a mechanism via interconnection, connecting to something larger than the self, or self-abnegation, voluntarily subordinating yourself to something greater than the self. Finally, *cultural and interpersonal sense-making* has been found as a mechanism to meaningful work (Rosso, Dekas, and Wrzesniewski, 2010) and relates to sociocultural factors and the social environment that shape the meaning people make of different work aspects.

It depends on the individual which mechanisms are used. While one employee would try to exert more control over a work situation that evokes anxiety (self-efficacy mechanism), someone else could deal with the same situation by giving him or herself over to something or someone else (mechanism of transcendence), for example faithfully following a transformational leader. In conclusion, there is a vast individual diversity not only in *what* creates meaningful work but also *how* meaning is shaped.

NATIONAL CULTURE AND MEANINGFUL WORK

Taras, Rowney, and Steel (2009) suggest that cultural definitions share four assumptions. This section will, however, focus on two of the assumptions due to their possible applicability to employees' experiences of meaningful work. First, culture is an intricate multilevel construct, which may comprise (but not be limited to) individual, organizational, and national culture (see Erez and Gati, 2004). It is important to explicitly state the level of analysis when referring to culture (Kwantes and Glazer, 2017), and not assume that cultural aspects on one level will universally apply to every other level. For instance, Hofstede (1980) indicated that work-related values (as a measure of culture) should be assessed from a national level, as the same values may not be applicable in the individual context. Therefore, proclaiming that every Chinese person is collectivistic simply because they belong to the Chinese culture would be a fundamental ecological misconception (Hofstede, 1980), as the description of a culture and the description of an individual embedded within that culture are two distinct concepts (Kwantes and Glazer, 2017). This is illustrated by other cultural models (Bond et al., 2004; Schwartz, 1999; Trompenaars, 1993), where the number of cultural dimensions varies according to the level of assessment (national vs. the individual level).

Furthermore, culture is multifaceted, which may manifest materially (e.g. clothing, food) or non-materially (e.g. language, values). Although we acknowledge other cultural facets, this section will focus on values, as virtually all existing instruments have quantified culture from a values perspective. Values are easier to measure than other cultural facets, especially from a national perspective. In a review of 121 culture measures, Taras, Rowney, and Steel (2009) established that 5/13 percent of those instruments are theoretically similar to the dimensions proposed by Hofstede (1980, 2001). Based on this notion, culture from a national level is best explained by Hofstede's (1980, 2001) five dimensions, that rank countries based on their aggregate scores on individualism, masculinity, power distance, uncertainty avoidance, and long-term orientation. A sixth dimension, indulgence, was later added by Minkov (2007). From the preceding discussion, one can thus conclude that culture is a multilevel, multifaceted concept. Therefore, in the generalization of findings, one should be cautious about creating comparisons across cultural levels and facets (Kwantes and Glazer, 2017).

Second, culture is relatively stable (Taras, Rowney, and Steel, 2009). Although it may be more accurate for specific cultural aspects than others, research (e.g. Inglehart and Welzel, 2005) suggests that national culture is susceptible to change. For instance, using Hofstede's (1980) framework, specific countries may significantly shift from being at one end of the continuum (masculine) to the other end of the continuum (feminine) due to a combination of environmental changes. This is illustrated by Fernandez et al. (1997), who assessed Hofstede's (1980) dimensions twenty-five years later. Some findings from their study showed that the United States of America shifted on two (lower uncertainty avoidance and masculinity) of the original four dimensions, while Japan (higher uncertainty avoidance), Mexico (higher individualism), and Germany (lower masculinity) also shifted on at least one dimension. Therefore, it is suggested that managers should focus on determining value profiles through primary data at the individual level, rather than depend on country aggregates (Fernandez et al., 1997).

From research by Markus and Kitayama (1991) and Triandis (1989), cultures are thought to influence self-concepts along an independent (individualistic) to interdependent (collectivistic) continuum. In independent cultures, individuals may enhance their self-images because the self is emphasized as an individual agent (Heine, Kitayama, and Lehman, 2001). Interdependent cultures emphasize the self as part of a communal network and individuals may criticize their self-images (Heine et al., 1999). People from independent cultures seem to focus on success and self-enhancement (Heine et al., 1999), while those from interdependent cultures tend to place a higher value on effort and strive for self-improvement. Steger et al. (2008) found that people in the USA were less inclined to search for meaning in life when they experience it. In contrast, people in Japan were more inclined to search for meaning when they experience more meaning in life.

A significant study has been reported by the Meaning of Working International Research Team (MOW, 1987). The leading concept in this project was work centrality, which is defined as "a general belief about the value of working in one's life" (MOW, 1987: 17). To assess meaning of work, respondents had to answer how important work was for them, and how important it was in relation to other life roles (leisure, community life, religion, and family). The results showed that 86 percent of all subjects would continue to work even if they had sufficient money to live in comfort for the rest of their lives. Furthermore, work was second in importance among the five life roles. Only family was rated higher. Differences between countries were about 1.5 times larger than between occupational groups.

CONCLUSION

Indeed, the contemporary organization of work, which is increasingly precarious, sometimes unpaid, and frequently subject to coercive practices, is generating a crisis of meaning, as organizations fail to connect to social and environmental purposes.

If people still aspire to work which is useful, interesting, expressive, or in some other way valuable, worthwhile, and dignified, this raises questions about how we arrange economic and organizational practices to promote such work.

In line with the findings of Cheung, van de Vijver, and Leong (2011), it is vital to use a combined etic and emic approach, which brings together methodological rigor and cultural sensitivity to research meaningful work in different cultures and countries. Such an approach is helpful in delineating the universal and culture-specific aspects of meaningful work and its antecedents. Meaningful work must be understood not only in universal terms (i.e. an etic perspective) but also in terms of each culture (an emic perspective). The cultural context of meaningful work must be unpacked in a given society to fully understand the construct.

The findings of various studies on individual diversity and their relationship to the experience of meaningful work strongly suggest that to experience optimal levels of meaningful work, one size does *not* fit all. Organizations should incorporate measures of individual differences and personalize strategies to fit the individual if they want to get the most out of strategies to improve meaningfulness at work. Individual characteristics, such as the generation someone belongs to, can give important clues on what can give meaning and how meaning is shaped.

Assessing meaningful work from a national culture perspective could be problematic, as national culture fails to account for factors such as within-culture variability, acculturation, the changing nature of cultural aspects (e.g. values), and cultural tightness or looseness. Although national culture may influence workplace attitudes and behaviors (to a greater extent in culturally tight nations and among older, more educated men), familiarity with an employee's nationality is insufficient to predict his or her organizational functioning in modern times (Taras, Steel, and Kirkman, 2011). The world has become a global village. Countries have different subcultures that vary from the dominant national culture (Kwantes and Glazer, 2017). Consequently, geographical borders in cross-cultural research are losing relevance (Taras, Rowney, and Steel, 2009), as workforces are continually diversifying. Since national and regional culture aggregates are becoming outdated, a stronger emphasis should be placed on individual-level analysis (Taras, Rowney, and Steel, 2009), especially in culturally loose nations (e.g. Ukraine) where cultural values are expected to have lower influence in predicting employee outcomes (Taras, Steel, and Kirkman, 2011). Furthermore, national culture's predictive power is also significantly weaker in explaining individual-level outcomes (e.g. an employee's psychological meaningfulness) than group-level outcomes (Taras, Steel, and Kirkman, 2011). In a re-analysis of Hofstede's data, Gerhart and Fang (2005) established that nationality explained a low percentage (only 2–4 percent) of variance in individual values, while organizational (in relation to country) differences accounted for a higher percentage explained in cultural values. Although national culture may still influence an employee's experiences of meaningful work, we suggest that individual and organizational cultural factors will play a more significant role.

Minkov and Hofstede (2012) found that there is little empirical support for the objection that the concept of nation is compromised by cultural diversity within some countries and similarities across national borders. However, Poortinga (2011) maintains that it is risky to treat nations as uniform cultures. There is weakness in conceptualizing culture solely based on clustering individual values and beliefs (Smith, 2011). From an organizational research perspective, it is necessary to consider the extent to which shared understandings of a context exist. Given the divergence of methods in the Hofstede et al. (1990) and House et al. (2004) studies, it is difficult to provide a definitive answer on the extent to which national and organizational cultures match. It might be useful to compare characteristics of culture based on aggregated values with characteristics based on aggregated ratings of cultural practices (Smith, 2011).

Various challenges exist regarding cross-cultural comparisons. These challenges include conceptual equivalence, measurement invariance, and response styles. First, measurement invariance of measures of meaningful work (and its antecedents and outcomes) has not been studied sufficiently. Therefore, it is difficult to make cross-cultural comparisons of meaningful work. It is not only essential to assess equivalence of meaningful work measures for different cultures, but also for different age and gender groups. Lack of measurement invariance limits the conclusions that can be reached from between-group comparisons (Steger, Oishi, and Kashdan, 2009).

Difficulties might arise when comparing constructs (e.g. meaningful work) across cultural bounds (Kahneman and Krueger, 2006; Mathews, 2012). For example, concerning self-reports, North Americans may engage in self-serving biases such as self-enhancement more than East Asians (Diener, Oishi, and Lucas, 2003). In East Asian societies such as Japan, personal modesty and suppression of positive affect are important social values, and one should not boast about one's success or declare one's well-being too strongly (Mathews, 2012). Smith (2011) warns that language used in surveys may often lead to an underestimation of cultural differences. Organizations might prefer to administer surveys in English. However, this might result in the distortion of responses of non-English speakers toward responses that are typical of English speakers.

FUTURE DIRECTIONS

Future research should employ longitudinal and experimental designs to study the following questions: What are the specific factors that affect meaningful work in distinct organizational and national cultures? Do multicultural identity and social inequity affect the experiences of meaningful work? What are the implications of globalization for meaningful work? How does meaningful work affect functioning in different cultures? A shortcoming in cross-cultural research in organizations is that most of the studies have focused on business organizations rather than on governments, schools, hospitals, and non-governmental organizations (Smith, 2011). There has also been a preoccupation with contrasts between North America and Asia (Steger, 2017). Future research on meaningful work should be inclusive and focus on all the above mentioned contexts.

To study culture, Poortinga (2011) argued in favor of the study of conventions in specific communities to understand individuals' behavior. He points out that individuals' motives behind their behavior might be based on constraints—in law-bound rules—on the one hand, and affordances, or those options open to an individual from which he or she can choose, on the other. These affordances and constraints or rules are what inform decisions on how to act, think, and feel. An individual's cognition, behavior, and affect again crystallize into practices and mentalities which are often unique to a particular community of people. Conventions include overt actions, beliefs, and ways of dealing with problems. When conventions are more or less independent of each other, this implies that only limited psychological organization of cultural differences needs to be presumed.

References

Allen, P. (2004). "Welcoming Y." *Benefits Canada*, 28(9), 51–6.

Asik-Dizdar, O. and Esen, A. (2016). "Sensemaking at work: Meaningful work experience for individuals and organizations." *International Journal of Organizational Analysis*, 24(1), 2–17.

Baruch, Y. (2004). *Managing Careers: Theory and practice*. London: Pearson Education.

Baumeister, R. F. (1991). *Meanings of Life*. New York: Guilford.

Berg, J. M., Dutton, J. E., and Wrzesniewski, A. (2013). "Job Crafting and Meaningful Work." In B. J. Dik, Z. S. Byrne, and M. F. Steger (eds.), *Purpose and Meaning in the Workplace*, pp. 81–104. Washington, DC: American Psychological Association.

Berg, J. M., Wrzesniewski, A., and Dutton, J. E. (2010). "Perceiving and responding to challenges in job crafting at different ranks: When proactivity requires adaptivity." *Journal of Organizational Behavior*, 31(2–3), 158–86.

Bond, M. H., Leung, K., Au, A., Tong, K.-K., Reimel de Carrasquel, S., Murakami, F., et al. (2004). "Culture-level dimensions of social axioms and their correlates across 41 cultures." *Journal of Cross-Cultural Psychology*, 35, 548–70.

Bonebright, C. A., Clay, D. L., and Ankenmann, R. D. (2000). "The relationship of workaholism with work–life conflict, life satisfaction, and purpose in life." *Journal of Counseling Psychology*, 47(4), 469–77.

Brodbeck, F. C., Hanges, P. J., Dickson, M. W., Gupta, V., and Dorfman, P. W. (2004). "Societal Culture and Industrial Sector Influences on Organizational Culture." In R. J. House, P. J. Hanges, M. Javidan, P. W. Dorfman, and V. Gupta (eds.), *Culture, Leadership and Organizations: The GLOBE study of 62 societies*, pp. 654–68. Thousand Oaks, CA: Sage.

Cardador, M. T., Pratt, M. G., and Dane, E. I. (2006). "Do callings matter in medicine? The influence of callings versus careers on domain specific work outcomes." Paper presented at the Positive Organizational Scholarship Conference, Ann Arbor, MI.

Cheung, F. M., van de Vijver, F. J. R. and Leong, F. T. L. (2011). "Toward a new approach to the study of personality in culture." *American Psychologist*, 66, 593–603.

Claes, R. and Ruiz-Quintanilla, S. A. (1993). *Work Meaning Patterns in Early Career*. CAHRS Working Paper #93-22. Ithaca, NY: Cornell University, School of Industrial and Labor Relations, Center for Advanced Human Resource Studies.

Clegg, C. and Spencer, C. (2007). "A circular and dynamic model of the process of job design." *Journal of Occupational and Organizational Psychology*, 80(2), 321–39.

Costa, G., Åkerstedt, T., Nachreiner, F., Baltieri, F., Carvalhais, J., Folkard, S., et al. (2004). "Flexible working hours, health, and well-being in Europe: Some considerations from a SALTSA project." *Chronobiology International*, 21(6), 831–44.

Curlin, F. A., Dugdale, L. S., Lantos, J. D., and Chin, M. H. (2007). "Do religious physicians disproportionately care for the underserved?" *Analysis of Family Medicine*, 5(4), 353–60.

de St. Aubin, E. (2013). "Generativity and the Meaning of Life." In J. A. Hicks and C. Routledge (eds.), *The Experience of Meaning in Life*, pp. 241–55. Netherlands: Springer.

Delle Fave, A., Brdar, I., Wissing, M. P., and Vella-Brodrick, D. A. (2013a). "Sources and motives for personal meaning in adulthood." *The Journal of Positive Psychology*, 8(6), 517–29.

Delle Fave, A., Wissing, M. P., Brdar, I., Vella-Brodrick, D. A., and Freire, T. (2013b). "Cross-cultural Perceptions of Meaning and Goals in Adulthood: Their Roots and Relations with Happiness." In A. S. Waterman (ed.), *The Best Within Us: Positive psychology perspectives on eudaimonia*, pp. 227–45. Washington, DC: American Psychological Association.

Diener, E., Oishi, S., and Lucas, R. E. (2003). "Personality, culture and subjective well-being: Emotional and cognitive evaluations of life." *Annual Review of Psychology*, 54, 403–25.

Erez, M. and Gati, E. (2004). "A dynamic, multi-level model of culture: From the micro level of the individual to the macro level of a global culture." *Applied Psychology: An International Review*, 53, 583–98.

Fernandez, D. R., Carlson, D. S., Stepina, L. P., and Nicholson, J. D. (1997). "Hofstede's country classification 25 years later." *Journal of Social Psychology*, 137(1), 43–54.

Fouché, E., Rothmann, S., and van der Vyver, C. (2017). "Antecedents and outcomes of meaningful work among school teachers." *SA Journal of Industrial Psychology/SA Tydskrif vir Bedryfsielkunde*, 43(0), a1398. Available at: https://doi.org/10.4102/sajip.v43i0.1398 [accessed June 28, 2018].

Gerhart, B. and Fang, M. (2005). "National culture and human resource management: Assumptions and evidence." *The International Journal of Human Resource Management*, 16(6), 971–86.

Giacalone, R. A., Jurkiewicz, C. L., and Fry, L. W. (2005). "From Advocacy to Science: The Next Steps in Workplace Spirituality Research." In R. F. Paloutzian and C. L. Park (eds.), *Handbook of the Psychology of Religion and Spirituality*, pp. 515–28. New York: Guilford.

Heine, S. J., Kitayama, S., and Lehman, D. R. (2001). "Cultural differences in self-evaluation: Japanese readily accept negative self-relevant information." *Journal of Cross-Cultural Psychology*, 32, 434–43.

Heine, S. J., Lehman, D. R., Markus, H. R., and Kitayama, S. (1999). "Is there a universal need for positive self-regard?" *Psychological Review*, 106, 766–94.

Hill, P. L., Turiano, N. A., Mroczek, D. K., and Burrow, A. L. (2016). "The value of a purposeful life: Sense of purpose predicts greater income and net worth." *Journal of Research in Personality*, 65, 38–42.

Hofstede, G. (1980). *Culture's Consequences: International differences in work-related values*. Beverly Hills, CA: Sage.

Hofstede, G. (2001). *Cultures Consequences: Comparing values, behaviors, institutions and organizations across nations*, 2nd edn. Thousand Oaks, CA: Sage.

Hofstede, G., Neuijen, B., Ohayv, D. D., and Sanders, G. (1990). "Measuring organizational cultures: A qualitative and quantitative study across twenty cases." *Administrative Science Quarterly*, 35, 286–316.

Hoole, C. and Bonnema, J. (2015). "Work engagement and meaningful work across generational cohorts." *SA Journal of Human Resource Management/SA Tydskrif vir Menslikehulpbronbestuur*, 13(1), 1–11.

House, R. J., Hanges, P. J., Javidan, M., Dorfman, P. W. and Gupta, V. (eds.) (2004). *Culture, Leadership and Organizations: The GLOBE study of 62 societies*. Thousand Oaks, CA: Sage.

Inglehart, R. and Welzel, C. (2005). *Modernization, Cultural Change and Democracy: The human development sequence*. New York: Cambridge University Press.

Kahneman, D. and Krueger, A. B. (2006). "Developments in the measure of subjective well-being." *Journal of Economic Perspectives*, 20(1), 3–24.

Kitayama, S. and Markus, H. R. (2000). "The Pursuit of Happiness and the Realization of Sympathy: Cultural Patterns of Self, Social Relations, and Well-being." In E. Diener and E. M. Suh (eds.), *Culture and Subjective Well-being*, pp. 113–61. Cambridge, MA: MIT Press.

Kobau, R., Sniezek, J., Zack, M. M., Lucas, R. E., and Burns, A. (2010). "Well-being assessment: An evaluation of well-being scales for public health and population estimates of well-being among US adults." *Applied Psychology: Health & Well-Being*, 2(3), 272–97.

Kompier, M. (2005). "Dealing with Workplace Stress." In C. L. Cooper (ed.), *Handbook of Stress Medicine and Health*, pp. 349–74. London: CRC Press.

Kwantes, C. T. and Glazer, S. (2017). *Culture, Organizations, and Work: Clarifying concepts*. Cham: Springer.

Lan, G., Okechuku, C., Zhang, H., and Cao, J. (2013). "Impact of job satisfaction and personal values on the work orientation of Chinese accounting practitioners." *Journal of Business Ethics*, 112(4), 627–40.

Lang, F. R. and Carstensen, L. L. (2002). "Time counts: Future time perspective, goals, and social relationships." *Psychology and Aging*, 17(1), 125–39.

Leana, C. R., Mittal, V., and Stiehl, E. (2012). "Organizational behavior and the working poor." *Organization Science*, 23(3), 888–906.

Lips-Wiersma, M. (2002). "The influence of spiritual "meaning-making" on career behavior." *The Journal of Management Development*, 21(7), 497–520.

Lips-Wiersma, M., Wright, S., and Dik, B. (2016). "Meaningful work: Differences among blue-, pink-, and white-collar occupations." *Career Development International*, 21(5), 534–51.

Major, V. S., Klein, K. J., and Ehrhart, M. G. (2002). "Work time, work interference with family, and psychological distress." *Journal of Applied Psychology*, 87(3), 427–36.

Markus, H. R. and Kitayama, S. (1991). "Culture and the self: Implications for cognition, emotion, and motivation." *Psychological Review*, 98, 224–53.

Mathews, G. (2012). "Happiness, culture and context." *International Journal of Well-being*, 2, 299–312.

Minkov, M. (2007). *What Makes us Different and Similar: A new interpretation of the World Values Survey and other cross-cultural data*. Sofia, Bulgaria: Klasika y Stil Publishing House.

Minkov, M. and Hofstede, G. (2012). "Is national culture a meaningful concept? Cultural values delineate homogeneous national clusters of in-country regions." *Cross-Cultural Research*, 46(2), 133–59.

Miranda-Chan, T. and Nakamura, J. (2015). "A generativity track to life meaning in retirement: Ego-integrity returns on past academic mentoring investments." *Work, Aging and Retirement*, 2(1), 24–37.

MOW International Research Team (1987). *The Meaning of Working*. London: Academic Press.

Poortinga, Y. H. (2011). "Research on Behaviour and Culture: Current Ideas and Future Projections." In F. J. R. van de Vijver, A. Chasiotis, and S. Breugelmans (eds.), *Fundamental*

Questions in Cross-cultural Psychology, pp. 545–78. Cambridge: Cambridge University Press.

Pratt, M. G. and Ashforth, B. E. (2003). "Fostering Positive Meaning at Work." In K. S. Cameron, J. E. Dutton, and R. E. Quinn (eds.), *Positive Organizational Scholarship: Foundations of a new discipline*, pp. 309–27. San Francisco, CA: Berrett-Koehler.

Ragins, B. R. and Dutton, J. E. (2007). "Positive Relationships at Work: An Introduction and Invitation." In J. E. Dutton and B. R. Ragins (eds.), *Exploring Positive Relationships at Work: Building a theoretical and research foundation*, pp. 3–25. Mahwah, NJ: Lawrence Erlbaum Associates.

Rosso, B. D., Dekas, K. H., and Wrzesniewski, A. (2010). "On the meaning of work: A theoretical integration and review." *Research in Organizational Behavior*, 30, 91–127.

Rothmann, S. and Haṃukangandu, L. (2013). "Psychological meaningfulness and work engagement among educators of Zambia." *SA Journal of Education*, 33(2), 1–16.

Schnell, T. (2011). "Individual differences in meaning-making: Considering the variety of sources of meaning, their density and diversity." *Personality and Individual Differences*, 51, 667–73.

Schwartz, S. H. (1999). "A theory of cultural values and some implications for work." *Applied Psychology: An International Review*, 48, 23–47.

Schwartz, S. H. (2011). "Values: Cultural and Individual." In F. J. R. van de Vijver, A. Chasiotis, and S. M. Breugelmans (eds.), *Fundamental Questions in Cross-cultural Psychology*, pp. 463–93. Cambridge: Cambridge University Press.

Shweder, R. A. (1990). "Cultural Psychology: What Is It?" In J. W. Stigler, R. A. Shweder, and G. Herdt (eds.), *Cultural Psychology: Essays on comparative human development*, pp. 1–43. Cambridge: Cambridge University Press.

Smith, P. B. (2011). "The Cultural Context of Organizational Behavior." In F. J. R. van de Vijver, A. Chasiotis, and S. Breugelmans (eds.), *Fundamental Questions in Cross-cultural Psychology*, pp. 494–517. Cambridge: Cambridge University Press.

Steger, M. F. (2017). "Creating Meaning and Purpose in Work." In L. Oades, M. F. Steger, A. Della Fave, and J. Passmore, (eds.), *The Wiley-Blackwell Handbook of Psychology of Positivity and Strengths-based Approaches at Work*, pp. 60–81. London: Wiley-Blackwell.

Steger, M. F. and Dik, B. J. (2010). "Work as Meaning." In P. A. Linley, S. Harrington, and N. Page (eds.), *Oxford Handbook of Positive Psychology and Work*, pp. 131–42. Oxford: Oxford University Press.

Steger, M. F., Dik, B. J., and Duffy, R. D. (2012). "Measuring meaningful work: The Work and Meaning Inventory (WAMI)." *Journal of Career Assessment*, 20, 322–37.

Steger, M. F., Kawabata, Y., Shimai, S., and Otake, K. (2008). "The meaningful life in Japan and the United States: Levels and correlates of meaning in life." *Journal of Research in Personality*, 42, 660–78.

Steger, M. F., Littman-Ovadia, H., Miller, M., Menger, L., and Rothmann, S. (2013). "Engaging in work even when it is meaningless: Positive affective disposition and meaningful work interact in relation to work engagement." *Journal of Career Assessment*, 21(2), 348–61.

Steger, M. F., Oishi, S., and Kashdan, T. B. (2009). "Meaning in life across the life span: Levels and correlates of meaning in life from emerging adulthood to older adulthood." *The Journal of Positive Psychology*, 4, 43–52.

Stillman, T. F., Baumeister, R. F., Lambert, N. M., Crescioni, A. W., DeWall, C. N. and Fincham, F. D. (2009). "Alone and without purpose: Life loses meaning following social exclusion." *Journal of Experimental Social Psychology*, 45, 686–94.

Suh, E. M. and Choi, S. (2018). "Predictors of Subjective Well-being Across Cultures." In E. Diener, S. Oishi, and L. Tay (eds.), *Handbook of Well-being*. Salt Lake City, UT: DEF Publishers.

Sullivan, S. C. (2006). "The work–faith connection for low-income mothers: A research note." *Sociology of Religion*, 67(1), 99–108.

Taras, V., Rowney, J., and Steel, P. (2009). "Half a century of measuring culture: Approaches, challenges, limitations, and suggestions based on the analysis of 112 instruments for quantifying culture." *Journal of International Management*, 15, 50–75.

Taras, V., Steel, P., and Kirkman, B. (2011). "Three decades of research on national culture in the workplace: Do the differences still make a difference?" *Organization Dynamics*, 40(3), 189–98.

Tenney, E. R., Poole, J. M., and Diener, E. (2016). "Does positivity enhance work performance? Why, when, and what we don't know." *Research in Organizational Behavior*, 36, 27–46.

Triandis, H. C. (1989). "The self and social behavior in differing cultural contexts." *Psychological Review*, 96, 506–20.

Trompenaars, F. (1993). *Riding the Waves of Culture: Understanding cultural diversity in business*. London: The Economist Books.

van de Vijver, F. J. R. (2011). "Bias and Real Differences in Cross-cultural Differences: Neither Friends nor Foes." In F. J. R. van de Vijver, A. Chasiotis, and S. Breugelmans (eds.), *Fundamental Questions in Cross-cultural Psychology*, pp. 235–58. Cambridge: Cambridge University Press.

van de Vijver, F. J. R. and Leung, K. (1997). *Methods and Data Analysis for Cross-cultural Research*. Newbury Park, CA: Sage.

van Hemert, D. (2011). "Frameworks for Explaining Cross-cultural Variance: A Meta-analytical Examination of their Usefulness." In F. J. R. van de Vijver, A. Chasiotis, and S. Breugelmans (eds.), *Fundamental Questions in Cross-cultural Psychology*, pp. 116–33. Cambridge: Cambridge University Press.

Ward, S. J. and King, L. A. (2016). "Poor but happy? Income, happiness, and experienced and expected meaning in life." *Social Psychological and Personality Science*, 7(5), 463–70.

Ward, S. J. and King, L. A. (2017). "Work and the good life: How work contributes to meaning in life." *Research in Organizational Behavior*, 37, 59–82.

Wong, I. A., Wan, Y. K. P., and Gao, J. H. (2017). "How to attract and retain Generation Y employees? An exploration of career choice and the meaning of work." *Tourism Management Perspectives*, 23, 140–50.

Wrzesniewski, A. and Dutton, J. E. (2001). "Crafting a job: Revisioning employees as active crafters of their work." *Academy of Management Review*, 26(2), 179–201.

Wrzesniewski, A., McCauley, C., Rozin, P., and Schwartz, B. (1997). "Jobs, careers, and callings: People's relations to their work." *Journal of Research in Personality*, 31, 21–33.

Yeoman, R. (2014). "Conceptualising meaningful work as a fundamental human need." *Journal of Business Ethics*, 125, 235–51.

CHAPTER 26

BRINGING POLITICAL ECONOMY BACK IN

A Comparative Institutionalist Perspective on Meaningful Work

MARC THOMPSON

INTRODUCTION

THE nature and purpose of work are core to the foundational debates in political economy and underpin traditional and heterodox debates in economics since the times of Adam Smith and Karl Marx. However, political economy perspectives are largely missing from the recent resurgence of interest in meaningful work which has been influenced by psychology, organizational behavior, political theory, and philosophy, among others. Drawing on comparative political economy and in particular the comparative institutionalist literature, this chapter seeks to redress this imbalance and bring political economy, and in particular comparative institutionalism, back into the current debates on meaningful work.

The purpose of this chapter is to encourage greater dialogue between comparative institutionalism and meaningful work, thereby opening up new insights and questions related to the role of the socio-political context in shaping the opportunities for meaningful work. Comparative institutionalism is not one coherent and integrated body of work. Rather, there are different schools and each one places emphasis on different mechanisms and processes that might explain institutional variety across nations. These schools open up valuable insights into the opportunities for meaningful work in different societies and, from a normative perspective, point to different public policy agendas, if the wider opportunities for meaningful work are to be taken seriously.

As a consequence, the chapter addresses a number of questions. First, to what extent is the potential for meaningful work afforded by socio-political institutions in different countries? Second, what empirical evidence is there that the opportunity for meaningful work is more fairly distributed in some societies than others, and why? Third, what specific institutions may be more important than others in undergirding the potential for more meaningful work? Fourth, what are the implications for public policy in the future? Finally, I consider how the predominant focus on the micro- and to some extent meso-dynamics of meaningful work can be integrated in a socio-political macro-level perspective. This can open up new questions about the type of society we want to live in and the role of work in that society. As such, questions of power and interests become foregrounded.

The chapter is structured as follows. First, I return to the question of meaningful work, the main focus of the Handbook, and underline its simultaneous subjective and objective qualities and how they are interrelated. The bias toward subjective experiences is noted and the need to re-engage with the material objective qualities of work asserted. I then turn to discuss the spillover effects from meaningful work, both in how it can contribute to human flourishing and also in how broader political institutions can facilitate meaningful work opportunities. I then move on to outline the different schools of institutionalism and make some initial observations on the insights they provide, but also the implications for future research on meaningful work. I then consider the current research informed by these perspectives and their implications and end the chapter by outlining strategies for institutional change that support more opportunities for meaningful work.

What is Meaningful Work?

The purpose of this Handbook is to provide multiple theoretical perspectives on the concept of meaningful work, thereby expanding the concept and making it more amenable to further conceptual and empirical investigation. One of the desired outcomes is to establish not only the multidimensional nature of the construct, but also to deepen insights into its multilevel nature and the interlinkages between dynamics at different levels and how these interact to shape the subjective and objective character of meaningful work. But what is meaningful work?

The current debate differentiates between meaning "in" work and the meaning "of" work. The former takes a psychological or philosophical perspective, arguing that meaning is a process which can be shaped by a range of factors such as personality, drive, and values. This approach is core to the work of Pratt, Pradies, and Lepisto (2013), who propose three orientations to gaining meaning and fulfillment through work—the first, a craftsmanship orientation which values doing work well for its own sake, the second, a serving orientation which values work as a drive to help others, and finally a kinship orientation which values work that creates bonds among people working together. There is debate as to whether one orientation is sufficient to create a meaningful work experience, and other writers such as Steger (2012) have argued that all three orientations need to be present for meaningful work to exist. In particular, Steger emphasizes the importance of a broader purpose which may not need to be present in all three orientations. This debate is largely anchored in the subjective experience of work and largely fails to consider the objective conditions of work that can underpin or facilitate meaningful work.

Ciulla (2018, but also see Bowie, 2018) addresses this gap and makes a helpful distinction between what she calls the "moral conditions" of work and the subjective experience of meaningful work. By moral conditions she is referring to opportunities for fair pay, equal treatment, personal growth and development, autonomy, voice, freedom and dignity at work, among others. These are seen as important contextual building blocks for meaningful work to be experienced and can be articulated in actual practices. However, these conditions do not necessarily guarantee that it will be experienced because individuals have different preferences and values and while the moral conditions may be favorable, the process of meaning-making may not be either sought or available to every individual. This distinction echoes Wolf's observation that meaningful work is created (a bit like a chemical reaction) when "objective attractiveness meets subjective attractiveness" (Wolf, 2010). The important point here is that in order for the "reaction" to take place work needs to contain certain attributes to help trigger the reaction. This suggests that meaningful work is the product of a mutual process wherein organizations have a responsibility to provide the moral conditions and the individual has the responsibility to take advantage of these conditions to live a meaningful life, of which work is an important part. In this sense, meaningful work can be seen as the product of a social exchange and as a consequence raises issues about power, interests and the responsibilities of different actors.

Yeoman (2014) develops further the idea of the moral conditions of meaningful work, anchoring it in a political theory perspective, arguing that meaningful work is a fundamental human need. The consequence of this line of argument is that there is a societal obligation to "insure that all work is structured for meaningfulness" (ibid.). Yeoman makes a further important contribution when she argues that the implicit norm shaping liberal democracies is that meaningful work is seen, predominantly, as an individual preference which "may or may not be expressed in any particular conception of the good life." In other words, in the spirit of liberal neutrality, there is no socio-political commitment to ensuring meaningful work as a human right and, consequently, there is no social responsibility to structure work in order to meet its requirements. People can find meaning in other activities and not necessarily work, and liberal neutrality would be against compelling people to undertake meaningful work. She argues furthermore that the ways in which society arranges work is "unjust, because it unfairly allocates and unnecessarily constrains the kind of work which is most likely to enable individuals to satisfy their fundamental human interests." This leads to a further step in her argument that society should provide "institutional guarantees" to provide opportunities for meaningful work for all citizens. This points to the importance of the socio-political context in which work is designed and developed, which is the core focus of this chapter.

In summary, meaningful work can be interpreted as the product of individual preferences and is subjectively experienced. However, in order for experienced meaningfulness in work to increase, the objective conditions of work need to be developed to enhance this opportunity and all actors have responsibilities to render work meaningul. Lastly, the moral conditions of meaningful work are enabled not only through the appropriate practices but also the individual's perception of the ability to realize their values through those practices, which raises issues of power, dignity and mutual respect at work.

So, what are these practices? Taking the various perspectives on meaningful work from political theory, philosophy, psychology, organizational behavior, and employee relations, a number of domain areas can be delineated in which a range of appropriate practices are manifest. These are: autonomy, fair treatment, recognition and voice, personal growth and development, non-alienation, and freedom. Autonomy at work, one of these domains, can be defined as the degree of control and discretion that employees have over their work. Greater autonomy, in turn, fosters the ability of individual employees to behave according to their own values and goals and connects directly to the role of power in shaping meaningful work. I now turn to consider how autonomy has been addressed through research.

There have been various attempts to develop measurement approaches for autonomy in empirical work. Breaugh (1985, 1999), for example, developed a multidimensional conceptualization of autonomy and proposed that it has three specific facets: *work method autonomy* (the degree of discretion individuals have regarding the procedures and methods used in their work); *work scheduling autonomy* (the control they have over the sequencing and timing of their tasks); and *work criteria autonomy* (individuals' ability to influence the criteria used to evaluate their performance). He developed a psychometric scale to capture these three aspects. Psychometric measurement is one means of capturing whether organizations enact practices which can lead to valued autonomy. However, such measures focus on the extent to which workers experience these dimensions rather than whether they operate through specific practices at the micro-institutional level. Other approaches use data (mostly from managerial respondents but occasionally workers as well) which ask for the presence and coverage of actual practices that are argued to facilitate greater autonomy at work (Burchell et al., 2014). These might distinguish between task- or job-based autonomy practices such as quality circles and company-level practices such as works councils. As one can see, each domain area in and of itself raises complex empirical challenges if we take the importance of measuring both subjective and objective conditions simultaneously.

Each of the other domain areas can also be refined further in terms of practices and measures to substantiate their presence and effect among workers. For example, there is a considerable body of theoretical and empirical work that explores fairness (e.g. Folger and Cropanzano, 1998). This work has differentiated three aspects of fairness: (1) procedural (does the individual feel that the process has been fair?); (2) distributive (do they feel that the outcome of the process is fair?); and (3) interactional (do they feel that the quality of the relationship with their superior or organization involved in the decision has been fair?). Fairness can be measured at the individual experience level but also at the level of organizational practices.

At the level of practices, procedural fairness might consist of rights to appeal decisions and the presence of arbitration or dispute resolution methods. At the experience level it is the extent to which people feel that they have been fairly treated or that workers as a whole in the organization are fairly treated. This tension between the material practices and subjective experiences is a critical point as research on meaningful work develops. It raises important issues about the role of institutions in shaping not only behavioral but also cognitive schemas.

As an example of how this may play out, Frege and Godard (2014) explored the extent to which employers' practices on job quality were linked to civic principles such as freedom, fairness, justice, dignity, and democratic empowerment. They found that while the perception of the overall attainment of these principles was similar in both Germany and the USA, the German workers had much higher expectations that these civic principles would be met (i.e. more critical subjectivities) than their counterparts in US firms. When they controlled for the actual practices (such as work councils), they found that German workers had much more positive outcomes. In other words, while being objectively better off in terms of their institutional environment, this was masked by their more critical subjective standards. US workers in comparatively weak institutional environments were more acritical. Societal institutions may therefore have an important role to play in shaping subjectivities.

This important difference between the institutional guarantees embedded in the access to practices and workers' subjective feelings is something we return to later in the chapter. The critical point here is the extent to which institutions supporting aspects of meaningful work (voice, autonomy, personal growth and development), in and of themselves, develop higher levels of awareness of these fundamental human needs and shape subjective feelings.

THE SPILLOVER EFFECTS
OF MEANINGFUL WORK

While the domain of work can be structured to afford more opportunities for meaningfulness to develop, there is a body of literature which argues that the nature of work is important for the quality and character of wider citizenship. Pateman (1970) argued that the habit of democratic participation and citizenship is in part influenced by people's experiences of work. This reflects much earlier insights by John Stuart Mill (1848) and Alfred Marshall (1890), who were both convinced that good working conditions can improve workers' behavior as citizens through developing higher mental faculties. Building on this insight, Pateman argued specifically that opportunities for more participation in decision-making at work has the potential to spill over into higher levels of democratic participation. Some have argued that this entails a radical restructuring of corporate governance and ownership to create more employee-owned and cooperative firms (Greenberg, 1986), while others contend that a more limited version of greater employee involvement in decision-making can confer the same advantages (Carter, 2006).

Pateman, herself, distinguishes between pseudo, partial, and full workplace participation. Pseudo participation refers to the plethora of management-initiated schemes designed to persuade workers to accept decisions that have already been made. Partial participation involves a process whereby two or more parties influence each other, but final power to decide rests with one party (management) alone. Full participation gives each individual member equal power to determine the outcome of decisions. It is only when full participation is possible that the spillover effects into civil society are manifest, and these participation rights are most likely to be present in governance arrangements such as cooperative ownership. Unfortunately, this model of ownership is not very widespread in capitalist societies.

There is also the possibility of reverse spillover effects wherein societies that structure their democratic processes to be more participative thereby create a strong culture of participation and involvement that in turn can create expectations and preferences for similar opportunities in the workplace. As a consequence, institutional environments may be important in shaping citizenship behaviors. Comparative institutional theory (which has several variants, discussed later) is a helpful perspective to understand these dynamics. From this perspective, nations are characterized not only by their dominant legal/institutional arrangements but also by the dominant "logics of appropriateness" (March, 1994: 57–8). These logics can embody deeply ingrained norms that help shape and define the nature, functioning, and legitimacy of institutions. These in turn have important implications for how work is organized and managed. In societies where there are strong institutionalized worker representative rights through mechanisms such as works councils, and significant statutory protection against dismissal, we might expect to find higher levels of worker involvement in decision-making, greater autonomy, and workers happier with the levels of fair treatment experienced in their workplace. It is the wider socio-political context that matters and it matters more in some societies than others because of the history of power struggles between capital and labor and how these played out over time. We now turn to consider the different approaches to comparative institutionalism.

Comparative Institutionalism and Meaningful Work

Thus far, I have argued that meaningful work has both subjective and objective moral dimensions, and that if it is to be more widely experienced, there needs to be greater attention paid to the moral conditions of work. This is because moral conditions are institutionalized in practices that workers experience every day, not just their subjective orientations or preferences. It is through the interaction of the objective attractiveness of the work context with the subjective experience that opportunities for meaningful work are enabled and sustained. Comparative institutionalism is a promising theoretical perspective that can broaden our understanding of these dynamics in different national contexts.

In the context of meaningful work, it can also provide greater insights into the multi-level, interdependent, and recursive nature of institutions, practices, and experiences. As Greif (2006: 11) has observed, "institutions provide the cognitive, coordinative, informational and normative micro-foundations of behaviour" but there are different ways of understanding institutional dynamics and how they influence behavior.

This is reflected in the varieties of comparative institutionalism, each of which privileges different factors in institutional environments and how they impact on work and employment. The challenge of institutional change is a significant contemporary debate that resonates across all the different schools. As meaningful work is an accomplishment, shaped by norms, values, and cultural preferences, action and agency become more important to understand, and in particular how these vary across countries. Is change possible, or are the institutional forces holding current norms in place too embedded to prevent significant change? Are the opportunities for the greater experience of meaningful work destined to be more limited in certain contexts than others? If change is possible, what are the levers that might be more helpful to deploy in some contexts rather than others?

Comparative institutionalism can open up powerful new questions such as these that can shape and revitalize the future research and policy agenda on meaningful work. Furthermore, by bringing political economy back in, I shed new light on questions generated by other disciplinary perspectives discussed in this Handbook.

I briefly summarize these different variants, focusing primarily on the aspects that are most relevant to our concern with meaningful work. There are four broad schools of institutional theory: (1) rational choice, (2) historical, (3) sociological, (4) constructivist or discursive.[1] Later in the chapter, we will consider the existing empirical evidence on domains of meaningful work that draws on the different schools of comparative institutional theory.

Rational Choice Institutionalism

Rational choice institutionalists base their approach on a specific set of behavioral assumptions (Hall and Taylor, 1996). First, actors have a fixed set of preferences or tastes, behave entirely instrumentally in order to achieve these preferences, and do so in a highly calculated and strategic way. Second, they postulate that actors' behavior is not driven by a set of impersonal historical processes but by instrumental reasons, and a calculus based on how the other actors in the system are likely to react to their claims. Researchers in this domain tend to use game theory and the Prisoners' Dilemma to model potential outcomes. The role of institutions in this context is to structure such

---

[1] See Morgan and Hauptmeier (2014) for application of these four varieties of institutional theories to employment relations.

gaming behavior in a way that is more optimal for the whole system than for any specific interest group. In other words, how can "gains from exchange" be designed into rules governing systems? As Hall and Taylor (1996) succinctly put it, "what prevents the actors from taking a collectively superior course of action is the absence of institutional arrangements that would guarantee complementary behaviour by others." This echoes Yeoman's (2014) observation that institutional guarantees are necessary for meaningful work to flourish.

In the context of meaningful work, this opens up questions about the institutional environments that are better suited to achieving mutual gains for different actors in a system or organizational setting. In the employment relations literature, the strategic choice framework of Kochan, McKersie, and Cappelli (1984) is an example of this mode of thinking. Their analysis of changes in employment relations in the USA which shaped workers' organizational work experiences, delineated how employers participated in union avoidance and de-collectivizing of labor relations. Employers sought to re-establish their preference for a unilateral right to manage in a changing context of increased global competition. This also saw a parallel process of firms innovating in work practices at a local level outside of the collective bargaining institutions. The assumption here is that whereas context changes, the preferences of capital and labor and their agents are relatively stable and constant. However, the theory also sees potential for change coming from significant exogenous shocks such as economic crises or wars. Consequently, a punctuated equilibrium model of change is permitted in an otherwise stable set of institutional dynamics.

Rational choice institutionalism is largely informed by economic thinking and sees the organization primarily through the lens of transaction costs economics. Social values are underplayed and often seen as contaminating the model, which raises questions about the extent to which this perspective is helpful in connecting with meaningful work as a fundamental human need constituted by substantive normative commitments (Yeoman, 2014).

Of most relevance to our interest in meaningful work is the connection in rational choice institutionalism with collective action and the behavior of groups (Olson, 2009). For Olson, organizational activity is a collective action dilemma wherein structures, incentives, and processes need to be developed to harness the capacity of individuals to coordinate for mutual advantage. Olson's main concern was to explain why it was so difficult to generate collective action around new norms. In his theory, the free-rider, or free-riding groups are seen as one of the main barriers to the provision of collective goods. Why should individuals participate in action when they can benefit from the actions of a few?

The implications for research on meaningful work, from this perspective, is that if meaningful work is considered as a collective good, gaining commitment to the new norms will be challenging because of the entrenched nature of preferences. Change is only likely to happen as a result of crises or significant exogenous shocks and there is a strong likelihood that the original preferences of capital and labor may reassert themselves over time.

Historical Institutionalism

Hall and Taylor (1996), in their review of institutional theories, distinguish between "calculus based" and "cultural based" approaches. In the latter perspective,

> institutions provide moral or cognitive templates for interpretation and action. The individual is seen as an entity deeply imbricated in a world of institutions, composed of symbols, scripts and routines, which provide the filters for interpretation, of both the situation and oneself, out of which a course of action is constructed. Not only do institutions provide strategically-useful information, they also affect the very identities, self-images and preferences of the actors.

While historical institutionalism also incorporates several of the ideas of rational choice institutionalism (inertia, path dependence, and lock-in as a result of complementarities in institutional settings), it also seeks to integrate cultural dynamics, interpreted as institutions shaping skills, education, and governance. An important conceptual model was developed by Hall and Soskice (2001) in their "Varieties of Capitalism" approach. This identified two broad forms of capitalism—coordinated market economies (CMEs) such as Germany and the Nordic countries, and liberal market economies (LMEs) such as the UK and the USA. In a further elaboration, Gallie (2007) introduced the concept of "employment regime theory," which focuses on how the relative power of employers and workers is mediated by the state and the institutions involved in this process (financial, educational, welfare regimes, and national employment policies and trade unions). This took a more differentiated approach, distinguishing four institutional regimes: Social Democratic (Denmark, Sweden, Finland), Continental (Austria, Belgium, France, Germany, Netherlands, and Luxembourg), Liberal (UK and Ireland), and Southern European (Greece, Italy, Portugal, and Spain).

Both models emphasize that skills and training systems, finance structures, and collective bargaining arrangements privileged certain types of institution which shaped the experience of work in different contexts. For example, a number of researchers have argued that CMEs are more likely to develop high-skill, high-paid, and high-quality/price products whereas LMEs will compete on low-skill, low-wage, and low-quality/price products. In other words, the nature of the institutions is critical in shaping actors' strategies in how work is configured. From the perspective of the moral conditions of meaningful work, there is a greater likelihood of this developing in CMEs where collective bargaining and worker participation rights are institutionalized. Hall and Soskice's (2001) descriptive model suggests that these dominant logics and path-dependent institutional configurations are reasonably stable and there is strong inertia against change.

However, more recent authors in this perspective, while recognizing path-dependence and institutional lock-in via the complementarities of different systems (training, finance, collective bargaining, etc.), do see the potential for change. They do not see the preferences of actors as pre-given but as formed through institutions and through the micro-level adaptations of institutions (Streeck and Thelen, 2009). Institutions are not the product of some grand bargain between actors but are continually being adapted and changed in order to maintain the dominant institutional logic and maintain the value of their interests and assets.

This model of incremental adaptation opens up the space for actors to embrace agency and explore potential new futures. History is not a straitjacket and preferences are not fixed; rather, actors have the potential to imagine different future pathways and not have their actions fully predetermined by existing institutions. For example, the emergence of dualism in labor markets and employment in France and Germany is argued to have developed as trade unions and employers sought to deal with the pressures of globalization. In dual employment systems, there is a core of employees who have high wages and high levels of security and employment rights, and a secondary peripheral employment model characterized by low pay, high levels of insecurity and low skills, and often only temporary or part-time work.

Palier and Thelen (2010) argue that in both France and Germany some unions, employers, and the state decided that attacking core workers would lead to too much social unrest and instead introduced reforms (such as Hartz IV in Germany) which enabled the opening up of a secondary labor market with less protection and lower pay and lower skilled work. However, institutional arrangements in CMEs can also temper and shape the nature of work and employment in specific sectors. Building on a tradition of same-sector comparative institutional studies, Doellgast (2012) found that German national labor institutions exerted strong constraints on how managers could restructure work compared to managers of call centers in the USA. In Germany, unions were able to negotiate greater investment in skills and discretion in tasks.

The same "moral conditions" of work are therefore not available to every worker in these different institutional regimes, as the costs of responding to exogenous global economic pressures fall more heavily on certain groups than others. Institutional arrangements also place constraints on firms in how they can configure work in response to exogenous shocks. In the context of research on meaningful work, we can see how the material experiences of work are shaped by the national institutions which create varied opportunities for meaningful work.

Sociological Institutionalism

Sociological institutionalism challenges the rational choice model, which implies a structural functionalist interpretation of institutions in that they embody the optimal preferences of different actors in the system. Instead, building on March and Olsen (2011), social actors' behavior is motivated by a "logic of appropriateness" and the institutions that do emerge, do so because they have legitimacy among a broad set of actors. Scott (2003) argues that a number of mechanisms ensure stability in institutional orders: shared cognitive schemas and norms, accompanied by regulative processes to ensure that there is no deviation from these norms. These practices are argued to constitute particular institutional logics (Thornton and Ocasio, 2008) that operate in a particular field of activity such as professional service firms, manufacturing, government, or international organizations. The concept of "field" as an organizing device is important and there is considerable debate about the boundaries of fields and how these change over time. Thus, any study of meaningful work would need to first be situated within its appropriate "field" as a first step in understanding the institutional logics and emergent tensions.

Researchers from this perspective are interested in how institutions are adopted, diffused, disrupted, and maintained. In terms of reproduction, this perspective takes a multilevel approach and is interested in understanding the origins of change within institutionalized fields. This has given rise to the concept of "institutional work" and there is some debate on the scale of purposive agency available to actors seeking to change institutions. The perspective emphasizes the importance of cultural phenomena in institutional life and privileges discourse and meaning structures as sources of legitimacy. Suchman (1995) distinguishes between different sources of legitimacy. Pragmatic legitimacy occurs when fields adopt new practices based on evidence that they work elsewhere. Normative legitimacy happens when a practice is deemed to be a good thing in one field and therefore can be legitimately tried in another field.

Sociological institutionalism's primary focus on "fields" means it has tended to ignore or at least pay insufficient attention to national institutional systems or configurations of complementary institutions at that level. This is partly due to its contention that there are multiple potential logics across fields and change can be the consequence of actors in one field (say healthcare) importing a practice such as "lean thinking" from another field (manufacturing). This has given rise to a wave of interest in the idea of "institutional entrepreneurs" whose key work is framing and reframing interpretations of such innovations. They act as "bricoleurs," drawing on a range of features in the field and across fields such as meaning structures, identities, and narratives to embed new practices. In a further development, Fligstein and McAdam (2012) have integrated social movement theory as a way to understand how power and political influence are used to shape institutional renewal and change.

Historical and rational choice institutionalists would be more interested in the extent to which specific national systems adopt, adapt, or resist innovations due to path dependency, inertia, and institutional complementarities that create "lock-ins," as well as the consequences of training, collective bargaining, and financial systems on change. Therefore, they would question the extent to which the concept of "institutional logics" is really transferable across different socio-political contexts, as similar institutions can lead to such heterogeneity across contexts (Hotho and Saka-Helmhout, 2017). Sociological institutionalism opens up a range of interesting questions and also methodological choices when conducting research on meaningful work. Where does change come from? What are the dynamics? How is commitment to new practices established?

Constructivist Institutionalism

This more recent variant of institutionalism draws heavily on its historical institutionalist antecedent, but is characterized by a frustration with its process mapping approach and is motivated by the need to understand how to change institutions once formed

(Hay, 2006). At the core of this approach is the role of ideas in institutional change. This can cover worldviews, beliefs, values, identities, and norms. Hall (1993), a key figure in comparative institutional theory, drawing on his own experiences, argued that ideational change invariably precedes institutional change.

This has shaped an interest in "ideational path dependence" of institutions. Ideas are seen to be potentially decoupled from institutions and can become change agents in their own right. The empirical interest is in understanding the processes and mechanisms that can lead to the hegemony of a new set of ideas. An important contribution to this debate is the magisterial work on the rise of neoliberal ideology and the role of the Mont Pelerin society in the creation of a network of relational resources, key people, and institutions that promulgated free market ideas which subsequently transformed global and national economies and institutions (Mirowski and Plehwe, 2009). With current growing levels of inequality, the rise of populism, fears about automation, global pollution, and climate change, there is arguably a new space for ideational contestation to emerge about not only the future of the economy but also the future of work.

Hall (1993) sees a constructivist perspective as helpful in understanding the possibilities for change at a governance level and in particular through public policy interventions. He argues that new ideas have to contend with the "policy paradigms" of policymakers, who are generally constrained by a perceived set of legitimate policy techniques, mechanisms, and instruments that effectively limit the new policy goals. Similar to other branches of institutionalism, constructivists see the greatest potential for change at times of crisis. The importance of imprints from the past and old ideas limiting futures was beautifully summarized by John Cage, the innovative composer, who was asked why people are afraid of new ideas. His response was that he was more afraid of the old ones, as these tended to persist despite new circumstances and often reasserted themselves.

If we see meaningful work as a new idea and anchored in moral conditions, embedded in new practices and generative of new norms, constructivist institutionalism opens up a rich set of questions and insights. What needs to happen or be mobilized in order to win ideational contestations? How can actors navigate institutional lock-ins and open up spaces for new ideas to take root, and how do old ideas persist or constrain the new ideas' emergence? How do ideas change over time in order to achieve legitimacy in different contexts? What are the longer term consequences of these new ideas on practices—are they truly generative of new behaviors?

Given that institutionalists are interested in the multilevel dynamics, a concept such as Lean production systems is interesting to explore as they are enacted at the micro level in firms but are also shaped by broader macro-institutions. The debate between Berggren and Adler (Adler and Cole, 1993; Berggren, 1994) on NUUMI (a GM–Toyota joint venture which used Lean) and Volvo in Sweden (which used a team-based assembly approach) revealed, among other things, the power of global production systems driving out models that were developed in a specific institutional context. However, later work also shows that there is both divergence and convergence in how such systems operate, with national institutions shaping the nature and scope of adoption.

Given that meaningful work is an emergent construct with a plurality of definitions and meanings (see current volume), future research, from a constructivist perspective may be challenging but also valuable as the construct gains traction and becomes embedded in different ways in different contexts. A constructivist view would see this Handbook and the academic networks emerging around meaningful work as one of the institutional actors in a wider interconnected world of idea brokers (management consultants, media, trade associations, etc.) and framers (the PR communities and world of twitter, snapchat, and for the older generation, as my daughter reminds me, Facebook). These actors in turn can shape the dialogue of decision-makers (politicians, bureaucrats, and managers) and the wider public in their role as voters, consumers, and investors (Campbell, 2004).

ILLUSTRATIVE EMPIRICAL EVIDENCE

After reviewing the different schools of thought in comparative institutionalism and reflecting on their implications for a future research agenda connected to meaningful work, I now turn to particular studies that link specifically to some of the key attributes of the moral conditions of meaningful work: autonomy, discretion, and voice. This is not an exhaustive review, which is beyond the scope of this chapter, but rather an illustration of research that connects with the meaningful work agenda in a comparative institutionalist framing.

Autonomy and Discretion at Work

Esser and Olsen (2011), drawing on individual-level data from 13,414 workers from nineteen countries, analyzed this using the Varieties of Capitalism and Gallie's Employment Regime theory or Power Resources approach. While the broad focus was on explaining job quality from a comparative institutional perspective, the study looked specifically at autonomy and job security. Their main interest was to explore which particular institutional features explain higher levels of both across institutional typologies.

They found that the highest levels of job autonomy were in Nordic countries and the lowest in Transition countries (e.g. Czech Republic, Poland, and Slovakia) and Southern European Countries (Greece). The correlation with Nordic countries is now a well-established empirical fact with several studies confirming this relationship (e.g. Holman, 2003 Gallie, 2007). Esser and Olsen's (2011) study found additionally that individual attributes were also associated with lower levels of job autonomy (being female, working part-time, belonging to a lower socio-economic class and education) and skill-specific training systems were strongly associated with more job autonomy, which supports the Varieties of Capitalism model. However, union power was one of the most important differentiators, with strong unions being linked to higher levels of autonomy. They argue that the "power of unions may improve quality of working life by constraining the actions of employers."

A second relevant recent study, Holman and Rafferty (2018), draws on the European Working Conditions Survey (EWCS) to explore whether institutional regimes vary in the extent to which they foster job discretion over time, using survey data from 1995 to 2015. They note that strong unions and active labor market policies may result in the steady accumulation of job discretion over time. Thus, they would expect to see social democratic regimes (Denmark, Sweden, and Finland) to be most effective at fostering job discretion and Southern European regimes (Portugal, Italy, Spain, and Greece) less likely to do so. Their analysis extends the work of Esser and Olsen (2011) by bringing a more sophisticated occupational analysis, and their longitudinal data allowed them to explore dynamics over time. They drew on current debates on skill biased and routines biased skills change to explore whether there was occupational divergence or convergence.

While they noted polarized decline in job discretion generally, it was non-routine clerical occupations which suffered the lowest levels of decline while routine clerical occupations suffered the largest decline. The fastest pace of decline was experienced by those in Southern European, Liberal, and Continental regimes with Social Democratic regimes experiencing the slowest decline. For manual employees, job discretion has remained at very low levels over this time. Overall, Holman and Rafferty (2018) find that "current institutional arrangements do not foster job discretion for a significant number of employees and are widening inequalities in working conditions." As with previous studies, they point to union power and in particular the specific strategies of unions in social democratic regimes:

> trade unions in social democratic regimes seek to promote better forms of work organizations through collective agreements, policy initiatives and collaborations with governmental and employer organizations to a far greater extent than trade unions in other European regimes.

So, it is not just unions that can make a difference but the strategies of unions and how they work with stakeholders (employers and the state) to create more meaningful work. In Nordic regimes socio-political factors are configured in a way that enables more sustained attention to the possibilities for creating meaningful work opportunities. These involve higher levels of trust between employers, unions, and state agencies that can support shared learning and the diffusion of innovative practices.

Overall Job Quality

Job quality is a broad concept which can embrace several dimensions. It is at the core of studies seeking to understand differential experiences of work across institutional contexts. The most advanced study to date is that by Green and Mostafa (2012) which developed a robust measure that included four indices: earnings, prospects, working time quality, and intrinsic job quality. However, the study, based on the European Working Conditions Survey, did not permit an overall measure of job quality as the four indices, although conceptually robust individually, did not have a high level of intercorrelation. Furthermore, the four indices did not all move in the same directions according to institutional context, which illustrates the strength of a decomposed measure. In some countries (within the EU 27), some measures increased while others simultaneously declined. Also, the indices developed are not based on subjective preferences or experiences, rather they are based on self-reported features of jobs that are associated with worker well-being. As such, the survey takes account of the "object attractiveness" side of the equation of meaningful work, referred to earlier (Wolf, 2010). This is important as the bulk of studies focus on subjective experiences, which while important, are susceptible to considerable bias, for example the risk of adaptive preferences, where people adjust to poor-quality work experiences and rationalize these as a normal state of affairs (Burchell et al., 2014). Challenges also confront those trying to measure the objective attractiveness of work: "despite solid theoretical and empirical foundation, no consensus was reached as to what exactly constitutes a 'good job' or how best to operationalize the idea in a synthetic or compound measure" (Burchell et al., 2014).

Analyzing the 2010 EWCS data, based on twenty-seven countries, Green and Mostafa found: "that 14% of jobs in Europe are high-paid good jobs; 37% are well-balanced good jobs; 29% are poorly balanced jobs; and 20% are poor quality jobs." In further analysis, based on these data but supplemented with EWCS data going back to 1995 and tracking developments in fifteen countries, Green et al. (2013) found that it was social corporatist countries (Denmark, Finland, and Sweden) that had the highest levels of job quality and that this persisted over time. This points to the path-dependent nature of institutional arrangements and how they respond to and shape globalization pressures.

IMPLICATIONS FOR MEANINGFUL WORK

One of the challenges for those seeking to develop meaningful work from a philosophical debate to a material discussion of the lived experiences of workers and the context of workplace practices, is how to take account of meaningful work in empirical studies. The bulk of studies in the meaningful work field are predominantly in the subjective experiences space. It is only recently that attention has begun to turn to the study of workplace practices and understanding the objective attractiveness side of the equation. The empirical studies cited in the previous section, and others referred to in the chapter, capture several dimensions of meaningful work and employ both subjective and objective measures. However, there is still considerable work to do, to develop measures of meaningful work that are not only robust at the organizational level but can also be used across national contexts. As we have seen with the ILO's Decent Work campaign, developing such measures is challenging at a global level. Comparing economies which are highly affluent and developed to others where there are "institutional voids" in areas such as skills, training, employer coordination, low or non-existent levels of worker representation and limited legal protection for workers, presents many challenges.

CONCLUSIONS

The purpose of this chapter is to argue for an institutionalist perspective on meaningful work and in particular the value of a comparative approach. One constraint on the future development of the meaningful work field is a lack of consensus on a common definition of the construct and how to capture eudemonic dimensions. As Wolf comments, work should allow people the opportunity to "contribute to something bigger than oneself," but capturing this in practices is clearly a challenge. Opportunities for voice and involvement in decisions that affect the organization's purpose and direction is clearly one avenue to pursue, but again these practices need to be balanced by subjective experience. We know that many employers offer opportunities for employee involvement but these are often pseudo forms of involvement, seeking compliance rather than involvement and quite often undermining commitment rather than generating it.

Subjective experiences are in themselves an insufficient basis to move the field of meaningful work forward and research needs to integrate both subjective and objective approaches. This debate is somewhat similar to the one preoccupying sociologists, labor economists, and psychologists in relation to the quality of work. However, theoretical and empirical work is much more advanced here and a comparative institutionalist perspective is well anchored. It is the case that the measures developed to understand job quality are also relevant to the meaningful work construct and can be integrated and built on. The challenge is balancing the growing cottage industry of micro-level studies seeking to perfect better measures with the need to develop measures that can be used across contexts.

Context is a theme that has been largely absent from the academic debate on meaningful work (apart from a focus on occupations) but as the job quality research is showing, it can be critical in explaining the factors important in shaping both subjective experiences of work and also the material practices at organizational level. Returning to one of my initial questions, the chapter has illustrated the importance of socio-political institutions shaping the opportunities for meaningful work, if we take evidence discussed on autonomy, discretion, and indices of job quality into account. Institutions play a critical role in shaping norms, expectations, meanings, identities, and beliefs about what practices are legitimate. They are generative motors that create stability and meaning, and can support collective action among societal actors toward goals of mutual advantage.

The evidence reviewed shows that social democratic countries are more likely to develop the institutional arrangements that create more opportunities for meaningful work. If you want a future for your children where they have more opportunity for meaningful work, consider moving to a Nordic country. However, these countries also have high-discretion jobs where heavy workloads and antisocial hours can also be a problem (Holman, 2012).

What about the rest of us, living in other employment regimes or varieties of capitalism? The issue here is what needs to change in order to reorient these economies onto a pathway to meaningful work. The current evidence seems to be quite clear: address the power imbalance between employers and workers through strengthening collective bargaining institutions at a national, industry, and workplace level. Second, create an enabling state that supports the development of institutional contexts that allow employers, unions, and state agencies to focus on developing a greater awareness that creating meaningful work is a choice and is possible. Third, from a social constructivist perspective, develop social movements that combine academics, practitioners, consultants, media, and state agencies to tilt the ideational path dependence more toward meaningful work. The Nordic countries were very effective in such approaches during the 1970s and 1980s, when various programs around the quality of working life were established. These were effective in providing demonstrators and pilot initiatives that established the proof of the concept. They also created a climate of expectations about work quality and undergirded the development of new norms. Much in the way that the Mont Pelerin Society built networks of support among key actors in business, politics, and the media to promulgate neoliberalism, it may be important to take a similar long-term approach to changing the rules of the game when it comes to meaningful work. Of course, this is not the only route to change. All forms of institutionalism allow for radical exogenous shocks that can shift societies onto new pathways. What will the next economic crisis bring?

REFERENCES

Adler, P. S. and Cole, R. E. (1993). "Designed for learning: A tale of two auto plants." *Sloan Management Review*, 34(3), 85–94.

Berggren, C. (1994). "Nummi vs. Uddevalla." *Sloan Management Review*, 35(2), 37–49.

Bowie, N. E. (2018). "Dignity and Meaningful Work." In R. Yeoman, C. Bailey, A. Madden, and M. Thompson (eds.), *The Oxford Handbook of Meaningful Work*, pp. 36–50. Oxford: Oxford University Press.

Breaugh, J. A. (1985). "The measurement of work autonomy." *Human Relations*, 38(6), 551–70.

Breaugh, J. A. (1999). "Further investigation of the work autonomy scales: Two studies." *Journal of Business and Psychology*, 13(3), 357–73.

Burchell, B., Sehnbruch, K., Piasna, A., and Agloni, N. (2014). "The quality of employment and decent work: Definitions, methodologies, and ongoing debates." *Cambridge Journal of Economics*, 38(2), 459–77.

Campbell, J. L. (2004). *Institutional Change and Globalization*. Princeton, NJ: Princeton University Press.

Carter, N. (2006). "Political participation and the workplace: The spillover thesis revisited." *The British Journal of Politics and International Relations*, 8(3), 410–26.

Ciulla, J. B. (2018). "The Moral Conditions of Work." In R. Yeoman, C. Bailey, A. Madden, and M. Thompson (eds.), *The Oxford Handbook of Meaningful Work*, pp. 23–45. Oxford: Oxford University Press.

Doellgast, V. (2012). *Disintegrating Democracy at Work: Labor unions and the future of good jobs in the service economy*. Ithaca, NY: Cornell University Press.

Esser, I. and Olsen, K. M. (2011). "Perceived job quality: Autonomy and job security within a multi-level framework." *European Sociological Review*, 28(4), 443–54.

Fligstein, N. and McAdam, D. (2012). "A Political–cultural Approach to the Problem of Strategic Action." In D. Courpasson, D. Golsorkhi, and J. Sallaz (eds.), *Rethinking Power in Organizations, Institutions, and Markets*, pp. 287–316. Bingley: Emerald Group Publishing Limited.

Folger, R. G. and Cropanzano, R. (1998). *Organizational Justice and Human Resource Management*, Vol. 7. Thousand Oaks, CA: Sage.

Frege, C. and Godard, J. (2014). "Varieties of capitalism and job quality: The attainment of civic principles at work in the United States and Germany." *American Sociological Review*, 79(5), 942–65.

Gallie, D. (2007). "Production regimes and the quality of employment in Europe." *Annual Review of Sociology*, 33, 85–104.

Green, F. and Mostafa, T. (2012). *Trends in Job Quality in Europe*. Luxembourg: Publications Office of the European Union.

Green, F., Mostafa, T., Parent-Thirion, A., Vermeylen, G., van Houten, G., Biletta, I., and Lyly-Yrjanainen, M. (2013). "Is job quality becoming more unequal?" *ILR Review*, 66(4), 753–84.

Greenberg, J. (1986). "Determinants of perceived fairness of performance evaluations." *Journal of Applied Psychology*, 71(2), 340–2.

Greif, A. (2006). *Institutions and the Path to the Modern Economy: Lessons from medieval trade*. New York: Cambridge University Press.

Hall, P. A. (1993). "Policy paradigms, social learning, and the state: The case of economic policymaking in Britain." *Comparative Politics*, 25(3), 275–96.

Hall, P. A. and Soskice, D. W. (eds.) (2001). *Varieties of Capitalism: The institutional foundations of comparative advantage*. Oxford: Oxford University Press.

Hall, P. A. and Taylor, R. C. (1996). "Political science and the three new institutionalisms." *Political Studies*, 44(5), 936–57.

Hay, C. (2006). "Constructivist Institutionalism." In R. Rhodes, S. Binder, and B. Rockman (eds.), *The Oxford Handbook of Political Institutions*, pp. 56–74. Oxford: Oxford University Press.

Holman, D. (2003). "Call Centres." In D. Holman, T. Wall, C. Clegg, P. Sparrow, and A. Howard (eds.), *The New Workplace: A guide to the human impact of modern working practices*, pp. 115–34. Chichester: John Wiley & Sons.

Holman, D. (2012). "Job types and job quality in Europe." *Human Relations*, 66(4), 475–502.

Holman, D. and Rafferty, A. (2018). "The convergence and divergence of job discretion between occupations and institutional regimes in Europe from 1995 to 2010." *Journal of Management Studies, 55(4), 619–47.*

Hotho, J. and Saka-Helmhout, A. (2017). "In and between societies: Reconnecting comparative institutionalism and organization theory." *Organization Studies*, 38(5), 647–66.

Kochan, T. A., McKersie, R. B., and Cappelli, P. (1984). "Strategic choice and industrial relations theory." *Industrial Relations: A Journal of Economy and Society*, 23(1), 16–39.

March, J. G. (1994). "The Evolution of Evolution." In J. Baum and J. Singh (eds.), *Evolutionary Dynamics of Organizations*, pp. 39–50. New York: Oxford University Press.

March, J. G. and Olsen, J. P. (2011). "The Logic of Appropriateness." In R. E. Goodin (ed.), *The Oxford Handbook of Political Science*, pp. 478–97. Oxford: Oxford University Press.

Marshall, A. (1890). *Principles of Economics*. Routledge.

Mill, J. S. (1848). *Principles of Political Economy With Some of Their Applications to Social Philosophy*, 467–74. Manchester: George Routledge and Sons.

Mirowski, P. and Plehwe, D. (2009). *The Road From Mont Pelerin: The making of the neoliberal thought collective*. Cambridge, MA: Harvard University Press.

Morgan, G. and Hauptmeier, M. (2014). "Varieties of Institutional Theory in Comparative Employment Relations." In A. Wilkinson, G. Wood, and R. Deeg (eds.), *The Oxford Handbook of Employment Relations: Comparative employment systems*, pp. 190–221. Oxford: Oxford University Press.

Olson, M. (2009). *The Logic of Collective Action*, Vol. 124. Cambridge, MA: Harvard University Press.

Palier, B. and Thelen, K. (2010). "Institutionalizing dualism: Complementarities and change in France and Germany." *Politics & Society*, 38(1), 119–48.

Pateman, C. (1970). *Participation and Democratic Theory*. Cambridge: Cambridge University Press.

Pratt, M. G., Pradies, C., and Lepisto, D. A. (2013). "Doing Well, Doing Good, and Doing With: Organizational Practices for Effectively Cultivating Meaningful Work." In B. Dik, Z. S. Byrne, and M. F. Steger (eds.), *Purpose and Meaning in the Workplace*, pp. 173–96. Washington, DC: American Psychological Association.

Scott, W. R. (2003). "Institutional carriers: Reviewing modes of transporting ideas over time and space and considering their consequences." *Industrial and Corporate Change*, 12(4), 879–94.

Steger, M. F. (2012). "Experiencing Meaning in Life: Optimal Functioning at the Nexus of Well-being, Psychopathology, and Spirituality." In P. Wong (ed.), *The Human Quest for Meaning: Theories, research, and applications*, pp. 165–84. New York: Routledge.

Streeck, W. and Thelen, K. (2009). "Institutional Change in Advanced Political Economies." In B. Hancke (ed.), *Debating Varieties of Capitalism: A reader*, pp. 95–131. Oxford: Oxford University Press.

Suchman, M. C. (1995). "Managing legitimacy: Strategic and institutional approaches." *Academy of Management Review*, 20(3), 571–610.

Thornton, P. H. and Ocasio, W. (2008). "Institutional Logics." In R. Greenwood, C. Oliver, K. Sahlin, and R. Suddaby (eds.), *The Sage Handbook of Organizational Institutionalism*, pp. 99–128. London: Sage.

Wolf, S. (2010) *The Meaning of Life and Why it Matters*. Princeton, NJ: Princeton University Press.

Yeoman, R. (2014). "Conceptualising meaningful work as a fundamental human need." *Journal of Business Ethics*, 125(2), 235–51.

....

CHAPTER 27

THE MEANINGFUL CITY

Toward a Theory of Public Meaningfulness,
City Institutions, and Civic Work

....

RUTH YEOMAN

DISCOVERING MEANINGFULNESS IN THE CITY

....

THE value of meaningfulness has been applied to work and life, and to some degree to organizations. This chapter attempts to explore the limits of meaningfulness by examining the prospects for meaningfulness in large-scale social and economic entities. At a juncture when ecosystem challenges threaten to overwhelm organizations acting alone, investigating the relevance of meaningfulness to social cooperation at a system-level offers new perspectives on what it means to live a life we have reason to value, and how to design institutions, practices, and work which support our search for meaning. In a speculative attempt to apply meaningfulness to ecosystems arrangements, I bring meaningfulness into a philosophical inquiry of the city. Cities are manifestations of human organizing at astonishing scale and complexity. By the year 2030, 60 percent of the global population will be urban dwellers (Webb, 2014). Such escalating urban growth makes urgent a critical assessment of claims that "the existence of the city or polis [is] necessary for human flourishing and political action" (ibid.). Cities are indispensable actors in efforts to address acute social, environmental, and economic challenges. However, these efforts are frequently conducted while looking through the techno-bureaucratic lens of smart, sustainable, and participatory cities This ends up neglecting moral concerns related to rights, justice, and the common good. The lives and voices of city dwellers and visitors are marginalized and silenced in the economic competition between global cities, and between cities and their regions.

In this chapter, I seek to show that the value of meaningfulness can help describe a philosophy of the city which connects normatively desirable social organization (governance, institutions, associations, etc.) to the lives and work of city people. I start with the observation that, as sites of human civilization and flourishing, cities provide

richly diverse sources of meanings which may be incorporated into the meaningfulness of lives. This is particularly the case when city living requires us to exercise our
human capabilities in a complex system of social cooperation. Thus, Wendell Holmes
proposes a productive connection between richly experienced human lives and
extended human efforts:

> the chief worth of civilisation is just that it makes the means of living more complex;
> that it calls for great and combined intellectual efforts, instead of simple, uncoordi-
> nated ones, in order that the crowd may be fed and clothed and housed and moved
> from place to place. Because more complex and intense intellectual efforts means a
> fuller richer life. They mean more life. Life is an end itself, and the only question as
> to whether it is worth living is whether you have enough of it.
>   Oliver Wendell Holmes, Jr. (see Jacobs, 1961)

Of course, cities can also stunt human flourishing when they generate modes of organizing which stifle lives through relationships of domination, exploitation, and exclusion.
Guided by Wendell Holmes, we might ask: what would it mean for all city people to
experience the richly complex ways of being and acting which are generative of a life
worth living? In this chapter, I use the concept of the Meaningful City to argue that
justice in the pursuit of meaningfulness requires city people to be invested with equal
status and capabilities for meaning-making. These allow people to not only craft
meaningful lives, but also to mobilize the social cooperation needed to solve wicked
problems. I show that widespread capabilities and status for meaningfulness requires
an infrastructure of city-level meaningfulness, consisting of meaning-promoting city
institutions which harness civic work into a politics of meaningfulness aimed at producing the common good.

The city is a social achievement (Amin, 2006). Cities are created by city dwellers and
visitors exercising their human capabilities for world-building—capabilities which are
generative of meaningfulness when they are used in contributions structured by
autonomy, freedom, and dignity. Honig (1993: 112) argues that "human beings denied
the opportunity to exercise their world-building capacities live an impoverished life, a
life that is somehow less human, a life without freedom, without happiness." Participating in world-building is a route to meaningfulness when people are involved in worthwhile activities which draw on diverse sources of meaning, and from which city life
emerges. In the Meaningful City, access to the capabilities and opportunities for world-
building is provided by institutional arrangements which invest city people with the
rights and responsibilities for city-making by involving them in the joint activities of
social cooperation. This includes the civic work needed to discover, curate, and reproduce the culture, history, and character of the city. By engaging in civic and other kinds
of work, people form the capabilities for contributing to solving social and environmental problems, thereby providing themselves—and each other—with resources for forging
meaningfulness in life and in work. However, inviting people to take up their responsibilities for world-building is legitimate only when city-making immerses people in
activities which they experience as emotionally compelling and judge to be morally

valuable, important, or in some way significant. In other words, when such activities are structured by the value of meaningfulness.

People increase meaningfulness in their lives when they engage with city institutions, organizations, and associations which are replete with diverse sources of positive meanings. Cities afford an abundance of meaningfulness when they offer city people various means and routes to contribute their different perspectives into the conscious curation of a common-pool resource of public meanings. In order to play their part in gathering, arranging, and cultivating the raw material of culture, history, economy, and politics into this common-pool resource, city people must be members of networks, organizations, and institutions which allow them to exercise their human capabilities for world-building, and to become confident in their status as equal co-authorities in meaning-making. At a city level, this includes participating in the collective determination of what rules and public values will govern the social cooperation needed to maintain the life of the city, and ensuring that the institutions of social cooperation are just. Unjust city institutions can hinder the experience of meaningfulness: they can degrade or silence positive sources of meaning, distort the formation of human capabilities for world-building, or undermine the entitlements of meaning-makers. Therefore, concerns for justice in the city extend to a moral inquiry into how power imbalances can congeal into dominating relationships which permit privileged individuals, groups, or organizations to appropriate the interactive processes of meaning-making, stunt meaning-making capabilities, or deny the meaning-making status of others.

In this chapter I aim to provide a philosophical sketch of the city which is concerned with justice in the generative activities of city people, and how these activities contribute to the meaningfulness of work and lives. These activities constitute the civic work needed to create and maintain the common good of the city, and are consistent with justice when they are structured by the moral value of meaningfulness (see Figure 27.1). I proceed as follows: first, I identify how smart, sustainable, and participatory models of the city have neglected human values, and show that this can be repaired by developing a philosophy of the city which attends to meaningfulness in the lives and work of city people. Second, I describe the value of meaningfulness, identifying the harmful effects of alienation in experiencing meaningfulness, and using an ethic of care to remedy alienation in the work of social cooperation. Third, I apply the value of meaningfulness to the concept of the Meaningful City, arguing that contributing to city-making is generative of meaningfulness in work and life when processes of meaning-making are just. Finally, I propose that an ethico-normative infrastructure is needed to promote city-level meaningfulness. This includes three core elements: *public meaningfulness* or a common-pool resource of positive meanings, bounded by a horizon of liberal democratic values, from which people draw to make the city and to craft meaningful lives and work; membership of *the society of meaning-makers*, which invests people with the status and capabilities needed to be world-builders; and *agonistic republicanism* to foster positive difference-making and encourage a culture of civic emotions which goes beyond respect to knowing one other as "distinct persons with a life of our own to lead" (Yeoman, 2014a: 153; see also Yeoman, 2014b).

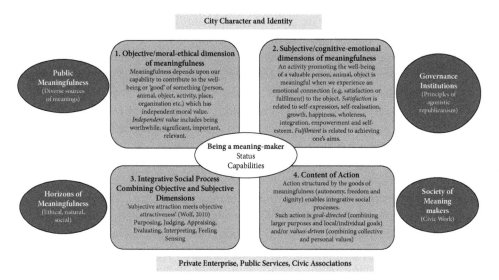

FIGURE 27.1 Ethico-normative infrastructure of the Meaningful City

LIMITS TO TECHNO-BUREAUCRATIC VISIONS OF THE CITY

Initiatives to promote smart, sustainable, and participatory cities are predominantly understood in technological and procedural terms. Meijer et al. (2016) describe the smart city as "a utopian vision of a city that produces wealth, sustainability, and well-being by using technologies to tackle wicked problems." Their claim is that, by bringing technology and urban governance together, smart cities will integrate economic development and public service delivery; direct investment to achievable projects with high practical impact; and foster widespread participation of businesses, community groups, and residents (Meijer and Rodríguez Bolívar, 2016). However, smart city projects have been limited by insufficient attention to the part played by human agency and public values in technological development. Agency is conceived in human capital terms which focuses on how smart cities can attract and mobilize smart people, rather than considering how designing for autonomy—understood in terms of political and personal self-determination—can foster the human development of all who contribute to making the city, thereby promoting "the feeling that we are all owners and equally responsible for our city" (Angelidou, 2014). A sense of ownership is inculcated when all city people are invited to take part in institutions which embody a diversity of public values, not just those related to production and economic growth, and where deliberative procedures permit a plurality of perspectives. This includes using expressive variety to establish connections between human values and public value creation (see Jørgensen and Bozeman, 2007).

A more granular approach to human agency and public values in city-making, which takes account of power relations and inequalities, can be found in the work of Saskia Sassen (2005). Sassen argues that the concept of the Global City and the Global-City Region addresses the emergence of new economic and organizational units arising from the process of globalization: "The global city and the network of these cities is a space that is both place-centered in that it is embedded in particular and strategic locations; and it is transterritorial because it connects sites that are not geographically proximate yet are intensely connected to each other" (ibid.: 39). These new organizational units consist of the specialized centralizing functions (finance, information, and operational) which are needed to run the global economy. Sassen challenges the assumption that global forces are irresistible, and so the impact of these specialized functions on the city and its region cannot be shaped, adapted, or otherwise subjected to the agency of affected stakeholders. She claims that, by making use of neglected categories of place and work process, new capabilities for "global operation, coordination and control contained in the new information technologies and in the power of transnational corporations" will generate *practices* which can be modified to serve human development. Attentiveness to how people are related to the city through place and work shows us that much of what the city does is not hypermobile, but embedded in and dependent on low-skilled, low-income jobs. The categories of place and work help us to examine power relations and inequality in "the actual work of managing, servicing and financing a global economy," revealing the city as a site of claims to justice and inclusion.

Sassen evokes entitlements in the form of "rights to place" which provide an "opening for new forms of citizenship," and addresses the question, "Whose City is it?" Her analysis challenges us to consider how the terms of social cooperation shape city lives. Injustices in the work of social cooperation foster experiences of alienation, lack of belonging, and a sense of meaninglessness. Consequently, the answer to the question, "Whose city?" often becomes "my city from which you are excluded," making people feel as if they have become "strangers in their own land" (Hochschild, 2016). This sense of alienation erodes social connections, undermines the possibility of a "shared normative order," and fosters feelings of disrespect and misrecognition (Gidron and Hall, 2017). For example, in his work on "The Glasgow Effect," Professor Harry Burns found "premature mortality" and widespread health inequalities in young and middle-aged people whose families had experienced the disruption of deindustrialization and the consequences of poor planning decisions in housing and industrial policy (*Inside Health*, 2018). Adverse childhood experiences led to socially determined causes of mortality such as drugs, alcohol, suicides, violence, and accidents. People presenting with alcoholism at Burns's surgery would not give up drinking. His patients would tell him, "[I] don't care, life is not very nice... drink makes me feel better" (ibid.). The remedy for this, Burns argues, is "to tackle the social, environmental and economic dislocation felt by people" (ibid.). However, this will require policymaking to ensure that "*all* the public sector... work together to help people regain a sense of purpose and meaning in life," including innovations in social cohesion which move away from "doing things *to* people, rather than doing things *with* people" (ibid.). Repairing chronic and systemically embedded alienation requires the reintegration of people into social cooperation, giving them something to do which matters and which makes a contribution to the world.

Techno-bureaucratic approaches to city-making can help mitigate chronic alienation if they are joined with a politics of meaningfulness which encourages people to participate in meaning-making. A politics of meaningfulness helps us to understand how rights to place are related to duties to make the city, where the experience and satisfactions derived from discharging such duties are part of what it means to live a meaningful life. Duties to make the city include contributing to the work of meaning-making which generates and maintains the sources of positive meanings needed for public meaningfulness at a city level. But if they are to be constitutive of meaningfulness, contributions to making the city must be worthy of human effort, and this demands that the structures, processes, and practices of human organizing be just. Before considering this claim in more detail, I describe the value of meaningfulness and apply it to the concept of the Meaningful City.

THE VALUE OF MEANINGFULNESS

Many contemporary philosophers argue that feelings of desire or satisfaction are insufficient for a meaningful life, which must additionally include objectively valuable goods and activities. Drawing on this view, I have argued elsewhere that we construct meaningfulness when we appropriate to our lives objects (including, for example, ideas, activities, people, animals, places, and organizations) which are independently valuable and toward which we foster positive emotional connections by caring about and contributing to the good for such objects (Yeoman, 2014a). Our interactions with valuable objects promote meaningfulness when they are structured by a capabilities component and a status component. The capabilities component is realized through the formation of capabilities for judging the value or worth of things and forging affective attachments to them. Jointly, these capabilities provide us with the ability to craft meaningful lives. In other words, we establish, justify, and legitimate the meaning content of our lives when we participate in collective judgments concerning the value of objects and discharge our responsibilities of care toward those objects. The status component grounds our entitlement to be recognized as equal co-authorities in meaning-making. Endowed with this status, we learn to see ourselves as the authors of our actions and entitled to speak up in public deliberation concerning our interpretations of the value, significance, and meaning of such actions, including whether they are worthy of our involvement.

This yields a conceptual structure for meaningfulness which integrates the objective/ethical-moral perspective on the significance of those things we appropriate to the meaningfulness of our lives with the subjective/cognitive-emotional experience of being connected to, belonging to, being involved with something at a deeply emotional level. Notably, Susan Wolf's (2010) hybrid account describes meaningfulness as a value where meaningfulness arises when "subjective attraction meets objective attractiveness."

The experience of meaningfulness is more likely to occur when a person becomes actively connected to a worthy object; that is, something or someone of value. This is frequently the case when we belong to organizations or participate in practices constituted by worthwhile, valuable objects which demand from us a moral response. Through such organizations and practices, we engage with others in interactive encounters of judging, attending, appraising, caring, and evaluating. These constitute the integrative social processes by which we bring together the objective and subjective dimensions of meaningfulness and establish the cognitive and emotional pathways through which we craft meaningfulness in our lives and work.

Our capacity to experience meaningfulness is increased by the plurality of meaning sources we bring to bear in our lives. Schnell (2011) identifies a connection between meaningfulness and sources of meaning, such that meaningfulness is more likely to be experienced when individuals are engaged with "density and diversity of sources of meaning" (ibid.: 667), which orientate individuals beyond the self. Lips-Wiersma and Wright (2012) describe how meaningfulness arises from "dynamic processes of seeking wholeness through addressing the relationship between multiple sources of meaning" (ibid.: 658). Braybrooke (1998a; see also Braybrooke, 1998b) argues that the experience of an increased richness of needs is an advanced condition of human development which obliges society to expand human capabilities (ibid: 22). At its best, city living provides a complex exterior richness which matches our need for interior richness, consistent with the conditions needed for experiencing meaningfulness across a whole life.

Alienation and Meaningfulness

Yet there is no denying that cities often disconnect people from valuable projects and objects. In a restatement of Wolf's hybrid account of meaningfulness, Evers and van Smeden (2016) advance a "fitting valuing" version of meaningfulness such that "meaning rises when subjective valuing meets objective valuableness" and where "life is meaningful in virtue of actively pursuing objectively valuable projects that one cares about" (ibid.: 367). Evers and van Smeden argue that "many people who long for meaning do not simply long for doing good but also for a kind of connectedness to the good they do" (ibid.: 369). But it is not uncommon for people who may be doing good things to also experience a sense of emotional separation and distance from their activities.

This experience of disconnection is one aspect of what we mean by alienation. Cities are potent sites of alienation because urban social relations tend toward indifference, misrecognition, and exclusion. For instance, new forms of work such as platform capitalism foster relationships of domination and exploitation, rendering people vulnerable to relational harm which divides them from their moral and emotional orientations to valuable objects. In her analysis of work in Parisian factories of the 1920s, Weil observes how the "existence of other men" (Weil, 2006 [1955]: 90) presses the worker into a relation of dependence, so that "his own life escapes not only out of his hands, but also out of the control of his intelligence; judging and resolution no longer have anything to which to apply themselves; instead of contriving and acting, one has to stoop to pleading or threatening" (ibid.: 91; see Yeoman, 2014a). People subjected to degrading treatment of this kind are thwarted in their capacity for world-building and denied opportunities to make their contribution to complex challenges which are morally important and emotionally engaging.

This echoes with a recent account of alienation by Jaeggi (2014), who argues that alienation can be understood as a sense of not having oneself at one's command, of being distanced from one's most important commitments, and particularly of not "being able to understand oneself as the author of one's own actions." In other words, alienation is an impaired relationship to the world or "a relation of relationlessness" (ibid.). This arises from: first, meaninglessness as a distorted ability "meaningfully to *identify* with what one does and with those with whom one does it," and second, powerlessness as "the inability to exert *control* over what one does—that is, the inability to be, individually or collectively, the subject of one's actions" (ibid.). This can lead to an emotional condition whereby a person can feel himself to be "a stranger in the world that he himself has made" (MacIntyre, 1953: 23). Jaeggi (2014) proposes that alienation may be overcome through a productive praxis or "way of relating practically to the world" (ibid.: 38) which restores "productive relations, as open processes in which appropriation always means both the integration and transformation of what is given" (ibid.: 1). Such productive relations are conducive to the experience of meaningfulness because they may overcome the feeling that one's world is constituted by dominating and inescapable forces over which one has no control. When civic work in smart and sustainable city initiatives is designed to encourage people to exercise voice and share responsibility for joint action and outcomes, the prospects for connections and relationships which lead to positive meaning-making is increased. In this way, city institutions can consciously multiply morally valuable opportunities for people to contribute to the productive practices needed for world-building. Indeed, the existence and accessibility of such opportunities is a precondition of people accepting their duties to join together in social cooperation.

Caring and Meaningfulness

What scope do city institutions have for creating attractive opportunities to participate in world-building? One route is through the ethical requirement to have a care for the well-being of self, others, animals, objects, etc (see Yeoman, 2014a). Engaging in caring practices generates the productive relations and affective orientations needed to overcome alienation by restoring our sense of being authors of morally legitimate actions which promote the good for valuable objects. Frankl makes this point:

> Human behaviour is really human to the extent to which it means acting into the world. This, in turn, implies being motivated by the world. In fact, the world toward which a human being transcends itself is a world replete with meanings that constitute reasons to act and full as well of other human beings to love.   (Frankl, 2004: 93)

Frankfurt (1982: 250) argues that loving is a powerful source of universal meaning—"locating the source of meaning in the activity of loving renders opportunities for meaningful life much more readily accessible." He goes on to say that this requires us to find something we are capable of caring about. By engaging in acts of care toward whatever objects it is possible for us to care about, we establish the value of those objects—we make them worth caring about and in the process we make ourselves into creators of value. In complex systems bounded by regulation and accountability, finding things to care about and acting with care toward such things is not something we leave purely to individual preference or judgment. Wolf (2002: 237) situates her objective valuing in a pluralistic framework "against the background assumption that the facts about our value are likely to be highly pluralistic and complex and that in consequence our approach to questions of objective value should be tolerant and open-minded." The presence of background assumptions, or a horizon of values and meanings, does not preclude the possibility for contestation and challenge as to what constitutes objective value, but they do demand that we evaluate the impact our different interpretations have on valuable objects which are in our care.

Meaning-making understood in this way is a public and not simply a private activity. I have argued elsewhere with regard to meaningful work that "the search for meaningfulness [is not] a purely personal affair for which we have no collective responsibility, because [...] social structures can inhibit or support meaning-making capabilities, rendering us more or less vulnerable to the harms of non-meaningful work, and unfairly distributing the available range of positive values" (Yeoman, 2014a: 25–6). Moral evaluation is required wherever we think there may be an unfair distribution of burdens and benefits. In this case, justice matters when social structures supporting capabilities for meaningfulness and grounding our status as meaning-makers become subordinated to elite interests, or are made available only to specific groups and individuals. This can stimulate a politics of meaningfulness via struggles to secure public recognition for the legitimacy of one's meanings and values. In urban contexts, such a politics can be made productive at the institutional level by applying the hybrid value of meaningfulness to the conscious, deliberative formation of public meaningfulness, or the many sources of positive meanings derived from public practices and civic work which are bounded by a horizon of liberal democratic values.

THE MEANINGFUL CITY

What are the associational and institutional conditions for people to undertake the civic work needed to make the city—work which also has the structure for meaningfulness? I suggest that identifying such conditions requires a normative evaluation of the circumstances under which people enter into social cooperation, including why they need to do so in the first place. Classical philosophy identifies clear connections between the city and human flourishing. Socrates argues that the origins of the city lie in human vulnerabilities to hunger and homelessness (see Meagher, 2008). Need motivates people to gather together into a division of labor in order to secure "the condition[s] of life and existence" (Plato, in Meagher, 2008). But this produces injustices when "the original healthy city is no longer sufficient" (ibid.: 30) and the pursuit of diversity and novelty causes people to "exceed the limit of necessity, and give themselves up to the unlimited accumulation of wealth" (ibid.: 31). In Plato's city, justice is attained through dialogic reflection and inquiry, and is therefore a social achievement proceeding from "the city in process of creation" (ibid.: 25), a process which is instigated "out of the needs of mankind" (ibid.). The process of creating the city begins when "partners and helpers are gathered together in one habitation" (ibid.: 26) and are joined by the recognition of mutual needs for food, dwelling, and clothing which are "the condition of life and existence" (ibid.: 26). In so doing, they develop the specialized activities required to produce the goods which maintain the life of the city. Hence, the possibility of justice is intimately connected to the ethical features of contributing one's knowledge, craft, and skill into the social cooperation necessary for meeting needs, mitigating vulnerabilities and enabling flourishing.

The provision of goods such as food, shelter, health, and security remain a potent entry point for city-making. Cities depend on complex systems of production and supply which are exposed to risk and fragility. Complex harms such as climate change, terrorism, and inequalities affect all city people, potentially providing the basis for dialogic reflection and inquiry when searching for just solutions. This often demands high levels of cooperation and coordination. In maintaining such efforts, practices of mutual aid and mutual relationships become a source of positive meaning and value. Jane Jacobs argues that "dynamic cities" are characterized by mutual rather than competitive relationships. She goes on to say that "cities have the capability of providing something for everybody, but only when they have been created by everybody" (Jacobs, 1961). But needs satisfaction extends beyond distributive justice in the provision of material goods to our needs for culture, society, autonomy, and recognition. Producing the goods for both survival needs and human flourishing require processes which must themselves be subject to the standards of justice. With respect to meaningful lives and work, this is especially the case when some are prevented from acquiring or exercising the complex capabilities needed for contributing to city-making (Gomberg, 2007). The right to make one's contribution through activities which pass ethical tests of dignity, autonomy, and freedom provides content to Lefebvre's right to the city and "right to urban life" (1996 [1968]: 158) which derives from his idea of the city as an oeuvre, a work of art, craft, and skill maintained by the daily activities of city people (see Attoh, 2011). In other words, justice in the social cooperation needed to make the city involves people in discharging duties to organize. But asking people to accept such duties is legitimate only when the associated activities are structured by the objective and subjective dimensions of meaningfulness, thereby allowing people to connect emotionally to things that matter and giving them a sense of significance and purpose.

JUSTICE IN THE CITY

City-level meaningfulness is rooted in history, culture, and identity, but is evolved through the present actions of city dwellers and visitors. Through the activities of their members, cities produce social richness and sources of meaning which expand the possibilities for human acting and being. They hold out "the promise of the good life lived jointly with fellow citizens" (Dahl, 1967). However, cities are also replete with inequalities and exclusions, generating concerns for justice not only in material distribution but also in the social, economic, and environmental goods needed for human expressiveness. Persson and Savulescu (2013: 110) argue that unequal access to the goods of meaningfulness means that "some people's lives are often less meaningful than the lives of others through no fault or voluntary choice of their own. Under such conditions, it seems unfair or unjust that the former lead less meaningful lives than the latter." Injustice in the distribution of meaningful lives is remedied when the processes and practices of city-making are designed to promote the formation of the capabilities and status needed by city people to make their contribution to world-building.

Justice in city-making depends on people being uninhibited in their exercise of capabilities for world-building, provided that doing so does not exploit or harm the ability of others to do likewise. This includes permitting each person to offer their different perspectives into the creation and maintenance of the meaning-systems on which world-building depends. However, the meanings and values constituting meaning-systems are often conflicting, negative, and power-laden, especially when some seek to constrain the variety of meanings by closing down on certain meanings or controlling the take-up of meanings. Diminishing the common-pool resource of positive meanings in this way limits the possibilities for meaningful lives, reducing the scope for what Rawls (1999 [1971]) calls "conceptions of living." Justice must therefore be concerned with equal access to public meaningfulness as an urban common which is constituted by a plurality of positive meanings. The diversity, depth, and quality of public meaningfulness is maintained by the activities of city people in a system of social cooperation.

Rawls (1999 [1971]) describes how the terms of social cooperation determine the conditions and possibilities for individual lives: "social cooperation is necessary to our development as persons, the realization of our reasoning and moral powers, the development of our social capacities, and our having a conception of the good" (Freeman, 2007: 421). The terms of cooperation are created out of values and meanings. When social cooperation is maintained by impoverished meaning-systems which confine the range of public values to a monovocal scale such as efficiency, productivity, and shareholder maximization, then we should not be surprised if the result is poor-quality work in the form of low wages, voicelessness, or lack of dignity. To improve the terms of social cooperation, we need a shared language which is forged out of the many kinds of vulnerabilities experienced by city people. Enriching our understanding of injustice involves pluralizing the range of public values by involving people in the construction and interpretation of meanings. Participation in meaning-making is enabled by a basic structure of institutions to which the principles of justice can be applied (Rawls, 1999 [1971]). These institutions are fair when they foster inclusive participation procedures in which people, in their role as meaning-makers, are able to amend and authorize the values, meanings, and rules governing collective action. There are, however, many ways in which the values, rules, and meaning-systems of complex social entities such as cities can be co-opted to serve the interests of some and to disadvantage others. Meanings can be manipulated or appropriated by powerful elites; people can voluntarily alienate their meaning-making capacities to avoid the personal efforts demanded by public meaning-making; relationships based on domination can result in meanings being exploited or silenced. Thus, the social interactions needed for institutional meaning-making can be marked by injustice even before a basic structure has been established.

The social interactions which make possible social cooperation can be more or less fair: Abizadeh (2007) argues that social cooperation is fair when it is "a *fair* or *just* system of social interaction." He shows that it is social interaction which must be subject to justice, and that the basic structure is the route by which this is achieved: "a basic structure is the indispensable means by which a system of social coordination or interaction could become a fair system of social cooperation" (ibid.: 329). In other words, justice applies not only once a basic structure has come into being, but also to the social interactions which exist *prior* to the basic structure. These social interactions create, maintain, and repair the institutions and organizations of the basic structure needed for social cooperation: "organizations are sites of continuously changing human action and organization is the making of form, the patterned unfolding of human action" (Tsoukas and Chia, 2002: 577). The continued existence of the basic structure depends on the meaning-making efforts generated by just social interactions. Social interactions which are productive of positive meanings require inclusive procedures and practices enabling the articulation, interpretation, assessment, and selection of meanings and values.

Hence, meaning-making efforts can be more or less productive of meaningfulness to the extent that interactive social processes are subject to principles of justice. Therefore, ensuring that some lives are not rendered meaningless through no fault of their own depends on justice being applied not simply to social interaction per se, but more precisely to the *processes* of unfolding joint action which make possible complex entities such as cities. These processes are the same processes by which people integrate the objective and subjective dimensions of meaningfulness. However, consistent with the normative construct of meaningfulness, requiring people to engage in such processes is legitimate only when the activities involved pass the tests of autonomy, dignity, and freedom. Thus, social interaction is just when the social processes needed to produce the institutions, associations, and practices of collective action are structured for meaningfulness. When social interaction is just, we will have established the legitimate basis for requiring us to make our contribution to social cooperation because, by so doing, we enhance not only the diverse sources of meanings needed for city-making but also enrich the resources we have to craft meaningful lives and work.

AN INFRASTRUCTURE OF CITY-LEVEL
MEANINGFULNESS

I propose that manifesting city-level meaningfulness, consistent with the demands of justice, requires institutions capable of fostering: first, a common-pool resource of public meaningfulness; second, a society of meaning-makers; and third, public deliberation orchestrated by principles derived from agonistic republicanism.

Public Meaningfulness

To foster meaningful lives and work, cities require a resource of public meaningfulness which is sufficiently capacious to shelter a plurality of meanings and values. Such diversity of meanings is produced from the collective efforts of people to make the city across its social, political, cultural, and economic domains. This makes public meaningfulness a particular kind of discursive space and hence a type of urban commons, where urban commons include "public infrastructures as well as public spaces, places of culture and education, cafés, the street and the street corner along with the capacity to make and unmake these spaces" (Vrasti and Dayal, 2016). Justice in the making and unmaking of city spaces depends on inclusiveness in the interpretation of public meanings and values. Fostering interpretive diversity in meanings and values enriches civic work, especially where activities are constituted by the goods of meaningfulness; that is, freedom, autonomy, and dignity. Civic work structured by meaningfulness ensures that the contributions of city people to the work of social cooperation is morally worthy and emotionally attractive. Social cooperation also invests people with duties to care for things which matter, but only when the activities involved are non-alienating, non-dominating, and dignified.

I develop the following understandings of the objective and subjective dimensions of public meaningfulness. Objective value is derived from the creation and preservation of publicly valuable goods which are needed to affirm life values and form human capabilities for world-building. Subjective attachment is provided by the satisfactions of joining together to create the organizations we need to fulfill our responsibilities to care for publicly valuable goods.

With respect to the objective dimension of public meaningfulness, I make use of Noonan's (2012) materialist ethics, which draws on McMurtry's (2011) life-values philosophy to connect values, needs and the common good in complex social organization. Noonan (2012) argues that "all value is *rooted* in that which is required to maintain and develop life and its sentient, cognitive, imaginative and creative-practical capacities." This is the "life-ground of value" connecting the human being to the natural and social worlds where "the good for each individual is to satisfy her life-requirements in ways that enable her to contribute back to the fields of natural life-support and social life-development" (ibid.).

Vulnerabilities, limitations, and needs arising from life systems provide the objective ground for evaluating what really matters. The human vocation is "to be of living worth" and "to do what is of value to others and meaningful to oneself" (McMurtry, 2011: 15). This suggests that we can increase our personal prospects for a meaningful life when we contribute to the production of life goods: "The good of human vocation is the ultimate life good for human beings in community insofar as it enables and obliges people to contribute to the provision of universal life goods consistent with each person's enjoyment of them" (ibid.). Fulfilling our human vocation depends on our collective ability to produce "civil commons" which are the social and material bases of rights and justice. These social bases are "any and all social constructs which enable universal access to human life goods without which people's capacities are always reduced or destroyed," and include human-made goods and culture, as well as "what is given by nature." Each person requires access to life goods on the same basis as every other person. Providing one another with life goods is objectively valuable and a morally legitimate use of our human capacities. In this way, participating in the production of life goods is a source of objective meaning and value.

The subjective dimension of public meaningfulness is related to a sense of connectedness and ownership that arises when we feel ourselves to be the authors of our acts of care for publicly valuable goods. Systematic materialist ethics sets out universal responsibilities to create "comprehensive meaning and value across the spectrum of life-requirements and capacities," and to accept duties of world-building for which we need to form and exercise life capabilities: "human life is not just bread and sex but the self-conscious expression and enjoyment of capacities for creation and world-building which have no real analogues in the rest of nature" (Noonan, 2012). Discharging such duties through joint activity is a potent source of satisfaction and fulfillment, consistent with the subjective dimension of meaningfulness. Braybrooke (1998b: 55) identifies the human desire to "play a recognised role in a joint human activity"; Sherman (1993: 278) argues that we engage with others in common pursuit because "we simply value doing things for their own sake" and "we value creating a shared world and the mutuality that is defined by our interactions. The pleasure of mutuality at the expansion of self that comes with it is part of human flourishing" (ibid.). Through the experience of shared endeavor, we create "a sense of tracking something with one another, of creating a sense of unity through attunement to each other other's moves" (ibid.). Meaningful work and lives are promoted when city institutions foster inclusive opportunities for subjectively attractive joint action aimed at creating and caring for objectively worthwhile goods—such as the urban commons needed for life value.

The Society of Meaning-makers

Cities come into being through the joint meaning-making efforts of their many members. These efforts foster meaningfulness when people offer into meaning-making encounters their diverse interpretations of meanings and values. In urban contexts, intersubjective encounters suitable for positive meaning-making will depend on a form of social relations which Young (1990: 264) describes as "the being together of strangers." When people "interact within spaces and institutions they all experience themselves as belonging to, but without those interactions dissolving into unity or commonness" (ibid.). Being together in this way helps city people to experience an urban bond which involves "sharing one's separateness with others, of together affirming the value of having radically different values, of having skateboarders and readers share a common space" (Conlon, in Meagher, 2008: 207). Young argues that city living requires people to work out how to share decision-making power, and how to design a division of labor which prevents the reproduction of severe social inequalities consequent on the institutionalization of domination and oppression. People are protected from dominating and oppressive relationships when they are acknowledged by others to be members of a society of meaning-makers in which each person is invested with the status of co-authorities in meaning-making, entitled to speak up concerning interpretive differences, and equipped with the capabilities for objective valuing and subjective attachment.

As members of a society of meaning-makers, city people acquire rights to the capabilities and standing they need to discharge their duties to make the city. Potentially, these duties are sources of positive meanings, and therefore productive of meaningfulness. Raz (1989: 14) makes duties and rights part of a broader theory of well-being, consisting of the "successful pursuit of worthwhile activities." Well-being depends on being able to access common goods such as "the general atmosphere of toleration and kindness that prevail in human relations among the inhabitants of a city" (ibid.: 9). The common goods needed for well-being are created by people exercising duties which are specific to the nature of the good they have made part of their lives: "duties make goods" and "they make activities and relationships such as friendship into the goods they are" because "the duty is (an element of) a good in itself" (ibid.: 19). In the city, having such duties may stem the alienation arising from a lack of significance and purpose, resulting from not having anything to do which really matters. In accepting rights to the city, each city person acquires important responsibilities to make her contribution to the production of the many urban commons which embody vital life values. Having such duties enriches our lives—Raz says of duties that "but for their presence our lives would be considerably impoverished" (ibid: 21). Capability-building to discharge duties of city-making can be a target for city policymaking. This includes helping people to fulfill their duties by sponsoring the institutions and organizations through which capabilities for world-building may be formed, and by encouraging people to become participants in social practices "which establish and mark out patterns of interactions between people" (ibid.: 190). As we have seen, these social interactions are the precondition of social cooperation to which principles of justice must be applied.

Agonistic Republicanism

To be a member of the society of meaning-makers is to be a participant in difference-making. But difference-making is often a source of tension and strain, sometimes anger and even violence, which can inhibit or distort the productive pluralism needed to create sources of positive meanings. City-level meaningfulness requires an institutional framework for difference-making which facilitates the just social interactions needed to maintain public meaningfulness as a type of urban common. I suggest that agonistic republicanism is able to supply institutional approaches to collective self-determination which preserve interpretive variety in the many meaning sources of the city.

Agonistic republicanism combines the contestation and struggle of agonistic politics with republican self-determination which harnesses difference-making for the common good. This requires democratic innovation which is attentive to unavoidable difference while also "enabling cooperation under conditions of enduring dissent" (Westphal, 2014). By facilitating difference and guarding against premature closure of meanings, agonistic practices overcome power-laden processes of consensus building which marginalize and silence forms of expression based on emotion and partiality. Institutional features such as mini-publics provide for expressive diversity, and facilitate inclusion. At its best, agonistic democracy is committed to emancipation which "involves an expansion of the acceptable range of identities and social practices available to human beings" (Wingenbach, 2011), but avoids the breakdown of cooperation between those who hold to different conceptions of living.

However, to ensure that difference-making serves the production of public meaningfulness, a pluralistic order requires a horizon of values. In other words, difference-making should be channeled through structured practices and institutional arrangements which, while enriching encounters between strangers, avoid provoking oppositional clashes. This is where republicanism can provide a framework for agonist encounter. The central concern of republicanism is self-government in the public realm for the common good. In Cicero's words (Cicero, 1999: 18), "the commonwealth [res publica] is the concern of a people, but a people is not any group of men assembled in any way, but an assemblage of some size associated with one another through agreement on law and community of interest." What constitutes the common good will be viewed from a plurality of often conflicting perspectives. These perspectives can be harnessed into difference-making for public meaningfulness when each person is recognized as being an authority in naming and speaking, and having the deliberative status to argue for their understanding of the common good (White, 2011). Responsible difference-making aimed at creating urban commons can help foster a form of critical republicanism which Khan (2013: 321) describes as an "immanent critique of existing institutions that identifies forms of domination and oppressive practices in order to transform them." This requires a contestatory form of democracy where interactions do not put one "at the mercy of another" (Pettit, 1997: 4). Rather, people encounter one another through non-dominating relationships permitting them to experience themselves as free persons. That is, persons invested with a standing in relation to others such that "they are fit to be held responsible; they do not act under pressure or duress or coercion or whatever" (Pettit, 2001: 65). Such persons possess a particular kind of freedom as "discursive control" (ibid.), which is the ability to take part in rational discourse combined with the "relational capacity that goes with enjoying relationships that are discourse-friendly" (ibid: 70). When allied with expressive variety, freedom as discursive control can mitigate alienation arising from not feeling ourselves to be the authors of our actions.

Republican self-government is pluralized by agonistic approaches which foster interpretive diversity. However, to be generative of productive difference, agonistic republicanism requires a form of expressive reason-giving in encounters between people which acknowledges the role of emotions. Nussbaum (2013) argues that social stability requires a culture of public emotions which combines principles and institutions with moral sentiments. Emotions are forms of thinking which direct us to what we care about, and why we care about it; they are "concerned with value, they see their object as invested with value or importance" (Nussbaum, 2001: 30). In this way, they provide information about how we need to respond in order to have a care for how well the target of our emotions is doing. In public deliberation, we rely on mutual respect to carry the burden for positive relationships between deliberators. However, respect has become so formalized that it is now a way of avoiding knowing anything of importance about the subject. Nussbaum (2013) argues that respect is unstable because it encourages people to worry about status and hierarchy—respect does not lie sufficiently "deep in the human heart" (ibid.: 43). In other words, respect is a weak form of emotional connection, and insufficient for establishing a public meaningfulness capable of mitigating alienation and social fragmentation.

Aristotle hints at the fragility of impartial respect for maintaining social bonds. In critiquing Plato's ideal city, Aristotle says that impartiality is too "watery emotion" for binding citizens together, saying that "there are two things above all that make people love and care for something, the thought that it is all theirs, and the thought that it is the only one they have. Neither of these will be present in that city" (Aristotle, *Politics*). To forge the society of meaning-makers, we need emotional orientations toward one another which attend to our distinctiveness as individuals and which train us for evaluating the worth of things by directing our emotions to the common good. For Nussbaum, "all the major emotions are 'eudaimonistic', meaning that they appraise the world from the person's own viewpoint and the viewpoint, therefore, of a worthwhile life" (2013: 11; see also 2001). Evaluative emotions direct us to what is of vital importance; they provide content and information on the nature of significance and the interaction between sources of meaning. In the Meaningful City, evaluative emotions are also public emotions when they are linked to "a definite set of normative goals" (Nussbaum, 2013: 16) which are derived from the shared resource of public meaningfulness. Nussbaum identifies two capacities needed to cultivate evaluative public emotions: "the capacity of concern for others and its relationship to the capacity for imaginative play" (ibid.: 20). I adopt these as necessary for establishing the society of meaning-makers which is invested with the capacity to produce public meaningfulness. This capacity is exercised through public institutions constituted by the features derived from agonistic republicanism. Hence, in the Meaningful City, difference-making is ordered by practices of expressive reason-giving, which train people to experience evaluative emotions. In this way, people come to understand how their commitments to caring for worthy objects are constitutive of their urban commons, or those shared resources of the public realm which are needed for city living and which provide the basis for lives to be experienced as meaningful.

CONCLUSION

I have proposed how the value of meaningfulness may be applied to large-scale entities, such as cities. A philosophical sketch of the institutional framework needed for city-level meaningfulness is outlined. These features are susceptible to empirical investigation and may be used to evaluate to what extent urban contexts have the capacity to promote meaningfulness in lives and in work. A "bifocal approach" (Wiener, 2017) combining normative and empirical perspectives is recommended. This would include investigating how values, norms, and meanings are generated at different scales and across different stages in meaning-making (see Wiener, 2017). Ethnographic methods could be employed, as well as participatory learning where multiple stakeholders are involved in experiments aimed at generating the institutional conditions for establishing public meaningfulness and a society of meaning-makers. Deliberative experiments encouraging expressive reason-giving in communicative action, for example, could test principles of agonistic republicanism. This could draw on ideas such as Kohlbacher et al's (2014) concept of "super-diversity" which has been applied to challenges of pluralism in Viennese urban neighborhoods and could be adapted to identifying rich sources of positive meanings in the discovery phase of participatory research. With respect to the values which inhere in public meaningfulness, an example is Argent LLP's use of "the principles for a Human City" in assessing social and economic impact in London's Kings Cross Development.[1] Two contrasting examples of an emerging society of meaning-makers are: the CODALoop project in Amsterdam which encourages citizens to gather and discuss the meanings that energy-related initiatives have for them[2] and the UK's Preston City which supports citizens in creating an inclusive economy based on cooperative ownership in order to retain wealth in the city.[3] These cases suggest the presence of already existing elements of the Meaningful City which have the potential to be harnessed to provide empirical support for a general model.

REFERENCES

Abizadeh, A. (2007). "Cooperation, pervasive impact, and coercion: On the scope (not site) of distributive justice." *Philosophy and Public Affairs*, 35(4), 318–58.
Amin, A. (2006). "The Good City." *Urban Studies*, 43(5–6), 1009–23.

[1] http://www.onlondon.co.uk/redeveloping-kings-cross-an-evaluation-of-the-story-so-far/
[2] https://www.codaloopamsterdam.org/
[3] http://clok.uclan.ac.uk/14526/1/Co-operative%20activity%20PrestonREPORT%20copy.pdf

Angelidou, M. (2014). "Smart city policies: A spatial approach." *Cities*, 41(S1), S3–S11.

Attoh, K. A. (2011). "What kind of right is the right to the city?" *Progress in Human Geography*, 35(5), 669–85.

Braybrooke, D. (1998a). "Two Conceptions of Needs in Marx's Writings." In D. Braybrooke, *Moral Objectives, Rules, and the Forms of Social Change*, pp. 15–33. Toronto: University of Toronto Press.

Braybrooke, D. (1998b). "The Meaning of Participation and of Demands for It." In D. Braybrooke, *Moral Objectives, Rules, and the Forms of Social Change*, pp. 54–84. Toronto: University of Toronto Press.

Cicero. (1999). "On the Commonwealth." In J. Zetzel, *Cicero: On the Commonwealth and On the Laws*, pp. 1–104. Cambridge: Cambridge University Press.

Dahl, R. (1967). "The city in the future of democracy." *American Political Science Review*, 61(4), 953–64.

Evers, D. and van Smeden, G. E. (2016). "Meaning in life: in defense of the hybrid view." *Southern Journal of Philosophy*, 54(3), 355–71.

Frankfurt, H. (1982). "The importance of what we care about." *Synthese*, 53, 257–72.

Frankl, V. E. (2004). "Logos, Paradox, and the Search for Meaning." In A. Freeman, M. Mahoney, P. DeVito, and D. Martin (eds.), *Cognition and Psychotherapy*, pp. 83–100. New York: Springer.

Freeman, S. (2007). *Rawls*. London and New York: Routledge.

Gidron, N. and Hall. P. A. (2017). "Populism as a Problem of Social Integration." Paper presented at the Annual Meeting of the American Political Science Association, San Francisco, September 1, 2017.

Gomberg, P. (2007). *How to Make Opportunity Equal: Race and contributive justice*. Malden, MA: Blackwell Publishing.

Hochschild, A. R. (2016). *Strangers in Their Own Land: Anger and mourning on the American right*. New York: New York Press.

Honig, B. (1993). *Political Theory and the Displacement of Politics*. Ithaca, NY: Cornell University Press.

Inside Health. (2018). BBC Radio 4, 24 January. Available at: http://www.bbc.co.uk/programmes/b09nvrst [accessed February 8, 2018].

Jacobs, J. (1961). *The Death and Life of Great American Cities*. New York: Vintage Books.

Jaeggi, R. (2014). *Alienation*. New York: Columbia University Press.

Jørgensen, T. B. and Bozeman, B. (2007). "Public values: An inventory." *Administration & Society*, 39, 354–81.

Kahn, G (2013). "Critical republicanism: Jürgen Habermas and Chantal Mouffe." *Contemporary Political Theory*, 12(4), 318–37.

Kohlbacher, J, Schnell, R, Reeger, U, and Franz, Y (2014). *Super-diversity and Diversity Related Policies: Baseline Study Vienna*. Vienna: Austrian Academy of Sciences Institute for Urban and Regional Research.

Lefebvre, H. (1996 [1968]). *Writings on Cities*. Oxford: Blackwell.

Lips-Wiersma, M. and Wright, S. (2012). "Measuring the meaning of meaningful work. Development and validation of the comprehensive meaningful work scale (CMWS)." *Group and Organization Management*, 37(5), 655–85.

MacIntyre, A. (1953). *Marxism: An interpretation*. London: SCM.

McMurtry, J. (2011). "Human rights versus corporate rights: Life value, the civil commons and social justice." *Studies in Social Justice*, 5(1), 11–61.

Meagher, S. M. (2008). *Philosophy and the City: Classic to contemporary writings*. New York: State University of New York Press.

Meijer, A. and Rodríguez Bolívar, M. P. R. (2016). "Governing the smart city: A review of the literature on smart urban governance." *International Review of Administrative Sciences*, 82(2), 392–408.

Meijer, A. J., Ramon Gil-Garcia, J., and Rodríguez Bolívar, M. P. (2016). "Smart city research: Contextual conditions, governance models, and public value assessment." *Government Information Quarterly*, 55(1), 255–77.

Noonan, J. (2012). *Materialist Ethics and Life-Value*. Montreal and London: McGill-Queen's University Press.

Nussbaum, M. C. (2001). *Upheavals of Thought: The intelligence of emotions*. Cambridge: Cambridge University Press.

Nussbaum, M. C. (2013). *Political Emotions: Why love matters for justice*. Cambridge, MA and London: Belknap Press of Harvard University Press.

Persson, I. and Savulescu, J. (2013). "The Meaning of Life : Science, Equality and Eternity." In T. Uehiro (ed.), *Ethics for the Future of Life: Proceedings of the 2012 Uehiro-Carnegie-Oxford Ethics Conference*, pp. 109–24. Oxford: Oxford Uehiro Center for Practical Ethics, University of Oxford.

Pettit, P. (1997). *Republicanism: A theory of freedom and government*. Oxford: Oxford University Press.

Pettit, P. (2001). *A Theory of Freedom: From the psychology to the politics of agency*. Cambridge: Polity Press.

Rawls, J. (1999 [1971]). *Theory of Justice*. Oxford: Oxford University Press.

Raz, J. (1989). "Liberating duties." *Law and Philosophy*, 8(1), 3–21.

Sassen, S. (2005). "The global city: Introducing a concept." *The Brown Journal of World Affairs*, XI(2), 27–40.

Schnell, T. (2011). "Individual differences in meaning-making: Considering the variety and sources of meaning, their density and diversity." *Personality and Individual Differences*, 51, 667–73.

Sherman, N. (1993). "The virtues of common pursuit." *Philosophy and Phenomenological Research*, 53(2), 277–99.

Tsoukas, H. and Chia, R. (2002). "On organizational becoming : Rethinking organizational change." *Organization Science*, 13(5), 567–82.

Vrasti, W. and Dayal, S. (2016). "Cityzenship: Rightful presence and the urban commons." *Citizenship Studies*, 20(8), 994–1011.

Webb, D. (2014). "Urban common property: Notes towards a political theory of the City." *Radical Philosophy Review*, 17(2), 371–94.

Weil, S. (2006 [1955]). *Oppression and Liberty*. London and New York: Routledge.

Westphal, M. (2014). "Applying Principles of Agonistic Politics to Institutional Design." Paper presented at the European Consortium for Political Research (ECPR) General Conference, University of Glasgow, September 3–6.

White, S. (2011). "The Republican critique of capitalism." *Critical Review of International Social and Political Philosophy*, 14(5), 561–79.

Wiener, A. (2017). "Agency of the governed in global international relations : Access to norm validation." *Third World Thematics: A TWQ Journal*, 2(5), 709–25.

Wingenbach, E. (2011). *Institutionalizing Agonistic Democracy: Post-foundationalism and political liberalism*. Farnham and Burlington: Ashgate.

Wolf, S. (2002). "The True, the Good, and the Lovable: Frankfurt's Avoidance of Objectivity." In S. Buss and L. Overton (eds.), *Contours of Agency: Essays on Themes from Harry Frankfurt*, pp. 227–44. Cambridge, MA and London: MIT Press.

Wolf, S. (2010). *Meaning in Life and Why It Matters*. Princeton, NJ: Princeton University Press.

Yeoman, R. (2014a). *Meaningful Work and Workplace Democracy: A philosophy of work and a politics of meaningfulness*. London: Palgrave Macmillan.

Yeoman, R. (2014b). "Conceptualising meaningful work as a fundamental human need." *Journal of Business Ethics*, 125(2), 235–51.

Young, I. M. (1990). *Justice and the Politics of Difference*. Princeton, NJ: Princeton University Press.

INDEX

Note: Tables, figures, and boxes are indicated by an italic *t*, *f*, and *b* following the page number.